Indicators

of Children's

Well-Being

Indicators

of Children's

Well-Being

Robert M. Hauser
Brett V. Brown
William R. Prosser
editors

Russell Sage Foundation
New York

The Russell Sage Foundation

Library of Congress Cataloging-in-Publication Data

Indicators of children's well-being / edited by Robert M. Hauser, Brett V. Brown, William R. Prosser.

    p. cm.

  Includes bibliographical references and index.

  ISBN 0-87154-386-9

  1. Child welfare—United States. 2. Children—United States—Social conditions. 3. Children—United States—Economic conditions. 4. Children—Health and hygiene—United States. 5. Social Indicators—United States. 6. Health status indicators—United States.

I. Hauser, Robert Mason. II. Brown, Brett. III. Prosser, William.

HV741.I537 1997   97-13242

362.7'0973—DC21   CIP

Text design by Suzanne Nichols.

RUSSELL SAGE FOUNDATION
112 East 64th Street, New York, New York 10021
10 9 8 7 6 5 4 3 2

To the dedicated social scientists who have created our statistical system and make it work.

Contents

Foreword: Thomas J. Corbett   xix
Preface: Matthew Stagner   xxiii

PART I.   **OVERVIEW**   1

Chapter 1:   **Indicators of Children's Well-Being: A Review of Current Indicators Based on Data from the Federal Statistical System**   3
Brett V. Brown

Chapter 2:   **Criteria for Indicators of Child Well-Being**   36
Kristin A. Moore

PART II.   **HEALTH**   45

Chapter 3:   **Population Indicators of Prenatal and Infant Health**   47
Paula Lantz and Melissa Partin

Chapter 4:   **Health Indicators for Preschool Children, Ages One to Four**   76
Barbara L. Wolfe and James Sears

Chapter 5:   **Health Indicators for Preadolescent School-Age Children**   95
Barbara Starfield

Chapter 6:   **Adolescent Health Indicators**   112
Arthur B. Elster

PART III.   **EDUCATION**   123

Chapter 7:   **Indicators for School Readiness, Schooling, and Child Care in Early to Middle Childhood**   125
Deborah A. Phillips and John M. Love

Chapter 8:   **Indicators of High School Completion and Dropout**   152
Robert M. Hauser

Chapter 9:   **Postsecondary and Vocational Educations: Keeping Track of the College Track**   185
Thomas J. Kane

Chapter 10:   **Indicators of Educational Achievement**   208
               Daniel Koretz

PART IV.   **ECONOMIC SECURITY**   235

Chapter 11:   **Indicators of Children's Economic Well-Being
               and Parental Employment**   237
               Susan E. Mayer

Chapter 12:   **Longitudinal Indicators of Children's Poverty and
               Dependence**   258
               Greg J. Duncan and Leslie Moscow

Chapter 13:   **Parental Employment and Children**   279
               *Judith R. Smith, Jeanne Brooks-Gunn, and
               Aurora Jackson*

PART V.   **POPULATION, FAMILY, NEIGHBORHOOD**   309

Chapter 14:   **Demographic Change and the Population of
               Children: Race/Ethnicity, Immigration, and
               Family Size**   311
               Dennis P. Hogan and David J. Eggebeen

Chapter 15:   **Family Structure, Stability, and the Well-Being of
               Children**   328
               Gary D. Sandefur and Jane Mosley

Chapter 16:   **The Influence of Neighborhoods on Children's
               Development: A Theoretical Perspective and a
               Research Agenda**   346
               *Frank F. Furstenberg, Jr., and Mary Elizabeth
               Hughes*

Chapter 17:   **Potential and Problems in Developing
               Community-Level Indicators of Children's
               Well-Being**   372
               Claudia J. Coulton

PART VI.   **SOCIAL DEVELOPMENT AND PROBLEM
               BEHAVIOR**   393

Chapter 18:   **Indicators of Positive Development in Early
               Childhood: Improving Concepts and Measures**   395
               J. Lawrence Aber and Stephanie M. Jones

Chapter 19:   **Indicators of Problem Behavior and Problems in
               Early Childhood**   409
               John M. Love

Chapter 20:   **Positive Indicators of Adolescent Development:
Redressing the Negative Image of American
Adolescents**   428
*Ruby Takanishi, Allyn M. Mortimer, and
Timothy J. McGourthy*

Chapter 21:   **The Status of Adolescent Problem Behavior
Indicators**   442
Bruce P. Kennedy and Deborah Prothrow-Stith

PART VII.   **WHITHER INDICATORS?**   455

Chapter 22:   **Potential and Problems in Developing Indicators
on Child Well-Being from Administrative Data**   457
Robert M. Goerge

Chapter 23:   **Context and Connection in Social Indicators:
Enhancing What We Measure and Monitor**   472
Marc L. Miringoff and Marque-Luisa Miringoff

Chapter 24:   **Children in Dire Straits: How Do We Know
Whether We Are Progressing?**   483
William R. Prosser and Matthew Stagner

                Index   501

Contributors

ROBERT M. HAUSER is Vilas Research Professor of Sociology and affiliate at the Institute for Research on Poverty, University of Wisconsin, Madison. He is also a member of the National Academy of Sciences.

BRETT V. BROWN is research associate at Child Trends, Inc., Washington, D.C.

WILLIAM R. PROSSER is senior policy analyst who is retired from the Office of the Assistant Secretary for Planning and Evaluation, U.S. Department of Health and Human Services, Washington, D.C.

J. LAWRENCE ABER is director of the National Center for Children in Poverty at the School of Public Health, Columbia University.

JEANNE BROOKS-GUNN is Virginia and Leonard Marx Professor of Child Development and Education at Teachers College, Columbia University.

THOMAS J. CORBETT is associate director of the Institute for Research on Poverty and assistant professor at the School of Social Work, University of Wisconsin, Madison.

CLAUDIA J. COULTON is professor of social welfare and codirector of the Center for Urban Poverty and Social Change at the Mandel School of Applied Social Sciences, Case Western Reserve University.

GREG J. DUNCAN is professor of education and social policy and research affiliate at the Institute for Policy Research, Northwestern University.

DAVID J. EGGEBEEN is associate professor of human development and family studies and sociology, and research scientist at the Population Research Institute, Pennsylvania State University.

ARTHUR B. ELSTER is director of the Department of Adolescent Health at the American Medical Association, Chicago.

FRANK F. FURSTENBERG, JR., is Zellerbach Family Professor of Sociology at the University of Pennsylvania.

ROBERT M. GOERGE is associate director and research fellow of the Chapin Hall Center for Children, University of Chicago.

DENNIS P. HOGAN is Robert E. Turner Distinguished Professor of Population Studies, and director of the Population Studies and Training Center at Brown University.

MARY ELIZABETH HUGHES is a postdoctoral fellow at the National Opinion Research Center, University of Chicago.

AURORA JACKSON is assistant professor at the School of Social Work, Columbia University.

STEPHANIE M. JONES is research associate at the National Center for Children in Poverty, School of Public Health, Columbia University.

THOMAS J. KANE is associate professor of public policy at the John F. Kennedy School of Government, Harvard University.

BRUCE P. KENNEDY is director of public health practice at the School of Public Health, Harvard University.

DANIEL KORETZ is senior social scientist at the RAND Institute on Education and Training, Washington, D.C.

PAULA LANTZ is assistant professor at the School of Public Health, University of Michigan, Ann Arbor.

JOHN M. LOVE is senior fellow at Mathematica Policy Research, Inc., Princeton, New Jersey.

SUSAN E. MAYER is associate professor at the Irving B. Harris Graduate School of Public Policy Studies, University of Chicago.

TIMOTHY J. MCGOURTHY is research assistant at the Carnegie Commission on Resolving Deadly Conflict, Washington, D.C.

MARC L. MIRINGOFF is director of the Institute for Innovation in Social Policy, Fordham University.

MARQUE-LUISA MIRINGOFF is professor of sociology at Vassar College.

KRISTIN A. MOORE is president of Child Trends, Inc., Washington, D.C.

ALLYN M. MORTIMER was program associate of the Carnegie Corporation of New York.

LESLIE MOSCOW is a doctoral candidate in the Department of Economics and research affiliate of the Institute for Policy Research, Northwestern University.

JANE MOSLEY is associate research scientist at the National Center for Children in Poverty, School of Public Health, Columbia University.

MELISSA PARTIN is research scientist at the Minnesota Department of Health, Minneapolis.

DEBORAH A. PHILLIPS is director of the Board on Children, Youth, and Families, Institute of Medicine, National Research Council, Washington, D.C.

DEBORAH PROTHROW-STITH is professor of public health practice at the School of Public Health, Harvard University.

GARY D. SANDEFUR is professor of sociology and affiliate at the Institute for Research on Poverty, University of Wisconsin, Madison.

JAMES SEARS is a doctoral candidate in the Department of Economics, University of Wisconsin, Madison.

JUDITH R. SMITH is associate professor in the Graduate School of Social Services, Fordham University, and research associate at the Center for Young Children and Families, Teachers College, Columbia University.

MATTHEW STAGNER is senior policy analyst in the Office of the Assistant Secretary for Planning and Evaluation, U.S. Department of Health and Human Services, Washington, D.C.

BARBARA STARFIELD is University Distinguished Service Professor and professor of health policy in the School of Hygiene and Public Health, Johns Hopkins University.

RUBY TAKANISHI is president of the Foundation for Child Development, New York.

BARBARA L. WOLFE is director of the Institute for Research on Poverty and professor of economics and preventive medicine at the University of Wisconsin, Madison.

ACLU: American Civil Liberties Union
ACOG: American College of Obstetricians and Gynecologists
ACS: American Communities Survey
AFCARS: Adoption and Foster Care Reporting System
AFDC: Aid to Families with Dependent Children
AHS: American Housing Survey
AIDS: Acquired Immune Deficiency Syndrome
AMA: American Medical Association
APNUC Index: Adequacy of Prenatal Care Utilization Index
ASPE: Office of the Assistant Secretary for Planning and Evaluation
BLS: Bureau of Labor Statistics
BPI: Behavior Problems Index
CANDO: Cleveland Area Network for Data Organization
CBCL: Child Behavior Checklist
CCD: Common Core Data (U.S. Department of Education)
CDC: Centers for Disease Control and Prevention
CDF: Children's Defense Fund
CEX: Consumer Expenditures Survey
CHAMPUS: Civilian Health and Medical Program of the Uniformed Services
CHIP-AE: Child Health and Illness Profile-Adolescent Edition
CPI: Consumer Price Index
CPI-U: Consumer Price Index for Urban Consumers
CPI-U-XI: Consumer Price Index for Urban Consumers-XI
CPS: Current Population Survey
CSSP: Center for the Study of Social Policy
CU: Consumer Units
DHEW: Department of Health, Education, and Welfare
DHHS: Department of Health and Human Services
DWI: Driving While Intoxicated
ECLS: Early Childhood Longitudinal Survey
ELBW: Extremely Low Birth Weight
ESEA: Elementary and Secondary Education Act
ETS: Educational Testing Service
FAMIS: Family Assistance Management Information Systems
FARS: Fatal Accident Reporting System
GAIN: Greater Avenues for Independence Program
GDP: Gross Domestic Product
GED: Graduate Equivalency Diploma
GNP: Gross National Product
GPRA: Government Performance and Results Act

GUI: Graphical User Interface
HDC: Hospital Discharge Survey
HIV: Human Immunodeficiency Virus
HMO: Health Maintenance Organization
HOME: Home Observation Measure of the Environment
HSB: High School and Beyond
ICD: International Classification of Diseases
IEA: International Association for the Evaluation of Achievement
IMR: Infant Mortality Rate
IPDS: Integrated Postsecondary Education Data System
IRP: Institute for Research on Poverty
ITBS: Iowa Test of Basic Skills
ITED: Iowa Test of Educational Development
JTPA: Job Training Partnership Act
KERA: Kentucky Educational Reform Act
LMP: Last Menstrual Period
MCHB: Maternal and Child Health Bureau
MIS: Management Information System
MMIS: Medicaid Management Information Systems
MTFS: Monitoring the Future Survey
NAEP: National Assessment of Education Progress
NCANDS: National Child Abuse and Neglect Data System
NCCAN: National Clearinghouse on Child Abuse and Neglect Information
NCCS: National Child Care Survey
NCES: National Center for Education Statistics
NCHS: National Center for Health Statistics
NCVS: National Crime Victimization Survey
NDB: Kids Count National Data Book
NEGP: National Educational Goals Panel
NELS: National Education Longitudinal Survey
NHANES III: the third National Health and Nutrition Examination Survey
NHANES: National Health and Nutrition Examination Survey
NHES: National Household Education Survey
NHIS: National Health Interview Survey
NHIS-CHS: National Health Interview Survey—Child Health Supplement
NHSDA: National Household Survey on Drug Abuse
NHTSA: National Highway Traffic Safety Administration
NIS: National Immunization Survey
NICHD: National Institute of Child Health and Human Development
NLS: National Longitudinal Study of High School Class
NLSY: National Longitudinal Study of Youth
NLSY-M/C: National Longitudinal Survey of Youth—Mother-Child Data
NMIHS: National Maternal and Infant Health Survey
NNS: National Natality Survey
NPSAS: National PostSecondary Student Aid Surveys
NSC: National Survey of Children
NSFG: National Survey of Family Growth
NSFH: National Survey of Families and Households
OBE: Obstetricians Best Estimate
OECD: Organization for Economic Cooperation and Development
OERI: Office of Educational Research and Improvement
PCE: Personal Consumption Expenditures

PCE-A: Personal Consumption Expenditures-A
PHS: Public Health Service
PPVT: Peabody Picture Vocabulary Test
PPVT-R: Peabody Picture Vocabulary Test-Revised
PSID: Panel Study of Income Dynamics
PTA: Parent Teachers Association
PUMS: Public Use Microdata Sample
QALYS: Quality of Adjusted Life Years Scale
RAND HIS: RAND Health Insurance Study
SARS: School Archival Records Search
SAS: Statistical Analysis System
SASS: School and Staffing Survey
SAT: Scholastic Assessment Test (formerly the Scholastic Aptitude Test)
SES: Socioeconomic Status
SF-36: Short Form-36
SIDS: Sudden Infant Death Syndrome
SIPP: Survey of Income and Program Participation
SPCU3: Survey of Parents of Children Under Three
SPD: Survey of Program Dynamics
SSI: Supplemental Security Income
SSN: Social Security Number
STD: Sexually Transmitted Disease
TANF: Temporary Assistance for Needy Families
TSA: Trial State Assessment
UCDATA: University of California Data Archive and Technical Assistance
UCR: Uniform Crime Reports
UI: Unemployment Insurance
UNICEF: United Nations International Children's Education Fund
WHO: World Health Organization
WIC: Women, Infant, and Child Program
YRBS: Youth Risk Behavior Survey
YRBSS: Youth Risk Behavior Surveillance System

Foreword

Thomas J. Corbett

THOUGH THE PAPERS in this volume have been updated since first prepared for a national conference in 1994, the conference versions would have been timely and relevant had they been published in their original form. This is so because the challenges of developing, introducing, and using quality indicators of children's well-being, always daunting, are virtually timeless.

An increased sense of urgency surrounds the task of developing indicators of children's well-being. Powerful reform themes in the United States are transforming the management and governance of social policy. For example, national welfare reform became a reality in 1996 with the Personal Responsibility and Work Opportunity Reconciliation Act, a piece of legislation passed amid furious claims and counterclaims about its effects. Opponents saw in the act a dire future for disadvantaged children, while proponents with equal conviction argued that the reform would reverse several decades of decline in child well-being.

Welfare reform is merely one expression of a larger transformation in social policy governance, best reflected in what is termed the "devolution" movement. Simply put, devolution consists of a shift in the locus of program authority from more inclusive levels of government to levels closer to the problems being addressed (for example, from the national government to states to local communities). Devolution, proponents argue, will increase the flexibility afforded states to design, coordinate, and administer social programs affecting children, youth, and their families.

Similarly, the "reinvention" movement in government intends to shift public-sector management from a focus on process and inputs—what organizations and programs do—to a focus on outcomes—what organizations and programs accomplish. This new focus purportedly gives managers greater freedom to restructure the ways they shape and deliver services with the goal of enhancing efficiency and effectiveness. Taken together, these movements potentially will alter policymaking and policy management by facilitating the emergence of outcomes-based accountability strategies, systems-wide coordination and integration efforts, performance-based competitive service models, and public-sector privatization and democratization schemes.

The common thread that runs through all of these transformations is the premise that performance, not process, counts. All of the design and management strategies and the fundamental changes in the policy revolution focus on achieving certain results rather than merely guaranteeing exposure to certain services or opportunities or obligations. This focus on outcomes and results suggests, in fact requires, an advanced use of what we broadly think of as social indicators.

It may seem serendipitous that the insights and perspectives summarized in this volume are being available at this critical juncture. The conference, and this volume, did not emerge out of thin air, however. They are the product of a lengthy intellectual process involving many actors. In 1990, I was asked by colleagues at the University of Wisconsin to solicit a small planning grant for a project that ultimately would produce a report on the status of children in Wisconsin. This request, resulting in what came to be known as the WisKids project, funded by the Annie E. Casey Foundation and several Wisconsin groups, acquainted me with the promises and perils of preparing reports on children's circumstances.

I learned that the problems with indicators of well-being are several. A fine and ever shifting line exists between *informing* society about social conditions and *influencing* current policy discussions. Data on indicators are expensive and sometimes difficult to obtain, so we often rely on what is available rather than what is needed. Some domains, or areas of interest, are well covered, whereas indicators in other domains for all practical purposes do not exist. There are many pitfalls in the collection and interpretation of indicators. Every step in the process of using social indicators—selection, collection, mode of presentation, choice of baseline or comparative data—is partly subjective and thus open to second-guessing. It became clear that preparing indicators well would require a serious intellectual effort.

Robert Hauser, then director of the Institute for Research on Poverty (IRP), and I initiated a series of discussions on the topic of indicators. By the summer of 1993 the Institute, the Office of the Assistant Secretary for Planning and Evaluation (ASPE) in the U.S. Department of Health and Human Services, and Child Trends, Inc., had agreed to organize three events over the next two years: a planning workshop to think through the issues related to indicators of child well-being; a national conference to seriously explore the intellectual and practical challenges; and a follow-up conference directed at effecting practical action. The first workshop took place in November 1993, the national conference in November 1994. Although the final conference did not take place, a number of activities consequent to the large conference are described in the preface to this volume.

Many people have played critical roles in this process. At ASPE, William Prosser (now retired) and Matthew Stagner made important contributions, with ongoing support from Ann Segal and Wendell Primus, who was then Deputy Assistant Secretary. At IRP, Robert Hauser completed the bulk of the conference-planning work. At Child Trends, Kristin Moore and Brett Brown were active players. Other individuals made critical contributions: V. Jeffery Evans, at the Center for Population Research of the National Institute of Child Health and Human Development; Deborah Phillips, director of the Board on Children and Families at the National Academy of Sciences; and William O'Hare, Associate Director of the KidsCount project at the Annie E. Casey Foundation. Dawn Duren, a key staff member at IRP, skillfully transformed the individual papers into a single volume of uniform format. In particular, Elizabeth Evanson was instrumental in bringing the project to fruition.

The project has been sustained because all of those involved realized that change inevitably involves opportunity and risk. Shifting the responsibility for social welfare programs from the federal government to the states opens up possibilities for great innovation and experimentation. At the same time, it puts children at considerable risk. This is not an argument against the changes taking place; rather, it is an argument for investing in the capacity to measure the well-being of vulnerable populations, particularly children, as reform is realized. The gap in time between discussion of performance-driven, accountable systems and their actual implementation is very great.

Whether children fare well or poorly in the context of all the changes taking place is an empirical, not a normative, question. But it will remain normative, partisan, and probably inconclusive if we do not have the data on which to decide the issue. This volume is a start, although much remains to be done. A generation or so ago, during President Lyndon Johnson's War on Poverty, the litmus test by which new policies were judged was, What does it do for the poor? Today, perhaps a new litmus test is emerging: What does it do for the children? This volume may help us advance to the place where we can answer that question.

Preface

Matthew Stagner

THIS VOLUME IS based on papers originally presented at a conference, "Indicators of Children's Well-Being," held at the Hughes Conference Center of the National Institutes of Health in November 1994. This conference brought together some of the nation's premier social scientists representing a wide range of disciplines. The conference was sponsored by the Institute for Research on Poverty at the University of Wisconsin–Madison; the Office of the Assistant Secretary for Planning and Evaluation, U.S. Department of Health and Human Services; the National Institute of Child Health and Human Development; the Annie E. Casey Foundation; and Child Trends, Inc.

The conference organizers planned to take stock of the current state of measuring child well-being and to challenge social scientists within and outside government to improve such measurement. They wanted to build on over two decades of work on child indicators—work which, though it had many successes, had lost some of its momentum. As a way to build on this history, authors were asked to address the state of child indicators in their fields of expertise, to assess the prospects for improved indicators in the short run, and to discuss the resources and methods required to develop a more comprehensive set of indicators in the long run. The conference was attended by ninety people, including the authors of the chapters in this volume and other representatives of federal agencies, private foundations, child-oriented nonprofit organizations, and the academic research community.

The conference was held at a time when many social scientists and policymakers who are concerned with the condition of children in the United States also were concerned that current methods of measuring child well-being were inadequate. In part, this inadequacy came from changes in the operation and role of government, such as performance-driven management, which challenges policymakers to develop clear goals and measure progress toward them.

Organizers of the conference should be pleased at the results—represented both by the work contained in this volume and the activities that followed the conference. The work in this volume speaks for itself. It marks a major step forward in the understanding of measures of child well-being. And it challenges all of us to take steps to improve that measurement.

Since 1994, several activities in Washington have moved the federal statistical agencies toward improved ongoing measurement of the well-being of children. Some states have undertaken improvements as well.

Three activities in particular have kept up the momentum for improved child indicators at the national level. First, the Office of the Assistant Secretary for Planning and Evaluation, U.S. Department of Health and Human Services, has created an annual publication entitled *Trends in the Well-Being of America's Children and Youth*. This publication includes many indicators recommended by the researchers at the 1994 conference, as well as additional measures. The *Trends* reports measure the condition of children annually and challenge the federal statistical system to improve and expand the array of available measures.

Second, the Federal Interagency Forum on Child and Family Statistics—founded near the time of the 1994 conference—continued the work begun at the conference. The forum fosters coordination, collaboration, and integration of federal data collection on children and the reporting of children's conditions. In April 1997, President Clinton signed Executive Order No. 13045, which formally establishes the Federal Interagency Forum and requires an annual report to the president on the condition of children. The first of these reports was presented in the summer of 1997. As the essays in this volume demonstrate, gaps in the federal statistical system limit our capacity to monitor the well-being of our nation's children. The forum is working to identify and fill those gaps, as well as to improve the reporting of what we do know about the condition of children.

Finally, the Family and Child Well-Being Research Network of the National Institute of Child Health and Human Development also continues the work of the conference. Researchers affiliated with the Network continue to explore areas of children's life that require better measurement. They are developing new sets of questions for federal surveys that will better capture the status of children. And they are examining better ways to use existing data resources to report on the condition of children.

This volume will bring to a new audience the ideas that were developed at the 1994 conference and will foster further dialogue on the condition of children as policymakers face new challenges. The improvement of the national monitoring of child well-being remains of paramount importance, both as a model for state and local monitoring of child well-being and in and of itself as a crucial federal function. The concepts, recommendations, and analyses presented here will serve as a guidepost to the field as we seek to understand—and improve—child well-being in the United States.

Part I

Overview

Indicators of Children's Well-Being: A Review of Current Indicators Based on the Federal Statistical System

Brett V. Brown

THIS ESSAY WAS written to familiarize participants of the 1994 Conference on Indicators of Children's Well-Being with the variety of indicators of children's well-being currently in use that are based on federal data. The indicators reviewed here were culled from existing federal government and private publications which feature descriptive measures of children's well-being that are available through the federal statistical system. This review does not exhaust all of the important measures of child well-being that are available from the vast federal statistical system, nor does it tap the full range of measures that could be created. Rather, the collection represents a listing of the available measures that one or more organizations thought important enough to publish as indicators of child well-being.

The review has been organized to correspond to the following topics: health; education; economic security; population, family and neighborhood; and social development and problem behavior. For each of the topics, indicators and their characteristics are listed and summarized in the tables which appear in the appendix. The characteristics covered in the tables include a description of the variables; the age groups for which they are available; their periodicity; the geographic levels at which the indicators can be produced (that is, national, state, and local); and the data source from which the indicator is constructed. The tables also list indicators discussed by the authors whose work is represented in this volume.

In the text the following items are reviewed for each of the five areas: the major data sources from which most of the indicators are constructed; the indicators themselves; and any obvious limitations of the existing set of indicators in each area. Where appropriate, new developments within the federal statistical system that may address one or more of these limitations are also identified.

In compiling this collection of indicators, I have not used a rigid definition of "indicator." The only hard and fast criterion used is that the data on which the measure is based must be gathered on a regular basis so that trends can be tracked over time. This has left by the wayside many valuable measures of child well-being that appear in one-time surveys sponsored by the federal government. There are many desirable characteristics that an indicator should have (see Kristin

Moore's contribution to this volume), but at a minimum a measure must be taken at regular intervals if it is to function as a social indicator.

CHILD HEALTH
Sources of Data

Data related to child health are relatively detailed and abundant. There are four major federal sources of data that offer periodic measures of child health in the federal statistical system. The National Vital Statistics System offers data from birth and death registries. Information contained in birth certificates includes basic physical and health characteristics of the infant at the time of birth, selected demographic characteristics of child and parent(s), and information on prenatal care. Most of these data are available on an annual basis down to the county level for the entire United States.

The National Health Interview Survey (NHIS) is a large annual survey (over forty thousand households in 1996) that monitors the health status, health-care utilization, and health-related behaviors of the U.S. population. The survey has recently undergone a substantial redesign, which will be fully implemented in 1997. In the redesign, a great deal of attention has been paid to maintaining trend data for key health measures. The survey is funded and designed by the National Center for Health Statistics.

The Youth Risk Behavior Survey (YRBS) is a survey of students in grades nine through twelve. It gathers a great deal of unique data on teen behaviors, practices, and attitudes on a range of important topics, especially health-related behavior. The survey was first done in 1990, again in 1991, and has been fielded every second year since. There is a national survey, and separate state and city surveys as well. In 1995, thirty-nine states and sixteen cities participated. At present, nearly two-thirds of the state and city surveys are based on representative samples of their populations. The survey was developed by the Division of Adolescent and School Health, Centers for Disease Control and Prevention.

The National Health and Nutrition Examination Survey (NHANES) collects detailed medical and biometric data on members of the United States noninstitutional population. It gathers information through personal interviews, physical examinations, and clinical and laboratory tests. Three NHANES surveys have been fielded to date, covering the years 1970 to 1974, 1976 to 1980, and 1988 to 1994.

These major data sources allow for separate reporting of most indicators for narrow age groups, and for the larger race/ethnicity groups (white, African American, and Hispanic). In addition, indicators from the Vital Statistics System can be produced for Asian/Pacific Islanders and Native American populations. Vital Statistics estimates also are routinely produced for distinct subgroups within the Hispanic and Asian/Pacific Islander populations.

Appendix table 1.1a lists child health and related indicators that have been derived from federal data sources and which appear in one or more publications of indicators reviewed for this essay. The indicators have been sorted into four categories: mortality, health conditions, health care, and health-related behavior. The table also includes measures discussed by other authors in this volume which are not discussed here.

Mortality

Simple mortality rates often are reported for all children under age eighteen, and for five-year age groups. In addition, within the first year of life, rates are commonly reported for neonatal (first twenty-eight days following birth) and post-neonatal groups.

Mortality indicators also are commonly reported by major causes of death. Common causes of death reported for infants and young children include sudden infant death syndrome (SIDS), congenital anomaly, and unintentional injury. For adolescents, rates of "violent death" (a combination of car accident, homicide, and suicide) are most often reported, though some publications also report mortality by type of violent death. Because most of the mortality indicators are taken from the death registries of the Vital Statistics System, they are available at national, state, and local levels on an annual basis.

Health Conditions

A number of health condition indicators are reported for newborns, due in large part to the abundance of information available from birth certificates.[1] Two composite indicators based on birth certificate data, the healthy birth index and the children's health index, have been reported in recent national Kids Count reports. (See appendix table 1.1a for definitions.) Other indicators taken from this data source include low birth weight (under 5.5 lbs.), very low birth weight (under 3.3 lbs), and whether the child was born with a congenital anomaly.

Health conditions commonly reported as indicators for children of all ages include HIV/AIDS, child abuse, measles, obesity, lead levels in the blood, children limited by chronic health conditions, and developmental delays. Among adolescents, indicators related to health condition include rates of venereal disease (syphilis, gonorrhea), whether the youth has seriously contemplated suicide within the last year, and rates of victimization from violent crime.

Health Care

Indicators of children's health-care receipt include the presence (or absence) and type of (public or private) health insurance coverage, immunization rates among two-year-olds, the proportion of children lacking a usual source of care, the number of physician and dental visits within the past year, and rates of late or no prenatal care. Most of these measures are available on an annual or semiannual basis for all age groups of children. Measures of health care receipt below the national level are more limited, consisting of prenatal care (available at the state and local levels), immunization among two-year-olds[2] and health insurance coverage rates (available at the state level).

Health-Related Behavior

Indicators of health-related behavior among adolescents are relatively abundant, and include the proportion of teens who are sexually active, the proportion of sexually active teens using varied methods of contraception, cigarette smoking,

problem drinking, use of illegal drugs, riding with a drunk driver, physical exercise, nutrition, and use of a bicycle helmet.[3] Major sources for this information
include the Youth Risk Behavior Survey and the Monitoring the Future Survey
(described in this chapter). In addition, the National Survey of Family Growth
provides information on sexual activity and contraceptive measures, and the National Household Survey on Drug Abuse provides data on drug use. Regularly
reported indicators of health-related behavior for children prior to adolescence
are scarce, and have been limited primarily to safety belt and bicycle helmet use.

Major Limitations of Existing Health Indicators

There are several significant limitations to the existing set of indicators of child
health. First, indicators of child health-related behavior appear to be limited
primarily to adolescents, and, among those, to adolescents attending school. Both
the Youth Risk Behavior Survey and the Monitoring the Future surveys are
limited to adolescents attending school. The National Survey of Family Growth
and the National Household Survey on Drug Abuse cover adolescents who are
not in school, but they do not cover some important health-related behavior, and
are limited to the national level.

Second, institutionalized children are underrepresented in the current collection of child health indicators. Of the major sources of health indicator data
identified above, only the Vital Statistics System regularly collects data on institutionalized children. This is a significant limitation, since children are commonly institutionalized for health-related reasons.

Third, indicators of health care receipt at the state and local levels are limited.
The most complete data of this sort relates to prenatal care. State data on immunization among two-year-olds recently became available through the National
Immunization Survey, but it is unclear whether this survey will continue past
1998. State-level indicators of health insurance coverage are produced using the
Current Population Survey, but they have large standard errors, making them of
limited use for identifying all but the largest changes in coverage rates.

EDUCATION

Sources of Data

Four federal databases provide data for most of the indicators related to children's
education. The National Assessment of Educational Progress (NAEP) is a biennial survey measuring the educational achievement and related behavior of children in the fourth, eighth, and twelfth grades. Surveys are produced every other
year for the nation and for states that have volunteered to participate in the
program. The national assessment has been conducted since 1969, and the state
assessments since 1990. In 1996, forty-four states participated in the survey.
Reading and math skills are assessed every two years. Skills in other areas including science, writing, history, and geography have been assessed on a more occasional basis.

The National Household Education Survey (NHES) is a nationally representative biennial survey with a rotating set of topical modules that are repeated
periodically. These include modules on school readiness, school safety and disci-

pline, early childhood program participation, parental involvement, citizenship, and civic participation. The survey began in 1991. The original survey design called for an annual survey with topical modules repeated every three years. Since the switch to the biennial design, it has not been determined how often the modules will be repeated.

The School Enrollment Supplement to the Current Population Survey (CPS) is fielded annually in October. This nationally representative survey provides data on current and recent enrollment status, highest grade completed, diplomas received, and type of school. Schooling data are gathered on all persons ages three and over in each household. The survey, begun in 1946, represents our best source of long-term trend data in this area.

The Schools and Staffing Survey (SASS) is a survey of schools, teachers, and administrators. It was first fielded in 1987, and is repeated every three to five years. Estimates are produced for the nation as a whole, and for each of the fifty states. Over nine thousand schools are involved in all. Each sample school provides aggregate data of the demographic characteristics of their student population in addition to detailed information on school programs, finances, staff characteristics, and other social characteristics of the school. Its potential as a source of data for indicators relating to the qualities of children's school environment is only beginning to be explored.

Appendix table 1.2a lists indicators of educational well-being that have been derived from federal data sources and which appear in one or more of the publications of indicators reviewed for this chapter. The indicators have been divided into four categories: enrollment, achievement/proficiency, education-related behaviors and characteristics, and school characteristics.

Enrollment

Among prekindergarten children, enrollment indicators include rates of preprimary and center-based enrollment among all such children ages three and over, and rates of Head Start enrollment among the eligible population. In the middle years, the focus changes to children who have repeated a grade, or who are behind the appropriate grade for their age. Among teens and postteen youth, indicators focus on rates of high school dropout and graduate rates, and rates of on-time graduation. Indicators of college attendance and degree receipt are also produced.

Achievement/Proficiency

Most of the indicators of scholastic achievement come from the NAEP, and are available for children in the fourth, eighth, and twelfth grades. Children have been rated according to their level of accomplishment in each of the subject areas covered, including math, reading, writing, science, history, and geography.[4] Separate indicators are reported by sex and for major race/ethnicity groups, including whites, blacks, Hispanics, Asian/Pacific Islanders, and Native Americans.

In addition, each year many college-bound high school students take the Scholastic Aptitude Test (SAT). Scores are available separately for the verbal and math sections of the exam. Average scores are available for national, state, and local areas. Scores are often reported by sex, and for the major race/ethnicity groups.

Education-Related Behavior and Characteristics

The NHES provides a number of indicators of school readiness among pre-kindergarten and kindergarten children, including the proportion who are read to daily; regularly told stories in the household; taken to the library one or more times per month; engage in art or music activities with an adult household member; and who engage in other learning activities such as a concert, museum visit, zoo, household chores, or a discussion of family history. Among three- to seven-year-olds, the NHES also determines the proportion who have ever had learning disabilities.

For older children (grades four, eight, and twelve), the NAEP provides data from which a number of positive and negative indicators of education-related behavior have been calculated, including the proportion who average a particular number (one or more, two or more) of hours of homework per night, read ten or more pages per day, watch six or more hours of television per day, or were absent from school three or more days in the previous month. In addition, NAEP provides data for determining the proportion of students in the three age groups who have positive general attitudes toward mathematics and science.

School Characteristics

A commonly reported indicator of children's school environments is the average annual expenditure per student. Though the federal government does collect and publish a great deal of information about the characteristics of schools, little of this information has made its way into publication efforts featuring indicators of child well-being. Recently, however, the Annie E. Casey Foundation's Kids Count project has sponsored the development of an innovative indicator of school environments reflecting the proportion of children attending "troubled schools." These are defined as schools with significant student behavioral, conduct, or staff morale problems as reported by school administrators in the Schools and Staffing Survey. This is a valuable source of data on the school environments experienced by children, one from which additional valuable indicators potentially could be developed.

Major Limitations of Existing Education Indicators

The federal statistical system currently supports a large and comprehensive collection of periodically measured indicators of children's educational well-being. In addition, new topical modules being fielded periodically as part of the NHES (early childhood program participation, parental involvement, citizenship and civic participation modules) are expanding that coverage in new and informative directions.[5]

One significant weakness in the current set of education indicators is the lack of measures on the quality of children's school environments. The Schools and Staffing Survey offers an existing source from which additional indicators of this sort may be constructed. In addition, the NHES early childhood program module may provide important data regarding the quality of preschool environments.

ECONOMIC SECURITY
Sources of Data

Five federal surveys provide data for most of the indicators related to children's economic security. The decennial census provides information on income receipt, employment, and housing quality. Though this information is not as detailed as in the other surveys, the census is unique in providing the capability to produce estimates for small geographic areas (down to the block group) and for relatively small population subgroups (for example, Native Americans) that are not as well represented in the smaller and more frequently fielded federal surveys.

The Income and Demographic Supplement of the Current Population Survey (CPS), fielded each March, is a large annual cross-sectional survey of the United States noninstitutionalized population involving over fifty thousand households. National-level estimates can be produced separately for narrowly defined age groups and major race/ethnicity subgroups with this survey. State-level indicators often can be produced by combining three to five consecutive years of data, although such estimates usually cannot be produced for age or race subgroups, and the estimates for smaller states have large standard errors (Pollard and Riche 1994). A special CPS supplement on child support is fielded in April of every other year, providing detailed data on child support arrangements and receipt.

The Survey of Income and Program Participation (SIPP) is a continuous longitudinal survey that has been fielded since 1983. Households are interviewed every four months. Income, program participation, and employment measures are recorded for each month, and are more detailed and somewhat more accurate than those taken in the CPS, whose measures refer to the previous year. Special child care, child support, and child well-being topical modules have been fielded on a regular basis. Prior to 1996, each panel was followed for thirty months. Beginning in 1996, however, households are being followed for fifty-two months.

The Panel Study of Income Dynamics (PSID) is a longitudinal survey to study the determinants of economic well-being and program usage among U.S. families. The survey began in 1968 with a sample of approximately four thousand eight hundred households, and has followed these households and their descendants annually since that time. It is a unique source of data which can be used to construct economic indicators of well-being that cover the entire period of childhood (see Duncan and Moscow this volume).

The American Housing Survey is a biennial survey that monitors the quality and quantity of America's housing stock. In addition to the national survey, there are individual representative surveys of over forty major metropolitan areas. Each metropolitan area is surveyed once every four years. In addition to extensive information on the quality and cost of the physical residence and characteristics of the neighborhood, basic demographic and income data are gathered on the residents of each household. Thus, indicators of children's housing and neighborhood quality can be constructed from this data source.

Appendix table 1.3a contains a listing of existing indicators of children's economic well-being that are currently available through the federal statistical system. They have been sorted into four categories: poverty/income, income support

programs, employment, and housing. Except where noted on the table, all measures described are available on an annual basis at the national level. Indicators
based on data from the CPS can be produced for states by the five-year averaging
method described above, with its attendant limitations. Indicators of children's
economic security below the state level are available only every ten years from the
census. Virtually all of the indicators represented can be produced for age-
specific subgroups.

Poverty/Income

Existing indicators of child poverty include extreme poverty (below 50 percent of
the official poverty line), poverty, and various definitions of "near poverty," ranging from 125 percent to 200 percent of the poverty line. Such poverty indicators
are virtually always based on the official federal poverty line. Indicators of household income are most often expressed as median or mean levels of annual income. Finally, there are a number of common indicators based on the receipt of
income from particular sources. Most of these are reflective of participation in
federal income support programs. Exceptions are the indicators related to receipt
of child support, which include the "proportion of eligible families not receiving
child support payments" and the "proportion of mother-headed families receiving
child support" within the previous year. Data on other nonfederal sources of
income (for example, earnings, investment income) are widely available through
the federal statistical system, but have not been developed as indicators of children's economic well-being.

Government Support Programs

Indicators related to government support programs include the proportion of
children living in families who have participated in the following programs: Aid
to Families with Dependent Children (AFDC), Food Stamps, Medicaid, subsidized or public housing, energy assistance, and free or reduced-price lunches.
Typically there are separate indicators for each type of program, though useful
composite indicators reflecting participation in multiple programs or any of several programs certainly could be constructed. In 1996, AFDC was ended and
replaced with the Temporary Assistance for Needy Families Block Grant (TANF).
It is unclear whether a TANF-based measure comparable to AFDC receipt can
be constructed, though it seems unlikely.

Employment

These include both parental employment measures and measures of employment
among older children. Indicators of parental employment include the proportion
of children where all residential parents are in the workforce, the proportion of
children with no parents working, and the proportion for whom no parents are
fully employed (working full time, full year). These indicators reflect concerns
about both family economic stability, and the absence of parental/child time due
to parental labor force activity. Often such indicators are given separately by the
age of the child, with particular attention paid to the experience of younger
children (less than age one, three, or six).

Youth employment-related indicators that have been used include a straight unemployment rate among sixteen- to nineteen-year-olds, and the proportion who are idle (not in school, not at work or in the military). These are often reported separately by gender.

Housing

Indicators of housing quality that have been produced include the proportion of children living in crowded conditions (less than one room per person), living in houses with inadequate plumbing or kitchen facilities, living in relatively expensive housing (with housing costs exceeding 50 percent of family income), and living in housing with moderate to severe physical problems.

Major Limitations of Existing Indicators of Economic Security

A major limitation of existing indicators of children's economic well-being is the lack of regularly updated measures below the national level. With the exception of some housing data for selected metropolitan areas, measures of children's economic well-being are not available between decennial censuses below the state level. Even at the state level, indicators can be produced only by combining multiple years of CPS data, and are not very sensitive to change. This is a significant shortcoming of the existing federal statistical system, since such information is often needed for economic and government program planning. The Census Bureau is developing a survey that would provide such estimates annually for all states and places with populations over two hundred and fifty thousand. Estimates down to the census tract level could be produced every five years. Called the American Communities Survey (ACS), it will include most of the information on the decennial census long form. This survey may replace the decennial census long-form questions altogether. It is currently being field-tested and is expected to be fully operational by 2000.

Until recently, a second major limitation has been the lack of longitudinal indicators of economic well-being even at the national level. Measures which look at multiyear poverty and income-support program use are superior to single-year measures in identifying children whose families are under prolonged financial stress (Duncan et al. 1994). However, as a direct result of the recommendations from the essay by Duncan in chapter 12 of this volume, such measures have been constructed using data from the PSID, and have been included in an annual federal report on child well-being (Brown and Stagner 1996).

POPULATION, FAMILY, AND NEIGHBORHOOD CHARACTERISTICS
Sources of Data

The indicators included in this section are primarily descriptive, demographic measures. The four primary data sources for these indicators are the decennial census, the Current Population Survey Income and Demographic Supplement, the Survey of Income and Program Participation, and birth certificate data from the Vital Statistics System. Each of these data sources has been described in this essay. In addition, estimates of the number of children are generated each year by the Population Estimates Branch of the U.S. Bureau of the Census. Appendix table 1.4a contains a listing of existing indicators of children's demographic, family structure, and neighborhood characteristics that are available through the federal statistical system.

Child Characteristics

Indicators of basic child characteristics include the number of children, the percent within each major race/ethnicity group (white, black, Asian/Pacific Islander, Native American, and Hispanic), the percent who changed residences in the previous year,[6] and the percent who are linguistically isolated.[7] Children as a percent of the total population has also been used as an indicator.

Family and Household Characteristics

Common indicators related to family structure and living arrangements include the proportion of children living in two-parent and single-parent families, with stepparents, and with neither parent, in subfamilies within multigeneration households, and in institutions or group headquarters. Recent changes in the decennial census and the Current Population Surveys allow one to estimate the percentage of children living with a parent who is cohabiting, though one cannot determine whether the cohabitant is also the biological parent of the child.

There are in addition several family indicators related to birth and family formation including the percent of births to unmarried women, to teens, to unmarried teen women, and the rate of second births to unmarried teen mothers. In addition, a composite indicator called the New Family Index reports the percent of first births to women with less than twelve years of schooling who are unmarried and under the age of twenty.[8] It is an indicator of the proportion of new families that are high risk.

Neighborhood Characteristics

The decennial census provides census tract characteristics related to income and poverty, welfare use, employment, family structure, educational attainment, and other population measures. To date, two such indicators have appeared in publications featuring indicators of child well-being. The first is the proportion of children living in high poverty areas (40-plus percent). The second is the proportion living in "severely distressed neighborhoods," defined as neighborhoods with values one or more standard deviations beyond the mean level in at least four of the following five characteristics: poverty, female-headed families, high school dropouts, males unattached to the labor force, and families receiving public assistance.[9]

Major Limitations of Existing Indicators of Population, Family, and Neighborhood

The federal statistical system provides a great deal of data from which a broad array of useful child and family demographic indicators can be constructed, and which can be presented for age and race/ethnicity subgroups. There are two significant limitations, however. First, between decennial censuses, the data do not support indicators for places below the state level, and state-level indicators can be constructed only by combining multiple years of CPS data. This problem will be largely addressed once the American Communities Survey is fully operational.

A second significant limitation is the lack of longitudinal indicators. Such indicators can reflect changes in family structure or residential stability over time, which are known to be negatively related to child well-being (Coleman 1988; Hetherington and Clingempeel 1992). The SIPP may be able to support some such indicators when it expands to four and one-half years of coverage per cohort. The PSID is another potential source of data which could be used to construct such measures. Some valuable longitudinal family indicators may require retrospective marriage and residential histories such as those taken in the National Survey of Families and Households.

SOCIAL DEVELOPMENT AND PROBLEM BEHAVIOR
Sources of Data

Indicators in this area would include age-appropriate measures of psychosocial development and measures of both prosocial and antisocial or problem behavior. The major federal sources of data for such indicators include the National Household Education Survey, the Youth Risk Behavior Survey, the National Household Survey on Drug Abuse, and Monitoring the Future. The first two data sources have been described in this essay. Monitoring the Future is an annual survey of a nationally representative sample of high school students. It has interviewed twelfth-grade students since 1975, and eighth- and tenth-grade students since 1991. The survey focuses on questions concerning drug use; delinquency; crime victimization; aspirations related to schooling, work, and family formation; and attitudes concerning such topics as race relations and the government.

The National Household Survey on Drug Abuse is a national survey of drug use that includes a special sample of twelve- to seventeen-year-olds. It has been fielded every one to three years since 1971, and is now scheduled to be repeated annually. The survey gathers information on lifetime, past, and current drug use, as well as frequency of use for all illicit drugs, cigarettes, and alcohol.

In addition to these data sources, the FBI's Uniform Crime Report system provides some data on youth arrests, and the National Survey of Family Growth provides data on sexual and fertility behavior for females ages fifteen to nineteen.

Appendix table 1.5a lists and provides descriptive information on indicators of child social development and problem behavior which are based on federal data sources and which appeared in one or more of the publications reviewed for this essay.

Prosocial Behavior and Attitudes

Available indicators in this area have been limited primarily to the behavior and attitudes of teens. Existing indicators of prosocial behavior include the percent of teens who participate in organized sports, who regularly attend church, and who do the following activities on a daily basis: read, see friends, perform household chores, play music, do art, or write. Indicators related to attitudes and beliefs include the proportion who report that their peers approve and support hard work and good behavior, those who hold a variety of positive life goals as being extremely important (for example, success in work, good family life, strong friendships, community involvement), and the proportion who are concerned about national problems such as crime, drugs, hunger and poverty, race relations, nuclear war, economic problems, and pollution.

Problem Behavior and Attitudes

Indicators of teen problem behavior include measures of drug use, delinquency and violence, and sexual activity. Measures related to drug use include the proportion who regularly smoke cigarettes, who binge drink, who have driven drunk, and who have used various other controlled substances (for example, cocaine, crack, marijuana, or LSD) within the last thirty days. The proportion reporting peer approval for such behavior is also reported. Indicators related to violence include the proportion of teens who have carried a weapon to school, or who have been in a fight within the last thirty days, and the proportion of ten- to seventeen-year-olds arrested for violent crimes within the past year. Indicators related to sexual activity include the proportion who are sexually experienced, who are sexually active, the number of partners, and the proportion who have had unprotected intercourse within the past year.

The Behavior Problems Index (BPI) is a composite indicator of problem behavior—based parent report. It is a twenty-eight-item scale developed by Nicholas Zill and James Peterson, and is based on the Achenbach Behavior Problems Checklist (Achenbach and Edelbrach 1981) and other child behavior scales. Versions of the scale differ by age group, and have been developed for children as young as age four. The BPI has been asked in 1981 and 1988 as part of the Child Health Supplement to the National Health Interview Survey (NHIS). A four-item measure also based on Achenbach's work has been included in the recently redesigned National Health Interview Survey.

Major Limitations of Existing Measures of Social Development and Problem Behavior

Of all of the categories of indicators reviewed in this chapter, this is the area in which the most work remains to be done. The most striking limitation of the current set of indicators of children's social development and problem behavior is the lack of measures for children prior to their teen years. And yet this is an area in which a great deal of measurement work has been done, both on direct measures of social development in early childhood, and on measures of family functioning and the home environment that are known to affect a child's social development and well-being (Zaslow, Brown, Coiro, and Blumenthal 1994; Love, Aber, and Brooks-Gunn 1994; Phillips and Love 1994). Though measures of this sort have appeared in previous federally sponsored surveys (including the National Survey of Children, the National Survey of Families and Households, and the National Longitudinal Survey of Youth), until very recently none have been incorporated into surveys that are to be repeated on a regular basis.

The National Center for Health Statistics has been considering incorporating some social development and family functioning measures into a NHIS child and family topical module as part of its NHIS redesign. This module, should it develop, will not be fielded before 1998 at the earliest. In addition, the school-readiness supplement to the NHES, which is scheduled to be repeated every few years, contains a number of social-development-related measures for children age three through seven that can serve as the basis for new, regularly reported indicators for young children.

A second limitation has to do with inadequate coverage of the teen population. Many of the current indicators of social development and problem behavior for teens are based on data sources that include only those teens who are still in school. While the YRBS and Monitoring the Future are valuable sources of data, they do not provide information on the very teens who are the most likely to be experiencing difficulties in these areas: those who have dropped out of school. It is important that these or other surveys, such as the NHIS, be expanded to gather regular measurements of this sort for all teens.[10]

Finally, the existing set of indicators of prosocial behavior and attitudes requires further development. Historically, considerably more time and effort have been devoted to conceptualizing and tracking negative behavior and attitudes than positive ones (see Moore 1994). Both conceptual work, determining which positive and behavioral attitudes are most important, and further data development are needed in this area.

APPENDIX

Table 1.1a   Indicators of Children's Well-Being: Available Measures from the Federal Statistical System, and Measures Discussed in This Volume: Child Health (Mortality, Health Conditions, Health Care, and Related Behavior)

Indicator	Approximate Age Group in Years				Periodicity of Measures	Geographic Level[a]	Source[b]	Chapters
	0–18	0–5	6–11	12–18				
Mortality								
1. Neonatal and post-neonatal mortality rates (per 1,000 live births)		X			annual	N,S,L	vital stats	Lantz
2. Fetal mortality rate (per 1,000 live births + fetal deaths)		X			annual	N,S,L	vital stats (fetal death report)	Lantz
3. Child mortality rate from all causes	X	X	X	X	annual	N,S,L	vital stats	
4. Teen violent death rate (accident, suicide, homicide) (ages 15–19) together and by type of death				X	annual	N,S,L	vital stats	
5. Mortality rate by cause of death (including medical vs. accidental)[c]	X	X	X	X	annual	N,S,L	vital stats	Starfield Elster
6. % of 9th- to 12th-graders who have attempted suicide in the past 12 months				X	semiannual	N,S*,L*	YRBS	
Health conditions								
7. Child Health Index: % of births rated positively on all four of the following indicators: APGAR score 9+; birth weight of 2500+ grams; gestational age of 37+ weeks; mother received prenatal care in first trimester of pregnancy		X			annual	N,S,L	vital stats	
8. Children's Health Index: % of children born with 0,1,2,3+ of the following risk factors: late or no prenatal care; low maternal weight gain(< 21 lbs.); having 3 or more siblings; mother smoked while pregnant; mother drank alcohol while pregnant; birth < 18 months from previous birth		X			annual	N,S,L	vital stats	

Table 1.1a   *Continued*

Indicator	Approximate Age Group in Years				Periodicity of Measures	Geographic Level[a]	Source[b]	Chapters
	0–18	0–5	6–11	12–18				
9. Rates of communicable diseases[d]	X	X	X	X	annual	N,S,L	CDC	Starfield
10. Rates of iron-deficiency anemia	X	X	X	X	irregular	N	NHANES	Starfield
11. Rate of elevated blood lead levels	X	X	X	X	irregular	N	NHANES	Starfield
12. Low birth weight (< 5.5 lbs.), and very low birth weight (< 3.3 lbs.)		X			annual occasional occasional	N,S,L	vital stats NNS NMIHS	Lantz
13. Proportion of births with low Apgar scores		X			annual occasional occasional	N,S,L	vital stats NNS NMIHS	Lantz
14. Proportion of births with congenital anomalies		X			annual occasional occasional	N,S,L	vital stats NNS NMIHS	Lantz
15. Proportion of infants admitted to Neonatal Intensive Care Unit		X			annual		HDC	Lantz
16. Incidence of vaccine-preventable diseases during infancy		X						Lantz
17. Global assessment of child's health (excellent, good, etc.)		X	X		annual	N	NHIS	Wolfe Starfield Takanishi
18. Play limited by health condition		X			annual	N	NHIS	Wolfe
19. Child abuse/neglect rate: reported or confirmed cases per 1,000 children	X	X	X	X	annual	N,S	NCANDS	Lantz
20. Incidence of AIDS in children and youth (0–13, 14–19, 20–24)	X	X	X	X	annual	N,S,L*	CDC	
21. Rate of syphilis, gonorrhea in 15- to 19-year-olds				X	annual	N,S,L	CDC	
22. % of 9th- to 12th-graders who have seriously considered suicide in past 12 months				X	semiannual	N,S*,L*	YRBS	Kennedy
23. Incidence of measles in children under age 18	X				annual	N,S,L	CDC	
24. % children who are limited by chronic health conditions	X	X	X	X	annual	N	NHIS	Starfield
25. % of children ever experiencing a delay in growth or development	X	X	X	X	1982, 1988	N	NHIS-CHS	Lantz Wolfe
26. Annual victimization rate among youth ages 12 to 17 from violent crime				X	annual	N,S*	NCVS	

(Table continues on p. 18.)

Table 1.1a *Continued*

Indicator	Approximate Age Group in Years				Periodicity of Measures	Geographic Level[a]	Source[b]	Chapters
	0–18	0–5	6–11	12–18				
27. Motor skills acquisition during infancy		X						Lantz
28. Cognitive development during infancy		X						Lantz
29. % of high school seniors who report being very happy				X	annual	N	MTFS	
30. Pregnancy complications (e.g., gestational diabetes, preeclampsia)		X			annual occasional occasional	N,S,L	vital stats NNS NMIHS	Lantz
31. Low maternal weight gain during pregnancy (under 16 lbs)		X			annual occasional occasional	N,S,L	vital stats NNS NMIHS	Lantz
32. Maternal use of tobacco, alcohol, and other drug use during pregnancy[e]		X			annual occasional occasional	N,S,L	vital stats NNS NMIHS	Lantz
33. Percent of teens who have had a pregnancy[f]				X				Elster
Health care								
34. % of children covered by health insurance (public,private,none)	X	X	X	X	annual	N	CPS-March	Wolfe
35. % of children with no physician visits in last 12 months	X	X X	X	X	annual occasional	N N	NHIS NHES	Mayer Wolfe
36. % of children with a usual source of health care (e.g., doctor's office, clinic)	X	X X	X	X	annual occasional	N N	NHIS NHES	Elster Wolfe
37. Number of physician visits per year.	X	X	X	X	annual	N	NHIS	
38. % preschool children who have not seen a dentist in the past year		X			occasional	N	NHES	
39. % of live births to mothers receiving prenatal care in first trimester		X			annual occasional occasional	N,S,L	vital stats NNS NMIHS	Lantz
40. % of live births to mothers receiving late or no prenatal care		X			annual occasional occasional	N,S,L	vital stats NNS NMIHS	Lantz
41. Measures of adequacy of prenatal care (Kessner and Kotelchuck indexes)[g]		X			annual occasional occasional	N,S,L	vital stats NNS NMIHS	Lantz
42. Rate of full immunization (ages infant, two, five, teens)[h]		X X		X	annual annual	N N,S	NHIS NIS	Lantz Wolfe Elster
43. % of children with accidental injuries requiring medical attention	X	X	X	X				Wolfe
44. Rate of teens seen in the emergency room with an intentional or unintentional injury				X			CDC	Elster

Table 1.1a   *Continued*

Indicator	Approximate Age Group in Years 0–18	0–5	6–11	12–18	Periodicity of Measures	Geographic Level[a]	Source[b]	Chapters
45. % of teens who have had a preventive visit during which they were screened for sexual behavior, use of tobacco products, and use of alcohol and other drugs				X				Elster Kennedy
46. Hospitalizations for ambulatory sensitive conditions (i.e., preventable or treatable through good primary care)	X	X	X	X			HDC	Starfield
Health-related behavior								
47. % of teens who drink alcohol (daily, in previous month)				X	semiannual	N,S*,L*	YRBS	Elster Kennedy
48. % of 9th- to 12th-graders who are sexually active				X	semiannual	N,S*,L*	YRBS	Kennedy
49. Rate of birth control use, by type, among 9th- to 12th-graders				X	semiannual every 6 years	N,S*,L* N	YRBS NSFG	Kennedy
50. % of 9th- to 12th-graders who have driven drunk (or with a drunk driver) in the past 30 days				X	semiannual	N,S*,L*	YRBS	Elster Kennedy
51. % of teens who have carried a weapon to school in last month				X	semiannual	N,S*,L*	YRBS	Elster Kennedy
52. % of teens who smoke daily (or regularly)[i]				X	semiannual 1–3-year intervals	N,S*,L* N	YRBS NHSDA	Elster Kennedy
53. % teens who have had unprotected intercourse at last episode[j]				X	semiannual	N	YRBS	Elster Kennedy
54. % of children who regularly use seat belts	X	X	X	X	annual semiannual	N N,S*,L*	NHIS YRBS	Takanishi Kennedy
55. Rate of bicycle helmet use			X	X	annual semiannual	N N,S*,L*	NHIS YRBS	
56. % of homes containing unlocked and loaded guns	X	X	X	X				Starfield
57. Excessive television viewing	X	X	X	X	semiannual	N,S	NAEP	Starfield
58. % of teens getting adequate sleep				X				Takanishi
59. % 9th- to 12th-graders with a healthy diet[k]				X	semiannual	N,S*,L*	YRBS	Takanishi
60. Criminal victimization of youth ages 12–20				X	annual	N	NCVS	Mayer

Source: Prepared by Child Trends, Inc.

[a]N = Nation, S = State, L = Local Area, S* = Selected States, L* = Selected Local Areas

[b]Government entities administering the state and local surveys are not required to make information from the surveys public, though most of them do. National-level information is available through the Centers for Disease Control and Prevention
[c]Including death from alcohol-related vehicle crash for teens
[d]Currently, reporting is incomplete
[e]Problems with underreporting on use of illegal drugs
[f]Can be calculated from administrative data on births and abortions
[g]Combine timing and total number of visits, while adjusting for gestational age.
[h]NIS survey covers two-year-olds only
[i]See table 1.5a for additional measures
[j]YRBS asks about last year rather than last episode
[k]A measure would have to be constructed from the diet questions in the YRBS

Table 1.2a Indicators of Children's Well-Being: Available Measures from the Federal Statistical System, and Measures Discussed in the Conference Papers: Education and Child Care (Enrollment, Achievement/Proficiency, Related Behavior, School Characteristics, and Child Care)

Indicator	Approximate Age Group in Years				Periodicity of Measures	Geographic Level[a]	Source[b]	Chapters
	0–18	0–5	6–11	12–18				
Enrollment								
1. % of pre-K 3- to 5-year-olds enrolled in center-based programs		X			semiannual	N	NHES	
2. Preschool enrollment rate of 3- to 4-year-olds		X			annual	N	CPS-Oct	
3. % of eligible children enrolled in head start		X			semiannual	N	NHES	
4. % of children ages 6 to 7 who have repeated 1st or 2nd grade			X		semiannual	N	NHES	Phillips
5. % students ages 7 to 17 who are behind age-for-grade	X		X	X	annual	N	CPS-Oct	
6. % of 14- to 17-year-olds enrolled in school				X	annual	N	CPS-Oct	
7. % of 18- to 24-year-olds who are high school dropouts				X	annual	N	CPS-Oct	
8. % of 19- to 20-year-olds who lack a high school credential					annual	N	CPS-Oct	
9. Proportion of 21- to 22-year-olds who have completed high school[c]					annual	N	CPS-Oct	Hauser
10. Proportion of 10th- to 12th-graders who dropped out of high school during the past year[d]				X	annual	N	CPS-Oct	Hauser
11. On-time graduation (the % of 9th-graders who graduate from high school four years later)				X	annual	N, S	CCD	
12. Average net cost of college tuition for low-, middle-, and high-income students (net of grants)[e]								Kane
13. Average annual earnings foregone by students ages 18–24 attending college[f]							CPS, all months combined	Kane

Table 1.2a *Continued*

Indicator	Approximate Age Group in Years 0–18	0–5	6–11	12–18	Periodicity of Measures	Geographic Level[a]	Source[b]	Chapters
14. Long-term payoff to postsecondary education of various sorts								Kane
15. Percent of postsecondary students enrolled in two-year, four-year, and vocational schools						N	CPS-Oct	
Achievement/proficiency								
16. Approaches to learning (e.g., task persistence, impulse control, attentiveness, curiosity, creativity, cooperativeness, and independence)[g]	X	X						Phillips
17. Proportion of kindergartners who are "unready" for kindergarten[h]		X			occasional	N	NHES	Phillips
18. Emergent literacy and numeracy development[i]		X			occasional	N	NHES:93	Phillips
19. Reading and math achievement for 4th-, 8th-, and 12th-graders: % of children demonstrating proficient or advanced achievement in these areas			X	X	semiannual	N,S*	NAEP	Phillips
20. Reading and math achievement ages 5–12[j]			X		semiannual	N	NLSY PSID	Smith
21. Science and writing achievement for 4th-, 8th-, and 12th-graders: % of children demonstrating proficient or advanced achievement in these areas			X	X	every 4 years	N,S*	NAEP	Phillips
22. U.S. history and geography achievement for 4th-, 8th-, and 12th-graders: % of children demonstrating proficient or advanced achievement in these areas			X	X	every 4–6 years	N,S*	NAEP	Phillips
23. Average SAT scores for college-bound high school seniors (math and verbal)				X	annual	N,S,L	ETS	
Related behavior and characteristics								
24. % of children ages 3–5 who are read to (every day, frequently) by a parent or household member		X			occasional	N	NHES	Phillips
25. % pre-K children ages 3–5 who are told stories 3+ times per week by a parent or household member		X			occasional	N	NHES	

(Table continues on p. 22)

Table 1.2a   *Continued*

Indicator	Approximate Age Group in Years				Periodicity of Measures	Geographic Level[a]	Source[b]	Chapters
	0–18	0–5	6–11	12–18				
26. % pre-K children ages 3–5 who were taken to the library 1+ times in the last month		X			occasional	N	NHES	
27. % pre-K children who engaged in songs, music, or art with parent or other household member in last month		X			occasional	N	NHES	
28. Learning opportunities: % of pre-K children ages 3–5 whose parents regularly engage them in the following activities: play, concert, art gallery, museum, zoo, errands, household chores, discussion of family history or ethnic heritage, events sponsored by community or religious groups		X			occasional	N	NHES	
29. Parental involvement in school and school-related activities	X	X		X	occasional	N	NHES	Phillips
30. Number of hours of homework each day (4th, 8th, and 12th grade)			X	X	semiannual	N,S*	NAEP	
31. % students reading 10+ pages per day (4th, 8th, and 12th grade)			X	X	semiannual	N,S*	NAEP	
32. % students absent 3+ days in previous month (4th, 8th, and 12th grade)			X	X	semiannual	N,S*	NAEP	Phillips
33. % students watching 6+ hours of television per day (4th, 8th, and 12th grade)			X	X	semiannual	N,S*	NAEP	
34. % of children ages 3+ who ever had learning disabilities		X	X	X	1982, 1988	N	NHIS-CHS	
		X			occasional	N	NHES	
35. % of high school seniors who intend to go to college				X	annual	N	MTFS	
36. % of students with positive attitudes toward mathematics, sciences (4th, 8th, and 12th grade)			X	X	semiannual	N,S*	NAEP	
School characteristics								
37. Where English is not the primary language, proportion of children who are instructed in their native language		X			occasional	N	NHES	Phillips

Table 1.2a   *Continued*

Indicator	Approximate Age Group in Years				Periodicity of Measures	Geographic Level[a]	Source[b]	Chapters
	0–18	0–5	6–11	12–18				
38. % of children in troubled schools, defined as schools with significant student behavioral, conduct, or staff morale problems			X	X	every 3–4 years	N,S	SASS	
39. Proportion of children exposed to bilingual education			X	X				Phillips
40. Average expenditures per student			X	X	annual	N,S	CCD	
Child care								
41. Quality of care		X						Phillips
42. Stability of care		X			annual	N	SIPP (child-care module)	Phillips Smith
					annual	N	NLSY	
43. Type and mix of child care[k]		X			annual	N	SIPP	Smith
44. Proportion of eligible children in early intervention programs		X						Phillips
45. Proportion of children under age 13 in latchkey situations			X		annual	N	SIPP (child-care module)	Phillips
46. Ratio of child-care costs to family income		X			annual	N	SIPP (child-care module)	Phillips
47. Proportion of parents who are satisfied with their child-care arrangements		X						Phillips
48. Proportion of children from non-English-speaking homes who have access to providers that speak the home language		X						Phillips
49. Amount of time parent spends with child on a typical day	X	X	X	X	one-time	N	PSID	Smith
50. HOME environment scale		X	X		semiannual	N	NLSY	Smith
51. Child care caregiver's educational background		X			annual one-time	N	NLSY PSID	Smith
52. Adult/child ratio in child care setting		X			annual one-time	N	NLSY PSID	Smith

Source: Prepared by Child Trends, Inc.

[a]N = Nation, S = State, L = Local Area, S* = Selected States, L* = Selected Local Areas

[b]Government entities administering the state and local surveys are not required to make information from the surveys public, though most of them do. National-level information is available through the Centers for Disease Control and Prevention

[c]Hauser recommends using three-year moving averages for stability. Author recommends combining "12th grade, no diploma" with high school graduates

[d]Author recommends combining "12th grade, no diploma" with high school graduates

[e]Could be produced through annual surveys of state financial aid offices, who could calculate the level of aid available to students with standard low-income, medium-, and high-income profiles

[f]Kane has worked out a formula to estimate this

[g]Phillips suggests teachers' ratings as the means to collect this information efficiently

(*Table notes continue on p. 24.*)

[b]Questions include whether kindergarten was repeated, and whether child received any special help with reading, math, speech, learning disability, or English as a second language

[i]Phillips offers the PPVT and Early Screening Inventory as possible measures for future surveys

[j]PIAT Achievement

[k]Type of organized care, and informal care by relationship to provider

[l]Based on data from time diary

Table 1.3a   Indicators of Children's Well-Being: Available Measures from the Federal Statistical System, and Measures Discussed in This Volume: Economic Security (Poverty/Income, Support Programs, Employment, Housing and Other Consumption)

Indicator	Approximate Age Group in Years				Periodicity of Measures	Geographic Level[a]	Source[b]	Chapters
	0–18	0–5	6–11	12–18				
Poverty/income								
1. % of children in poverty	X	X	X	X	annual	N	CPS-March	
					annual	N	SIPP	
					decennial	N,S,L	Census	Mayer
2. Average monthly poverty rate for children	X	X	X	X	annual	N	SIPP	Duncan
3. Multiyear rates of poverty for children	X	X	X	X	annual	N	SIPP	Duncan
					annual	N	PSID	
4. Rates of transitions into and out of poverty[c]	X	X	X	X	annual	N	SIPP	Duncan
5. % of children at or near poverty (<150% or <200% of poverty line)	X	X	X	X	annual	N	CPS-March	
					annual	N	SIPP	
					decennial	N,S,L	Census	
6. % of children in extreme poverty (<50% of poverty line)	X	X	X	X	annual	N	CPS-March	
					annual	N	SIPP	
					decennial	N,S,L	Census	
7. Median income of families with children	X	X	X	X	annual	N	CPS-March	
					annual	N	SIPP	Mayer
					decennial	N,S,L	Census	
8. Percent of children in high-income households.	X	X	X	X	annual	N	CPS-March	
					annual	N	SIPP	
					decennial	N,S,L	Census	
9. % of eligible families *not* receiving child-support payments					annual	N	CPS-April	
					annual	N	SIPP	
10. % of mother-headed families receiving child support or alimony					annual	N	CPS-April	
					annual	N	SIPP	
11. Percent of children's households containing selected durables	X	X	X	X	annual	N	CEX	Mayer
Government support programs								
12. % of children in families receiving AFDC or food stamps in past year	X	X	X	X	annual	N	CPS-March	
					annual	N	SIPP	
13. Average monthly rate of AFDC recipiency for children	X	X	X	X	annual	N	SIPP	Duncan
14. Multiyear rates of AFDC receipt for children	X	X	X	X	annual	N	SIPP	Duncan
					annual	N	PSID	
15. % of children in families receiving food stamps in past year[d]	X	X	X	X	annual	N	CPS-March	Duncan
					annual	N	SIPP	

Table 1.3a   *Continued*

Indicator	Approximate Age Group in Years				Periodicity of Measures	Geographic Level[a]	Source[b]	Chapters
	0–18	0–5	6–11	12–18				
16. % of children in families in subsidized or public housing	X	X	X	X	annual annual	N N	CPS-March SIPP	Duncan
17. Rate of intergenerational welfare dependence[e]	X				annual	N	PSID	Duncan
18. % of children in families receiving energy assistance in past year	X	X	X	X	annual annual	N N	CPS-March SIPP	Duncan
19. % of children receiving free or reduced-price lunches	X	X	X	X	annual annual	N N	CPS-March SIPP	Duncan
20. Percent of children in families receiving any means-tested federal support	X	X	X	X	annual annual	N N	CPS-March SIPP	
Employment (parent and youth)								
21. % of children less than age (1,3,6,18) where both parents or only parent are working	X	X	X	X	annual annual decennial	N N N,S,L	CPS-March SIPP Census	
22. % of children less than age (1,3,6,18) whose mothers are in the labor force	X	X	X	X	annual annual decennial	N N N,S,L	CPS-March SIPP Census	
23. % of children with no parents in the labor force	X	X	X	X	annual annual decennial	N N N,S,L	CPS-March SIPP Census	
24. Average hours worked per week by parents (both mother and father)	X	X	X	X	annual	N N	CPS-March SIPP	Smith Mayer
25. Percent of children with 1+ parents working long hours (50+ hours per week)	X	X	X	X	annual annual	N N	CPS-March SIPP	
26. Number of job changes in the previous year[f]	X	X	X	X		N	NLSY	Smith
27. Occupational complexity of parents' jobs[g]	X	X	X	X		N	CPS	Smith
28. Parental unemployment rate by reason for and length of unemployment	X	X	X	X		N	CPS	Smith
29. % of children where no parent is fully employed (full time, full year)	X	X	X	X	annual annual	N N	CPS-March SIPP	
30. Percent of fathers who are: in the labor force; unemployed; employed	X	X	X	X	annual	N	CPS-March	Mayer
31. Percent of mothers who are: in the labor force; unemployed; employed	X	X	X	X	annual	N	CPS-March	Mayer

(*Table continues on p. 26.*)

Table 1.3a   *Continued*

Indicator	Approximate Age Group in Years				Periodicity of Measures	Geographic Level[a]	Source[b]	Chapters
	0–18	0–5	6–11	12–18				
32. Level of maternal job satisfaction	X	X	X	X	annual	N	NLSY	Smith
33. Length of maternal leave taken		X			annual one-time	N	NLSY PSID	Smith
34. Average hours per week of parental time available to children[h]	X	X	X	X	annual	N	CPS-March	Mayer
35. % of youth ages 16–19 who are unemployed				X	annual annual	N N	CPS-March SIPP	
36. % of youth ages 16–19 who are idle in a given week (not in school and not at work)				X	annual annual	N N	CPS-March SIPP	
37. Youth's attitudes toward work				X	annual	N	NLSY	Smith
Housing and other consumption								
38. % of children living in crowded conditions (<1 room per person)	X	X	X	X	semiannual decennial	N,L* N,S,L	AHS Census	
39. % of children living in houses without complete plumbing or kitchen facilities	X	X	X	X	semiannual decennial	N,L* N,S,L	AHS Census	
40. % of children living in inadequate housing (severe or moderate physical problems)	X	X	X	X	semiannual	N,L*	AHS	Mayer
41. % of children in families where housing costs exceed 50% of family income	X	X	X	X	semiannual decennial	N,L* N,S,L	AHS Census	Mayer
42. % of families that sometimes do not have enough to eat[i]	X	X	X	X		N	SIPP	Mayer
43. Annual average consumption of children's families, for each income quintile	X	X	X	X	annual	N	CEX	Mayer

Source: Prepared by Child Trends, Inc.

[a]N = Nation, S = State, L = Local Area, S* = Selected States, L* = Selected Local Areas
[b]Government entities administering the state and local surveys are not required to make information from the surveys public, though most of them do. National-level information is available through the Centers for Disease Control and Prevention
[c]Based on monthly data from SIPP. Some methodological work needed to determine optimal measurements. Rates of transition by cause (e.g., marriage, fertility, work, etc.) should also be developed
[d]Duncan recommends rates of transitions onto and off of each major assistance program. He also recommends that entrances and exits be tracked by events associated with the transition
[e]This measures the proportion of persons receiving welfare as adults who were also on welfare as children
[f]This is a measure of employment stability. Separate rates for full-time and part-time job changes are recommended
[g]Higher levels of job complexity among mothers have been shown to be beneficial to children
[h]Can measure total hours per family with children, or hours per child. The two produce very different trends
[i]This may not be regularly asked

Table 1.4a   Indicators of Children's Well-Being: Available Measures from the Federal Statistical System, and Measures Discussed in This Volume: Population, Family, and Neighborhood

Indicator	0–18	0–5	6–11	12–18	Periodicity of Measures	Geographic Level[a]	Source[b]	Chapters
Population characteristics								
1. Number of children	X	X	X	X	annual	N	CPS-March	
					annual	N	SIPP	
					decennial	N,S,L	Census	
2. Children as a percent of the total population	X	X	X	X	annual	N	CPS-March	
					annual	N	SIPP	
					decennial	N,S,L	Census	
3. % of children in major race/ethnicity groups[c]	X	X	X	X	annual	N	CPS-March	Hogan
					annual	N	SIPP	
					decennial	N,S,L	Census	
4. % of children who have moved within the last year, by type of move (intracounty, intercounty, interstate)	X	X	X	X	annual	N	CPS-March	
5. % of children who are linguistically isolated, defined as living in a household where no one age 14 or older speaks English exclusively or very well			X	X	decennial	N,S,L	Census	
6. % of children who are immigrants[d]	X	X	X	X	annual	N	CPS-March	Hogan
					decennial	N,S,L	Census	
7. % of children < age 5 in child care		X			annual	N	SIPP	
Family and household characteristics								
8. Number of children in household	X				annual	N	CPS-March	Hogan
					annual	N	SIPP	
					decennial	N,S,L	Census	
9. % of children in each of the following living situations: married couple, stepparent, cohabiting parents, single female parent, single male parent, no parent[e]	X	X	X	X	annual	N	CPS-March	Sandefur
					annual	N	SIPP	
					decennial	N,S,L	Census	
10. Noncustodial parent: legal custody arrangements, proximity, time spent with child	X	X	X	X	annual	N	CPS-April	Sandefur
					annual	N	SIPP	
11. Adult/child or parent/child ratio	X				annual	N	CPS-March	Sandefur
					annual	N	SIPP	
					decennial	N,S,L	Census	
12. % of children living in institutions or group quarters	X	X	X	X	decennial	N,S,L	Census	

(*Table continues on p. 28.*)

Table 1.4a   *Continued*

Indicator	Approximate Age Group in Years				Periodicity of Measures	Geographic Level[a]	Source[b]	Chapters
	0–18	0–5	6–11	12–18				
13. % of children living in related and unrelated subfamilies	X	X	X	X	annual annual decennial	N N N,S,L	CPS-March SIPP Census	
14. % of households with children	X	X	X	X	annual annual decennial	N N N,S,L	CPS-March SIPP Census	
15. % of children who ever lived in foster care	X							Sandefur
16. % of children who are living in foster care					annual	N	NCANDS	
17. % of children who went to live with someone other than their parents for 1+ months in previous year	X	X	X	X				Sandefur
18. % births to unmarried women				X	annual	N,S,L	vital stats	
19. % teen births to unmarried teen females				X	annual	N,S,L	vital stats	
20. Teen birth rate (ages 15–17, 18–19)				X	annual	N,S,L	vital stats	
21. Second births to teen females: rate per 1,000				X	annual	N,S,L	vital stats	
22. New family index: (% first births to women with <12 years schooling, unmarried, and under age 20)		X		X	annual decennial	N,S,L N,S,L	vital stats Census	
23. Child abuse (physical, emotional, sexual) and neglect (substantiated cases)[f]	X	X	X	X	annual	N,S	NCANDS	Sandefur
Neighborhood characteristics								
24. % of children living in severely distressed neighborhoods, defined as census tracts 1+ standard deviations beyond the mean level in 4 of 5 characteristics: poverty, female-headed families, high school dropouts, males unattached to the labor force, and families receiving public assistance	X	X	X	X	decennial	N,S,L	Census	
25. % who live in high poverty neighborhoods (40+ percent poor)	X	X	X	X	decennial	N,S,L	Census	

Table 1.4a   *Continued*

Indicator	Approximate Age Group in Years				Periodicity of Measures	Geographic Level[a]	Source[b]	Chapters
	0–18	0–5	6–11	12–18				
26. % of high school se-niors who would not want to live in an area where most of the neighbors were of other races				X	annual	N	MTFS	
27. Neighborhood dem-ographic composi-tion (e.g., family structure, education levels, income, wel-fare use, mobility status, employment rates)	X	X	X	X	decennial	N,S,L	Census	Furstenberg
28. Neighborhood phys-ical infrastructure (e.g., quality of housing, percent rentals, presence of graffiti)[g]	X	X	X	X	biennial	N,L*	AHS	Furstenberg
29. Neighborhood insti-tutions.[h] Outside: availability of police, social welfare, health clinics, libraries. In-side: local busi-nesses, churches, community centers	X	X	X	X				Furstenberg
30. Degree of social or-ganization: social capital (shared norms, reciprocal obligation networks), dysfunctional orga-nization (deviant culture, gangs)[i]	X	X	X	X				Furstenberg

Source: Prepared by Child Trends, Inc.

[a] N = Nation, S = State, L = Local Area, S* = Selected States, L* = Selected Local Areas

[b] Government entities administering the state and local surveys are not required to make information from the surveys public, though most of them do. National-level information is available through the Centers for Disease Control and Prevention

[c] Recommended categories: for Census: non-Hispanic white, black, Latino (nonblack), Asian and Pacific Islander, and Native American for CPS: nonblack non-Hispanics, nonblack Hispanics, and blacks

[d] Hogan recommends including both foreign-born and native-born of foreign-born parent(s)

[e] Only SIPP allows for identification of stepparent and cohabiting parent families

[f] Conflict Tactics Scale and Child Abuse Potential Inventory recommended as measures for future surveys

[g] Graffiti measures not available through AHS

[h] Should include measures of presence, parental awareness, and use

[i] Very difficult to measure

Table 1.5a   Indicators of Children's Well-Being: Available Measures from the Federal Statistical System, and Measures Discussed in This Volume: Social Development and Problem Behavior

Indicator	Approximate Age Group in Years				Periodicity of Measures	Geographic Level[a]	Source[b]	Chapters
	0–18	0–5	6–11	12–18				
Prosocial behavior and attitudes, and positive development								
1. % 0–3-year-olds with trusting relationship with primary caregiver		X						Aber
2. % of children with a sense of basic security (ages 0–3)[c]		X						Aber
3. % of children who are actively curious, exploratory, and inquisitive (ages 2–5)		X						Aber
4. % of children who are self-regulating (ages 4–7)[d]			X					Aber
5. % of children who are suitably flexible in adjusting to new environments			X					Aber
6. % of children with good conflict resolution and interpersonal problem-solving skills[e]			X					Aber
7. % of children with strong, positive self-image (competent, efficacious)[f]			X					Aber
8. Rate of participation in organized sports among teens				X	semiannual	N,S*,L*	YRBS	Takanishi
9. Frequency of church attendance among high school seniors				X	annual	N	MTFS	
10. % high school seniors for whom religion plays an important role in their lives				X	annual	N	MTFS	
11. % of high school seniors who believe that the following life goals are extremely important: being successful at work; having strong friendships; having a good family life; having lots of money; making a contribution to society; working to correct social inequities; being a leader in the community				X	annual	N	MTFS	

Table 1.5a   *Continued*

Indicator	Approximate Age Group in Years				Periodicity of Measures	Geographic Level[a]	Source[b]	Chapters
	0–18	0–5	6–11	12–18				
12. % of high school seniors who often worry about the following national problems: crime and violence; drugs; hunger and poverty; race relations; nuclear war; economic problems; pollution				X	annual	N	MTFS	
13. % of high school seniors who see friends, read, do sports, work around the house, play music, do art, or write on a daily basis				X	annual	N	MTFS	
14. % of children in grades 6–12 reporting peer approval of hard work and good behavior				X	occasional	N	NHES	
15. % of youth age 18 who are registered to vote[g]				X	annual	N	CPS-Oct	Takanishi
16. % of youth who perceive socioeconomic opportunities, and believe that they can attain them[h]				X				Takanishi
17. % of youth who have high aspirations for postsecondary education				X				Takanishi
18. Mental health: capacity to cope with stress, and to engage in personally meaningful activities				X				Takanishi
19. % of youth involved in postsecondary education[i]				X				Takanishi
20. Knowledge and skills for making choices about responsible parenthood[j]				X				Takanishi
21. Citizenship knowledge				X	occasional	N	NHES	Takanishi
Problem behavior, attitudes, and outcomes								
22. % of children with high rates of behavior problems, as measured by the Behavior Problems Index (BPI)	X	X	X	X	1982, 1988	N	NHIS-CHS NLSY	Love Smith
23. % of children with learning disabilities	X	X	X	X				Love
24. % of children with developmental delays	X	X	X	X				Love

(*Table continues on p. 32.*)

Table 1.5a   *Continued*

Indicator	0–18	0–5	6–11	12–18	Periodicity of Measures	Geographic Level[a]	Source[b]	Chapters
25. % of youths ages 10–17 arrested for violent crimes in the past year				X	annual	N,S	UCR	Kennedy
26. % 9th- to 12th-graders who have carried weapons (knife, gun, club) in last 30 days				X	semiannual	N,S*,L*	YRBS	Kennedy
27. % of teens who were in a fight in the last 30 days				X	semiannual	N,S*,L*	YRBS	Kennedy
28. Cigarettes: % of teens who smoke cigarettes regularly				X	1–3-year intervals / annual / semiannual	N / N / N,S*,L*	NHSDA / MTFS / YRBS	Elster Kennedy
29. Problem drinking: % of teens who have had 5 or more drinks in a single evening in the last 30 days				X	1–3-year intervals / annual / semiannual	N / N / N,S*,L*	NHSDA / MTFS / YRBS	Elster Kennedy
30. Substance abuse: % of teens who have used illicit drugs (e.g., marijuana, cocaine, crack, LSD, PCP, ecstasy, mushrooms, speed, ice, heroin, or pills) without a prescription, in the last 30 days				X	1–3-year intervals / annual / semiannual	N / N / N,S*,L*	NHSDA / MTFS / YRBS	Kennedy
31. % of teens who have had unprotected intercourse within the last year				X	semiannual	N,S*,L*	YRBS	Elster Kennedy
32. % of teens who are sexually active				X	semiannual	N,S*,L*	YRBS	Kennedy
33. Number of sexual partners				X	semiannual / every 6 years	N / N	YRBS / NSFG	Kennedy
34. Teen abortion rate[k]				X	annual	N,S*	CDC Allen Guttmacher	Kennedy
35. % of teens who report peer approval of smoking tobacco, drinking alcohol				X	annual / occasional	N / N	MTFS / NHES	

Source: Prepared by Child Trends, Inc.

[a]N = Nation, S = State, L = Local Area, S* = Selected States, L* = Selected Local Areas
[b]Government entities administering the state and local surveys are not required to make information from the surveys public, though most of them do. National-level information is available through the Centers for Disease Control and Prevention
[c]Measures include home-based and center-based Q-Sort
[d]California Q-Sort as a suitable measure
[e]Possible measures include the Attributional bias scale, and the social problem-solving measure
[f]Possible measure: PCCS child assessment
[g]May have to look at a wider age range to get subgroup data
[h]Such questions are in the NLSY
[i]No specific age group was specified.

[1]Areas would include knowledge about child development, parenting skills, basic human reproduction, birth control, prenatal health, STDs, threats to good health, knowledge of social and family-planning services
[2]Not all states report

NOTES

1. Birth certificate forms have, with minor exceptions, been standardized across the fifty states and the District of Columbia. Differences in data quality across states do remain, however.

2. Annual estimates of immunization rates for two-year-olds for each of the fifty states have been produced since 1994 based on data from the National Immunization Survey, a joint project of the National Center for Health Statistics and the National Immunization Program of the Centers for Disease Control and Prevention.

3. Indicators related to cigarette smoking, alcohol consumption, and substance abuse are listed in table 1.5a of the appendix, titled Social Development and Problem Behavior.

4. State assessments have been limited to math, reading, writing, and science.

5. In addition, data to be collected in the Early Childhood Longitudinal Survey, a one-time special survey sponsored by the Department of Education, will also meet the need for better data on school readiness and achievement among young children.

6. Frequent residential moves have been associated with subsequent academic and other difficulties (Coleman 1988).

7. Linguistic isolation is defined as any child age five or over living in a household where there is no person age fourteen or over who speaks English only or very well.

8. This indicator was originally developed by Christine Nord and Nicholas Zill for the national Kids Count Report (Annie E. Casey Foundation 1993).

9. See Annie E. Casey Foundation 1994, for details.

10. This was done on a one-time basis in 1992, when questions from the Youth Risk Behavior Survey were added to the National Health Interview Survey. The questions were given to a nationally representative sample of all children ages twelve and over, regardless of student status.

REFERENCES

Achenbach, T. M., and C. S. Edelbrock 1981. "Behavior Problems and Competencies Reported by Parents of Normal and Disturbed Children Aged Four through Sixteen." *Monographs of the Society for Research in Child Development* 46 (188): 1–82.

Annie E. Casey Foundation. 1993. *Kids Count Data Book: State Profiles of Child Well-Being*. Baltimore, Md.: Annie E. Casey Foundation.

———. 1994. *Kids Count Data Book: State Profiles of Child Well-Being*. Baltimore, Md.: Annie E. Casey Foundation.

Brown, Brett, and Christopher Botsko. 1996. *A Guide to State and Local-Level Indicators of Child Well-Being Available Through the Federal Statistical System*. Baltimore, Md.: Annie E. Casey Foundation.

Brown, Brett, and Matt Stagner, eds. 1996. *Trends in the Well-Being of America's Children and Youth*. Washington, D.C.: U.S. Department of Health and Human Services, Assistant Secretary for Planning and Evaluation.

Center For Health Economics Research. 1993. *Access to Health Care Key Indicators for Policy*. Princeton, N.J.: The Robert Wood Johnson Foundation.

Center for the Study of Social Study. 1994. *A Start-Up List of Outcome Measures with Annotations*. Washington, D.C.: Center for the Study of Social Study.

Child Trends. 1993. *Researching the Family: A Guide to Survey and Statistical Data on U.S. Families.* Washington, D.C.: Child Trends, Inc.

Children's Defense Fund. 1994. *The State of America's Children Yearbook 1994.* Washington, D.C. Children's Defense Fund.

Coleman, J. 1988. "Social Capital in the Creation of Human Capital." *American Journal of Sociology* 94: s95–s120.

Duncan, G., J. Brooks-Gunn, and P. K. Klebanov. 1994. "Economic Deprivation and Early-Childhood Development." *Child Development* 62 (2): 296–318.

Hernandez, Don. 1993. *We the American Children.* Washington: U.S. Government Printing Office for U.S. Department of Commerce.

Hernandez, D., and D. Myers. 1980. *America's Children Resources from Family, Government, and the Economy.* New York: Russell Sage Foundation.

Hetherington, E. M., and W. G. Clingempeel. 1992. "Coping with Marital Transitions: A Family Systems Perspective." *Monographs of the Society for Research in Child Development* 57 (227): 2–3.

Love, J., L. Aber, and J. Brooks-Gunn. 1994. *Strategies for Assessing Community Progress Toward Achieving the First National Education Goal.* Princeton, N.J. October 1994.

Maternal and Child Health Bureau. U.S. Department of Health and Human Services. 1993. *Child Health USA '92.* Washington: U.S. Government Printing Office.

Moore, K. 1994. "Criteria for Indicators of Child Well-Being. Paper presented at the Conference on Indicators of Children's Well-Being, Bethesda, Md. (November 17–18, 1994).

———. 1991. *A State-by-State Look at Teenage Childbearing in the U.S.* Flint, Mich.: The Charles Stewart Mott Foundation.

Moore, K., and M. A. Snyder. 1994. *Facts at a Glance.* Washington, D.C.: Child Trends, Inc.

National Center for Child Abuse and Neglect. U.S. Department of Health and Human Services. 1994. *Child Maltreatment 1992: Reports from the States to the National Center on Child Abuse and Neglect.* Washington: U.S. Government Printing Office.

National Commission on Children. 1993. *Just the Facts: A Summary of Recent Information on America's Children and Their Families.* Washington, D.C.: National Commission on Children.

National Education Goals Panel. 1993. *The National Education Goals Report, Volume One: The National Report.* Washington, D.C.: National Education Goals Panel.

National Education Goals Panel. 1993. *The National Education Goals Report, Volume Two: State Reports.* Washington, D.C.: National Education Goals Panel.

Nord, C., and N. Zill. 1994. *Running in Place: How American Families Are Faring in a Changing Economy and an Individual Society.* Washington, D.C.: Child Trends, Inc.

Phillips, D., and J. Love. 1994. *Indicators for School Readiness, Schooling, and Child Care in Early to Middle Childhood.* Paper presented at the Conference on Indicators of Children's Well-Being. Bethesda, Md. (November 17–18, 1994).

Pollard, K. M., and M. F. Riche. 1994. "The Current Population Survey and Kids Count: A Report to the Annie E. Casey Foundation." Working Paper. Washington, D.C.: Population Reference Bureau.

The Population Reference Bureau. 1992. *The Challenge of Change: What the 1990 Census Tells Us About Children.* Washington, D.C.: Center for the Study of Social Policy.

Schorr, L., F. Farrow, D. Hornbeck, and S. Watson. 1994. *The Case for Shifting to Results-Based Accountability.* Washington, D.C.: Center for the Study of Social Policy.

United Way of America. 1993. *Standards for Success: Building Community Supports for America's Children.* Alexandria, Va.: United Way of America.

U.S. Department of Education. 1993. *Youth Indicators: Trends in the Well-Being of American Youth.* Washington: U.S. Government Printing Office.

U.S. Department of Health and Human Services. 1990–1991. *Chronic Disease and Health Promotion: 1990–1991*. Youth Risk Behavior Surveillance System. Reprints from the MMWR. Atlanta, Georgia, National Center for Chronic Disease Prevention and Health Promotion.

U.S. House of Representatives, Committee on Children, Youth and Families. 1989. *U.S. Children and Their Families: Current Conditions and Recent Trends, 1989*. Washington: U.S. Government Printing Office.

Zaslow, M., B. Brown, M. J. Coiro, and C. Blumenthal. 1994. *Assessing Family Functioning in Community-Level Interventions for Families and Children*. Washington, D.C.: Child Trends, Inc.

2

Criteria for Indicators of Child Well-Being

Kristin A. Moore

ARE THE CIRCUMSTANCES of children growing worse, or not?[1] Are U.S. families falling apart, or not?

How people answer these questions will vary substantially, depending upon where they live, their economic situation, their age, their personal values, their political party affiliation, and whether their focus is on trends in children's health, education, income, or family size.

Yet, one could ask similar questions about the economy and get relatively consistent answers from different people. The economy, like the family, is diverse and complex. Different regions enjoy quite different levels of prosperity, and different industries have quite varied earnings situations and prospects for the future. Yet, we have a set of economic indicators that are quite widely accepted as markers of the country's well-being: the rate of inflation, the Gross National Product (GNP), the unemployment rate, the Dow Jones average, and the poverty rate, for example. Our common understanding of these indicators guides public policy, influences the directions of private organizations, and affects individual decisionmaking as well. We take economic indicators seriously, even when real concerns exist about their validity (Ruggles 1990). Indeed, considerable resources are invested in maintaining and monitoring economic indicators. Information is updated regularly, and trends are reported monthly in some cases.

The status of economic indicators stands in stark contrast to indicators of child well-being, where, despite earlier efforts (see Watts and Hernandez 1982; Select Committee on Children, Youth and Families 1989), we continue to lack not only a clear set of reliable, valid, up-to-date indicators but a consensus regarding what it is desirable to track. What set of measures can be developed that reflects a public consensus and that reliably and fully track the well-being of children and families with children? This task is, of course, the mission of this volume. To serve this mission, we need a concrete goal. Specifically, we need to think through what a system of indicators about children ought to look like.

As an initial attempt at this task, I have developed a series of criteria for child indicators. I have not tried to rank their importance, and I recognize that it may not be possible to make maximum use of them all, particularly in the short run. They are put forward to provide a common point of departure.

Table 2.1   Criteria for Indicators of Child Well-Being

1. Comprehensive coverage. Indicators should assess well-being across a broad array of outcomes, behavior, and processes.
2. Children of all ages. Age-appropriate indicators are needed at every age from birth through adolescence and covering the transition into adulthood.
3. Clear and comprehensible. Indicators should be easily and readily understood by the public.
4. Positive outcomes. Indicators should assess positive as well as negative aspects of well-being.
5. Depth, breadth, and duration. Indicators are needed that assess dispersion across given measures of well-being, children's duration in a status, and cumulative risk factors experienced by children.
6. Common interpretation. Indicators should have the same meaning in varied population subgroups.
7. Consistency over time. Indicators should have the same meaning across time.
8. Forward-looking. Indicators should be collected now that anticipate the future and provide baseline data for subsequent trends.
9. Rigorous methods. Coverage of the population or event being monitored should be complete or very high, and data collection procedures should be rigorous and consistent over time.
10. Geographically detailed. Indicators should be developed not only at the national level, but also at the state and local level.
11. Cost-efficient. Although investments in data about U.S. children have been insufficient, strategies to expand and improve the data system need to be thoughtful, well planned, and economically efficient.
12. Reflective of social goals. Some indicators should allow us to track progress in meeting national, state, and local goals for child well-being.
13. Adjusted for demographic trends. Finally, to aid with our interpretation of indicators, indicators, or a subset of indicators, should be developed that adjust for changes in the composition of the population over time that confound our ability to track well-being. Alternatively, indicators should be available for population subgroups that are sufficiently narrow to permit conclusions within that subgroup.

CRITERIA FOR SOCIAL INDICATORS OF CHILD WELL-BEING

The first criterion for a set of child indicators is comprehensiveness.

- Indicators should assess well-being across a broad array of outcomes, behavior, and processes.

Indicators that assess only one domain or type of well-being provide an incomplete and potentially biased perspective on the development and well-being of families and children. For example, while childhood mortality from communicable diseases has declined markedly, sexual activity and substance abuse pose new risks to adolescents. Similarly, while SAT scores have declined over time, improving only marginally for some subgroups, housing conditions have improved substantially for most families.

Thus, a strong set of indicators needs to include measures from varied domains, including:

- population composition and geographic distribution; fertility; mortality;
- physical health and safety; access to health care; nutrition;
- mental health; access to treatment or counseling;

- educational attainment and cognitive achievement; school and nonschool cognitive stimulation and learning experiences;
- economic well-being; housing adequacy; assets; receipt of public transfers;
- behavior problems, such as delinquency and substance abuse; positive behavior; attitudes; goals;
- family structure; contact with an absent parent (if any) and extended family members; child support; parent-child interaction and time use; children in institutions and foster care;
- workforce behavior of parents and children; child care for children; job-related benefits; and
- the child's school and neighborhood environment.

The concepts covered within each domain can and sometimes need to be represented by numerous indicators. The same domain can be examined with a focus on assets and strengths or deficits and problems. In addition, indicators are needed for children of varied ages. This leads to our second criterion.

- Age-appropriate indicators are needed at every age from birth through adolescence and covering the transition into adulthood.

Both the measures chosen and the data collection strategies employed need to vary for children of different ages. Infants, children in elementary school, and teenagers differ dramatically, and different indicators are needed to capture this variation. For example, accidents and safety in the home are indicators that are more relevant for preschoolers, while motor vehicle accidents and substance abuse are more relevant for teenagers.

The kinds of data required from younger children generally must be supplied by parents—for example, recent medical care, accidents, and behavior problems. However, child assessments have been conducted in the homes of young children age three and even younger by specially trained survey interviewers. Teachers become an excellent source of data once children reach school age. Parents continue to be an important source of information about the family into the teen years, but increasingly it is essential to query youth themselves. The need to interview teens is most obvious for risk-taking behavior such as substance abuse, sexual activity, and delinquency. However, even for more neutral topics, such as time spent watching television, the older youth is likely to provide more accurate data than the parent.

It is also important, if child indicators are to be a part of public discussion and policy debate, that they make sense to a lay audience. This leads to the third criterion:

- Indicators should be easily and readily understood by the public.

We cannot expect policymakers and the general public to spend much time mastering complex measures of well-being. Ideally, comprehension should be instantaneous. It should be possible for a person with an average education more or less to read a sentence and understand the trend.

Of course, it is not possible to cover every topic with simple and readily accessible measures. Hence, it often will be necessary to have a set of relatively more complex measures that can be mastered with a moderate level of effort to supplement the set that is broadly disseminated in the media. Even on the more complex level, however, indicators should have face validity. We do not want to divert attention away from explaining the meaning of the trends to explaining and justifying the indicator itself.

It is the case, of course, that many economic indicators lack face validity. Over time, however, people have become used to measures such as "the poverty rate" and the GNP and believe they understand them. So we should not allow ourselves to be driven to suggesting only the most obvious and simple indicators. We can also work to educate the public, the media, and policymakers.

The American press tends to highlight negative trends, and the American public tends to show particular concern about negative trends. The focus on bad news and failures may account in part for the public's pessimism regarding families and children and the widespread belief that programs to enhance outcomes are ineffective. Therefore:

• Indicators should assess both positive and negative aspects of well-being.

The government itself, because it is organized to identify needs and to address and solve problems, tends to collect data on problems, such as crime, disease, and death. So we hear about trends in drug use, violence, and sexual activity; but we rarely hear about the commitment of youth to recycling, the work youth do around the house or outside, close parent-child relationships, or the time that youth spend volunteering. We do not even hear much about neutral items, such as whether kids receive an allowance, and how much it is. Yet parents rarely content themselves only with the aspiration that their children not do drugs or avoid prison. Most parents have positive aspirations that their children will be useful, well-adjusted, and happy.

To provide a more balanced perspective, new measures need to be developed and new data need to be collected. Possible constructs include community involvement, recycling, volunteering, religious practice and activities, exercise and sports, activities in school clubs, reading and participation in cultural affairs, family activities, and work done in the home.

The lives of children are complex and multifaceted. Our indicators should reflect the complexities of children's lives. We know that long-term poverty is more problematic than short-term spells of poverty. We know that cumulative risks undermine child development more than a single risk. And we know that average values do not reflect the diversity experienced by children from varied backgrounds. Therefore, our fifth criterion is:

• Indicators are needed that assess dispersion across given measures of well-being, the duration that children spend in a given status, and which assess cumulative risk factors experienced by children.

Measures of duration can be developed to assess how long children live in varied statuses, for example, how long they have lived in poverty, the years they spend in a single-parent family, the months or years that they suffer from a chronic condition, or the time they live with both biological parents. For this task, longitudinal data are generally required. It is possible to develop longitudinal indicators from retrospective data, but the quality of the data diminishes as the interval lengthens. In fact, indicators assessed annually or biennially produce higher quality data than indicators based on data collected every five or six years (Moore and Glei 1993).

Several studies have demonstrated that children experiencing more than one risk factor face very elevated probabilities of poor outcomes (Sameroff, Seifer, Barocas, Zax, and Greenspan 1987; Moore, Nord, and Peterson 1989). However, few indicators assessing the proportion of children facing multiple risks are currently available. The data required to estimate multiple risks can come from demographic variables, such as income, parent education, and family structure; but they might also be based on measures of family processes, such as monitoring of the child's activities, parent/child joint activities, and parent involvement in school events. A very strong measure of risk could be developed on the basis of duration in multiple risk statuses, for example, the number of years a child lived in a single-parent family in poverty with four or more siblings.

Having developed these (and other) complex indicators of child well-being and risk, it is useful to go beyond universally reporting the proportion at the bottom or the average status of children. It is valuable to emphasize heterogeneity, to illustrate the varied experiences that contemporary children have living in advantageous or disadvantaged circumstances. It is as helpful to know, for example, trends in the proportion of children in environments with no or only one major risk factor, as it is to know trends in the proportion of children growing up encumbered by multiple risks.

Whether a particular indicator measures well-being over the short-term or the long-term, whether it assesses single or multiple risks, the meaning of the indicator should be comparable for persons in varied social groups. This is the sixth criterion:

• Indicators should have the same meaning in varied societal groups.

Infant mortality is a tragedy that can be measured and tracked with considerable and comparable accuracy across racial, educational, and income groups. Whether the same can be said for other topics such as attitudes about gender roles, discipline patterns, aspirations, and religiosity is an empirical question.

Little methodological research has been conducted to examine whether these kinds of indicators hold the same meaning across different groups. This is unfortunate because these are areas where American society seems to be undergoing substantial change, and these changes may have important implications for family life and children's development. In the short run, reliance on behavioral indicators represents the most cautious approach. For example, rather than assessing religious belief (a nebulous concept), it may be necessary to focus on a more tangible indicator and assess actual attendance at religious observances or services. Measures of behavior in general will be less susceptible to different meanings across societal groups than measures of feelings and attitudes. However, methodological research is needed to develop solid measures of attitudes, values, and goals, as well as behavior.

The seventh criterion is particularly important if our goal is to develop a set of indicators that can be used into the next century:

• Indicators should have the same meaning over time.

Where social indicators are concerned, it is a real challenge to develop indicators that hold their meaning across the decades. Such a fundamental measure as the proportion married, for example, has changed as formal marriage has been postponed but often been replaced by cohabitation. This change over time affects not only indicators of marriage and family structure but measures of fertility, such as the nonmarital birth rate. For some measures, such as family structure, researchers can go back and reanalyze data to provide a consistent measure over time. In the case of remarriage, for example, household records can be searched to identify cohabiting partners for a measure of family structure. However, similar reanalyses are not possible with vital statistics data.

As social conditions change, it is often tempting to abandon existing measures in favor of new indicators that more accurately describe contemporary society. In many cases, new measures are essential. The cost is that we cannot track trends if we change measures. A compromise in strategy is to collect information that permits tracking of both the original and the new indicator.

An example can be provided from work on adolescent sexual activity. Available indicators do not distinguish between voluntary and involuntary initiation of sex. However, research indicates that a substantial proportion of the first sexual experiences of girls is involuntary (Moore et al. 1989). Whether first sex is voluntary or coerced has, of course, substantial implications for services and policy, and it seems imperative that surveys collect information that makes a distinction between voluntary and nonvoluntary sexual initiation. To change the definition of sexual debut, however, destroys historical continuity and makes it impossible to assess trends in adolescent pregnancy among those at risk of pregnancy. Thus, collecting data that permit analysts to construct both the traditional and new indicators seems imperative. If it is not feasible to collect such extensive data on a regular basis, it should be possible to collect the data needed to maintain the historical measure on an intermittent basis.

This discussion leads to the eighth criterion:

• Indicators should be collected now that anticipate the future and provide baseline data for subsequent trends.

Society is becoming more technological and international. The availability of complex technology in the home, such as high-powered personal computers, laser printers, and educational games, is now a critical component of parenting that may give middle-class children a tremendous lead over low-income children. Similarly, travel to foreign countries and mastery of foreign languages and customs are becoming more common for families and for students in some school programs. Also, postsecondary education outside of college settings has become widespread, and such training can have important implications for employment and income.

We all know that these kinds of changes are occurring. Unfortunately, data over time with rigorous and consistent definitions and methods are not available to document such trends. We need to think about other changes occurring that seem likely to continue and to begin now to develop measures that can provide a baseline for the future.

The ninth criterion requires little elaboration:

• Coverage of the population or event being monitored should be complete or very high; data collection procedures should be rigorous and should not vary over time.

Response rates in American surveys have declined over the years, and this decline poses an issue for the continuity of some data series. Recently, the Office of Management and Budget has opposed payment of incentives to respondents, one strategy which might increase response rates. Consideration of the response rate in a survey should affect whether that survey is viewed as a source of indicator data.

Changes in data collection methods can also affect reporting. For example, reporting of substance abuse by teens is higher when they are able to enter data directly into a laptop computer. This methodological improvement thus appears to enhance data quality for highly sensitive topics. At the same time, however, changing over to this new method may undermine trend data. It is essential, of course, to improve methods and procedures for collecting data, but we must develop methods for calibrating the new measures with old measures, or intermittently repeat the old measures, if we are to maintain the integrity of a series of social indicators.

• Indicators should be developed not only at the national level, but also at the state and local level.

In order to assess the effect of changes in services and policies, and of social, ecological, and economic variations at the state and local level, indicators are needed that track the status and well-being of families and children at levels of geographic and political aggregation below the national level. In particular, measures are needed at the state level. With education organized at the local level, even state-level data are inadequate. At present, the vital statistics system and the decennial census provide the primary sources of local area data. As state agencies computerize and upgrade their record keeping, state child support, welfare, health, and education data systems may generate much useful information at the state and substate level that can be used to track family and child well-being.

Investments in data regarding children and families have been modest, relative to public and private expenditures on data collection for other groups such as the elderly, for current consumption, or on other social problems such as the savings and loan crisis. Hence, it is assumed that some spending increases are appropriate, especially in view of current concerns regarding the well-being of U.S. children. Yet with a substantial federal deficit and high taxpayer resistance to new taxes, ways to hold down the cost of obtaining and processing indicators data must be considered thoughtfully.

• While cost should not be the driving force behind decisionmaking, planners should consider cost as design decisions are made.

Costs can be minimized by employing data from social indicators that were originally collected for other purposes, as was done with the AFDC Quality Control Survey, where data were collected primarily to monitor welfare fraud and mistakes. This can also be done by piggybacking a child module onto surveys being conducted for other purposes, such as the child module being developed for the Survey of Income and Program Participation, conducted to assess income and employment and the receipt of income supports and services among individuals and families. Similarly, the child health supplements added periodically to the National Health Interview Survey provide information on children's physical health not elsewhere available. In addition, data collected for analytic purposes, such as the National Longitudinal Survey of Youth, a labor force survey, and the National Educational Longitudinal Survey conducted by the Department of Education, also can be analyzed to provide cross-sectional indicator data.

Indicators should also reflect societal goals and support the efforts of policymakers to assess progress toward meeting national goals, such as school readiness, economic self-sufficiency, and comprehensive health care. The twelfth criterion reflects this need:

- Indicators should help track progress in meeting national goals for child well-being.

Because many programs and policies are initiated and managed at the state and local level, it is also important to measure and track indicators of child well-being at these levels. Currently in the United States, sustained attention is focused on health care and welfare receipt. Efforts to improve indicators of child well-being should inform these policy efforts. Similarly, concern with violence, drug use, scholastic achievement, immunization, and adolescent pregnancy argue for up-to-date information on these topics.

Since indicators cannot be developed for every aspect of children's behavior, choices must be made. Indicators should focus on issues of general or substantial importance to the public, program providers, and policymakers. Alternatively, indicators, or at least a subset of indicators, should be weighted according to the importance or salience of an item to the public or by the proportion of the public affected by a trend. Victory over rare congenital diseases represents an important event for the families affected, but to compile social indicators it is more useful to assess trends in more widespread conditions, such as low birth weight, sexually transmitted diseases, and accidents, that affect large numbers of individuals.

Finally, to aid with our interpretation of indicators:

- New indicators, or a subset of indicators, should be developed that adjust for changes in the composition of the population over time that can confound our ability to track well-being. Alternatively, indicators should be available for population subgroups that are sufficiently narrow to permit tracking within that subgroup.

The composition of the population affects our interpretation of trend data. For example, the United States has experienced a substantial influx of Hispanic persons into the country and simultaneously has seen the white teen birth rate rise. Since 90 percent of all Hispanics are classified as white by the vital statistics system, separating non-Hispanic whites from Hispanics shows that much of the increase in the white teen birth rate in the 1980s was due to increased numbers of Hispanic teens. Only if the data are analyzed by race and ethnicity simultaneously is this subtle but important difference apparent.

Similarly, trends in SAT (Scholastic Aptitude Test) scores have been a source of substantial concern in the United States, as college-bound high school students, with some exceptions, have tended to score lower than students did several decades ago. When the data are analyzed adjusting for changes in the composition of the student body taking the SAT, some of this negative trend can be explained. It is important to know that some of the change can be explained by changes in demographic composition, but it is also important to know that not all of the change is explained by changes in composition.

Hence, when trends are evident that are particularly puzzling or troubling, reanalyzing the data within narrow population groups or using multivariate methods can be very helpful in explaining the meaning of these trends.

SUMMARY

In the United States, efforts to develop, tabulate, and disseminate social indicators regarding children and families have moved forward erratically. There appears to be a renewed interest at the present time in assessing the circumstances in which children are growing up. Traditional indicators are receiving new attention, and an effort is being made to develop a richer set of indicators. Developing a complete and rigorous set of measures appropriate to the next century is a challenging task; but if one believes that the well-being of children is as crucial to the nation as the well-being of the economy, then it is appropriate to direct the needed talent, energy, and resources to the task.

NOTE

1. For an earlier version of this chapter see Moore 1995.

REFERENCES

Moore, Kristin A. 1995. "Criteria for Social Indicators of Child Well-Being." *Eurosocial* 56: 7–13.

Moore, Kristin A., and Dana Glei. 1993. *Memorandum.* Unpublished raw data. Washington, D.C.: Child Trends, Inc.

Moore, Kristin A., Christine W. Nord, and James L. Peterson. 1989. "Non-Voluntary Sexual Activity among Adolescents." *Family Planning Perspectives* 21(3): 110–14.

Ruggles, Patricia. 1990. *Drawing the Line: Alternative Poverty Measures and Their Implications for Public Policy.* Washington, D.C.: The Urban Institute Press.

Sameroff, Arnold, Ronald Seifer, Ralph Barocas, Melvin Zax, and Stanley Greenspan. 1987. "Intelligence Quotient Scores of Four-Year-Old Children: Social-Environment Risk Factors." *Pediatrics* 79: 343–50.

Select Committee on Children, Youth and Families. 1989. *U.S. Children and Their Families: Current Conditions and Recent Trends, 1989.* Washington, D.C.: U.S. Government Printing Office.

Watts, Harold W., and Donald J. Hernandez. 1982. "Child and Family Indicators: A Report with Recommendations." Report of the Advisory Group on Child and Family Indicators of the Advisory and Planning Committee on Social Indicators. Washington, D.C.: Social Science Research Council.

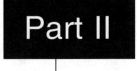

Part II

Health

3

Population Indicators of Prenatal and Infant Health

Paula Lantz and Melissa Partin

AT THE PRESENT time, approximately four million babies are born in the United States each year (National Center for Health Statistics 1993; Guyer et al. 1995). The health and well-being of these babies and their mothers is of critical importance. It is commonly accepted that the foundation for all aspects of life (physical, social, and emotional) is laid during its earliest stages. Children are indeed the future, and their well-being before birth and during infancy are of great importance to that future. In addition, the health status and well-being of pregnant women and their infants says much about a society, for healthy children imply a healthy society. Many statistics and other indicators of prenatal and infant health are part of common, everyday language and are used to compare health conditions for mothers and infants across population subgroups and across nations as well. For example, the fact that the rate of infant mortality in the United States ranks well behind most other developed countries and some underdeveloped countries is well known and a source of great national concern (Haub and Yanagishita 1991).

The purpose of this chapter is to discuss aggregate information and indicators that can be used to assess the health and well-being of children during the prenatal period and infancy. We begin by presenting a comprehensive list of prenatal and infant health indicators and discussing the major sources of information on these indicators. We next identify a set of three priority or key indicators from the comprehensive list of indicators and provide a justification for their selection. We then evaluate the three key indicators with regard to their availability, quality, and usefulness for measuring prenatal and infant health status. As part of this discussion, we present an assessment of the strengths and limitations of each key indicator and provide recommendations for improved data collection.

PRENATAL/INFANT HEALTH INDICATORS AND PRIMARY DATA SOURCES

To compile a list of important indicators of prenatal and infant well-being, several sources of information were used. These sources included: scientific literature from medicine, public health, and the social sciences; the United States Public Health Service's goals and objectives for the year 2000, as outlined in *Healthy People 2000: National Health Promotion and Disease Prevention Objectives* (hereafter referred to as Year 2000 objectives) (1990); and materials and reports prepared by child advocacy groups (Children's Defense Fund 1992, 1994; The Carnegie Task Force on Meeting the Needs of Our Youngest Children 1994).

Table 3.1 displays a list of important direct indicators of prenatal and infant well-being (that is, those measures which describe various aspects of the health status and well-being of mothers and fetuses during the prenatal period and of babies during infancy). The list of indicators presented in table 3.1 is by no means exhaustive. Additional indicators and measures have been used to assess aspects of prenatal and infant well-being and to identify health risks during these time periods. The indicators included in our list were selected based on the following criteria: each indicator definition is clear, objective, and measurable; each indicator's definition remains consistent across population subgroups and has remained relatively stable over time; and each indicator is generally understood by the public. As a group, the indicators assess well-being across a wide range of outcomes, processes, and behavior, and include both positive and negative measures of well-being.

The majority of the information and measures used to assess prenatal and infant health in the United States are derived from three types of data: vital registration data; medical records data (including patient medical charts, patient laboratory and procedure records, patient billing records, and hospital discharge data); and survey research data. All of these data sources are available in a variety of formats (including in combined forms) at the national, state, and local level (National Center for Health Statistics 1993; Gable 1990). Table 3.2 provides a list of specific sources of data for each of these categories. Although our focus primarily is on national data sources, it is important to emphasize that many states

Table 3.1   List of Direct Indicators of Prenatal and Infant Health

Key direct indicators
Measures of infant mortality
Measures of low birth weight
Measures of prenatal care utilization
Other direct indicators of prenatal health
Fetal mortality rates
Measures of maternal health during pregnancy
   Rate of maternal pregnancy complications
   Maternal weight gain during pregnancy
   Maternal tobacco, alcohol, and other drug use during pregnancy
Apgar scores
Congenital anomaly rates
Measures of infant morbidity
   Proportion of infants admitted to Neonatal Intensive Care Unit
   Incidence rates of illnesses during infancy
   Immunization rates
   Incidence rates of infant abuse and neglect
Measures of growth and development
   Measures of physical growth (height/weight) during infancy
   Measures of motor skills acquisition during infancy
   Measures of cognitive development during infancy

Table 3.2   Sources of Data for Indicators of Prenatal and Infant Health

Type of Data	Major Data Sources
Vital registration data	State and local data from birth certificates, death certificates, and fetal death reports
	National data from National Vital Statistics Program
	National linked files of live births and infant deaths
Medical records data	Local patient medical charts
	Local patient laboratory and procedure records
	Local patient billing records
	State hospital discharge data
	National Hospital Discharge Survey
Social survey data	State and local surveys
	National Survey of Family Growth
	National Longitudinal Survey of Youth
	National Health Interview Survey
	National Health and Nutrition Examination Survey
Combined data sources	National Natality Surveys
	National Maternal and Infant Health Survey

also have excellent data sources for assessing prenatal and infant health at the state, county, or local level. For example, many state centers for health statistics link their birth and death certificates to produce state-specific information on birth outcomes. In addition, most states aggregate hospital discharge information that is used to compare data on perinatal hospital diagnoses, lengths of stay, treatment costs, and outcomes across geographic regions and subpopulations within the states.

We will be discussing the various data sources in greater detail in our presentation below. However, it is important to note that several measures of prenatal and infant health (including our three key indicators) can be attained from vital registration data alone. The strengths of vital record data are that coverage for all births and deaths is nearly complete, data collection methods and forms are similar across geographic regions and sociodemographic groups, and much work has already been invested in assessing and improving data quality. A main concern regarding vital registration data is that the quality of some of the data elements on birth and death certificates is suspect. Studies have found quality problems associated with a variety of data elements, including length of gestation, obstetric complications, medical interventions during pregnancy, and reports of the use of alcohol and other drugs during pregnancy (Carver et al. 1993; David 1980; National Center for Health Statistics 1985; Frost et al. 1984; Kramer et al. 1988; Oates and Forrest 1984; Parrish et al. 1993; Piper et al. 1993). An additional concern is that the turnaround time for indicator availability is lengthy (typically three years behind data collection).

INDICATORS OF HIGHEST PRIORITY FOR PRENATAL AND INFANT HEALTH

The following three indicators from the list of direct indicators in table 3.1 were selected as being the most important for assessing prenatal and infant well-being in the United States: measures of infant mortality, low birth weight, and prenatal care utilization. These key indicators were selected as being of highest priority for several reasons. *First*, they are meaningful across population subgroups, cultures, and nations. One cannot imagine dissent from the opinions that pregnant women deserve adequate prenatal care, and babies ought to be born mature and healthy and survive through infancy and beyond. Indeed, these indicators are already widely reported and used to assess prenatal and infant health in a variety of formats, including national surveillance data prepared by government agencies, the Year 2000 health promotion/disease prevention objectives, the reports and materials prepared by child advocacy groups, and academic maternal and child health research. *Second*, data collection methods for these indicators, overseen by the National Vital Statistics System (National Center for Health Statistics 1993) are similar in all states, and have remained relatively stable over time. Comparable data for all three indicators are available at the national, state, and local levels, and can be broken down by race, maternal age, and other factors. *Finally*, and most importantly, the indicators are sensitive measures of the health and well-being not only of the infants themselves, but also of the communities in which they live.

Because it reflects medical technology, hygiene, and sanitation systems, and the availability and use of both preventive and clinical health services, the *infant mortality* rate is a widely used indicator of development and the overall health of a society. Although infant death is relatively rare in the industrial world, comparisons across developed countries can be informative. As mentioned previously, the United States has one of the highest infant mortality rates in the developed world (Schieber et al. 1991; Haub and Yanagishita 1991; Howell and Blondell 1994). Why, in a country where the average citizen enjoys a higher standard of living than in most other developed countries, do we have such a high infant mortality rate? While differences in data quality and the definition of live births have been cited as potential explanations for this poor United States ranking, persistent inequalities in the distribution of social and health care resources also may be to blame. For example, research on race differences in infant mortality suggests that the persistent African American disadvantage in infant mortality may be explained in part by differences in access to prenatal care and other societal resources (Partin 1993; Strobino et al. 1995). In summary, although infant mortality is rare in the United States, it can be an elucidating and quite useful indicator of both overall infant health and sociodemographic differences in health resource distribution.

Low birth weight is generally used as an indicator of infant frailty. The validity of this measure as an indicator of frailty is well documented. Low birth weight is one of the strongest determinants of infant mortality (McCormick 1985; Tompkins 1985; Rogers 1989; Cramer 1987; Eberstein et al. 1990). Indeed, the 2,500 gram cutoff for low birth weight is the conventional comparison precisely because studies of birth-weight-specific mortality have demonstrated that infant mortality rates rise sharply when birth weight lies below this level (Kramer 1987; Saugstad 1981). In addition to being a strong predictor of infant mortality, low birth weight is also associated with greater morbidity in the first few years of life (Hackman et al. 1983; Hayes 1987), with certain neurological and developmental handicaps (Hayes 1987; Harvey et al. 1982; Westwood et al. 1983), and with cognitive capacity, adaptive skills, and scholastic performance (McCormick et al. 1992; Baker et al. 1989; McCormick 1985).

Prenatal care presumably improves pregnancy outcomes by serving as a screening mechanism for high-risk pregnancies. If measures to prevent poor outcomes are to be effectively invoked, high-risk pregnancies must be identified early and monitored regularly. Prenatal care may also improve pregnancy outcomes by modifying certain maternal behaviors (such as smoking, drinking, and poor nutritional habits) that may threaten the healthy development of the fetus. Some studies investigating the association between prenatal care and pregnancy outcomes have shown that mothers lacking adequate prenatal care are more likely to deliver low birth weight infants (Eisner et al. 1979; Greenberg 1983; Leveno et al. 1985; Kotelchuck 1994b) and experience infant death (Leveno et al. 1985) than mothers who have had at least some prenatal care. However, uncertainties remain as to whether these patterns are genuine or the artifact of various selection processes confounding the association between prenatal care use and birth outcomes (Frick and Lantz 1996). Despite the uncertainties regarding the true effects of prenatal care on outcomes, measures of prenatal care utilization are an essential compliment to the other two priority indicators. While infant mortality and low birth weight measure infant health outcomes directly, to the extent that prenatal care use represents access to and use of medical care resources in our society, it serves as an indicator of the various processes through which these outcomes are achieved.

Before moving forward with our discussion of the priority indicators, we would like to emphasize that there are some limitations and risks associated with using broad population-level statistics as indicators of such multidimensional concepts as prenatal and infant health. In using simple indicators to describe the health state of large segments of the population, we do run the risk of oversimplifying complex situations and problems. In turn, especially if the indicators become widely known and used among health professionals, policymakers, and the public at large, the result can be programmatic/policy responses that narrowly focus on the indicators rather than on the complexity of the problem. Such policy responses run the risk of being inappropriately simplistic or too limited in their scope—that is, they are "quick fixes" or aimed only at one small component of a problem. This is of special concern regarding the labeling of prenatal care utilization as an important indicator of prenatal health. Prenatal care has been a major focus of public health policies aimed at improving maternal health and birth outcomes in the United States (Sardell 1990). However, despite this strong policy focus, the large body of research on this topic has failed to provide clear and consistent evidence that improving a population's use of prenatal care will actually lead to improved birth outcomes (Kramer 1987; Alexander and Korenbrot 1995; Groutz and Hagay 1996; Fiscella 1996). Thus, our choice of prenatal care use as an important indicator of prenatal health does not mean that we view prenatal care as a primary predictor of birth outcomes or that we endorse a public health policy focus on prenatal care as a means to improve infant health and birth outcomes. Much more research needs to be done in these areas. Rather, our choice reflects the widespread belief that every pregnant woman deserves adequate medical attention during pregnancy for myriad aspects of her physical and emotional health and the health of the baby, regardless of the impact of that attention on general indicators used for birth outcomes (birth weight, gestational age, and survival).

In the sections to follow, we describe in detail the state of each of the three priority indicators and the various ways in which the indicators are produced and used. We also address three questions for each indicator: how is the indicator currently measured?; how should the indicator be produced?; and how can improved measures be produced over the next decade?

Measures of Infant Mortality

How Is Infant Mortality Currently Measured?   Infant mortality is a measure of infants' survivability through the first year of life. The infant mortality rate (IMR) is a ratio of the number of deaths to children under the age of one compared to the number of live births during a specified time period (usually a year). The crude or conventional IMR can be defined as follows (Shryock and Siegel 1976):

$$\frac{\text{deaths to children} < 1 \text{ year of age during the year}}{\text{live births during the year}} \times 1,000$$

The majority of infants who die during the first year do so during the first weeks of life (McCormick 1985). In addition, the causes of death for those babies dying very early in infancy differ significantly from those dying later during this time period. Thus, the overall infant mortality rate is often broken down into two component parts: the neonatal mortality rate and the postneonatal mortality rate. The *neonatal mortality rate* measures the level of death during the first four weeks of infancy (that is, less than 28 days of age). The *postneonatal mortality rate* measures the level of death after the first month (that is, between 28 and 364 days of age). The neonatal mortality rate is used as a measure of endogenous mortality, since the majority of neonatal deaths are due to causes that are congenital or endogenous to the mother and/or baby (that is, prematurity or congenital defects). Alternatively, the postneonatal mortality rate has been used as a measure of exogenous mortality, since a higher proportion of postneonatal deaths are due to causes of death which are external to the mother and child (that is, nonintentional injury, respiratory infections). However, as improvements in perinatal medicine have extended the survival time of infants born very ill, the assumption that postneonatal deaths are primarily due to exogenous causes has become less valid.

Cause-of-death-specific neonatal and postneonatal mortality rates by race and ethnicity provide useful information for assessing the racial/ethnic differences in the timing and causes of infant death. Also useful are infant mortality rates by birth weight categories and gestational age in weeks. Trends in both of these indicators are useful for many types of assessments, including the tracking of improvements in perinatal medicine.

The data used to compute measures of infant mortality (and other indicators of prenatal and infant health) come from vital records. The registration of births and deaths is required by law in all states and territories of the United States. All states, therefore, have vital registration data on births and deaths that can be assessed at the state, county, or municipal level. National data on births and infant deaths are available through the National Vital Statistics System, a data collection effort of the National Center for Health Statistics (NCHS) (Perrin 1974). It is generally accepted that at least 99 percent of all live births and deaths are captured in the national vital records system (National Center for Health Statistics 1993, 1991; Frost et al. 1982).

United States standard certificates for live births, deaths, marriages, and divorces, and standard reports for induced termination of pregnancy and fetal deaths are periodically revised (in approximately ten-year cycles). The standard certificates/reports represent the minimum data needed to produce comparable national, state, and local vital statistics. The most recent revisions were implemented in 1989 (National Center for Health Statistics 1991; Freedman et al. 1988; MacFarlane 1989). It is believed that these changes have improved the quality of the data gathered and provided new and increased opportunities for research on birth outcomes (Taffel et al. 1989; Freedman et al. 1988; Luke and Keith 1991). Nearly all the registration areas for which NCHS publishes data were using the revised standard forms by January 1, 1989 (National Center for Health Statistics 1991).

In addition to housing separate files containing annual birth and death certificate information, NCHS also links vital records for research on infant mortality. The national linked file of live births and infant deaths is comprised of linked birth and death records for infants born in a given calendar year who died before their first birthday (National Center for Health Statistics 1993). Two years worth of vital statistics data are required for the construction of the linked file, since infant deaths can occur during the year of birth and the year after. The match completeness for the linked files is high (98 percent for the 1983–1987 files) (National Center for Health Statistics 1993). This national file can be used to assess prenatal and infant health at the state and local level as well.

State and county infant mortality statistics typically are produced on an annual basis and disseminated by state centers for health statistics. National infant mortality statistics are also produced on an annual basis and are published in a variety of places including various NCHS reports, the *Health, United States* series, and the *Morbidity and Mortality Weekly Report*. The turnaround time for the production of annual infant mortality statistics is generally between two and four years.

Infant mortality statistics can be produced with information from infant death certificates and a count of the number of live births during the same time period. With this information, infant mortality rates by cause of death and by timing of death (neonatal versus postneonatal) can be computed. If the number of live births is available by race and ethnicity, race- and ethnic-specific infant mortality rates can also be produced. When death certificate information is combined with data from birth certificates, infant mortality rates can be assessed by birth weight, timing and use of prenatal care, and other relevant factors on the birth certificate. Thus, files which link birth and death certificate data provide a rich source for producing measures of infant mortality across a variety of sociodemographic groups (National Center for Health Statistics 1985; Zahniser et al. 1987).

Birth certificate coverage of live births and death certificate coverage of infant deaths are believed to be quite high (U.S. National Office of Vital Statistics 1978; Frost et al. 1982; Kleinman 1986; Lambert and Strauss 1987). Nevertheless, concerns regarding the underreporting of fetal, perinatal, and infant deaths have been documented (Kleinman 1986; David 1986; Williams et al., 1986). Even a small number of unreported out-of-hospital births and deaths can have a substantial impact on mortality rates for racial, ethnic, or other subpopulations (Kleinman 1986). The main quality concerns regarding infant mortality indicators, however, involve cause of death information and race identification on death certificates.

Several studies have found discrepancies in cause of death information when autopsy results are compared with the cause of death codes on corresponding death certificates (Kircher et al. 1985; Schottenfeld et al. 1982; Carter 1985). With regard to infant deaths, it is believed that cause of death statistics from death certificates underestimate deaths due to a number of diseases and underlying conditions, including congenital anomalies (Minton and Seegmiller 1986), child abuse and neglect (McClain et al. 1993), and the impact of a short gestation (Carver et al. 1993). The problems associated with cause of death information on death certificates are believed to be related to several factors. First, the immediate function of the death certificate is legal (that is, to permit transfer of the body and to initiate appropriate claims). Thus, the document is usually completed as quickly as possible and is rarely edited or modified by autopsy or other subsequent findings (Kircher et al. 1985; Carter 1985; Buetow 1992). Second, the majority of physicians have no training in the purpose and process of death certification (Comstock and Markush 1986). Third, physicians are not routinely queried about incomplete diagnoses, unlikely sequences, or missing information (Comstock and Markush 1986; Rosenberg 1989). Finally, with regard to the underestimation of infant deaths due to short gestation, it has been argued that biases in World Health Organization (WHO) selection rules allow other immediate causes of death (such as infectious diseases like sepsis) to have a higher priority over short gestation (Carver et al. 1993).

There is also empirical evidence that there are data quality problems associated with the coding of race and ethnicity on birth and death certificates. At least two studies have documented inconsistencies in the coding of race and ethnic information on birth and death certificates (Kennedy and Deapen 1991; Hahn et al. 1992). These studies found that because the majority of infants classified differently at birth and death are coded as a nonwhite race or ethnicity on birth certificates, but as non-Hispanic white on the death certificate, infant mortality estimates among minority groups that are based on death certificate information may be anywhere between 3 percent to 50 percent lower than estimates using birth certificate race/ethnicity data. Improvements in the coding of race/ethnicity on birth and death certificates need to be made (Kennedy and Deapen 1991; Hahn et al. 1992; Nakamura et al. 1991; Becerra et al. 1991). In addition, however, the issues of multiracism and how definitions of race and ethnicity have changed over time also need to be acknowledged and addressed if statistical indicators involving race are to be meaningful (Wright 1994).

Since much research on infant mortality is conducted on files which link birth and death certificates, the quality of information on birth certificates is also of importance. Studies have found birth certificate data on birth weight, APGAR scores, maternal education, and other sociodemographic variables to be of relatively high quality (Brunskill 1990; David 1980; National Center for Health

Statistics 1985; Jepson et al. 1991; Oates and Forrest 1984; Piper et al. 1993; Querec 1980). There is some evidence, however, that birth certificate data on gestational age, prenatal care utilization, maternal health complications, and congenital anomalies and abnormal conditions of the newborn do have some problems related to quality (Alexander et al. 1991; Alexander et al. 1990; Carver et al. 1993; David 1980; National Center for Health Statistics 1985; Frost et al. 1984; Hexter et al. 1990; Kramer 1988; Parrish et al. 1989; Piper et al. 1993; Querec 1980). It was hoped, based on previous studies, that the 1989 revision of the Standard Certificate of Birth would improve the quality of these items through the provision of the check box format (Frost et al. 1984; National Center for Health Statistics 1991; Taffel et al. 1989).

Infant mortality rates are produced from vital registration data. This does not mean, however, that other sources of information are not useful or essential to the study of infant mortality. Information from alternative sources can augment the data available through the vital records system. For example, linking vital records with hospital discharge information can provide data on the costs associated with caring for premature infants who eventually die (Hexter et al. 1990; Parrish et al. 1993). In addition, information from survey questionnaires provides rich opportunities for researchers to investigate explanations for observed sociodemographic differentials in infant death. For example, Geronimus et al. (1991) used data from the National Health and Nutrition Examination Survey to investigate the hypothesis that racial differences in the age-specific prevalence of health conditions associated with maternal pregnancy complications (that is, hypertension) may explain some portion of long-observed racial differences in pregnancy outcome.

How Should Infant Mortality Rates Be Produced?   As mentioned above, national, state, and local rates typically are produced for a calendar year. The production of annual infant mortality statistics seems sufficient, and we see no reason to increase or decrease this rate of production. The distinction between neonatal and postneonatal mortality continues to be important, thus we recommend that infant mortality rates for these two different age groups continue to be produced. In addition, infant mortality data for population subgroups are very important. Sociodemographic differentials (both levels and trends) are very elucidating and are considered to reflect differences in lifestyle, access to medical care, and health-related knowledge, attitudes, and practices. We recommend that, at a minimum, national and state infant mortality rates be produced by race/ethnicity and maternal age. In addition, cause-specific infant mortality rates also should be produced on an annual basis. In all cases, new annual statistics should be compared with previous years to identify trends in both levels and patterns of infant mortality.

Analyses of trends in infant mortality rates should include adjustments for several other concurrent trends, such as changes in the distribution of births by maternal age, race, and parity. All of these demographic changes can have an impact upon crude infant mortality rates and/or their interpretation. For example, since blacks have a higher rate of infant mortality than whites, the overall infant mortality rate is influenced by the proportion of births to black mothers. In addition, analyses of trends in infant mortality rates have attempted to adjust for changes in maternal behavior and social policy in addition to changes in demographics. For example, attempts have been made to adjust or explain the widening of the black/white infant mortality gap by incorporating into trend analyses information on the decreased availability of abortions for low-income women (Partin and Palloni 1994).

Statistical modeling and estimation are essential to improve our understanding of the sociodemographic differentials in infant mortality. Thus, data which allow for sophisticated modeling and controls are crucial. Currently, some of the best data available for this purpose are the national linked birth and death certificate files and the special natality surveys (National Center for Health Statistics 1993, 1985; Sanderson et al. 1991; Overpeck et al. 1992).

How Can Improved Indicators Be Produced over the Next Decade?

While an impressive system for the collection of infant mortality data is currently in place, several areas of improvement have been noted. First, although the Vital Statistics System plays a valuable and indispensable role in the production of infant mortality statistics, further study is needed to evaluate the reporting completeness of this system. Out-of-hospital births and deaths and the nonuniform application of definitions of live births and fetal death could contribute to the underreporting of infant deaths (Kleinman 1986). Additional research is needed to better evaluate the reporting problems and the degree of reporting completeness in the death registration system.

Second, cause of death information on death certificates should be improved. The following interventions have been recommended: increased training opportunities and education regarding death certificate completion, including training in how to use the *International Classification of Diseases* and WHO selection rules for physicians (Carter 1985; Rosenberg 1989); querying of physicians regarding questionable or suspect cases, which provides ongoing education and feedback and in turn improves the quality of cause of death information (Hopkins et al. 1989); and initiation of a two-part death certificate. The first part of such a certificate would include only demographic information and provide a quick way to register the death, while the second part would include an investigation form to be completed at a later date by qualified certifiers (Salmi et al. 1990). In addition, Carver et al. (1993) recommend that WHO selection rules be modified to allow short gestation priority over immediate causes of infant death.

Third, the quality and consistency of infant race/ethnicity coding on birth and death certificates need to be improved. Several of the suggestions we have mentioned (increased training, initiation of a two-part death certificate) may also improve the quality of race, ethnicity, and other sociodemographic information on the death certificate. Another way to improve the quality of data on race/ethnicity would be to rely on maternal reports rather than observation from the physician or other health professional. Fourth, faster turnaround time is needed for information from the linked birth/death certificate files. The increasing use of the electronic transfer of data may assist in this process. Fifth, in addition, continued opportunities are needed to augment vital registration data by linking it with medical records information and/or survey questionnaire data. For instance, detailed information on maternal socioeconomic status and community-level variables that can be linked with vital records information is needed to further investigate the complex interaction of race, social class, and neighborhood in regard to infant mortality and other birth outcomes.

Sixth, to assist in analyses of trends in infant mortality rates and their determinants, local, state, and federal agencies reporting on vital events should supply complete documentation of any changes in data collection, manipulation, or reporting practices that may artifactually influence rates and their trends. For instance, birth certificate format revisions or changes in definitions of variables (that is, what constitutes a "live birth," or how specific race and ethnic minority groups are defined) should be provided in footnotes. Similarly, the names of the specific states on which national figures are based should be footnoted when not all states are included in the information reported.

Finally, research also is needed to identify data collection and definitional issues that might be related to cross-national differences in infant mortality. Additional data are needed to determine what portion of the observed higher level of infant mortality in the United States is due to procedural or methodological differences in the way the indicator is produced (Howell and Blondell 1994).

Measures of Low Birth Weight

How Is Low Birth Weight Currently Measured?   While low birth weight is most commonly represented in terms of the proportion of infants born at weights less than 2,500 grams (or approximately 5.5 pounds), measures distinguishing very low birth weight infants (less than 1,500 grams) from moderately low birth weight infants (1,500–2,499 grams), and low birth weight due to intrauterine growth retardation from low birth weight due to premature delivery (before 37 weeks gestation) are also widely employed. The low birth weight "rate" refers to the percent of live births delivered at weights less than 2,500 grams in a given time period (usually a year). Measures of low birth weight distinguishing between premature and growth-retarded (or "small for gestational age") infants have been variously defined. The most common definition involves a simple trichotomy where infants born both before 37 weeks gestation and at weights less than 2,500 grams (labeled "premature low birth weight"), and infants born at or after 37 weeks gestation and at weights less than 2,500 grams (labeled "intrauterine growth-retarded low birth weight") are distinguished from infants of normal weight and gestation. Some health professionals and researchers have focused on more detailed definitions of the joint distribution of gestational age and birth weight. These more detailed definitions are frequently based on published fetal growth curves, such as those produced from an early study of births delivered in a Colorado hospital (Lubchenco et al. 1966), which summarize variation in the birth weights of infants delivered at various gestational ages. This information from the distribution of birth weights among infants delivered at various ages is commonly used to categorize infants into percentiles of birth weight for gestational age. More recently it has been argued, however, that an infant's birth weight should be expressed not in terms of divergence from some absolute standard, but rather in terms of standard deviations from population-specific mean birth weights for gestational age (Wilcox and Russell 1990).

The individual investigator's decision regarding which measure of low birth weight to employ will be guided not only by the level of detail desired but also by the quantity and quality of the data available. For instance, investigators with only sparse data available will want to rely on less detailed definitions. For reasons we will delineate, definitions of low birth weight conditioned on gestational age should not be used unless resources are available to meticulously clean gestational age data for missing and implausible values.

The primary source of data on low birth weight is the birth certificate. Data on registered births are published annually by the National Center Statistics in Vital Statistics of the United States, and in the Monthly Vital Statistics series under the title of "Advance Report of Final Natality Statistics" (see, for instance, National Center for Health Statistics 1991). The latter summaries provide various information on birth weight including: the proportion of births delivered in 500 gram birth weight categories by race and age of the mother; and the proportion of infants born at very low, low, and high (4,000 grams or more) weights by maternal race and Hispanic origin. Since the 1989 revisions in the birth certificate, NCHS has published a new report entitled "Advance Report of Maternal and Infant Health Data." Along with a variety of other useful information on maternal and infant health, this report includes tabulations of: the percent low birth weight by smoking status, age, and race of the mother; and the percent low birth weight by maternal weight gain during pregnancy, period of gestation, and race of mother. National trends in low birth weight incidence can easily be examined with the use of the *Health, United States* series, which publishes national-level data on the incidence, prevalence and distribution of a variety of health-related behavior and outcomes over time, and is also updated annually by NCHS (see, for instance, National Center for Health Statistics 1993). In addition to the above sources of national-level data, most states provide county-specific information on the annual proportion of births delivered at weights less than 2,500 grams.

While vital records data provide the only continuous source of data on low birth weight, periodic sources of data include: medical records matched with samples of births from local hospitals; maternal reports of pregnancy histories obtained from social surveys such as the National Survey of Family Growth and the National Longitudinal Survey of Youth; the National Natality Surveys; and the 1988 National Maternal and Infant Health Survey. The advantages of the periodic sources of data we have mentioned over vital registration data are that: they enable the examination of low birth weight by subgroups such as family income and poverty status that cannot be identified in published vital statistics data; and since individual records can be identified, they enable detailed analyses of the distribution and determinants of low birth weight that could not be completed using aggregate-level data alone. Furthermore, prior to 1989, these periodic surveys were the only source of data enabling the examination of the incidence of low birth weight by maternal health and health-related behavior during pregnancy.

The quality of low birth weight data varies according to source. While certainly not error free (Horwitz and Yu 1984; Romm and Putnam 1981), medical records are generally considered the gold standard for data of clinical importance. Examinations of the quality of data on low birth weight therefore frequently focus on comparing data obtained from the birth certificate with data recorded on medical records, using either the proportion of cases agreeing on both sources or the sample *kappa* statistic as the measure of reliability. In general, these studies suggest that the data obtained from birth certificates is of quite respectable quality. For instance, studies comparing birth weight data obtained from the birth certificate with birth weight data obtained from medical records report levels of agreement between the two sources ranging from 87 to 100 percent (Buescher et al. 1993; Querec 1980; Piper et al. 1993; National Center for Health Statistics 1985).

Studies examining the validity of maternal reports of birth weight have focused on comparing these reports with data obtained from the birth certificate. As with the studies comparing birth certificate and medical record data on birth weight, these studies suggest the quality of the birth weight data obtained from maternal reports is quite high, reporting levels of correspondence between the two sources ranging from 70 to 96 percent (Gayle et al. 1988; Tilley et al. 1985). Most studies interested in maternal and child health outcomes seek maternal report data within nine months of delivery, but some studies rely on data recalled potentially years after the birth of a child. Investigators relying on maternal reports of low birth weight should be aware that the quality of maternal recall data generally tends to deteriorate over time (Oates and Forrest 1984).

While this discussion suggests that the available data on birth weight is of relatively high quality, it is not without its limitations. Researchers have identified several shortcomings of birth weight data. The first shortcoming involves the suspected underreporting of live births delivered at extremely low (that is, less than 500 grams) weights. While it is presumed that the United States more completely reports very low birth weight infants than other countries (Howell and Blondel 1994), some misreporting of these extremely low birth weight infants as stillbirths likely still occurs in our vital registration system. For this reason, infants weighing less than 500 grams are frequently excluded from analyses. The second shortcoming of available birth weight data involves the selective accuracy of data obtained from the birth certificate and maternal reports. Gayle et al. (1988) found that lower accuracy of birth weight reporting was associated with high-risk profiles (low birth weight, preterm delivery, low Apgar scores, multiparity, low maternal education, black race, unmarried marital status, and young maternal age). This nonrandom accuracy of birth weight data may bias the results of analyses comparing birth weight across various population subgroups. The third shortcoming of birth weight data involves the common response bias of digit preference. David (1980) found in his analysis of 1975–1977 North Carolina birth certificates that the distribution of recorded birth weights demonstrated heaping at every quarter pound. This heaping should be taken into consideration when researchers are grouping birth weight into categories. To minimize biases, cut points should be made such that the range of birth weight in each category is centered around peaks in reporting. The final shortcoming of birth weight data involves errors occurring while the data from the birth certificate is key entered into computerized records. Brunskill (1990) identified three common types of errors in the coding of birth weight during key entry: confusion of ounces for pounds; mistaken reading of one pound as eleven pounds; and errors in the placement of the decimal. All three of these reporting errors lead to systematic overreporting of extremely high birth weight infants and underreporting of very low birth weight infants.

The results from studies estimating the quality of birth weight data obtained from various sources suggest that while the simple dichotomous measure of low birth weight which distinguishes between infants delivered at weights less than 2,500 grams from those delivered at weights of 2,500 grams or more may be less precise than more detailed definitions, it does produce higher levels of correspondence in responses across various data collection instruments. The results of Gayle et al. (1988) suggest that individuals employing data from either birth certificates or maternal reports collected within nine months of delivery can rely on at least 98 percent of cases being accurately categorized into low birth weight and normal birth weight categories. If definitions of birth weight conditioned on gestational age are preferred, however, data quality may be seriously compromised. The most common estimate of gestational age employed—the number of weeks between the date of delivery and the date of the last menstrual period (LMP) reported by the mother—suffers from some serious limitations. While this measure is the estimate provided on the standard birth certificate, it frequently produces high proportions of missing or incomplete information (Alexander and Cornely 1987; David 1980) and tends to display low levels of accuracy at the extremes of the gestational age distribution (Kramer et al. 1988; David 1980). While ultrasound images are believed to provide more accurate estimates of gestational age than LMP data, the former estimate cannot be ascertained accurately for mothers receiving no prenatal care, and it is considered inaccurate for mothers receiving their first prenatal care visit in the third trimester of pregnancy. Since not all pregnant women receive prenatal care before the third trimester, and some never receive any prenatal care (National Center for Health Statistics 1993), sole reliance on ultrasound estimates of gestational age can lead to selective missing information and consequently biased results. The obstetrician's best estimate (OBE) of gestational age, which is based on both ultrasound images and LMP estimates when both are available, and LMP only when ultrasound images are not available, provides an attractive alternative to the sole reliance on either LMP or ultrasound measures. Inclusion of this estimate of gestational age on the birth certificate would likely improve the coverage and quality of available gestational age information.

The various methods of collecting data on birth weight afford different advantages and disadvantages. An important advantage of birth certificate data on birth weight is that it is collected continuously and disseminated annually, and therefore allows the examination of trends in incidence of low birth weight over time. Since low birth weight is a relatively rare event in the United States (typically 7 to 8 percent of births are delivered at low weights), birth certificate data also afford the advantage of providing enough cases to analyze differences in the distribution and determinants of low birth weight across various subgroups of the population. An important disadvantage of birth weight data obtained from both birth certificates and medical records is the potential for errors in the classification of mothers and infants into racial and ethnic subgroups. Since the information on maternal and infant race and ethnicity recorded on both the birth certificate and medical record may be determined by the observation of a physician or other health professional rather than a maternal report, these data are likely a less valid measure of these characteristics than measures obtained from maternal reports. We have discussed other problems associated with race/ethnicity coding on vital records. A disadvantage in birth weight data shared by all three sources (birth certificates, medical records, and maternal reports) is the questionable quality of gestational age data. If definitions of birth weight conditioned on gestational age are preferred, data quality may seriously be compromised.

How Should Low Birth Weight Indicators Be Produced?   Aggregate figures of the incidence of low birth weight are currently summarized annually by both states and National Centers for Health Statistics for various subpopulations as described earlier. The availability of such continuous data on the incidence of low birth weight across various subgroups of the population is essential to the careful surveillance of infant health, and for the monitoring of progress of national and local groups toward reaching Year 2000 objectives for infant health. The currently available disaggregations of low birth weight by severity (very low and moderately low) are particularly important. Research on low birth weight suggests that the determinants and consequences of these categories of birth weight differ, and that improvements in very low birth weight have lagged far behind improvements in moderately low birth weight over time (Kleinman and Kessel 1987). The distribution of low birth weight according to maternal age, race, and health behavior should also continue to be disseminated. The substantial black-white gap in low birth weight has persisted for decades, and has actually widened rather than narrowed in recent years (Partin and Palloni 1994). Subgroup information on race is particularly essential for tracking progress toward the national Year 2000 low birth weight goals. To help narrow the race gap in low birth weight, the Year 2000 objectives for absolute declines in low birth weight for blacks are greater than those targeted for whites.

Careful adjustment of low birth weight indicators for trends in other factors such as changes in the distribution of maternal age, marital status, and education at birth, or changes in maternal health-related behavior, requires subgroup data on low birth weight not currently available in aggregate form. However, investigators can use published data on the characteristics of live births over time, in combination with regression analyses of the effects of these characteristics on low birth weight, to estimate the fit between various demographic trends and changes in low birth weight. This approach was recently used, for instance, to demonstrate the sensitivity of low birth weight trends to changes in fetal death rates over time (Partin and Palloni 1994).

While much progress toward understanding the correlates and determinants of low birth weight has been made in the last thirty years, efforts to reduce low birth weight in this country have fallen short of expectations. If progress is to be made in reducing low birth weight, research on patterns and determinants of low birth weight must continue. The continued timely creation and availability of rich, nationally representative natality surveys such as those produced by the NCHS most recently in 1980 and 1988 is essential to this endeavor.

How Can Improved Indicators Be Produced over the Next Decade?
While detailed information on the incidence and distribution of low birth weight is readily available at both the state and national level, and has been shown to be of particularly high quality, the discussion in this chapter suggests the need for improvement in several areas. First, high proportions of missing data and low

levels of accuracy are important limitations of available gestational age data. David (1980) has offered the following suggestions for improving the coverage and accuracy of these data. Efforts should focus on improving gestational age reporting performance in the hospitals that tend to produce the records with the most errors. This might be done by instructing hospitals not to edit their gestational age data (that is, reporting gestations that do not fit the clinical pattern as unknown). Partial information on gestational age also should be salvaged. Presently, if only month and year of LMP appear on the birth certificate, completed weeks of gestation generally is coded as unknown. These LMP data, while incomplete, could be useful, and are present in most cases lacking full LMP data (David 1980). In addition, standardized data surveillance programs at the state level could improve the completeness and accuracy of the birth files by checking unrealistic values for keying errors and by providing feedback on a regular basis to reporting hospitals about their performance in providing raw data. Finally, keystroke errors (for example, confusing one pound for eleven pounds and misplacements of decimal points) might be minimized if birth weight pounds and ounces were recorded on separate lines or in separate boxes on the birth certificate (Brunskill 1990).

Second, the underreporting of very low birth weight infants continues to compromise the quality of birth weight data. The standardized surveillance programs at the state level suggested by David (1980) for improving the coverage and quality of gestational age data could also be used to promote more accurate and thorough documentation of very low birth weight infants. Third, the nonrandom accuracy of low birth weight and gestational age data may bias comparisons across population subgroups. Providing feedback on a regular basis to reporting hospitals about their performance in providing complete raw data for various populations subgroups with typically high rates of missing data could help promote higher quality data. Finally, as mentioned previously, changes in data collection, data manipulation techniques, and reporting practices that may have an impact on trends should be well documented in published reports on low birth weight.

Measures of Prenatal Care Utilization

How Is Prenatal Care Utilization Currently Measured?   Prenatal health care refers to pregnancy-related services provided between conception and delivery, and may include monitoring the health status of the mother and fetus; providing information to foster optimal maternal health, dietary habits, and hygiene; and providing appropriate psychological and social support. Prenatal care utilization has been measured in a variety of ways in the published literature, including such operationalizations as a dichotomous indicator of whether or not any care was received, the total number of visits made, the month in which the first visit was made, or the trimester of the first visit. Because information on the timing of the first prenatal care visit and the total number of prenatal care visits received represent the aspects of prenatal care most readily available to investigators, prenatal care is most often defined as a function of one or both of these pieces of information. The most common definition of prenatal care employed by investigators that combines these two pieces of information is the Kessner Index. This definition of prenatal care adjusts the number and timing of prenatal care visits to gestational age, which is important since women who deliver prematurely have less "opportunity" to visit prenatal care providers. The Kessner Index groups mothers into categories of "inadequate," "intermediate," and "adequate" care according to recommendations from the American College of Obstetricians and Gynecologists (ACOG) regarding the periodicity of visits (American College of Obstetricians and Gynecologists 1974). While several researchers have criticized the Kessner Index for its lack of detail (Alexander and Cornely 1987; Kotelchuck 1994a), it continues to be the most widely used measure of prenatal care.

Many investigators have assigned cases with missing information on any one of the items making up the Kessner Index to the "inadequate care" category. Modifications in the treatment of missing values on gestational age have been explored by other researchers with some success. For instance, many researchers have dealt with the problem of missing information on the exact day of the last menstrual period by assigning the fifteenth day of the month to that value. Studies employing this procedure suggest it does not substantially bias the direction of results (Binkin et al. 1985; Alexander et al. 1985).

While considerable effort has been expended to arrive at valid measures of both the timing and quantity of prenatal care obtained by mothers, little attention has been paid to the distribution and content of the prenatal care visits obtained. As pointed out by Alexander and Cornely (1987), one disadvantage of the Kessner Index described above is that "women who initiate their first visit early, who do not return for care until late in pregnancy, and who do so because of complications resulting in a flurry of visits prior to delivery, would be indistinguishable from women making the same number of visits in an orderly fashion." They suggest future research consider the spacing of prenatal care visits along with the timing of the first visits and total number of visits. Other investigators are pushing for measures which consider the adequacy of content, as well as timing and quantity, in measures of prenatal care (Petitti et al. 1991; Hansell 1991; Kogan et al. 1994a; Kogan et al. 1994b). Individual investigators' decision as to which definition will best suit their purposes will be shaped not only by the degree of accuracy desired, but also by the quality and availability of data on the various aspects of prenatal care.

In 1994, Kotelchuck published a new method for assessing the adequacy of prenatal care utilization (Kotelchuck 1994a). This index—called the Adequacy of Prenatal Care Utilization Index (or APNCU Index)—was developed in response to some of the limitations of the Kessner Index. This new index measures prenatal care on two distinct and independent dimensions: the adequacy of the initiation of prenatal care (broken down by the month prenatal care began rather than trimester), and the adequacy of the amount of prenatal care received once care has begun (measured as a percent of the number of ACOG-recommended prenatal care visits received during the time under care). The two dimensions are combined into a single summary index with the following four categories: adequate plus, adequate, intermediate, and inadequate. Using data from the 1980 National Natality Survey, a comparison of the APNCU Index with the Kessner Index revealed that 28.5 percent of women received different ratings, with the majority receiving a poorer rating on the APNCU Index (Kotelchuck 1994a). Thus, Kotelchuck asserts that previous estimates of prenatal care in the United

States may have overestimated its level of adequacy (Kotelchuck 1994a, 1994b). Wise (1994) describes Kotelchuck's index as introducing important technical improvements over its predecessors, providing a picture of the potential impact of prenatal care over the entire pregnancy period. However, the computing involved with determining APNCU ranks for individual women is extensive and somewhat complex. Thus, analysts who want to use this measure of prenatal care use are encouraged to get copies of the Statistical Analysis System (SAS) code that Kotelchuck has made available (Kotelchuck 1994a).

As with most other indicators of prenatal and infant health, the primary source of data on prenatal care is the birth certificate. Information on the timing of the first prenatal care visit and the total number of visits obtained by mothers in various subgroups extracted from birth certificates appear in the NCHS Monthly Vital Statistics Report, the annual natality volumes of Vital Statistics of the United States, and in the *Health, United States* series. In 1993, this volume included tabulations of the proportion of live births to mothers receiving early (initiated in the first trimester), late (initiated in the third trimester) or no prenatal care in 1970, 1975, and 1980–1991. Additionally, most states provide county-specific information on the proportion of births to mothers receiving late or no prenatal care in their annual vital statistics summaries.

While the continuously recorded birth certificate information described above is often more readily available to investigators, various periodic sources of data on prenatal care may be preferred by investigators desiring more detailed subgroup information. Periodic sources include the various national surveys mentioned previously. The richest subgroup data available on prenatal care measures comes from the 1972 and 1980 National Natality Surveys. These surveys combined information on the timing of the first prenatal care visit and the total number of prenatal care visits obtained from the birth certificate, medical records, and maternal reports, and are one of the few sources of maternal and infant health data which provide information on income and poverty status. An important advantage of these surveys is the ability to compare data on prenatal care obtained from various sources. Two important disadvantages of these surveys are the fact that they are now somewhat dated and that the maternal survey information on poverty was collected only for married mothers.

The 1988 National Maternal and Infant Health Survey (NMIHS) is an important source of information on the content of early prenatal care visits and includes information on the poverty status of both married and unmarried mothers (Sanderson et al 1991). In addition, information on the timing of prenatal care can also be obtained from the National Survey of Family Growth (NSFG). As with the NMIHS, the NSFG collected information on poverty status from both married and unmarried mothers. A less frequently exploited source of information on prenatal care is the National Longitudinal Survey of Youth. The longitudinal nature of this data set enables comparisons of care-seeking patterns among women with different profiles not possible in other data sources. For instance, analyses examining the effect of complications in prior pregnancies to prenatal care sought in the current pregnancy are possible with this data source, and might be helpful in resolving remaining questions regarding the extent of selection into prenatal care.

As mentioned previously, although some studies suggest that prenatal care is a significant determinant of both prenatal and infant health, several methodologi-cal problems continue to impede research on the relationship between prenatal care and birth outcomes (Fiscella 1995; Alexander and Korenbrot 1995; Peoples-Shep et al. 1988). An important issue here is that the validity of the prenatal care measures most commonly employed may be severely limited. Since there have not been any carefully conducted clinical trials of the efficacy of prenatal care, investigators have had to test the extent to which prenatal care actually represents an indicator of favorable health inputs with the data available (primarily that from the birth certificate). When randomized clinical trials are not feasible (as is the case with prenatal care, which is so much a part of common obstetric practice that it cannot ethically be withheld from mothers), a rigorous test requires careful standardization and sophisticated modeling.

While aggregate measures of the timing and quantity of prenatal care visits are readily available, using these measures in the absence of any adjustments may leave investigators with invalid measures. Arriving at valid measures, however, requires surmounting several methodological challenges. The first challenge stems from the fact that the number of prenatal care visits obtained by the mother is restricted by the length of gestation. This simultaneity of prenatal care and gestational age (often referred to as the "preterm bias" effect) makes it diffi-cult for the investigator to distinguish whether the length of gestation was cut short because the number of prenatal care visits was inadequate, or whether the number of prenatal visits was cut short as a result of a short gestation caused by other factors. One way to disentangle these associations is to define prenatal care as a function of the length of gestation. This is the approach used to create the Kessner and APNCU indices. Another solution involves using the predicted number of prenatal care visits expected by a given gestational age (for example, thirty-seven weeks), which is estimated from a model for prenatal care demand, in the model assessing the effects of prenatal care on pregnancy outcomes (Guilky et al. 1989; Frick and Lantz 1996).

The second challenge to arriving at a valid measure of prenatal care involves the fact that, because the amount of prenatal care obtained represents at least in part behavioral choices of the mother, any observed association between prenatal care and health outcomes may be due partially, if not entirely, to self-selection. There are several different selection processes that may be occurring (Frick and Lantz 1996), including both favorable selection (women at a low risk for a nega-tive birth outcome are more likely to be adequate users of care) and adverse selection (women at high risk for a negative birth outcome are more likely to be high/adequate users of care). The most common strategy employed for correcting for selection processes which both inhibit and promote the use of prenatal care is the instrumental variable approach. This approach corrects for the selective na-ture of prenatal care by regressing the number of prenatal care visits (or some other indicator of prenatal care) on various exogenous factors that serve as instru-ments for identifying the unobserved characteristics of the mother, which are both related to the pregnancy outcome and to the amount of prenatal care the mother seeks (see Frick and Lantz 1996, for a thorough explanation and review of this literature). The success of this approach in adjusting for the biases intro-duced by these unobserved factors is of course contingent upon obtaining a suita-ble array of instruments. One requirement is that the equation predicting the demand for prenatal care include an assortment of exogenous factors which are associated with the amount of prenatal care received but not with the outcome of the pregnancy itself. Investigators have generally relied on information describing the availability of care, such as number of prenatal care clinics in the area and distance to the closest clinic, to satisfy this requirement. The results from the studies published to date suggest that selectivity in the use of care does exist, and that the predominant process is one of adverse selection (Rosenzweig and Schultz 1983; Guilky et al. 1989; Joyce 1994; Grossman and Joyce 1990). These results imply that analyses which fail to control for selection processes in the use of prenatal care will underestimate the effect of care on birth outcomes. There are, however, analytical challenges associated with this type of research, and the potential biasing effects of positive selection (which have been evidenced in a few studies) cannot be ignored (Frick and Lantz 1996).

In addition to the formidable obstacles to obtaining valid measures of prenatal care, a number of other factors threaten the overall quality of available prenatal care measures. The most serious threat to the quality of prenatal care data is the high proportion of cases with missing information on prenatal care and gestational age (Alexander et al. 1991; Forrest and Singh 1987; Piper et al. 1993). The reliability of prenatal care measures is also called into question by studies finding low levels of correspondence in prenatal care information obtained from different sources (Buescher et al. 1993; Querec 1980; Forest and Singh 1987; Piper et al. 1993). Lantz and Penrod (1996) found considerable disagreement across the three data sources in the 1980 NNS with regard to individual women's use of prenatal care, and that this type of measurement error leads to significant attenuation bias in estimates of the impact of prenatal care on birth weight. A final threat to the quality of the most commonly employed measures of prenatal care are the limitations of gestational age data. While efforts to control for the preterm bias effect are a necessary step in arriving at valid measures of prenatal care, investigators should carefully inspect gestational age information for non-random patterns of missing data and implausible values.

Because of the wide availability of prenatal care utilization information (from birth certificates and other data sources), the adequacy of prenatal care received is often equated with the adequate utilization of care, as defined by the Kessner or APNCU indices. While we do not equate the adequate utilization of prenatal care with the overall adequacy of care received, it is important to emphasize that this discussion has focused on prenatal care utilization rather than other dimensions of this service such as the content of the care, the quality of the care, the continuity of care providers during the course of the pregnancy, and the comprehensiveness of services offered. Unfortunately, data on these dimensions of care are difficult to obtain, and methodological approaches to their measurement are not well developed. Additional research is needed to improve and expand the conceptualization of prenatal care beyond its mere utilization, and to measure the relative importance of these additional dimensions on maternal and infant health outcomes (Peoples-Shep et al. 1996; Maloni et al. 1996; Groutz and Hagay 1995).

No source or definition of prenatal care utilization is flawless. For instance, while measures of prenatal care conditioned on gestational age and corrected for potential self-selection are thought to be more valid than uncorrected measures, they make much greater demands on data typically limited by high proportions of missing data and low levels of quality. The birth certificate may be the preferred source of information for investigators seeking a continuous source of temporal data, but suffers the disadvantage of providing less subgroup detail than most periodic sources of information. If the distribution and determinants of prenatal care, or the association between prenatal care and birth outcomes is of primary interest, investigators may want to turn to more detailed sources of data such as the National Natality Surveys, the NMIHS, the NSFG, or the NLSY. Although the natality surveys provide the richest data available on prenatal care, combining reports from birth certificates with those from medical records and maternal interviews, the most recent wave (1980) is now quite dated. The 1988 National Maternal and Infant Health Survey provides more timely data, but the medical record section of the survey containing detail on the distribution and content of prenatal care visits has not been released for public use due to a low response rate from medical providers. Investigators interested in a prospective source of information can turn to the NLSY, but will have to rely on maternal reports of somewhat limited prenatal care data.

How Should Prenatal Care Indicators Be Produced?   State- and national-level data on prenatal care are generally summarized by prevalence measures of the proportion of women delivering in a given year that received prenatal care during their pregnancy. Information on whether care was received and the trimester in which the first visit was made should continue to be made available by maternal age, race/ethnicity, and other key sociodemographic characteristics. However, given the dependence of prenatal care receipt on the gestational length of pregnancies, measures of prenatal care standardized by gestational age also should be provided in addition to the currently available unstandardized measures. Standardized measures will allow investigators to distinguish subgroup differences and temporal trends in prenatal care receipt from patterns due to gestational age. Since the proper measurement of prenatal care may require statistical modeling and adjustments beyond the scope of many investigators, the availability of these standardized measures likely will be invaluable to investigators lacking the resources to estimate standardized measures of prenatal care themselves.

How Can Improved Indicators Be Produced over the Next Decade?   Of the three priority indicators of prenatal and infant health discussed here, prenatal care represents the indicator with the greatest overall need for improvement. The shortcomings of existing prenatal care data delineated in this discussion reflect a lack of knowledge about prenatal care. In order to determine where to focus our efforts for arriving at improved indicators of prenatal care, we need to strengthen our understanding of the association between prenatal care and favorable health outcomes and of variations in this association across racial and other sociodemographic groups. Relatedly, we need additional research to identify important components of prenatal care in addition to utilization patterns. For example, we need to examine the content of prenatal care closely to identify those components most essential to ensuring healthy outcomes for both the mother and fetus (Nagey 1989). We also need to examine the distribution of prenatal care visits across gestational age to determine the patterns most likely to ensure healthy outcomes. Finally, further research must also be conducted to better understand the potential for selection bias in specific populations (Frick and Lantz 1996).

In addition to strengthening our understanding of prenatal care, the following suggestions should help us achieve better indicators of prenatal care utilization in the future. First, what a prenatal visit actually represents needs to be defined more clearly. This will help to achieve a more reliable and valid measure of prenatal care. For example, it is currently unclear whether a visit for a pregnancy test should be considered as the first prenatal care visit. Second, missing information on prenatal care visits and gestational age needs to be reduced. Doing so in all data sources will greatly enhance the quality of data on prenatal care. The current amount of missing data on these factors has a great impact on the distribution of these variables. Third, improvements in the overall quality of gestational age data are desperately needed. As mentioned previously, inclusion of the obstetrician's best estimate of gestational age on the birth certificate likely would improve greatly the quality of available gestational age information. Reductions in the amount of missing information in gestational age data can be achieved via the guidelines recommended by David (1980) and mentioned in this chapter. In addition, standards for cleaning gestational age data published by NCHS for implausible values would be invaluable. Finally, in addition to the unstandardized measures of prenatal care utilization currently available, NCHS should provide measures of prenatal care standardized for gestational age, with the resulting standardization protocols made available for others to emulate.

SUMMARY AND CONCLUSIONS

By focusing on priority indicators of prenatal and infant health, our discussion of measures is admittedly incomplete. We make no explicit mention, for instance, of a wide variety of *indirect* indicators of prenatal and infant well-being (those measures and markers that are linked to or associated with prenatal and infant health and are therefore indirectly related to the well-being of very young children). Examples of indirect indicators include unintended pregnancy rates, teen pregnancy rates, maternal mortality rates, breast-feeding rates and practices, postpartum substance abuse rates, antenatal care issues (such as rates of screening for genetic disorders and other disabling conditions), socioeconomic issues such as the proportion of pregnant women and infants living in poverty, and the proportion of pregnant women and infants without health insurance. Although we did not select any of these indirect indicators as being among the priority indicators, they are nonetheless greatly important to health and well-being during the prenatal and infant time periods.

As suggested in this chapter, there are numerous indicators available to those who wish to assess the status of prenatal and infant health in the United States. Both direct and indirect indicators of health status are available at the local, state, and national level. Overall, the state of indicators for prenatal and infant health is impressive, reflecting the historic interest that government, public health (including researchers), child advocates, and the general public have had in using various statistical indicators as measures of the health and social well-being of children in our society. In addition, the state of prenatal and infant health indicators reflects the advanced state of our national and state vital registration systems.

The state of the three priority indicators (measures of infant mortality, low birth weight, and prenatal care utilization) has been discussed in great detail. Although these indicators are already widely used to assess levels, trends, and patterns in prenatal and infant health, each indicator is currently experiencing its own set of problems related to data quality and data dissemination. Some of these problems are in need of further study and investigation before detailed recommendations for improvement can be made. Conversely, other problems have been studied to the extent that concrete recommendations for improvement have been made, and efforts to improve existing data now can be implemented. David (1980) has argued that some of the shortcomings in vital registration data on prenatal and infant health will not improve significantly until the dramatic differences in the access to and use of medical care between mothers with accurate and inaccurate data have been addressed. For this to be accomplished, health professionals must develop a greater proficiency at bridging the communication barriers that separate them from socioeconomically disadvantaged clients. This is a formidable yet crucial challenge.

In the United States, there is a vast array of resources available to those who want to document and/or investigate the determinants of prenatal/infant health and illness. National vital records data and national surveys provide researchers with a plethora of opportunities for investigation. The third wave of the National Health and Nutrition Examination Survey, with its oversampling of children under the age of thirty-six months, will provide new and unique data on the health status of infants on a national level. Increased research activity also could be realized at the state and local level, taking advantage of vital statistics and medical records data currently available. In addition, however, we believe that some of the most important research that needs to be done is that which will offer instruction on how to move beyond the mere production of statistical indicators and measures. Specifically, research is needed to guide the process of transforming indicators and related research findings into policy and programmatic recommendations that address the many dimensions and complex nature of maternal and infant health problems in our society. Only then will the assessment and production of prenatal and infant health indicators result in the larger goal of actually improving the health and well-being of children in our society.

REFERENCES

Alexander, G. R., and D. A. Cornely. 1987. "Prenatal Care Utilization: Its Measurement and Relationship to Pregnancy Outcome." *American Journal of Preventive Medicine* 3: 243–53.

Alexander, G. R., and C. C. Korenbrot. 1995. "The Role of Prenatal Care in Preventing Low Birth Weight." *The Future of Children* 5(1): 103–20.

Alexander, G. R., M. E. Tompkins, J. M. Altekruse, and C. A. Hornung. 1985. "Racial Differentials in the Relation of Birth Weight and Gestational Age to Neonatal Mortality." *Public Health Reports* 100: 539–47.

Alexander, G. R., M. E. Tompkins, and D. A. Cornely. 1990. "Gestational Age Reporting and Preterm Delivery." *Public Health Reports* 105: 267–75.

Alexander, G. R., M. E. Tompkins, D. J. Peterson, and J. Weiss. 1991. "Source of Bias in Prenatal Care Utilization Indices: Implications for Evaluating the Medicaid Expansion." *American Journal of Public Health* 81: 1013–16.

American College of Obstetricians and Gynecologists. 1974. *Manual of Standards in Obstetric-Gynecological Practice.* Chicago: American College of Obstetricians and Gynecologists.

Baker, D. J. P., C. Osmond, P. D. Winter, B. Margetts, and S. J. Simmond. 1989. "Weight in Infancy and Death from Ischaemic Heart Disease." *Lancet* 9: 578–80.

Becerra, J. E., C. J. R. Hogue, H. K. Atrash, and N. Perez. 1991. "Infant Mortality Among Hispanics: A Portrait of Heterogeneity." *Journal of the American Medical Association* 265: 217–21.

Binkin, N. J., R. L. Williams, C. T. R. Hogue, and P. M. Chen. 1985. "Reducing Black Neonatal Mortality: Will Improvement in Birth Weight Be Enough?" *Journal of the American Medical Association* 253: 372–75.

Brunskill, A. J. 1990. "Some Sources of Error in the Coding of Birth Weight." *American Journal of Public Health* 80: 72–73.

Buescher, P. A., K. P. Taylor, M. H. Davis, and J. M. Bowling. 1993. "The Quality of the New Birth Certificate Data: A Validation Study in North Carolina." *American Journal of Public Health* 83: 1163–65.

Buetow, S. A. 1992. "The Perinatal Autopsy: Its Conduct and Reporting in Australia." *Medical Journal of Australia* 156: 492–94.

Carnegie Task Force on Meeting the Needs of Young Children. 1994. *Starting Points: Meeting the Needs of Our Youngest Children. The Report of the Carnegie Task Force on Meeting the Needs of Young Children.* New York: Carnegie Corporation of New York.

Carter, J. R. 1985. "The Problematic Death Certificate." *New England Journal of Medicine* 313: 1285–86.

Carver, J. D., R. J. McDermott, N. H. Jacobson, K. M. Sherin, K. Kanarek, et al. 1993. "Infant Mortality Statistics Do Not Adequately Reflect the Impact of Short Gestation." *Pediatrics* 92: 229–32.

Children's Defense Fund. 1992. *The State of America's Children Yearbook 1992.* Washington, D.C.: Children's Defense Fund.

———. 1994. *The State of America's Children Yearbook 1994.* Washington, D.C.: Children's Defense Fund.

Comstock, G. W., and R. E. Markush. 1986. "Further Comments on Problems in Death Certification." *American Journal of Epidemiology* 124: 180–81.

Cramer, J. 1987. "Social Factors and Infant Mortality: Identifying High Risk Groups and Proximate Causes." *Demography* 24: 299–322.

David, R. J. 1980. "The Quality and Completeness of Birth Weight and Gestational Age Data in Computerized Birth Files." *American Journal of Public Health* 70: 964–73.

———. 1986. "Did Low Birth Weight Among U.S. Blacks Really Increase?" *American Journal of Public Health* 76: 380–84.

Eberstein, I., C. Nam, and R. Hummer. 1990. "Infant Mortality by Cause of Death: Main and Interaction Effects." *Demography* 27: 413–30.

Eisner, V., J. V. Brazie, M. W. Pratt, and A. C. Hexter. 1979. "The Risk of Low Birth Weight." *American Journal of Public Health* 69: 887–93.

Fiscella, K. 1995. "Does Prenatal Care Improve Birth Outcomes? A Critical Review." *Obstetrics and Gynecology* 85(3): 468–79.

Forrest, J. D., and S. Singh. 1987. "Timing of Prenatal Care in the United States: How Accurate Are Our Measurements?" *Health Services Research* 22: 235–53.

Freedman, M. A., G. A. Gay, J. E. Brockert, P. W. Potrzebowski, and C. J. Rothwell. 1988. "The 1989 Revisions of the U.S. Standard Certificates of Live Birth and Death and the U.S. Standard Report of Fetal Death." *American Journal of Public Health* 78: 168–72.

Frick, K. D., and P. M. Lantz. 1996. "Selection Bias in Prenatal Care Utilization: An Interdisciplinary Framework and Review of the Literature." *Medical Care Research and Review* 53(4): 371–96.

Frost, F., T. Jennings, and P. Starzyk. 1982. "Completeness of Infant Death Registration for Very Low Birth Weight Infants: Washington State 1978–1979." *American Journal of Public Health* 76: 740–41.

Frost, F., P. Starzyk, S. George, and J. F. McLaughlin. 1984. "Birth Complication Reporting: The Effect of Birth Certificate Design." *American Journal of Public Health* 74: 505–6.

Gable, C. B. 1990. "Reviews and Commentary: A Compendium of Public Health Data Sources." *American Journal of Epidemiology* 131: 381–94.

Gayle, H. D., R. Yip, M. J. Frank, P. Nieburg, and N. J. Binkin. 1988. "Validation of Maternally Reported Birth Weights Among 46,637 Tennessee WIC Program Participants." *Public Health Reports* 103: 143–47.

Geronimus, A. T., H. F. Anderson, and J. Bound. 1991. "Differences in Hypertension Prevalence Among U.S. Black and White Women of Chidbearing Age." *Public Health Reports* 106: 393–99.

Greenberg, R. S. 1983. "The Impact of Prenatal Care in Different Social Groups." *American Journal of Obstetrics and Gynecology* 145: 797–801.

Grossman, M., and T. J. Joyce. 1990. "Unobservables, Pregnancy Resolutions, and Birth Weight Production Functions in New York City." *Journal of Political Economy* 98: 983–1007.

Groutz, A., and Z. J. Hagay. 1995. "Prenatal Care: An Update and Future Trends." *Current Opinion in Obstetrics and Gynecology* 7: 452–60.

Guilky, D. K., B. M. Popkin, J. S. Akin, and E. L. Wong. 1989. "Prenatal Care and Pregnancy Outcome in Cebu, Phillipines." *Journal of Development Economics* 30: 241–72.

Guyer, B., D. M. Strobino, S. J. Ventura, and G. K. Singh. 1995. "Annual Summary of Vital Statistics—1994." *Pediatrics* 96: 1029–39.

Hackman, E., I. Emanuel, G. van Belle, J. Daling. 1983. "Maternal Birth Weight and Subsequent Pregnancy Outcome." *Journal of the American Medical Association* 250: 2016–19.

Hahn, R. A., J. Mulinarc, and S. M. Teutsch. 1992. "Inconsistencies in Coding of Race and Ethnicity Between Birth and Death in U.S. Infants." *Journal of the American Medical Association* 267: 259–63.

Hansell, M. J. 1991. "Sociodemographic Factors and the Quality of Prenatal Care." *American Journal of Public Health* 81: 1023–28.

Harvey, D., J. Prince, J. Bunton, C. Parkinson, and S. Campbell. 1982. "Abilities of Children Who Were Small-for-Gestational-Age Babies." *Pediatrics* 69: 296–300.

Haub, C., and M. Yanagishita. 1991. "Infant Mortality: Who's Number One?" *Population Today* March: 6–9.

Hayes, C. D. ed. 1987. "Risking the Future: Adolescent Sexuality, Pregnancy, and Childbearing," vol. 2. *Working Papers*. National Academy of the Sciences Panel on Adolescent Pregnancy and Childbearing. Washington D.C.: National Academy Press.

Hexter, A. C., J. A. Harris, P. Roeper, L. A. Croen, P. Krueger, and D. Gant. 1990. "Evaluation of the Hospital Discharge Diagnoses Index and the Birth Certificate as Sources of Information on Birth Defects." *Public Health Reports* 105: 296–307.

Hopkins, D. D., J. A. Granty-Worley, and T. L. Bollinger. 1989. "Survey of Cause of Death Query Criteria Used by State Vital Statistics Programs in the United States and the Efficacy of the Criteria Used by the Oregon Vital Statistics Program." *American Journal of Public Health* 79: 570–74.

Horwitz, R. I., and E. C. Yu. 1984. "Assessing the Reliability of Epidemiologic Data Obtained from Medical Records." *Journal of Chronic Disease* 37: 825–31.

Howell, E. M., and B. Blondell. 1994. "International Infant Mortality Rates: Bias From Reporting Differences." *American Journal of Public Health* 84: 850–52.

Hutchkins, V., S. Kessel, and P. Placek. 1984. "Trends in Maternal and Infant Health Factors Associated with Low Birth Weight, U.S., 1972 and 1980." *Public Health Reports* 99: 162–72.

Jepson, H. A., M. L. Talashek, and A. M. Tichy. 1991. "The Apgar Score: Evolution, Limitations, and Scoring Guidelines." *Birth* 18: 83–92.

Joyce, T. J. 1994. "Self-Selection, Prenatal Care, and Birth Among Blacks, Whites and Hispanics in New York City." *Journal of Human Resources* 29: 762–94.

Kennedy, R. D., and R. E. Deapen. 1991. "Differences between Oklahoma Indian Infant Mortality and Other Races." *Public Health Reports* 106: 97–100.

Kircher, T., J. Nelson, and H. Burdo. 1985. "The Autopsy as a Measure of Accuracy of the Death Certificate." *New England Journal of Medicine* 313: 1263–69.

Kleinman, J. C. 1986. "Underreporting of Infant Deaths: Then and Now." *American Journal of Public Health* 76: 365–66.

Kleinman, J. C., and S. Kessel. 1987. "Racial Differences in Low Birthweight." *New England Journal of Medicine* 317: 749–53.

Kogan, M. D., G. R. Alexander, M. Kotelchuck, and D. A. Nagey. 1994a. "Relation of the Content of Prenatal Care to the Risk of Low Birth Weight: Maternal Reports of Health Behavior Advice and Initial Prenatal Care Procedures." *Journal of the American Medical Association* 271: 1340–45.

Kogan, M. D., M. Kotelchuck, G. R. Alexander, and W. E. Johnson. 1994b. "Racial Disparities in Reported Prenatal Care Advice from Health Care Providers." *American Journal of Public Health* 84: 82–88.

Kotelchuck, M. 1994a. "An Evaluation of the Kessner Adequacy of Prenatal Care Index and A Proposed Adequacy of Prenatal Care Utilization Index." *American Journal of Public Health* 84: 1414–20.

———. 1994b. "The Adequacy of Prenatal Care Utilization Index: Its U.S. Distribution and Association with Low Birth Weight." *American Journal of Public Health* 84: 1486–88.

Kramer, M. S. 1987. "Determinants of Low Birth Weight: Methodological Assessment and Meta-Analysis." *Bulletin of the World Health Organization* 5: 663–737.

Kramer, M. S., F. H. McLean, M. E. Boyd, and R. H. Usher. 1988. "The Validity of Gestational Age Estimation by Menstrual Dating in Term, Preterm, and Postterm Gestations." *Journal of the American Medical Association* 260: 3306–8.

Lambert, D. A., and L. T. Strauss. 1987. "Analysis of Unlinked Infant Death Certificates from the NIBS Project." *Public Health Reports* 102: 200–204.

Lantz, P. M., and J. R. Penrod. 1996. "Measurement Error in Prenatal Care Utilization: Evidence of Attenuation Bias in Birth Weight Estimation." *Robert Wood Johnson Foundation Scholars in Health Policy Research Working Paper Series.* Boston, Mass.: Boston University.

Leveno, K. J., F. G. Cunningham, M. L. Roark, S. D. Nelson, and M. L. Williams. 1985. "Prenatal Care and the Low Birth Weight Infant." *Journal of Obstetrics and Gynecology* 66: 599–605.

Lubchenco, L. O., C. Hansman, and E. Boyd. 1966. "Intrauterine Growth in Length and Head Circumference as Estimated from Live Births at Gestational Ages from Twenty-six to Forty-two Weeks." *Pediatrics* 37: 403–8.

Luke, B., and L. G. Keith. 1991. "The United States Standard Certificate of Live Birth: A Critical Commentary." *Journal of Reproductive Medicine* 36: 587–91.

MacFarlane, A. 1989. "Commentary: Revised U.S. Certificate of Birth: A View from England." *Birth* 16: 193–95.

Maloni, J. A., C. Y. Cheng, C. P. Liebl, and J. S. Maier. 1996. "Transforming Prenatal Care: Reflections on the Past and Present with Implications for the Future." *Journal of Obstetric, Gynecologic and Neonatal Nursing* 25: 17–23.

McClain, P. W., J. J. Sacks, R. G. Froehlke, and B. G. Ewigman. 1993. "Estimates of Fatal Child Abuse and Neglect, United States, 1979–1988." *Pediatrics* 91: 338–43.

McCormick, M. 1985. "The Contribution of Low Birth Weight to Infant Mortality and Childhood Morbidity." *New England Journal of Medicine* 312: 82–89.

McCormick, M., J. Brooks-Gunn, K. Workman-Daniels, J. Turner, and G. Peckham. 1992. "The Health and Development Status of Very Low Birth Weight Children at School Age." *Journal of the American Medical Association* 267: 2204–8.

Minton, S. D., and R. E. Seegmiller. 1986. "An Improved System for Reporting Congenital Malformations." *Journal of the American Medical Association* 256: 2976–79.

Nagey, D. A. 1989. "The Content of Prenatal Care." *Obstetrics and Gynecology* 74: 516–28.

Nakamura, R. M., R. King, E. H. Kimball, R. K. Oye, and S. D. Helgerson. 1991. "Excess Infant Mortality in an American Indian Population, 1940–1990." *Journal of the American Medical Association* 266: 2244–48.

National Center for Health Statistics. 1991. "Advance Report of Final Natality Statistics, 1991." *Monthly Vital Statistics Report* 42 (Suppl).

———. 1993. *Health, United States, 1993.* Hyattsville, Md.: Public Health Service.

National Center for Health Statistics, L. A. Fingerhut, and J. C. Kleinman. 1985. "Comparability of Reporting Between the Birth Certificate and the 1980 National Natality Survey." *Vital and Health Statistics*, series 2, no. 99. Washington: U.S. Government Printing Office for the Department of Health and Human Services.

National Center for Health Statistics, G. C. Tolson, J. M. Barnes, G. A. Gay, and J. L. Kowaleski. 1991. "The 1989 Revision of the U.S. Standard Certificates and Reports." *Vital and Health Statistics*, series 4, no. 28. Washington: U.S. Government Printing Office for the Department of Health and Human Services.

Oates, R. K., and D. Forrest. 1984. "Reliability of Mothers' Reports on Birth Data." *Australian Pediatric Journal* 20: 1858–1860.

Overpeck, M. D., H. J. Hoffman, and K. Prager. 1992. "The Lowest Birth Weights and the U.S. Infant Mortality Rate: National Center for Health Statistics 1983 Linked Birth/Infant Death Data." *American Journal of Public Health* 82: 441–44.

Parrish, K. M., V. L. Holt, F. A. Connel, B. Williams, and J. P. LoGerfo. 1989. "Variations in the Accuracy of Obstetric Procedures and Diagnoses on Birth Records in Washington State, 1989." *American Journal of Epidemiology* 138: 119–27.

Partin, M. R. 1993. "Explaining Race Differences in Infant Mortality in the United States." Ph.D. diss., University of Wisconsin–Madison.

Partin, M. R., and A. Palloni. 1994. "Accounting for Recent Increases in Low Birth Weight among African Americans." Paper presented at the annual meetings of the Population Association of America. Miami, Fl. (May 1994).

Peoples-Sheps, M. D., V. K. Hogan, and N. Ng'andu. 1996. "Content of Prenatal Care During the Initial Workup." *American Journal of Obstetrics and Gynecology* 174: 220–26.

Peoples-Sheps, M. D., W. D. Kalsbeek, and E. Siegel. 1988. "Why We Know So Little About Prenatal Care Nationwide: An Assessment of Required Methodology." *Health Services Research* 23: 359–80.

Perrin, E. B. 1974. "The Cooperative Health Statistics System." *Health Services Research* 89: 13–15.

Petitti, D. B., R. A. Hiatt, V. Chin, and M. Crougan-Minihane. 1991. "An Outcome Evaluation of the Content and Quality of Prenatal Care." *Birth* 18: 21–25.

Piper, J. M., E. F. Mitchel, M. Snowden, C. Hall, M. Adams, and P. Taylor. 1993. "Validation of 1989 Tennessee Birth Certificates Using Maternal and Newborn Hospital Records." *American Journal of Epidemiology* 137: 758–68.

Querec, L. J. 1980. "Comparability of Reporting on Birth Certificates and National Natality Survey Questionnaires." *Vital and Health Statistics*, series 2. no. 83. Washington: U.S. Government Printing Office for the Department of Health and Human Services.

Rogers, R. 1989. "Ethnic and Birth Weight Differences in Cause-Specific Infant Mortality." *Demography* 26: 335–44.

Romm, F. J., and S. M. Putnam. 1981. "The Validity of the Medical Record." *Medical Care* 19: 310–15.

Rosenberg, H. M. 1989. "Improving Cause of Death Statistics." *American Journal of Public Health* 79: 563–64.

Rosenzwieg, M. R., and T. P. Schultz. 1983. "Estimating a Household Production Function: Heterogeneity, the Demand for Health Inputs, and Their Effects on Birth Weight." *Journal of Political Economy* 91: 723–46.

Salmi, L. R., F. Dabis, and T. McKinley. 1990. "Quality of Death Certificates: Studying or Burying." *American Journal of Public Health* 80: 751–52.

Sanderson, M., P. J. Placek, and K. G. Keppel. 1991. "The 1988 National Maternal and Infant Health Survey: Design, Content and Data Availability." *Birth* 18: 26–32.

Sardell, A. 1990. "Child Health Policy and U.S.: The Paradox of Consensus." *Journal of Health Politics, Policy and Law* 15: 271–304.

Saugstad, L. F. 1981. "Weight of All Births and Infant Mortality." *Journal of Epidemiology and Community Health* 35: 185–91.

Schieber, G., J. Pullier, and L. M. Greenwald. 1991. "Health Care Systems in Twenty-Four Countries." *Health Affairs* 10: 22–38.

Schottenfeld, D., M. Eaton, S. C. Sommers, D. R. Alonso, and C. Wilkinson. 1982. "The Autopsy as a Measure of Accuracy of the Death Certificate." *Bulletin of the New York Academy of Medicine* 58: 778–94.

Shryock, H. S., and J. S. Siegel. 1976. *The Methods and Materials of Demography.* 1976. Orlando, Fl.: Academic Press, Inc.

Strobino, D., P. O'Campo, K. C. Schoendorf, et al. 1995. "A Strategic Framework for Infant Mortality Reduction: Implications for 'Healthy Start.'" *Milbank Memorial Fund Quarterly.* 73(4): 507–33.

Taffel, S. M., S. J. Ventura, and G. A. Gay. 1989. "Revised U.S. Certificate of Birth—New Opportunities for Research on Birth Outcomes" *Birth* 16: 188–93.

Tilley, B. C., A. B. Barnes, E. Bergstrahl, D. Labarthe, K. Noller et al. 1985. "A Comparison of Pregnancy History Recall and Medical Records: Implications for Retrospective Studies." *American Journal of Epidemiology* 121: 269–81.

Tompkins, M. E., G. R. Alexander, K. L. Jackson, C. A. Hornung, J. M. Altenkruse, et al. 1985. "The Risk of Low Birthweight. Alternative Models of Neonatal Mortality." *American Journal of Epidemiology* 122: 1067–79.

U.S. Department of Health and Human Services. 1990. *Healthy People 2000: National Health Promotion and Disease Prevention Objectives.* Washington: U.S. Government Printing Office for the U.S. Department of Health and Human Services.

U.S. Public Health Service. 1989. *Caring for Our Future: The Content of Prenatal Care.* Washington: U.S. Government Printing Office.

Wilcox, A. J., and I. Russell. 1990. "Why Small Black Infants Have a Lower Mortality Rate Than Small White Infants: The Case for Population-Specific Standards for Birth Weight." *Journal of Pediatrics* 116: 7–10.

Williams, R. L., N. J. Binkin, and E. J. Clingman. 1986. "Pregnancy Outcomes Among Spanish Surname Women in California." *American Journal of Public Health* 76: 387–91.

Wise, P. H. 1994. "What You Measure Is What You Get: Prenatal Care and Women's Health." *American Journal of Public Health* 84: 1374–75.

Wright, L. 1994. "One Drop of Blood." *The New Yorker* 25: 46–55.

Zahniser, C., G. Halpin, W. Hollinshead, S. Kessel, and A. Koontz. 1987. "Using Linked Birth and Infant Death Files for Program Planning and Evaluation: National Infant Mortality Surveillance Workshop Lessons." *Public Health Reports* 102: 211–16.

Health Indicators for Preschool Children,
Ages One to Four

Barbara L. Wolfe and James Sears

PER CAPITA HEALTH-CARE expenditures on young children are lower than those on any other age group.[1] Although preventive care is critical for preschoolers, children between the ages of one and four experience low rates of acute and chronic illnesses, and they are studied less than are their younger (infant) and older (school-aged) counterparts. Immunization rates are the one aspect of preschoolers' health which has recently received substantial attention, an exception that is partially attributable to the sudden increase in the incidence of measles in 1990 (see, for example, Lewit and Mullahy 1994; Goldstein, Kviz, and Daum 1993).

Children aged one to four are a particularly vulnerable group. They rely almost entirely upon others (adults) to meet their needs and make decisions on their part. Over time, successive cohorts of preschool-age children have experienced social and economic events that have significant implications for their development. Several changes in particular over the last two decades suggest that recent cohorts of preschoolers are not doing well: the poverty rate for children has been increasing since the early 1970s, and the proportion of children growing up in single-parent families has increased. This makes the paucity of indicators for preschool-age children surprising.

Public opinion suggests that children's well-being is a primary public concern. According to a 1993 article by Susan Nall Bales, recent surveys tell us that:

> The public wants children to be a top priority for government spending. . . . twenty-four percent chose it as their top priority. . . . [F]or 61 percent . . . it was among their top three priorities for tax dollars. . . . Children's access to health care is more important to the public than other key children's issues. . . . There is a clear mandate for government to do more for children. . . . Americans are so concerned about children that they will even support new taxes. (Bales 1993: 186–187)

A major change across cohorts of preschoolers is the declining number of those with a parent at home full-time. From 1940 to 1989 the proportion of five-year-olds with a parent who could supply full-time care dropped from 84 to 52 percent (Hernandez 1994). Among children aged zero to five the proportion living with a full-time homemaker decreased from 78 to 32 percent over four decades, from the 1940s to the 1980s (Hernandez 1994). Sixty-five percent of children under five were in day care outside of their home in 1991.

The poverty rate of children under six stood at 23.7 percent in 1995, down from the recent high of 25.7 percent in 1992, but up from 18 percent in 1966 and from a low of 16 percent in 1973 (March Current Population Survey various years.) The Medicaid program provides health insurance to the majority of children living in poverty. Nearly 86 percent of children who were under age eleven and below the poverty line received Medicaid in 1993 (Dubay and Kenney 1996). Near-poor children (those with family incomes between 100 and 133 percent of poverty) are more likely to lack insurance altogether; Dubay and Kenney find that 15.8 percent of near-poor children under age eleven were uninsured for the year 1993, as compared with 8.1 percent of young children living in poverty. These same authors estimate that 45 percent of the children ages birth to five who lack health insurance are actually eligible for Medicaid.

As states change the welfare system from one that provides cash assistance to one that requires work, young children will surely be affected. They are likely to spend reduced time with parents, more time in child care and, for some, in minimum-cost child care that may be of poor quality. For many, family income will be reduced. Added family stress from these changes may also lead to increases in maltreatment of young children, increases of family moves, more density in living arrangements, increased risks of emotional and physical harm as well as an increase in the probability of homelessness. For some, their parent's satisfaction of work may mean an improvement in emotional well-being if not material standard of living. But all of these are simply conjectures; we need to monitor the state of our young children as never before, at least those who are part of our low-income (vulnerable) population.

The question of great importance is, What has been (or will be) the impact of these changes in terms of children's well-being? The answer requires data on outcomes, which are generally more difficult to measure than inputs. If a clear, strong relationship is established between an input and an outcome, data on the input can serve as a proxy for an outcome. Unfortunately, in most cases we have not collected adequate data to establish these links in such a way as to give researchers confidence in the input-outcome relationship. Collection of such data is therefore part of the task facing those of us interested in monitoring children's well-being (Hernandez 1994).

In this chapter we report on measures of health collected for children aged one to four, recommend construction of three measures concerning health status and two concerning access to medical care, and argue that these dominate other possible indicators. We then discuss the steps required to obtain information for these indicators, providing some alternatives that vary with health-care policy.

In the discussion that follows we make use of three criteria to judge measures of child health:

1. *Variability:* the ability to detect changes over time and differences across populations.

2. *Validity:* actual measurement of what is intended to be measured.

3. *Reliability:* freedom from error (and related to this, sensitivity—that is, the probability of detecting true cases).

To illustrate: the sex-adjusted mortality rate for children one to four is an objective and readily available statistic which is quite *reliable* (free of error). However, because that mortality rate is very low, it has limited *variability* and hence is unlikely to detect most of the changes in the health of children. Given this, it is not a very useful or *valid* indicator of overall child health. We also regard the difficulty of gathering information on the indicator as an important consideration in the task of evaluating and recommending indicators. Surveys which require combinations of provider and parental responses are not only very expensive but may fail to yield publicly available data sets in a timely manner. Furthermore, they may be selective of certain populations who have a regular provider and/or who are reachable by phone.

CURRENT COLLECTION OF INDICATOR INFORMATION

Four surveys collect data on the health of preschool-age children with some degree of regularity: the National Ambulatory Medical Care Survey (NAMCS), the National Health and Nutrition Examination Survey (NHANES), the National Health Interview Survey (NHIS), and the National Medical Expenditure Survey (NMES). These are household-based surveys, except for the NHANES, which includes data from physical examinations. Some NMES data also are corroborated with provider-based information. Only the NAMCS and the NHIS are collected annually. While most NHIS child health data are only available for years in which a special child health topical module has been included, current plans call for questions about children to be added to the basic NHIS questionnaire beginning in 1997. In the future the State and Local Area Immunization Coverage and Health Surveys (SLICHS) may become another valuable source of annual child health information. So far, only the immunization portion of the SLICHS, called the National Immunization Survey, has been fielded (beginning in 1994).

Several other sources of child health information currently exist, but these are not collected regularly or only provide information on particular aspects of child health. The Rand Health Insurance Study (Rand HIS) contributes to our knowledge of children's health status, but it is not current. The National Longitudinal Survey of Youth (NLS-Y) collected data on the children of respondents to the National Longitudinal Survey, but these are children born to women of a narrow age range and hence may not be generally representative of preschool-age children generally. The Survey of Parents of Children Under Three (SPCU3), conducted by the Princeton Survey Research Associates and DataStat for the Commonwealth Fund, is a onetime survey of more than two thousand parents of children under three years of age; it asks only limited questions in terms of health status as compared to more detailed questions on insurance coverage and health care utilization. Data sources which provide limited types of child health information include the U.S. Immunization Survey, the Pediatric Nutrition Surveillance System, the National Survey of Families and Households (NSFH), the National Hospital Discharge Survey, and the Survey of Income and Program Participation (SIPP).

For purposes of discussion, we divide indicators of child health into the following broad categories: overall health status, medical care utilization, impairments, and other medical conditions. We also consider how some environmental factors influence child well-being through child care experiences and the incidence of accidental injuries. Overall health status may be gauged by a general measure of health, by activity limitations, days in bed, and anthropometric measures. Medical care utilization may include measures of use and measures of access or coverage. Impairments comprise physical impairments and emotional or behavioral impairments. The set of tables in this chapter provides details on the information collected in these categories, and their sources. Only the most recent surveys are included.

Overall Health Status

These measures of general health include social measures that deserve serious consideration as indicators for preschool-age children (see table 4.1).

The parent's or caretaker's impression of the overall health of the child is often summed up as excellent, good, fair, or poor. This is a common categorization of health for all age groups, which is easy to collect and has been validated for certain older age groups (see Maddox and Douglas 1973; Fylkesnes and Forde 1991). It has not been well validated for this young age group. It is subjective on the part of parents/caretakers.

The ability of the child to engage in ordinary play activities is analogous to the absence of a work limitation for an adult. Questions about play typically focus on whether health reasons prevent the child from participating in normal activities for his or her age. Physical location (for example, urban versus rural, small apartment, or dangerous neighborhood) may influence opportunities and therefore affect responses.

Anthropometric measures include the child's height, weight, and weight for height. These are objective measures and hence are attractive. They are normally collected as part of a physical examination and are included in patient records. The National Center for Health Statistics has established standards for height by age and weight for height that can be used to capture such significant deviations as "stunted" or "wasted," meaning that a child's height for age or weight for height is less than the 5th or 10th percentile. These indicators are typically used for comparisons across races (see, for example, U.S. Department of Health and Human Services 1986, p. 22). The chief limitation is that they are not sensitive to most changes in health status. Nevertheless, they do provide some indication of the well-being of poor children relative to other children. Using NHANES, for example, researchers find that among two- to five-year-old boys (girls), those in poor families are about twice (thrice) as likely to be stunted as those in nonpoor families (Montgomery and Carter-Pokras 1993).

Most of the other measures described in table 4.1 are poorer indicators of child health. Those related to perceived vulnerability and resistance to illness have little appeal as measures of overall health because they depend on the parents' expectations (norms), the child's exposure to illness, and the presence of siblings. Bed days or preschool days missed depend not only on the child's health but also on the parents' normal activities (that is their opportunity cost of keep-

(Text continues on p. 82)

Table 4.1 Measures of Overall Health Status

Measure	Description	Source
Health status	Excellent, good, fair, or poor (respondent's impression)	NMES, RAND HIS, NHANES III, NHIS core, NLS-Y, SPCU3
	Excellent, very good, good, fair, or poor (physician's impression)	NHANES III
	Worry about child's health: not at all, little, some, great deal (past 3 months)	NMES
	Health caused pain/distress: not at all, little, some, great deal (past 3 months)	NMES
	Resists illness very well (definitely F, mostly F, mostly T, definitely T) (T or F)	NHIS child questionnaire (1988, 1991), RAND HIS
	Never been seriously ill (definitely F, mostly F, mostly T, definitely T) (T or F)	NMES
	Catches things "going around" (definite F, mostly F, mostly T, definite T) (T or F)	NHIS child, RAND HIS
		NMES
	Less healthy than other children (T or F)	NHIS child, RAND HIS
	Usually recovers quickly when sick (T or F)	NHIS child, RAND HIS
	Ever so sick you thought might die (T or F)	NHIS child
		NHIS child, RAND HIS
Play limitations	Able to take part at all in usual play activities (current)	NHIS core, NHANES III
	Able to take part at all in usual play activities (past 3 months)	NMES
	Has condition that limits play activities	NLS-Y
	Kind or amount of play activities limited by impairment or health problem (current)	NHIS core, NHANES III
	(past 3 months)	NMES
	Kind or amount of ordinary play limited by health	RAND HIS
	Health keeps from taking part in ordinary play	RAND HIS
	Needs more help than usual for age in eating, dressing, bathing, or using toilet because of health	RAND HIS
	Limited in any way by impairment or health problem	NMES

Bed days	Stayed in bed because of illness or injury (past 2 weeks)	NHIS core
	Days in bed > $1/2$ day due to illness or injury (past 2 weeks and year)	NHIS core
	Days in bed > $1/2$ day due to illness or injury (since last interview)	NMES
Anthropometric measure	Height and weight without shoes, age	NMES, NHANES III, NHIS core, Pediatric Nutrition Surveillance System (low-income only), NLS-Y
	Low (5th percentile) height-for-age, low weight-for-height, and high (95th percentile) weight-for-height	Pediatric Nutrition Surveillance System
	Body measurements including head and upper arm circumferences and triceps skinfold	NHANES III
Abbreviations used in tables	CPS	Current Population Survey
	NAMCS	National Ambulatory Medical Care Survey
	NHANES III	National Health and Nutrition Examination Survey
	NHIS	National Health Interview Survey
	NLS-Y	National Longitudinal Survey of Youth
	NMES	National Medical Expenditure Survey
	NSFH	National Survey of Families and Households
	Rand HIS	RAND Health Insurance Study
	SIPP	Survey of Income and Program Participation
	SPCU3	Survey of Parents of Children Under Three

ing the child in bed or at home). Bed days or days at home may reflect the proportion of mothers who work rather than the child's health. A parent's occupation may also influence reported bed or school days missed. This class of indicators is neither valid nor reliable.

Medical Care Utilization

Use of medical care is among the most commonly collected data on health. In this category we include ambulatory or outpatient visits, hospitalization, and insurance coverage. Several of these measures are presented in table 4.2. Medical care is an input into the production of health; at best, it serves as a health proxy. More use may be associated with poorer health (greater need for care), yet it may also indicate adequate access, leading to improved health. For a utilization measure to act as a valid health indicator, one of these effects must clearly dominate the other.

Two measures of ambulatory care visits are often encountered: whether over some specified period the child has seen (or had any form of contact with) a provider and whether the child has a regular source of care. Unless the role of "well child" visits is understood, these measures alone cannot be viewed as valid indicators of good or poor health. When data on diagnoses or specific health conditions are collected, the utilization of providers for particular conditions may provide a more sensitive and valid set of health proxies. Choosing an appropriate recall period poses a dilemma for all such data: poor recall of long-ago events may lead to unreliable measures, but a short reference period limits variability. Diagnostic-specific information is likely to convey useful information regarding access to medical care; however, the small proportion of children with any particular diagnosis limits its validity as an overall indicator of child health. It may be useful as an indicator for a particular subgroup of children defined in terms of some preexisting health condition.

Data on hospitalizations include number of inpatient stays, length of stay, and rate of hospitalization by diagnosis. These measures tend to be reliable and easy-to-collect indicators of poor health, but they contain limited information. Too few children experience hospitalizations in any year for these data to provide a comprehensive measure of child health. However, a comparison of hospital utilization to physician utilization may be informative. Children in poor families have been observed to use less ambulatory care and more hospital care than children in wealthy families, suggesting that they do not receive care until later in the course of their illness (U.S. Department of Health and Human Services 1989).

Insurance coverage is another possible measure of child health. It is commonly collected, has varied substantially over time, and has historically revealed striking differences among racial and income groups. Studies have repeatedly shown that insurance coverage is linked to utilization, so it does capture an important factor that is likely to influence access to care (Manning et al. 1987).

Vaccinations prevent illness; they are easier to observe than the incidence of illness. Information on vaccinations is collected both from individuals answering questionnaires and from provider surveys. The goal of immunization is the prevention of illness, and the success rate is extremely high. As such it is a potentially useful indicator of child health and one that has historically exhibited

(Text continues on p. 85.)

Table 4.2 Medical Care Utilization

Measure	Description	Source
Visits and calls	Seen or talked to medical doctor about child (past 2 weeks)	NHIS core
	Seen or talked to medical doctor or assistant about child (past year)	NHIS core
	Time since seen or talked to MD or assistant about child	NHIS core
	Is there a usual place (doctor's office, clinic, etc.) for routine care?	NHIS child (1988, 1991), NHIS access to care (1993, 1994), SPCU3
	Is there a usual place where child goes when sick or injured?	NHIS child, NHIS access to care
	Is there a place child usually goes for routine care, advice, or when sick?	NHANES III
	Is there a particular medical person child sees when sick?	NHIS child, NHIS access to care, NHANES III
	Is there a particular medical person who usually gives advice over phone?	NHIS child, NHIS access to care
	Time since last routine care visit (<6 mo., 6 mo.–1 yr, 1–2 yrs., >2 yrs.)	NHIS child
	Time since last saw or talked to health professional about (<1 yr, 1–2 yrs., . . .)	NHANES III
	Doctor visits since previous interview	NMES
	Other medical practitioner visits since previous interview	NMES
	Nurse, physician assistant visits since previous interview	NMES
	Phone calls to medical doctor about child since previous interview	NMES
	Rate of visits by diagnosis category	NAMCS
Hospitalization	Outpatient visits since previous interview	NMES
	Emergency room visits since previous interview	NMES
	Different times overnight in hospital in past year	NHIS core
	Inpatient stays since previous interview	NMES
	Times overnight in hospital in life (except birth)	NHANES III
	Rate of hospitalization by diagnosis	National Hospital Discharge Survey

Table 4.2 *Continued*

Measure	Description	Source
Insurance	Medicare, Medicaid, any employer based, any other (current and previous year)	CPS
	Medicare, Medicaid, CHAMPUS/CHAMPVA, other public, any private, HMO coverage	NMES
	Medicare, Medicaid, CHAMPUS/CHAMPVA, HMO, and any coverage	NHIS insurance (1986, 1989, 1993, 1994)
	Medicare, Medicaid, CHAMPUS/CHAMPVA, employer private, other private coverage (current and since initial interview)	SIPP
	Medicare and other coverage	NHANES III
	Medicaid, employer-provided coverage, HMO, PPO, uninsured	SPCU3
	Medicaid and any insurance	NLS-Y
	Medicaid coverage and any use in past year	NHIS topics (1988, 1989, 1991–1994)
		NMES
	Whether card available	NMES
Vaccinations	Diphtheria, tetanus, or pertussis (DPT); red measles; german measles; mumps; polio by mouth	NHANES III
	Tetanus including DPT	U.S. Immunization Survey (1985 and earlier)
	DPT (# doses), measles, mumps, rubella, and polio (# doses)	NHIS Immunization (1991–1994), National Immunization Surveys
	DPT, measles, Haemophilus influenzae type b, polio, hepatitus b	U.S. Immunization Survey, NHIS Immunization
	Whether vaccination card available	*Statistical Abstracts*, using 1991 NHIS
	Vaccination up-to-date for age	*Health United States*, using U.S. Immunization Survey
	% immunized (measles, mumps, rubella, DPT, polio) out of people referring to immunization records	

dramatic variation. If based on parental responses, reliability is limited, however, and validity over time depends on an unvarying recommended immunization schedule. (The recent Children's Vaccine Initiative of the U.S. government has been very successful in increasing the rate of immunizations of children birth to four in the last few years, for example).[2]

Impairments

This set of measures, which are presented in table 4.3, includes problems with regard to sight, hearing, growth, and mental functioning, as well as physical impairments. It is likely to have long-run impacts on school performance and acceptance by peers, but it may be unreliable to the extent that emotional, developmental, and learning problems require professional diagnosis. If a child does not go to a medical care provider or a psychological testing group, the parents may be ignorant of their child's condition and hence unable to convey the "true" information on development. The remaining impairment indicators are likely to be reliable and valid, but the low incidence of impairments limits their ability to convey significant changes in the health status of the one- to four-year age group.

Other Medical Conditions

Another set of indicators concerns acute and chronic conditions (see table 4.4). Chronic measures that are likely to have long-term and significant consequences for a child include heart problems, diabetes, frequent diarrhea or colitis, and significant allergies. However, they share the drawback mentioned for impairments: identification may require contact with a provider. One could imagine that reported health status might appear to deteriorate (the number of conditions might grow), when what actually occurs is a rise in physician contact and a corresponding increase in the probability of diagnosis and treatment. Another problem with both acute and chronic conditions is that they are not adjusted for severity. A final drawback is that a count of conditions may be deceiving, since not all conditions are similar in their implications for child health.

Information on acute conditions is more typically included among the utilization indicators than in direct measures of acute problems. One exception is the third National Health and Nutrition Examination Survey, NHANES III, which provides an indicator of iron deficiency anemia. While this measure may be useful for international comparisons, rates of anemia are unlikely to exhibit much variation for groups of preschoolers within the United States.[3]

Environmental Factors

Health status is linked to countless environmental factors, ranging from violence within the community to the quality of adult supervision to whether or not the parents smoke in the home, as well as parental use or abuse of a variety of other substances. Because many of these environmental influences are viewed as "norms" by the people who experience them, they are unlikely to be fully reflected in parental assessments of child health or play limitations, nor can we hope to address every one of them individually. Instead, we include child care in

(*Text continues on p. 88.*)

Table 4.3 Impairments

Measure	Description	Source
Sight	Blindness	NHIS child (1988, 1991), NMES
	Blindness in one or both eyes	NHIS core
	Wears glasses or contact lenses	NHIS child, NHANES III, NMES
	Difficulty seeing even with glasses	NHIS child, NHIS disability (1994), NHANES III, NMES
	Recognizes familiar people at 2 or 3 feet with glasses	NMES
	Serious difficulty seeing	NLS-Y
	Ever had vision tested	NHANES III
Hearing	Deafness	NHIS topics (1988, 1990, 1991), NMES
	Deafness in one or both ears	NHIS core
	Wears hearing aid	NHIS topics (1988, 1990, 1991), NHANES III, NMES
	Difficulty hearing even with hearing aid	NMES
	Hears some things with hearing aid	NMES
	Serious hearing difficulty	NLS-Y
	Ever had trouble hearing, which lasted more than short period	NHANES III
	Ever had hearing tested	NHANES III
Development	Delay in growth or development (When? Seen doctor? Taken medicine?)	NHIS child
	Emotional or behavioral problem lasting more than 3 months (When? Seen doctor? Taken medicine?)	NHIS child

	Has problem or delay in physical development (and whether doctor or health care professional has mentioned this problem)	NHIS disability
	Has problem or delay in emotional or mental development (and whether doctor or health care professional has mentioned this problem)	NHIS disability
	Learning disability (When? Seen doctor? Taken medicine?)	NHIS child
	Seen doctor/counselor for any emotional, developmental, or behavioral problem (When was last time?)	NHIS child
	Learning disability, minimal brain dysfunction, hyperkinesis or hyperactivity, serious emotional disturbance, mental retardation	NLS-Y
	Learning disability or mental retardation	NHIS disability
	Doctor said mentally retarded	NHANES III
	Respondent feels child is fast, slow, or about on time in development	National Survey of Families and Households
Physical impairments	Permanent impairment, stiffness or deformity of back, foot, leg, fingers, hand, or arm (specify)	NHIS child
	Missing finger, hand, arm, toes, foot, leg (specify)	NHIS child
	Crippled, orthopedic handicap	NLS-Y
	Part of body affected by perceived disability	NHIS disability

Table 4.4   Other Medical Conditions

Measure	Description	Source
Number of conditions	Eleven chronic conditions including heart problem, anemia, allergies	NMES
	Nine chronic conditions identified by MD, including heart disease, epilepsy	NHANES III
	About 30 chronic listed, with space to enter other condition	NHIS child (1988, 1991)
	Any perceived disability mapped to a chronic condition if possible	NHIS disability (1994)
	Seven acute, including diarrhea, flu/virus, stomachache, earache, fever	NMES
	Anemia (acute)	NHANES III
Information about each condition	Had at least 3 months (If not, is it obviously permanent?)	NHIS child
	Days in bed >1/2 day due to condition (past 12 months)	NHIS child
	Taken medication for condition (past 12 months)	NHIS child
	Surgery for condition (past 12 months)	NHIS child
	Pain or discomfort or upset (all the time, often, once in a while, never)	NHIS child
	Bothered by condition (great deal, some, very little)	NHIS child
	How long ago condition first noticed	NHIS disability
	How long ago saw doctor for condition	NHIS disability
	Saw doctor for condition (30 days acute, 12 months chronic)	NMES, NHANES III

our final set of indicators (see table 4.5) and try to capture the effects of other environmental factors through measures of safety and accidental injury.

Although child care is clearly not valid as a measure of overall health status, it may serve as a measure of parental time spent with children. It could also be viewed as a control for acute illness since, in general, children are exposed to more disease in child care outside the home than at home. The questions asked are directed at child care quality, and quality may influence child well-being.

The NHIS has been the only national survey to gather a substantial amount of information relating to child safety. Recent NHIS topical modules have included questions on firearm storage, use of child safety seats, smoke detectors, ipecac syrup, and radon gas. The only aspect of child safety addressed regularly by administrative data is the injured that require the use of emergency rooms or an inpatient visit; this, however, may limit the data to severe injuries and may reflect a variety of issues of access. The use of accidents as a health indicator presents some of the problems already mentioned for other types of medical conditions. Any count of accidents must combine conditions of varying degrees of seriousness. Even if a count is limited to injuries which require the attention of a physician, it will still reflect varying propensities to seek medical care. Nonetheless, rates of accidental injury are expected to have some validity for the comparison of health risks across populations.

Table 4.5   Health Effects of Environmental Factors

Measure	Description	Source
Accidental injuries	Accidents, injuries, and poisonings in past year	NHIS child (1988, 1991)
	Three most recent accidents	NLS-Y
	Causes of recorded accidents	NLS-Y
	Resulting conditions (for example, broken bones, burns, poisoning)	NHIS child, NLS-Y
	Place where accident occurred (for example, home, day care, street)	NHIS child, NLS-Y
	Whether any disabling condition is the result of an accident	NHIS disability (1994)
Safety	Use of child safety seats (most of time, sometimes, occasionally, never)	NHIS topics (1988, 1990, 1991)
	(Seldom or never, sometimes, nearly always, always)	NMES
	Ipecac syrup in home	NHIS health promotion (1990)
	Whether respondent has telephone number of poison control center	NHIS health promotion
	Lead paint in home	NHIS environmental health (1991)
	Household air tested for radon gas	NHIS topics (1991, 1993, 1994)
	Number of working smoke detectors in home	NHIS Year 2000 objectives (1994)
	Number of firearms in home (loaded, locked up, taken apart)	NHIS Year 2000 objectives
	Ammunition in home (with firearm, locked up)	NHIS Year 2000 objectives
Child care	School, preschool, day care center, babysitter, day camp, relative (specify), other (time spent past 4 weeks)	NHIS child, NLS-Y
	Whether child care usually in home	NHIS child, NLS-Y
	Whether caretaker received special training	NHIS child, NLS-Y
	How often main child care arrangement changed in past year	NHIS child
	School, day care center or preschool, relative, at nonrelative home, other (typical secondary arrangement for work week)	SIPP
	Number of adults and children present during child care	NLS-Y
	Whether child's grandparent, child's sibling, other relative, babysitter, day care provided care while respondent worked (past week)	NSFH
	Hours provider cared for child while respondent worked (past week)	NSFH
	Whether provider cares for child in home	NSFH

POTENTIAL INDICATORS FOR WHICH DATA
HAVE NOT BEEN COLLECTED

We have seen that information on a wide range of child health indicators is collected regularly. We might wish to see some measures collected in a different manner, but almost no aspect of child health has been entirely ignored. As suggested above, safety is one health-related area that has received relatively little attention. The hazards to young children for which more data would be useful include bathing without supervision and open stairways. Accidental injuries, which have been the subject of survey questions, reflect many of the same health risks as safety hazards. Safety hazards would have the advantage of being much more common than resulting injuries, but survey respondents might be unaware of or unwilling to acknowledge such hazards.

Lead poisoning is a child health concern which has not been (and probably can never be) accurately assessed with national survey data. The Centers for Disease Control reduced the level of blood lead concentrations calling for intervention from twenty-five micrograms per deciliter in 1985 to ten micrograms per deciliter in 1993 (National Research Council 1993). Such low doses of lead are measurable, given strict quality control, but testing is generally limited to high-risk groups (pregnant women and young children among the poor).

Parental use of drugs and tobacco also may influence the health of children, either through the physical quality of the environment or through resulting parental behavior. However, establishing a causal link remains problematic given the difficulty of gaining accurate assessments of parental substance use and the long term involved until the influence can be measured in terms of impact on a child's health.

RECOMMENDATIONS FOR FUTURE DATA COLLECTION

Considering all available measures and the type of research that we might wish to do, the following five indicators seem desirable:

- parental evaluation of overall health: excellent, good, fair, or poor;
- whether or not the child can engage in normal play activities for age, and if not, whether play is limited by health or impairment;
- whether the child is covered by health insurance, and if so, what type;
- whether the child is vaccinated according to recommended standards for age; and
- number of accidents requiring medical treatment (a visit to the hospital) and the cause of each such accident.

If we could add a sixth, it would be height for age and weight for height (or length) measured by a person who conducts the survey or who accompanies the primary "surveyor." This indicator has been gathered at long intervals by the NHANES. Given the expense involved in conducting this sort of survey, we cannot recommend collecting weights and heights more frequently. However, if health data should be gathered from providers for other reasons, we would like to see these statistics included.

Our first recommended indicator is the "excellent, good, fair, poor" measure that is so commonly collected across age groups. The advantages of this measure are that it is easily collected, commonly used, and readily understood (even if the difference between excellent and good is not clear, the difference between either of these and poor is quite apparent). This overall health indicator is likely to be most useful when collected in conjunction with work and income data, as in the NLS-Y; it would be useful to learn whether labor market behavior is influenced by the presence of children with poor health and whether health status varies with family income.

A second indicator with desirable properties is whether the child is limited in the kind or amount of play activities in which he or she can participate. Surveys regularly collect this information with the typical stipulation that the play limitation be the result of health or an impairment. Play activities also could be limited by space constraints or a lack of time on the part of the caretaker. In such cases the limitation would still seem to be an indicator of "poor health," though in a broad sense rather than a narrow medical one. Accordingly, we would recommend that child health surveys include one question regarding ability to engage in normal play activities for age and use a follow-up question to ascertain the role of health or impairments in causing any limitations.

Play limitations and parental categorization of health status share two major drawbacks as overall measures of health: they are dependent on the norms of the society in which they are asked, and they do not indicate whether health problems are medically treatable. The first of these disadvantages is inherent. If average health status in a society improves, expectations will rise, and overall trends in parental health evaluations over time will be invalid. However, these measures still may be valid for judging whether the health of various racial or income groups converges or diverges over time. Fylkesnes and Forde (1991) find a "striking gap" between conditions which affect self-reported health status and conditions which are medically treatable. The second drawback may be partly addressed by follow-up questions. Over the next decade, we would like to see follow-up questions developed that would inquire whether play limitations and poor or fair health were primarily the results of permanent impairments, self-limiting ailments such as colds, or treatable conditions.

Until or unless we have universal health insurance coverage, another indicator that provides useful information is whether or not a child has health insurance. Coverage is correlated with access to medical care; without coverage children may not get adequate medical attention for any health conditions they develop. A decrease in the proportion of children covered suggests a deterioration in access to medical care and hence deterioration of the quality of life for young children. Parents should be asked whether the child is covered under Medicaid, a parent's coverage through employment, other private coverage, CHAMPUS or other government programs, or is not covered by any form of health insurance. It would also be useful to know whether the child has had the same coverage for the last six months. This will provide information on the extent, nature, and stability of coverage. This information is quite easy to collect and can be collected whenever parental information on coverage is asked, as in the Current Population Survey. The type of coverage conveys information augmenting the simple "yes, no" response, since access may be reduced, especially access to specialists, if coverage is provided publicly rather than privately.

A good deal of attention has been paid to the proportion of children who are vaccinated. (It is really the *only* measure for this age group that has received attention.) The typical vaccination issue facing researchers is what fraction of children are up to date on their immunizations at age two. Virtually all children eventually receive immunizations because of school entry requirements. Vaccinations represent prevention as well as access to medical care. They are our best indicator of preventive care because "well child" visits are difficult to count or clarify. A problem is that, because parental response is not reliable,[4] this measure really depends on administrative data. If a system were developed in which vaccination data were routinely reported to the Public Health Service, this information could be made readily available and serve as a form of administrative data on child health. This could be provided on a state or county basis and could be used to identify areas where service is significantly under par for the preschool-age population. Although such a system theoretically could be implemented on a nationwide basis within the next decade, we believe a more realistic goal would be to make the administrative immunization data available for a large sample of counties within ten years.

Finally, we believe that accidental injuries requiring medical treatment may reflect environmental influences on health that are not captured in the other measures we have suggested. The easiest method to gather information on accidents would be by survey. Serious accidents are relatively rare, but we do not anticipate that parents would have difficulty remembering them. Accordingly, we recommend a recall period of a full year. Accident data also could be gathered from emergency room records, but one would need a reliable estimate of the number of children in the area served by the hospital in order to interpret them. Studies in New York City (Szapiro 1989) provide evidence that children in poorer areas have more hospital admissions for poisonings, fractures, traumatic stupra, and coma. We have no such data nationwide or by age or race. A comparison of estimates could provide insights into the accuracy of parent-provided data and the feasibility of using hospital records.

CONCLUSION

What would we gain by collecting, on a regular basis, these indicators of child health for those aged one to four? Parents' evaluation of their children's overall health, the proportion of children who can engage in play, and the proportion of children who had an accident that required medical treatment are all *outcome* measures. When disaggregated by income, race, or geographic location they will provide us with real measures of children's well-being. They will allow us to track whether children's well-being is improving or deteriorating or both depending upon the group of children studied. But these indicators are also useful to study the relationship between inputs and outcome. On an aggregate (county) basis we can study the relationship between each of these outcome measures and availability of medical care, of health insurance coverage, of average income, such neighborhood factors as proportion of high school dropouts, proportion of female-headed households, and such policy variables as the required hours of work of single parents, the extent of the safety net, the time-limit for receipt of cash transfers and so forth. Similar studies can be done using individual data in a structural model to ask questions regarding the impact of poverty, of insurance, of parental time, of mother's actual work, of benefits in kind such as food stamps, parental education, and age of mother on children's health. With such data, we can learn far more regarding the determinants of child health. With such knowledge, public policy can be better directed.

The remaining two indicators (insurance coverage and vaccinations) represent inputs into the health of the child which public policy can influence. If we can establish a causal link to health outcomes, we will have an important policy tool to improve the well-being of children aged one to four.

NOTES

1. While published data are tabulated for varying age groups, Evans and Friedland (1994) estimate that children between the ages of one and ten have the lowest health expenditures.

2. Launched in 1990, the goal of this initiative is to increase the immunization of children. Two agencies, the Public Health Service and the Agency for International Development, are involved. The national initiative focuses on five areas that range from improving vaccines to decreasing the cost of immunization to outreach.

3. This is not to suggest that anemia poses negligible risks for all age groups. Earl (1993) recommends that infants not receiving iron-fortified formula be screened for iron deficiency at age nine months. He also suggests that children with such other risk factors as poverty or abuse be prescreened between the ages of six and nine.

4. Goldstein, Kviz, and Daum (1993) found that one-third of parents who reported their children fully immunized without consulting immunization cards were incorrect. Immunization cards improved response accuracy for those who had them, but possession of a card was positively correlated with having immunizations.

REFERENCES

Bales, Susan N. 1993. "Public Opinion and Health Care Reform for Children." *The Future of Children* 3(2): 184–97.

Dubay, Lisa C., and Genevieve M. Kenney. 1996. "The Effects of Medicaid Expansions on Insurance Coverage of Children." *The Future of Children* 6(1): 152–61.

Earl, Robert. 1993. *Iron Deficiency Anemia: Recommended Guidelines for the Prevention, Detection, and Management Among U.S. Children and Women of Childbearing Age*. Washington, D.C.: National Academy Press.

Evans, Alison, and Robert B. Friedland. 1994. "Financing and Delivery of Health Care for Children." Background paper. Washington, D.C.: National Academy of Social Insurance Advisory Committee on Reforming American Health Care Financing: Policy and Administrative Choices.

Fylkesnes, K., and O. H. Forde. 1991. "The Tromso Study: Predictors of Self-Evaluated Health: Has Society Adopted the Expanded Health Concept?" *Social Science and Medicine* 32(2): 141–46.

Goldstein, Karen P., Frederick J. Kviz, and Robert S. Daum. 1993. "Accuracy of Immunization Histories Provided by Adults Accompanying Preschool Children to a Pediatric Emergency Department." *Journal of the American Medical Association* 270(18) November: 2190–94.

Hernandez, Donald J. 1994. *America's Children: Resources from Family, Government, and the Economy*. New York: Russell Sage Foundation.

Lewit, Eugene M., and John Mullahy. 1994. "Immunization of Young Children." *The Future of Children* 4(1): 236–47.

Maddox, G., and E. Douglas. 1973. "Self-Assessment of Health: A Longitudinal Study of Elderly Subjects." *Journal of Health and Social Behavior* 14: 87–93.

Manning, W., J. P. Newhouse, and N. Duan. 1987. "Health Insurance and the Demand for Medical Care: Evidence from a Randomized Experiment." *American Economic Review* 77: 251–77.

Montgomery, L., and O. Carter-Pokras. 1993. "Health Status by Social Class and/or Minority Status: Implications for Environmental Equity Research." *Toxicology and Industrial Health* 9(5): 729–73.

National Research Council. 1993. *Measuring Lead Exposure in Infants, Children, and Other Sensitive Populations*. Washington, D.C.: National Academy Press.

Szapiro, N. 1989. "Children, Poverty and Hospital Care in New York City." In *Poverty and Health in New York City*, edited by M. I. Krasner. New York: United Hospital Fund of New York.

U.S. Department of Health and Human Services. 1986. *Health USA*. Washington: Government Printing Office.

————. 1989. *Child Health USA*. Washington: Government Printing Office.

World Health Organization Working Group. 1986. "Use and Interpretation of Anthropometric Indicators of Nutritional Status." *Bulletin of the World Health Organization* 64: 929–41.

5

Health Indicators for Preadolescent School-Age Children

Barbara Starfield

THE LONG AND honorable tradition of public health and vital statistics in the United States has provided the country with a wealth of information on the health status of its population and on trends over time in these characteristics. With new imperatives for greater accountability of the new health services systems, and with increasing evidence of inequity in the distribution of resources across the population, new types of data with new types of data systems are likely to be required.

This chapter first will review the purposes for which health status measures are intended. Second, the different types of health status measures and the sources of data that can provide them are presented. Third, the major types of existing measures are discussed, along with their strengths and limitations and the uses to which they are put. Fourth, major existing health indicators are presented along with the extent of their use. Finally, the chapter discusses those measures that are likely to be most useful in the future. No attempt in this chapter is made to review or suggest indicators that assess access to, use of, or performance of the health services system or parts of it. Such indicators of access, use, or quality, although important, are not considered "health status" indicators.

PURPOSES OF HEALTH STATUS MEASURES

There are four major purposes for health status measures:

- To characterize the health of communities and of the nation as a whole, to permit comparisons with other communities and with comparably industrialized countries in order to assess the adequacy of the health system in meeting major needs of the population;

- To compare the health of major subgroups of the population in order to detect systematic differences in health;

- To enable evaluations of the adequacy of specific health care interventions and the impact of interventions designed to improve health status; and

- To serve as the basis for planning and targeting services in order to meet important health needs.

TYPES OF HEALTH STATUS MEASURES

Health status measures are of two major types: health indicators and composites of health status that are expressed as profiles or indices.

Health indicators are measures of specific aspects of health status that are assumed to represent the general state of health in the population. Death rates, low birth weight ratios, teenage pregnancy rates, reportable disease rates, and immunization rates are examples of health indicators.

Health status profiles are more comprehensive representations of health that are composed of several aspects (usually known as domains) that are aggregated to form a pictorial representation. They usually represent various aspects of physical ability or performance, mental and emotional characteristics, and social behavior or interaction. Profiles are generally used to characterize individuals rather than populations, although they can be aggregated to populations.

Health indices are measures of health that assign a quantitative score to each of a number of components (either indicators or the domains of a profile) in order to derive a single score that enables rapid comparison of different population groups.

Health indicators are generally obtained from ongoing data collection on deaths, births, hospitalizations, and morbidity as reported in regular national health interview surveys (such as the National Health Interview Survey, the National Hospital Discharge Survey, and the CDC Risk Behaviors Survey).

Health profiles may be obtained either from health interviews that tap the important domains, from health information systems that include data on various domains, or from a combination of both. Since profiles are a relatively new concept in health status assessment, there are few examples of their use. Case-mix measures, which take information from health information systems in managed health systems, provide profiles of the burden of diagnosed morbidity in different population groups served by these organizations. The Johns Hopkins Ambulatory Care Case Mix System (Starfield et al. 1991), for example, has demonstrated generally similar profiles of health among individuals served by large employer-based health systems, but heavier burdens of morbidity experienced by populations enrolled in Medicaid plans (Starfield 1991). Over the past decade, profiles of the health of children that are comparable in concept to these developed earlier for adults (such as the Sickness Impact Profile and the SF-36) (Bergner et al. 1981; Stewart and Ware 1992) are receiving attention. For example, the Child Health and Illness Profile-Adolescent Edition (CHIP-AE) (Starfield et al. 1992; Starfield et al. 1995) is currently being used by a variety of health plans and health services researchers in their attempts to characterize the health of the populations with whom they are concerned.

Health indices are generally calculated from a set of health indicators, although they are equally amenable to use with data collected from special data collection efforts. Examples of health indices are QALYS—Quality of Adjusted Life Years Scale (Kaplan et al. 1987; Stein et al. 1990).

The strengths of the health indicator approach include the widespread availability of those that are relatively easy to obtain, the generally standard way in which they are obtained, and their demonstrated usefulness in documenting systematic differences in health across different populations. For example, the relatively poor position of the United States among Western industrialized nations is readily demonstrated by the use of several standard health indicators, and the disparities across the nations are greater the younger the age group that is compared (Starfield 1993). The United States ranks last among eleven comparable nations with regard to percent of births that are low birth weight, last in neonatal mortality, eighth in postneonatal mortality, and eleventh in infant mortality as a whole. It ranks fifth to seventh, depending on the particular age and sex group, among seven comparable nations, in child death rates resulting from accidents and injuries, and it ranks fourth to fifth, depending on age and sex group, among the same seven countries ranked for death rates resulting from medical causes. Rates for indicators in adulthood, including age-adjusted death rates at age twenty, years of potential life lost before age sixty-five (which also includes preventable deaths in infancy and childhood), and age-adjusted death rates, show generally similar poor performance (although not as large as in infancy and childhood), whereas indicators of health at age sixty-five place the United States in the middle of the rankings. It is only for age eighty that the U.S. position approaches top ranking.

The limitations of indicators as the major method for characterizing the health of populations have to do with the policy decisions that they generate, which often are directed at the development of programs to address only the particular problem reflected in the indicator. As a result, U.S. health policy is often designed to address, in piecemeal fashion, the deficiencies in care associated with the particular indicator: immunization campaigns for low immunization rates, or funds for targeted prenatal care programs where low birth weight ratios are high. That is, performance on an indicator is often interpreted as a deficiency in that particular aspect of the health system, rather than as a reflection of a more generalized problem that is also influencing other but unmeasured health characteristics. As a result, policy decisions often provide piecemeal solutions to a more widespread problem in the organization and financing of services. For example, low birth weight ratios are usually interpreted as an effect of poor access to prenatal services, when in reality they may be a result of poor access to comprehensive primary health care services long antedating pregnancy.

The profile approach is designed to remedy the limitations of the indicator approach. Population groups that are found to be at a disadvantage across a range of domains can be identified and targeted for the enhancement of programs that would address comprehensively the myriad of problems that are concentrated in those populations. Moreover, profiles make it easier to detect interrelationships between different areas of health and thus to help in the elucidation of factors that predispose to poor health or, conversely, enhance the likelihood of good health. Comprehensive planning for services is facilitated and the assessment of impact is more focused on general areas rather than on specific indicators of health that may or may not be representative of health in general.

The profile approach is limited in that there are few existing instruments that have been tested for reliability and validity, although some are currently being planned or tested. Second, there is little precedent for the use of this type of measure on a widespread scale and little understanding of its potential. Methods for assuring comparability of data collection do not yet exist, and there are no well-developed methods for aggregating individual profiles into community profiles.

The strength of the index approach is its conceptual simplicity. Different countries or different communities can be scored, with higher scores representing a different level of health status than lower scores. Such an approach might be particularly useful when interest lies more in documenting differences in health status rather than the causes of those differences. Limitations of the index approach include the assumption that intervals between successive item scores represent equivalent differences in health. One method of overcoming this limitation is to weight component scores for their perceived importance by expert judgments or consumer valuations (Patrick and Bergner 1990). Another limitation is that a single score gives no information on specific types of deficits in health status; in order to inform policy decisions, the subsequent exploration of components of the index is required for this purpose.

CURRENT HEALTH INDICATORS

Table 5.1 lists the four major sources of health indicators and the particular indicators that they produce.

Vital statistics have the longest history of use, and they have the advantage that standard definitions are in place not only nationally but also, for the most part, internationally. This source of data provides information on death rates, by age and race, for International Classification of Diseases (ICD)-coded causes of death, which can be aggregated to produce the categories of interest.

Data on hospital discharges, by coded cause of hospitalization, have been available from a sample of U.S. hospitals and for all hospitals in some states for several years. Data in these information systems identify health problems that should have been prevented by adequate ambulatory care.

Interview data have been collected in the United States for almost forty years and some studies of reliability and validity were carried out during the early years of the development of the survey methods. When conducted under the aegis of the National Center for Health Statistics, methods of administration are standardized, with good quality control. Also, analysis generally follows a standard pattern which facilitates comparisons over time when the questions are the same (as they usually are). Computerized entry of data at the point of its collection speeds analysis time so that information from the surveys is available more quickly than in the past. Interview data yields information on reported chronic conditions, reported limitations of activity associated with these conditions, reported restriction of activity associated with acute illnesses, reported completeness of immunizations, reported health behavior, and reported physical fitness. The Child Health Supplement also elicits some information on emotional and behavior problems. The major disadvantage of interview surveys is the unknown reliability and validity of information obtained by self-reporting, particularly when the survey has not been independently validated.

Examination data, as obtained by the NHANES (National Health and Nutrition Examination Survey) and its predecessor HES (Health Examination Survey), provide information on the frequency of occurrence of abnormalities that are reflected in anatomical or physiological findings. These surveys generally also include selected laboratory tests that permit estimates of the prevalence of conditions such as anemia (including iron-deficiency anemia), elevated blood-lead

Table 5.1   Sources of Information for Health Indicators

Vital Statistics and Surveillance Data
   Death rates by age group
   Death rates for injuries/accidents, by type and aggregated
   Death rates for medical causes, by type and aggregated
   Deaths from sentinel conditions (conditions that should never or only rarely occur when health
     services are adequate)
Hospitalizations, by diagnosis
Interview Data
   Reported chronic conditions
   Reported restrictions of activity, by nature of acute illness
   Reported limitations of activity, by degree of interference with major or visual activities
   Reported behavior problems
   Reported health behavior
   Reported physical fitness
   Reported completeness of immunizations
   Reported overall health as excellent, very good, good, fair, or poor
   Health Profiles
Examination Data
   Physical examination findings of manifested abnormalities
   Laboratory examinations
     Anemia
     Elevated blood-lead levels
     Skin testing for allergies
Data from Clinical Information Systems
   Reportable diseases
     Communicable diseases
   Case registers
     Cancer registers
     Congenital metabolic disease (Cystic Fibrosis)
   Diagnosed morbidity/disability
     Diagnoses, individual and aggregated by type
     Hospital discharges, by diagnosis

levels, and allergies as manifested by skin tests. The major problem with physical examinations is their poor reliability, even when conducted by physicians. It has been estimated that two physician examiners agree only about 15 percent of the time on the presence or absence of an abnormality (Starfield, unpublished data).

Data from Clinical Information Systems

Information potentially available from clinical sources includes rates of communicable diseases, cancer incidence and prevalence rates, and rates of congenital metabolic disease (such as cystic fibrosis), as well as all diagnoses that are recorded in the process of providing services. Although most existing ambulatory health care systems have not coded diagnoses made by health care providers, it is likely that this situation will change in the future. The imperative of managed care organizations to monitor utilization and quality of care is generating interest in the development and application of case-mix measures that depend upon ICD-coded diagnoses.

Table 5.2 lists the most commonly used indicators according to the aegis under which they have been collected. The U.S. National Health Surveys, Canadian health surveys, and two major U.S. states are represented, as are a Canadian province, the Organization for Economic Cooperation and Development (Europe), and the compilations prepared by the Bureau of Maternal and Child Health (MCH) and by the Annie Casey Foundation (Kids Count). Of the data collection efforts, only the Vital Statistics System and the U.S. National Health Interview Survey (NHIS) are ongoing on a regular basis, although the NHIS Child Health Supplement (the source of much of the indicated information) is collected sporadically. The U.S. National Health and Nutrition Survey is irregularly periodic. (In fact, there have been only three such surveys since their inception in the early 1960s.) The compilations (Maternal and Child Health Bureau and Casey Foundation) depend on the availability of other sources of information.

Although other types of data often are obtained, only those in the table are population-based. Other indicators are derived from services data and therefore cannot be generalized to produce population rates. These include but are not limited to such indicators as rates of serious behavior problems in schools (whose populations do not include individuals excluded from or otherwise not in public schools as a result of behavior problems), and manifestations of undernutrition deriving from individuals seen in facilities such as Women, Infants, and Children clinics. Data based upon use of health-related facilities may systematically underestimate the frequency of problems in the population because they exclude individuals who are not receiving services even though they may need them. They also fail to represent whole populations because they include information only on population groups eligible for their services.

The amount of information on preadolescent children is far less than that available for infants and preschool children; for the latter population group it is common to have information on neonatal and postneonatal mortality rates, low birth weight rates, and immunization rates, in addition to the types of information available for older children. However, a variety of types of data is at least potentially available, which makes it possible to accomplish some of the aims of health status indicators *if* the data are being consistently and regularly collected.

EXAMPLES OF THE USE OF HEALTH INDICATORS
International Comparisons

Table 5.3 provides some international comparisons of death rates and rates of activity restriction and limitation as published by the National Center for Health Statistics and the OECD, respectively. This information derives from special studies and no time trends are available. However, table 5.3 demonstrates the potential of such data were they periodically available.

Comparisons by Socioeconomic Status

Data by family income or parental education are consistently available only from national health interview and national health examination surveys. As a result, many of the indicators in table 5.2 that are obtained by other means do not allow

(*Text continues on p. 104.*)

Table 5.2 Preadolescent School-Age Child—Indicators Used in Selected Publications (United States and Canada)

	Bureau of Maternal and Child Health	Kids Count	New York State	Washington State	Canadian Institute of Child Health	Province of Manitoba**	Organization for Economic Cooperation and Development	U.S. National Health Surveys and Vital Statistics
Periodicity	Annual	Annual	?	?	Occasional	?	Occasional	Regular/Irregular
Age aggregation								
Death rates	✓	✓	✓	✓	✓		✓	✓
Injuries	✓		✓	✓	✓	✓	✓	✓
Medical causes						✓	✓	✓
Sentinel Indicators								
Communicable diseases			✓	✓				✓
Iron-deficiency anemia								
Lead poisoning	✓		✓					✓
Restricted activity by acute illness								✓
Limitations of activity	✓		✓		✓	✓		
Mental health	✓		✓		✓		✓	✓
Child abuse*	✓		✓					

Table 5.2 *Continued*

	Bureau of Maternal and Child Health	Kids Count	New York State	Washington State	Canadian Institute of Child Health	Province of Manitoba**	Organization for Economic Cooperation and Development	U.S. National Health Surveys and Vital Statistics
Pediatric AIDS*	✓		✓					
Physical fitness	✓			✓				
Dental caries				✓				
Behavior problems				✓				
Hospitalizations, by diagnosis								✓
Obesity			✓			✓		
Health behaviors					✓***			✓****
Overall health†					✓			✓

Note: Specifically absent from any of these published data sources are: under-nutrition, health-protecting behaviors such as bicycle helmets, gun exposure, or smoke detectors, or specific diseases or conditions other than communicable diseases.

Source: Maternal and Child Health Bureau 1994; New York State–Bureau of Child and Adolescent Health 1989; Manitoba Center for Health Policy and Evaluation 1994; Institute for Public Policy Management 1992; Canadian Institute of Child Health 1989; Annie E. Casey Foundation 1994.

* All child ages combined   ✓ indicator used in publicaton
** All data expressed as Standard Mortality Ratios (not age stratified)   ? Unknown
*** e.g., physical activity, smoking, drinking, child restraints
**** seat belts

†Reported by parental respondent as excellent, very good, good, fair, poor

Table 5.3   Child Health Indicators: International Comparisons, 1985

					Country				
	Australia	Canada	Great Britain	France	Federal Republic of Germany	Japan	Netherlands	Sweden	United States
Deaths per 100,000 population									
age 5–9									
Female	20	19	18	21	22	15	18	11	21
Male	30	26	22	28	24	27	22	20	28
age 10–15									
Female	16	20	19	19	17	13	19	15	21
Male	29	31	29	30	23	20	29	17	35
Disability and activity limitation (age 0–15)									
Disability days (per person per year)	14	9	17				11		12
Bed days (per person per year)	4	4					3		5
Activity restriction due to long-standing conditions (percent of population)	3	3	6		1		2		4

Source: National Center for Health Statistics 1989; Fingerhut 1989; Organization for Economic Cooperation and Development 1986

Table 5.4   Child Health and School Attendance, 1991

Ratings	School Days Absent	Excellent/Very Good Health (% of population)
Poor	6.4	64.0
Near-poor	5.0	74.7
Nonpoor	4.9	87.4

Source: Original analysis of the 1991 National Health Interview Survey by the Center for Health Economics Research. Access to Health Care Indicators for Policy, November 1992.

for comparisons by social class. Table 5.4 presents information derived from special analyses of data in the National Health Interview Survey. In contrast to the data from the survey itself, which are published by income groups, social class is categorized into three groups (poor, near-poor, and nonpoor).

Time Trends

Since hospitalizations provide utilization data, inferences as to population rates of problems is fraught with potential bias. However, if access to inpatient care is generally available to all members of the population, and if hospital admission policies do not change over time, trends in hospitalization rates from different causes can be considered to reflect the frequency of these problems in the population. For example, rates of hospitalization for tonsillectomy and adenoidectomy have fallen over time, most likely as a result of changing hospital admission policies and medical practice rather than changes in the frequency of disease. On the other hand, rising rates of admission for the diagnosis of asthma probably are a reflection, at least in part, of increasing morbidity from asthma, because the data are consistent with rising rates as obtained by other methods (Starfield 1991). Time trends for limitations of activity resulting from chronic illnesses, as obtained from the National Health Interview Survey, also show that the number of children unable to perform their major activity (play or going to school) due to a chronic condition has increased over time, especially among six- to sixteen-year-olds (as compared with birth- to five-year-olds) (Starfield 1991).

SUGGESTIONS FOR THE FUTURE

Table 5.5 presents a summary of health indicators recommended for preadolescent school-age children, according to thirteen criteria. The first eleven of these criteria are derived from Moore (1994); the twelfth takes into consideration the likelihood that the indicator directly reflects health system characteristics amenable to change, or the extent to which it provides at least the potential for elucidating the relationship between the cause of the health concern and its manifestation. The thirteenth addresses the potential for international comparisons. The indicators reflect a reasonably broad spectrum of health status, although neither mental health problems nor states of risk and resilience (characteristics of health that influence, negatively or positively, subsequent health) are well represented.

Table 5.5 Recommendations for Indicators, by Desirable Criteria, Preadolescent School-Age Children

	Hospitalizations for Ambulatory Care Sensitive Conditions	Death Rates Total and Cause, by Aggregatable Type Ages 5–7, 8–10, 11–14, 15–17	Limitations and Restrictions of Activity, Total and by Morbidity Burden	Specific Condition: Communicable Diseases, Iron-Deficiency Anemia, Blood-Lead Levels, Morbidity Burden
Comprehensive Coverage	Selected indicators represent preventable mortality, preventable morbidity, impact of morbidity on functional status			
Potential to track across ages	good	good	good	good
Clear and comprehensible	good	good	good-moderate	good
Positive/negative	negative	negative	negative	negative
Common interpretation	yes	yes	yes (maybe less for international comparisons)	yes
Consistency over time	yes	yes	yes (with standard instrument)	yes
Reliability/validity	yes	yes	yes	yes
Geographic detail	high-moderate	high-moderate (given periodic availability of data source)	poor (with existing data)	variable
Cost efficient	high	high	moderate-low	high
Reflective of social goals	high	high	high	variable
Adjustable for demographic characteristics/SES	only at ecological level (community of residence)	only at ecological level (community of residence)	high	high
Relationship to health system characteristics a potential for linkage between cause and effect	high	moderate	moderate	
Availability for international comparisons	no	yes	no	no

Four indicators are recommended given the current state of availability and feasibility:

- Death rates, from vital statistics, presented in total and by cause, aggregated into deaths resulting from accidents and injuries and those resulting from "medical" causes;

- Limitations of activity, from the National Health Interview Survey, total and by morbidity burden;

- Hospitalizations for conditions sensitive to primary care, obtained from hospital discharge data, total and by individual ICD-coded diagnosis; and

- Indicator conditions, obtained from the various sources noted in this chapter and including communicable disease incidence rates, prevalence of iron-deficiency anemia, prevalence of elevated blood-lead levels, and burdens of morbidity as diagnosed in clinical facilities.

Each of the indicators received a high rating for most of criteria; other indicators not listed in table 5.2 would receive lower ratings for most of the criteria.

Hospitalizations for conditions sensitive to good primary care and therefore preventable by such care is a relatively new indicator of health status. It is potentially available universally, since it depends only on the availability of discharge data that contain ICD-coded data. Such information, while not universally available now, will become increasingly available as imperatives for cost containment and accountability increase. Such an indicator has considerable potential for characterizing differences in health, particularly those that are amenable to medical intervention, since the data can be aggregated according to geographic areas distinguished by their social characteristics (such as median income). Rates of admissions for all types of these illnesses (severe ear, nose, and throat infections, bacterial pneumonia, asthma, gastroenteritis, cellulitis, urinary tract infection, dehydration, iron-deficiency anemia) are much higher among populations living in low-income areas (Center for Health Economics Research 1993). The potential of this indicator to demonstrate international differences is suggested by a recent study (Casanova and Starfield 1994), which showed that rates of admission for these types of conditions among children in Valencia, Spain (where access to care is universally provided), do not vary by social characteristics of areas of residence, as they do in the United States as a whole and in specific U.S. areas that have been studied.

Death rates have the considerable advantage of being widely available for international and intranational comparisons. They already have shown their usefulness for this and other purposes; time trends are relatively easy to obtain. A major limitation of this indicator is the relative rarity of deaths in childhood, so that comparisons among population groups too small to permit stable estimates of rates are not possible. But since the data are available for each year, aggregation over a period of more than one year can make the estimates more stable and permit interpretation in populations that are otherwise too small. Another limitation is the unavailability of individual data on social class, which makes it impossible to use these rates to assess systematic differences in deaths or cause of death by class except at the ecological level (where characteristics of the place of residence are assigned to deaths in that community).

Data on limitations of activity linked to acute illness require information from health interview surveys that currently are conducted only on the basis of national sampling. These national samples permit regional estimates but not state estimates. As more states recognize the usefulness of health interview surveys, the capacity for data collection at the state level, and perhaps even at the substate level, will facilitate the collection of such information periodically. Table 5.6 presents information obtained from the National Health Information Survey; it combines data from the chronic conditions checklist with information about restriction of activity. The major disadvantage of this indicator is its unavailability internationally. Limitations of activity as a result of chronic conditions is also a potentially useful measure.

The recommended specific indicator conditions, while generally fulfilling all criteria to a relatively high degree, are limited by their current unavailability. Since potential feasibility of data collection varies with the indicator, each will be discussed separately.

Communicable Diseases   While reporting systems and data compilation by the Centers for Disease Control make these indicators very useful, their potential is limited by the unavailability of associated sociodemographic characteristics and by incomplete reporting. They are particularly useful in reflecting the adequacy of the health system in providing immunizations to prevent these conditions. Therefore, efforts to improve reporting rates should be continued, and efforts should be made to obtain information about sociodemographic characteristics, either of the individual with the disease or by area of residence of the individual.

Iron-Deficiency Anemia and Elevated Blood-Lead Levels   Information on both of these conditions is available from the National Health and Nutrition Examination Survey, which tests for their presence. The usefulness of such information has been demonstrated by the analysis of time trends in blood levels among children in the United States over the past several decades (Morbidity and Mortality Weekly Report 1994a, 1994b). Unfortunately there is currently no possibility of international comparisons, since other countries do not routinely collect such data. The major problem with these data is the irregularity with which the survey is conducted. It would be helpful if national policy led to greater regularity of these surveys.

Morbidity Burdens   The imperative for accountability within new organizational arrangements for health services delivery will stimulate the development of information systems that collect information on diagnoses made during the course of clinical care. As health care organizations take on responsibility for defined populations over a period of time, there will be a need for case-mix systems that provide a basis for higher reimbursements to facilities with sicker populations. These case-mix systems are likely to be based on demonstrated morbidity as well as on age, gender, and social class (Starfield et al. 1991; Weiner et al. 1991). As a result, it will be possible to characterize populations by the burdens of diagnosed morbidity. These methods characterize morbidity burdens, including those associated with mental health, as various combinations of different types of diagnoses experienced in a year. Their use demonstrates generally

Table 5.6   Additional Recommendations for Indicators, by Desirable Criteria, Preadolescent School-Age Children

	Major Health Risks (For Example, Unlocked Loaded Guns in Household, Television Viewing)	Sense of Well-Being and Overall Health (For Example, Ratings of Overall Health and Self-Esteem)	Behavior Problems Checklist
Comprehensive Coverage		increases comprehensiveness	
Potential to track across ages	good	good	poor
Clear and comprehensible	good	good	good
Positive/Negative	negative	positive	negative
Common interpretation	yes	yes	yes
Consistency over time	yes	yes	probably
Reliability/Validity	probably	yes	yes
Geographic detail	yes	yes	poor, with existing data
Cost efficient	high-moderate	high-moderate	high (given periodic availability of data source)
Reflective of social goals	high	moderate (?)	high
Adjustable for demographic characteristics/SES	high	high	high
Relationship to health system characteristics a potential for linkage between cause and effect	moderate	moderate	moderate
Availability for international comparisons	no	no	no

similar levels of overall burdens of morbidity among children enrolled in HMOs but higher morbidity of poor children (those enrolled in Medicaid) (Starfield 1991). With the increasing sophistication of information systems, enrollment files (with sociodemographic information) and clinical data can be merged to permit the analysis of morbidity burdens by social class and other sociodemographic characteristics. This information is not likely to be available internationally, or even nationally (at least for a long time). However, efforts to begin such an approach should be encouraged and supported as investments in future health indicators for children.

Table 5.6 provides three additional types of indicators that are recommended for consideration, along with ratings based on the criteria. The first concerns mental health problems. Since these problems are among the most common health concerns in the population, they should be included in any set of health indicators. The Child Health Supplement of the National Health Interview Survey contains a set of questions directed at eliciting the frequency of behavioral and affective problems in the population of children. While research is needed on the usefulness of these indicators for planning health services or evaluating their impact, their inclusion in the core set of indicators provides a more appropriate balance to the current sole focus on the physical manifestations of health. The second, behavior that influences subsequent health, is potentially available from interviews. The two particular sorts of behavior provided as examples (unlocked loaded guns and television viewing) both have been demonstrated to influence health; both have been tested and found to have adequate reliability and validity (Starfield et al. 1995). The third additional indicator concerns self-perceptions of health, which have also been shown to be useful. Perceived well-being reported as excellent, very good, good, fair, or poor is a standard question in the National Health Interview Survey. Responses to this question have been shown to be predictive of subsequent health in adults, although no studies have been conducted concerning children. Responses to the question have been found to be related to social class, in children as well as adults, with more disadvantaged individuals reporting poorer health. Both self-perceived health and self-esteem have been shown to have moderate correlations with other aspects of health in the adolescent health profile (Starfield et al. 1995), although studies of younger children have not yet been done.

Technical Considerations

All of the suggested indicators should be produced by individual year of age, aggregated for ages five to seven, eight to ten, eleven to fourteen, fifteen to seventeen, and for five to ten and eleven to seventeen, to provide information about specific developmental stages of childhood.

Presentation of information by social class would be facilitated if standard classifications were adopted. Instead of income categories, or specification by poor, near-poor, and nonpoor, data might be aggregated according to those in the lowest 10th percentile of income in the population, those from the 11th to 24th percentile, 25th to 49th percentile, 50th to 70th percentile, and 71st percentile and above. This would have the advantage of standardizing comparisons across population groups that differ in income because of geographic factors.

Since information on the distribution of wealth in various countries is often depicted in this way, the collection of data in this manner would permit the analysis of data concerning equity in distribution of health in addition to that of social welfare.

Periodicity of information is less important than regularity of scheduling for its collection. In general, every five years (except for those items that are currently collected more frequently) seems appropriate, although new types of information systems (such as those derived from clinical facilities) should have information on-line and be very easy to produce continuously. Health examination surveys should be carried out regularly, at least once every five to ten years.

These suggested indicators represent a reasonable and practical set for the near future. Developmental efforts recently completed or currently under way will provide, within five to ten years, more comprehensive profiles of health to complement the indicators suggested above. Combined with other indicators that reflect the state of access to health services and their actual and perceived quality, they should move the country forward to a new generation of data systems that are better suited to the planning and evaluation of societal policies and programs.

REFERENCES

Annie E. Casey Foundation. 1994. *Kids Count Data Book: State Profiles of Child Well-Being*. Greenwich, Ct.: Annie E. Casey Foundation.

Bergner, M., R. Bobbitt, W. Carter, B. Gibson. 1981. The Sickness Impact Profile: Development and Final Revision of a Health Status Measure. *Medical Care* 19: 787–805.

Canadian Institute of Child Health. 1989. *The Health of Canada's Children: A Canadian Institute of Child Health Profile*. Ottawa, Canada: Canadian Institute of Child Health.

Casanova, C., and B. Starfield. 1995. "Hospitalizations of Children and Access to Primary Care: A Cross-National Comparison." *International Journal of Health Services* 25(2): 283–94.

Center for Health Economics Research. 1993. *Access to Health Care: Key Indicators for Policy*. Princeton, N.J.: Robert Wood Johnson Foundation.

Fingerhut, L. 1989. "Trends and Current Status in Childhood Mortality, United States 1980–85." *Vital and Health Statistics*, series 3, no. 26. Washington: U.S. Government Printing Office for National Center for Health Statistics, U. S. Department of Health and Human Services.

Institute of Public Policy Management. 1992. *The State of Washington's Children*. Seattle, Wa.: University of Washington.

Kaplan, R., and J. Anderson. 1987. The Quality of Well-Being Scale: Rationale for a Single Quality of Life Index. In *Quality of Life: Assessment and Application,* edited by S. Walker and R. Rosser. Proceedings of the Centre for Medicine Research Workshop held at the CIBA Foundation, London.

Manitoba Centre for Health Policy and Evaluation. 1994. *Population Health: Health Status Indicators. Vol. 1* Manitoba, Canada: University of Manitoba.

Maternal and Child Health Bureau. 1994. *Child Health USA '93*. USDHHS no. HRSA-MCH-94-1. Washington: U.S. Government Printing Office for the U.S. Department of Health and Human Services.

Moore, K. 1994. "Criteria for Indicators of Child Well Being." Paper presented at the Conference on Indicators of Children's Well-Being. Rockville, Md. (Nov. 17–18, 1994).

Morbidity and Mortality Weekly Report. 1994a. "Blood Lead Levels—United States 1988–1991." *Morbidity and Mortality Weekly Report* 43(30): 545–48.

Morbidity and Mortality Weekly Report. 1994b. "National Health and Nutrition Examination Survey." *Morbidity and Mortality Weekly Report* 43(30): 546.

New York State–Bureau of Child and Adolescent Health. 1989. "Maternal, Child and Adolescent Profile." Albany, N.Y.: New York State Department of Health.

Organization for Economic Cooperation and Development. 1986. "Living Conditions in Organization for Economic Cooperation and Development Countries." *Social Policy Studies* (3).

Patrick, D., and M. Bergner. 1990. "Measurement of Health Status in the 1990s." *Annual Review of Public Health* 11: 165–83.

Starfield, B. 1991. "Childhood Morbidity: Comparisons, Clusters, and Trends." *Pediatrics* 88(3): 519–26.

———. 1993. "Primary Care." *Journal of Ambulatory Care Management* 16(4): 27–37.

Starfield, B., M. Bergner, M. Ensminger, A. Riley, S. Ryan, P. McGauhey, A. Skinner, and S. Kim. 1993. "Adolescent Health Status Measurement: Development of Child Health and Illness Profile." *Pediatrics* 91(2): 430–35.

Starfield, B., A. W. Riley, B. F. Green, M. E. Ensminger, S. A. Ryan, K. Kelleher, S. Kim-Harris, D. Johnston, and K. Vogel. 1995. "The Adolescent Child Health and Illness Profile: A Population-Based Measure of Health." *Medical Care* 33(5): 553–56.

Starfield, B., J. Weiner, L. Mumford, and D. Steinwachs. 1991. "Ambulatory Care Groups: A Categorization of Diagnoses for Research and Management." *Health Services Research* 26(1): 53–74.

Stein, R. E. K. and D. J. Jessop. 1990. "Functional Status II(R). A Measure of Child Health Status." *Med Care* 28(11): 1041–55.

Stewart, A., and J. Ware. 1992. *Measuring Functioning and Well-Being: The Medical Outcomes Study Approach.* Durham, N.C.: Duke University Press.

Weiner, J., B. Starfield, D. Steinwachs, and L. Mumford. 1991. "The Development of a Population Oriented Case-Mix Measure for Application to Ambulatory Care." *Medical Care* 29(5): 452–72.

6

Adolescent Health Indicators

Arthur B. Elster

A CRITICAL FIRST step in identifying a set of indicators for assessing health and well-being is to determine the possible uses of such indicators. What are the advantages and what are the disadvantages? Above all else, we must ensure that we "do no harm."

It is reasonable to assume that health indicators measured accurately, regularly, and across a broad spectrum of the population can be a valuable mechanism for tracking progress toward achieving identified national goals. Used in this fashion, health indicators can help guide program planning, research, and education.

Selected health indicators for children and adults have been used in this manner for many years. Although there are many examples, two widely accepted indicators are those used to monitor prenatal care and pregnancy outcome, and an index used to monitor adult health risk behavior.

Cesarian section rates and percent of women who enter prenatal care in the last trimester are often used as indicators of the adequacy of prenatal care. Low birth rate, infant mortality, and whether the newborn went to an intensive care unit have been used as indicators of pregnancy outcome. These indicators meet several important criteria that have made their use widely accepted: they can be measured routinely and universally from birth certificates without additional financial cost, and they have a high degree of face validity. Health advocates have used these two sets of indicators to successfully lobby for increased governmental funding for obstetrical and prenatal nutrition programs. The growth of the Women, Infant, and Child (WIC) Program during the period of reduction in funding for social programs that occurred in the 1980s and the recent expansion of Medicaid to cover pregnancy and infant care are good examples of how health indicators can be used to promote health and well-being.

Another set of indicators has been used to monitor adult health risk behaviors. Developed by the Centers for Disease Control and Prevention (CDC), the Behavioral Risk Factor Survey includes eight sorts of behavior linked to the ten leading causes of premature death among adults (Marks et al. 1985). State data are collected and reports are published by the CDC. This index provides a mechanism for not only tracking changes in adult preventive behavior over time, but also for comparing the health of adults among various states and regions.

Most indicators used to monitor adolescent health focus on problem behavior. Use of alcohol, drugs, and tobacco; adolescent pregnancy, live births, and abortion; and homicide comprise the majority of adolescent health indicators that are monitored and reported to the public on a regular basis. Contextual factors and health-promoting behaviors are not measured as regularly as are health risk behaviors (Zill and Daly 1993). Probably the two most widely used indicators of adolescent health are data from the Youth Risk Behavior Surveillance System (YRBSS) conducted by the CDC and the Monitoring the Future surveys conducted by the University of Michigan

The YRBSS was developed by the CDC in 1988 to "identify and periodically monitor important health behaviors among youth" (Kann et al. 1993). The survey targets six types of behavior: behavior that results in unintentional and intentional injuries; alcohol and other drug use; sexual behavior that results in HIV infection, other sexually transmitted diseases, and unintended pregnancy; tobacco use; dietary behavior; and physical activity. Surveys are conducted through most state departments of education and large local educational agencies. Representative high schools in the community are chosen and all students in these schools are surveyed. The strengths of the YRBSS are that it monitors both health risk behaviors and two health-promoting behaviors; it includes a national representative sample of youth; and it is conducted on a relatively frequent basis. The major problem with the YRBSS is that it is conducted through state and local departments of education; it is excluded from some states, while other states refuse to include questions on sexuality.

Monitoring the Future is a national survey of high school seniors that has been conducted annually since 1975 by the University of Michigan's Institute for Social Research (Johnson et al. 1993). Funded by the National Institute on Drug Abuse, this survey tracks alcohol and drug use attitudes and behavior among high school seniors. These findings are reported annually and have served to increase awareness of substance abuse among adolescents. The strengths of this survey are that it includes a national representative sample of youth and that the results have become the standard for tracking adolescent drug usage. The major drawbacks are that it surveys only students who are still enrolled in school and that it focuses on a relatively narrow range of health problems.

Surveys, such as the National Longitudinal Survey of Youth and the National Health and Nutrition Examination Survey, measure a broad range of health issues including some that relate to adolescents. However, since these surveys are not ongoing or else completed only periodically, their use in developing adolescent health indicators may be limited. There are various other national surveys, such as the National Hospital Ambulatory Medical Care Survey and several reproductive health surveys that provide valuable information for constructing adolescent health indicators (Zill and Daly 1993).

The discussion so far has been on how health indicators are used to monitor conditions selected as high national priority. Although probably unintended, health indicators also can impact society by setting standards or at least influencing the way people think about issues. This can have both a positive and a negative influence on shaping public opinion and concern. For example, reporting on distinctions among special populations, such as racial and ethnic groups and adolescents, has had a positive effect on bringing to the public's attention the fact that our society is heterogeneous with different health care needs.

If health indicators presumably can have a positive effect on program development and public perception, what then are the potential or real ways that indicators can be harmful to adolescents? There are at least three ways. One is the way that indicators, as described previously, negatively can influence public opinion. For example, the current use of adolescent health indicators to track problem behavior tends to distract from the many types of positive behavior exhibited by adolescents. In addition, the negative and aggregate manner in which findings are reported tends to hide the fact that most adolescents are relatively uninvolved in problem behavior and that most serious problems cluster among only a sub-population of adolescents. The negative implication of indicators probably serves to further emphasize society's view that all adolescents have problems. By focus-ing on problem behavior, health indicators fail to help society develop more nurturing attitudes toward youth.

A second way that use of health indicators may be problematic is that data can lead to erroneous interpretations, especially in light of the atheoretical manner in which indicators are often constructed. For example, for years the National Cen-ter for Health Statistics has reported children and youth data according to age categories that run counter to developmental principles. Research on adolescent pregnancy and parenthood, and on other issues, has been hampered by this ap-proach because data hide critical age distinctions. Thus, combining data of youth twelve to fourteen for purposes of reporting is logical and appropriate, while combining data of youth fifteen to nineteen obscures important distinctions be-tween school-age and older adolescents.

A third way indicators are problematic is that they cannot accurately reflect complex behavior. Although select indicators reliably may measure health condi-tions that have discrete outcomes, such as the rate of low birth weight infants, categorical measures are excessively reductionist. Single health indicators cannot possibly measure complex health issues that have poorly defined antecedent pro-cesses or whose meaning is abstract. This is especially problematic for adolescents in that the health of this population is reflective of factors in multiple physical, psychological, and social domains. Monitoring the rate of drinking among ado-lescents is a good example. Although illegal before age twenty-one, drinking apparently alarms many people only when adolescents are involved in motor vehicle deaths while under the influence of alcohol. By focusing predominantly on alcohol consumption, indicators as currently reported and used understate the role that alcohol plays in adolescent morbidity and mortality, education and vo-cational underachievement, and social dysfunction.

In summary, because of rapid physical, social, psychological, and behavioral changes associated with adolescence, identifying an appropriate set of indicators to measure adolescent health and well-being is a difficult task. The types of measures that could be tracked are many. Unfortunately, some of the most prom-inent health issues affecting adolescents have become highly politicized. In many ways, adolescents are a mirror of our society in that their behavior mimics adult behavior. What we dislike about adult behavior, such as infidelity, alcohol abuse, drug abuse, and excessive violence yet are unwilling to take a strong stand against, we can project on our adolescents. Because of the risk that adolescent health indicators can be used punitively, great care must be taken when selecting the type of issues to measure, the ways in which the data will be analyzed, and the types of reports that will be produced.

After reviewing the ways in which they can be used, the next step in identify-ing a set of health indicators is to provide a working definition of health and to describe special issues of health that relate to adolescents. Assumptions will be presented in this chapter that could form the foundation for identifying adolescent health indicators. Finally, a scheme for organizing health indicators will be presented along with the results of a survey of national experts regarding their choice of health indicators for adolescents.

WHAT ARE PARAMETERS OF ADOLESCENT HEALTH?

Broadly defined, health is the maximal obtainable state of physical and emotional well-being. Health, therefore, is not an outcome of life, but a major resource for life. Identifying a set of indicators that measure adolescent health requires an understanding of how health is conceptualized and determined; the fact that health indicators for adolescents are both an outcome and an antecedent; and that the current nature of adolescent morbidity necessitates a greater emphasis on prevention.

Health as a State of Equilibrium

Adolescents' level of health is determined by their current state of physical equilibrium with their internal and external environment and their potential to maintain that balance. Adolescents need the reserve and resources to cope with environmental influences and to keep this balance. Physical and emotional disorders; personal behavior, such as alcohol and drug use, unsafe sexual practices, and possession of guns; family dysfunction; and dangerous community and school environment are threats to this equilibrium. Based on this concept, it is understandable why involvement in multiple health risk behavior is a greater threat to equilibrium than a single health risk.

Using this definition, health and the factors that promote health encompass a broad band of issues. From the medical perspective, health practitioners need to expand their practice to think more of the role that sociological factors play in influencing health. From the sociological perspective, health researchers need to broaden their concepts to include the manner and degree in which medical conditions influence a person's ability to function in society. Working groups that bring together an eclectic collection of health scientists, economists, social and behavioral scientists, and education specialists provide a good opportunity to take a comprehensive look at health and the most reliable and valid indices to measure health.

The Dual Nature of Health Indicators

Because of rapid growth and development, adolescent health indicators serve both as an outcome measure of earlier changes, as well as a measure of how well young people are preparing themselves for a healthy adult life. For example, whether or not a young adolescent participates in sexual intercourse results, in part, from earlier psychological factors. This same behavior, however, is also an indicator of future reproductive health. In addition, some indices might have immediate implications, while others affect health only many years later. Understanding the dual nature of health indices for adolescents is important for determining what measure to include in a package of indicators.

Even in its simplest form, a set of adolescent health indicators would need to focus on conditions that threaten current health equilibrium as well as those that threaten future health. In a more expanded mode, the set of indicators might include factors that precede or even predict conditions that threaten health.

The Changing Focus of Health Indicators

Changes in the nature of adolescent morbidity and mortality over the past several decades have resulted in greater attention directed at health risk behavior and the prevention of this behavior. Whereas thirty years ago most adolescent morbidity and mortality was due to natural causes, today the leading causes of death among adolescents are related to preventable, personal behavior—motor vehicle accidents, homicide, and suicide (Gans et al. 1990). Until recently, initiatives have addressed categorical issues, such as alcohol use, unintended pregnancy, and tobacco use. Although this approach has led to important discoveries and to the growth of special interest groups for both research and services, it also has had some unfortunate consequences. Specifically, efforts highly focused on categorical conditions have led to scholarly separatism; attention that is directed at the problem, rather than on the adolescent as a person or the family and community as an integrated unit; an atheoretical approach to the analysis of adolescent health; a politically polarizing sensationalism of health risk behavior that leads society to perceive the period of adolescence as dominated by problem behavior and family discord; and an overshadowing of disease prevention at the expense of health promotion.

The measurement of adolescent health behavior is complicated by several important developmental issues:

1. Some degree of behavioral experimentation is normal and expected. The challenge is how to use relatively simple indices that distinguish experimental, nonproblematic behavior from behavior that is destructive.

2. The significance of various types of health risk behavior varies by developmental age, the culture in which the adolescent lives, and political decisions. For example, most health professionals would agree that sexual intercourse at age twelve is problematic, while intercourse at age sixteen may not be problematic depending on emotional maturity and the other factors. However, within a religiously conservative community, intercourse at age sixteen probably indicates a greater willingness to deviate from community standards than does the same act in less conservative communities. For most adolescent health risk behavior, with smoking one of a few exceptions, there is a lack of clear national priorities for the goals of prevention. Because of this, the relevance of certain behavior, such as sexual intercourse and alcohol use, varies depending on sociopolitical decisions.

3. Although adolescents identify similar health concerns as do adults, the priority they ascribe to these issues differs (Millstein 1993). Like adults and health professionals, adolescents are concerned about the leading morbidities, such as

substance abuse and the consequences of sexual behavior. Unlike adults and health professionals, however, adolescents are even more concerned about problems related to appearance (weight and acne), emotional states (anxiety and depression), interpersonal relationships (how they get along with parents, friends, teachers), school (school work), and physical complaints (for example, headaches and dental problems). If one reason for identifying and measuring health indicators is to help guide prevention efforts, and not merely to have them serve as a barometer, then more will need to be known about how adolescents perceive risk and health.

CRITERIA FOR INCLUSION

Based upon the previous discussion, several criteria have been chosen to direct the selection of adolescent health indicators:

1. The indicators must focus directly on the adolescent, not on indirect enabling or disabling factors of the family or community. Although these other factors provide important clues to better understand causality and to direct research, with the limited number of indicators that can be chosen it is more important to assess the adolescent directly.

2. The indicators must be justifiable according to either the degree of burden of suffering experienced by adolescents or else their economic burden to society. Indicators should focus on conditions amenable to either primary or secondary preventive interventions. With a limited number of indicators that can be tracked over time, care should be taken to chose only those measures that, if improved, will produce the most good for the most people.

3. The indicators must be measurable and, to have the greatest impact, easily understood by society. Meeting this criterion will be tricky. The tendency will be to chose indicators that are simple and universally measured on a routine basis. Because of the complexity of issues involved, there are no clear markers of adolescent health that are as easily followed as those for pregnancy and infancy. The ideal situation would be to measure adolescent indicators annually because of the rapid and substantial psychosocial changes that youth experience. In reality, there will need to be a compromise between choosing health measures that are relevant and choosing measures that are assessed by existing health surveys.

4. The indicators must be amenable to reporting by various distinctions that are consistent developmentally. As a minimum, these should include age, gender, race/ethnic group, and preferably, family characteristics. Care should be taken to ensure that the package of indicators are balanced and include health-promoting factors as well as markers of health problems.

As a basis for the justification of health indicators, the conceptual framework developed by the Public Health Service (PHS) in its document, *Healthy People 2000: National Health Promotion and Disease Prevention Objectives*, was used (U.S. Public Service 1990). In this report, the PHS identified 298 health objectives in 22 separate priority areas. The purpose of having health objectives is to guide public research, education, and services toward reducing preventable death, disease, and disability. Approximately seventy of these objectives related directly to adolescents and have been published by the American Medical Association (AMA) (American Medical Association 1991).

The PHS Year 2000 objectives are divided into three groups, those that address health status, those that address risk reduction and health promotion, and those that address health services. *Health status* measures relate to current disease, death, or disability; *risk reduction* indicators relate to reducing the prevalence of risks to health or to increasing behavior known to reduce such risks; and *service* indicators relate to increase comprehensiveness, accessibility, and/or quality of preventive services and preventive interventions.

These three categories were used to organize possible adolescent health indicators. This distinction serves both to organize the health objectives and to promote the integration of efforts among federal and private health initiatives that might use health indicator data.

Once criteria and organizational structure were identified, the next step in identifying a set of adolescent health indicators was to use current epidemiological data and data on health services to identify a list of possible measures that could be included in each category (see tables 6.1–6.3). This list was compiled by reviewing existing papers and source books that describe markers of adolescent health and well-being. The most commonly used markers were included in the list.

Next, a group of national experts was asked to rank the markers in each of the three categories as to how useful each was as a health indicator. Experts were chosen who represented a range of professional disciplines.[1] The average rank for each category was computed. Indicators that were closely aligned were collapsed to produce the final listing (see table 6.4).

Table 6.1   Health Status Indicators

1. Rate of teens who are obese
2. Rate of teens who diet frequently
3. Rate of teens who have iron-deficiency anemia
4. Rate of teens with genital gonorrhea infections
5. Rate of teens who have had a pregnancy
6. Rate of teens seen in emergency rooms with a self-inflicted injury or overdose
7. Number of teens seen in emergency rooms with alcohol- or drug-related injury
8. Rate of teens who die from an alcohol-related motor vehicle crash
9. Days missed from school/work during the past year
10. Rate of teens with a chronic condition that results in some loss of ability to conduct normal physical, social, or recreational activities
11. Days hospitalized during the past year for conditions with preventable relapses, such as asthma and diabetes mellitus
12. Mortality rate, broken down by cause of death
13. Rate of victimization of violent crime
14. Percent of teens treated for emotional or behavioral problems in the past 12 months
15. Percent of teens who had an accident, injury, or poisoning in the past 12 months
16. Percent of teens with indicators of anxiety or depression

Table 6.2   Risk Reduction and Health Promotion Indicators

 1. Rate of teens who smoke daily
 2. Rate of teens who drank alcohol during the past month
 3. Rate of teens who drink alcohol daily
 4. Rate of teens who drove a motor vehicle after drinking during the past month
 5. Rate of teens who disapprove of tobacco, alcohol, and drug use
 6. Arrest rates for alcohol- or drug-related violations
 7. Rate of illicit substance use during the past month
 8. Rate of teens who have had sexual intercourse
 9. Rate of teens who used a condom at last intercourse
10. Rate of teens who carry a weapon to school
11. Rate of teens who participate in daily school physical education
12. Rate of teens who consume three or more servings daily of foods rich in calcium
13. Rate of teens who have at least one meal a day with their parent
14. Rate of teens who have discussed AIDS with their parents
15. Rate of teens who participate in an extracurricular activity
16. Rate of teens who value sexual restraint

CONCLUSION

A paradigm based upon the PHS Year 2000 Health Objectives was used to select groups of indicators for tracking adolescent health. This approach produces three types of indicators: health status measures, risk reduction and health-promotion measures, and health services. Based upon the rankings of a national group of experts, a small number of indicators were selected for each of the three categories. The recommended health indicators for adolescents are:

Health Status: number of teens seen in emergency rooms with an intentional or unintentional injury.

Table 6.3   Health Service Indicators

 1. Rate of teens with completed immunization (diphtheria-tetanus booster, second measles-mumps-rubella, hepatitis B virus vaccine)
 2. Rate of teens who had a routine (preventive service) visit in the last year
 3. Rate of teens who had a dental exam during the past year
 4. Rate of teens who have a primary health care provider or a clinic that serves as a "health care home"
 5. Rate of teens who know that they can receive confidential health services related to reproductive health; physical or sexual abuse; and alcohol and drug problems
 6. Rate of sexually active teens who had pelvic exam (females) or genital exam (males) during the past year
 7. Rate of teens who used psychological services during the past year
 8. Rate of teens who are screened about sexual behavior
 9. Rate of teens who are screened about use of tobacco products
10. Rate of teens who are screened about use of alcohol and other drugs
11. Rate of teens who are covered by either public or private health insurance

Table 6.4   Top Rankings by Category of Indicators

Ranking	Health Status
#1	Number of teens seen in the emergency room with an intention or unintentional injury
#2	Mortality rate, broken down by cause of death, including deaths from alcohol-related motor vehicle crash
#3	Rate of teens who have had a pregnancy

Ranking	Risk Reduction and Health Promotion
#1 (tie)	Rate of teens who drink alcohol daily
	Rate of teens who drove a motor vehicle after drinking during the past month
	Rate of teens who carry a weapon to school
#2 (tie)	Rate of teens who smoke daily
	Rate of teens who had unprotected sexual intercourse at last episode

Ranking	Service
#1 (tie)	Rate of teens with completed immunizations
	Rate of teens who have a primary health care provider
#2	Rate of teens who have had a preventive service visit during which time they were screened for sexual behavior, use of tobacco products, and use of alcohol and other drugs

Risk Reduction and Health Promotion:
   rate of teens who drink alcohol daily;
   rate of teens who drove a motor vehicle after drinking during the past month;
   and
   rate of teens who carry a weapon to school.
Health Services:
   rate of teens with completed immunizations; and
   rate of teens who have a primary health care provider.

These indicators emphasize the importance of violence and injury to the health and well-being of adolescents and to society. They also underscore the causative role of alcohol in adolescent morbidity. Completed immunizations and having a primary health care provider are rather straightforward and traditional health service indicators that have inherent validity.

For the most part, these six indicators already are monitored on a regular basis currently. The number of teens seen in emergency rooms for injury is measured by the National Ambulatory Medical Care Survey (Nelson and Stussman 1994). This annual survey, which was first done in 1992, includes data from a national probability sample of emergency rooms. The risk reduction and health promotion indicators can be obtained from the YRBSS and the Monitoring the Future surveys (Kahn et al. 1993; Johnson et al. 1993). The health service indicators can be obtained from the National Medical Care Utilization and Expenditure Survey and the National Health Interview Survey (Bloom 1990; Butler et al. 1985). Taken together, these indicators produce a well-rounded picture of adolescent health and well-being.

NOTE

1. The Expert Panel consisted of Charles Irwin, M.D.; Anne Petersen, Ph.D.; Barbara Ritchen, R.N., M.S.N.; John Schowalter, M.D.; Barbara Starfield, M.D.; and Laurie Zabin, Ph.D.

REFERENCES

American Medical Association. 1991. *Healthy Youth 2000: National Health Promotion and Disease Prevention Objectives for Adolescents.* Chicago, Ill.: American Medical Association.

Bloom, B. 1990. "Health Insurance and Medical Care: Health of Our Nation's Children, United States, 1988." Advance Data from vital and health statistics, no. 188. Hyattsville, Md.: National Center for Health Statistics.

Butler, J. A., W. D. Winter, J. D. Singer, and M. Wenger. 1985. "Medical Care Use and Expenditure among Children and Youth in the United States: Analysis of a National Probability Sample." *Pediatrics* (76): 495–507.

Gans, J. G., D. A. Blyth, A. B. Elster, and L. L. Gaveres. 1990. *America's Adolescents: How Healthy Are They?* Chicago, Ill: American Medical Association.

Johnson, L. D., P. M. O'Malley, J. G. Bachman, and J. Schulenberg. 1993. "The Aims, Objectives, and Rationale of the Monitoring the Future Study." *Monitoring the Future* Occasional Paper 34. Ann Arbor, Michigan: University of Michigan, Ann Arbor.

Kann, L., W. Warren, J. L. Collins, and L. J. Kolbe. 1993. "Results from the National School-Based 1991 Youth Risk Behavior Survey and Progress Toward Achieving Related Health Objectives for the Nation." *Public Health Reports* 108 (suppl) 1: 47–67.

Marks, J. S., G. C. Hogelin, E. M. Gentry, J. T. Jones, K. L. Gaines, M. R. Lorman, F. L. Trowbridge. 1985. "State-Specific Prevalence Estimates of Behavioral Risk Factors." *American Journal of Preventive Medicine* 1985; 1: 1–8.

Millstein, S. G. 1993. "A View of Health from the Adolescent's Perspective." In *Promoting the Health of Adolescents: New Dimensions for the Twenty-First Century,* edited by Millstein, S. G., A. C. Petersen, and E. O. Nightingale. New York: Oxford University Press.

Nelson, C. R., and B. J. Stussman. 1994. "Alcohol-Related and Drug-Related Visits to Hospital Emergency Departments: 1992 National Hospital Ambulatory Medical Care Survey." Advance data from vital and health statistics, no 251. Hyattsville, Md.: National Center for Health Statistics.

U.S. Public Health Service. 1990. *Healthy People 2000: National Health Promotion and Disease Prevention Objectives.* Washington: U.S. Government Printing Office.

Zill, N., and M. Daly, eds. 1993. *Researching the Family: A Guide to Survey and Statistical Data on Families.* Washington, D.C.: Child Trends, Inc.

Part III

Education

7

Indicators for School Readiness, Schooling, and Child Care in Early to Middle Childhood

Deborah A. Phillips and John M. Love

A NATIONAL CONSENSUS has recently reemerged regarding the importance of education, fueled in part by a perception that our schools are not doing an adequate job of preparing an educated citizenry for the twenty-first century. At the same time, national attention has been riveted on notions of outcome accountability for a variety of reasons, ranging from frustration with the regulation of inputs to hopes that a reliable accountability system might provide persuasive evidence of the effectiveness of interventions for children and their families (Schorr 1994). As a result, indicators that assess and track the school readiness and schooling of our nation's children are likely to become a particularly salient component of any effort to construct national indicators for children. Indeed, they likely will be used not only to track children's well-being, but also to assess the success or failure of our recent national experiment in school reform. A recent report from the Department of Education, *Education Counts: An Indicator System to Monitor the Nation's Educational Health* (National Household Education Survey 1991) states that "if the broad reform movement is to succeed, the United States must develop a comprehensive educational indicator information system."

The development of this system is beyond the purview of this chapter. Indeed, its indispensability for a successful school reform effort is highly questionable. Indicators, in general, seldom offer appropriate tools for purposes of evaluation. On the other hand, an accepted and valid set of indicators can be a highly effective device for public communication and a significant lever for change. As such, efforts to construct a set of school readiness indicators that expands the richness, depth, and rigor of our understanding of children's well-being, and enables us to chart their educational progress from the child care through the middle school years, warrant substantial attention.

OUR APPROACH TO IDENTIFYING INDICATORS

A disclaimer is in order at the outset. Our training as developmental psychologists and our experience with program evaluation have prepared us to capture the contexts and complexity of children's lives, to search for explanations of the trends that characterize these lives, and to mistrust data that get far removed from the observational methods that our fields have labored long to develop and refine. Indicators, in contrast, emphasize simplicity, are designed to monitor rather than to understand children's development, and, by design, do not rely on labor-intensive data collection methods.

We have, as a result, adopted an approach to the task of identifying indicators that draws upon our conceptual understanding of what to measure and then considers how best to quantify these concepts in the form of indicators. Specifically, we draw upon our knowledge of the developmental and evaluation literatures to identify dimensions of family and child well-being relevant to child care and early schooling that are most predictive of positive child outcomes in the short and long term. We then discuss the implications of this empirical evidence for indicator data. In effect, we start with the goal of developing a set of indicators that measures the "right things," as noted by Brandon (1992).

In some instances, this approach points to a critical facet of development, such as "approaches to learning," for which no reliable indicator-type data sources presently exist. We hope, however, that our conceptual starting point will guard against the temptation to identify straightforward, easy-to-collect indicators that may be useless for policy purposes, or even misleading. We are particularly concerned about the tendency, over time, for indicators to take on a life of their own; to reify—rather than simply to reflect—the important parameters of child and family well-being. The strength of indicators is that they focus attention on critical issues. But, if we focus attention on the wrong issues, or on unreliable sources of information about the right issues, then we run the risk of misdirecting both public attention and public policy.

Consider the assessment of child care quality—the aspect of child care that is most strongly predictive of children's well-being (in contrast to use, type, or duration of child care). Several large surveys (for example, the National Household Education Survey and the National Longitudinal Survey of Youth) have asked parents to report on quality features of their child care arrangements (staff-child ratios, total numbers of children, and staff qualifications). The reliability and validity of these reports, particularly for group care arrangements, are entirely unproven, and, for retrospective reports, are most likely very poor. Rather than propose an indicator based on parent reports of quality, we suggest searching for other child care indicators that can be assessed accurately.

In the domain of educational outcomes, we face a special challenge posed by the strong association in the United States between educational achievement and the demographic characteristics of the families whose children are being assessed, particularly their levels of maternal education. As a result, indicators of academic achievement could easily allow a state or school district to proclaim that its particular brand of education reform is especially effective—or to be subjected to criticism as ineffectual—when changing community demographics, rather than improved educational programs, could account for aggregate improvements or declines in school performance indicators. We strongly recommend that any subnational or longitudinal reporting of educational outcomes be accompanied by information about (or adjustments for) the socioeconomic status and ethnic composition of the population under consideration, in order to guard against such misattributions.

SCHOOL READINESS

The concept of school readiness is central to each of the sets of indicators addressed in this chapter and thus offers an appropriate point of departure. We care about school readiness because, as a nation, we are becoming increasingly concerned about the fact that children enter kindergarten with widely differing levels of preparation and, therefore, differing levels of functioning (see Bradburn 1994). This causes us, on the one hand, to look back in time at variation in the resources and experiences to which children are exposed prior to school entry. Child care is included in this chapter because it is now perceived as an environment that, among its other goals, should help to prepare children for school. We also look ahead to children's differential progress through the school system which is now viewed as a function, in part, of their uneven status at school entry. Thus, the middle childhood years are included because this is presumably a useful point at which to take stock of the adequacy with which we have prepared children for school.

Conceptualizing School Readiness

Although any one of these premises is open to debate (for example, child care should be a place where children play, free of the pressures of being prepared for school), we have chosen not to delve into the intricacies of these controversies. We cannot, however, so quickly bypass the controversy that has surrounded the current state of knowledge and debate about the concept of school readiness itself. In practice, the selection of indicators involves the selection of social goals. Moreover, because of the political significance of social indicators, we are appropriately cautioned to assure that they are accepted and readily understood by the public (Moore 1994).

Efforts to conceptualize school readiness, while widespread, are in their infancy and characterized by controversy. Two important tensions, with relevance to constructing indicators, are particularly prominent. The first concerns the distinction between school readiness and learning readiness. School readiness is generally approached as a school entry measure—a fixed standard of development sufficient to enable children to fulfill school requirements and to absorb the curriculum content (Kagan 1994). This stands in contrast to concepts of learning readiness that acknowledge the fluid and cumulative nature of development, and typically adopt a more idiosyncratic than normative perspective. This is possible, in part, because concepts of learning readiness are not tied to a specific set of institutional requirements or expectations. Indeed, some assert that all children are born ready to learn even though not all are ready for school.

The second tension exists between the prevailing emphasis on children's readiness for school (the child outcome focus) and the relative inattention presently being paid to the extent to which schools are ready for the children they are now receiving and responsible for educating (the institutional focus). This tension derives from the concerns of many that assessments of young children's readiness will be misused to "blame" children and their families for low levels of early learning. In fact, at least a portion of responsibility should lie with schools that vary in the extent to which they are receptive places for young children with differing characteristics and backgrounds (see Love, Aber, and Brooks-Gunn 1994). Stated more constructively, efforts to promote the early success of children in school surely entail offering children beneficial early inputs and experiences (ranging from good nutrition to good books) and making certain that the classrooms and teachers they first encounter are receptive and affirming of their backgrounds, capabilities, and interests.

For the task at hand, we have been asked to focus on indicators that pertain directly to child outcomes and children's well-being (and to avoid indicators of institutional or jurisdictional performance). We strongly recommend, however, that a comprehensive effort to develop childhood indicators include indicators of schools' readiness for the diverse populations of young children they now must educate.

Measuring School Readiness

The status of efforts to develop measures of school readiness is rudimentary, at best. And they too are immersed in controversies such as the appropriateness of such assessments for minority language children, and their role in determining school entry and tracking for very young children. This is murky and value-laden territory.

Yet charged by the president and the fifty state governors in 1990 to assure that "by the year 2000 all children in American will start school ready to learn" (a goal that was lent the weight of law with the recent passage of the Goals 2000 legislation), a number of states have been designing and implementing their own readiness assessment systems. At the national level, the National Center for Education Statistics is supporting the development of a new assessment of readiness through the Early Childhood Longitudinal Survey (ECLS) (West 1992). One of the primarily rationales for this survey, which is projected to go into the field in 1998, is "the scarcity of data on children's preparation for school, their transition into school, and their progress through the primary and elementary grades" (Bradburn 1994). Focusing primarily on children in kindergarten through fifth grade, the ECLS includes a cohort of Head Start children. Although, as a longitudinal survey, the ECLS will not provide an ongoing source of indicator data, it does offer a rare opportunity to develop indicators of school readiness, early schooling and child care, including quality of care for center-based arrangements.

In addition, the Office of Educational Research and Improvement (OERI) in the U.S. Department of Education is being reorganized to better fulfill its mission, which includes monitoring the state of education. The new OERI is structured around five national research institutes, including the National Institute on Early Childhood Development and Education and the National Institute on Student Achievement, Curriculum, and Assessment (Office of Educational Research and Improvement 1994). The domain of readiness, schooling, and child care indicators bears directly on the agendas of these new institutes. Given the importance of data from the Department of Education for the indicators that we discuss, some coordinated planning would be highly desirable.

Most recently, Love and his colleagues (Love, Aber, and Brooks-Gunn 1994) have proposed an assessment system to help schools, communities, and states determine how effectively they are supporting and promoting children's school readiness. This system is designed to be implemented by most school districts in the context of their kindergarten registration procedures. If fully implemented, it too would offer a rich source of indicator data at district, state, and national levels of aggregation.

Absent the ECLS and the assessment system proposed by Love et al., we must fall back on current conceptualizations of school readiness and adapt them to our present purposes. Most fundamentally, conceptions of school readiness acknowledge the vast amount of school-relevant learning that occurs long before formal instruction is introduced at school entry. Empirical documentation of the significance of early learning has focused on early literacy acquisition (Hakuta and D'Andrea 1992; Snow 1983), but growing evidence is now revealing the importance of early experience for numerical knowledge as well (Case and Griffin, 1990; Griffin, Case, and Sandieson 1992; Siegler and Robinson 1982). Beyond the acquisition of early concepts and knowledge (for example, the alphabet and the number line), a large literature has documented the many ways in which children's home environments instill the behavioral and motivational repertoires that enable children to enter school eager and ready to learn (Entwisle and Alexander 1990; Stipek 1988). Accordingly, a central challenge is that of deciphering those aspects of children's preschool experiences that will provide a valid portrait of their preparation for school.

Once a child enters school, the assessment of readiness has received more attention, compared to the preschool period. Of particular relevance to our task is the work of the Goal 1 Technical Planning Group of the National Education Goals Panel (December 1993). The Planning Group has identified five dimensions that encompass the wide range of abilities and experiences on which early learning and development depend. Each dimension includes a number of criteria for assessment. These are:

Physical well-being and motor development:
- physical development (rate of growth and physical fitness)
- physical abilities (gross and fine motor skills, oral motor skills, and functional performance)

Social and emotional development:
- emotional development (feeling states regarding self and others, including self-concept; the emotions of joy, fear, anger, grief, and so forth; and the ability to express feelings appropriately, including empathy and sensitivity to the feelings of others)
- social development (cooperation, understanding the rights of others, ability to treat others equitably, ability to distinguish between incidental and intentional actions, willingness to give and receive support, ability to balance one's own needs with those of others, creating opportunities for affection and companionship, and ability to solicit and listen to other's points of view)

Approaches toward learning:
- predispositions (gender, temperament, cultural patterns, and values)

- learning styles (openness to and curiosity about new tasks and challenges, task persistence and attentiveness, a tendency for reflection and interpretation, and imagination and invention)

Language usage:

- verbal language (listening, speaking, social uses of language, vocabulary and meaning, questioning, creative uses of language)
- emerging literacy (literature awareness, print awareness, story sense, and writing process)

Cognition and general knowledge:

- knowledge (physical knowledge, logico-mathematical knowledge, and social-conventional knowledge)
- cognitive competencies (representational thought problem-solving, mathematical knowledge, and social knowledge)

In this chapter, we narrow the lens to encompass the final three dimensions. (See chapters 4, 5, 18, and 19, this volume, for discussion of the other dimensions.)

Indicators of School Readiness

Drawing upon the National Education Goals Panel's (NEGP) conceptualization of readiness and the research literature on this topic, we suggest that indicators of school readiness focus on exposure to reading at home; exposure to prenumeracy experiences at home; approaches to learning; emergent literacy and numeracy development; proportion of kindergartners deemed "unready" for kindergarten; parental attitudes and expectations; and access to some instruction in the child's native language. The home environment provides the focus for this section of the paper; children's child care environments are discussed in the next section. Table 7.1 presents the proposed list of school readiness indicators, distinguishing between those that are currently available and those that need to be developed.

Exposure to Reading at Home   Children's preliteracy interactions in the home have been found repeatedly to differentiate children who are readily able to acquire age-appropriate information at school entry from those who are not. Specifically, a large and sophisticated literature has documented the predictive role that children's exposure to environments rich in discourse and literacy experiences plays in their reading levels at kindergarten and first grade (Dickinson and Beals 1994; Goldenberg 1987). The extent to which these experiences are provided to children is, in turn, affected by maternal education and parents' views about how children learn to read, write, and use numbers. Opportunities to acquire literacy skills at home, nevertheless, provide a highly valid proximal indicator of educationally significant early experiences.

Some of the most important aspects of these opportunities would be difficult to capture with indicators, including the extent to which parents depart from simply reading the text to engage children in conversations about the text and the extent to which children are encouraged to talk about past and future events.

Table 7.1   Indicators of School Readiness

Indicator	Current Sources	Future Prospects
Exposure to reading at home	NHES: 93	NHES: 95/96
		SIPP Child Module
		NLSY-MC
		ECLS
Exposure to prenumeracy experiences		NHES: 95/96
		ECLS
Approaches to learning	Love et al. 1994	ECLS
Emergent literacy and numeracy	NHES: 93	NHES: 95/96
development	Prospects Study	SIPP Child Module
		ECLS
		Love et al. 1994
		State/local level data
Proportion of kindergartners "unready"	NHES: 93	NHES: 95/96
for kindergarten		SIPP Child Module
		State/local level data
Parental attitudes/expectations		NHES: 95/96
		ECLS
		Survey of Program Dynamics
Access to instruction in native		NHES: 95
langauge		OECD
		Schools and Staffing Study

But, the number of books in the home, particularly the number of children's books, and parents' reports of time spent reading children's books to their children have been found to offer reasonable proxies for the home literacy environment.

Current indicators could be developed from the National Household Education Survey: 93. This telephone survey of a representative sample of households with three- to seven-year-olds, sponsored by the Department of Education and first implemented in 1991, asked parents a series of questions about home activities that are relevant to the early reading environment. These include:

• whether the child pretends to read;

• number of children's own books in the home;

• frequency of reading to the child;

• frequency of storytelling; and

• rules governing content and hours of children's television viewing (may bear on opportunities for reading experiences at home).

Factor analyses of data from the 1991 wave of the NHES, carried out by Zill and colleagues (Zill, Stief, and Coiro 1992), identified four scales focusing on activities with the child at home; activities with the child outside the home; educational materials in the home; and rules about television viewing. The scales show good internal consistency and may offer an alternative to reliance on individual items.

This (or similar) information will be obtained in the NHES:95, and we understand that the NHES may be planning a parent component in the 1996 wave. Subsequent assessments will occur at two-year intervals. The child well-being module of the SIPP (in the field) also asks parents of children who are infants through five-year-olds about the frequency of reading to the child at home, and a set of questions about television viewing (rules about what shows, total hours, and how early/late the child can watch). One note on this new module is in order: it is not clear whether this will be an ongoing component of the SIPP. We would like to highlight the importance of repeating this module on a regular schedule.

Each wave of the mother/child module of the National Longitudinal Survey of Youth (NLSY) includes a modified version of the Home Observation Measure of the Environment (HOME) Scale—a well validated and widely used assessment of the home learning environment. The mother-child supplement is a biennial survey, beginning in 1986, of the children of a nationally representative sample of women age fourteen to twenty-one when they were first interviewed in 1979. The children are assessed beginning at age three and interviewed directly beginning about age ten. These data are limited, however, by the basic design of the NLSY. Most notably, the older children are children of early childbearers and the younger children are children of later childbearers. The NLSY eventually will include children of older and younger childbearers at each age and, as such, will prove more useful as a possible source of indicator data.

Finally, we recommend that the development of the ECLS protocol be observed carefully as a potentially valuable "testing ground" for each of the readiness constructs that we have identified. We will reemphasize this point only in those instances where we want to recommend that a particular construct not presently highlighted in the plans for the ECLS be seriously considered for inclusion in this study.

Exposure to Prenumeracy Experiences   A parallel literature has focused on identifying the home experiences that distinguish children who come to school with an intuitive sense of numbers and how they work from those who do not. While not as well developed as the knowledge base about preliteracy experiences, beneficial prenumeracy experiences include board games and card games that involve numbers, as well as the engagement of children in conversations and other activities that associate number with quantity (for example, sorting laundry or picking up toys) and teach children to think in terms of a mental number line. It is not simply the act of counting that matters, it is exposure to the functions and meaning of counting.

The challenge for an indicators project is one of identifying meaningful indicators from among the array of important experiences that have been identified. We are not aware of any current representative data sources that inquire about prenumeracy experiences, and we propose that this be a priority for the development of new indicators data. An appropriate focus, parallel to indicators that capture books (resources) and reading (experiences), would be on the availability of counting games and toys (resources) and time spent playing with/explaining numbers to children as distinct from simply getting them to count to ten. These are admittedly far more complicated questions for parents to answer than those regarding literacy, and substantial work would be entailed in developing reliable and valid indicators. But, a growing literature on children's math achievement suggests that the effort would have large payoffs.

The NHES: 93 included a question regarding the frequency of playing with games and toys at home, as well as one inquiring about how high the child can count. Perhaps, in future waves, a probe about the types of games could be added, and the query about counting could be replaced with a more meaningful item regarding numeracy experiences. The opportunity provided by the NHES to ask about prenumeracy experiences in the context of other questions about parent-child activities in the preschool years is well worth exploring.

Approaches to Learning   As important for school achievement as children's early exposure to school-related concepts and skills is the early encouragement of their motivation to acquire and marshal this knowledge as they progress through school. Behaviors such as task persistence, impulse control, and attentiveness are likely to improve children's adjustment to structured elementary school classrooms (Benasich, Brooks-Gunn, and McCormick 1992; Lee, Brooks-Gunn, Schnur, and Liaw 1990). The development of enhanced self-regulatory abilities (such as delay of gratification and impulse control) predicts academic competence (SAT scores) more than a decade later (Mischel 1984). "Personal maturity" in preschool, which includes a large self-regulatory component, predicts achievement in reading and math in elementary school (Entwisle et al. 1987).

Children's approaches toward learning include curiosity, creativity, independence, cooperativeness, and persistence. This construct calls attention to the important distinction between children's repertoire of skills and knowledge, on the one hand, and their engagement in learning and self-concept as a learner, on the other hand. The Goal 1 Technical Planning Group identifies four components of "approaches toward learning": openness to and curiosity about new tasks and challenges; task persistence and attentiveness; a tendency for reflection and interpretation; and imagination and invention. This group further speculates that "approaches toward learning is the least understood dimension [of school readiness], the least researched, and perhaps the most important." We agree.

Other investigators have focused on somewhat different, but closely related, components of a child's approach to learning. Bronson (1994) has emphasized the "ability to carry out developmentally appropriate goal-oriented tasks in an independent, self-regulated manner." Component behaviors include "selecting tasks appropriate to one's level of skill, organizing task-relevant materials, using effective task attack strategies, resisting distraction, trying repeatedly (persisting) when necessary, and, ultimately, completing tasks successfully." Bronson has developed a detailed observational measure that captures these constructs. Aber and his colleagues (Aber, Molnar, and Phillips 1986) have used the term "disposition to learn" and emphasize the inseparability of cognitive from socioemotional, motivational, and personality development, particularly during the preschool and early school years. Notions of self-regulatory behavior, as described above, are also featured prominently in this literature, with the preschool years identified as a particularly sensitive stage for their development (Aber et al. 1986).

Valid measurement of these constructs entails labor-intensive methods: classroom observations of children or the administration of a set of child assessments. Such measures exist (such as Torrance's Thinking Creatively in Action and

Movement measure for three- to eight-year-olds, 1981), but are not likely to be widely enough used to form the basis for a representative set of indicators. Teacher ratings can be used (for example, proposed self-control and cooperation subscales of the Social Skills Rating System, for their assessment system, Love et al., 1994; Gresham and Elliott 1990) and offer a more practical source of indicator data. This is clearly a topic that warrants a high priority for the development of improved indicators.

We would like to make a particularly strong case for instrument development in this area in conjunction with the ECLS. This survey affords a rare opportunity to measure approaches toward learning, although inclusion of such assessment is not presently a priority. We believe that an investment of this sort now, given the timing of the ECLS, would reap substantial benefits for future efforts to track important indicators of school readiness.

Emergent Literacy and Numeracy Development   These indicators would serve to capture, at school entry and during the early elementary years, the skills and knowledge in literacy and math that beneficial home preliteracy and prenumeracy experiences have been found to foster. Language is central to learning in all domains of achievement, and is also the dimension of early learning that kindergarten teachers identified as the area where most "unready" children have difficulty (Boyer 1991).

Measurement of literacy development is not straightforward. Ideally, it would encompass aspects of form (structure or syntax, including recognition of the alphabet), content (meaning or semantics; the ability to comprehend), and function (the use of language to communicate; to acquire information)—each of which has its own developmental timetable. For our present purposes, two commonly accepted domains of emergent literacy require consideration: verbal language, including listening, speaking, social uses of language, and vocabulary and meaning; and literacy, including literature awareness, print awareness, story sense, and writing processes (see National Educational Goals Panel 1993).

A special challenge in this area concerns children whose primary language is not English—a sizeable and growing share of the preschool and elementary school population (see Phillips and Crowell, 1994). Whatever shape efforts to track literacy take, it will be critical to include immigrant and non-English-speaking children, as is partially the case with the Department of Education's *Prospects* study of Chapter I services (Department of Education 1993), which includes Spanish-speaking children.

Numerical-mathematical knowledge is also heavily stressed in elementary school curricula. As with literacy skill, striking differences are found in the mathematical understandings that children bring to school (see, for example, Griffin, Case, and Siegler 1992). A significant number of low-income children, for instance, have been unable to tell which of two numbers (six or eight) is bigger or smaller or which number (six or two) is closer to five. Yet this is precisely the knowledge on which the solving of first-grade addition and subtraction problems is dependent. The concern here is that many children enter school without knowledge that their teachers assume they have, and then are left behind as their early school instruction departs from a baseline that they have never reached.

Measurement of early number knowledge is at a more rudimentary stage than is the case with early literacy knowledge. The major challenge is that many children are able to count, but they do not have a sense of the "number line"—of how numbers relate to quantity and to sequencing—which is, in fact, the critical numeracy knowledge at school entry. A child's ability to count actually can camouflage the absence of adequate numerical knowledge.

At the time of kindergarten entry, there is sparse data from which to draw national indicators of literacy and numeracy knowledge. The NHES: 93 (and presumably NHES: 95 and/or the 1996 parent survey) asks parents about their children's knowledge of color names and the alphabet, about whether the child can write his/her first name, and how high the child can count. We are not confident of the validity of these data, and question whether counting per se is a useful indicator of numeracy knowledge. The child well-being module to the SIPP may contain some relevant items in the future.

A major assessment of the cognitive skills and abilities of children exposed to Chapter I services is being conducted by the Department of Education (Puma et al. 1993). This study, called Prospects: The Congressionally Mandated Study of Educational Growth and Opportunity, is following thirty thousand students across the United States in grades one, three, and seven for five years. Its purpose is to evaluate the long-term effects of exposure to Chapter I services. In addition, a subset of these students is being observed in classroom settings. At a minimum, the ECLS should examine the protocol for this study so that some parallel data are collected. The Prospects study may also be a current source of indicator data regarding literacy and numeracy skill, albeit for only a segment of the population. A real strength of this study is its inclusion of immigrant and non-English-speaking students who speak Spanish.

Again, one of the most promising prospects for improved indicators is the Early Childhood Longitudinal Study (ECLS). This will offer the opportunity to assess children's readiness in the Head Start and kindergarten cohorts. In their strategy for a district-level kindergarten entry assessment system, Love et al. (1994) propose use of the Early Screening Inventory (Meisels, Wiske, Henderson, Marsden, and Browning 1988) as a source of information on expressive (verbal) language, verbal reasoning, and knowledge of colors, letters, numbers, and writing. Vocabulary development (for example, the Peabody Picture Vocabulary Test) is also a useful correlate of early literacy development (see Cazden, Snow, and Heise-Baigorria 1990). It would not be very difficult to design a set of useful items to assess early math knowledge, either incorporating or modifying assessments used in empirical research (see Griffin, Case, and Siegler 1992, for example).

We further suggest that state-level kindergarten assessment data be examined as a possible source of indicator data. Many states have developed a battery of kindergarten screening tests, some of which are highly regarded (see, for example, the nationally normed Tests of Early Math Ability and analogous tests in reading, writing, and language, developed by nationally recognized researchers in each area). Many states, in addition, are engaged in efforts to construct their own assessments of school readiness.

Proportion of Kindergartners Deemed "Unready" for Kindergarten A readiness indicator that has high face validity, but may be more a reflection of differing school practices than of child well-being, concerns the proportion of kindergarten-age children who are deemed "unready" for kindergarten. Some of these children are placed in transition kindergarten programs or are asked to repeat kindergarten; others are assigned to special education services in kindergarten.

The NHES: 93 asks parents to report whether their child attended one or two years of kindergarten, and whether the child received any special help in school for reading, arithmetic, speech, a learning disability, or English as a second language. Relevant information will be available from the child well-being module of the SIPP, which asks parents of six to eleven-year-olds if their child has repeated a grade, including kindergarten.

The consistency and validity of state- and district-level data regarding the educational status of kindergartners also warrant careful attention. The School Archival Records Search (Walker et al. 1991) offers a uniform system for obtaining information from school records about children's school experiences. Data collection includes information regarding school attendance, achievement, retention, in-school and outside referrals for academic or disciplinary causes, placements outside the regular classroom or for special services, and negative narrative comments.

Parental Attitudes and Expectations   Once children enter school, dimensions of parenting such as parental monitoring (Crouter et al. 1990; Dishion 1990; Zill and Nord, 1994), positive mutual participation (Bradley, Caldwell, and Rock 1988; Moorehouse 1991), and parental involvement in the child's schooling (Alexander and Entwistle 1988) become important predictors of children's motivation and performance in school. Parental expectations regarding their child's school performance are also correlated with schooling outcomes (Stipek 1988). For very young ages, however, most parents (and children) hold high educational expectations, thereby generating only minimal variability.

It appears that the deployment of expectations, in the form of actual involvement (help with homework, taking the child to the library, getting to know teachers), is the more potent and discriminating indicator for young children (although the NHES: 93 reveals that nearly three-quarters of students in the third to fifth grade had parents who showed at least a moderate level of school involvement). The fact that the parent takes the time to get involved communicates to the child that she/he considers school important and is likely to indicate that the parent provides other forms of encouragement and support for learning outside of school (Zill and Nord 1994).

The NHES: 95 will ask parents who are using Head Start, a prekindergarten program, or other group care program if they worked at the child's program in the last month. We are not aware of any other source of nationally representative data that reflect this construct at the prekindergarten- or kindergarten-age levels. Perhaps the ECLS, or the proposed Survey of Program Dynamics of the U.S. Bureau of the Census, will provide pertinent information.

Access to Instruction in the Child's Native Language   Estimates of the number of students in U.S. schools with limited English proficiency range from 2.3 million (U.S. Department of Education 1992) to much higher (Stanford

Working Group 1993). The current influx of new immigrant groups, some of whom also have relatively high rates of birth, will fuel continued growth in the number of students who enter school with little or no English proficiency.

These trends pose new opportunities, but also serious challenges, to United States educational institutions, including the early childhood programs that lay the foundation for children's school experience and achievement (see Phillips and Crowell 1994). In California, for example, a recent study of four hundred child care centers revealed that only 4 percent enrolled children from a single racial group (Chang 1993). Nationwide, estimates suggest that 20 percent of the children enrolled in Head Start speak a language other than English (Kagan and Garcia 1991). In the Washington, D.C., public schools, over one hundred languages are now represented.

Coinciding with these demographic trends, research now suggests that some degree of consistency in young children's exposure to their native language may be important for their later linguistic development and learning. Specifically, children younger than five years old are still acquiring the basic grammatical and phonological aspects of their first language. It appears that students can more readily become literate in a second language once literacy has been established in the home language (Snow 1992). Moreover, if English is introduced at a very young age to a non-English-speaking child, proficiency in the home language can be disrupted, with possible adverse consequences for the child's communication with parents and the home community.

For these reasons, we feel that it is extremely important to include consideration of language issues in any contemporary discussion of readiness, child care, and schooling indicators. The NHES: 95 contains questions concerning the language spoken at home and the language of the child's caregiver/teacher. In addition, the Organization for Economic Cooperation and Development (OECD), with support from the National Center for Education Statistics, has recently published *Education at a Glance*, which summarizes thirty-eight educational indicators from the OECD countries (OECD 1993). Among these indicators is information on the percentage of children who say they usually speak the same language in school and at home. The information is based on a special survey conducted by the International Association for the Evaluation of Educational Achievement (IEA) and the Educational Testing Service (ETS), and includes only nine- to fourteen-year-olds. We recommend that a down-age extension of this information be developed for future use in the child and family well-being indicators project.

Pertinent data could be obtained by adding questions about language of instruction and languages of students in the Schools and Staffing Surveys (school survey and teacher survey) conducted by the National Center for Education Statistics. This unified set of surveys profiles the nation's elementary and secondary school system, with the third administration conducted during the 1993 to 1994 school year. The school survey includes information about student characteristics and about types of programs and services offered. The teacher survey collects data from teachers regarding their education, training, and teaching experience, among other things. The proposed Survey of Program Dynamics of the U.S. Bureau of the Census may also offer a source of information about languages used at school.

Priority Indicators

We propose three priority indicators. First, given strong evidence regarding the importance of early reading experiences for later success in school, and the growing policy interest in programs that promote these experiences (for example, parent education, Early Head Start, Even Start), we include exposure to reading at home as a priority indicator. However, because exposure itself (differentiated from *where* the exposure occurs) appears to be the important variable, we encourage efforts to collect comparable data regarding preliteracy experiences *across* the home and child care settings that children inhabit prior to school entry.

Second, few would dispute the importance of capturing indicators of children's earliest school performance in the areas of literacy and number knowledge. Early performance is a powerful predictor of later performance, and offers a useful proxy for the extent to which children are coming to school with the types of skill and knowledge that teachers typically expect and often assume as a point of departure for formal instruction.

Third, given the rapid diversification of the preschool population, substantial evidence regarding the importance *during the early years of language development* of support for the child's native language, and the availability of a data source (NHES: 95), we recommend the inclusion of access to *some* instruction in the native language for children whose primary language is not English as a critical indicator of "readiness." This recommendation is not intended to detract from the importance of assuring that young children receive instruction in English— an aim that many non-English-speaking parents appear to endorse for their children. Rather, we interpret the current literature to suggest that abrupt and discontinuous shifts from one language at home to another language at school may interfere with young children's first- and second-language development. This may become less important at later stages of schooling, although we would like to see some consideration given to bilingualism among older children in light of the diverse population and global economy in which today's generation of students will need to function productively.

Finally, we repeat our recommendation that the development of indicators of attitudes toward learning be a high priority for the future, with special attention paid to the opportunities that the ECLS provides along these lines. As we consider the future, access to educational technology at home and in preschool and kindergarten settings should be added to the list of readiness indicators. We believe that this topic will become increasingly important for children's preparedness for school, as well as for considerations of equal access to resources that facilitate success in school.

CHILD CARE

Children in the United States are negotiating the transition from home to school at younger ages than was true even a decade ago. Most children's initial exposure to a school-like setting used to occur when they entered kindergarten or first grade. Today, preschool and child care environments are playing this role in the lives of growing numbers of youngsters. As of 1990, 55 percent of low-income children aged three to five were enrolled in a school, child care center, or Head

Start program (Brayfield, Deich, and Hofferth 1993); 40 percent of all three- and four-year-olds were in some form of group care or preschool program as of 1991 (Casper, Hawkins, and O'Connell 1994). State and national welfare reform initiatives are likely to fuel substantial growth in these numbers, including growth in the number of infants and toddlers in nonmaternal care settings.

At the same time, there has been growing recognition that the precursors of school success are found in the earliest years of life and that substantial learning occurs before children first encounter formal academic instruction. It is not surprising, then, that child care and preschool are no longer seen simply as a place where children play and have fun with their age-mates. Concerns about the educational attainment of the country's children have refocused attention on early childhood settings as places where children also get ready for school.

The educational significance of children's early care and preschool settings was prominently affirmed in 1990 when the president and the fifty state governors established the first of six national educational goals: "By the year 2000 all children in America will start school ready to learn." Assuring that "all children will have access to high quality and developmentally appropriate preschool programs that help prepare children for school" was identified as one of three objectives that accompanied the goal statement. In this context, it is critical that there be a close articulation between indicators of children's well-being across the preschool and school-age years.

Fortunately, there is a substantial research literature on the developmental consequences of child care from which to discern the "right things" to include in a national effort to assess and track children's well-being. Unfortunately, however, scant attention has been devoted to translating this empirical literature into a list of indicators. A preliminary effort was recently launched to develop a set of indicators of "improved results of the childhood care and education system" (Galinsky, personal communication, August 1994). But to date, this initiative has not attempted to map its set of twenty-four proposed indicators onto available data sources. Further, most prior efforts to develop a set of education indicators curiously, though predictably, have bypassed the preschool years, with the notable exception of the post-1990 initiative of the NCES reported in *Education Counts* (National Center for Education Statistics 1991).

Indicators for Child Care

What aspects of child care warrant national attention in the context of an indicators project? Research evidence on child care indicates that the well-being of children depends primarily on the quality and continuity of their care settings and providers (Hayes, Palmer, and Zaslow 1990). For low-income children, access to Head Start, school-sponsored prekindergarten programs, and other early intervention programs appears to be developmentally advantageous, at least in the short term. For school-age children, the absence of child care during hours when their parents cannot provide supervision is associated with adverse developmental outcomes, particularly for children under age thirteen who live in urban areas (Long and Long 1981; Coleman, Robinson, and Rowland 1990; Posner and Vandell 1994). Parents' inclinations and ability to provide these features of care for their children, in turn, depend on issues of access/eligibility and of cost.

Finally, recent evidence suggests that when parents perceive they are using arrangements that constitute their preferred choices, then their own efforts to attain economic self-sufficiency are affected (Meyers 1993).

Thus, indicators of child well-being that relate to child care should focus on six general areas: quality of child care settings and providers; stability of care; access to early intervention programs on behalf of eligible populations; proportion of children under age thirteen in latchkey situations; costs of care relative to family income; and parent choice. It is also worth noting that the third, fifth, and sixth areas also raise critical issues regarding equity of access to decent child care options—a relatively neglected perspective on child care that richly deserves attention in this project.

Table 7.2 presents our proposed list of child care indicators. Two dimensions of care are conspicuously absent from our list: use of child care and type of care. Despite public anxiety regarding the dramatic shift from mother care to other care (and, specifically, to market care) that has characterized the last two decades, research has repeatedly demonstrated that the use/nonuse of child care is not meaningfully associated with young children's development. Similarly, given the wide range of quality that characterizes every type of care, children's well-being does not appear to be differentially affected by the type of child care in which they are enrolled (for example, center, family day care home, relative). As noted above, it is not whether or where children are being cared for that matters; it is how well.

Quality/Characteristics of Care   Quality of care is a heterogeneous construct, although most evidence suggests that "good things go together" in child care. We stress indicators of trained and educated staff, child-staff ratios and group size, staff salaries, and, for home-based settings, regulatory status and connection to provider networks. These are the quality variables, from among the large repertoire of quality indices that have been assessed, that have shown the most consistent and strongest associations with children's development in both center-based and home-based child care settings (Galinsky et al. 1994; Hayes, Palmer, and

Table 7.2   Child Care Indicators

Indicator	Current Sources	Future Prospects
Quality of care		ECLS
		State regulatory data
Stability of care	SIPP Child Care Module	NHES: 95
		SIPP Child Module
Proportion of eligible children in early intervention programs		Survey of Program Dynamics State/local level data
Proportion of children in latchkey situations	SIPP Child Care Module	
Child care costs: family income	SIPP Child Care Module	NHES: 95
Parent choice	SIPP Child Module	NHES: 95/96

Zaslow 1990; Helburn, et al. 1995; Whitebook, Howes, and Phillips 1989). Data sources that are worth exploring and developing in this regard include state regulatory data and a possible downward extension of the protocol that is being planned for the Early Childhood Longitudinal Survey.

There are no ongoing sources of nationally representative data on child care that we feel confident recommending as a current source of indicators of child care quality. Although some national data sets include maternal reports of ratios and provider training (for example, NHES and NLSY), we are not confident of the validity or reliability of these data. Even self-reports of ratios from center directors, let alone mothers, have been found to be poorly associated with observational data (Phillips et al. 1994). Given the importance and likely weight that would be given to indicators of child care quality, we feel that it is important to wait for the development of reliable indices.

Stability of Care   Children who have experienced multiple changes in child care providers and arrangements prior to school entry show poorer developmental outcomes in both the short and long term (Cummings 1980; Howes 1988). It follows that one of the most important indicators of children's well-being in the context of child care cannot be captured with "snapshot" data. Rather, it is important to capture the patterning of care over the early childhood years.

These are difficult data to obtain given that their most reliable source is prospective accounts of children's concurrent and sequential child care arrangements. As a shortcut, however, we feel that it is worth obtaining mothers' counts of the total number of child care arrangements that they used for each child prior to kindergarten entry. Ideally, a variable that controls for the duration of children's reliance on child care, such as the average number of arrangements per year, would also be constructed. These indices are being collected prospectively in the National Institute of Child Health and Development (NICHD) Study of Early Child Care and data regarding their validity and predictive power will soon be available (see the National Institute of Child Health and Development Early Child Care Network 1994).

The child care module of the Survey of Income and Program Participation (SIPP) will provide information about the total number of arrangements and changes in arrangements during the past twelve months. The pertinent questions are currently asked only of working mothers, but in the next wave will be expanded to include nonworking mothers and nonwork hours for all mothers. An additional improvement would involve asking specifically about the number of concurrent *and* sequential arrangements since the child was first placed in nonmaternal child care. The NHES: 95 includes questions that inquire about simultaneous care arrangements. Although parents may not be entirely accurate, we expect that the relative ranking of families using very few, a moderate number, and a high number of arrangements could be derived from parent reports.

Proportion of Eligible Children in Early Intervention Programs   We include this variable for two reasons. First, three major studies now have documented the higher quality of care that characterizes Head Start, Chapter I, and other school-sponsored early childhood programs compared to community-based child care programs, particularly those that do not receive substantial public subsidies (Helburn et al. 1995; Layzer, Goodson, and Moss 1993; Phillips et al. 1994). Numerous studies examining the outcomes associated with early intervention programs, including Head Start, have documented their positive short-term (and sometimes long-term) effects on school achievement. Enrollment in these programs may, therefore, serve as a proxy for access to quality child care settings.

Second, given our national commitment to supporting several early intervention programs for low-income children (for example, Head Start, Early Head Start, Chapter I prekindergarten, Even Start), it strikes us as highly appropriate to obtain estimates of the proportion of eligible children served.

It is a challenge, however, to obtain an accurate estimate of the proportion of eligible children in early intervention programs. The biggest problem concerns the fragmentation of data sources and the difficulty of obtaining an unduplicated count of eligible children in Head Start, various child care programs, state prekindergarten, and so on. The NHES: 93 and NHES: 95 (program participation interview) inquire separately about children's enrollment in Head Start and other center/nursery school/preschool/prekindergarten programs. The child module of the SIPP employs the same strategy of distinguishing Head Start from other group programs. Currently, respondents are asked only about the two most frequently used arrangements, so some programs are likely to be missed. Future rounds of data collection for the SIPP will inquire about all arrangements.

The OECD data contain an indicator titled, "net rates of participation in early childhood education." Based on data provided by each participating country, this indicator includes information on the age at which, and number of years in which, children aged two to six years typically participate in early childhood education. If there is interest in assuring that our indicators facilitate international comparisons, this data source is worth exploring.

For the future, the proposed Survey of Program Dynamics is a logical focal point for the collection of relevant indicators. We also suggest that the availability and validity of state- and district-level data on prekindergarten enrollments be explored given that the majority of states now supplement federal programs with state-subsidized prekindergarten programs for low-income children.

Proportion of Children Under Age Thirteen in Latchkey Situations   As of 1991, more than 1.6 million five- to fourteen-year-olds regularly spent time alone before and after school (Casper et al. 1994). The research literature on the developmental effects of self- or latchkey care is not wholly consistent. Children in suburban settings, where self-care is most common, do not appear to be harmed when left to care for themselves after school, although longitudinal evidence for outcomes such as substance abuse and sexual activity is not available. To the extent that negative effects are found, they tend to be restricted to urban samples and children under age thirteen. Thus, we propose that the proportion of children under age thirteen in latchkey situations be included among the list of child care indicators. It is worth noting that we consider this indicator to be closely tied to the issues of parental supervision and involvement that are discussed in the sections on readiness and schooling.

Data are currently available for this indicator. The child care module of the SIPP provides national data on the number of children of employed mothers who cared for themselves for some part of the time their mothers were working. Ideally, we would obtain data regarding "unsupervised time" for all children and for all hours. This hope may materialize when the SIPP child care module expands to include nonworking mothers and nonwork hours.

Costs of Care Relative to Family Income   As a nation, it is important to consider whether we are tolerating extremely inequitable situations, particularly with respect to parents' ability to secure the resources needed for their children's healthy development. Concern is widespread regarding children's access to health care, for example. We submit that it is also important to consider equity of access to child care, particularly in light of current evidence of wide disparities in child care expenditures between poor and nonpoor families. As of 1991, employed mothers living in poverty who paid for child care spent an average of 27 percent of their monthly family income on it, compared with 7 percent for nonpoor women (Casper et al. 1994; Hofferth, Brayfield, Deich, and Holcomb 1991).

We propose that available data regarding the proportion of families paying for child care and, among those who pay, the proportion of family income spent on child care be included among the indicators of child care that we track at the federal level. These data are currently available from the child care module of the SIPP. The NHES: 95 also includes questions about child care fees.

Parental Choice   Recent evidence suggests that the success with which welfare-dependent mothers complete job training and placement programs hinges in part on their perceptions that their children are in child care arrangements of their choice. Meyers and her colleagues report that mothers in California's program Greater Avenues for Independence (GAIN) who wished they could use a different child care provider were over twice as likely to drop out of the program than were mothers who were satisfied with their provider (Meyers 1993). Further, substantial evidence has now documented that about one-quarter of all mothers using child care wish they could change arrangements and that up to half of low-income, single, or teen-age mothers report a desire to change.

These data not only document surprisingly high levels of dissatisfaction with child care, and reveal another possible source of income-based inequity in our child care system, but they point to a useful approach for assessing satisfaction with care—an issue that has eluded effective assessment for years. When asked directly about satisfaction with child care, the vast majority of mothers report that they are highly to quite satisfied. These recent data suggest that we may obtain more valid reports from mothers if we ask them whether they are using arrangements that constitute their first choice, or whether they would prefer to change providers.

We are not aware of any nationally representative data sources that assess parents' reliance on child care of their choice, and with which they are comfortable. Plans are in place, however, to add such a question to the child well-being module of the SIPP. The same could be done with the NHES 1996 parent survey.

Priority Indicators

We propose three indicators for our short list. First, we include the proportion of eligible children who receive early intervention programs. Our rationale is three-fold: substantial federal and state resources are spent on early intervention programs; these programs appear to offer higher quality care than the typical child care arrangements that low-income children receive; and they can reap positive outcomes for children. We would not want this indicator to provide an incentive to "water down" the quality of these services in order to serve yet more eligible children.

To guard against this, we include indicators of quality of care as our second priority—despite the lack of an available data source. This should be a top priority for "future prospects" with serious attention paid to both the addition of a preschool cohort to the ECLS to provide national data on quality of care and an exploration of state-level child care licensing data to provide state and substate indicators. Until reliable indicators of child care quality become available—a long-range goal—we propose that improved questions aimed at capturing the stability and choice of care be added to the SIPP and NHES. These data could serve as interim indicators that are closely linked to children's well-being in child care.

Third, to assure attention to issues of equity, we include the proportion of family income spent on child care as a family-level indicator that is currently available.

EARLY SCHOOLING

There is no agreed upon demarcation between the assessment of school readiness and that of schooling outcomes, although it is logical to consider the postkindergarten years as falling within the purview of schooling indicators. Here again, other chapters in this volume are highly relevant, most notably that on achievement outcomes, but also those by Love (chapter 19), Aber (chapter 18), and Brooks-Gunn (chapter 13) that capture nonacademic aspects of schooling.

We focus our discussion on the important transition that characterizes schooling around grades three and four—often considered the transition from primary to elementary school—for two reasons. First, the school curriculum undergoes an important shift at this stage from one that emphasizes the acquisition of skills (reading, writing, computation) to one that begins to emphasize the use of these skills (reading for comprehension, writing for communication, functional uses of numbers). Accordingly, it is our recommendation that indicators of schooling, focused on this period, should attempt to capture the functional uses of knowledge, rather than just the amount of knowledge that a given child has acquired.

Second, this halfway point between school entry and middle school has been identified as a particularly vulnerable period for schooling outcomes. Labeled the "third grade slump," it is not uncommon for some children who have been performing adequately through second grade to experience decrements in achievement around third and fourth grade, presumably as a result of the change in pedagogy.

Indicators for Early Schooling

Once children enter the elementary school years, aggregate data are available to assess achievement and school functioning. Although we focus on third- and fourth-graders, we emphasize topics that we believe have relevance for all school-age children. Of course, the specific indicators that capture each topic will vary with the age of the child (that is, a child's engagement in school will manifest itself somewhat differently in elementary school and in high school). There is also fairly wide agreement about aspects of schooling that are important to capture. These include: achievement; progress in school (proportion of children at grade level, rates of grade failure/retention, placements in remedial classes or gifted classes, receipt of special education services); engagement in school (absenteeism, extracurricular activities); and parental involvement/participation. We also discuss bilingualism as a potentially important area for the future development of indicators. Although we focus on national data, schooling indicators are particularly amenable to documentation with state and local data—an important issue for future exploration. Table 7.3 presents our proposed list of indicators of early schooling.

Achievement Indicators of school achievement should be linked to the educational goals of the nation, and whatever assessments are used to track progress on these goals should be among our national indicators. As these assessments are being developed, the National Assessment of Educational Progress (NAEP) offers the most obvious source of indicator data regarding student achievement, particularly given its fourth-grade starting point.

We appreciate the difficult debate that has recently accompanied efforts to set achievement levels in conjunction with the NAEP (basic, proficient, advanced levels of achievement), but consider it important to work toward some indicator that captures criterion-referenced levels of knowledge. We further encourage consideration of functional measures of achievement, beginning at the third- to fourth-grade level and continuing throughout the child's schooling. By "functional" we mean to capture the difference between having acquired a body of knowledge (knowing how to read and comprehend text) and putting this knowledge to use (using books to acquire knowledge and understanding).

Table 7.3 Indicators of Early Schooling

Indicator	Current Sources	Future Prospects
Achievement	NAEP	ECLS
		NEGP initiatives
		State/local level data
Progress in school	NHES: 93	SIPP Child Module
	Profiles Study	NHES: 95/96
		ECLS
		Survey of Program Dynamics
Engagement in school	NHES: 93	ECLS
	SIPP Child Module	Survey of Program Dynamics
Parental involvement/participation		NHES: 96
		ECLS
		Survey of Program Dynamics
Bilingualism		NHES: 95
		OECD
		ECLS

Progress in School   Beyond measures of achievement, school functioning is most commonly assessed through measures of grade failure/retention, placements in remedial classes or gifted classes, and receipt of special education services. These measures track the share of children who are showing patterns of progress in school that depart from the typical range. They are another obvious candidate for inclusion in a set of schooling indicators. One of the major decisions to be made concerns the source of data on which this project should rely: parents, teachers, or records. Ideally, convergent evidence from multiple data sources would be used.

Among the current sources of data are: the NHES: 93, which asks parents about grade repetition and receipt of special help (we are unsure about whether gifted classes are included); the Child Module of the SIPP, which asks parents about grade repetition, placement in gifted classes, and school suspension; and the *Profiles* study, which also contains relevant items on children in schools in low-income districts. The Schools and Staffing Surveys may also contain pertinent information.

In the future, the ECLS will surely include information on children's progress in school. In addition, the NHES: 95 includes comparable information to that in the 1993 protocol, and the proposed Survey of Program Dynamics will collect relevant data.

Engagement in School   This construct becomes much more important once the child passes beyond the elementary years, and can be assessed with negative measures of absenteeism, as well as with positive measures of participation in extracurricular activities and special roles in school. At the elementary level, absenteeism is important to track because it has a direct effect on children's opportunity to learn. Variation in attendance, however, is probably affected more by health and other factors beyond the child's control than by the child's interest in school during these early years.

The ECLS will likely be a useful source of data on young children's school attendance. For current data, the NHES: 93 School Safety and Discipline component (interviews with parents of children in grades three through twelve and youth in grades six through twelve) includes information about participation in extracurricular activities, suspensions, and problems in school, as does the SIPP Child Well-Being Module. The proposed Survey of Program Dynamics would also collect such information.

Parental Involvement/Participation   Parental involvement in schooling is actually a somewhat ill-defined construct. Although it is difficult to be "against" parental involvement, the literature in this area remains unclear about exactly what forms and amounts of parental involvement really matter for children. To illustrate the conceptual confusion, consider the time parents spend helping the child with homework. It is entirely possible that parents who spend relatively large amounts of time involved with homework will have children who do relatively well in school. Alternatively, at least some parents who provide substantial help with homework may do so because their child is doing poorly in school or is resisting homework. Another issue that generates debate is whether it is involvement with the child at home or involvement in the school setting (or both, since they are likely correlated) that constitutes the most predictive form of involvement. Finally, there may be cultural differences in how parents express their commitment and engagement with their child's schooling.

Nevertheless, for the reasons already discussed in this chapter (see readiness), we propose that patterns of parent involvement in schooling are important to capture. Recent evidence that, during the postelementary years, parent involvement in the child's school setting predicts children's academic standing, classroom conduct, and rates of suspension even when related family factors are controlled (Zill and Nord 1994), provides additional support for our position. Relevant behavior would include the parents' familiarity with the child's teacher, their perceptions of the school's receptivity to their involvement, number of times they have visited the child's teacher/classroom (school and nonschool hours) for positive or routine reasons (excluding visits occasioned by the child's negative conduct), attendance at Parent Teachers Association (PTA) and other policy-oriented meetings, and other roles assumed in conjunction with the school (such as volunteer work and parent committees). Unfortunately, we are not aware of any current data sources that inquire about relevant behavior, although the NHES 1996 parent interview may include relevant information. The ECLS may provide a vehicle for the development of indicators of parental involvement and the Survey of Program Dynamics may offer a future source of ongoing indicator data.

Bilingualism   As discussed earlier in this essay (see child care indicators), today's children will need to be prepared to achieve, contribute, work, and parent in a multicultural society and global economy. Exposure to a language other than English (for English speakers) and support for native languages among children whose first language is not English strike us as very basic indicators of the extent to which our nation's schools are preparing children for this future. Thus, we recommend inclusion of an indicator of children's exposure to non-English instruction among the set of schooling indicators that are developed in conjunction with this new initiative. The NHES: 95 may be a source of pertinent information and the OECD indicators should also be reviewed with this indicator in mind.

Priority Indicators

We propose that three indicators be included on the priority list: achievement; progress in school; and parent involvement. The first two are probably not controversial; we include the third because it focuses on a positive outcome, embraces a family-level indicator, and is receiving growing empirical support as an important predictor of children's school achievement.

CONCLUSIONS

This chapter covers a broad territory. We have focused more on the early childhood and "readiness" stages of development than on the indicators of schooling during the elementary years. We strongly suggest that our recommendations for indicators be placed in the context of the other chapters in this volume that focus on schooling outcomes and encompass the full range of factors—cognitive, social, health—that predict and reflect success in school.

As a final note, we address the question of a schedule for indicators data collection. Our approach emphasizes major developmental and institutional transitions in children's lives. These occur when children first encounter school-like settings and curricula, first enter formal school settings, and at the third and fourth grade. Therefore, we recommend collection of readiness, child care, and early schooling data at these transition points, for which it is important to recognize that chronological age is an imperfect proxy. This translates into assessments of three-year-olds (when a substantial share of children in out-of-home settings are in group care/education settings), kindergarten-age children (at kindergarten entry), and third- or fourth-graders.

The opinions expressed in this paper are those of the authors only. They do not reflect the views of our home institutions. The authors wish to thank Richard Murnane and Don Hernandez for their insightful comments on an earlier draft of the paper.

REFERENCES

Aber, J. L, J. Molnar, and D. Phillips. 1986. "Action Research in Early Education." Report prepared for the Foundation for Child Development. New York: Foundation for Child Development.

Alexander, K. L., and D. R. Entwisle. 1988. "Achievement in the First Two Years of School: Patterns and Processes." *Monographs of the Society for Research in Child Development 53* (2, serial no. 218). Chicago: University of Chicago Press.

Benasich, A. A., J. Brooks-Gunn, and M. D. McCormick. 1992. *Behavioral Problems in the Two-to-Five Year-Old: Measurement and Prognostic Ability.* Educational Testing Service. Princeton, N.J.: Unpublished manuscript.

Boyer, E. 1991. *Ready to Learn: A Mandate for the Nation.* Princeton, N.J.: Carnegie Foundation for the Advancement of Teaching.

Bradburn, N. M. 1994. "Outline of Issues Report for Early Childhood Educational Study." Working Paper. Chicago, Ill.: National Opinion Research Center.

Bradley, R. H., B. M. Caldwell, and S. L. Rock. 1988. "Home Environment and School Performance: A Ten-Year Follow-Up and Examination of Three Models of Environmental Action." *Child Development* 59: 852–67.

Brandon, R. N. 1992. *"Social Accountability: A Conceptual Framework for Measuring Child/Family Well-Being."* Paper prepared for the Center for the Study of Social Policy. Washington, D.C.: Center for the Study of Social Policy.

Brayfield, A. A., S. G. Deich, and S. L. Hofferth. 1993. *Caring for Children in Low-Income Families. A Substudy of the National Child Care Survey, 1990.* Washington, D.C.: Urban Institute.

Bronson, M. D. 1994. "The Usefulness of an Observational Measure of Young Children's Social and Mastery Behaviors in Early Childhood Classrooms." *Early Childhood Research Quarterly* 9: 19–43.

Case, R., and S. Griffin. 1990. "Child Cognitive Development: The Role of Central Conceptual Structures in the Development of Scientific and Social Thought." In *Developmental Psychology: Cognitive, Perceptuo-Motor and Psychological Perspectives,* edited by C. A. Hauert. Amsterdam, The Netherlands: Elsevier.

Casper, L., M. Hawkins, and M. O'Connell. 1994. *Who's Minding the Kids?* Statistical Brief 94-5. Washington: U.S. Government Printing Office for U.S. Department of Commerce.

Cazden, C. B., C. E. Snow, and C. Heise-Baigorria. 1990. *Language Planning in Preschool Education*. Unpublished paper prepared for the Consultative Group on Early Childhood Care and Development. New York: United Nations International Children's Education Fund.

Chang, H. 1993. *Affirming Children's Roots: Cultural and Linguistic Diversity in Early Care and Education*. San Francisco, Calif.: California Tomorrow.

Coleman, M., B. Robinson, and B. Rowland. 1990. "Children in Self-Care: An Examination of Research Confounds." *Children and Youth Services Review* 12: 327–39.

Crouter, A. C., S. M. MacDermid, S. M. McHale, and M. Perry-Jenkins. 1990. "Parental Monitoring and Perceptions of Children's School Performance and Conduct in Dual- and Single-Earner Families." *Developmental Psychology* 26: 649–57.

Cummings, M. E. 1980. "Caregiver Stability and Day Care." *Developmental Psychology* 16: 31–37.

Department of Education. 1993. *Prospects: The Congressionally Mandated Study of Educational Growth and Opportunity: The Interim Report*. (July) Washington: U.S. Government Printing Office.

Dickinson, D. K., and D. E. Beals. 1994. "Not by Print Alone: Oral Language Supports for Early Literacy Development. In *Emergent Literacy: From Research to Practice*, edited by F. DeLancy. New York: Praeger Publishers.

Dishion, T. J. 1990. "The Family Ecology of Boy's Peer Relations in Middle Childhood." *Child Development* 61: 874–92.

Entwisle, D. R., and K. L. Alexander. 1990. "Beginning School Math Competence: Minority and Majority Comparisons." *Child Development* 61: 454–71.

Entwisle, D. R., K. Alexander, A. Pallas, and D. Cadigan. 1987. "The Emergent Academic Self-Image of First-Graders. *Child Development* 58: 1190–206.

Galinksy, E., C. Howes, S. Kontos, and M. Shinn. 1994. *The Study of Children in Family Child Care and Relative Care*. New York: Families and Work Institute.

Goldenberg, C. 1987. "Low-Income Hispanic Parents' Contributions to Their First-Grade Children's Word-Recognition Skills." *Anthropology and Education Quarterly* 18: 149–79.

Griffin, S., R. Case, and R. Sandieson. 1992. "Synchrony and Asynchrony in the Acquisition of Everyday Mathematical Knowledge: Towards a Representational Theory of Children's Intellectual Growth." In *The Mind's Staircase: Exploring the Central Conceptual Underpinnings of Children's Theory and Knowledge*, edited by R. Case. Hillsdale, N.J.: Erlbaum Press.

Griffin, S., R. Case, and R. Siegler. 1992. *Rightstart: Providing the Central Conceptual Prerequisites for First Formal Learning of Arithmetic to Students at Risk for School Failure*. Department of Education, Clark University. Unpublished manuscript.

Hakuta, K., and D. D'Andrea. 1992. "Some Properties of Bilingual Maintenance and Loss in Mexican Background High-School Students." *Applied Linguistics* 13: 72–99.

Hayes, C., J. Palmer, and M. Zaslow, eds. 1990. *Who Cares for America's Children: Child Care Policy for the 1990s*. Washington, D.C.: National Academy Press.

Helburn, S., M. L. Culkin, J. Morris, M. Mocan, C. Howes, L. Phillipsen, D. Bryant, R. Clifford, D. Cryer, E. Peisner-Feinberg, M. Burchinal, S. L. Kagan, and J. Rustici, J. 1995. "Cost, Quality, and Child Outcomes in Child Care Centers." Executive Summary. Boulder, Colo.: University of Colorado.

Hofferth, S. L., A. Brayfield, S. Deich, and P. Holcomb. 1991. *National Child Care Survey, 1990*. Washington, D.C.: Urban Institute Press.

Howes, C. 1988. "Relations Between Early Child Care and Schooling." *Developmental Psychology* 24: 53–57.

Kagan, S. L. 1990. "Readiness 2000: Rethinking Rhetoric and Responsibility. *Phi Delta Kappan* (December): 272–79.

Kagan, S. L., and E. Garcia. 1991. "Educating Culturally and Linguistically Diverse Preschoolers: Moving the Agenda." *Early Childhood Research Quarterly* 6: 427–43.

Gresham, F., and S. Elliott, S. 1990. *The Social Skills Rating System*. Minn.: American Guidance Service.

Layzer, J. I., B. D. Goodson, and M. Moss. 1993. *Life in Preschool: Final Report of the Observational Study of Early Childhood Programs, Vol. 1.* Washington: U.S. Government Printing Office for U.S. Department of Education.

Lee, V., J. Brooks-Gunn, E. Schnur, and T. Liaw. 1990. "Are Head Start Effects Sustained? A Longitudinal Comparison of Disadvantaged Children Attending Head Start, No Preschool, and Other Preschool Programs." *Child Development* 61: 495–507.

Long, L., and T. Long. 1981. *Latchkey Children: The Child's View of Self Care.* Washington, D.C.: Catholic University. Mimeo.

Love, J. M., J. L. Aber, and J. Brooks-Gunn. 1994. *Strategies for Assessing Community Progress Toward Achieving the First National Educational Goal.* Princeton, N.J.: Mathematica Policy Research, Inc.

Meisels, S. J., M. S. Wiske, I. W. Henderson, D. B. Marsden, and K. G. Browning. 1988. *ESI 4–6: Early Screening Inventory for Four- Through Six-Year-Olds.* Rev., 3rd ed. New York: Teachers College Press.

Meyers, M. K. 1993. "Child Care in JOBS Employment and Training Program: What Difference Does Quality Make?" *Journal of Marriage and the Family* 55: 767–83.

Mischel, W. 1984. "Convergences and Challenges in the Search for Consistency." *American Psychologist* 39: 351–64.

Moore, K. 1994. *New Social Indicators of Child and Family Wellbeing for the Twenty-First Century.* Working Paper. Washington, D.C.: Child Trends, Inc.

Moorehouse, M. J. 1991. "Linking Maternal Employment Patterns to Mother Child Activities and Children's School Competence." *Developmental Psychology* 27: 295–303.

National Center for Education Statistics. 1991. "Education Counts: An Indicator System to Monitor the Nation's Educational Health." Report of the Special Study Panel on Education Indicators. Washington, D.C.: Department of Education.

National Education Goals Panel. 1993. "Reconsidering Children's Early Development and Learning: Toward Shared Beliefs and Vocabulary." Draft Report to the National Education Goals Panel from the Goal 1 Technical Planning Group. Washington, D.C.: National Education Goals Panel.

National Institute of Child Health and Development Early Child Care Network. 1994. "Child Care and Child Development: The NICHD Study of Early Child Care." In *Developmental Follow-up: Concepts, Domains, and Methods*, edited by S. L. Friedman and H. C. Haywood. San Diego, Calif.: Academic Press, Inc., 373–96.

Office of Educational Research and Improvement. 1994. *Reinventing the Office of Educational Research and Improvement.* Washington, D.C.: Office of Educational Research and Improvement.

Organization for Economic Cooperation and Development. 1993. *Education at a Glance: OECD Indicators.* Paris, France: Organization for Economic Cooperation and Development.

Phillips, D., and N. Crowell. 1994. *Cultural Diversity and Early Education.* Washington, D.C.: National Academy Press.

Phillips, D., M. Voran, E. Kisker, C. Howes, and M. Whitebook. 1994. "Child Care for Children in Poverty: Opportunity or Inequity?" *Child Development* 65: 472–92.

Posner, J. K., and D. L. Vandell. 1994. "Low-Income Children's After-School Care: Are There Beneficial Effects of After-School Programs?" *Child Development* 65: 440–56.

Schorr, L. B. 1994. "The Case for Shifting to Results-Based Accountability." Paper written for the Improved Outcomes for Children Project. Washington, D.C.: Aspen Institute.

Siegler, R. S., and M. Robinson. 1982. "The Development of Numerical Understandings." In *Advances in Child Development and Behavior*, edited by H. W. Reese and L. P. Lipsitt. N.Y.: Academic Press.

Snow, C. E. 1992. "Perspectives on Second-Language Development: Implications for Bilingual Education." *Educational Researcher* 21: 6–19.

———. 1983. "Literacy and Language." *Harvard Educational Review* 53: 165–89.

Stanford Working Group. 1993. *Federal Education Programs for Limited-English-Proficient Students: A Blueprint for the Second Generation.* Stanford, Calif.: Stanford University.

Stipek, D. 1988. *Motivation to Learn: Theory to Practice.* Englewood Cliffs, N.J.: Prentice-Hall.

U.S. Department of Education. 1992. "The Condition of Bilingual Education in the Nation: A Report to the Congress and the President" Washington (June 30, 1992).

Walker, H. M., A. Block-Pedego, B. Todis, and H. Stevenson. 1991. *School Archival Records Search.* Longmont, Colo.: Sopris West Inc.

West, J. 1994. *Early Childhood Longitudinal Study Kindergarten Cohort.* Washington, D.C.: National Center for Education Statistics.

Whitebook, M., C. Howes, and D. Phillips. 1989. "Who Cares? Child Care Teachers and the Quality of Care in America." Final report of the National Child Care Staffing Study. Oakland, Calif.: Child Care Employee Project.

Zill, N., and C. W. Nord. 1994. *Running in Place: How American Families are Faring in a Changing Economy and an Individualistic Society.* Washington, D.C.: Child Trends, Inc.

Zill, N., T. Stief, and M. J. Coiro. 1992. *Scalability and Reliability of Home Environments Items from the 1991 National Household Education Survey.* Child Trends, Inc., Washington, D.C. Unpublished manuscript.

8

Indicators of High School Completion and Dropout

Robert M. Hauser

WHETHER OR NOT a person has completed high school would appear a simple matter of fact, yet there are diverse indicators of high school completion and diverse opinions about trends and differentials therein. In this chapter, I note the importance of high school graduation as a national goal and as an indicator of prospects for successful adulthood. I review several ways of taking stock of high school graduation and the implications of these methods for assessment of trend. Then I turn to a more systematic review of indicators of high school dropout or completion. I suggest explicit conceptual and methodological criteria to evaluate indicators, but—more important—I focus on the usefulness of alternative indicators in highlighting important national and subnational trends and differentials.

The highly publicized National Goals for Education (U.S. Department of Education 1990) have proclaimed 90 percent high school completion by the year 2000 among six primary goals. A report of the Department of Education notes uncertainty about what marks high school graduation, how the goal can be reconciled with state-to-state variation in graduation requirements, and what populations, at what ages, should be defined as at risk of graduation (Tomlinson et al. 1993: 2).[1] The 1994 report of the National Educational Goals Panel (1994) states the goal is to "increase the percentage of nineteen- and twenty-year-olds who have a high school credential to at least 90 percent," and the report finds that high school completion is one of six areas in which "no significant changes in national performance have occurred." As of 1992, "the nation is already very close to achieving the 90 percent target," for 87 percent of nineteen- and twenty-year-olds have completed high school. According to the report, completion rates were 91 percent among whites, 81 percent among African Americans, and only 65 percent among Hispanics, so we must "make serious efforts to close the persistent gap in completion rates between White and minority students."[2] In its 1995 and 1996 reports, the National Educational Goals Panel (1995; 1996) made essentially the same observations, but referred them to the percentage of eighteen- to twenty-four-year-olds who had completed a high school credential. It is not clear what "90 percent high school completion" actually means.

SOME CONSEQUENCES OF HIGH SCHOOL DROPOUT

While the public perception of high school dropout as a social problem has been widespread for at least thirty years (Schrieber 1967), recent years have brought increasing evidence that the failure to complete high school is associated with problems in employment, earnings, family formation and stability, civic participation, and health. For example, figure 8.1 shows trends and differentials in employment rates of persons twenty-five to thirty-four years old, by sex and educational attainment, from the early 1970s to the middle 1990s.[3] In every year and among women and men, employment varies directly with completed schooling. Moreover, from the early 1970s to the mid-1990s, the differential in employment grew between dropouts (here defined as those with nine to eleven years of schooling) and either high school or college graduates. Men and women differ in the sources of the growing differential. Among men, employment has been very high and stable among college graduates, while it has declined, both among high school graduates and, to an even greater extent, among dropouts. Among women, employment has increased among dropouts as among all women, but the growth has been greater among high school and college graduates. In the early 1970s, a male dropout was about thirty percentage points more likely to be employed than a female college graduate. By the early 1990s, a college woman was at least ten percentage points more likely to work outside the home than was a male dropout.

Figure 8.1   Employment Rates of Persons Twenty-Five to Thirty-Four Years Old, by Sex and Educational Attainment

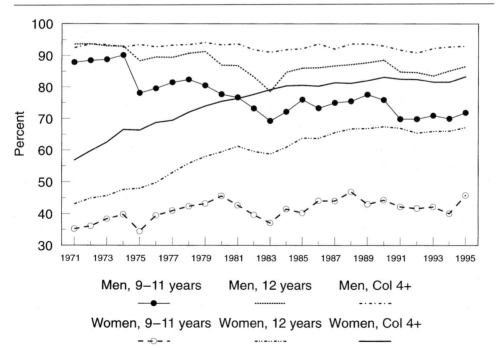

Source: Compiled by the author from March Current Population Surveys.

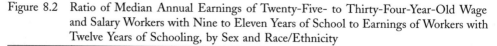

Figure 8.2   Ratio of Median Annual Earnings of Twenty-Five- to Thirty-Four-Year-Old Wage and Salary Workers with Nine to Eleven Years of School to Earnings of Workers with Twelve Years of Schooling, by Sex and Race/Ethnicity

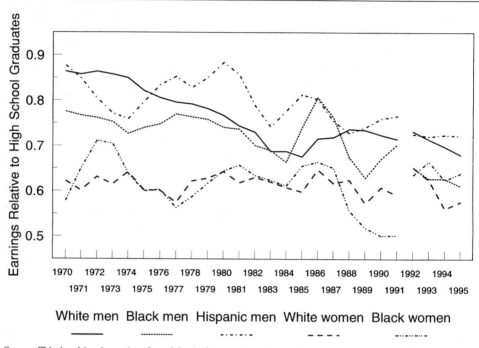

Source: Tabulated by the author from March Current Population Surveys (three-year averages).

Just as the earning power of high school graduates has declined relative to that of college graduates (Murphy and Welch 1989; Murnane and Levy 1993; Hauser 1993), so has the earning power of high school dropouts fallen relative to that of high school graduates. Indeed, the economic consequences of dropping out of high school have never been so severe. Among men and women wage and salary workers, dropouts make substantially less than high school graduates (figure 8.2).[4] Over the past two decades, the earnings of white male dropouts declined from 85 percent to less than 75 percent of the earnings of white high school graduates.[5] Among African American and Hispanic men, the time series is far more variable, but there also appears to be some evidence of a decline in earnings relative to high school graduates. Among women, there is no obvious long-term trend in the relative earnings of high school dropouts, but the differential hovers around a level of 0.6. That is, women high school graduates earn about two-thirds more than dropouts.

Illustrative differentials between dropouts and graduates could be elaborated endlessly. For example, electoral participation by high school dropouts is less than among high school graduates, and the gap has widened since the mid-1960s (National Center for Education Statistics 1994). Failure to obtain at least a high school diploma looks more and more like the contemporary equivalent of functional illiteracy. High school dropout indicates a failure to pass minimum thresholds of economic, social, or political motivation, access, and competence.

TRENDS IN HIGH SCHOOL DROPOUT

Since the middle 1980s, there has been a steady stream of new reports about the familial and economic origins of high school dropout (McLanahan 1985; Ekstrom et al. 1986; Krein and Beller 1988; Astone and McLanahan 1991; Haveman, et al. 1991; Sandefur et al. 1992; Hauser and Phang 1993). The National Center for Education Statistics (NCES) now produces annual reports on trends and differentials in high school dropout (Frase 1989; Kaufman and Frase 1990; Kaufman et al. 1991; Kaufman et al. 1992; McMillen et al. 1993; McMillen et al. 1994; McMillen and Kaufman 1996). Thus, the association of high school dropout with educational and economic deprivation, minority status, and family disruption is well documented, as are global trends in various measures of high school dropout.

Overused as it may be, Charles Dickens's line, "It was the best of times, it was the worst of times," neatly captures the range of public views about high school dropout (Dickens 1989). At the least, the times are confusing. According to the Children's Defense Fund (1994), "Every 5 seconds of the school day a student drops out of public school." Moreover, "no significant progress has been made nationally since 1985 in reducing the proportion of students who drop out before completing high school. In 1991, 12.5 percent of all young people ages sixteen through twenty-four who were not enrolled in school did not have a high school diploma or its equivalent, up slightly from 12.1 percent in 1990." This text garbles the concept on which the quoted figures are based. It should read, "In 1991, 12.5 percent of all young people ages sixteen to twenty-four were not enrolled in school and did not have a high school diploma or its equivalent." I have re-created this series in figure 8.3, by age, from 1967 to 1994. Within age subgroups, there would appear to be some year-to-year unreliability, but it would be hard to ignore the long-term downward trend from the late 1970s to the middle 1980s. The rise in dropout from 1990 to 1991 noted by the Children's Defense Fund might have been a minor, year-to year fluctuation.[6] It is impossible to determine the trend between 1991 and 1992 because that is just when major changes were made in the definition and measurement of high school completion in the Current Population Survey. The two more recent annual reports of the Children's Defense Fund (1995; 1996) make no reference to trends in high school dropout, but the data from 1992 to 1994 do not suggest that there has been any subsequent decline.

One might draw an equally negative inference by consulting another source, the annual *Kids Count Data Book 1994* of the Annie E. Casey Foundation (1994). One of ten key *Kids Count* indicators, the percentage of youths graduating from high school on time, declined regularly from 71.6 percent in 1985 to 68.8 percent in 1991.[7] In its state rankings, higher on-time graduation rates are presumably better than lower on-time graduation rates, yet the overall rate of on-time graduation declined nationally, even as some other indicators of high school completion were increasing. In 1995, the *Kids Count Data Book* adopted a new definition of high school dropout, the percentage of sixteen- to nineteen-year-old youths who were neither high school graduates nor enrolled in school (Annie E. Casey Foundation 1995). While on-time graduation had declined since the mid-1980s, the new measure of dropout also declined, from 10.5 percent in 1985 to 9.3 percent in 1992.[8]

Figure 8.3   Persons Who Were Not Enrolled in School and Had Not Graduated from High School, by Age

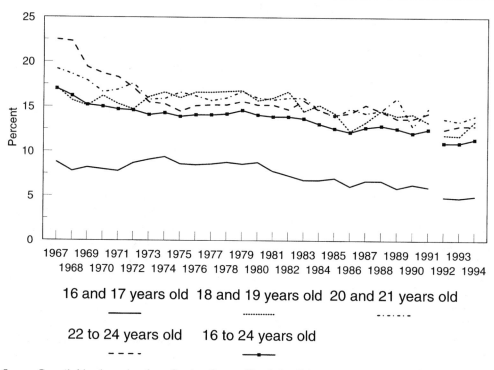

16 and 17 years old 18 and 19 years old 20 and 21 years old

22 to 24 years old   16 to 24 years old

Source: Compiled by the author from October Current Population Surveys.

The 1994 edition of the *Condition of Education* opens with the good news that, "Overall high school dropout rates have gradually decreased. The differences between dropout rates for blacks and whites have also narrowed. . . . This is encouraging because schools provide young people with the opportunity to explore their interests and develop their talents. It is also encouraging because staying in school is an important indication that a young person is learning to be a productive member of U.S. society and is less likely to suffer from poverty and unemployment" (National Center for Education Statistics 1994: iii). The NCES report is based largely on the annual dropout rates proposed by Robert Kominski (1990) of the U.S. Bureau of the Census, which I have reproduced in figure 8.4 to figure 8.6 with extensions to 1994.[9]

Annual dropout rates increased from the late 1960s to the late 1970s, but they began to decrease after 1978. Indeed, the percentages of high school students in grades ten to twelve who dropped out, by failing either to enroll in two successive years or to complete high school, declined steadily from a peak of 6.7 percent in 1978 down to 4.0 percent in 1990. The rates among young men and women have followed very similar trajectories. If anything, women appear to have enjoyed greater chances of remaining in high school than men through most of the past twenty years (figure 8.4). Among whites, the annual dropout rate declined from 6.1 percent in 1978 to 3.8 percent in 1990, and among Afri-

Figure 8.4   Year-to-Year Dropout Rates of High School Students in Grades Ten to Twelve, Ages Fifteen to Twenty-Four, by Sex

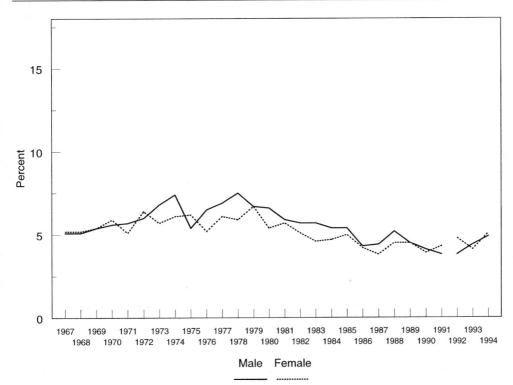

Male   Female

Source: Compiled by the author from October Current Population Surveys.

can Americans, it declined from 9.5 percent to 6.3 percent (figure 8.5). Among Hispanics, dropout rates have been much higher, and the decline in dropout has been less, from 10.0 percent in 1978 to 7.7 percent in 1990.[10]

Moreover, the gap between youth from high- and low-income families declined from the late 1970s to the early 1990s. In 1978, year-to-year dropout was 17.1 percent in the lowest fifth of family income and 3.0 percent in the highest fifth of family income (figure 8.6). By 1990, the dropout rate was 9.3 percent in the lowest fifth of family income and 1.1 percent in the highest fifth of family income (National Center for Education Statistics 1994; McMillen et al. 1994).

There was a subtle difference in the overview of high school dropout and school completion in *The Condition of Education 1995* (National Center for Education Statistics 1995), which reported that "most of these changes occurred before the mid-1980s." This report extended the series of annual dropout rates through 1993, again with no adjustment for the post-1991 procedural changes. It also introduced a time series of educational attainment at ages twenty-five to twenty-nine from the March Current Population Survey, clearly showing breaks between data collected up to and after 1991. The discussion of those series mentions both their gradual rise and the proximity of high school completion rates to the national goal of 90 percent. The discussion of dropout and school completion

Figure 8.5   Year-to-Year Dropout Rates of High School Students in Grades Ten to Twelve, Ages Fifteen to Twenty-Four, by Race/Ethnicity

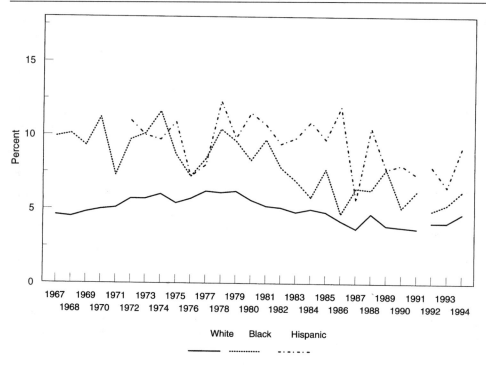

Source: Compiled by the author from October Current Population Surveys.

in *The Condition of Education 1996* is similar to that in the 1995 edition, but a new series was introduced, the percentage of persons aged sixteen to twenty-four who had not completed high school and were not enrolled in school (National Center for Education Statistics 1996). The report also mentions the possibility that school re-entry and GED examination could account for rising high school completion at ages twenty-five to twenty-nine.

Are high school dropout rates really rising or falling? Or is there no clear pattern? Are we moving toward the national goal of 90 percent high school completion? Or does it remain a distant possibility? My reading of the evidence is more consistent with that of the National Center for Education Statistics than that of the National Educational Goals Panel, the Children's Defense Fund, or—before 1995—the Annie E. Casey Foundation. However, conflicting interpretations could readily be drawn from alternative measures of school leaving, and post-1990 changes in the measurement of educational attainment have made trend assessments more difficult. In the following discussion, I examine and compare some of the measures of high school dropout and completion or non-completion that are now in wide use and offer my suggestions for improving them.

Figure 8.6   Year-to-Year Dropout Rates of High School Students in Grades Ten to Twelve, Ages Fifteen to Twenty-Four, by Family Income

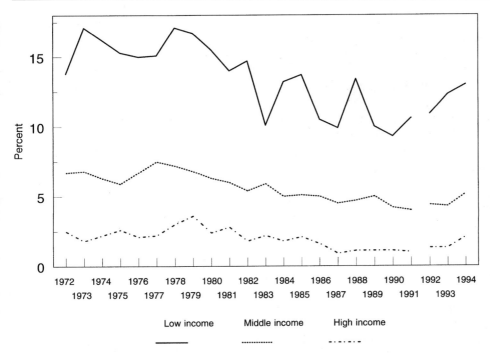

Source: Compiled by the author from October Current Population Surveys.

INDICATORS OF HIGH SCHOOL COMPLETION AND DROPOUT

I focus on six key, desirable characteristics of indicators of high school completion or dropout. First, an indicator should have face validity. A positive indicator should rise when conditions are improving and fall when they are getting worse. Second, an indicator should be conceptually sound. It should be consistent with a reasonable understanding of the process or processes that it purports to measure. It should pertain to a well-defined population and set of events. It should be understandable to the public at large. Third, it must be possible to ascertain the indicator comparably for different populations, for example, racial or ethnic subgroups, political or administrative units, or time periods. Fourth, an indicator should be timely, and in two different ways. It should tell us about outcomes of the educational process as early in the course of schooling as it is feasible to think of them as essentially complete, and it should be measured and disseminated soon afterward. Fifth, an indicator should be statistically reliable, so we can know whether things are really getting better or worse. Sixth, it should be possible to analyze the sources of trends and differentials in the indicator. That is, it should not merely be of self-evident diagnostic value, but it should be possible to link the indicator to other relevant data.

Schooling is a process that takes place across time, and students may and do move into and out of school, before as well as after they reach the age at which enrollment is no longer compulsory. While educational attainment is, in principle, cumulative and irreversible, students may attend grades without completing their requirements, and grade repetition is commonplace. For these reasons, it is important to distinguish between measures or indicators of high school completion and measures or indicators of enrollment, dropout, or other activities that may contribute to, but are not the same as school completion or school-leaving. For example, students may drop out and reenter school repeatedly, or they may leave school altogether and earn high school credentials without ever reenrolling. Moreover, because of typical patterns of age-grading in enrollment, the same measure of high school completion may have very different interpretations at younger and older ages. At age seventeen, the percentage of youth who have graduated from high school is more an indicator of the speed of age-grade progression than of ultimate completion, while the same measure at age twenty-four is a sound indicator of eventual high school graduation.

HIGH SCHOOL COMPLETION

Figure 8.7 shows the trend in high school completion by race/ethnicity and sex over the past three decades. The measure is the percentage of persons aged twenty-five to twenty-nine who completed twelve or more years of school, as reported in March Current Population Surveys. Ages twenty-five to twenty-nine are old enough to cover almost all persons who complete high school. There are few differences in high school completion by sex within the three largest race/ethnic groups (white, black, and Hispanic). Blacks began this period, in the middle of the civil rights revolution, well below the level of high school completion that Hispanics had achieved in the early 1970s, when we first began to measure their attainments. By the middle 1970s, white attainment stabilized at about 85 percent, and continued growth among African Americans has brought them close to the completion rate among whites.

What are the advantages and disadvantages of this indicator? It is conceptually sound, one of the measures that the NCES refers to as a "status" indicator. It depends on two counts, the total population of interest (by age) and the total population who completed high school. Thus, the numerator depends on the measurement of educational attainment or years of completed schooling. As measured since the early 1940s, educational attainment can be measured with high reliability in social surveys, either directly or by proxy (Bielby et al. 1977). It is measured regularly in the monthly Current Population Survey (CPS).

The wobbly trend lines for blacks and Hispanics in figure 8.7, which I have not attempted to smooth out, suggest that, for minority populations, there is substantial statistical unreliability from year to year in the CPS measure of attainment. In the fall of 1996, there was a great deal of publicity about observed similarity in this indicator between blacks and whites. In the March 1995 Current Population Survey, 87.4 percent of twenty-five- to twenty-nine-year-old whites and 86.5 percent of twenty-five- to twenty-nine-year-old blacks had completed high school (U.S. Bureau of the Census 1996; Lawton 1996). However, a closer look at the components of these statistics suggests that the black-white

Figure 8.7   Percentage of Persons Aged Twenty-Five to Twenty-Nine Completing Twelve or More
Years of Schooling, by Race/Ethnicity and Sex

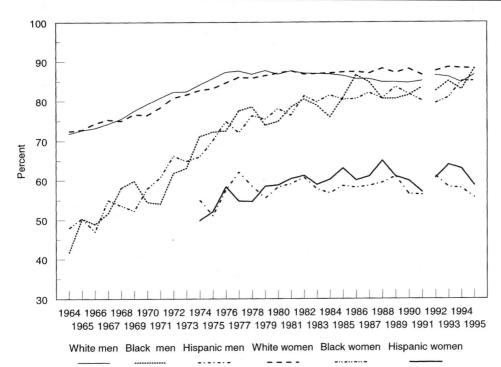

Source: Compiled by the author from March Current Population Surveys.

"convergence" should be viewed with some skepticism. The observed rates of
high school completion were higher among whites than blacks. The Census Bureau found only that "there is no statistically significant difference." Also, the
high school completion rate among twenty-five- to twenty-nine-year-old black
men was estimated to rise from 82.9 percent in 1994 to 88.1 percent in 1995. A
true increase this large from one year to the next is not credible, given the three-
year overlap between the cohorts aged twenty-five to twenty-nine in 1994 and in
1995.

While it is usually reported only for persons in the March Annual Demographic Survey, the reliability of this indicator could readily be increased, either
by smoothing the series across years or by pooling data from other months of the
CPS—for example, from the October samples, whose membership never over-
laps with that of the March samples. As noted earlier, the Annie E. Casey Foundation has adopted both of these strategies in its new state and national estimates
of dropout among sixteen- to nineteen-year-old youths. One of the persistent
problems in the tabulation and reporting of data from Current Population Surveys is that they are almost always reported in CPS month by calendar year units,
and this fails to take advantage of the essential comparability of the surveys from
month to month and year to year.

Because educational attainment is cumulative and irreversible, in principle we could improve the reliability of historic series by combining data for older and younger persons, classified by age within survey cross-sections. There are two limitations to the last of these possibilities: first, that reports from older individuals tell us about the increasingly distant past and, second, that there appears some tendency for older adults to exaggerate their levels of completed schooling. Thus, efforts to estimate educational differentials by intercensal survivorship have sometimes yielded negative mortality at higher levels of schooling.

A serious problem with this indicator is that it is not timely, at least in the first sense noted earlier. By the time the population reaches ages twenty-five to twenty-nine, most people are seven to twelve years beyond the modal age at high school completion. Thus, the measure is, at best, about a decade behind the realities of school progression and dropout. It is valuable when we choose to look back at the progress, or lack thereof, among major social and economic groups. Once observed, we can obtain this indicator in timely fashion. Data from the March Current Population Survey are regularly available in the fall of the year in which they were collected. Thus, in principle, a decade-old measure of trends in high school completion can be examined within six months of its collection.

THE CHANGING STATISTICAL DEFINITION OF GRADUATION

Another serious issue in the use of this indicator pertains to recent changes in the conceptualization and measurement of educational attainment, both in the U.S. Census of Population and in the Current Population Survey. In the United States, if not elsewhere, it used to be easy to ascertain educational attainment. It was sufficient to ask, "What was the highest grade of school that . . . completed?" and provide numeric categories ranging from zero to seventeen or more. In the Current Population Survey (CPS), a most useful distinction was added (Kominski and Adams 1994): "What is the highest grade or year of regular school . . . has ever attended? Did . . . complete that grade (year)?" This two-part question made it clearer that the question was about regular (academic) schooling. Moreover, it was possible in principle to measure school dropout among those who had attended, but not completed a grade. Over the years, the upper range of responses was expanded, and by 1991, the CPS recorded as many as twenty-six years of schooling.

Following a similar change in the 1990 census, the CPS introduced a new, single educational question early in 1992: "What is the highest level of school . . . has completed or the highest degree . . . has received? The sixteen CPS codes and response categories for the new item are displayed in figure 8.8 (Kominski and Adams 1994). The new CPS educational attainment question and its responses differ in several ways from the old item and its response categories. First, it eliminates the probe distinguishing between the highest grade attended and the completion of that grade. Second, responses below the level of secondary school have been grouped. Third, a new category, "twelfth grade, no diploma" has been added. Fourth, the category for completion of high school now specifically identifies both high school graduation and obtaining a high school equivalent, such as the GED. Fifth, major changes have been introduced in the classification of schooling beyond high school completion. These are now based on credentials, rather than on the completion of numbers of years of schooling.

Figure 8.8   The 1990-Basis CPS Educational Attainment Classification

What is the highest level of school X has completed or the highest degree X has received?

Code	Level of Schooling Completed
31	Less than first grade
32	1st, 2nd, 3rd, or 4th grade
33	5th or 6th grade
34	7th or 8th grade
35	9th grade
36	10th grade
37	11th grade
38	12th grade, no diploma
39	High school graduate—high school diploma or the equivalent (For example, GED)
40	Some college but no degree
41	Associate degree in college—Occupational/vocational program
42	Associate degree in college—Academic program
43	Bachelor's degree (For example: BA, AB, BS)
44	Master's degree (For example: MA, MS, MEng, MEd, MSW, MBA)
45	Professional school degree (For example: MD, DDS, DVM, LLB, JD)
46	Doctorate degree (For example: PhD, EdD)

Among other rationales for the new item, the Bureau of the Census states that the old system led to uncertainty in the classification of high school graduates because persons who had equivalent credentials were supposed to be counted as completing twelve years of school, but often were not so classified. This has become an increasingly important matter because some localities require a final graduation test or certification; thus, it is possible to complete twelve years of regular schooling without earning a diploma (Kominski and Adams 1994). One might expect that, over time, the new CPS educational attainment item will supplant older survey items. I hope that this will not happen. In my opinion, it was clearly desirable to change to a system in which postsecondary credentials were measured explicitly, but the new CPS item fails to obtain important information, especially about high school completion.[11]

The collapse of several grade levels below high school has made it impossible to follow age-grade progression at younger ages.[12] Neither can we examine school completion closely among recent immigrant populations or among populations with learning disabilities. In populations with low levels of schooling, the collapse will remain problematic—for example, at older ages or when it is necessary to ascertain educational attainments in past generations.

The new CPS item has made it more difficult to measure completion of the twelfth grade, despite the Census Bureau's distinction between "twelfth grade, no diploma" and "high school graduate—high school diploma or the equivalent." A cross-tabulation of educational attainment under the new and old systems, which was carried out using the February 1990 Current Population Survey, suggests that elimination of the previous "completion" probe accounts in part for nearly four million individuals who are classified by the new item as nominally having "completed" twelve years of school without a high school diploma or its equivalent (Kominski and Adams 1994).[13] This is problematic, for we do not know whether the category of twelfth grade nongraduates is an artifact of survey methodology or an indication of the application of new standards of academic achievement. Indeed, there are disagreements about how persons with "twelfth grade, no diploma" should be classified. The Census Bureau classifies such persons as nongraduates, and this appears to have affected published time-series. In a match between old and new attainment items in the Current Population Survey samples of March 1991 and March 1992,[14] Jaeger (1993) found that 55 percent of persons who reported "twelfth grade, no diploma" in 1992 had reported completing twelve years of school in 1991. Thus, Jaeger recommends combining the new "twelfth grade, no diploma" and "high school graduate" categories into a single category of twelve years of schooling. Taking a statistical compromise, Mare's (1995) analysis of educational trends from 1980 to 1990 allocates the "twelfth grade, no diploma" responses to dropout and completer categories in proportion to their shares in a cross-classification of the two items obtained in the February 1990 Current Population Survey.

Despite its proliferation of categories, the new educational classification fails to distinguish individuals who completed twelve years of school from those who achieved high school equivalency, yet there is strong evidence of differences between regular high school graduates and the growing number of individuals with GEDs (Cameron and Heckman 1992). If the "twelfth grade, no diploma" category makes sense, I think that it makes more sense to place GED holders in that category than to combine them with regular graduates. It would make even more sense for public policy if GED-holders were reported separately.

Finally, despite or perhaps because of its failure to measure certification directly, the old educational questions come far closer than the new question to telling us how people spent their time during their formative years. That is, the old educational attainment questions tell us more about the process of growing up than how far a person went in school. Post-1992 data suggest that there are aggregate discrepancies in rates of high school completion between the old and new measures. For example, the new measure leads to much larger estimates of year-to-year dropout in the twelfth grade (McMillen et al. 1994).

In my judgment, it will be best if the new CPS education questions are not used as a model in other surveys. I hope that the Bureau of the Census will modify its question soon, if possible before rather than in conjunction with the census of 2000. A novel question that was evidently designed within the severe constraints of the decennial census form need not have been adopted with minimal changes in the CPS. I recommend that researchers continue to use the old CPS question to ascertain educational attainment, preferably including the probe about completion of the highest grade attended. A separate question or questions should be used to measure the highest diploma, equivalency credential, or degree obtained.[15]

HOW EARLY CAN WE MEASURE HIGH SCHOOL COMPLETION?

Might it be possible to ascertain the completion of high school at an earlier stage in the life history of cohorts and thus overcome the problem of timeliness in attainment measured at ages twenty-five to twenty-nine? Figure 8.9 provides some evidence about this. I have taken educational attainment from March Current Population Surveys for six two-year age groups from 1972 to 1993: ages nineteen to twenty (the key age identified by the National Educational Goals Panel before 1995), twenty-one to twenty-two, twenty-three to twenty-four, twenty-five to twenty-six, twenty-seven to twenty-eight, and twenty-nine to thirty.[16] The data are arrayed relative to the year in which each cohort reached ages nineteen to twenty, so a vertical reading of the overlapping segments of the graph shows the growth of high school completion within cohorts from one age to the next.

These series suggest three observations. First, two-year cohorts are too narrow to provide reliable data from a single Current Population Survey, even for the total population. There is far too much "wobble" in the series displayed in figure 8.9. To put this more concretely, the lowest of the three series corresponds to the indicator used initially by the National Educational Goals Panel (but without

Figure 8.9   High School Completion of Selected Cohorts, by Age

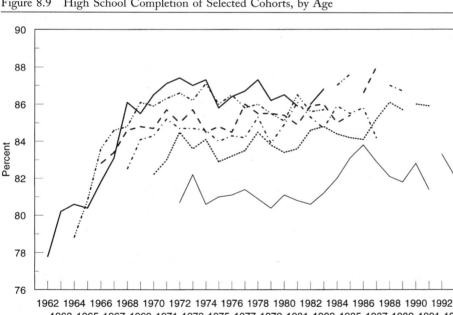

Year at Which Cohort Reached Ages 19–20

Ages 19–20 Ages 21–22 Ages 23–24 Ages 25–26 Ages 27–28 Ages 29–30

Source: Compiled by the author from October Current Population Surveys, as reported by McMillen, Kaufman, and Whitener (1994).

excluding persons still enrolled in secondary school). Even for the total population, the standard error of a point estimate of the percentage completing high school is 0.76 percentage points at ages nineteen to twenty. This is far too large for the measure to be useful in detecting likely true changes from one year to the next. The unreliability is even greater in minority populations: In 1993 the standard errors are 2.59 percentage points among non-Hispanic blacks and 4.31 percentage points among Hispanics (McMillen et al. 1994). Thus, using the rule of thumb that a difference or change of two standard errors is statistically reliable, we should have to observe year-to-year changes of about 2 percentage points in the total population, 7 points among blacks, and 12 points among Hispanics before we could conclude that high school completion had really changed significantly.[17] In the October 1993 CPS, the standard error of the difference between completion rates of nineteen- to twenty-year-old blacks and whites is about 2.7 percentage points, and in the case of Hispanics and whites, the standard error of the difference is about 4.5 percentage points. This indicator is a crude instrument indeed.

Major features of the series appear more clearly in moving averages (not shown). There are large gaps between levels of attainment in each cohort at ages nineteen to twenty with those at any older age. If a great deal of educational growth occurs between ages nineteen to twenty and twenty-one to twenty-two, it is questionable whether the younger age is appropriate for the target of our national goal. Moreover, since ages at high school completion are increasing along with attainment levels (Hauser and Phang 1993), it would appear to make sense, for reasons of substance as well as reliability, to extend the upper end of the age range for which high school completion is measured.

There are relatively small gaps between completion levels at successive ages above twenty-one. Roughly speaking, the gap between ages nineteen to twenty and ages twenty to twenty-one is about as large as that between ages twenty to twenty-one and ages twenty-nine to thirty. That is, even if we must wait until close to age thirty to learn how far a cohort will ultimately go in school, we can learn substantially earlier—if not by age twenty—how many in a cohort will complete high school. Thus, following the 1993 NCES report on high school dropout, I would suggest that ages twenty-one to twenty-two are an appropriate range for assessments of progress in the completion of high school, provided the sample is large enough to yield reliable estimates (McMillen et al. 1994). An extension of the upper age range would increase the reliability of the estimate, but decrease its timeliness.

Another striking feature of figure 8.9 is the sharp discontinuity in high school completion rates between 1991 and 1992, when the new CPS education measure was introduced, especially at ages nineteen and twenty. It is not clear what features of the new measure are responsible for this disjuncture. It could be sampling variability, but my guess is that the exclusion of nondiploma-holding twelfth-grade completers may be compensated by GED completion at older ages, but not at younger ages.

The estimates of high school completion used by the National Educational Goals Panel differ from those displayed in figure 8.9 in one important respect, that persons still enrolled in secondary school have been excluded from the denominator of the percentages. That adjustment would raise the series for nineteen- to twenty-year-olds much closer to those for the same cohorts at older ages.

In 1995 the National Educational Goals Panel substituted high school completion by ages eighteen to twenty-four for its earlier indicator of completion by ages nineteen and twenty, while continuing to exclude persons who were still enrolled in secondary school from the denominator of the rate. This redefinition presumably increased the statistical reliability of the indicator, but it did so by lowering as well as increasing the age range. In my opinion, the decision to include eighteen-year-olds may have been unwise. The problem is that a large share of eighteen-year-olds who are "on track" will not have completed their senior year of high school when enumerated in the October CPS. From 1987 to 1994, 24 to 28 percent of eighteen-year-old youth were enrolled in high school in October. The enrollment rates were even higher among minorities—31 to 38 percent among blacks and 23 to 44 percent among Hispanics.

Consequently, despite the adjustment of eliminating students in secondary school from the denominator of the rate of high school completion, the percentage of high school graduates is usually lower at age eighteen than at older ages. Figure 8.10 shows the series of high school completion in the October CPS at ages eighteen and nineteen to twenty from 1987 to 1994. High school completion at age eighteen is usually well below that at ages nineteen and twenty throughout the series, especially for the two minority groups.[18] Thus, inclusion of eighteen-year-olds in the assessment of the National Educational Goals tends to reduce the estimate of eventual high school completion among minorities relative to its value among non-Hispanic whites.

Figure 8.10   Conditional High School Completion, by Age, Race, and Ethnicity

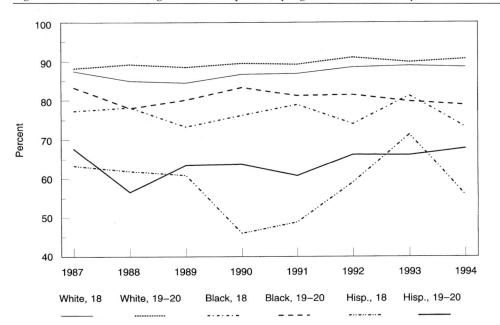

Source: Compiled by the author from October Current Population Surveys. Based on persons not enrolled in elementary or secondary school.

SUBNATIONAL ESTIMATES OF HIGH SCHOOL COMPLETION

Figure 8.11 shows another piece of evidence relevant to the age at which high school completion is ascertained. The data are percentages completing high school or more (using the official version of the new census concept), ascertained at ages twenty to twenty-four and twenty-five to twenty-nine in the Census of 1990 (U.S. Bureau of the Census 1994). Obviously, across states, there is a close relationship between rates of attainment observed at those two ages. The linear correlation is 0.96. Moreover, while a comparison of rates at the two ages confounds maturation with change, it is suggestive that there is very little change in high school completion rates by states between ages twenty to twenty-four and twenty-five to twenty-nine. The average increase is just 0.4 percentage points. Thus, in order to increase the reliability of subnational comparisons, it would appear reasonable to focus status measures of high school completion on the period when cohorts reach ages twenty to twenty-four.

In its latest annual dropout report, the National Center for Educational Statistics has, for the first time, reported high school completion among eighteen- to twenty-four-year-olds by state, using data from the October CPS (McMillen and Kaufman 1996). As in the 1995 and 1996 reports of the National Educational Goals Panel, persons still enrolled below the college level have been excluded from the base of these rates, and the state percentages have been reported as three-year averages, for 1989 to 1991 and for 1992 to 1994. The break between the two state series corresponds to the change in the census measure of

Figure 8.11   Percentage Completing High School at Ages Twenty to Twenty-Four, by Completion at Ages Twenty-Five to Twenty-Nine for States: April 1990

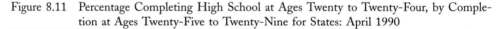

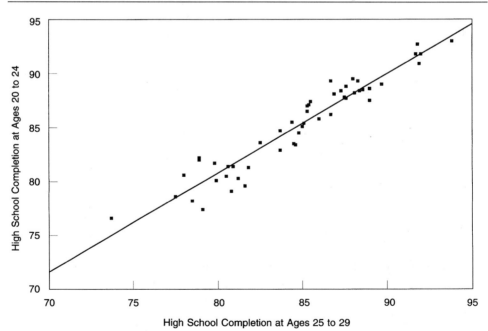

High School Completion at Ages 25 to 29

Source: Tabulated by the author from the 1990 Census of Population (U.S. Bureau of the Census 1994).

high school completion, so the two sets of state averages are not strictly comparable. All the same, it is instructive to ask whether the data are reliable enough to
detect change at the state level. My examination of the estimates suggests that
differences in state rates of high school completion will be detected reliably only
in large states undergoing rapid change. For example, while the average absolute
change in high school completion rates between 1989 to 1991 and 1992 to 1994
was 2.3 percentage points, the average standard error of state-level differences
was 2.8 percentage points. Only six states experienced statistically significant
changes in high school completion between the earlier and later periods. Moreover, while the correlation across states of high school completion rates in the
1990 census was very high, 0.96, between ages twenty to twenty-four and
twenty-five to twenty-nine, it was much lower between the census and CPS
series centered on 1990, 0.87. While both the age groups and graduation concepts differ in the latter case, I would expect a higher level of correlation—on the
order of that in the two sets of census rates—if the CPS series were sufficiently
reliable.

TIMELY HIGH SCHOOL COMPLETION

The pre-1995 measure of timely high school completion in the *Kids Count Data
Book* (1994) would appear to have serious defects, as well as some advantages.
The measure is obtained by dividing the number of public high school graduates
in the reference year by the public ninth-grade enrollment four years earlier, with
some adjustments for secondary students not classified by grade and for inter-
state migration. One advantage is that the measure is available annually by state.
A second advantage is that it is timely, in the sense that it pertains to a standard
of accomplishment early in the life of each cohort. On the other hand, there
appears to be a substantial lag in the availability of the measure for publication.
The 1994 *Kids Count Data Book* reported rates of on-time high school completion in 1991.

There are more serious problems with the measure of timely school completion. I have already noted that it shows steady annual declines during a period
when other measures show increasing rates of high school completion (but at
older ages). As we approach an upper limit of high school completion, how
should we weigh the advantage of timeliness (by age) against eventual completion?

Second, the indicator of timely school completion does not appear to measure
the same thing, from state to state, that we observe in percentages of high school
completion in the census. For example, I have looked at state-level correlations
between the timely completion rates in 1985 and in 1990 with the census completion rates at ages twenty-five to twenty-nine and twenty to twenty-four
(which correspond, roughly, with graduation in 1985 and 1990). These intercor-
relations are distressingly low. The four correlations range from 0.68 to 0.78,
which are low indeed at that aggregate level. Moreover, the correlation of the
timely completion indicator from 1985 to 1990 is 0.89, which suggests either
that differential change in aggregate high school completion rates is quite rapid,
or that the underlying data are unreliable.

Third, state-level high school completion rates for all population groups combined do not adequately portray state-to-state differentials in completion among major race/ethnic groups. I have looked at state-to-state correlations among percentages completing high school in the 1990 census at ages twenty to twenty-four and twenty-five to twenty-nine among the five race-ethnic groups recognized in the federal statistical system. The state-level correlations within the same race/ethnic group, but between age groups, are relatively large in the case of the larger race/ethnic groups: 0.96 among non-Hispanic whites, 0.94 among blacks, and 0.93 among Hispanics. They are much lower in the two smaller minority groups: 0.77 among American Indians and 0.65 among Asian and Pacific Islanders.[19] The state-level correlations among black and non-Hispanic white rates range from 0.27 to 0.38; the state-level correlations among non-Hispanic white and Hispanic rates range from -0.13 to -0.04; and the state-level correlations among black and Hispanic rates range from 0.26 to 0.40. Also, the correlations between the rates for non-Hispanic whites and for American Indians range from 0.06 to 0.29, while those between non-Hispanic whites and Asian and Pacific Islanders range from -.05 to 0.14. Given this level of inconsistency in state-level completion rates among the major race/ethnic groups, it is reasonable to wonder how much guidance for public policy is provided by aggregate, annual state-level high school completion data. For example, one might ask whether we can learn more about high school completion in a state among blacks, Hispanics, American Indians, or Asian and Pacific Islanders by looking at current state-level completion rates or by looking at group-specific rates in the preceding decennial census.

The Annie E. Casey Foundation (1995) has fortunately adopted a new measure of high school dropout, the percentage of sixteen- to nineteen-year-old youth who are neither enrolled in school nor high school graduates. In each year the new measure is aggregated across all monthly Current Population Surveys from September to May—the months in which schools are in session—and the Foundation reports a three-year average, rather than an annual figure, both at the national and state levels. The measure is heterogeneous in one important respect, namely, that it includes younger ages at which high school graduation is unlikely to have occurred. However, this should present no problem if it is read as an (inverse) indicator of age-appropriate activity, rather than strictly as a measure of high school completion.

ANNUAL DROPOUT OR PERSISTENCE RATES

The most novel and widely adopted indicator arising from the recent national interest in high school dropout is the annual dropout rate proposed by Kominski (1990):

> By using current and prior enrollment statuses, along with information on years of school completed, it is possible to identify those individuals who were enrolled a year ago, are not enrolled now, and have not completed high school. These individuals are identified as high school dropouts in the past year. The formula for the 1-year rate from grade X is $A/(A + B)$, where A is the number of persons with grade $(X-1)$ completed who were enrolled in school last year and are not currently enrolled and B is the

number of persons with grade X completed who were enrolled last year and are currently enrolled. In computing the rate for the 12th grade, a modification is necessary, since many persons who successfully complete grade 12 will not be enrolled in the fall following graduation. In this case the value for B is the number of persons who were enrolled in the previous fall and who graduated in the spring (as determined from a question that asks high school graduates for their year of graduation).

Such rates can be ascertained each year from the October Current Population Survey, and the series can easily be extended back in time.[20] Among rates that are available annually and for major population subgroups, this comes closest to recognizing that high school completion is a process that may involve repeated moves out of and back into school. Another important advantage of the annual dropout rates is that they condition on prior school enrollment. Thus, unlike "status" measures of dropout, they are not directly affected by the presence of immigrants who have had no exposure to schooling in the United States.

At the same time, the definition of the annual dropout rate is less than ideal because it combines persons who do not continue from one grade to the next in the survey year with persons who drop out from the next higher grade level during the academic year preceding the survey, as if they were in the same cohort. It also fails to identify return enrollees among this year's students at each grade level. Despite these problems, the definition is useful, perhaps more so than definitions based upon grade completion and enrollment by a specific age, which fail to account for variation in age-grade progression.[21] Perhaps to increase its reliability as well as to limit the number of data series that need be displayed, the annual dropout rates are usually aggregated across grades ten to twelve. This also partly overcomes the conceptual problem in cohort coverage mentioned previously.

Because the construction of annual dropout rates by the Bureau of the Census has, since 1992, rested on the official distinction between "twelfth grade, no diploma" and "high school graduate (or equivalent)," there has been a substantial change in the annual rate of high school dropout in the twelfth grade. This series, originally presented by McMillen, Kaufman, and Whitener (1994), is reproduced in figure 8.12. Obviously, the changing treatment of twelfth-grade dropout is a major break in the series, and analysts should be most cautious in using the published series.[22] While one may accept or reject the new Census definition of high school completion, there would appear to be a conceptual inconsistency between the definitions of grade completion at the tenth- and eleventh-grade levels, which remain purely nominal, with that at the twelfth-grade level, which now excludes persons who did not earn a high school diploma or equivalent. As the unit record data from October Current Population Surveys are released publicly, it would be useful, at least for the next few years, to construct an alternative series that will hew more closely to the old definition of twelfth-grade completion, that is, by including "twelfth-grade, no diploma" with "high school graduate."[23]

An important advantage of the annual dropout measure, at least as defined for persons nineteen and younger, is that dropout status can be linked to many other characteristics of the household in which the student lives, which is—at those

Figure 8.12   Year-to-Year Dropout Rates of High School Students Aged Fifteen to Twenty-Four, by Grade Level

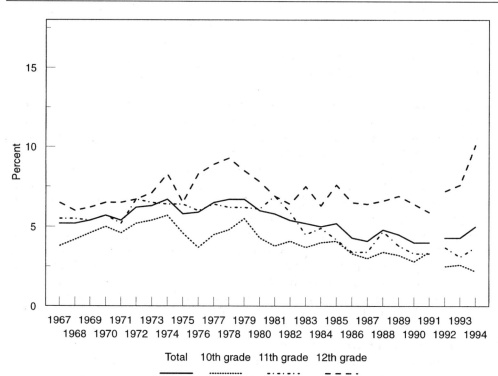

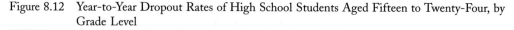

Source: Compiled by the author from October Current Population Surveys.

ages—almost always a parental or quasi-parental household. Thus, for example, the Census Bureau annually reports dropout rates of dependent family members fifteen to twenty-four years old by age, sex, race, Hispanic origin, and family income (Kominski and Adams 1993, table 8). Hauser, Jordan, and Dixon (1993) have created a uniform file of October Current Population Surveys from 1968 to 1991 in which the characteristics of youths are matched with those of their households, including the social and economic characteristics of the householders.[24] Hauser and Phang (1993) report a logistic regression analysis of trends in high school dropout based on the uniform October files in which family background factors include sex, age, grade level, dependency status, metropolitan locations, region, sex of householder, number of children in the household, educational attainment of householder, occupational status of householder, family income, and housing tenure. These data make it possible to describe the changing social and economic composition of high school cohorts as well as the implications of those changes for high school completion. Over the period 1968 to 1990, the uniform CPS file includes approximately ninety-five thousand whites, fifteen thousand blacks, and sixty-four hundred Hispanics. Thus, the October CPS data invite multivariate analysis, and the list of regressors is far richer than those used in official statistical series.[25]

Again, the link between dropout or continuation and characteristics of the (parental) household is the presumption that the student lives with parents or parent surrogates. In general, nondependency is greater among women than men, and greater among Hispanics than among whites or blacks. The older the person and the higher the grade level, the less likely that a youth is dependent. When an individual is living independently, household income may well be an effect, rather than a source of high school dropout, continuation, or completion. So far as high school completion is concerned, I think that the link between children and parental households should be regarded as questionable no later than age twenty, and perhaps by age nineteen. Thus, I am highly skeptical of the suggestion by McMillen, Kaufman, and Whitener (1994) that the inverse relationship between dropout and income, regardless of dependency status, shows there is no problem in arraying "status" dropout rates at ages fifteen to twenty-four by household income.

The major limitation of the annual dropout (or persistence) rates is the obverse of their most attractive feature. They pertain to dropout or completion or a single grade in a single year or to dropout or completion aggregated across three grade levels in a single year. Thus, as suggested in some of the series presented earlier, the data are rather thin, and simple disaggregations of rates, including those presented in official publications, are subject to a great deal of sampling variability. On the other hand, if one is willing to think of year as a variable, rather than as an obligatory unit for aggregation, analysis, and reporting, or if one is willing to assume relative constancy in the effects of some social and economic characteristics across limited periods of time, for instance, by aggregating or smoothing data across years, we can readily obtain a far richer understanding of the sources of trends and differentials in dropout.

For example, figure 8.13 shows estimated annual high school dropout rates by grade level, sex, and race/ethnicity from 1973 to 1989.[26] The estimates are based upon a logistic regression model that includes main effects on dropout of grade level, sex, and race/ethnicity; interaction effects between grade level and sex, race/ethnicity and sex, and race/ethnicity and grade level; and interaction effects between year and grade level and between year and race/ethnicity. This model has the effect of smoothing the data, for it does not include the three-way interaction effects of dropout with grade level, sex, and race/ethnicity or any of the higher-order interaction effects of dropout with year and grade level, sex, or race/ethnicity. All of these higher-order interaction effects were tested and found not to be statistically significant. Thus, the model estimates distinct trends in dropout by grade level and race/ethnicity, but not by sex, and the trends for combinations of grade level and race/ethnicity are combinations of the trends for each grade level and each race/ethnicity. The model increases statistical power, that is, it decreases standard errors, for the significant contrasts.

Figure 8.13 shows the trends in annual high school dropout rates by race/ethnicity within each of six combinations of sex and grade level.[27] Dropout rates are consistently higher with each successive grade level and, among blacks and Hispanics, they are substantially higher at the twelfth-grade level than at the tenth or eleventh grades. Among whites at all grade levels there was a steady decline in high school dropout during the 1980s. Among blacks, dropout rates were generally lower in the 1980s than in the 1970s. The trends are less clear among Hispanics, but the data suggest an increase in dropout through the early to middle

Figure 8.13   Annual High School Dropout, by Race/Ethnicity: Tenth- to Twelfth-Grade Males and Females

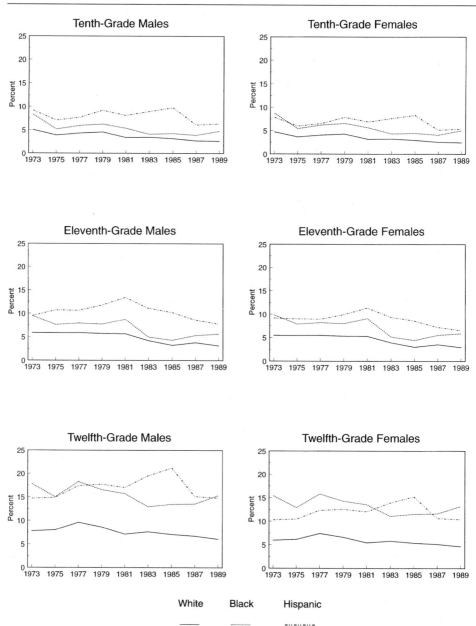

Source: Tabulations from October Current Population Surveys by Hauser and Phang (1993).

1980s, followed by a decline to the level of the middle 1970s. In each combination of grade level and sex, rates of dropout are almost always highest among Hispanics, followed by African Americans; dropout rates are lowest among whites. However, black and Hispanic dropout rates are similarly high at the twelfth-grade level, where the gap between the minority groups and whites is larger than in the tenth or eleventh grade. Fewer than 10 percent of white men or women have dropped out of school in any year or grade level since the early 1970s. Among blacks, fewer than 10 percent drop out of school at the tenth or eleventh grade, but about 15 percent drop out in the twelfth grade. Among Hispanics, about 10 percent drop out in the tenth and eleventh grade, but 15 percent or more of men and 10 to 15 percent of women drop out in the twelfth grade. At the twelfth-grade level, there is also a higher rate of dropout among men than among women in each racial/ethnic group.

In figure 8.14, under similar assumptions about interactions between race/ethnicity, sex, grade-level, and year, the annual dropout rates have been adjusted for effects of social background, both within and between years.[28] Thus, the model permits comparisons of dropout rate across years, within and among race/ethnic groups. The rates have been normed in two ways. First, they pertain to dropout among dependent youth, not to all high school students.[29] Second, rates of dropout are normed so the predicted rates among dependent black youth (of each sex and at each grade level) are set equal to the corresponding observed rates. By virtue of this normalization, the dropout rates of whites and of Hispanics can be said to pertain to youth in those groups with the average social background characteristics of blacks.

The striking finding in figure 8.14, which does not depend on the normalization of the dropout rates, is that controls for social background reverse the observed ordering of dropout rates between whites and blacks or Hispanics, especially in the 1970s. That is, when social background is controlled, whites have the highest propensity to drop out of high school, followed by Hispanics and then blacks. Moreover, by the end of the 1980s, and primarily because of a steady improvement among whites, there was a substantial convergence in dropout rates among the three racial/ethnic groups. That is, one need not invoke culture, academic ability, motivation, or discrimination to account for observed racial/ethnic differences in high school dropout; they are fully explained by easily observable factors of social and economic origin. Moreover, to the degree that we must offer some explanation of differences in dropout beyond the obvious, the problem is not to explain higher dropout among minorities, but to explain it in the majority population. One possibility is that economic opportunities outside of school were greater for whites than for minorities. This would account both for the higher net rates of dropout among whites and—because of the global decline in the labor market opportunities of dropouts—for the convergence of white dropout rates with those among minorities.

There are real limits to our ability to disaggregate annual dropout rates. For example, I have not been successful in constructing useful time-series of these rates from the CPS data by state or for major metropolitan areas.[30] However, I believe that further analytic work, using status rates, say, for twenty- to twenty-four-year-olds, as well as temporal aggregations of annual dropout rates, may prove fruitful.

Figure 8.14   High School Dropout Adjusted for Social Background: Tenth- to Twelfth-Grade Men
and Women, by Race/Ethnicity

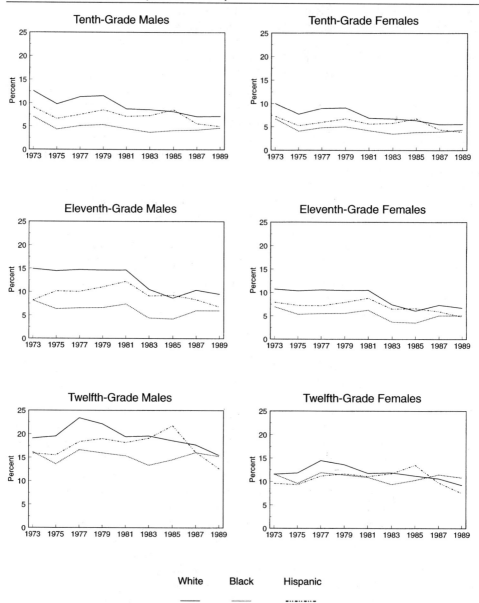

Source: Tabulations from October Current Population Surveys by Hauser and Phang (1993). All graphs are plotted for dependents with the characteristics of average black males or females at each grade level.

COHORT RATES

The annual dropout reports of the National Center for Education Statistics suggest a distinction among "event," "status," and "cohort" rates. The reports use the latter term primarily to refer to rates of dropout or high school completion in the major longitudinal studies carried out by the NCES, that is, the High School and Beyond surveys of the early 1980s (HSB) and the National Educational Longitudinal Study of 1988 (NELS: 88). Generically, NCES says that, "Longitudinal or cohort analyses are based on repeated measures of a group of individuals." In *Dropout Rates in the United States: 1993*, cohort rates are illustrated by comparison of dropout status in repeated CPS cross-sections, as well as by reference to the longitudinal studies (McMillen et al. 1994). In my opinion, the distinction between "cohort" and "event" or "status" rates has not been cleanly drawn, nor has the NCES used the available longitudinal data in its annual reports as well or as thoroughly as one might hope.

For example, the annual dropout rates discussed in the preceding section would qualify as "cohort" rates, as those are described in the NCES reports, because they depend upon longitudinal observation. To be sure, the initial condition—enrollment in the prior year—is ascertained retrospectively, but that does not alter the concept. Thus, there is little difference in concept between annual dropout rates from the CPS and the eighth- to twelfth- or tenth- to twelfth-grade dropout rates from NELS, except the latter are based upon a longer period of observation. This is not to say that reported findings (and comparisons of findings) from HSB and NELS: 88 are unimportant, but merely that they do not offer any conceptual advantage relative to the CPS. The difference seems smaller yet when one considers the large array of social background variables that are available in the CPS, but not used in the dropout reports, as well as the richer set of variables available in the longitudinal studies that have not been used in the annual reports.

One area in which the longitudinal studies could be most valuable, and the NCES reports are incomplete, is the relationship between academic performance and school dropout. The National Educational Goals call on us to improve academic performance as well as school retention. There is an obvious relationship between academic success and retention, which is glossed through references to motivation, effort, and engagement of students (Office of Educational Research and Improvement 1993). There may well be tradeoffs between growth in academic standards and growth in school retention. Unlike the Current Population Survey, the major national longitudinal studies do contain good measures of academic achievement. Yet the NCES dropout reports contain almost no information about the relationship between academic performance and school retention or dropout. For example, in *Dropout in the United States: 1994*, dropout from NELS: 88 is reported by sex, race/ethnicity, self-reported reasons for dropping out, poverty level, family composition, and presence of an own child in the home (McMillen and Kaufman 1996). The report presents no direct evidence about the relationship between academic performance or grade retention and school dropout. In my opinion, this is a deplorable omission.

Elsewhere I have suggested that the value of the national longitudinal studies could be increased substantially, at relatively low cost and without sacrificing analytic utility, if the observations were spread out over the decade on an annual or biennial basis (Hauser 1991). I have seen no progress toward this in the past few years, but I believe that it remains an attractive goal. Briefly put, by spreading observations across calendar years, rather than "bunching" them in cohort samples drawn once per decade, we can accumulate samples of analytic utility equal to those presently available. At the same time, we could obtain readings of trends in the process of schooling on a regular basis, rather than once per decade. A redesign of the national longitudinal surveys also should include oversamples of large, minority populations that will be large enough to monitor trends within those groups, as well as among non-Hispanic whites or the total population. Thus, improvements in the design, as well as in the use, of longitudinal educational data could contribute to educational policy with respect to high school dropout and completion.

RECOMMENDATIONS

Ultimate high school completion can be measured well in cohorts that have passed the age of twenty. Thus, there is little reason to wait for cohorts to reach the traditional age of twenty-five to twenty-nine at which CPS time-series of educational attainment have been reported for decades. For the U.S. population as a whole and for very large subpopulations, for example, non-Hispanic whites or all women, there should be an annual time-series of high school completion at ages twenty to twenty-four, based on the March Current Population Survey. In my opinion, and despite the additional statistical reliability that might be gained, it would be unwise to extend the lower age limit downward; it should definitely not include eighteen-year-olds. Even if persons still enrolled in elementary or secondary school are eliminated from the denominator, a younger extension of the age range will tend to exaggerate attainment differences between majority and minority groups.

Without access to public use microdata files, the population estimates for these series are readily available in *Current Population Reports* or in unpublished tabulations of the Bureau of the Census. For smaller subpopulations, for example, non-Hispanic blacks or Hispanics, annual estimates from the March CPS are not reliable enough to permit valid inferences about change on a year-to-year basis. The Census Bureau or other appropriate agencies should consider providing multiyear composite estimates of this series for subpopulations, just as it does in the case of state-level estimates of the poverty rate.

Alternatively, since educational attainment is available for all cases in the CPS, annual estimates could be aggregated across all CPS rotation groups in each year. I do not know whether such annual aggregations from the CPS would be sufficiently reliable, that is, whether one could in that way avoid taking averages across calendar years. For example, this series could be produced annually at the state level, but the experiment with a similar series by the NCES suggests that even three-year averages across a single month of the CPS would not yield statistically reliable intercensal estimates. A third viable possibility for aggregation of state-level estimates—beyond aggregation across months and years—would be to extend the age-range of state-level estimates, that is, to report high school completion by ages twenty to twenty-nine, rather than by ages twenty to twenty-four.

Of course, an upward extension of the age range would reduce the timeliness of the estimates.

In addition to measuring high school completion, we ought to have more timely and proximate measures of progress toward high school completion. At the national level, the time-series on year-to-year dropout of fifteen- to twenty-four-year-olds in grades ten to twelve, based on the October Current Population Survey, is probably the best available indicator. However, there is no way to disaggregate this indicator for major subpopulations within survey years. By definition, coverage for each year is limited to only three grade cohorts, and—given present survey procedures—the series can be obtained only from the October CPS and not in other months. The existing series are of very low reliability at any level of disaggregation, as indicated, for example, by large year-to-year fluctuations in the dropout rates of Hispanics. The one viable possibility for extending the use of the annual dropout rate is greater use of model-based estimates, which are not commonly used in public statistical reports. Since multiyear averages are—in an important sense—model-based, I hope that their use will lead to reports based on more powerful models.

Annual dropout rates are not only statistically unreliable, but they focus narrowly on school-leaving, which is only one aspect of the dropout phenomenon. Thus, there is an important need for other indicators of the process of early school-leaving. In my opinion, the percentage of current dropouts among sixteen- to nineteen-year-old youth that was adopted recently by the Annie E. Casey Foundation for its *Kids Count* reports is the best alternative. While it is a status measure, rather than a rate, it does reflect the share of the late adolescent population which is not making progress toward high school graduation. The population base—four age cohorts—is not much wider than that of the annual dropout rate, but the measure can be ascertained and aggregated across nine months of the CPS in each calendar year. Thus, month-to-month and year-to-year aggregation can each be used to increase its statistical reliability.

FUTURE PROSPECTS

In closing, I want to comment briefly on two other ways in which data on school dropout and retention may be measured in future. The first is the use of administrative records. An ambitious effort is now underway to obtain comparable measures of high school dropout across states and across time through the Common Core of Data (CCD), an annual survey of state-level educational agencies (McMillen et al. 1994; McMillen and Kaufman 1996). During 1991–1992, an effort was made by forty-three states to participate in this new program, but only fifteen states reported data that were consistent with the specified definitions of school enrollment and dropout. By 1993–1994, seventeen states submitted data of adequate quality (McMillen and Kaufman 1996). These administrative data depend on the ability of local and state agencies to determine whether or not a student who has left a school has subsequently reenrolled elsewhere. The goal of the program is to report "the number and rate of event dropouts from public schools by school districts, states, major subpopulations, and the nation . . . by grade for grades seven to twelve, by sex and by sex within race/ethnicity categories" (McMillen et al. 1994). This is an ambitious and laudable undertaking. If it is successful, it will obviously fill in many of the intercensal gaps in reports of school dropout and retention for state and local areas. However, given the difficulty of imposing standard definitions across localities and states and of linking school-leavers to reenrollment, I suspect that it will be a long time before this project yields nationally useful cross-section or time-series estimates.

The Census Bureau's plans for continuous measurement are another distant, but attractive possibility for the improvement of educational indicators below the national level. Briefly, the Bureau is hoping to introduce a very large national sample survey operation, perhaps with as many as two hundred fifty thousand households per month. This would eventually replace the long form in the decennial census of population, and it would be designed to produce reliable data for very small areas, such as census tracts, when the data are accumulated over a three- to five-year period. Assuming that the content of this survey would be similar to that of recent decennial censuses or to the March Current Population Survey, it would present very rich possibilities for estimation of school dropout and completion on a regular basis, well below the national level. Very serious design and operational issues must be addressed before continuous measurement becomes a reality, but it does offer the possibility of vast improvement in our ability to monitor the process of schooling.

This research was supported in part by grants from the Office of the Assistant Secretary for Planning and Evaluation, U.S. Department of Health and Human Services; from the National Institute on Aging; and from the Spencer Foundation. It was carried out using facilities of the Center for Demography and Ecology at the University of Wisconsin–Madison, for which core support comes from the National Institute of Child Health and Human Development, and facilities of the Institute for Research on Poverty, which is supported by a grant from the Office of Assistant Secretary for Planning and Evaluation, U.S. Department of Health and Human Services. I thank Linda Jordan, James A. Dixon, Taissa S. Hauser, Julia Gray, and Yu Xie for assistance in the preparation and documentation of the Uniform October Current Population Survey file, 1968–1990. Those data are available from the Interuniversity Consortium for Political and Social Research. I thank Jennifer C. Day of the U.S. Bureau of the Census for providing unpublished tabulations from the Current Population Survey.

NOTES

1. Indeed, as discussed later, the National Educational Goals Panel recently changed its criterion of high school completion from 90 percent at ages nineteen and twenty to 90 percent at ages eighteen to twenty-four.

2. According to the *Report* these rates are based on data from the October 1992 Current Population Survey, and "Persons still enrolled in high school were not included in the calculation" (National Educational Goals Panel 1994: 133). I was initially unable to reconcile the figures in the 1994 *Report* with data on school enrollment and completion by age in 1992 reported by the U.S. Bureau of the Census (1993: table 3). The *Report* uses "Whites" to refer to "Non-Hispanic Whites" and "Blacks" to refer to "Non-Hispanic Blacks," but without documenting either convention, for the quoted figures are reported by McMillen, Kaufman, and Whitener for those population groups (1994).

3. The employment rate is just the ratio of employed persons to the total population in the specified group; that is, it ignores labor force status. These persons are old enough so differentials in age between recent dropouts and graduates should not much affect employment differentials; indeed, for dropouts and graduates of the same age, experience is inverse to schooling.

4. Graduates are individuals with exactly twelve years of schooling or a high school diploma or equivalent. Data for Hispanic women are unreliable and are not shown.

5. The earnings of white male high school graduates have also declined in real terms.

6. The recency of the data in the spring 1994 report of the Children's Defense Fund (CDF) would appear to be about a year off, relative to the availability of data. The CDF series ends in 1991 yet, by the fall of 1994, the National Center for Education Statistics (NCES) reported dropout rates for 1993 from the same source, the October Current Population Survey (McMillen et al. 1994).

7. The 1994 *Kids Count Data Book* notes, "This measure is not the same as a dropout rate. Some of those who fail to graduate on time are dropouts, but others are simply falling behind their peers. It is worth noting, however, that those who fall behind age/grade norms are more susceptible to dropping out eventually" (1994).

8. The new *Kids Count* dropout measure is admirably unique among education indicators drawn from the Current Population Survey, in that it is based on nine months of data for each year, from September through May, and the reported figures are based on three-year averages.

9. Because of the post-1991 change in the CPS measure of high school dropout, I show a break in each series between 1991 and 1992. *The Condition of Education 1994* reports data for 1992 and notes but makes no adjustment for the change in procedure.

10. Because of unreliability in the data for blacks and Hispanics, these estimates are based on three-year averages of the reported annual rates through 1990.

11. Other problems with the new CPS education item fall outside the scope of this discussion.

12. This problem was exacerbated in the 1990 Census because there was no separate question on the grade level of persons currently enrolled in school. That is, grade level had to be inferred from educational attainment. Because the educational attainment question grouped some levels of schooling and elided the distinction between attending and completing a grade, it was not a suitable tool for the analysis of age-grade progression.

13. A cross-classification of the two items by age might be instructive. That is, if the Bureau's understanding of the sources of the noncertified twelfth-grade completers is correct, noncertification should occur much more often among younger than older persons.

14. There is 50 percent overlap, year to year, in CPS samples for the same month.

15. One reasonably good series is used by the National Opinion Research Center in its General Social Survey.

16. These data are reported by McMillen, Kaufman, and Whitener (1994, appendix C).

17. The estimates assume independence from year to year in samples with equal standard errors. This overstates sampling error, for the overlap of CPS samples from one year to the next reduces variability in estimates of change. However, even if there were sampling error in only one of any two adjacent years, we should have to see a shift of about 1.5 percentage points in the white population, 5.2 points in the black population, and 8.6 points in the Hispanic population before we could conclude that anything had changed from one year to the next.

18. This series is based on published tables in *Current Population Reports*, rather than on the special tabulations reported by McMillen, Kaufman, and Whitener (1994) because the latter tabulations are not disaggregated by single years of age. In figure 8.10, the data for whites refer to the counts for non-Hispanic whites, but Hispanics have not been excluded from the counts for blacks.

19. I assume that the low correlations among American Indians and Asian and Pacific Islanders can be attributed to the very small size of these populations in some states.

20. For example, these are the rates shown in figures 8.4 to 8.6 for years since 1967, aggregated across grades ten to twelve. The series can be extended back to 1967, except in the case of Hispanics.

21. For further discussion of the conceptualization and measurement of high school dropout, see Kominski (1990) and Pallas (1989).

22. There is also a minor break in the series between 1986 and 1987, when new editing rules were adopted. The effect of the change was to reduce dropout rates by about 0.5 percentage points.

23. The effect of the changing definition is especially large among overage students covered by the annual dropout concept, that is, persons aged twenty to twenty-four, and there is scarcely a blip in the series below age twenty. Thus, an alternative to revising the definition of high school completion used in the series would be to limit the dropout rate to students aged fifteen to nineteen.

24. This file is available from the Interuniversity Consortium for Political and Social Research.

25. In *Dropout Rates in the United States: 1994* marginal event dropout and persistence rates are presented by sex, race/ethnicity, family income, region, and metropolitan status. Time series of rates are presented only by race/ethnicity and by age. More detailed time-series were presented in earlier years, for example, by McMillen, Kaufman, and Whitener (1994).

26. These are reproduced from Hauser and Phang (1993).

27. The six panels of this and the next figure are prepared to the same scale in order to facilitate comparison.

28. Social background includes all of the variables mentioned earlier that are available in the uniform October CPS files.

29. This is a norming assumption; it does not mean that the model pertains only to dependent youth. Data for nondependent youth have been used to estimate effects of dependency status, sex, year, grade level, race/ethnicity, and regional and metropolitan location.

30. The October CPS data are reported separately and consistently for seventeen very large metropolitan areas from 1968 to the present. It was not possible, for reasons of confidentiality, to identify all states until the mid-1980s, but most states are identifiable in each survey year.

REFERENCES

Annie E. Casey Foundation. 1994. *Kids Count Data Book: State Profiles of Child Well-Being, 1994.* Baltimore, Md.: Annie E. Casey Foundation.

———. 1995. *Kids Count Data Book: State Profiles of Child Well-Being, 1995.* Baltimore, Md.: Annie E. Casey Foundation.

Astone, Nan Marie, and Sara McLanahan. 1991. "Family Structure, Parental Practices, and High School Completion." *American Sociological Review* 56(3): 309–20.

Bielby, William T., Robert M. Hauser, and David L. Featherman. 1977. "Response Errors of Black and Non-Black Males in Models of the Intergenerational Transmission of Socioeconomic Status." *American Journal of Sociology* 82: 1242–88.

Cameron, Stephen, and James Heckman. 1992. "The Nonequivalence of High School Equivalents." University of Chicago, Unpublished manuscript.

Children's Defense Fund. 1994. *The State of America's Children Yearbook: 1994.* Washington, D.C.: Children's Defense Fund.

———. 1995. *The State of America's Children Yearbook: 1995.* Washington, D.C.: Children's Defense Fund.

———. 1996. *The State of America's Children Yearbook: 1996.* Washington, D.C.: Children's Defense Fund.

Dickens, Charles. 1989. *A Tale of Two Cities.* New York: Bantam Books.

Ekstrom, Ruth B., Margaret E. Goertz, Judith M. Pollack, and Donald A. Rock. 1986. "Who Drops Out of High School and Why? Findings from a National Study." *Teacher's College Record* 87(3): 356–73.

Frase, Mary J. 1989. "Dropout Rates in the United States: 1988." National Center for Education Statistics, Analysis Report 89-609. Washington, D.C.: U.S. Department of Education, Office of Educational Research and Improvement.

Hauser, Robert M. 1991. "Reply to Michael Gillespie's Comment on Models of Sibling Resemblance." *American Journal of Sociology* 97: 206–9.

———. 1993. "Trends in College Entry Among Blacks, Hispanics, and Whites." In *Studies of Supply and Demand in Higher Education*, edited by Charles Clotfelter and Michael Rothschild. Chicago, Ill.: University of Chicago Press.

Hauser, Robert M., and Taissa S. Hauser. 1993. *Current Population Survey, October Person-Household Files, 1968–1990: Cumulative Codebook.* Madison, Wisc.: Center for Demography and Ecology, Department of Sociology, University of Wisconsin–Madison.

Hauser, Robert M., Linda Jordan, and James A. Dixon. 1993. *Current Population Survey, October Person-Household Files, 1968–1990.* Madison, Wisc.: Center for Demography and Ecology, Department of Sociolgy, University of Wisconsin–Madison.

Hauser, Robert M., and Hanam Samuel Phang. 1993. *Trends in High School Dropout Among White, Black, and Hispanic Youth, 1973 to 1989.* Madison, Wisc.: Institute for Research on Poverty.

Haveman, Robert, Barbara L. Wolfe, and James Spaulding. 1991. "Educational Achievement and Childhood Events and Circumstances." *Demography* 28(1): 133–157.

Jaeger, David A. 1993. "The New Current Population Survey Education Variable: A Recommendation," Research Reports 93-289. The University of Michigan, Population Studies Center.

Kaufman, P., M. M. McMillen, E. Germino-Hausken, and D. Bradby. 1992. *Dropout Rates in the United States: 1991.* National Center for Education Statistics, Analysis Report 92-129. Washington, D.C.: U.S. Department of Education, Office of Educational Research and Improvement.

Kaufman, Phillip, and Mary J. Frase. 1990. *Dropout Rates in the United States: 1989.* National Center for Education Statistics, Analysis Report 90-659. Washington, D.C.: U.S. Department of Education, Office of Educational Research and Improvement.

Kaufman, Phillip, Marilyn M. McMillen, and S. Whitener. 1991. *Dropout Rates in the United States: 1990.* National Center for Education Statistics, Analysis Report 91-053. Washington, D.C.: U.S. Department of Education, Office of Educational Research and Improvement.

Kominski, Robert. 1990. "Estimating the National High School Dropout Rate." *Demography* 27(2): 303–11.

Kominski, Robert, and Andrea Adams. 1993. "School Enrollment—Social and Economic Characteristics of Students: October 1992." *Current Population Reports*, Series P-20, no. 474. Washington: U.S. Government Printing Office for U.S. Bureau of the Census.

———. 1994. "Educational Attainment in the United States: March 1993 and 1992." *Current Population Reports*, Series P-20, no. 476. Washington: U.S. Government Printing Office for U.S. Bureau of the Census.

Krein, Shelia Fitzgerald, and Andrea H. Beller. 1988. "Educational Attainment of Children from Single-Parent Families: Differences by Exposure, Gender, and Race." *Demography* 25(2): 221–34.

Lawton, Millicent. 1996. "Graduation-Rate Data Spur Questions About School Quality." *Education Week*, September 18, 1996, p. 6.

Mare, Robert D. 1995. "Changes in Educational Attainment, School Enrollment, and Skill Levels." In *State of the Union*, vol. 1, edited by Reynolds D. Farley. New York: Russell Sage Foundation.

McLanahan, Sara. 1985. "Family Structure and the Reproduction of Poverty." *American Journal of Sociology* 90(4): 873–901.

McMillen, M. M., and P. Kaufman. 1996. *Dropout Rates in the United States: 1994*. National Center for Education Statistics, Analysis Report 96-863. Washington, D.C.: U.S. Department of Education, Office of Educational Research and Improvement.

McMillen, M. M., P. Kaufman, E. Germino-Hausken, and D. Bradby. 1993. *Dropout Rates in the United States: 1992*. National Center for Education Statistics, Analysis Report 93-464. Washington, D.C.: U.S. Department of Education, Office of Educational Research and Improvement.

McMillen, M. M., P. Kaufman, and S. Whitener. 1994. *Dropout Rates in the United States: 1993*. National Center for Education Statistics, Analysis Report 94-669. Washington, D.C.: U.S. Department of Education, Office of Educational Research and Improvement.

Murnane, Richard J., and Frank Levy. 1993. "Why Today's High-School Educated Males Earn Less Than Their Fathers Did: The Problem and an Assessment of Responses." *Harvard Educational Review* 63(1): 1–20.

Murphy, Kevin, and Finis Welch. 1989. "Wage Premiums for College Graduates: Recent Growth and Possible Explanations." *Educational Researcher* 18(4): 17–26.

National Center for Education Statistics. 1994. *The Condition of Education 1994*. Washington: U.S. Government Printing Office.

———. 1995. *The Condition of Education 1995*. Washington: U.S. Government Printing Office.

———. 1996. *The Condition of Education 1996*. Washington: U.S. Government Printing Office.

National Educational Goals Panel. 1994. *The National Educational Goals Report: Building a Nation of Learners, 1994*. Washington: U.S. Government Printing Office.

———. 1995. *The National Educational Goals Report: Building a Nation of Learners, 1995*. Washington: U.S. Government Printing Office.

———. 1996. *The National Educational Goals Report: Building a Nation of Learners, 1996*. Washington: U.S. Government Printing Office.

Office of Educational Research and Improvement. 1993. *Reaching the Goals: Goal 2, High School Completion*, Technical Report. Washington: U.S. Government Printing Office for U.S. Department of Education.

Pallas, Aaron M. 1989. "Conceptual and Measurement Issues in the Study of School Dropouts." In *Research in the Sociology of Education and Socialization*, vol. 8. Greenwich, Conn.: JAI Press.

Sandefur, Gary D., Sara McLanahan, and Roger A. Wojtkiewicz. 1992. "The Effects of Parental Marital Status During Adolescence on High School Graduation." *Social Forces* 71(1): 103–121.

Schrieber, Daniel, Ed. 1967. *Profile of the School Dropout*. New York: Vintage.

Tomlinson, Tommy, Mary Frase, Donald Fork, and Rene Gonzalez. 1993. "Reaching the Goals: Goal 2, High School Completion." Technical Report. Washington, D.C.: Office of Educational Research and Improvement, U.S. Department of Education.

U.S. Bureau of the Census. 1993. "School Enrollment—Social and Economic Characteristics of Students: October 1992." *Current Population Reports*, series P-20, no. 474. Washington: U.S. Government Printing Office.

———. 1994. *Education in the United States*. Washington: U.S. Government Printing Office.

———. 1996. "Educational Attainment in the United States: March 1995." *Current Population Reports*, series P-20, no. 489. Washington: U.S. Government Printing Office.

U.S. Department of Education. 1990. "National Goals for Education." Washington: U.S. Government Printing Office.

9

Postsecondary and Vocational Education: Keeping Track of the College Track

Thomas J. Kane

THROUGHOUT THE 1980s, the value of a college education increased dramatically as the earnings prospects of high school graduates dimmed. As a result, the stakes have been raised in the debate over college costs, access to college, and the payoffs to different types of postsecondary education. While high school gradua-tion was the critical hurdle facing youth two decades ago, college attendance is increasingly the prerequisite for a decent standard of living today. Unfortunately, our data collection methods have failed to keep pace with these important devel-opments in the labor market, leaving us guessing about many crucial questions regarding the well-being of youth of college age. In the following chapter, I survey the most important measures related to postsecondary education. The discussion is organized around three primary areas of concern: access (who is enrolled in postsecondary education and in various types of institutions?); cost (how much are students and the state and federal government investing in post-secondary education?); and the payoffs to different types of education (how much does such an education seem to influence one's earning prospects later in life?). Each section contains a description of available data and suggestions for revising available measures.

The four primary recommendations are described as follows:

• Collect parental education and occupation information for young adults (ages sixteen to twenty-four) on the Current Population Survey (CPS).

Given the CPS household definition, it is not possible to match youth out-comes to parental characteristics once youth move out of the household. As a result, though real public tuition levels increased by 50 percent during the 1980s, the impacts on the gap in college entry for youth of varying socioeconomic back-grounds is unclear. Given the rising importance of college entrance for one's lifetime earnings prospects, this hole in our statistical system should be filled.

• Develop a small number of student profiles, specifying family income and sav-ings levels, and interview the state financial aid offices directly to learn about available state grants each year.

Recent tuition increases have highlighted the importance of keeping track of the costs of college attendance, which varies in important ways by state. Total spending levels for federal and state financial aid programs tell us little about the costs for any particular student. Further, state and federal benefit formulae may interact in unknown ways. The Department of Education interviewed fifty to seventy thousand students during the 1986–1987, 1989–1990, and 1992–1993 school years to learn about multiple program eligibility. A lower cost method that would allow for more frequent observations would involve surveys of state financial aid offices, asking them to calculate student aid eligibility for various types of students. The use of profiles would also improve the reporting of the results of these large surveys.

• Report estimates of the earnings foregone by students attending college.

Policymakers have typically focused upon tuition levels and financial aid data in considering the costs of a college education. However, there is a considerable amount of cost-sharing in higher education not reflected in tuition payments. Foregone earnings totaled more than fifty billion dollars annually (1991 dollars) since 1985, approximately nine times the size of Pell Grant spending in 1992. Further, these costs have declined throughout the 1980s as the earnings prospects of high school graduates have dimmed.

• Experiment with questions to distinguish prior attendance at two-year, four-year, and vocational schools as a supplement to the CPS educational attainment question.

Only a few panel data sets allow one to identify the distinct returns to different types of postsecondary education. These include the National Longitudinal Study of the High School Class of 1972, the latest follow-up of the High School and Beyond Survey, and the National Longitudinal Survey of Youth. While valuable, these surveys do not allow one to study potential differences in age earnings profiles beyond fourteen years after high school graduation. The much larger sample provided by the CPS may prove useful in measuring these payoffs more precisely, albeit without the benefit of standardized test scores and family background as regressors.

• Collect unemployment insurance (UI) wage record data for a targeted sample of urban youth attending urban high schools. The longitudinal surveys have typically missed a large proportion of the youth attending private vocational schools. With a more targeted sample, response rates may rise.

While we have known little about the payoffs to a community college education until recently, we know even less about the payoffs to training at proprietary schools. Yet these schools currently claim a fifth of Pell Grant and student loan funds. The large panel surveys have not succeeded in collecting transcript information from these institutions. Rather than attempting to collect transcript and earnings data for all the schools attended by a random sample of students from a particular high school class, we may be better off with a more targeted sample of youth from a much smaller number of urban high schools and concentrate our resources to achieve higher response rates from these institutions.

Each of these recommendations is discussed in more detail in this chapter.

MEASURING ACCESS: HOW HAS COLLEGE ENTRY VARIED BY FAMILY SOCIOECONOMIC STATUS?

The two primary sources of annual data on college enrollment are the Current Population Survey (CPS) and the fall enrollment estimates from the Integrated Postsecondary Education Data System (IPEDS). While the CPS estimates are drawn from responses to a household survey, the IPEDS estimates are based upon an annual census of U.S. postsecondary institutions. The following discussion outlines the advantages and disadvantages of each.

Integrated Postsecondary Education Data System

Since 1965, the National Center for Education Statistics has conducted an annual census of roughly four thousand institutions accredited at the college level (or that were not accredited but granting bachelor's degrees or higher). Since 1976, in an attempt to monitor college access by race, the Office of Civil Rights has also required institutions to report biennially enrollment of students by race and gender.

Despite their widespread use, the IPEDS enrollment data are misleading indicators of college entry. Total student enrollment conflates at least three distinct factors: the duration of college enrollment, college entry, and the size of the underlying population. For instance, as reported in table 9.1, the number of students enrolled in higher education increased by 18 percent between 1980 and 1994. (This increase was similar to the increase in college enrollment reported in the CPS household survey over the same period: 22 percent.) However, this understated the extent of the increase in college entry since the number of youth of traditional college age, eighteen to twenty-four, fell by 17 percent. As reported in table 9.1, the proportion of eighteen- to twenty-four-year-olds enrolled in college in the October CPS actually increased by 33 percent, almost twice as fast as the increase in total enrollment in the IPEDS.[1] Therefore, while the IPEDS data may be useful to the Department of Education for other reasons, it is not very informative regarding issues of college access (that is, the proportion of youth entering college).

Table 9.1   Distinguishing Between College Enrollment and Enrollment Rates: Institutional and Household Surveys

	1980	1993	% Change
Total fall enrollment in higher education:			
IPEDS survey of institutions	12.1 million	14.3 million	+18
CPS household survey	11.4	13.9	+22
College enrollment of 18–24-year-olds:			
CPS household survey	7.4 million	8.2 million	+11
Population 18–24	29.0	24.1	−17
Enrollment rate of 18–24-year-olds	25.6%	34.0%	+32

Sources: National Center for Education Statistics, *Digest of Education Statistics, 1996*, table 203; and Bruno and Curry 1996, tables A1 and A5.

The Current Population Survey

In October of each year, a supplement to the Current Population Survey questionnaire includes questions identifying the following characteristics:

- year of high school graduation;
- current enrollment status at a college, university, or high school;
- grade level of current enrollment; and
- type of college attended (public or private, two-year or four-year).

    The results of the October supplement are published annually as part of the Bureau of the Census P-20 Series. Although the data are much less frequently used, the CPS also collects monthly enrollment data for all sixteen- to twenty-four-year-old youth, indicating whether they are enrolled in high school or college and whether they are enrolled full-time or part-time.[2]

    The strength of the CPS relative to IPEDS is that one can observe those who are not enrolled in postsecondary institutions at the same time that one observes enrollment. Therefore, rates of enrollment of various groups—rather than simple enrollment counts—are calculable from the CPS data. For instance, one can calculate enrollment rates by age, race, region, and in many of the larger states.

    However, with the current CPS we cannot calculate enrollment rates by family socioeconomic status for students above age nineteen. The primary obstacle is the CPS definition of household. According to the CPS Interviewer's Manual, one is considered a member of a household even if one is temporarily absent from the home. Therefore, college students who periodically return to live at their family home are considered members of their parents' households. Unfortunately, one does not observe any parental information for those who move out of their parents' home but do not go to college. Therefore, family background information is missing when a youth moves out of the house permanently. Even worse, the data are missing for a nonrandom subset of youth: one is less likely to observe family background for the noncollege-bound because they are more likely to be considered a new household. Figure 9.1 reports the proportion of each age group who are the children of the reference person or are other relatives of the reference person (not spouse, brother/sister, parent) by age in the 1991 Current Population Survey. Over 80 percent of those age eighteen to nineteen are still considered dependent members of a household. Therefore, selection bias, though still a worry, may not be hopeless for this age group. However, for those over age nineteen, the selection problem becomes much worse as an increasing proportion of youth have set up their own households.

    Yet it would be extremely valuable to keep track of gaps in college access by family economic status, given concerns about rising public tuition levels. Figures 9.2 and 9.3 report the proportion of dependent eighteen- to nineteen-year-olds enrolled in college in each year by family income quartile and by race. Gaps in enrollment rates seemed to grow by race and by income quartile throughout the 1980s.

    According to the American Freshmen Survey, the average age of college freshmen has also increased over time, making it increasingly important that we be able to gauge changes in access beyond age eighteen to nineteen. Given the rising

Figure 9.1   Proportion Living as Dependent Members of Households

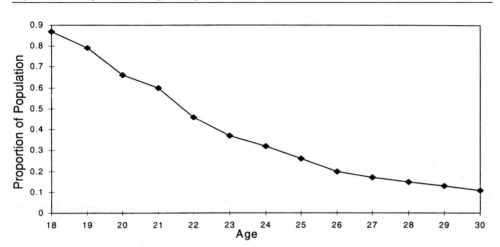

Source: 1991 Current Population Survey. Dependents include own children and other relatives who are not husbands, wives, parents, or siblings of reference person.

importance of delayed college entry and the higher stakes in evaluating changes in college access, it may be fruitful to directly collect data on parental occupation and education on the October questionnaire, rather than continue to infer family background from the responses of other household members. For instance, questions regarding highest educational attainment and occupational status of both parents of sixteen- to thirty-year-olds would provide valuable information with which to track access to college by family background even after a youth leaves the parental household.

Educational Attainment Versus College Enrollment

Enrollment rates are useful for measuring the stock of students at a point in time. However, we are primarily interested in flows, and particularly in knowing the proportion of a particular age group that had entered college or completed a degree by a particular age. The stock of college students will be sensitive to increases in part-time attendance and the timing of college entry. Changes in enrollment do not necessarily reflect changes in college entry. Reported educational attainment, rather than current enrollment status, provides an alternative measure of college enrollment rates.

Figure 9.4 reports estimates of the proportion of each cohort that reported being enrolled in college at age eighteen to nineteen and that had reported having attained some college at age twenty-three. Though both are from the CPS data, they are based upon independent samples of the same cohorts. At least on average, the two indicators have been consistent. However, there may still be higher rates of delayed entry among more economically disadvantaged youth. Indeed, if inadequate liquidity is one reason for lower entry rates among low-income youth, we would expect more delayed entry. Kane (1996) found such evidence using the NLSY data.

Figure 9.2 Enrollment Rates of Dependent Eighteen- to Nineteen-Year-Olds, by Family Income Quartile

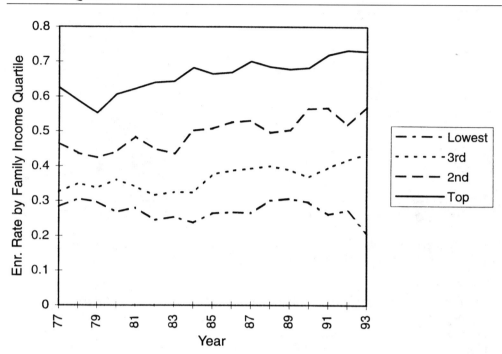

Source: Author's tabulations of October Current Population Survey, 1977 to 1993.

Figure 9.3 Enrollment Rates of Dependent Eighteen- to Nineteen-Year-Olds, by Race and Ethnicity

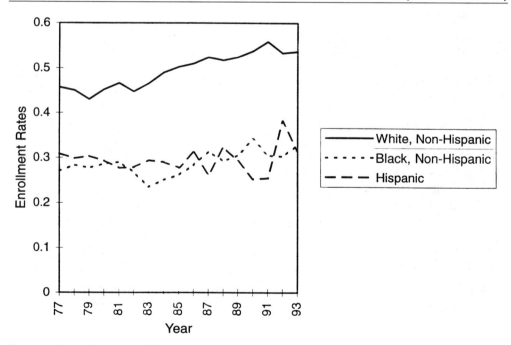

Source: Author's tabululations of October Current Population Survey, 1977 to 1993.

Figure 9.4   Enrollment at Age Eighteen to Nineteen and Eventual Attainment for Synthetic Cohorts

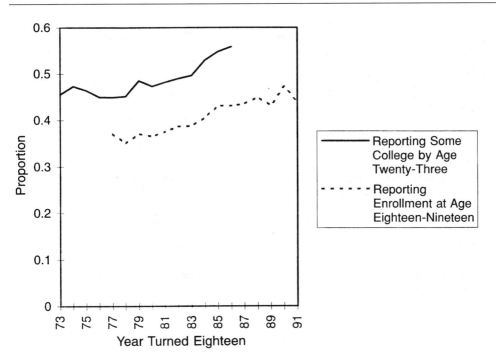

Source: Author's tabulations of October Population Survey, 1977 to 1993.

However, for the same reason discussed above, CPS data will not allow one to study educational attainment beyond high school by family socioeconomic status. There is no means for measuring family background for those who are no longer dependent members of households. The Department of Education has collected longitudinal data for large samples of the high school graduating classes of 1972, 1980, 1982, and 1992. Detailed family background data allow one to study educational attainment by family socioeconomic status. However, more than a decade has passed since the class of 1982 entered college. During that time, public tuition levels have risen more than 50 percent. Yet the impacts of these increases on high- and low-income youth remain largely unknown. As the critical threshold for economic success moves from the high school diploma to college entry and as increasing public tuition levels rise in importance, the federal statistical mission would be well served by collecting family background data at least for young adults of college entry age.

COLLEGE COSTS: IS "STICKER PRICE" A USEFUL INDICATOR?

Each year, tuition increases at public and private universities are the subject of prominent local and national headlines. However, to the extent that they inaccurately describe the prices paid by students and their families, such reporting may simply mislead students, parents, and policymakers. In this section, I evalu-

Table 9.2   "Sticker Price," Institutional Aid, and Net Price at Four-Year Colleges and Universities

Per full-time equivalent	Public Four-Year Colleges and Universities		
	1980	1993	% Change:
Gross tuition	$1,764	$ 3,129	+77%
Institutional aid	369	623	+69
Net tuition	1,395	2,506	+80

Per full-time equivalent	Private Four-Year Colleges and Universities		
	1980	1993	% Change
Gross tuition	$6,503	$10,523	+62%
Institutional aid	1,175	2,771	+136
Net tuition	5,328	7,752	+45

Source: Author's tabulations of the HEGIS/IPEDS database. Due to data limitations, all estimates combine both graduate and undergraduate students. Institutional aid includes both "merit-based" and "need-based" aid.

ate to what extent these "sticker prices" can be taken as an accurate measure of the costs of college enrollment. The "sticker price" may diverge from the actual cost to students for at least two reasons: institutional aid and state and federal means-tested aid.

Institutional Aid

The Integrated Postsecondary Education Data System asks colleges and universities to report expenditures on scholarship and fellowship aid to college students. The data for 1980 and 1993 are reported in table 9.2.[3] At public four-year institutions, institutional scholarship and fellowship aid (that is, price discounting) has been limited and generally grown proportionately with official tuition and fees. Between 1980 and 1993, gross public four-year tuition per full-time-equivalent student increased by 77 percent after accounting for inflation. Over the same period, institutional aid at public four-year institutions also increased by 69 percent. As a result, the "net price" charged per student increased only slightly faster than the official tuition increases.

At private four-year institutions, however, "sticker price" is an increasingly poor measure of the price actually paid by students and their families. Even though the gross tuition per full-time student rose by 62 percent over the period, the price discounts given to students in the form of scholarship and fellowship aid grew dramatically, by 136 percent. Even though the announced tuition increases at private institutions were nearly as large as the increases experienced at public institutions (62 percent versus 77 percent), the net price increases were much smaller at private institutions (45 percent versus 80 percent), due to the increasing price discounting at private institutions.

The data on institutional aid in the IPEDS survey suffer from at least three additional weaknesses. First, they combine graduate student aid with aid to undergraduates. Second, they include merit-based aid along with means-tested aid. Third, they provide data only on the sum of aid that is available, not the distribution of aid awards.

State and Federal Means-Tested Financial Aid

Institutional grant aid is not the only source of measurement error when using tuition to signal the direct costs of college. The Washington Office of the College Board has provided a useful public service in collecting and publishing data annually on the amount of spending on various state and federal programs over time. Figure 9.5 reports these figures for each year since 1970. Guaranteed student loans are the largest spending category. Although some proportion of these loans are subsidized in two ways—with below-market interest rates and deferred repayment—the implicit subsidy value of the loan programs is not typically reported. In fact, it is often difficult to compute, given the range of interest rates available in different programs.

Pell Grants (Basic Educational Opportunity Program) represent the largest means-tested grant program. As reported in figure 9.5, real spending on Pell Grants grew fairly steadily during the 1980s. However, these figures give a misleading impression of the amount of aid available to the neediest students. Changes in program rules—such as the exclusion of housing equity from asset values—have expanded the eligibility of middle-income students. A more useful measure of the amount of Pell Grant aid available to the neediest youth is the

Figure 9.5   Student Aid, by Source

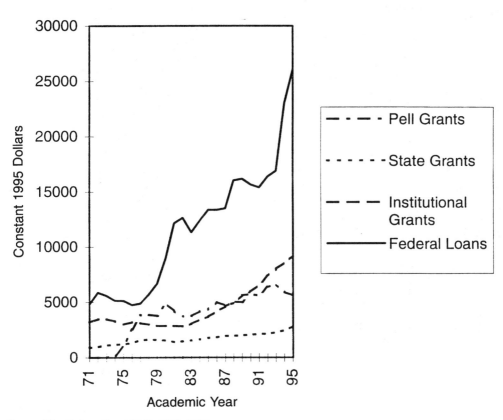

Source: The College Board 1983, 1994, 1996.

Pell Grant maximum award, which declined by 34 percent in real value between 1980 and 1995, as public tuition levels increased.

To supplement federal spending, a number of states have need-based grant programs. Figure 9.5 reported that these programs totaled roughly 2.8 billion dollars in 1994–1995, nearly one half the size of Pell Grants. Unfortunately, total need-based state grant spending does not tell us much about the costs of college enrollment for many of the same reasons that total Pell Grant program spending reveals little. Further, there is no single measure such as the maximum Pell award with which to summarize the costs of college enrollment. Aid programs differ dramatically across states. For instance, New York, Minnesota, and Vermont spent $294, $192, and $177 per eighteen- to twenty-four-year-old youth in means-tested state aid in 1992. In contrast, twenty-two states spent less than $25 per eighteen- to twenty-four-year-old youth in that year.[4] We need to learn more about the distribution of state grant aid and its interaction with federal aid programs.

National Postsecondary Student Aid Surveys

State, federal, and institutional financial aid programs overlap in ways that often are not obvious even to the policymakers involved. Benefit formulas and amounts vary across programs. Students may receive Pell Grant aid, state grant aid, and an institutional grant as well. Totaling the tuition amounts as well as grants received under various programs tells us only the average direct cost of a college education and reveals nothing about the distribution of costs. Yet it is the distribution of direct costs to students, particularly to those at the low end of the family income distribution, that concerns us.

To fill this gap, the Department of Education collected data from roughly sixty thousand college students during the 1986–1987 academic year, seventy thousand students in 1989–1990, and nearly eighty thousand students in 1992–1993.[5] The resulting reports contain estimates of the costs and types of aid received by a number of categories: public and private universities, two-year and four-year colleges, full-time and part-time students, race, family income level for dependent students. However, the published data are often difficult to interpret. For instance, it was not possible in the published tabulations to calculate the net tuition costs of students attending public and private four-year colleges for the years 1986–1987 and 1989–1990, after accounting for grant aid. As a first step, the results of these surveys could be published in a more cogent manner.

An Alternative Method of Reporting and Collecting Net College Cost Data

An alternative method of reporting the National Postsecondary Student Aid Surveys (NPSAS) data would involve the use of "student profiles." One could construct three different profiles: one for a representative disadvantaged youth, a "middle-income youth" and a "high-income youth." In specifying the profiles, one would want to specify and hold constant each of the characteristics relevant to state and federal financial aid. For instance, the disadvantaged youth may be attending a public two-year institution full-time, have poverty-level family income, two siblings not in college, one thousand dollars in personal savings, two thousand dollars in parental savings, and zero dollars in housing wealth. The "middle-income youth" may be chosen to represent the median of each of these characteristics, the "high-income youth" the 75th percentile. The mean direct costs faced by students with these profiles should then be reported by region or state (there is no such reporting in the NCES summary reports at this point) and over time. (If the sample sizes are small, one could use income and family size ranges.) The dollar figures, such as family income, would of course be indexed, but would not change with the distribution of family income of college students. The advantage of this approach is that it allows us to know precisely what is being held constant in making these comparisons.

A second advantage is that it would provide for a low-cost alternative in collecting data on state aid in the years between the national surveys. We may not need to interview sixty to seventy thousand students to learn about how different financial aid programs overlap. The National Association of State Scholarship and Grant Programs surveys its members annually, collecting data on total spending levels in various grant programs. However, as mentioned previously, the spending levels themselves need not reflect the benefits available to youth of any particular income level. Among other things, they would simply reflect differences in the income distributions across states. Therefore, the state financial aid authorities could be asked to calculate the aid available for each of the representative youths. With data on tuition costs, and knowing the Pell Grant rules, it would be a straightforward calculation to keep track of the direct costs of postsecondary education during the interim years as well as provide a check on the data collected in the NPSAS surveys. And it could be done without interviewing sixty to seventy thousand students each year. The only portion of direct costs that would be difficult to observe would be institutional aid, which tends to be low at public institutions. If public tuition levels are the price relevant to the marginal student, even this may not be an important limitation.

The NPSAS will continue to be valuable to the extent that some state aid programs are discretionary, campus-based programs, which, like institutional aid, would be missed in such a survey. Further, the NPSAS tells us about the aid actually received by students, not just their eligibility.

Foregone Earnings

In thinking about the costs of postsecondary education, higher education analysts have focused upon the components of the direct costs: tuition levels, direct subsidies by state and local governments, and financial aid. The statistics reported in the federal statistical digests reflect this perspective. However, one component of the costs of postsecondary education which is often ignored are the earnings foregone by the students themselves. Although they do not appear on any public budgets, such opportunity costs represent a large share of the costs of postsecondary education and they have been changing over time.

To estimate the size of these indirect expenditures, I estimated the following regression equation using earnings data for eighteen- to twenty-four-year-olds from the outgoing rotation groups for each month of the CPS:

$$y_i = X_i\beta + \delta_{ft}\textit{Enrolled in College FT}_i + \delta_{pt}\textit{Enrolled in College PT}_i + \epsilon_i$$

where X_i includes age dummies, race and gender dummies, and dummies for number of years of school completed. The dependent variable was reported average weekly earnings, including those with zero incomes. The sample consisted of high school graduates who were either enrolled in college or in the labor force. The coefficients on school enrollment, δ_{ft} and δ_{pt}, are rough estimates of the earnings foregone by those attending college full-time and part-time, respectively. Further, they are likely to be lower bounds, since one might have expected college students to have had higher earnings than noncollege-bound youth if they had not been enrolled themselves, given that the average college student has better high school performance, precollege ability test scores, and more favorable family backgrounds than the noncollege-bound.

Therefore, one could estimate the costs of college enrollment by multiplying δ_{ft} and δ_{pt} by the number of youth enrolled in college part-time and full-time. Table 9.3 contains the resulting estimates of opportunity costs and the earnings foregone per student. The earnings foregone by college students in a given year is estimated to total over fifty billion dollars (1991 dollars) in each year since 1985. Foregone earnings are roughly nine times the size of total Pell Grant spending in 1992 and considerably higher than the value of the state subsidies paid to postsecondary education. As these figures show, there is a considerable amount of cost-sharing by students in postsecondary education even beyond the tuition they pay.

Table 9.3   Estimating the Value of Earnings Foregone by College Students (1991 Dollars)

Year	Monthly Earnings Losses During College Enrollment: (std error)		Avg. Number of 18–24-Year-Old Youth Enrolled in College per Month: (millions)		Estimated Foregone Earnings (billions)
	Part-time	Full-time	Part-time	Full-time	
1985	−150 (16.7)	−815 (9.7)	.9	5.1	51.5
1986	−161 (18.1)	−833 (10.2)	.9	5.0	51.7
1987	−174 (17.5)	−862 (10.3)	1.0	5.1	54.8
1988	−184 (17.3)	−842 (10.6)	1.0	5.1	53.7
1989	−233 (16.7)	−895 (8.8)	.9	5.3	59.4
1990	−253 (15.5)	−878 (8.4)	1.0	5.3	58.9
1991	−281 (15.5)	−823 (8.4)	1.0	5.3	55.7

Note: All of the above were estimated using the sample of eighteen- to twenty-four-year-old high school graduates in the outgoing rotation groups of the CPS, 1985–1991. Average weekly earnings were converted into monthly earnings by multiplying by 4.33. Only those who were in school or were in the labor force were used in the sample. The separate specification for each year included gender, race, single year of age dummies, and dummies for years of education attended.

MEASURING THE PAYOFFS TO COLLEGE

The Current Population Survey has served well as an indicator of changes in the payoff to education. While the college–high school earnings differential grew after 1979, a number of published papers had noted the fact by the late 1980s.[6] Data published by the Bureau of the Census and the Bureau of Labor Statistics provide an opportunity to monitor earnings differences between college graduates and high school graduates. For instance, the January issue of *Employment and Earnings* and the annual census publication, *Money Income of Households, Families, and Persons in the United States*, provide readily available sources.

Identifying the Payoffs to Different Types of Postsecondary Education

However, our statistical system has performed much less well in identifying the returns to alternative types of postsecondary education. For instance, although they currently enroll over half of first-time freshmen, we have known very little about the economic payoffs to a community college education until recently. This has been a particularly regrettable gap in the literature, because community colleges enroll a disproportionate share of those students whose enrollment decisions are affected by state and federal financial aid policies.[7]

One important obstacle has been the lack of retrospective data on the type of postsecondary institution attended. While the October CPS asks *current* students to identify whether their schools are two-year or four-year colleges or vocational schools, one cannot distinguish between nonstudents who have attended a two-year or four-year institution. For fifty years between the 1940 and 1990 decennial census, the standard Bureau of the Census educational attainment question merely asked for the highest grade attended and whether the respondent completed that grade. A CPS supplement which asked respondents to identify the type of college attended should be considered. Such a question would require experimentation, however, because any particular student may have attended varying amounts of each type of school.

An alternative approach is to continue to rely upon the postsecondary transcript data collected for the high school classes of 1972 and 1982. (The latter became available in late 1994.) Recently, Kane and Rouse (1995b), Grubb (1993), and Hollenbeck (1993) have studied the payoffs to alternative types of postsecondary education using postsecondary transcripts provided by the National Longitudinal Study of the High School Class of 1972. Before controlling for family background and measured high school performance, Kane and Rouse (1995b) find that a full year of college credits (using thirty semester credits per year as a rule of thumb) increases male and female earnings by roughly 6 and 7–8 percentage points, respectively. After including family background, high school class rank, and standardized test scores, these estimates fall by 13–20 percent. Each year of schooling was associated with a 4–7 percent earnings differential fourteen years after high school. As mentioned earlier, the strength of the NLS-72 data is that it allows one to observe the distinct payoffs for two-year and four-year college credits. For those not completing college, Kane and Rouse estimate that a year at a two-year or four-year college would lead to a 6 percent and 3 percent increase in annual earnings for men, respectively, and a 7 percent and 10 percent increase in annual earnings for women. These differences in the payoffs to two-year and four-year college credits are not statistically significant. After correcting for computational errors in Grubb (1993),[8] one finds estimates of similar magnitude as reported by Kane and Rouse.

The high school class of 1972, upon whose experience most of the above evidence depends, graduated from high school more than two decades ago. Community colleges today are quite different. Certainly, among those completing associate degrees, there was a shift toward vocational subjects between 1972 and 1982, although the distribution seems to have stabilized after 1982.[9] Kane and Rouse (1995b) also report results from the National Longitudinal Survey of Youth, with youth who were aged fourteen to twenty-one in 1979. After controlling for family background, Armed Forces Qualifying Test scores, and work experience, even those who had attended community colleges without finishing had earnings 4–13 percent higher than similar high school graduates.[10]

The estimates from the ten-year follow-up of the high school class of 1982 will shed more light when those data are analyzed. Such long-term panel data have several advantages: they measure precollege differences in test scores and family background as potential regressors; they observe type of school contemporaneously with attendance and collect transcripts to lessen errors from self-reporting; they observe long-term earnings differences ten to fourteen years after high school. However, an important disadvantage is that they are costly data to collect. After these data from the high school class of 1982, we may not have another chance to observe the payoffs to different types of postsecondary education for another ten years, until the National Educational Longitudinal Survey of the class of 1992 conducts a long-term follow-up survey.

Identifying the Payoffs to Education for Dropouts and Short-term Students

Particularly because only a quarter of two-year college entrants from the class of 1972 completed an associate's degree and less than 40 percent went on to four-year colleges, questions regarding the value of degree completion are important. Indeed, approximately 40 percent of those who dropped out of community colleges did so after less than a semester in credits.

Beginning with the 1990 decennial census and the 1992 Current Population Survey, the Bureau of the Census changed the coding of educational attainment to reflect degree completion, rather than the number of years of schooling completed. This may seem to have been a step forward. But the Bureau of the Census simultaneously took an equally large step back. Unfortunately, precise information on the number of years of schooling completed by those not completing a college degree was lost in the transition. All those with "some college, no degree" were lumped together in one category.

However, when the new question was tested in the February 1990 Current Population Survey, it was possible to combine information on years of school completed with the degree attainment questions and ask whether those with two years of college and no degree earned any less than those with the same amount of schooling and an associate degree. Table 9.4 contains the tabulations of these data reported by Paul Siegel (1991) of the Bureau of the Census.[11] Inspecting the row corresponding to those with two years of college, it is evident that there were essentially no differences in earnings among those with no degree or an associate's degree. All three groups earned roughly twenty-eight thousand dollars per year in 1990. More recent work by Jaeger and Page (1996), using matched CPS data from 1991 (including the question regarding years of schooling completed) and 1992 (with data on degree completion), suggests larger academic associate (AA) degree effects for women and a bachelor of arts (BA) degree effects for men. There was also evidence of a BA effect for women.

The Bureau of Labor Statistics is currently experimenting with further revisions to the educational attainment data which would recapture the information on the number of years of schooling completed by those without degrees. Given the importance of observing the payoffs for short-term noncompleters, the new data will be eagerly awaited.

Value-Added Measures

Unfortunately, the CPS does not allow one to adjust for differences in family background and ability between degree completers, college dropouts, and other high school graduates. Further, even the results from the NLS-72 and the High School and Beyond depend upon the use of measures of family background, high school performance, and standardized test scores as regressors to control for any unobserved differences between two-year or four-year college students and high school graduates. These measures may only imperfectly capture the differences between high school graduates and college entrants. For instance, one common worry is that college graduates are simply more "motivated" and may have produced higher earnings anyway, even without entering college.

In other fields of social policy, experimental evaluation with random assignment has been the answer to the empirical quandary. Indeed, there have been two recent experimental evaluations of classroom training for youth. A subset of the sample in the Job Training Partnership Act (JTPA) evaluation received classroom training. The Jobstart evaluation provides another example. (For a summary of these findings, see Orr et al. 1994 and Cave et al. 1993.)

Though these results often have been interpreted as showing low payoffs for classroom training for disadvantaged youth, there is absolutely no basis in the data for such an inference. The "treatment" being evaluated is not classroom training per se. In the case of JTPA, the treatment was simply the addition of JTPA services to the current menu of options, which included attending the same community colleges used by the JTPA program, but funded by the Pell Grant program. As reported in Kane (1994b), the treatment group at the sixteen JTPA sites evaluated would have expected to have their tuition paid for at a local community college (receiving $277 more in Pell grant aid than the average tuition at these schools) and would pay $60 to attend a public four-year college in their state. Therefore, the direct costs of college entry were quite low for these youth in the absence of JTPA, given the availability of Pell Grants. This may explain the

(Text continues on p. 202)

Table 9.4 Mean Earnings by Years of College Completed and Degrees Received in the February 1990 Current Population Survey

Years of College Completed	No College	Reported Degree Attainment				
		Some College, No Degree	Occupational Associate's	Academic Associate's	Bachelor's	Master's
6+					$35,252	$42,091
					(1019)	(553)
5					35,276	40,145
					(835)	(1301)
4		$32,245	$31,135	$34,385	35,992	37,709
		(1771)	(1674)	(1998)	(312)	(2146)
3		30,224	29,735	30,845	30,923	
		(771)	(1025)	(1424)	(1930)	
2		28,928	28,139	28,558		
		(413)	(535)	(603)		
1		26,057	24,199			
		(348)	(1571)			
High school graduate	$23,858	25,802	23,310			
	(135)	(480)	(1374)			

After Including Gender, Race, and Age as Regressors

Years of College Completed	No College	Some College, No Degree	Occupational Associate's	Academic Associate's	Bachelor's	Master's
6+					$32,608 (837)	$38,772 (439)
5					33,102 (758)	37,909 (901)
4		$31,100 (1350)		$32,771 (1480)	34,124 (290)	35,036 (1592)
3		27,738 (634)	29,184 (1322)	29,813 (1377)	29,791 (1954)	
2		27,264 (413)	26,534 (660)	27,245 (674)		
1		24,056 (397)	23,988 (2042)			
High school graduate	22,070 (223)	24,382 (516)	23,339 (2116)			

Hypothesis Tests:
(p-values)

Years Zero within MA	.060	MA = BA within Years	.001
Years Zero within BA	.030	BA = Acad AA within Years	.660
Years Zero within Acad AA	.001	Ac AA = Occ AA within Years	.670
Years Zero within Occ AA	.010	Occ AA-No Deg within Years	.810
Years Zero within Some Coll	.000		

Source: Data are drawn from Paul M. Siegel, "Note on the Proposed Change in the Measurement of Educational Attainment in the Current Population Survey." U.S. Bureau of the Census, Draft, February 5, 1991. Standard Errors are in parentheses.

high enrollment rate of the control group. Even if there were a huge payoff to postsecondary education for some subset of eligible youth, we would have observed small effects of the "treatment" in these recent experiments.

In contrast, these studies often find payoffs to providing job search assistance. Rather than reflecting the relatively high payoffs to job search, such evidence may simply be due to the lack of availability of such services elsewhere.

Experimental evaluations will work in postsecondary education only if we are willing to deny access to postsecondary education to the control groups. This has not been done to date. However, the empirical challenges differ from those faced by welfare employment and training program evaluators. First, there are many more youth already participating in classroom training than there were welfare recipients in job search assistance. The costs of denying access are higher. Second, currently high enrollment rates among youth provide access to alternative forms of evidence, such as provided by the panel data discussed earlier. The value of the information gained through experiments is almost certainly lower, because there are alternative estimates. Third, there is exogenous variation in access to college due to state tuition differences and the distance of one's high school from the closest college. Both of these sources of variation could be exploited further (current examples are Kane and Rouse [1993] and Card [1994]), in addition to controlling for observed differences in family background and student test scores.

Other Approaches

Recent work by Jacobson, LaLonde, and Sullivan (1993), evaluating the payoffs to postsecondary training for displaced workers, provides another model. Rather than following a sample of high school graduates over time and eliciting data from all the postsecondary schools they attended, the authors collected the unemployment insurance wage records for a sample of displaced workers attending a particular community college in Pittsburgh as well as a sample from other displaced workers in the same area who did not.

One advantage of such an approach is that the task of tracking down transcripts from a number of different schools is lessened. Second, the strategy relies upon observing wages before and after college entrance, to allow the investigators to control for person fixed effects. Although this strategy may work for later college entrants, it does not serve well for students immediately after college since they have no wage history. Nevertheless, this approach may be quite helpful for studying private vocational schools, which have not been evaluated adequately with other data. This issue is discussed at more length in the next section.

PRIVATE VOCATIONAL SCHOOL STUDENTS

We are beginning to obtain better information on the characteristics of students enrolled in private, for-profit vocational schools or proprietary schools. Beginning in 1986, the IPEDS universe was expanded to include 5,694 private, for-profit, less than two-year institutions. Indeed, the Higher Education Reauthorization Act of 1992 required all institutions receiving financial aid to respond to the IPEDS survey, although that provision has not been enforced. By 1990, response rates of these institutions to the IPEDS enrollment queries was quite high, 92.6 percent. However, response rates have been much lower on the financial portion of the questionnaire, 65–70 percent.[12]

Using the 1987 IPEDS list of institutions as its universe, the 1990 NPSAS sample contained 8,065 students attending proprietary schools. Given that the response rates were quite high among these institutions (87 percent) (NCES 1992), we have a chance to learn something about the characteristics and methods of financing used by these students.[13] Beginning in the late 1980s, the October Current Population Survey also distinguished between proprietary school students and those attending two-year and four-year colleges. The CPS question in 1992 read as follows:

> Excluding regular college courses and on-the-job training, is . . . taking any business, vocational, technical, secretarial, trade or correspondence courses?

However, the question captured a different population than the IPEDS estimates. In the fall of 1992, the IPEDS data suggested that there were approximately 800,000 students enrolled in less-than-two-year institutions. In October 1992, 3.4 million respondents reported that they were taking vocational courses but were not enrolled in college.[14] It is not clear that this implies that the IPEDS data are grossly understated or if the CPS question is capturing those enrolled in courses offered by institutions other than proprietary schools. These potential inconsistencies deserve to be resolved by the Bureau of the Census and the Department of Education.

However, the situation is much worse for evaluating the payoffs to proprietary schools. The Department of Education monitors loan default rates, which are higher at proprietary schools than other types of postsecondary institutions. These have often been interpreted as suggesting that the education being provided at proprietary schools is not worth the tuition costs born by students. However, the higher default rates may simply be due to the socioeconomic backgrounds of the students attending the schools. This is precisely the same issue so often raised in the evaluation of K–12 schools: are low test scores measuring low value-added, or are they measuring the low starting point of their students?

Unfortunately, the panel data sets are not very useful in examining the payoff to a proprietary school education simply because the response rates from proprietary schools which have been asked to supply transcript information are quite low. In the NLS-72 transcript survey, the response rates for proprietary schools was 43 percent. Two-year and four-year colleges had response rates over 90 percent.[15] One reason for the difficulty is that the schools often close. Roughly a quarter of the nonresponse was confirmed to be due to school closings. Another problem is poor recordkeeping. Half of the nonreporting schools reported that the records were lost or destroyed. The transcript collection effort for the High School and Beyond sophomore cohort is ongoing. Despite efforts to keep response rates high, proprietary schools are projected to have response rates below two-thirds.

Rather than attempting to identify a nationally representative sample of high school students and then hunting down transcripts from the thousands of postsecondary institutions these students enter, an alternative strategy is to oversample high school students attending schools which are most likely to produce prospective proprietary school students and follow them. To the extent that many entrants may have sporadic employment histories before entry, the collection of high school grades or test scores would provide a more adequate basis for estimating value-added measures. Although the estimates may be less easily generalizable to proprietary schools outside these areas, the result is likely to teach us more about the payoffs to proprietary schools than the current system with its very low response rates.

SUMMARY AND CONCLUSIONS

Increasingly, college entry, rather than high school graduation, has become the focus of public concern, as the labor market has changed. Our statistical collection efforts should adapt to this change. There are five primary weaknesses in the current system:

- We cannot reliably observe differences in school and enrollment by family background beyond age nineteen. Socioeconomic differences in college entry rates and attainment should be monitored annually or biennially.

- While there is plentiful data on average college costs because we can observe total spending on various types of financial aid, we have traditionally known little about the distribution of net costs, particularly for low-income youth. Recent surveys of undergraduates have begun to fill the gap. However, they often have not been reported in a useful way. The chapter recommends the use of student profiles for collecting such data more frequently from state financial aid agencies.

- Foregone earnings are typically ignored in the calculation of the costs of postsecondary education. Yet this is the primary method by which youth share the costs of postsecondary education.

- We have poor data on the payoffs to alternative types of postsecondary education. Better data could be pursued with a CPS supplement asking respondents to report the type of schools attended—two-year, four-year, or proprietary school—rather than just the number of years of school completed.

- Proprietary schools receive considerable public resources but have received little public scrutiny. The traditional panel data sets (NLS-72, HSB, and NLSY) have not yielded considerable evidence. Given their importance, more targeted efforts should be directed at observing the payoffs at these institutions. Social experiments are not likely to help.

Our statistical system evolved when tuition was an adequate measure of the direct costs of college and when the differences among institutions were not as large. Now that the stakes have been raised by the rising value of a college education, we should invest more heavily in the data required to track access and affordability.

The author would like to thank Anthony Shen, who provided research assistance for this chapter.

NOTES

1. Bruno and Curry 1996, table A5.

2. All age groups over sixteen are asked about their primary activity during the previous week. "Attending school" is one of the possible responses. However, this category may miss those who are in school, but also working. All sixteen- to twenty-four-year-olds have been asked a separate question since 1984 identifying whether they are enrolled in school, regardless of what they consider to be their primary activity during the previous week. While one cannot distinguish two-year or four-year colleges or public and private institutions with these data, the base CPS questionnaire does provide a much larger sample over the course of a year than the October questionnaire alone.

3. The data in table 9.2 are drawn from author's tabulations of the IPEDS data.

4. These figures were drawn from Davis (1993).

5. For a detailed description of the results of these surveys, see the National Center for Education Statistics 1988, National Center for Education Statistics 1993a; National Center for Education Statistics 1993b; and National Center for Education Statistics 1995.

6. For a review of this literature, see Levy and Murnane (1992). They cite a number of the early papers in this burgeoning literature (Levy 1988; Murphy and Welch 1989).

7. Even though they account for roughly a quarter of Pell Grant spending and a fifth of guaranteed loan volume, these figures certainly underestimate the proportion of students who would not have gone to college in the absence of aid. Presumably, a higher proportion of four-year college-age recipients would have attended some college in the absence of aid. In simulations reported by Manski and Wise (1983), community college entrants accounted for two-thirds of those who would not have entered college in the absence of the Pell Grant program.

8. For a detailed description of these differences, see Kane and Rouse (1995a).

9. Grubb (1995) emphasizes the differences in labor market payoffs to "vocational" and "academic" credits completed in postsecondary institutions. In particular, he reports higher estimated payoffs to vocational credits for men and academic credits for women. However, despite the differences in these point estimates, tests of statistical significance would not lead one to reject the hypothesis that the payoffs were the same at conventional levels (although one could reject the hypothesis of similarity at the .10 level for men). As Grubb has pointed out, one's interpretation of these facts depends upon the null hypothesis being tested. There is simply too little evidence to settle the matter.

10. Grubb (1994) uses the Survey of Income and Program Participation to evaluate the returns to schooling. Although there is no family background or ability measure, the survey allows one to identify wage differentials by year of schooling completed and degrees received. Males with less than one year of college and no credential earned 4–12 percentage points more than high school graduates in 1984 and 1987. (The estimates in the lower end of this range are not statistically significant.) Males with one year of college earned 12–16 percent more than high school graduates. Females with one year of college earned 10 percent more than high school graduates, although the estimate is only marginally statistically significant.

11. Hungerford and Solon (1987) also report finding nonlinearities in the payoff to schooling at eight, twelve, and sixteen years of schooling.

12. These response rates were obtained during a phone conversation with Vance Grant of the National Center for Education Statistics.

13. For a more detailed description, see NCES 1993a.

14. Figures were drawn from U.S. Bureau of the Census 1993. *School Enrollment: Social and Economic Characteristics of Students, October 1992*, series P-20, no. 474, table 12, p. 47.

15. Jones, et al. 1986.

REFERENCES

Bloom, Howard S., Larry L. Orr, George Cave, Stephen H. Bell, Fred Doolittle, and Winston Lin. 1994. "National JTPA Study Overview: Impacts, Benefits and Costs of Title II-A." A Report to the U.S. Department of Labor (January).

Bruno, Rosalind R., and Andrea Curry. 1996. "School Enrollment—Social and Economic Characteristics of Students: October 1994 vs. U.S. Bureau of the Census." *Current Population Reports*, P20-487. Washington: U.S. Government Printing Office.

Card, David. 1993. "Using Geographic Variation in College Proximity to Estimate the Return to Schooling." National Bureau of Economic Research: Cambridge, Mass.: Working Paper 4483 (October).

Cave, George, Hans Bos, Fred Doolittle, and Cyril Toussaint. 1993. *Jobstart: Final Report on a Program for School Dropouts*. New York: Manpower Demonstration Research Corporation.

College Board. 1983. *Trends in Student Aid: 1963 to 1983*. New York: The College Board.

———. 1994. *Trends in Student Aid: 1984 to 1994*. New York: The College Board.

———. 1996. *Trends in Student Aid: 1986 to 1996*. New York: The College Board.

Davis, Jerry. 1993. *National Association of State Scholarship and Grant Programs, Annual Survey Report: 1992–1993 Academic Year*. Harrisburg, Pa.: Pennsylvania Higher Education Assistance Agency.

Griliches, Zvi. 1977. "Estimating the Returns to Schooling: Some Econometric Problems." *Econometrica* 45:1–22.

Grubb, W. Norton. 1993. "The Varied Economic Returns to Postsecondary Education: New Evidence from the Class of 1972." *Journal of Human Resources* 28(3): 365–82.

———. 1995a. "Postsecondary Education and the Sub-Baccalaureate Labor Market: Corrections and Extensions." *Economics of Education Review* 14(3): 285–99.

———. 1995b. "The Returns to Education and Training in the Sub-Baccalaureate Labor Market: Evidence from the Survey of Income and Program Participation." National Center for Research in Vocational Education, University of California at Berkeley. Report.

Hollenbeck, Kevin. 1993. "Postsecondary Education as Triage: The Consequences of Postsecondary Education Tracks on Wages, Earnings and Wage Growth." *Economics of Education Review* 12(3): 213–32.

Hungerford, Thomas, and Gary Solon. 1987. "Sheepskin Effects in the Returns to Education." *Review of Economics and Statistics* 69(1): 175–77.

Jacobson, Louis S., Robert Lalonde, and Daniel G. Sullivan. 1993. *The Costs of Workers Dislocation*. Kalamazoo, Mich: Upjohn Institute for Employment Research.

Jaeger, David, and Marianne Page. 1996. "Degrees Matter: New Evidence on Sheepskin Effects in the Returns to Education." *Review of Economics and Statistics* 78(4): 733–40.

Jones, Calvin, Reginald Baker, and Robert Borchers. 1986. *National Longitudinal Study of the High School Class of 1972, Postsecondary Education Transcript Study, Data File User's Manual*. Chicago, Ill.: National Opinion Research Center.

Kane, Thomas J. 1994a. "College Attendance by Blacks Since 1970: The Role of College Cost, Family Background and the Returns to Education." *Journal of Political Economy* 102(5, Oct.): 878–911.

———. 1994b. "Reconciling Experimental and Nonexperimental Estimates of the Returns to Schooling." Kennedy School of Government. Mimeo.

———. 1996. "College Cost, Borrowing Constraints and the Timing of College Entry." *Eastern Economic Journal* 22(2): 181–94.

Kane, Thomas J., and Cecilia Rouse. 1993. "Labor Market Returns to Two-Year and Four-Year College." Working Paper 4268, Cambridge, Mass.: National Bureau of Economic Research.

————. 1995a. "Comment on W. Norton Grubb, 'The Varied Economic Returns to Postsecondary Education: New Evidence from the Class of 1972.'" *Journal of Human Resources* 22(2): 205–21.

————. 1995b. "Labor Market Returns to Two-Year and Four-Year College." *American Economic Review* 85(3, June): 600–614.

Katz, Lawrence, and Kevin Murphy. 1992. "Changes in Relative Wages, 1963–1987: Supply and Demand Factors." *Quarterly Journal of Economics* 107(1, Feb.): 35–78.

Levy, Frank. 1988. "Incomes, Families and Living Standards." In *American Living Standards: Threats and Challenges*, edited by Robert Litan, Robert Lawrence, and Charles Schultze. Washington, D.C.: Brookings Institution.

Levy, Frank, and Richard Murnane. 1992. "U.S. Earnings Levels and Earnings Inequality: A Review of Recent Trends and Proposed Explanations." *Journal of Economic Literature* 30(3): 1333–81.

Manski, Charles F., and David A. Wise. 1983. *College Choice in America*. Cambridge, Mass.: Harvard University Press.

Murphy, Kevin, and Finis Welch. 1989. "Wage Premiums for College Graduates: Recent Growth and Possible Explanations." *Educational Researcher* (May): 17–26.

National Center for Education Statistics. 1988. *Undergraduate Financing of Postsecondary Education: A Report of the 1987 National Postsecondary Student Aid Study*. Washington, D.C.: Office of Educational Research and Improvement.

————. 1992. *Methodology Report for the 1990 National Postsecondary Student Aid Survey*. Washington, D.C.: Office of Educational Research and Improvement.

————. 1993a. *Profile of Undergraduates in U.S. Postsecondary Institutions: 1989–1990*. Washington, D.C.: Office of Educational Research and Improvement.

————. 1993b. *Financing Undergraduate Education: 1990*. Washington, D.C.: Office of Educational Research and Improvement.

————. 1993c. *Changes in Undergraduate Student Financial Aid: Fall, 1986 to Fall, 1989*. Washington, D.C.: Office of Educational Research and Improvement.

————. 1995. *Student Financing of Undergraduate Education, 1992–93*. Washington, D.C.: Office of Educational Research and Improvement.

Orr, Larry L., Howard S. Bloom, Stephen H. Bell, Winston Lin, George Cave, and Fred Doolittle. 1994. *National Job Training Partnership Act Study: Impacts, Benefits and Costs of Title II-A*. Draft report to the U.S. Department of Labor (March).

Siegel, Paul M. 1991. "Note on the Proposed Change in the Measurement of Educational Attainment in the Current Population Survey." Draft. U.S. Bureau of the Census (February).

U.S. Bureau of the Census. 1993. "School Enrollment—Social and Economic Characteristics of Students." *Current Population Reports*, series P-20, no. 474. Washington: U.S. Government Printing Office.

10

Indicators of Educational Achievement

Daniel Koretz

CONVENTIONALLY, "EDUCATIONAL ACHIEVEMENT" is used in social science to mean mastery of knowledge and skills or, more narrowly, performance on specific tests of knowledge and skills. Thus narrowly defined, achievement stands in contrast to "attainment," which typically is used to refer to the levels of schooling individuals complete. In keeping with this traditional if somewhat arbitrary usage, this chapter uses "indicators of educational achievement" to refer to some classes of educational tests—or, as it is now more fashionable to say, "assessments." The chapter considers recent trends in the uses made of achievement tests; characteristics of available achievement measures; limitations of the measures; issues that arise in building a system of achievement indicators; and some possible steps toward a stronger indicator system.

To understand achievement indicators, it is helpful to contrast them to other indicators of children's status, or to other social indicators more generally. Over the past decade and a half, I have worked intensively with diverse social indicators, including postsecondary enrollment rates, dropout rates, measures of progress through school, poverty rates, health-care utilization rates, and incidence and prevalence rates for various disabilities and mental illnesses. All pose vexing and, on better days, fascinating challenges pertaining to data collection, incomplete or missing data, operationalization of constructs, choice of metrics, choice of analytical frameworks, and so on. In many respects, however, achievement indicators stand out as particularly difficult. For a variety of reasons, achievement data tend to be sparser, less robust, and more expensive to obtain than data in many other areas, and they are routinely—indeed, systematically—misinterpreted by many of the key audiences for which they are produced. Moreover, at the present time, achievement data are frequently required to serve several distinct and even conflicting functions. As a consequence, the value of these data as indicators is degraded, and improvement of the indicator system is made more difficult. Some of the bases for these conclusions are discussed in this chapter.

In the following section, I will comment on the characteristics of indicators. I will then discuss current achievement measures and their limitations. In conclusion, I will discuss some of the implications for the construction of a better system of achievement indicators.

SOME CHARACTERISTICS OF INDICATORS

The characteristics of educational indicators have been the subject of extensive writings (Raizen and Jones 1985; Murnane and Raizen 1988; Shavelson, Mc-Donnell, Oakes, and Carey 1987), and to summarize that literature would go well beyond the scope of this chapter. However, for present purposes, it is important to note some important attributes shared by most educational indicators.

Perhaps most important, the basic function of indicators is *descriptive*—to describe, for example, the income distribution of households with children, the health status of impoverished preschoolers, the range of science course offerings in high schools, or the mean mathematics achievement of American eighth-graders. That does not mean that appropriate uses of indicators are restricted to simple univariate and bivariate statistics. However, it does mean that databases that are well designed, or at least efficiently designed, to provide indicators will often be poorly designed or even totally inadequate to support causal inferences.

Indicators are intended to provide descriptive information at various levels of aggregation, such as poverty rates among school-age children or relative trends in achievement among racial/ethnic groups. Data that are best suited to providing aggregate information are often not the best for providing individual data, and indeed, different levels of aggregation often call for different design decisions. As discussed in this essay, these design conflicts are acute in the case of achievement data.

Indicators are typically used to support very general, broad conclusions (Koretz 1992b). For example, for many purposes, one needs to know variations in price changes across categories of goods, but the Consumer Price Index (CPI) is not able to tell one that; it simply provides an overall index of inflation. Similarly, the poverty rate tells one nothing about changes in the income sources of poor people, but it does provide a useful if crude picture of trends in the overall incidence of poverty. Achievement indicators are no exception to this generalization. In using indicators, the public is interested in constructs such as "mastery of secondary school mathematics" or "mastery of the mathematics needed for technologically advanced occupations," not "mastery of quadratic equations" or even, in most cases, "mastery of elementary algebra." To be a suitable basis for indicators, an achievement test should be built with these broad inferences in mind.

Because of the broad conclusions that indicators are used to support, there is a pervasive tension in building indicators between comprehensiveness and the simplicity of reported data. Moreover, different approaches to simplification of the data will often produce apparently different answers. For example, trends in the *numbers* of minority and white youth enrolled in postsecondary education show somewhat different trends than do enrollment *rates*, because trends in the size of the cohorts—the denominator in the rates—vary across racial/ethnic groups (Koretz 1990). Such considerations, which are arguably more severe in the case of achievement indicators than many other types of indicators, are generally obscure to the lay audiences that are among the most important consumers of indicators.

Finally, unless they can be obtained from administrative data, indicators are most often drawn from broadly based, multipurpose social surveys. This is primarily because of the need for large, representative samples. One consequence, however, is that information pertaining to smaller groups or certain specific topics may be inadequate or totally lacking. This is particularly important in the case of achievement indicators, because they require sampling of tasks as well as sampling of individuals.

FUNCTIONS OF ACHIEVEMENT MEASURES

Achievement tests are currently used to serve three functions: *individual measurement; monitoring of groups, schools, or systems;* and *accountability.* Indicator data, including achievement indicators, are aggregate statistics used to describe the output of the educational system or its components and thus are one instance of the second of these functions. The functions are not entirely distinct in the real world. In particular, one reason policymakers want to monitor schools is to hold educators accountable. Nonetheless, these functions are to some degree inconsistent; in particular, some uses undermine the utility of test data as indicators.

Standardized achievement testing—meaning achievement testing in which tasks, administrative conditions, and scoring are made uniform—has a long history in the United States. Resnick (1982) identified the use of tests with published directions and uniform scoring and interpretation as early as the 1840s. The first standardized achievement test battery, the Stanford Achievement Test, was initially published in 1923 (Resnick 1982). The role of standardized testing grew markedly if erratically over the following years (for example, during the 1930s [Haney 1981]) and has been a staple of elementary and secondary education for decades.

The amount and purposes of achievement testing have changed dramatically over the past several decades (see Koretz 1992a). Although monitoring and accountability both provided an early impetus for achievement testing (Haney 1984), neither of these functions were salient for the first two decades after World War II. Rather, during those years, standardized tests were used primarily to assess individual students, and to a lesser degree to evaluate curricula (Goslin 1963; Goslin, Epstein, and Hallock 1965). Generally, tests were "low-stakes"— that is, the consequences of test scores were minor for most teachers and students.

The functions of achievement testing began to change in the second half of the 1960s. One critically important change was the enactment of the Elementary and Secondary Education Act (ESEA). Title I of ESEA authorized the federal compensatory education program and established achievement testing as a primary mechanism for monitoring and evaluating it. Title I programs were eventually established in the overwhelming majority of school districts, and its testing programs are widely considered to have had a seminal influence on testing throughout the elementary and secondary education system (Airasian 1987; Roeber 1988). A second milestone was the establishment of the National Assessment of Educational Progress (NAEP), a recurring assessment of the achievement of a nationally representative sample of youth. NAEP was originally intended solely as an indicator of achievement—that is, a source of descriptive information. Because its focus was all youth, NAEP originally sampled not students in given grades, but rather individuals of given ages, in or out of school. By virtue of its frequency, representative sampling, and broad content coverage, NAEP rapidly became the preeminent national indicator of educational achievement. As discussed later in this chapter, its functions are now changing, with substantial implications for a national indicator system.

The next step in the transformation of achievement testing was the growth of state-mandated "minimum-competency testing" in the 1970s (see Jaeger 1982). These testing programs aimed not merely to measure performance, but also to improve it. They did so by imposing on students serious consequences for failure. A majority of the minimum-competency tests implemented by the early 1980s were used as "exit exams" (to set a minimum standard for graduation from high school), while a smaller number were used as "promotional gates" (to determine eligibility for promotion between grades).

Close on the heels of the minimum-competency testing movement came the "educational reform movement" of the 1980s. Early in that decade, policymakers and the public became increasingly aware of weaknesses in the performance of American students. Debate about the decline in aggregate test scores that had begun in the mid-1960s (and which in fact had already ended; see Koretz 1986) belatedly intensified. NAEP revealed that many students were failing to master even rudimentary skills, and a number of studies showed that American students compared unfavorably with their peers in other nations. Growing concern was expressed in a spate of commission reports, the most important of which was *A Nation at Risk* (National Commission on Excellence in Education 1983).

This concern spawned a wave of reform policies, particularly at the state level, the most consistent theme of which was the growing use of standardized tests as accountability devices. For example, Pipho (1985) noted that "Nearly every large education reform effort of the past few years has either mandated a new form of testing or expanded uses of existing testing." This new testing was generally tied to consequences for students, educators, or entire school systems (Koretz 1992a). Overall, however, the reform movement exhibited a shift away from stakes for students and toward evaluations of entire schools or systems.

Evaluations of the testing programs of the reform movement are few, but the available evidence suggested that they could produce inflated test scores and degraded instruction (Koretz, Linn, Dunbar, and Shepard 1991; Shepard and Dougherty 1991). The programs rapidly fell into disfavor in the policy world and were replaced by a "second wave" of education reform that continues at present. The diverse programs of the second wave typically continue the reliance on accountability-oriented testing as the prime engine of educational improvement and continue the shift toward aggregate accountability and consequences for educators rather than only students. The current programs differ from their predecessors, however, in placing less reliance (in some cases, none at all) on traditional multiple-choice tests, using instead diverse "performance assessments." (The phrase is ubiquitous but has no common definition; it includes virtually anything that is not multiple-choice, including short constructed response questions, essays, portfolios, large-scale performance events, and group projects.) An archetype is the Kentucky Education Reform Act, or KERA. KERA established a school performance index that comprises both achievement tests and noncognitive measures, such as dropout rates. The tests, which are given by far the greatest weight in the index, originally included both multiple-choice tests and performance assessments; the former were dropped for several years but are currently being phased back in. KERA assigns substantial financial rewards and serious sanctions to schools on the basis of the amount of change they show on the index. Other states, such as Vermont, have instituted lower-stakes performance assessment systems in which the publication of district or school scores is expected to be a sufficient source of pressure.

For present purposes, an essential aspect of the testing programs of the 1980s and 1990s is that they use test scores for a wide range of purposes. Perhaps most important, they typically use the same tests to hold individuals accountable and to monitor progress. These roles of accountability and monitoring conflict because the latter can corrupt scores and thus undermine the value of scores as indicators. (This is discussed further in the section on corruption from behavioral response.)

The functions of aggregate monitoring and student-level feedback also conflict. Because of the broad inferences that are typically based on achievement indicators—for example, conclusions about changes in the mean "mathematics proficiency" of the nation's high school seniors—most experts agree that an assessment used as an aggregate-level indicator should be matrix-sampled. A matrix-sampled assessment includes far more items than an individual student can take, and each student is administered a sample of the items from the total assessment. This approach, used in NAEP, increases the breadth and utility of the assessment as an indicator (and also decreases the probability of teaching to the test that might corrupt the scores). At the same time, matrix sampling makes it harder or even impossible to obtain reliable and comparable scores for individual students. In state after state, however, policymakers, educators, and the public have expressed dissatisfaction with the resulting lack of student-level scores. (This was one reason why the governor of California terminated the state's nationally renowned performance-assessment program several years ago.) Assessments can be redesigned to provide student-level scores, but often at the cost of lessening the quality of the data for aggregate monitoring.

The following two sections, which discuss the characteristics of achievement measures and some of their limitations, should clarify some of the reasons why the uses of assessments often conflict.

THE NATURE OF TESTS

Lay observers often treat achievement test scores as synonymous with achievement. But in almost all cases of interest, achievement is a latent variable, and tests are an incomplete measure of it. Tests are sets of tasks designed to elicit behaviors reflecting that latent variable. Those sets of tasks are generally small samples of the "domain" of achievement they are designed to represent. Moreover, even if they are representative in terms of some ideal mix of content and skills, they are often somewhat unrepresentative in terms of formats and context, because some formats and contexts are difficult to include in tests. These sampling characteristics hold the key to many of the limitations of achievement indicators.

To illustrate the magnitude of this sampling problem, consider three domains of achievement: writing mechanics, vocabulary, and mathematics at grade twelve. The skills comprising writing mechanics are quite few. There are a limited number of rules governing, for example, punctuation or capitalization. Therefore, a test of writing mechanics can be a reasonably large sample of the relevant domain of knowledge and skills. At the other extreme, consider vocabulary. Studies indicate that reasonable fluency in most natural languages requires knowledge of literally thousands of words. Even adolescents, whose productive vocabulary often seems to be two orders of magnitude smaller, comprehend thousands of words. No one, however, is prepared to construct a vocabulary test comprising thousands of words, and no one would spend the time and money required to administer one if it were constructed. Hence tests of vocabulary are typically small—say, forty or sixty words. A test in a subject area such as mathematics may be less extreme than vocabulary, but it still represents a small sample. For example, the grade twelve NAEP test is cumulative; that is, it is intended to assess the range of mathematics skills that students are expected to have acquired by that point in their schooling, from simple arithmetic on up. Moreover, the NAEP is a broader test (in terms of the number and range of its items) than many others. Yet the NAEP grade twelve mathematics test in 1992 comprised only 179 items—an average of 15 items per year of schooling.[1]

The consequence of this limited sampling is that *scores on a test are only meaningful to the extent that one can generalize from them to mastery of the broader domain the test is used to represent.* No one cares whether some students know thirty of the specific words on a vocabulary test, while others know thirty-five. Rather, people care about differences in working vocabulary that are revealed by those differences in test performance. Similarly, when using NAEP as an indicator, few are interested in the specific items included in the tests, except to the extent that the items are illustrative. Rather, most observers are interested in what they can infer about students' mastery of elementary and secondary mathematics.

The current movement toward performance assessment has several ramifications for the adequacy of task sampling. On the positive side, this trend may result in reliance on a broader and less unrepresentative sampling of formats. To take a particularly uncontroversial example, adding direct tests of students' ability to write provides a more representative sampling of skills pertaining to writing than one would have from a multiple-choice test of language mechanics taken alone. On the negative side, greater reliance on performance assessment will likely exacerbate the problem of sampling of skills and knowledge, for two reasons. First, performance assessment tasks typically take much more time, so students can complete far fewer tasks per unit of time. Second, by virtue of their complexity, scores on performance tasks typically include a substantial amount of "task-specific variance." That is, scores are substantially affected by idiosyncratic characteristics of the tasks. The consequence is that performance generally correlates poorly across theoretically related performance tasks (Dunbar, Koretz, and Hoover 1991; Shavelson, Baxter, and Gao 1993). This is true even of essay tests of writing, which would appear on their face to have less task-specific variance than many current assessments in areas such as science, some of which entail hands-on work with materials and apparatus. Moreover, there is evidence that much of this task-specific variance is "construct-irrelevant"—that is, irrelevant to the latent variable of interest. Thus, performance assessment generally will increase the amount of time (and money) required to obtain a reasonable sample of a domain of interest. Wainer and Thissen (1993), in an analysis of open-ended and multiple-choice questions on Advanced Placement exams, humorously suggested quantifying this using measures labeled "reliamin" and "reliabuck"—unit reliability per minute or dollar—and concluded that even essay questions appreciably lower an examination's value on both measures. Therefore, performance assessment increases the pressure to rely on matrix-sampled assessments and increases the tension between providing aggregate data suitable for indicator use and individual-level data suitable for diagnosis or student-level accountability.

LIMITATIONS OF ACHIEVEMENT TESTS

Because of their characteristics, tests have a number of important limitations as measures of the latent construct of children's achievement. In this section, I will briefly describe three limitations that should be of central concern in building an indicator system.

The Problem of Limited Robustness Across Measures

Because tests are generally sparse samples from large and varied domains, results often vary among theoretically comparable measures. To put this variation into perspective, the simple correlations among well-built tests of a given domain are generally very high.[2] Despite these high correlations, however, results often do differ in important and often unanticipated ways from one test to another, particularly when statistics other than rankings of individual students are at issue.

One particularly tidy example of the lack of robustness across measures comes from the historical data maintained by the Iowa Testing Programs at the University of Iowa, which are the longest time series of internally consistent achievement data available for students in the United States. Almost all students in Iowa take the Iowa Tests of Basic Skills (ITBS) through grade eight and the Iowa Test of Educational Development (ITED) in grades nine through eleven. Thus, the ITED trends for grade nine represent almost exactly the same cohorts of students as ITBS trends for grade eight, but lagged by one year. Yet during the period of declining test scores (roughly the mid-1960s to the late 1970s), the mean scores of Iowa eighth-graders on the ITBS dropped roughly twice as much as did the scores of the same students on the ITED in grade nine (Koretz 1986).

Another, more timely example can be found in a study conducted by Linn, Kiplinger, Chapman, and LeMahieu (1992) for the New Standards Project, a national effort to develop new performance assessments that will shape instruction. Linn and colleagues examined the impact of having writing assessments scored by raters from different states. That is, students in each state wrote essays in keeping with the requirements of their own state assessments, and raters from that state used the assessment's scoring rubrics. Papers were also given to raters from other states who applied the scoring rubrics from *their* states rather than those from the students' own states. This was an attempt to discern whether locally developed rubrics can be made to reflect a common set of underlying standards. Linn and colleagues found that correlations were very high across sets of raters, but means were sometimes substantially discrepant. That is, raters from all states ranked students similarly, but they often differed in classifying their levels of performance.

The Problem of Limited Robustness Across Metrics

Another limitation of robustness is variation in results across alternative metrics. This variation can stem from the characteristics of the test itself, the choice of a scaling method, or characteristics of the distribution of scores.

More than most indicators, achievement tests lack a "natural" metric. By way of contrast, consider dropout rates. There are numerous ways to tabulate dropout rates, including the percentage of tenth-graders who fail to graduate on schedule (used in HSB and NELS) and the proportion of an age group (typically sixteen to twenty-four or eighteen to twenty-four) who are not enrolled and have not graduated (see National Center for Education Statistics 1988). These two indicators measure different things and provide very different pictures of dropout rates, both cross-sectionally and over time. But both are nonetheless variants of a single metric: a rate, with dropouts (variously defined) in the numerator and a relevant base cohort (variously defined) in the denominator.

The closest analog for an achievement test would be the percentage of items answered correctly—the standard measure for the scores of teacher-created tests that we all took during school. This ratio, however, has no clear meaning, because it is entirely a function of the specific items included on the test. For that reason, most large-scale assessments, such as commercial achievement tests and the National Assessment (for the past decade or so), avoid the percentage-correct measure and use instead one or more types of scaled scores. The commonly used scales, however, are not linear transformations of each other, and the conclusions one reaches can depend on the scale employed. Choice of scale can influence, for example, conclusions about relative trends in high- and low-achieving groups (Spencer 1983; Koretz 1986) and about changes in the variability of scores as students progress through school (Clemans 1993; Burket 1984; Hoover 1984a, 1984b, 1988; Yen 1988).

Even once a scale has been chosen, achievement indicators can present different pictures depending on which aspect of the distribution of scores is the focus of attention. For example, because the variance of test scores differs among states, the National Assessment shows that states rank differently in terms of means than in terms of their seventy-fifth percentiles (Linn, Shepard, and Hartka 1992; Mullis, Dossey, Owen, and Phillips 1991, 1993).

A lack of robustness due to metric shows up clearly in a class of indicators that could be called "representational indicators"—that is, indicators of the representation of different groups in specified ranges of the achievement distribution. An example would be the proportion of each racial/ethnic group falling into the top quartile or top decile of the distribution. In general, if scores are approximately normally distributed and have similar variances among groups, representational indicators will show progressively more extreme underrepresentation of low-achieving groups as the threshold for the indicator is raised. For example, the underrepresentation of African American students will typically be more severe in the top decile than in the top quartile. We have found that pattern in NAEP (Koretz and Lewis n.d.), and Hedges has found it in the NLS-Y (Hedges, personal communication). This pattern occasionally has been noticed in the lay world and sometimes has been cited as an indication that the educational system fails high-achieving minority students more than it fails minority students in general. While this conclusion may or may not be correct, it does not follow from the simple fact of greater underrepresentation at high levels of achievement. Rather, given certain common distributional characteristics, that pattern can stem from nothing more than a mean difference between groups.

The Problem of Corruption from Behavioral Response

Perhaps the single most vexing aspect of achievement tests for purposes of building indicators is their susceptibility to corruption from behavioral responses to measurement. This problem is not limited to achievement tests, of course. The nominal budget deficit under Gramm-Rudman-Hollings is an example of a corruptible measure. Those who followed budgetary matters during the 1980s frequently saw the Congress manipulating the Gramm-Rudman measure by doing such things as moving a military payday backward or forward to cross the October 1 start of a new fiscal year. This changed the official deficit figure for the target fiscal year but of course had no real effect on the latent variable of interest, the actual budget deficit. Another example appears to be airline on-time statistics. Airline flights are frequently on time, now that public attention is focused on that particular indicator, but this level of service appears to have been obtained in part by setting arrival times far later than actual flight time requires.

Achievement measures, however, are particularly susceptible to corruption. The mechanism of this corruption is inappropriate teaching to the test, also commonly called "coaching" or (outside the United States) "cramming." The dividing line between inappropriate and appropriate teaching to the test is hazy and the subject of intense debate, and to address it adequately would go beyond the scope of this chapter. The basic issue, however, is that if teaching is narrowed to focus on the specific content of the test, the test will become less representative as a sample of the achievement domain of interest. Scores then become inflated as measures of mastery of that domain. Quantitative research on the inflation of test scores is limited, but there is evidence that it can be large. One study found inflation of mathematics scores of roughly half an academic year by the spring of grade three (Koretz, Linn, Dunbar, and Shepard 1991).

The problem of inflated test scores indicates a fundamental conflict between two of the functions often assigned to large-scale assessments: accountability and monitoring. Accountability will typically induce teaching to the test. Steps can be taken (for example, use of a very broad, matrix-sampled test) to lessen inappropriately narrowed instruction and its deleterious effects on scores. However, it is unrealistic to expect that an accountability-oriented testing program can entirely avoid the inflation of scores. In contrast, accurate monitoring of aggregate trends in achievement—that is, maintenance of high-quality indicators—requires that achievement measures remain unsullied.

ISSUES IN BUILDING ACHIEVEMENT INDICATORS

A principal focus of this volume is the steps that should be taken to improve indicators of children's well-being. This section notes several recommendations for achievement indicators, some of which stem directly from the characteristics of achievement tests noted earlier.

Maintaining Multiple Indicators

Although the importance of multiple measures is nominally widely accepted, it is a principle often observed in the breach. Multiple measures are important throughout an indicator system because reliance on a single measure or a single database leaves the risk that substantive findings will be confounded with measurement effects stemming from the peculiarities of a sample, the specifics of a survey instrument, the operationalization of constructs, and so on. Use of multiple measures is particularly important for achievement measures, however, because of the sampling of tasks and the concomitant risk of variation among measures. The national indicator system currently includes too sparse a set of achievement measures.

Deciding on Levels of Aggregation

Existing national, state, and local assessment programs vary in the levels of aggregation at which they provide data. Various programs provide data at the levels of students, policy-relevant groups of students (such as racial and ethnic minorities), classrooms (or teachers), schools, local education agencies, intermediate education agencies, states, and regions. Currently, there is a clear trend at both the state and national levels to focus accountability pressures at the levels of schools and teachers. This is evident, for example, in the provisions of the recently reauthorized Title I program and in state education reforms in Kentucky, Maryland, Vermont, and elsewhere. This emphasis is reflected in the design of state assessment programs, which are increasingly employing matrix-sampled designs to obtain school- and district-level statistics.

The optimal levels of aggregation of course depend on the purposes of the assessment program. The goal of institutional accountability clearly suggests the need to maximize the quality of estimates at the levels of aggregation at which educational decisions are made. However, it is important to note that aggregate statistics may be important even if assessment data are to be used only for the descriptive purposes that are most appropriate for indicators. The National Assessment provides an example. Originally, NAEP was designed to provide only estimates at very high levels of aggregation: the nation as a whole, regions, racial/ ethnic groups, and so on. The NAEP sample design reflected this; samples within states were typically insufficient to provide reliable state-level estimates, and the samples in many schools were far too small to provide reliable school-level estimates. In the late 1980s, however, pressure for reliable state-level estimates increased, and Congress authorized additional NAEP samples to provide them. Currently, there is widespread interest in school-level descriptive information, such as differences in the performance of students in schools with high or low mean socioeconomic status (SES) or between students in certain types of classes. However, the sample design has not yet been altered in ways (such as imposition of minimum within-school sample sizes or adding classes as a stratum for sampling) that would support such statistics well.

Unfortunately, there are trade-offs among levels of aggregation that often go unrecognized in the policy world, and the priorities among uses of data are often a matter of disagreement. The trade-offs among levels of aggregation are of several kinds in the case of achievement indicators. Trade-offs involving *sampling of individuals* are similar to those pertaining to other indicators. For example, if NAEP were to increase within-school samples or introduce classroom-level sampling, the result would be a more highly clustered sample that is less efficient for estimates at higher levels of aggregation. This lower efficiency could be offset only by increasing the total sample and thus the total cost of the survey. Achievement indicators, however, are also affected by a variety of other trade-offs in choosing among levels of aggregation. For example, an assessment designed to provide high-quality aggregate estimates will often be matrix-sampled; this increases the breadth of the assessment and its efficiency for producing aggregate estimates, but at the cost of limiting or even precluding scores for individual students. Thus the quality of the assessment for providing information at any given level of aggregation depends largely on design decisions about sampling of both individuals and tasks—decisions that are made before the assessment is fielded. Similarly, lowering the level of aggregation increases the risk that scores will be corrupted by inappropriate teaching to the test (Koretz 1991). (For an excellent discussion of specific trade-offs that would be raised by reporting NAEP scores at the level of districts or schools, see Beaton 1992.)

Reporting by Subgroups

National achievement data are generally reported for a variety of subgroups. The National Assessment, for example, traditionally reported scores by race/ethnicity, region, parental education, and a much criticized composite urbanicity/SES measure. (This composite, called "size and type of community," classifies schools as "advantaged urban," "disadvantaged urban," "extreme rural," and so forth, based on type of community and the principals' estimates of the occupational profiles of parents. NAEP recently stopped using this as a reporting variable because of its methodological weaknesses.) State and local data are often reported for fewer subgroups; for example, some jurisdictions do not report separately for racial/ethnic subgroups.

Several limitations of the reporting of achievement by subgroups should be noted. First, reporting tends to be based on *a priori* and conventional classifications, sometimes without clear agreement about purposes. In the case of some subgroups that are of clear importance to policy (such as racial/ethnic breakdowns), this has not been problematic, but for other groupings, it has been. For example, there has been substantial debate about the background variables that should be collected by and used for the reporting of NAEP. That debate hinges on decisions not yet made about the most important purposes of the reporting by subgroups. For example, some observers would like NAEP to focus its measures on SES, but if NAEP is to report trends for schools facing particularly severe educational challenges, variables not typically considered part of SES, such as proficiency in English, may be essential.

Second, most achievement databases lack certain background variables that are potentially important for reporting. Few achievement databases, for example, include trustworthy data about household income. State and local achievement data generally have no household income data at all. (Variables such as the percentage of students receiving free or reduced-price lunch are often used as poor proxies for poverty rates.) Even the National Assessment has no income data, because it does not include a parent survey. Only occasional research-oriented data collection efforts provide reasonable income data. The few representative databases that provide good measures of poverty over time, such as the Survey of Program Participation or the Panel Study on Income Dynamics, lack achievement measures. Most achievement databases also lack information about the place of students' and parents' birth. At a time of rapid immigration, this is a serious shortcoming; it precludes not only reporting for immigrants, but also disentangling the achievement of new immigrants from trends in the performance of native-born students in the same racial/ethnic group. (For example, some observers suspect that the lack of consistent progress in the status dropout rate of Hispanics—in contrast to blacks—may reflect an influx of dropout-prone poor immigrants that obscures progress shown by native-born Hispanics.)

Third, achievement databases lack sufficient samples to report for certain potentially important subgroups. For example, for some purposes, it may be sufficient to treat "Hispanic" as a single category, but the limited available evidence suggests that patterns of achievement and attainment differ substantially among Hispanic ethnic groups. Similarly, it would be naive to expect poor immigrants from Southeast Asia to perform similarly to the ethnically different native-born Asian Americans, who typically show mean scores higher than those of Anglo students in some subject areas. Specific Hispanic or Asian subgroups, however, are mostly quite small, and a sampling rate that would provide reliable estimates for them generally would be prohibitive.

Adjusting Indicators for Compositional Differences

Achievement indicators are substantially influenced by adjustment for demographic differences. Adjustment has large effects on cross-sectional comparisons because of the typically large mean differences in scores between certain groups, particularly racial/ethnic groups. Time-series are affected by adjustment not only because of differential trends among groups (such as the now well-recognized relative gains of black students), but also because of immigration and group differences in fertility.

Whether achievement indicators should be adjusted for compositional differences, however, is currently a matter of intense debate in the policy community. On the one hand, it is widely recognized that failure to adjust for compositional differences will undermine the fairness of cross-sectional comparisons. On the other hand, many in the policy world argue that adjusting scores for factors such as differences in racial composition or poverty rates reifies current disparities in performance and undermines the currently widespread push for higher standards for all students. These arguments, for example, were recently raised in a dispute about whether National Assessment results should be adjusted to make comparisons among states "fair." Not surprisingly, research shows that state rankings are substantially influenced by differences in the composition of the student body (Linn, Shepard, and Hartka 1992). However, the decision of the National Assessment Governing Board was that scores should *not* be adjusted.

The common arguments against adjustment lose much of their force when the issue is trends in achievement rather than cross-sectional comparisons. Yet, oddly enough, changes in the composition of the student body are rarely taken into account when trends in achievement are discussed. Bracey is an exception; he has argued that trends in achievement represent a striking success when changes in the demographic composition of the student population are considered (Bracey, 1991). Bracey did not actually estimate the effects of demographic changes, however, and his assertion is overstated: demographic change can account for only a modest portion of the pervasive decline in achievement that occurred during the 1960s and 1970s (Koretz 1987, 1992c).

The importance of taking compositional changes into account is illustrated by recent trends in the SAT. The familiar trends in overall mean SAT scores are shown in figure 10.1, expressed as differences in standard deviations from the low point of 1980. Several years ago, Jaeger (1992) pointed out that the lack of improvement in the grand mean was attributable to compositional changes rather than a lack of progress within racial/ethnic groups. This can be seen, albeit not too clearly because of the large number of groups, in figure 10.2. The grand mean in mathematics was only 2 points higher in 1993 than in 1976—a difference that is small both substantively and in comparison to the fluctuations in the mean during the intervening years. During that period, however, the mean mathematics score in every racial/ethnic group other than the "other Hispanic" group increased more than the grand mean. The means for Mexican Americans and whites showed the smallest gains—only 4 and 5 points, respectively, but still double the gain in the grand mean. The mean for blacks increased by 11 points, the mean for Asian Americans increased 14 points, and the mean for Puerto Ricans increased 9 points. Changes in the mix of racial/ethnic groups in the test-taking population obscured these gains.

Figure 10.1   SAT Overall Mean Scores

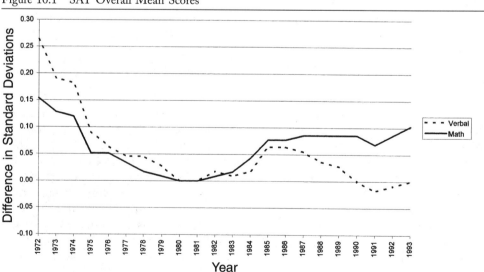

Figure 10.2   SAT Math Scores, by Subgroup

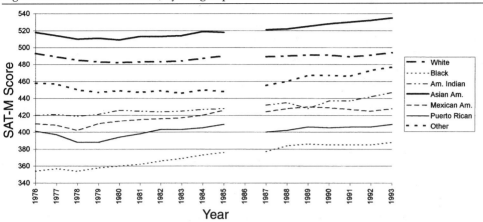

STATUS OF THE CURRENT INDICATOR SYSTEM

In the light of the importance of achievement measures and the large amount of testing undergone by American students, high-quality indicator data about achievement are surprisingly limited.

A Summary of Data Sources

Currently, debate about the performance of American students focuses on a small number of data sources. On the national level, data from the NAEP are the most salient, with lesser attention focused on college-admissions tests, occasional special studies, and international comparisons of achievement. At lower levels of aggregation, state and local data—in particular, scores on statewide assessments—are often prominent.

The following sections briefly note some of the strengths and weaknesses of major sources of achievement data. International studies raise a number of complex issues that are beyond the scope of this chapter, so they are not discussed.

The National Assessment of Educational Progress

The National Assessment has become the most salient source of data on the achievement of American students. For that reason, NAEP warrants more extensive discussion here than other databases.

NAEP's role as the leading achievement indicator is well justified. It is the only source of frequent data on the achievement of nationally representative samples of American students (table 10.1). It tests students in three grades (currently, forth, eighth, and twelth) in each biennial testing cycle. It covers a wider range of subject areas than most assessment programs, and its coverage within subjects is unusually broad. NAEP's content reflects a broadly based consensus

Table 10.1   Characteristics of Some Achievement Data Sources

	Sampling			Breadth	Validated	Useful for Trends	Potential for Corruption
	National	Ethnicity	School				
Main NAEP	Good	Good	Poor	High	Yes	No	Low
NAEP trend assessment	Good	Weak	Poor	Moderate	Yes	Yes	Low
College-admissions tests	Large, not representative	Large, not representative	Poor	Varies	Not as achievement indicator	Yes	Moderate
State and local assessments	NA	Varies	Varies	Varies	Some	Some	High
NCES longitudinal studies	Good	Good	Good	Moderate	Yes	No	Low

process. At all stages of the assessment—sampling, construction of the test, and the scaling and analysis of results—the NAEP is carried out with care and sophistication. Its methods, while arcane, are unusually well documented, and its data are always made available for secondary analysis. The entire assessment is subjected to an unusually extensive process of advice and criticism from a wide array of experts, including standing and ad hoc panels convened to advise the National Center for Education Statistics or the Educational Testing Service (the prime contractor for NAEP for the past decade) or to carry out congressionally mandated evaluative studies.

Yet for all its exceptional strengths, NAEP also has important limitations, many of which are poorly understood in the policy world and by the press.

The Gold Standard: Obscuring Problems of Robustness

Although NAEP is treated as the gold standard in much of the public debate—that is, it is considered to provide the most accurate data—it remains only one test, and consequently, its results are subject to the threats to robustness already noted. This is not a criticism of NAEP per se; no matter how carefully a test is built, it will always be subject to the possibility of limited robustness. Important results (either cross-sectional comparisons or trends over time) might be different if the test had a different mix of content, formats, or difficulty levels, or even a different type of administration. For example, black-white differences have sometimes varied across NAEP content areas within mathematics (Koretz and Lewis, n.d.). In addition, black students were more likely than whites to skip open-ended items, even after controlling for differences in total scores (Koretz, Lewis, Burstein, and Skewes-Cox 1992). Thus the mathematics assessment might show different racial/ethnic differences if the content or format mix were changed.

Threats to robustness will be exacerbated by the recent shift to reporting the proportion of students who reach a priori standards of performance. This trend, which is national in scope (it is embodied, for example, in new assessment programs in Kentucky and Maryland and was also a key part of California's (CLAS) assessment until Governor Pete Wilson terminated it), takes the form of "achievement levels" in NAEP. The three NAEP achievement levels, called Basic, Proficient, and Advanced, represent judgments about adequate achievement for each tested grade. Because these standards are judgmental, they are likely to vary if different panels of judges are used or if the judges are given a different process to follow. However, a review of a large number of articles about NAEP in the lay press in 1991—the first time achievement levels were used in reporting—found that the judgmental nature of the standards was rarely discussed, and its implications for the robustness of the results were not mentioned (Koretz and Deibert 1995/1996).

Limits of Sampling

The NAEP is to educational achievement what the Current Population Survey is to population characteristics: a general-purpose social survey the design of which represents a compromise among its many potential uses. One place these compromises becomes apparent is in NAEP's sampling design. One compromise was noted above: in the interest of efficiency for estimates at higher levels of aggregation, NAEP does not maintain within-school samples that would be appropriate for school-level analysis (table 10.1), and it does not sample on the basis of classrooms at all (even though educational practices vary greatly at the classroom level). Another compromise becomes apparent in the sampling of racial and ethnic minorities. In its assessments designed for cross-sectional comparisons (but not, as explained below, in its trend assessments), NAEP oversamples high-minority schools to obtain sufficiently large minority samples for robust estimates of statistics such as group means. However, even with this oversampling, NAEP obtains very small samples of high-achieving minority students—small enough that they are of no use for analyses of those groups. To obtain reasonably large samples of high-achieving minority students would require a substantially different design and the diversion of resources from other uses.

Compromises in NAEP's design are unavoidable. They have become a serious issue recently, however, because of the ever-expanding range of uses to which the policy community and others want to put the NAEP.

Weaknesses of NAEP Trend Estimates

Over time, NAEP will change along with expectations of what should be taught and learned. For example, the policy community currently wants more constructed-response testing and less reliance on the traditional multiple-choice format. This poses a dilemma for the assessment of trends. To alter the test too much runs the risk of confounding changes in the test with trends in performance. On the other hand, leaving the test unchanged renders it increasing irrelevant.

The 1986 NAEP assessment in reading—the second assessment using the test design and scaling procedures introduced by the Educational Testing Service when it took over operation of NAEP—produced an implausibly large decline in estimated average reading proficiency at ages nine and seventeen. This change, particularly at age seventeen, was far larger than any of the differences between two assessments since the inception of the reading assessments in 1971 (Beaton and Zwick 1990). Analysis suggested that changes in the measurement conditions (timing and item order) had added an unacceptable amount of error to the trend estimates (see Beaton and Zwick 1990). This led to the decision to separate NAEP into two assessments (Beaton and Zwick 1992): a main assessment, which is intended to document what students can do at a particular time and to monitor short-term trends; and a trend assessment, the primary purpose of which is to monitor longer-term trends. The main assessment continued to incorporate changes, while in the trend assessment, every effort has been made to maintain consistency over time.

Since then, trend and main assessments have grown quite distinct, but the differences between them—indeed, even the basic fact that they are not the same—are not widely understood among users of NAEP data. The trend results are among those given the greatest attention, but they are based on an assessment that is in many ways the poor cousin of the main NAEP assessment. The trend assessment, for example, has substantially sparser sampling of both items and students. It does not oversample high-minority schools. In addition, the trend assessment classifies students by age, while the main assessment (which samples by both grade and age) is reported primarily in terms of grades. The relationship between grade and age, however, has been changing over time. The two assessments also use different methods to delineate racial/ethnic groups: the main assessment relies on students' self-reports unless they are omitted or otherwise unusable, while the trend assessment uses the test administrators' guesses. The disparity between these methods is most extreme in grade four. For example, in mathematics in 1992, only 40 percent of the fourth-grade students classified as Hispanic by the method used in the main assessment were also classified as Hispanic by the method used in the trend assessment (Barron and Koretz 1996).

The practical consequences of these differences between the two NAEP assessments vary, but in one case they are clearly very important. As a result of the sample design of the trend assessment, NAEP's estimates of relative trends among racial/ethnic groups—one of the most important results of the NAEP assessment—have such large errors that in some instances only implausibly large changes could be statistically significant, and the magnitude of changes that reach significance can be estimated only very imprecisely (table 10.1; Barron and Koretz 1996).

College Admissions Tests

College-admissions test data, particularly the SAT (formerly the Scholastic Aptitude Test, now the Scholastic Assessment Test), have been used for years as an indicator of trends in student performance, and they still receive substantial attention, even though their inappropriateness for this use has been widely discussed. The SAT was neither designed to be nor validated as a measure of students' mastery of material taught to them during elementary and secondary education. (In contrast, the original American College Testing college-admissions tests were an adaptation of the Iowa Tests of Educational Development, a relatively difficult achievement test battery for students in grades nine through twelve.) Perhaps even more important, all college-admissions testing suffers from selectivity bias, in that students only take the tests if they chose to and can take it more than once if they wish (table 10.1). It is clear that the selectivity of the test-taking population is changing over time, but the nature of the changes are not clear and are difficult to ascertain fully. For example, one study (Beaton, Hilton, and Schrader 1977) used nationally representative data to estimate the effects of selectivity changes on SAT scores from 1960 through 1972, but I am not aware of any studies of comparable thoroughness addressing selectivity changes in more recent years. The lack of a clear estimate of the impact of selectivity changes severely limits the utility of college-admissions test data as an indicator.

Limitations of State, Local, and Private Data

Most achievement testing in the United States is conducted as part of state or local testing programs. Thus a key question is the adequacy of such data for use in an indicator system.

The usefulness of state and local achievement data in a national system of indicators is questionable. In earlier work (Koretz 1986, 1987), I made substantial use of state assessment data as a secondary source of data, to confirm or elaborate upon trends apparent in national data. However, as I noted then, the future utility of these data was in doubt even then, because the increased use of tests as accountability tools would likely lead to greater corruption or inflation of scores (table 10.1). More recently, Linn and Dunbar (1990) pointed out that many state and local testing programs have shown considerably more favorable trends than has NAEP and suggested that accountability pressures might help explain the disparity.

The utility of state data in an indicator system is also undermined by the rapid rate of innovation in state assessment programs. In response to the widespread view that teaching to multiple-choice tests damaged educational quality, many jurisdictions have been shifting rapidly to a greater reliance on various forms of performance assessment. Some of these forms, such as on-demand direct assessments of writing, have long been around and are well understood. Others push large-scale assessment into largely uncharted territory. An example is the portfolio assessment programs currently underway in Vermont and Kentucky, in which neither tasks nor administrative conditions are standardized. Another example is group tasks or hybrid group/individual tasks, such as those used in the Maryland assessment, in which part of an assessment task is carried out by a group and the rest is done individually. Research on the validity of these new assessments is only now being undertaken. Thus, whatever the mix of positive and negative effects on instruction of these changes in assessment (and there is evidence that it can have positive effects; see Koretz, Stecher, Klein, and McCaffrey 1994), they will lessen the usefulness of state data in a national indicator system, at least until validation work is completed.

Education Department Longitudinal Surveys

In the past two decades, the federal Department of Education has fielded three large, nationally representative longitudinal surveys: the National Longitudinal Study of the High School Class of 1972 (NLS), High School and Beyond (HSB), and the National Education Longitudinal Survey (NELS). NLS followed a single graduating cohort beginning in their senior year. HSB followed two cohorts, the high school classes of 1980 and 1982, and it followed the younger cohort beginning in tenth grade. NELS began with the class of 1994 when it was in eighth grade and recently completed its fourth biennial survey.

All of these longitudinal surveys include achievement measures. They provide nationally representative data, adequate sample sizes for racial/ethnic groups, and—unlike NAEP—adequate within-school sampling (table 10.1). However, for purposes of providing achievement indicators (as opposed to information on the correlates of achievement and achievement growth), these studies have two important weaknesses. First, the achievement batteries are much smaller than those of NAEP. Second, they are not designed to provide trend data across cohorts, and their achievement test batteries are therefore not necessarily comparable. The Education Department funded a post hoc study that equated the NLS and HSB test batteries and analyzed the nature of the changes in performance between the high school classes of 1972 and 1980 (Rock et al. 1985). However, to my knowledge, no comparable study has yet been undertaken with the HSB and NELS test data.

RECOMMENDATIONS FOR A STRENGTHENED INDICATOR SYSTEM

How might the national patchwork of achievement indicators be improved? In some areas, improvements in the quality of an indicator system may hinge largely on decisions about which new indicators would be most useful and which extant indicators could be jettisoned at least cost. In the case of educational achievement, however, strengthening the system of indicators would require more than a revised list of measures. It would require attention to the design and uses of the data systems in which achievement measures are embedded, the design of achievement measures themselves, and the methods of reporting the resulting data. Several recommendations that touch on each of these broad issues follow.

Distinguish the Functions of Achievement Data

If achievement indicators are to maintain their validity, and if funds for additional indicators are to be spent effectively, it will be necessary to distinguish the functions of indicator data clearly from the numerous other functions that achievement test data are expected to perform. First, it is essential that data used for indicators be protected from the potential for corruption that accompanies test-based accountability. Some people in the measurement field, myself included, have expressed concern that the use of NAEP for state comparisons may lead to its corruption. It is not clear whether this fear was warranted; state comparisons have been infrequent and may not have yet become salient enough to warrant efforts to teach to the test. However, it seems likely that the use of NAEP at the local level would pose substantially greater risks of corruption.

Second, it is necessary to clarify the distinction between data designed for descriptive purposes (even multivariate descriptive purposes) and data intended to support causal inferences. The misconception that NAEP-like data, cross-sectional and including only a weak set of potential covariates, can support causal inferences is widespread in the policy world. This was evident, for example, in the responses of policymakers and others to the first NAEP state comparisons. It arose again during the early stages of reauthorization of the Elementary and Secondary Education Act, when two senior Education Department employees informed congressional staff that they wanted a "NAEP-like" assessment of chapter 1 (now again Title I) students in order to gauge the program's effectiveness. As long as this confusion continues, it will be difficult to make sensible decisions about the allocation of resources in conducting NAEP and other data collection efforts.

Field More Overlapping Measures

The need for multiple measures of achievement is widely acknowledged in the profession even if often disregarded in practice. One reason for multiple measures is that they can assess a broader sample of the domains of interest than single measures. But at least as important is the threat to robustness noted above: even relatively similar measures that purport to assess the same constructs will sometimes provide substantially different answers. Moreover, as NAEP's 1986 reading results made clear, even well-designed assessments can occasionally produce unexpected, anomalous results. Multiple measures can provide an indication that a given pattern is robust enough to be trusted.

Fielding multiple, frequent, nationally representative assessments, however, would require a substantial and probably unrealistic increase in expenditures. A less costly alternative would be to field multiple assessments at varying frequencies. For example, NAEP could be maintained at its current biennial frequency, while other assessments, linked to NAEP but perhaps not entirely overlapping, could be conducted at less frequent intervals.

Mix Formats Carefully

Although the movement toward performance assessment is national in scope, assessment programs differ in the extent to which they place reliance on performance assessments and in the types of formats they employ. The NAEP has gradually increased its use of constructed-response items, including longer items that require more extensive use of language (for example, mathematics problems that require explanation of solutions). However, a large portion of the NAEP remains multiple-choice; in most subjects, the constructed-response items are relatively short; and all tasks are undertaken by individuals rather than groups. In contrast, many state programs have made much more dramatic shifts toward performance assessment.

The costs and benefits of various formats may not be the same for indicator systems and for accountability-oriented programs. In the context of state reforms such as those in Kentucky, Maryland, or Vermont, the quality of the measures is only one of several concerns; at least as important is the presumed positive effects—on instruction, and on learning—from using such assessments for accountability. Many proponents consider a decrement in reliability to be a reasonable price to pay for those incentives, and some would accept a decrement in some aspects of validity as well.

In the case of indicator data, however, the quality of measurement must be the prime concern. If forms of performance assessment are required to assess certain types of desired outcomes accurately, they should be included in the assessment. However, the breadth, reliability, and validity of the results must be maintained. At least for the time being, these requirements are likely to necessitate a substantial reliance on items that can be answered quickly and scored cheaply, including both multiple-choice and short constructed response items. Innovative formats may be included for experimentation and evaluation, but their results should only be used in reporting once they are adequately validated and if their benefits for purposes of monitoring outweigh their costs.

Field Complementary, Focused Data Collection

Because NAEP is designed to provide efficient estimates of performance for the American student population as a whole, it is not able to provide adequate estimates of many important aspects of achievement. And for reasons noted above, other data sources, such as college-admissions tests and state assessment data, provide inadequate supplements. For example, there are no nationally representative data providing an adequate view of trends in the performance of high-achieving high-school students. NAEP is not adequate for this purpose because of limited sampling of high-achieving students (particularly high-achieving minority students) and its dearth of test items appropriate for students at that level. College-admissions test data are inadequate for this purpose because of selectivity bias.

Therefore, to provide a stronger system of achievement indicators, large-scale broad-purpose surveys such as NAEP should be complemented with less frequent data-collection efforts focused on populations or topics that require different sampling of students or tasks. Both the content of these studies and their frequency are matters of judgment and disagreement. For example, in recent years, one very large and expensive supplement was added to NAEP: the Trial State Assessment (TSA), which provides achievement estimates for states and for a few subgroups within them. On the one hand, critics have argued that TSA may be a poor use of the large amount of money it requires, because it cannot support the causal inferences that many of its proponents want, will confirm many things that are widely known already (that states such as Minnesota and Iowa outscore states such as Louisiana and Mississippi), and lacks the ability to clarify whether the few surprising findings are really robust (Koretz 1991).

The limitations of NAEP TSA do not imply that it has no value. On the contrary, the TSA can clarify where problems of low achievement are most severe, even if it cannot explain those findings. Given NAEP's credibility, such findings might be very useful even if they are unsurprising to experts. Second, TSA could serve as an audit test, signaling when trends in scores on state-administered tests are grossly inflated.[3] However, the resources devoted to the TSA might be directed to other uses that could do more to strengthen a system of national indicators of achievement. In particular, those resources could be spent on targeted studies of important populations and topics that neither NAEP nor other current databases can address. The possibilities are numerous.

Studies of Special Populations   Complementary studies of specific populations poorly sampled by broad-purpose surveys such as NAEP and NELS could be valuable to policymakers and the public. Among the groups that might be appropriate focuses of such studies are high-achieving students, immigrant children (and children of immigrants), children with limited proficiency in English, disabled students, and ethnic groups that are too small for routine oversampling, such as various Hispanic groups and immigrant Asian groups. NAEP-like studies of at-risk populations could also be very valuable, albeit not for the program-evaluation function proposed by some advocates.

Complementary studies might also be used to provide a broader range of information about certain groups of students who are already adequately sampled for certain statistics. African American students provide a good example. Although NAEP currently provides a good cross-sectional estimate of the mean score of African American students, it offers only a fairly error-prone estimate of trends in that mean over time and virtually no useful information about high-achieving black students (because there are too few in the sample). Periodic larger samples of African American students could ameliorate some of these limitations.

Periodic special studies might also be used to provide reliable data at levels of aggregation that currently are not well supported by NAEP or other databases—for example, to provide robust estimates of achievement trends in different types of schools or to investigate changes in the instructional resources provided to students in different types of classes and schools.

Achievement Supplements to Longitudinal Surveys   The NELS, HSB, and NLS all include achievement measures, but NELS did not begin until eighth grade, and HSB did not begin until tenth. In addition, these surveys do not include the detailed measurement of income, program participation, and other important social constructs that are measured by longitudinal surveys like PSID and SIPP. An achievement supplement to one or more such surveys (which could use an adaptation of the NAEP item bank) could provide valuable information—for example, differences in achievement (rather than just attainment) between children who are poor long term and short term.

Studies of Different Achievement Constructs   Complementary, less frequent studies could also be used to provide measures of a wider array of achievement constructs. The infrequent national surveys of literacy in the young adult population provide a good example of one of the few such efforts already in place. It could be very useful, for example, to put in place a periodic survey of higher levels of high school mathematics and science—using items more difficult than most now in NAEP while avoiding the selectivity bias that plagues data such as the College Board Achievement Tests or American College Testing (ACT) college admissions tests.

Experiment with Multiple Metrics

Because different metrics often provide different views of patterns of achievement, it will often be important to present key findings about achievement using several different measures. For example, there are several reasons to complement mean or median differences among groups with "representational indicators," such as the proportion of students in each group falling into high quantiles or the proportion reaching high a priori standards. One reason is the fact that lay audiences will rarely understand the implications of a simple difference in central tendency for the proportion of students reaching a given threshold; another is that the policy world currently places great emphasis on the proportion of students reaching high standards. (There are also reasons not to report *only* the proportion of students reaching standards, including lesser precision of estimates and, in the case of unreliable measures, bias; see Koretz, Stecher, Klein, and McCaffrey 1994.)

However, recent experience (Koretz and Deibert 1995/1996) has shown that some current approaches to reporting are not effective with lay audiences. Some efforts are now under way to gain more understanding of the impact of alternative presentations on lay understanding of assessment results, but knowledge is still very limited. Accordingly, development of reporting metrics should be accompanied by an active program of research and evaluation.

Present Simple Statements of Confidence or Robustness

Because lay audiences comprise many of the key users of indicator data, the problem of finding a way to express degrees of confidence in terms they can understand affects all of the indicators under discussion in this volume. It is clear that simple statements of statistical significance are often found incomprehensible, but it remains less clear what alternative presentations might be more effective. In the case of assessment indicators, this problem is compounded by the relative importance of other, nonsampling threats to robustness, such as simple measurement error or potentially systematic differences attributable to the specifics of test construction. These nonsampling sources of error are rarely presented in reports of achievement indicators but should be, even when they cannot be quantified.

CONCLUSION

Many observers have commented on the enormous weight cognitive tests are given in American popular and policy debate, and the past twenty years have witnessed a great increase in the prominence and importance of test scores. In addition, some observers have commented on the large number of tests that American students take. Yet despite the frequency and salience of testing in this country, the range of data well suited to use in a national indicator system is surprisingly limited. Any number of steps to expand the stock of achievement indicators would be practical, but improvement will depend on a careful separation of the requirements of indicators from other uses of tests and on an agreement regarding the relative value of additional data of various sorts.

Notes

1. This count includes only the items in the main NAEP assessment that were scaled.

2. In fact, the correlations among tests of *different* domains are typically sizable as well. For present purposes, however, it is not necessary to go into the long-standing arguments about the meaning of these cross-subject correlations or of the general factor they imply.

3. However, to serve this function, state NAEP would have to be conducted differently. Specifically, limited resources would have to be used to assess the same subject areas reasonably frequently.

REFERENCES

Airasian, P. 1987. "State-Mandated Testing and Educational Reform: Context and Consequences. *American Journal of Education.* 95: 393–412.

Barron, S. I., and Koretz, D. M. 1996. "An Evaluation of the Robustness of the National Assessment of Educational Progress Trend Estimates for Racial/Ethnic Subgroups." *Educational Assessment* 3(3): 209–248.

Beaton, A. E. 1992. "Methodological Issues in Reporting NAEP Results at District and School Levels." Paper presented to the National Assessment Governing Board (October 2).

Beaton, A. E., T. L. Hilton, and W. B. Schrader. 1977. *Changes in the Verbal Abilities of High School Seniors, College Entrants, and SAT Candidates between 1960 and 1972.* New York: College Entrance Examination Board.

Beaton, A. E., and R. Zwick. 1990. "The Effect of Changes in the National Assessment: Disentangling the NAEP 1985–1986 Reading Anomaly" Report 17-TR-21. Princeton, N.J.: Educational Testing Service, National Assessment of Educational Progress.

———. 1992. "Overview of the National Assessment of Educational Progress." *Journal of Educational Statistics* 17: 95–109.

Bracey, G. 1991. "Why Can't They Be Like We Were?" *Phi Delta Kappan 73* (2, October): 104–17.

Burket, G. R. 1984. "Response to Hoover." *Educational Measurement: Issues and Practice* 3(4): 15–16.

Clemans, W. V. 1993. "Item Response Theory, Vertical Scaling, and Something's Awry in the State of Test Mark. *Educational Assessment* 1(4): 329–47.

Dunbar, S., D. Koretz, and H. D. Hoover. 1991. "Quality Control in the Development and Use of Performance Assessment." *Applied Measurement in Education* 4(4): 289–303.

Goslin, D. A. 1963. *The Search for Ability: Standardized Testing in Social Perspective.* New York: Russell Sage Foundation.

Goslin, D., R. R. Epstein, and B. A. Hallock. 1965. *The Use of Standardized Tests in Elementary Schools.* New York: Russell Sage Foundation.

Haney, W. 1981. "Validity, Vaudeville, and Values: A Short History of Social Concerns Over Standardized Testing." *American Psychologist* 36(10): 1021–34.

———. 1984. "Testing Reasoning and Reasoning about Testing." *Review of Educational Research* 54(4): 597–654.

Hedges, L. V. Personal communication, September 30, 1994.

Hoover, H. D. 1984a. "The Most Appropriate Scores for Measuring Development in the Elementary Schools: GE's." *Educational Measurement: Issues and Practice* 3(4): 8–14.

———. 1984b. "Rejoinder to Burket." *Educational Measurement: Issues and Practice* 3(4): 16–18.

———. 1988. "Growth Expectations for Low-Achieving Students: A Reply to Yen." *Educational Measurement: Issues and Practice* 7(4): 21–23.

Jaeger, R. M. 1982. "The Final Hurdle: Minimum Competency Achievement Testing." In *The Rise and Fall of National Test Scores*, edited by G. R. Austin and H. Garber. New York: Academic Press.

———. 1992. "World Class" Standards, Choice, and Privatization: Weak Measurement Serving Presumptive Policy. Vice-Presidential Address, Annual Meeting of the American Educational Research Association, San Francisco, Calif. (April 20, 1992).

Koretz, D. M. 1986. *Trends in Educational Achievement.* Washington: U.S. Government Printing Office for Congressional Budget Office, U. S. Congress.

———. 1987. *Educational Achievement: Explanations and Implications of Recent Trends.* Washington: U.S. Government Printing Office for Congressional Budget Office (August).

———. 1990. *Trends in the Postsecondary Enrollment of Minorities.* Santa Monica, Calif.: The RAND corporation (R-3958-FF).

———. 1991. "State Comparisons Using NAEP: Large Costs, Disappointing Benefits." *Educational Researcher* 20(3): 19–21.

———. 1992a. State and National Assessment. In *Encyclopedia of Educational Research*, 6th ed., edited by M. C. Alkin. Washington, D.C.: American Educational Research Association.

———. 1992b. *Validating and Evaluating Indicators of Mathematics and Science Education*, Report N-2900-NSF, Santa Monica, Calif.: The RAND Corporation.

————. 1992c. "What Happened to Test Scores, and Why?" *Educational Measurement: Issues and Practice* 11(4): 7–11.

Koretz, D., and E. Deibert. 1995/1996. "Setting Standards and Interpreting Achievement: A Cautionary Tale from the National Assessment of Educational Progress." *Educational Assessment* 3(1): 53–81.

Koretz, D., and E. Lewis. "Indicators of Achievement in Mathematics and Science." Working paper. Santa Monica, Calif.: The RAND Corporation.

Koretz, D. M., E. Lewis, L. Burstein, and T. Skewes-Cox. 1992. "Omitted and Not-Reached Items in Mathematics in the 1990 National Assessment of Educational Progress." Technical report to the National Center on Education Statistics. The RAND Corporation and UCLA, Center for Research on Evaluation, Standards, and Student Testing.

Koretz, D. M., R. L. Linn, S. B. Dunbar, and L. A. Shepard. 1991. "The Effects of High-Stakes Testing: Preliminary Evidence About Generalization Across Conventional Tests." Paper presented at The Effects of High Stakes Testing Symposium at the annual meetings of the American Educational Research Association and the National Council on Measurement in Education, Chicago, Ill. (April 1991).

Koretz, D. M., B. Stecher, S. Klein, and D. McCaffrey. 1994. "The Vermont Portfolio Assessment Program: Findings and Implications." *Educational Measurement: Issues and Practice* 13(3): 5–16.

Linn, R. L, and S. B. Dunbar. 1990. "The Nation's Report Card Goes Home: Good News and Bad about Trends in Achievement." *Phi Delta Kappan* 72(2, Oct.): 127–33.

Linn, R. L., V. L. Kiplinger, C. W. Chapman, and P. G. LeMahieu. 1992. "Cross-State Comparability of Judgments of Student Writing: Results from the New Standards Project." *Applied Measurement in Education* 5(2): 89–110.

Linn, R. L., L. Shepard, and E. Hartka. 1992. "The Relative Standing of States in the 1990 Trial State Assessment: The Influence of Choice of Content, Statistics, and Subpopulation Breakdowns." In *Assessing Student Achievement in the States: Background Studies*, National Academy of Education. Stanford, Calif.: Stanford University, National Academy of Education.

Mullis, I. V. S., J. A. Dossey, E. H. Owen, and G. W. Phillips. 1991. *The State of Mathematics Achievement: NAEP's Assessment of the Nation and the Trial Assessment of the States.* Washington, D.C.: National Center for Education Statistics.

————. 1993. *NAEP 1992 Mathematics Report Card for the Nation and the States*, no. 23-ST02. Washington, D.C.: National Center for Education Statistics.

Murnane, R., and S. Raizen. 1988. *Improving the Quality of Indicators of Science and Mathematics Education in Grades K-12.* Washington, D.C.: National Academy Press.

National Center for Education Statistics. 1988. *Dropout Rates in the United States*, no. 89-609. Washington, D.C.: U.S. Department of Education.

National Commission on Excellence in Education. 1983. *A Nation at Risk.* Washington, D.C.: U.S. Department of Education.

Pipho, C. 1985. Tracking the Reforms, Part 5: Testing—Can It Measure the Success of the Reform Movement? *Education Week* 4(35): 19.

Raizen, S., and L. V. Jones. 1985. *Indicators of Precollege Education in Science and Mathematics.* Washington, D.C.: National Academy Press.

Resnick, D. 1982. "History of Educational Testing." In *Ability Testing: Uses, Consequences, and Controversies, Part I*, edited by A. K. Wigdor and W. R. Garner. Washington, D.C.: National Academy Press.

Rock, D. A., R. B. Eckstrom, M. E. Goertz, T. L. Hilton, and J. Pollack. 1985. *Factors Associated with Decline of Test Scores of High School Seniors, 1972 to 1980.* Washington, D.C.: Center for Statistics, U.S. Department of Education.

Roeber, E. 1988. "A History of Large-Scale Testing Activities at the State Level." Paper presented at the Indiana Governor's Symposium on ISTEP, Madison, Ind. (February 10, 1988).

Shavelson, R. J., G. P. Baxter, and X. Gao. 1993. Sampling Variability of Performance Assessments. *Journal of Educational Measurement* 30(3): 215–32.

Shavelson, R. J., L. McDonnell, J. Oakes, and N. Carey. 1987. *Indicator Systems for Monitoring Mathematics and Science Education.* Santa Monica, Calif.: The RAND Corporation.

Shepard, L. A., and K. C. Dougherty. 1991. "Effects of High-Stakes Testing on Instruction." Paper presented at The Effects of High Stakes Testing Symposium at the annual meetings of the American Educational Research Association and the National Council on Measurement in Education, Chicago, Ill. (April 1991).

Spencer, B. 1983. "On Interpreting Test Scores as Social Indicators: Statistical Considerations." *Journal of Educational Measurement* 20(4): 317–33.

Wainer, H., and D. Thissen. 1993. "Combining Multiple-Choice and Constructed-Response Test Scores: Toward a Marxist Theory of Test Construction." *Applied Measurement in Education* 6(2): 103–18.

Yen, W. M. 1988. "Normative Growth Expectations Must Be Realistic: A Response to Phillips and Clarizio." *Educational Measurement: Issues and Practice* 7(4): 16–17.

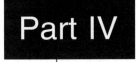

Part IV

Economic Security

11

Indicators of Children's Economic Well-Being and Parental Employment

Susan E. Mayer

IN CONTRAST TO measures of children's own outcomes, parents' income and employment are indirect indicators of children's well-being. The usefulness of indirect indicators depends on establishing their theoretical or empirical links to important outcomes of children. Poor children fare worse than rich children on nearly every outcome that social scientists have studied. This has lead to the conclusion among many policymakers and child advocates that low parental income hurts children's outcomes. Yet there is considerable disagreement about how much improving parents' income alone would help children. It is also not clear that raising parental income from say, ten thousand dollars to fifteen thousand dollars makes children better off if the median parent's income simultaneously rises from fifteen thousand dollars to thirty thousand dollars.

The likely effect of changes in parental employment is even more ambiguous. Children will benefit from their parents' working outside the home as long as the benefits of increased income outweigh the loss of their parents' time. Almost everyone believes that at least one parent should work in a two-parent family because the added income will outweigh the benefit of having two parents rather than one parent at home. Whether the second parent should work is a more complicated question, since it is not clear that the added income will outweigh the cost to children of having no parent at home for much of the day. The same question arises with respect to single parents.

This chapter is divided into two sections: one on indicators of economic well-being and one on indicators of parental employment. Each section describes both how children's well-being is related to the indicator and the available measures of the indicator.

INDICATORS OF ECONOMIC WELL-BEING

Parental income is a proxy for many factors that might affect children's outcomes. Two dominant models of the relationship between parents' income and children's outcomes emphasize different factors. The investment model holds that parents invest both time and money in their children's human capital. They do this especially by investing in their children's education, but also by purchasing health, good neighbors, and other goods and services that improve children's future well-being (Becker 1981). According to this model, children raised in affluent families are more likely to succeed than children raised in poor families because rich parents invest more in their children.

According to the good parent model, low parental income affects children by affecting parents' ability to be "good" parents. The "parental stress" version of this model holds that poverty is stressful and that stress diminishes parents' ability to be supportive, consistent, and involved with their children (McLoyd 1990).

The "role model" version of the good parents model holds that because of their position at the bottom of the social hierarchy, low-income parents develop values, norms, and behavior that cause them to be "bad" role models for their children. This is likely to be true for families experiencing long-term poverty who must adapt to their economic conditions. For families experiencing short-term poverty, parental stress may have a greater affect on parental behavior.

Both the investment model and the good parents model imply that as parents' income increases, children's outcomes improve, at least if other major influences stay more or less the same. Both models provide ambiguous predictions about what is likely to happen if parents' absolute income increases at the same time that their income declines relative to the incomes of other families. In principle, according to the investment model, growth in inequality could affect children's outcomes if higher demand among the rich increases the price of some goods. If, for example, the demand for postsecondary education increases as a result of income growth among the rich, poor children will be less likely to attend college even if their families' real income remains the same. If parental stress mostly depends on how much parents provide for their family, parents will experience less stress as their income rises. As a result their parenting practices will improve. If, on the other hand, parents' stress mostly depends on how they evaluate their living standard relative to the living standards of other families, parents will experience stress even when their own income grows, if it does not grow as fast as the income of others.

If the good parent model is correct, our goal should be to replace income measures with direct measures of parents' values, behavior, and psychological well-being, unless parental income is a very good proxy for these parental characteristics. If the investment model is correct, our goal should be to replace income measures with direct measures of the goods and services that contribute to children's success, unless income is a very good proxy for these inputs. If the relationship between income and the intervening processes that effect children's outcomes are weak, trends in children's outcomes will not necessarily follow trends in parents' income because other factors will affect these trends (Mayer 1997).

In the next part of this chapter I describe trends in several measures of parents' economic well-being. I begin with income-based measures because these are the most frequently used. But they are subject to many well-known flaws, so I also describe trends in how much families consume. Most people seem to agree that at a minimum children need adequate food, housing, and medical care in order to succeed. Therefore I describe trends in children's material living conditions. I know of no data that provide trends in parental stress or parenting behavior.

CHILDREN'S ECONOMIC WELL-BEING
Income-Based Measures

The first column in table 11.1 shows that the official poverty rate for children increased from 14.2 percent in 1969 to 19.6 percent in 1989. In 1992 the official child poverty rate was 21.8 percent. Most economic indicators, including poverty, are quite sensitive to the years one chooses to compare, since economic indicators are influenced by the business cycle. Business cycle peaks (assessed as peak years of Gross Domestic Product [GDP] growth) occurred in about 1969, 1973, 1979, and 1989, so this table shows business cycle peaks.

Social scientists have criticized the official poverty rate on many grounds (Citro and Michael 1995; Mayer and Jencks 1989; Ruggles 1990). Official poverty statistics compare each family's income to a poverty threshold developed by Mollie Orshansky in 1964. If a family's income falls below the threshold, it is classified as poor. But a family's annual money income is not, in fact, a very good measure of the resources available to families. This is true for many reasons:

- Many families seriously misreport their income in surveys. Errors are especially common at the top and bottom of the income distribution.

- Taxes, borrowing, and saving all vary substantially among families with the same income. As a result, families with the same annual income can spend quite different amounts during the year on goods and services.

- Even when families spend the same amount, the value of what they consume can vary because of differences in their ability to get free (or subsidized) goods and services. These noncash transfers can come from the government, from employers, or from friends and relatives.

- Families' resources also depend on what they already own. The "service flows" from owner-occupied housing and from automobiles bought in the past are especially important.

- Measures of income are usually adjusted for changes in prices in order to measure "real" income, or a constant level of purchasing power. But all price indexes embody hundreds of arbitrary decisions and compromises, some of which

Table 11.1   Trends in the Child Poverty Rate

Measure	1969	1979	1989	Change 1969–1989
Official poverty rate	14.2	16.4	19.6	5.4
Consistent thresholds				
CPI-U	15.2	16.8	19.6	4.4
CPI-U-X1	16.9	17.2	19.6	2.7
PCE-A	19.7	18.4	19.9	.2
Consistent thresholds, household	20.1	17.7	18.8	−1.3
Income, PCE-A				
Including noncash transfers	18.6	14.4	14.9	−3.7
Using census data	19.0	14.5	14.0	−5.0

Source: Jencks and Mayer 1996, table 1.

introduce systematic upward or downward bias (Boskin et al. 1996). If these biases persist, their cumulative effect can be substantial. Local variation in prices, especially for housing, also means that families that spend the same amount get more in some communities than in others.

- Families' needs for income differ depending on the size of the family, the health of family members, and other factors.
- The efficiency with which a family spends its money also influences the price it pays for goods or services of any given quality. A skilled shopper can buy a better car for ten thousand dollars or a better melon for two dollars than an unskilled shopper.

It is impossible to correct all these potential biases in measures of income. Christopher Jencks and I (Jencks and Mayer 1996) show that the increase in the official child poverty rate is exaggerated for at least three reasons: children's households now include more nonrelatives whose income is not included when the Census Bureau classifies children as poor; the official poverty threshold has risen faster than the true rate of inflation; and the growth of noncash transfers has raised many children's standard of living without raising their income. Table 11.1 summarizes our results.

The Census Bureau made several changes to the poverty thresholds over time. The second row in table 11.1 shows changes in the child poverty rate substituting consistent thresholds. These changes account for one percentage point of the increase in the child poverty rate between 1969 and 1989.

The official poverty thresholds are adjusted for changes in prices using the Consumer Price Index for urban consumers (CPI-U). Economists agree that the CPI-U overstated the annual inflation rate during the 1970s because of the way it computed housing costs. This problem was especially severe during the late 1970s when the cost of buying a new house increased faster than most other prices. In 1983 the error was corrected with the introduction of the CPI-U-X1. But earlier poverty statistics were not revised to reflect this correction. Using the CPI-U-X1 for all years reduces the increase in the child poverty rate between 1969 and 1989 to 2.7 percentage points.

Many economists prefer to measure price changes using the implicit price deflator for Personal Consumption Expenditures (PCE) in the National Income and Product Accounts. The implicit price deflator is difficult to interpret, however, because it does not describe the price of a fixed market basket of goods. The fixed-weight PCE index for the market basket that consumers bought in 1987 rose more slowly than the implicit price deflator. Jencks and I revised the 1987 PCE to take account of unmeasured depreciation in rental housing, substitution bias, and formula bias. We refer to this revision as the PCE-A. Substituting the PCE-A results in an increase in the child poverty rate of only .2 percentage points.

Official child poverty rates are based on the income of everyone living in a single housing unit who is related by blood, marriage, or adoption. Thus, if a woman and her child live with her boyfriend (and she is what the Census Bureau refers to as the "reference" person), the mother and child are counted as one family and the father is counted as a separate unrelated individual. If the mother's income is below the poverty threshold for a family of two, she and her child are classified as poor, regardless of how much money her boyfriend makes. As rates of cohabitation increase, this distinction may distort the true economic well-being of children. An alternative is to calculate poverty rates based on household income rather than family income. A household includes all the people who live in a single housing unit, regardless of their relationship to one another. The fifth line in table 11.1 shows that if we take into account the income of all household members and use the PCE-A to adjust for prices, the child poverty rate decreased 1.3 percentage points between 1969 and 1989. When we take into account the value of noncash means-tested transfers, such as food stamps, housing subsidies, and Medicaid, the child poverty rate declined 3.7 percentage points.

The official child poverty rate is based on data from the March Current Population Survey. All the poverty rates but the last row in table 11.1 are also based on CPS data. To test the sensitivity of the poverty rate to different data sources, the last row shows the child poverty rate calculated in the same way as row 6 but using data from the decennial census. It shows that the child poverty rate declined 5 percentage points between 1969 and 1989.

The trend in the child poverty rate is, thus, very sensitive to reasonable changes in the measurement of poverty and the data used to measure it.

One of the most important criticisms of the poverty line is that the equivalence scale used to adjust income for differences in household size reflects neither a sound theoretical nor empirical rationale. In fact, no one equivalence adjustment makes families equally well off in all respects. The size elasticity implied by the poverty thresholds is about .85 for families of three or more. This means that a 100 percent increase in family size requires an 85 percent increase in income to maintain the same level of economic well-being. The size adjustments of the poverty thresholds may be about right if we want the poverty line to be a proxy for material well-being (Mayer and Jencks 1989). Scales that try to equalize adults' subjective well-being require smaller adjustments for household size (Vaughn 1984; Rainwater 1974), while scales that try to equalize households' consumption require larger adjustments (Lazear and Michael 1980; van der Gaag and Smolensky 1981).

The size adjustment that would equalize children's cognitive test scores, or their chances of dropping out of high school, becoming a teenage mother or a single mother is greater than one (Mayer 1997). This means that family income must more than double to offset the effects of doubling family size. Thus if we intend for the poverty line to be a proxy for broader aspects of children's life chances, the size adjustments of the poverty thresholds might be too small. A family's size and its income should not be combined into one measure, such as a poverty rate, unless we are sure what we want to measure.

A poverty rate, however accurate, tells us only what has happened to children at the bottom of the income distribution. It does not tell us what has happened to average or affluent children. If children's well-being depends largely on their relative economic standing rather than absolute economic position, trends at the top of the income distribution may affect children at the bottom.

Table 11.2 shows trends in real household income of children (adjusted with the CPI-U-X1) using both CPS and census data. The mean of the third quintile is approximately the median income, so both census and CPS data show that the

Table 11.2   Mean Income (1994 Dollars) for Children's Households

	Income Quintile				
Income Measure	Lowest	Second	Middle	Fourth	Highest
Household income					
Census					
1969	11,485	26,314	36,668	48,264	84,919
1979	10,488	26,665	39,941	54,035	91,503
1989	9,554	25,739	40,036	56,857	102,913
CPS					
1969	13,173	26,727	36,558	47,687	77,201
1979	11,161	26,346	39,349	53,118	85,466
1989	9,662	24,813	39,421	56,420	95,961
1994	8,562	22,907	37,653	55,381	96,109
Per capita income					
Census					
1969	2,047	4,912	7,208	9,984	18,175
1979	2,277	5,793	8,799	12,194	21,304
1989	2,134	5,751	9,100	13,328	24,839
CPS					
1969	2,331	4,925	7,106	9,734	16,370
1979	2,399	5,783	8,745	12,136	19,815
1989	2,175	5,602	9,124	13,303	23,457
1994	1,955	5,207	8,711	13,143	23,458

Source: Computed by David Knutson. Income is adjusted for changes in prices using the CPI-U-X1. Means for the top quintile are biased downward due to top-coding.

income of the median child's household increased slightly during the 1970s and hardly changed during the 1980s.

The average size of children's households declined from 4.25 to 3.39 between 1969 and 1989, so families needed less money. The estimates in the first part of table 11.2 make no adjustment for differences in household size. The second part uses per capita income. Per capita income assumes that there are no economies of scale in larger households. These two alternative adjustments for size presumably bracket the "true" equivalence scale. In both census and CPS data, median per capita income increased in both the 1970s and the 1980s. In both data sets the increase in per capita median income was much greater than the increase in unadjusted median income. Much of the improvement in real per capita income is thus traceable to declining household size rather than rising money income.

Like trends in the poverty rate, trends in the median child's household income are sensitive to the way income is adjusted for changes in prices. Using the CPI-U, as most government publications do, the median child's household income hardly changed between 1969 and 1989 in the CPS. Substituting the PCE-A, the median child's household income increased 28.9 percent. The increases would be even greater for per capita income and for census data.

Table 11.2 shows that in the 1970s and the 1980s income unadjusted for household size grew for children whose households were in the top half of the income distribution and fell for those in the poorest fifth of the income distribution. CPS data show that per capita income fell during the 1970s for those in the poorest fifth of the income distribution, while census data show that per capita income grew among this group.

Because income grew at the top of the distribution, inequality grew regardless of the data set. However, it is unclear whether income growth at the top of the income distribution hurts children whose household income failed to grow. That depends on whether we think that relative or absolute economic well-being affects children.[1]

Over the past twenty years, tax rates fluctuated substantially, saving rates fell, prices changed, household size declined, cohabitation increased, and noncash transfers to children grew. In addition, more women worked, so consumers bought more goods and services in the marketplace and produced fewer at home. None of these changes are accurately accounted for in measures of income. Consequently, it might be a mistake to assume that measured parental income corresponds to the resources available to children.

Additional Measures of Economic Well-Being

How much families consume may be a better measure of available resources than income. The relationship between income and consumption depends on the savings rate, access to credit, taxes, and income volatility. If we are interested in children's well-being, we should probably focus exclusively on consumption that benefits children, but in practice there is no way of doing this. In Section I, therefore, I use data from the Consumer Expenditure Survey (CEX) to describe trends in the overall level of consumption in children's households.[2]

The measure of annual consumption used here includes total cash outlays for all items except the following: taxes;[3] purchases of stocks, bonds, and other investments; pension contributions; down payments and mortgage payments for owner-occupied housing; purchases of motor vehicles; interest; gifts. Consumption also includes the following noncash items: the estimated rental value of owner-occupied housing;[4] the estimated depreciation of motor vehicles;[5] and the estimated value of food bought with food stamps.[6] This measure of consumption is not ideal, but it should tell us more about the resources available to support children in any given year than the household's reported money income does.

The CEX income data are of poor quality, so I do not compare families' consumption with their income. Table 11.3 shows that between 1972 to 1973 and 1989 to 1990 consumption in the median child's household declined slightly even though both CPS and census data show that income increased. Consumption declined more among households with low consumption, but the decline was not as great as the decline in income reported in the census or in the CPS.

CPS data show that the poorest fifth of households with children reported incomes averaging 24.5 percent of median income in 1989. Using the CEX and categorizing households by consumption, the poorest fifth of children's households consumed 43.7 percent as much as the median child's household in 1989 to 1990. Annual consumption is thus far more equally distributed than annual income. That is partly because some households are only temporarily poor, allowing them to consume more than they take in during a given year, and because a large fraction of households with low reported income also have unreported income.

Table 11.3   Consumption in CEX Consumer Units with Children

Consumption Measure	Consumption Quintile		
	Bottom	Middle	Highest
Mean consumption			
1972–1973	14,828	31,327	59,238
1980–1981	13,804	30,639	57,834
1987–1988	12,465	30,115	60,379
1989–1990	13,029	29,783	62,952
Percent change			
1972–1973	− 12.1	− 4.9	6.3
Mean per capita consumption			
1972–1973	3,007	6,673	13,251
1980–1981	3,043	6,984	14,006
1987–1988	2,858	7,132	15,228
1989–1990	2,957	7,162	15,907
Percent change			
1972–1973	− 1.1	7.3	20.0

Source: Tabulations by Judith Levine and Scott Winship using data tapes provided by Bureau of Labor Statistics (BLS) and John Sabelhaus. Sample includes CUs with twelve months of expenditure data, weighted by the number of members under eighteen years of age. The unweighted number of CUs is 8,570 in 1972–1973, 1,395 in 1980–1981, 3,091 in 1987–1988, and 3,730 in 1989–1990.

Inequality in consumption also grew more slowly than inequality in measured income. Using CPS data and the CPI-U-X1 to adjust for price changes, the ratio of mean income among the poorest fifth of children's households to median income fell from 36 percent in 1969 to 24.5 percent in 1989. The ratio of mean consumption in the poorest quintile to the median fell from 47.3 percent in 1972 to 1973 to 43.7 percent in 1989 to 1990. This is partly because consumption did not decline as much as income in the bottom of the distribution and partly because consumption did not grow as much as income in the middle of the distribution. This conclusion also holds for per capita consumption.

Jencks and I (Jencks and Mayer 1996) compared the value of a consumer units' consumption with the poverty threshold for a family of the same size to create a measure of "consumption poverty." When we adjust consumption to 1992 dollars using the CPI-U-X1, consumption poverty rises from 11.9 percent in 1972 to 1973 to 13.4 percent in 1988 to 1990. Consumption poverty has thus risen less than official measures of income poverty.

Comparing consumption to income shows that:

• The median consumption of children's households declined 4.9 percent between 1972 to 1973 and 1989 to 1990. The median income of children's households increased over this time.

• Consumption is much more equally distributed than income.

• Consumption inequality grew between 1972 to 1973 and 1989 to 1990, but not as much as income inequality grew.

Because trends in consumption do not always parallel trends in income, and because consumption is probably a better measure than annual income of a household's resources, indicators of children's well-being would ideally include measures of their household's consumption. Unfortunately, the CEX is the only source of data on consumption and it is difficult to use.

If trends in income do not parallel trends in consumption, they also might not parallel trends in living conditions. In addition, trends in consumption might not parallel trends in living conditions because government effort on behalf of poor children increasingly has been in the form of noncash transfers that improve living conditions without families having to spend anything.

Judging by government expenditures, most Americans believe that adequate housing, food, and medical care are important living conditions. "Hardships" in these living conditions are themselves important indicators of children's well-being with considerable face validity.

The American Housing Survey collects data on numerous housing conditions, from design inadequacies such as not having central heat or not having a complete bathroom to maintenance problems such as having a leaky roof or peeling paint.[7] One technique for summarizing children's housing conditions is to simply count the number of housing problems that families have. Table 11.4 shows that between 1973 to 1975 and 1991 to 1993 the percent of children living in homes with no housing problems increased, and the percent living with as many as three problems declined.[8] For the median child these changes were small, so the average number of problems remained about the same. The reduction in housing problems was greater for low-income children than for middle-income children, even though income measured in both the CPS and census declined for the poorest children and increased for middle-income children.

This technique weights all problems equally: a family that lacks a complete bathroom has the same number of problems as a family that has a room with no electrical outlet, even though the first problem is probably a greater hardship

Table 11.4   Housing Problems by Parental Income

	Income Quintile		
Number of Problems	Bottom	Middle	Highest
Percent with no problems			
1973–1975	38.3	65.1	74.5
1981–1981	43.1	63.3	76.5
1991–1993	46.2	65.1	78.0
Percent with at least one problem			
1973–1975	27.7	23.8	19.4
1981–1981	26.9	25.2	18.8
1991–1993	28.9	25.6	18.0
Percent with at least three problems			
1973–1975	11.9	1.7	.6
1981–1981	8.9	1.2	.4
1991–1993	7.1	1.3	.3
Mean number of problems			
1973–1975	1.41	.52	.27
1981–1981	1.20	.55	.25
1991–1993	.96	.52	.27

Source: Tabulations by Joseph Swingle using the American Housing Survey.

than the second. An alternative might be to weight housing conditions by what families are willing to pay for them, using what social scientists usually refer to as a "rent equation." However, constructing weights in a consistent way over time is difficult and involves many decisions that are likely to be controversial.

Although housing problems declined, families with children were less likely to own their own home in 1990 than in 1970. The percent of children's households living in rental housing increased by 4.3 percent over this period. The increase was 11.3 percent for children in the poorest income quintile.

Income segregation has increased in cities (Jargowsky 1997) and many people believe that this has made neighborhoods less safe for children. Table 11.5 shows that in 1985 to 1989 parents were more likely than in 1973 to 1975 to say that crime was a problem in their neighborhood, and the increase was greater for low-income than high-income parents.

The National Crime Victimization Survey collects data on how many people were crime victims. These data show that between 1979 to 1981 and 1988 to 1990 reports of rape and robbery declined and reports of assault hardly changed among low-income children, even though their parents were more likely to report that crime was a problem in their neighborhood. Among middle-income children reports of rape and robberies declined, but reports of assaults increased.

Table 11.5   Trends in Crime, by Parental Income

Measure and Year	Income Quintile			Ratio Lowest/Middle
	Lowest	Middle	Highest	
Parents believe crime is a problem in neighborhood (%)				
1973–1975	18.9	16.1	16.2	1.17
1981–1983	25.8	19.8	19.4	1.30
1985–1989	30.2	20.7	16.7	1.45
1991–1993	36.3	23.7	20.1	1.53
Victimization rates/100,000 persons aged 12 to 20				
Rape				
1979–1981	467	163	117	2.87
1988–1990	268	118	87	2.27
1991–1992	297	102	131	2.91
Robbery				
1979–2981	1779	1095	1107	1.63
1988–1990	1498	625	968	2.40
1991–1992	1613	1060	1081	1.52
Aggravated assault				
1979–1981	2896	1770	1504	1.64
1988–1990	2743	1894	1363	1.45
1991–1992	3564	1864	1345	1.91
Simple assault				
1979–1981	4251	3094	3236	1.37
1988–1990	4587	3803	3352	1.21
1991–1992	5552	4896	3108	1.13

Source: Tabulations by David Harris using data from the National Crime Victimization Survey.

Crime rates did increase in 1991 to 1992 as did parents' likelihood of reporting that crime was a problem in the neighborhood.

Table 11.6 shows several additional measures of material well-being. Some of these, such as dishwashers, might be considered "luxuries." Others, such as having a telephone, might be considered necessities. If parents purchase goods and services in the order of their importance, families that have dishwashers are also likely to have other more basic material resources.

Children's households became more likely to have all these items except clotheswashers between the early 1970s and 1990. The likelihood that poor children's households had at least one motor vehicle hardly changed, but their chances of having at least two vehicles increased. This implies that there may

Table 11.6 Percent of Children with Selected Consumer Durables and Telephone Service, by Parental Income

	Income Quintile		
Measure and Year	Lowest	Middle	Highest
Motor vehicle			
1970	68.1	95.6	98.8
1980	68.4	95.7	98.4
1990	69.7	97.0	99.0
Change	1.6	1.4	.2
Two or more vehicles			
1970	16.6	44.4	74.8
1980	17.6	50.7	76.6
1990	25.8	75.3	92.9
Change	9.2	30.9	18.1
Telephone			
1970	63.9	91.7	98.5
1980	76.2	95.8	99.0
1990	74.2	96.5	99.5
Change	10.3	4.8	5.5
Clotheswasher			
1972–1973	67.4	91.6	97.5
1986–1987	62.3	90.4	97.7
1988–1990	58.3	89.5	98.0
Change	−9.1	−2.1	.5
Clothesdryer			
1972–1973	29.8	76.7	91.8
1986–1987	35.4	85.8	95.7
1988–1990	37.2	84.1	97.4
Change	7.4	7.4	5.6
Dishwasher			
1972–1973	5.2	32.5	72.9
1986–1987	9.3	49.7	85.4
1988–1990	12.9	49.4	85.9
Change	7.7	16.9	13.0

Source: Data on clotheswashers, clothesdryers, and dishwashers are from the Consumer Expenditure Survey (tabulations by Judith Levine and Scott Winship using tapes prepared by John Sabelhaus). These are shown by consumption quintiles. Data on motor vehicles and telephones are from the census and tabulated by David Knutson.

Table 11.7   Children's Annual Doctor Visits, by Parents' Income

Age and Year	Income quintile		
	Lowest	Third	Highest
No doctor visit last year (%)			
1970	37.9	28.6	21.4
1980	23.7	23.1	20.3
1982	25.0	23.9	18.3
1989	23.9	20.2	13.2
1993	20.6	18.8	12.8
Number of doctor visits last year			
1970	2.5	2.9	3.0
1980	3.0	3.0	3.0
1982	2.8	2.8	3.1
1989	3.1	3.1	3.7
1993	3.6	3.2	3.8

Source: Tabulations by David Knutson using Health Interview Survey public use data tapes. Unweighted cell sizes range from 987 to 8,072.

have been more mistakes in reported income among poor households in 1990 than in 1970. The improvement for low-income children was greater than for children in general.

Table 11.7 extends this analysis to a different domain, medical care. The estimates for 1970 and 1980 are comparable to one another, but not to the estimates for 1982 and 1989 because the Health Interview Survey was changed in 1982 in ways that affect these estimates.

Both the likelihood of visiting a doctor and the number of visits in a year increased for the median child in the 1970s and the 1980s. Both increased even more for low-income than middle-income children. Low-income children's access to physicians did not deteriorate, as one might have expected given the reduction in their parents' income.[9]

Summary of Economic Indicators

Social scientists and policymakers use parental income as a proxy for the resources available to children and for other aspects of children's home life, including parents' psychological well-being. As long as we are interested in what has happened to the economic well-being of the average child, all the measures covered in this chapter produce a relatively consistent story: income increased over the last two decades as did consumption and living conditions. However, the amount of the income increase is sensitive to the adjustment for prices, the adjustment for household size, and the data set used for the estimates. The degree of improvement in economic well-being also depends on whether we use income, consumption, or living conditions as an indicator. To the extent that the degree of change, rather than the direction of change, is important, multiple indicators will be needed to produce reliable information about the resources available to children.

If we are interested in the distribution of economic well-being, different measures and data sets can produce quite different conclusions. Conclusions about the growth in income inequality depend on the adjustments for households size. Trends on income inequality do not parallel trends in either inequality of consumption or inequality of material living conditions. This suggests that trends in income inequality also might not be a good proxy for trends in other aspects of children's home life. Consequently, no single measure can provide reliable evidence about changes in children's overall economic well-being, if by economic well-being we mean the material resources available to families.[10]

INDICATORS OF PARENTAL EMPLOYMENT

Americans have always believed that fathers should work. They are much more ambivalent about whether mothers should work. When parents work two things happen: their income increases, but the time that they have available to devote to their children and to home production decreases. Some people focus on the "time effect." They are alarmed at the increase in mothers' labor force participation because they fear that children of employed mothers are less likely than children whose mothers stay at home to be adequately supervised and nurtured. Others focus on the "income effect." They are alarmed at mothers who do not work enough to earn the money required to buy the things their children need.

Families in which mothers are employed average higher incomes than similar families in which mothers do not work outside the home. But the "income effect" of such work is usually exaggerated. The economic benefits of employment must be discounted by the value of lost home production (as well as the monetary costs associated with employment). Many studies have shown that home production has an important impact on economic well-being (Gottschalk and Mayer 1994). Gronau (1980) estimated that in 1973 the value of home production among white married-couple households was equal to 70 percent of households' money income after taxes. Gronau's estimates show that among households with young children, the loss of home production when the wife joins the labor force almost equaled her increased money earnings.

Furthermore, additional income may not benefit children as much as it benefits adults. Some evidence suggests that a greater proportion of family income goes to children in low-income than in high-income families (Lazear and Michael 1988). As income increases, additional income is "frosting on the cake," with greater benefits to adults than to children (Mayer 1977).

Americans have always believed that work builds character. Advocates of employment requirements for welfare recipients contend that employment not only increases income, but also reduces the depression, alienation, and lethargy that result from welfare dependency. According to this reasoning, working parents provide better role models than nonworking parents. The evidence that employment is improving for either middle-class or poor parents is sparse, however, so it provides little guidance about how to interpret trends in parents' employment.

The "time effect" of parental employment is also difficult to estimate. The effect of parental employment on children depends on the relative quality of care provided by parents and those who care for the children in their absence. If child care outside the home is worse than the care the parents could have provided, the child will suffer. If the care is better, the child will benefit. If the parental characteristics that help children are the same ones that employers value, and wages are a good indicator of the value of those characteristics, the care that children get in their parents' absence usually will be inferior to the care they would have received from their parents, because parents will not pay more for child care than their own wage. Nonparental child care might be as good as parents' care if the characteristics that are of value to children are not the same as those valued by employers, or if the child care or the parents' wages are subsidized. In that case parents could in principle purchase child care at a price higher than their own wage. In the United States child care is often subsidized by family members and less often by government. Neither theory nor empirical research on the relative merits of nonparental and parental child care provide strong evidence about how to interpret the relationship between parental employment and children's well-being. But they do suggest that in order to evaluate these trends, indicators of parental employment should be accompanied by indicators of what children do in their parents' absence. This is beyond the scope of this chapter.

Research on the effect of parental employment on children's socioemotional development, cognitive skills, and educational achievement is contradictory and subject to several methodological problems (see chapter 13, this volume). Most of this research relies on comparisons between working and nonworking parents that do not adequately account for all the differences between employed and not-employed parents that might affect children's well-being.

Empirical research is still too inconclusive to provide a strong rationale for interpreting the effect of changes in parental employment on children's well-being. Nonetheless, the increase in maternal employment has been one of the most important changes in the family over the last twenty years. Therefore, providing consistent indicators of parental employment may be useful. These indicators should capture the two implicit concerns of those who worry about parents' employment, namely the time that parents have available for their children and the income that they earn from employment. I discussed income (though not wages) in the previous section, so this section will concentrate on the first of these concerns.

In two-parent families the benefit of one parent working almost always outweights the costs of a child having one rather than two parents at home. Whether the second parent or a single parent should work is a more complicated question, since the added income benefit may not outweigh the cost of having no parent at home, at least for young children. If the family is poor without the second parent or a single parent working, the income effect might outweigh the time effect. These arguments imply we should provide separate indicators of parental employment by parents' marital status. Once children are school age, they are without their parents for several hours a day whether their parents work or not. As children get older any harmful effects of working parents will diminish. This implies that we should provide separate indicators by children's age.

The labor force participation rate is the most common indicator of parents' employment. But it may not be the best indicator. The labor force participation rate counts everyone who is working or unemployed as a "participant" in the labor force. An individual is counted as unemployed if he or she was not employed but made specific efforts to find employment within the previous four weeks. Therefore, the participation rate includes both people who are working and people who are not. It also gives equal weight to each adult: the participation rates tell us how many mothers and fathers participate in the labor force, but not how many children have mothers or fathers who are participants.

Table 11.8 uses CPS data to show trends in the percent of children whose fathers and mothers participated in the labor force by the marital status of their parents. Like income, labor force participation and employment are sensitive to business cycle fluctuations. Therefore I focus on changes between 1970, 1980, and 1990, which were fairly comparable points in the business cycle.

As is well known, labor force participation has increased a lot among mothers

Table 11.8   Labor Force Participation and Employment Among Parents

Measure and Year	Married Fathers	Married Mothers	Single Fathers	Single Mothers
Percent in labor force				
1970	93.9	37.5	81.9	51.3
1974	93.2	40.8	82.5	51.4
1976	92.6	44.1	80.6	54.9
1980	92.9	51.5	85.2	59.9
1985	92.6	57.6	85.3	59.0
1987	92.3	60.6	87.3	61.8
1990	92.3	62.9	83.9	61.9
1992	92.1	64.6	84.3	60.1
Change				
1970–1980	−1.0	14.0	3.3	8.6
1980–1990	−1.6	13.1	.9	.2
Percent unemployed				
1970	2.6	6.2	1.1	9.2
1974	3.0	5.6	6.0	8.8
1976	5.2	8.0	8.0	12.9
1980	4.7	6.0	10.1	12.2
1985	5.4	6.8	11.7	14.3
1987	5.0	5.6	9.7	13.6
1990	3.8	4.3	7.9	11.0
1992	6.2	5.5	9.5	13.4
Change				
1970–1980	2.1	−.2	9.0	3.0
1980–1990	.9	−.5	−.6	1.2
Percent employed				
1970	91.5	35.2	80.9	46.7
1974	90.4	38.5	77.5	46.9
1976	87.7	40.6	74.1	47.9
1980	88.6	48.4	76.6	52.6
1985	87.6	53.7	75.3	50.6
1987	87.7	57.2	78.8	53.4
1990	88.7	60.2	77.3	55.1
1992	86.4	61.1	76.3	52.1
Change				
1970–1980	−2.9	13.2	−4.3	−5.9
1980–1990	−2.2	11.8	−.3	−.5

Source: Tabulations by David Knutson using the March Current Population Survey file.

and changed little among fathers, and the increase among mothers has been greater among those who are married than among those who are single.

The unemployment rate for married fathers was 2.6 in 1970 and 4.7 in 1980. In 1990 the economy was stronger than in 1970 or 1980, but the unemployment rate for married fathers was 3.8 percent. Thus married fathers' unemployment rates appear to have increased slightly. Unemployment rates for single mothers also increased.

The employment rate is a better indicator than the participation rate of how many parents actually work. Employment rates declined more than labor force participation rates for fathers. Although the participation rates of single mothers increased somewhat, the proportion of single mothers actually working has declined since 1970.

Among parents who work, some work part-time and some work full-time, so employment status is not a good indicator of trends in either economic support or time with children. The first part of table 11.9 shows the number of hours worked by all parents in a week whether they worked or not. Because it concatenates changes in employment with changes in the hours that the employed work, it can be roughly interpreted as the trend in the hours that each parent was unavailable for child care and home production. The increase in mothers' hours of labor market work is more modest than one might imagine from changes in their labor force participation rate.

Table 11.9   Hours Parents Worked Last Week

Sample and Year	Married Fathers	Married Mothers	Single Fathers	Single Mothers
All parents				
1970	40.4	10.8	34.1	15.4
1974	39.4	11.8	31.5	16.1
1976	37.7	12.4	29.8	16.8
1980	38.0	15.3	31.2	18.8
1985	38.3	17.1	30.8	17.8
1987	38.3	18.4	32.1	19.1
1990	39.0	19.5	31.8	19.9
1992	38.1	20.3	30.8	18.6
Change				
1970–1980	− 2.4	4.5	− 1.9	3.7
1980–1990	1.0	5.2	− .4	− .2
Working parents				
1970	45.5	32.1	43.1	35.3
1974	45.2	32.3	42.7	36.0
1976	44.5	32.2	41.8	37.1
1980	44.5	32.6	42.5	37.2
1985	45.1	33.1	42.5	37.1
1987	45.0	33.6	42.7	37.2
1990	45.4	33.8	43.0	37.9
1992	45.3	34.6	41.5	37.2
Change				
1970–1980	− 1.0	.5	− .6	1.9
1980–1990	.8	1.2	.5	.7

Source: Tabulations by David Knutson using the March Current Population Survey.

The second part of table 11.9 shows the number of hours worked in a week among parents who worked. This is an indicator of changes in employment patterns among workers. Among workers the number of hours worked has hardly changed. Thus the increase in work hours among married mothers is mainly attributable to an increase in employment.

The amount of time that parents have available for their children is a function of how many parents are in the family and how much they work. The proportion of children's households with only one adult has increased. These households have fewer total hours to devote to both market work and home production than households with more than one adult. In additions, hours of labor market work increased for married mothers, which decreased the hours available for home production and child care.

Although we do not have good data on the number of hours that parents actually spend caring for their children or producing goods and services in the home that benefit their child, we can estimate changes in the time available to children by subtracting the amount of time that parents spend at work from the number of nonsleeping hours in the day (sixteen per parent). Thus a child living in a married-couple family in which one parent works eight hours a day, five days a week (forty hours per week), and the other parent does not work outside the home has in principle $7(16 \times 2) - 40 = 184$ hours to spend with their children and in other forms of home production that benefit the child. A single parent who works full-time has in principle $(7 \times 16) - 40 = 72$ hours per week to spend with her children and in other forms of home production.

These trends in nonworking hours are only an approximation of the hours parents really do spend with children. They do not take into account time spent commuting, in leisure, or in other activities that may not benefit children. They also do not take into account the quality of care that children receive in their parent's absence.

Table 11.10 shows that the amount of time parents could in principle spend with their children or in home production that benefits their children declined by 17.2 hours from 1970 to 1992. But because the number of children in families declined, the time available per child increased by 7.9 hours per week. Whether trends in overall time or time per child are more relevant to children's well-being is an empirical question. But the fact that parents actually had more time available per child in 1992 than in 1970 is contrary to what is usually inferred from labor force participation rates alone. There was almost no change in the per-child hours available to children under three-years-old.

If parents reduced leisure to make up for the time that they now spend in the labor market (or to make up for the absence of a spouse), these estimates would overstate children's loss of parental time. Data on home production from the PSID in table 11.11 show that parents spent 159 more hours per year in the labor market in 1987 than in 1976. But the hours that they spent in home production per year declined by 264 hours over this same period. This means that "leisure" increased by 105 hours. Parents apparently did not give up leisure to make up for the loss in time available for their children.

This data is consistent with evidence from time-use surveys in the United States reviewed in Juster and Stafford (1991). Between 1965 and 1981 the number of hours that women devoted to home production declined by an average of 11.3 hours per week (from 41.8 to 30.5). However, the number of hours that

Table 11.10 Potential Hours per Week Available for Children

Sample and Year	Per Child's Family	Per Child
All children		
1970	162.8	68.1
1974	159.9	72.0
1976	159.7	74.2
1980	154.0	77.5
1985	150.3	78.3
1987	148.7	78.3
1990	146.7	76.4
1992	145.6	76.0
Change		
1970–1992	−17.2	7.9
Children less than 3 years old		
1970	168.7	85.0
1974	166.3	92.0
1976	166.8	93.8
1980	161.7	93.5
1985	157.0	90.3
1987	154.9	89.6
1990	151.9	85.7
1992	150.9	85.9
Change		
1970–1992	−17.8	.9

Source: See table 11.8 and text for an explanation of how potential hours is calculated.

they spent in the labor market increased by an average of only 5.0 hours (from 18.9 to 23.9 hours per week). The result was a net decline of 6.3 hours per week devoted to combined home and market production (or a 6.3 hour increase in leisure). Time-use studies also show that while the number of hours that men

Table 11.11 Annual Hours of Housework and Market Work for Families with Children, 1976 to 1987

Year	Housework	Market Work	Total Hours
1976	1,778	2,534	4,312
1977	1,864	2,568	4,433
1978	1,853	2,606	4,459
1979	1,793	2,672	4,465
1980	1,808	2,639	4,447
1981	1,773	2,623	4,396
1983	1,702	2,500	4,202
1984	1,642	2,571	4,213
1985	1,589	2,706	4,295
1986	1,540	2,689	4,229
1987	1,514	2,693	4,207
Change			
1976–1987	−264	159	−105

Source: Tabulations by Tim Veenstra using the 1989 wave of the Panel Study of Income Dynamics. The sample is all households with children.

devote to home production is roughly a third of the number of hours women devote, men did increase their hours of home production by an average of 2.3 hours per week (from 11.5 hours to 13.8 hours) between 1965 and 1981. On average they decreased their market work by 7.6 hours per week, resulting in a net increase of 5.3 hours per week devoted to leisure.

If we are interested in parental employment as a proxy for parental time available to children, labor force participation rates may be misleading. The time that parents have available to spend with each child has not declined. In fact the number of hours that parents report spending in leisure has increased. Indicators of parents' employment must be balanced with indicators of what parents do when they are not working and the number of children that they have to care for. They should also be accompanied by indicators of what children do when they are not with their parents.

The section of this paper on income and material well-being is part of a long-term collaboration with Christopher Jencks. Many of the ideas and much of the analysis are the result of this joint work. However, errors that may appear in this paper are mine alone. This work would not have been possible without the research assistance of David Knutson, Judith Levine, David Rhodes, Joseph Swingle, Tim Veenstra, and Scott Winship. John Sabelhaus provided extracts of the Consumer Expenditure Surveys.

NOTES

1. Trends in annual income may not correspond to trends in permanent income. Studies show that using several years of parental income increases the intergenerational correlation of income (Solon 1993; Zimmerman 1993). Other studies show that using only one year of income seriously can underestimate the relationship of parental income to high school graduation (An, Haveman, and Wolfe 1992), and to children's cognitive test score, teenage childbearing, and educational attainment (Mayer 1997). This implies that trends in "permanent income" would be a better indicator of children's well-being. For this time period, trends in annual income appear to parallel trends in five-year income averages (Mayer 1997; Duncan et al. 1992).

2. The CEX provides data on what it calls "consumer units," not households. Consumer units are groups of individuals who live in the same household and either are related to one another or pool resources to purchase any two of the three categories of goods and services about which BLS inquires (food, housing, and "other expenses"). Since only 2 percent of households contain more than one consumer unit; I use the terms interchangeably in the text.

3. John Sabelhaus, who compiled much of the CEX data used here, found that the federal income tax liabilities in the 1980s public use data tapes were too low.

4. For owner-occupied housing, a home's rental value is based on the owner's estimate of the market value of the home, which was multiplied by the ratio of aggregate rental value to aggregate market value for all owner-occupied housing in the relevant year.

5. The estimate of vehicle depreciation is based on a regression equation that estimates a consumer unit's mean annual expenditure for purchases of motor vehicles. The independent variables in this equation were the household's total expenditures on other forms of consumption (which predicts vehicle expenditures better than income does) and the number of vehicles that the consumer unit owned. We used these predicted values to smooth year-to-year fluctuations in vehicle owners' outlays.

6. Because of data limitations, consumption does not include the value of other noncash transfers, such as federal housing subsidies, employer-financed health insurance, Medicare, Medicaid, or free child care.

7. The housing problems consistently measured over time in the AHS are incomplete plumbing (no full bath with exclusive use); no central heat; no sewer or septic system; no electrical outlet in one or more rooms; holes in floor; broken plaster or peeling paint; cracks in walls or ceiling; leaky roof; and crowding (more than one person per room).

8. In other work, I show that fewer children had each of these housing problems in 1991–1993 than in 1973–1975 and that the improvement was greater among poor children than among middle-income children. The exception to this rule is cracks in the wall or ceiling. But this problem increased for middle-class children as well. Low-income children were also more likely to live in rented housing, but so were middle-class children (Jencks and Mayer 1996; Mayer 1997).

9. The number of days that children limit their activity due to illness has also increased (Mayer and Jencks 1993). But even when health status is taken into account, the association between income and doctor visits decreased for children between 1982 and 1989. For an analysis of the relationship between doctor visits and parental income that controls self-reported health status, the presence of acute and chronic conditions, and bed days in the past year, see Mayer (1993).

10. Although not shown in this chapter, the conclusions about material living conditions are qualitatively the same regardless of the adjustment for household size.

REFERENCES

An, Chong-Bum, Robert Haveman, and Barbara Wolfe. 1992. "The 'Window' Problem in Studies of Children's Attainments: A Methodological Exploration." Discussion Paper 972-92. Madison, Wisc.: University of Wisconsin, Institute for Research on Poverty.

Becker, Gary. 1981. *A Treatise on the Family*. Cambridge, Mass.: Harvard University Press.

Boskin, Michael, Ellen Dulberger, Zvi Grilliches, Robert Gordon, and Dale Jorgenson. 1996. "Toward a More Accurate Measure of the Cost of Living." Washington, D.C.: Final Report to the Senate Finance Committee.

Citro, Constance, and Robert Michael, editors. 1995. *Measuring Poverty: A New Approach*. Washington, D.C.: National Academy Press.

Duncan, Greg, Timothy Smeeding, and Willard Rodgers. 1992. "Why Is the Middle Class Shrinking?" University of Michigan Survey Research Center. Unpublished paper.

Gottschalk, Peter, and Susan E. Mayer. 1994. "Changes in Home Production and Trends in Economic Inequality." University of Chicago. Unpublished paper.

Gronau, Ruben. 1980. "Home Production: A Forgotten Industry." *Review of Economics and Statistics* 62(3): 408–16.

Jargowsky, Paul. 1997. "Take the Money and Run: Economic Segregation in U.S. Metropolitan Areas." *American Sociological Review* 61: 984–98.

Jencks, Christopher, and Susan E. Mayer. 1996. "Do Official Poverty Rates Provide Useful Information about Trends in Children's Economic Welfare?" Northwestern University. Unpublished paper.

Juster, F. Thomas, and Frank Stafford. 1991. "The Allocation of Time: Empirical Findings, Behavioral Models and the Problems of Measurement." *Journal of Economic Literature* 24(2): 471–523.

Lazear, Edward, and Robert Michael. 1980. "Family Size and the Distribution of Real Per Capita Income." *American Economic Review* 70: 91–107.

———. 1988. *Allocation of Income Within the Household*. Chicago, Ill.: University of Chicago Press.

Mayer, Susan E. 1991. "Are There Economic Barriers to Seeing the Doctor?" University of Chicago, Harris School of Public Policy Studies. Unpublished paper.

———. 1997. *What Money Can't Buy*. Cambridge, Mass.: Harvard University Press.

Mayer, Susan E., and Christopher Jencks. 1989. "Poverty and the Distribution of Material Hardship." *Journal of Human Resources* 24: 88–114.

———. 1993. "Recent Trends in Economic Inequality in the United States: Income versus Expenditure versus Material Well-Being." In *Poverty and Prosperity in America at the Close of the Twentieth Century*, edited by Dimitri Papadimitriou and Edward Wolfe London. England: Macmillan.

McLoyd, Vonnie. 1990. "The Impact of Economic Hardship on Black Families and Children: Psychological Distress, Parenting and Socioemotional Development." *Child Development* 61: 311–46.

Rainwater, Lee. 1974. *What Money Buys: Inequality and the Social Meaning of Income.* New York: Basic Books.

Solon, Gary. 1992. "Intergenerational Income Mobility in the United States." *American Economic Review* June: 393–408.

van der Gaag, Jacques, and Eugene Smolensky. 1981. "True Household Equivalence Scales and Characteristics of the Poor in the United States." *Review of Income and Wealth* 28: 17–28.

Vaughn, Denton. 1984. "Using Subjective Assessments of Income to Estimate Family Equivalence Scales: A Report on Work in Progress." Washington, D.C.: Office of Research, Statistics, and International Policy, Social Security Administration.

Zimmerman, David. 1992. "Regression Toward Mediocrity in Economic Stature." *American Economic Review* June: 393–408.

12

Longitudinal Indicators of Children's Poverty and Dependence

Greg J. Duncan and Leslie Moscow

MONTHLY MEASURES OF unemployment and consumer-price inflation plus quarterly reports on aggregate disposable income are the best-known social indicators of household-sector well-being in most Western countries. Unique to the United States is the production of well-publicized annual reports on the extent of poverty among various groups, including children. The singular position of the United States in the routine compilation of poverty statistics results from a number of factors, including: a basic consensus that a comparison of a household's total income and its family-size-based "official" poverty threshold says something meaningful about whether individuals living in that household have a minimum level of material resources; a national statistical office brave enough to ask questions about income of a nationally-representative sample, coupled with a population willing and able to provide reasonably accurate responses to such questions; and a national psyche willing to absorb periodic reports of poverty indicators and eager to debate the policy implications of the statistics. These factors, combined with periodic reports on welfare receipt, health-insurance coverage, and related topics, produce a comparatively rich set of indicators of child-based economic deprivation in the United States.

Unfortunately, extensive research on the nature and consequences of economic deprivation in the United States yields many reasons to be dissatisfied with the current set of indicators of children's deprivation and dependence. Moynihan (1991) sees the problem of dependence in today's postindustrial society as comparable in scope to the problem of unemployment in the 19th and early 20th centuries. However, while progress toward meeting economic goals such as full employment or the elimination of poverty can be monitored with the help of periodic reports on the rates of unemployment and poverty, there is no routine set of indicators for tracking dependence. A National Research Council committee has proposed a new method for measuring income-based poverty (Citro and Michael 1995). Data from the Survey of Income and Program Participation (SIPP) suggest that the survey that is used to produce poverty indicators—the Current Population Survey (CPS)—undercounts annual income and therefore overcounts the poor (see, for example, U.S. Bureau of the Census 1991).[1] Research on expenditure-based indicators of deprivation reveals many troubling cross-sectional and time-series inconsistencies with income-based indicators (Mayer 1994).

The dearth of social indicators of welfare receipt and dependence led Congress to enact the Welfare Indicators Act of 1994, which called for the Secretary of the Department of Health and Human Services to produce annual reports containing indicators of dependence. As spelled out in DHHS's interim report, the passage of the Personal Responsibility and Work Opportunities Reconciliation Act of 1996 led the advisory panel to DHHS to call for indicators of both dependence and well-being. The interim report (U.S. Department of Health and Human Services 1996) was submitted in November, 1996; it is anticipated that the reports themselves will be published at one-year intervals beginning in the fall of 1997.

This chapter takes a longitudinal perspective in assembling its list of sources of dissatisfaction with current indicators of poverty and dependence and in making recommendations for change. It begins by outlining the problem of describing dynamic processes such as economic deprivation, welfare use, or unemployment experiences using either longitudinal or cross-sectional data. It then presents examples of longitudinal indicators for which timely data do not usually exist. It concludes with specific recommendations for indicators that could be produced with available data.

DESCRIBING DYNAMIC PROCESSES

The task of describing dynamic processes with any type of data, whether cross-sectional or longitudinal, is formidable. Figure 12.1 displays ten different possible patterns of "economic deprivation" over the twenty-two-year period from 1979 to 2001. The mixture of short- and long-term patterns is chosen to be roughly consistent with findings from the literature on periods of receipt of benefits from the Aid to Families with Dependent Children transfer program; the essential features of these patterns are similar to those found in connection with other aspects of economic deprivation such as poverty or, if the time scale were more compressed, unemployment.

The line labeled 1 depicts a period of continuous receipt over the entire twenty-two-year period. Individual 2 has a lengthy period of receipt that is divided into two spells, the first running from 1982 to 1988 and the second running for three years beginning in 1992. Individuals 4, 5, and 6 have only short, single spells, while the last four individuals have diverse experiences that could be described as intermediate in total length.

Important to note from these patterns are the following features:

- Experiences are very heterogeneous, with substantial fractions of individuals' welfare experiences lasting no more than two years and equally substantial fractions lasting for quite long periods.

- Repeated episodes are common, occurring in close to half of the cases and sometimes at wide intervals. Thus an analysis of individual spells (for example, the first spells of individuals 3 and 10) can provide a badly biased picture of the total scope of an individual's longer-run experience with deprivation or dependence.

The heterogeneity of AFDC experiences was documented by Bane and Ellwood (1983), who updated their findings in the 1994 book *Welfare Realities*. In

Figure 12.1   Generic Longitudinal Patterns of Deprivation or Dependence

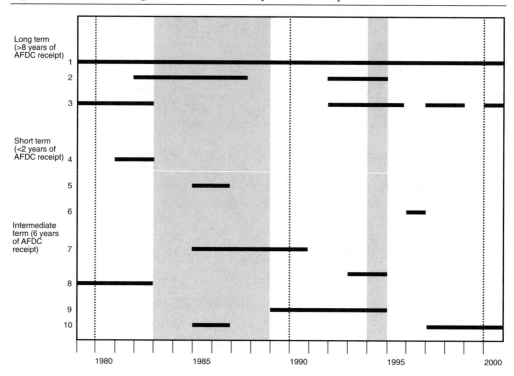

that book, they use data from the 1970s and 1980s to take a comprehensive look at the welfare experiences of first-time AFDC recipients by estimating the total number of years—regardless of the on-off patterns—that first-time recipients can expect to receive welfare over the twenty-five-year period following the point of first receipt. Their estimates show that:

- thirty-six percent of first-time AFDC recipients can expect to receive welfare for only one or two years;

- about 40 percent of first-time recipients can expect to receive it for a total of five years or more; and

- if ten years is taken as the definition of long-term receipt, then only about one in five (22 percent) first-time recipients will fit the long-term stereotype.

Duration of receipt for the Supplemental Security Program and the Food Stamp program is somewhat different from that of AFDC. Rupp and Scott (1995) estimate an expected lifetime program duration for Supplemental Security Income (SSI) for children and nonelderly adults of twenty-seven and ten years, respectively, as compared with an expected lifetime duration of about six years for AFDC recipients. Burstein (1993) estimates that individual spells of Food Stamps last twenty-two months, on average, but that individual spells are often followed by repeat spells.

Many first-time AFDC and Food Stamp recipients have quite short-term experiences, which suggests that for a substantial minority of recipients, the

AFDC and Food Stamp programs function as a kind of income insurance, providing transitory protection against income losses arising from a divorce, job loss, or other income-threatening event. These recipients use benefits for a short period of time, get back on their feet, and then leave the welfare system, never to return.

On the other hand, most first-time recipients do receive AFDC for more than two years, and about four in ten recipients receive welfare for at least five years. Thus, there are more than enough longer-term recipients to warrant investigating who they are and what might be done to shorten the likely length of their welfare spells.

AFDC and Food Stamp benefits are often provided in a series of discrete "episodes." More than one-third of first-time recipients have had more than one "spell" of AFDC.[2] In other words, among the women first starting to receive AFDC benefits, 35 percent will stop for periods lasting between several months and several years, but then return to the AFDC rolls for at least one more episode of receipt.

Multiple spells are common in both the Food Stamp and SSI programs as well. Rupp and Scott (1995) show that about one-quarter of adult SSI recipients and roughly one-half of child SSI recipients who end a spell of SSI receipt will begin another one within twelve months, and much smaller fractions will begin a second spell after periods of nonreceipt that exceed a year. Burstein (1993) reports that more than one-third of Food Stamp spells that end are followed by repeat spells within one year.

Bane and Ellwood (1994) stress the importance of these "cyclers" among the long-term AFDC recipients, pointing out that they constitute the majority of long-term recipients. Here again, the data on welfare dynamics challenge conventional wisdom in showing that most long-term recipients are not continuous recipients. Rather, the dynamics of welfare receipt produce an important subgroup of long-term recipients who do indeed leave the welfare rolls for work but then return.

Given the importance of repeat spells, we conclude:

• To the extent possible, indicators of long-term dependence should allow for the fact that welfare receipt often occurs in a series of discrete episodes.

Patterns such as those depicted in figure 12.1 can be linked to the demographic and other characteristics of the recipients. In the case of children, "childhood" and "early childhood" define important periods over which patterns of deprivation or dependence might be measured. In terms of figure 12.1, this amounts to superimposing a fixed-length window corresponding to the childhood period of interest. In the case of children born at the beginning of 1983, for example, a six-year window from birth to a child's sixth birthday would be represented by the six-year shaded portion of figure 12.1. In the case of individual 2, the birth occurs one year after the beginning of a spell of poverty or dependence for the mother. For individuals 1 and 9, the period of deprivation or dependence extends beyond the sixth birthday. And in the case of all individuals other than 4 and 5, the six-year window misses episodes of deprivation or dependence occurring later in childhood.

Our focus on children's indicators in this chapter dictates that compilations of data on these kinds of indicators use individual children where possible as the units of analysis. Because of the value of looking at children's outcomes by developmental stage, family-based measures are problematic. In addition, a family- or household-based analysis is troubling for longitudinal statistics since—given composition changes such as a divorce, in which some children remain in the custody of one parent and other children are in the custody of the other parent— it is ambiguous which new family is the "same" family as the old one (Hill and Duncan 1985). Using individual children as the analysis unit solves this problem since they retain a unique identity across time. In some cases, where individual-based measures are unclear or unavailable, families with children should be the unit of analysis.

- Where possible, individual children should be the unit of analysis.

Not apparent in figure 12.1 but also noteworthy is the importance of subannual detail on many welfare experiences, particularly short ones.

- Precise description of short-run experiences with poverty or welfare receipt usually requires data collected over subannual accounting periods.

For example, single-spell duration estimates based on monthly data from the Survey of Income and Program Participation show that many spells end within a single calendar year. According to data from the Census Bureau's Survey of Income and Program Participation, some 58 percent of AFDC spells, 66 percent of Food Stamp spells, but only 27 percent of SSI spells begun during 1991 or 1992 ended within twelve months (U.S. Bureau of the Census Web page 1997).

One subtle but very important distinction in understanding welfare dynamics is between the nature of individuals who *ever* receive welfare and individuals who are receiving welfare at *any given point* (Bane and Ellwood 1983). Since long-term recipients are much more likely to show up as recipients at any given time, the welfare caseload at any point contains many more long-term recipients than figures based on individuals ever receiving AFDC would suggest.[3]

Fewer than 10 percent of current AFDC recipients will have a total period of receipt (including multiple episodes as well as both past and future periods of receipt) of less than two years, while more than three-quarters will have periods of receipt extending for at least five years. In fact, more than half (57 percent) of the caseload can expect to be on the rolls for a decade or longer.

Which view of welfare recipients—"ever received" or "point-in-time"—is the "best" one? The answer to that question depends on the issue under discussion. For policies directed at families just starting to receive welfare, the "ever received" view, with its large numbers of short-term recipients, is the more relevant one.

Suppose, on the other hand, that the contemplated program would be targeted to people currently receiving AFDC benefits. In this case, the "point-in-time" view, with its overrepresentation of long-term recipients, is the more useful. "Point-in-time" caseload policies are directed at the set of welfare families with longer-term experience.

The distinction between "ever-on" and "point-in-time" sampling has implications for indicators of dependence and well-being. In particular, caseload-based sources of information about welfare recipients in a given year describe a very different group of recipients than do survey-based data that follow recipients as they begin to receive welfare. Survey data, unlike caseload data, follow the experience of individuals when they are both on and off of the welfare rolls. Since policy decisions require information about both kinds of samples, it is important to develop indicators of both groups. But it is also important for readers of the indicators reports to understand the sometimes confusing differences that will emerge from these two types of characterizations. Thus:

• Indicators of dependence should come from both "point-in-time" caseload sources as well as "ever-on" survey sources.

Deprivation and dependence have both *intra-* and *inter*generational dimensions. If the patterns of deprivation or dependence shown in figure 12.1 span both childhood and adulthood, then they can be taken to show both kind of patterns. Suppose, for example, that all of the individuals depicted in figure 12.1 became adults (in the sense of forming their own households and/or being eligible for receiving benefits on behalf of their own children) at the beginning of 1995. Deprivation or dependence spells prior to the beginning of 1995 refer to their parental households, while deprivation or dependence after 1995 reflect their own experiences as adults. Of the five individuals leaving poor or dependent families, two (numbers 1 and 3) continue to be poor or dependent, while one individual (number 6) who had not been poor or dependent during childhood became so shortly after reaching adulthood. These patterns are not inconsistent with the intergenerational literature, which points to heterogeneous experiences with positive but far from perfect correlations in economic status or welfare use across generations.[4]

The Importance of the Length of the Accounting Period and Observation Window

The ability of surveys and administrative data to describe patterns of deprivation or dependence is governed by the accounting periods over which such experiences are measured and the total length of their observation windows. In terms of patterns depicted in figure 12.1, the ideal data for describing welfare experiences would be month-by-month observations of individuals over the entire twenty-two-year period. The monthly detail would capture the short-run dynamics of deprivation, dependence, and program eligibility, which for many programs is based on a monthly accounting period, while the twenty-two-year coverage would provide information on multiple spells and minimize problems with the observations being censored by the beginning or end of the observation window.

Going from optimal to second-best data is not unproblematic, given the heterogeneity of experiences and competing demands for information about short- and longer-run dynamics. Indicators of short-run dynamics require data with a subannual accounting period. Even if collected over an observation window as short as one or two years, such data would be valuable for describing rates of transitions into and out of deprivation or dependence as well as events (for example, marital, employment-related) associated with those transitions. For welfare use it might be possible to gather reliable retrospective information about the duration of receipt or nonreceipt prior to the beginning of the survey period.[5]

This would enable analysts to classify spells observed during the observation window as first or subsequent spells, as well as to determine the length of censored spells.

Accurate description of longer-run dynamics requires a longer observation window, and not so much monthly detail. Gottschalk and Moffitt (1994) argue persuasively for the utility of "total time on" and "total fraction of income" measures of welfare use, in which the total number of years of welfare use and percentage of total income made up by welfare payments are calculated over a multi- (in their case, seven-) year observation period, without regard to the particular pattern of spells. Duncan (1984) and Duncan and Rodgers (1991) develop analogous measures for poverty.

The picture drawn by an observation window of, say, ten years, can be seen in figure 12.1 by taking the patterns observed between the lines drawn at the beginning of 1980 and 1990. Nine of the ten individuals whose experiences are depicted in figure 12.1 are caught by this ten-year window. There appear to be three short-term patterns of two years or less (individuals 4, 5, and 10) and three long-term patterns of five years or more (individuals 1, 2, and 7), which is not substantially different from the distribution of twenty-two-year patterns. Only one individual (number 10) is seriously misclassified in the sense that his second and longer spell is missed by the 1980–1990 window. Individual 10 *is* correctly classified if the observation window is taken literally—that is, his experiences during the decade of the 1980s were short-term.

Ellwood's (1986) analysis of long-term welfare experiences takes a different approach, in which the incidence and duration of first spells and the timing and length of subsequent spells are combined into a simulation model of total lifetime welfare experiences. Data requirements for this approach differ little from those of the "total time on" approach. In both cases one needs a long enough observation window, possibly supplemented with retrospective data, to identify first spells and gauge the length and distribution of first and subsequent spells.

WHAT DIMENSIONS OF ECONOMIC DEPRIVATION ARE MOST IMPORTANT?

Given that actual patterns of deprivation and dependence include both short-term and long-term experiences, it is useful to step back and ask: Under what circumstances should social policy and therefore social indicators attach importance to the duration of deprivation or dependence?

There are two ways of approaching this question. The first is to look at the extent to which current or contemplated policies take duration into account in their program rules. The distribution of effort in developing short- and longer-run indicators of deprivation and dependence should bear some correspondence to the distribution of short- and longer-run definitions of deprivation found in actual programs. If, for example, most programs opt for a monthly income-accounting period, then it would make sense from this perspective to develop at least some social indicators based on monthly data. Since the 1996 welfare reforms impose a twenty-four-month limit on the duration of receipt of welfare without employment and a sixty-month limit on the unconditional receipt of welfare, there is an obvious need for monthly information about welfare experiences that span periods of more than twenty-four months.

The second approach to thinking about the important features of duration of deprivation is to ask what difference duration and timing of deprivation make for children's development. If there are significant detrimental effects of longer-run poverty on children's IQs or academic achievement or on their welfare or labor-supply behavior when they become young adults, but no discernible effects from short-run poverty or welfare dependence, then social indicators should be less concerned with short-run episodes of deprivation or dependence than with longer-term experiences. And if the evidence indicates that poverty or welfare receipt affects development during early childhood but not during adolescence, then social indicators of childhood poverty and dependence should be especially concerned with descriptions of patterns during early childhood.

Program Design

With respect to the question of actual practice, it is clear that many social-assistance programs are aimed at fulfilling short-term needs—food or heating, for example—and that almost all means-tested programs in the United States rely on a monthly accounting period for the allocation of their benefits. Since programs do not take into account whether families with little incomes and few assets have had or will soon again have adequate levels of economic resources, at least some social indicators should be similarly unconcerned with the longer-term picture. Thus:

- The policy importance of short-term needs dictates that at least some social indicators of deprivation and dependence focus on "point-in-time" samples, monthly accounting periods, and short-term dynamics experiences.

Policy initiatives focused on curing long-term poverty or preventing long-term welfare dependence must make the distinction between the short and longer term, recognizing which poor people are most likely to remain poor as well as which of the long-term poor would profit most from these programs. Ellwood (1986) argues that it is most effective to target training programs designed to promote work-to-welfare transitions on employable "would-be" long-term poor or social-assistance recipients. His accounting period for lifetime welfare use—twenty-five years—is long indeed. Thus:

- Many policy issues focus on long-term poor or dependent families, dictating a need for long-run indicators.

Developmental Consequences

A different perspective is provided by evidence on the developmental consequences of short and long term deprivation and dependence. Does it really matter for children's development whether their childhood episodes of economic deprivation are short or longer term? Are a few years of deprivation sufficient to leave developmental scars, or is the longer-run level of resources of primary importance?

An impressive set of correlational evidence links the poverty status of families with various developmental outcomes for children (Children's Defense Fund

1994; Carnegie Corporation 1994; Huston 1991; Mayer 1997; Duncan and Brooks-Gunn 1997). Why should economic resources matter? Low levels of resources can render parents incapable of providing children with the necessary elements of successful childhood. Extreme poverty can make it difficult for parents to provide food and shelter; less extreme forms of financial hardship can make it difficult to provide enriching learning experiences either in the home or outside of it. All levels of deprivation may limit children's access to health care. Low levels of parental resources can lead to less parental involvement in children's developmental activities, social activities, and schooling, putting children at higher risk of difficulties in school, reduced accomplishments in elementary and high school, lower aspirations for college attainments, and higher risk of engaging in adult behavior such as sexual activity and independent living earlier than children otherwise would.

An illustration of the links in early childhood between family income and cognitive development is provided by Smith et al. (1997). They draw data from the National Longitudinal Survey of Youth and the Infant Health and Development Program—two studies that followed children from birth until middle childhood. After controlling for differences in the child's race, birth weight, age, and gender, and for the mother's education and family structure, they compare cognitive test score data on children with different levels of family income. Using children in families with incomes between 1.5 and 2 times the poverty line as the comparison group, they find that by age five, children growing up in deep poverty (with average incomes less than half the poverty line) scored 9–12 points lower on the cognitive tests. Since all of the tests of cognitive ability and achievement were independently normed with means of 100 and standard deviations of around 15, this difference is quite substantial. Children growing up in families with incomes between half of the poverty line and the poverty line had scores that were between 4 and 12 points lower than the reference group of nonpoor children. Other parts of their analysis suggested that increasing the incomes of children below or near the poverty line has a larger impact on ability and achievement than increasing the incomes of children in middle-class and affluent families.

More generally, the research on links between poverty and child development indicates that family economic conditions in early and middle childhood appear to be more important for shaping ability and achievement than do economic conditions during adolescence (Duncan and Brooks-Gunn 1997). As a consequence:

- Indicators of material deprivation such as low family income should be tabulated separately by age of the child, with the greatest concern accorded to young children living in families with incomes well below the poverty line.

Similar questions can be asked of the literature on welfare receipt. Does the length of parental dependence matter for children's outcomes? Theories of poverty have often included an intergenerational component, with anthropological studies arguing that children growing up in poor families and communities are likely to adopt the fatalistic and self-defeating attitudes and behavior of their parents (Lewis 1968). In the case of welfare use, it is also easy to imagine that characteristics of some recipient households—lack of attachment to the labor force and dependence on government income support—might convey to children the viability of similar kinds of lives in adulthood.

An obvious problem in drawing conclusions about the intergenerational consequences of parental welfare receipt is the need to adjust for other aspects of parental background and environment that may also affect a child's chance of subsequent success. Children from AFDC-dependent homes generally have fewer parental resources available to them, live in worse neighborhoods, go to lower-quality schools, and so forth. Any of these factors could have an effect on their accomplishments as adults that is independent of their parents' AFDC receipt.

Studies of effects of welfare receipt on early childhood outcomes using national data tend to find conflicting evidence (Yeung et al. 1996). In data from the NLSY, it appeared that welfare receipt was detrimental to the cognitive development of white children but not black children. A comparable analysis of data from the Infant Health and Development Program found no apparent effect of welfare on the cognitive development of whites, but larger effects for blacks. Nor was there consistency between the two data sets in an investigation of possible effects of welfare receipt on behavior problems of black and white children. It is clear that more research is needed on the question of whether and why welfare receipt affects the development of young children.

Studies relating parental welfare receipt during early adolescence to schooling and demographic behavior in late adolescence and early adulthood are more consistent in showing detrimental effects. For example, Gottschalk (1994) uses data on patterns of mother's welfare receipt *after* the daughter has left home to adjust for the effects of unobserved characteristics of mothers. After incorporating these adjustments, he finds for blacks but not for whites highly significant effects of parental welfare receipt on the chances that daughters will have AFDC-related births. Furthermore, the strongest effects are for parental receipt immediately prior to the daughter's possible fertility. Duncan and Yeung (1995) use similar methods and find detrimental effects of welfare on the completed schooling of children.

In sum:

- Evidence indicates a possible role for welfare receipt as a risk factor in childhood. Since the effects appear to vary according to the age of the child at the time of receipt, it is important that indicators of welfare receipt as a risk factor be geared to the age of the child.

All in all, both program considerations and developmental evidence suggest a need for both short- and longer-run indicators of deprivation and dependence. Many programs use a monthly income accounting period suggesting a need for short-run indicators, while many policies are geared toward assisting long-term and potential long-term recipients, suggesting a need for long-run indicators. There appears to be a growing consensus that both parental poverty and welfare use can have measurable effects on children's development. However, since there is insufficient evidence on the impact of the duration or timing of poverty or welfare use during childhood, both short- and longer-term indicators are clearly needed.

ARE CURRENT INDICATORS ADEQUATE?

Thus armed with an appreciation of the utility of both short- and longer-run indicators of deprivation and dependence, we turn to an assessment of our current stock of indicators.

The Current Population Survey

Most indicators of poverty come from the Census Bureau's Current Population Survey and are published in the annual volumes entitled *Poverty in the United States* (U.S. Bureau of the Census 1993). Each March CPS measures income and poverty thresholds over a single annual accounting period. The poverty status of all individuals and households in the sixty-thousand-household CPS sample is determined. Then, population weights are used to make the sample nationally representative and poverty rates are tabulated according to a myriad of demographic characteristics.

Recent years have seen numerous attempts to gauge the sensitivity of "official" poverty estimates to the method of inflation adjustment; the inclusion of noncash sources of income such as Food Stamps and Medicaid benefits; the proration of the poverty threshold to the composition of the family during the calendar year in which income was received; and so on. When the annual CPS data are placed side by side, they form a useful time series of snapshot pictures of the incidence of annual poverty dating back to the mid-1960s. These annual poverty indicators are released at the same time each year, amid great publicity, and often generate a productive discussion in editorials, opinion-page columns, and television reports.

When judged against our criteria for desirable properties of indicators of deprivation, how well does the CPS measure stack up? Unfortunately, not very well at all. In fact, were we starting from scratch in developing social indicators of economic deprivation, it would be hard to imagine selecting a worse indicator than one based on the CPS and an annual accounting period.

A first problem is the serious underreporting of transfer income in the CPS. The U.S. Bureau of the Census (1993, Table c-1) reports that the CPS accounts for only 71.6 percent of AFDC benefits, 89.0 percent of Supplemental Security Income, and 86.2 percent of other public assistance. As mentioned earlier, the CPS poverty rate is 30 percent higher than measured in the higher-quality SIPP data. It is puzzling that a 30 percent bias is not viewed with more concern than seems to be generated by the CPS bias.

A second problem with the CPS is that information about the makeup of the family and the family situation is measured at the time of the interview, while means-tested assistance is measured over the entire previous year. This creates a mismatch between those in the family at the time of the interview and those who benefited from assistance.

A third problem with the CPS measures of poverty and dependency is its annual accounting period, an example of which is depicted in figure 12.1 for the calendar year 1994. The window captures as poor half of the ten individuals who were ever poor over the twenty-two-year period, but its "point-in-time" nature leads it to miss short-term poor altogether. Thus, a twelve-month accounting period cannot be used to describe the distribution of experiences for the "ever-on" deprived.

The CPS measure for welfare dependency is slightly better. The survey asks whether an individual received any assistance in the previous year by program and the amount received. For AFDC, the CPS also asks the number of months in which assistance was received. Therefore, the short-term recipients are not missed altogether. However, because the CPS does not ask in *which* months AFDC was received, the subannual pattern of dependency cannot be determined.

More generally, a twelve-month accounting period is not ideal as either a short- or long-run poverty indicator. It is not short enough to capture month-to-month dynamics important for program participation; nor is it long enough to capture the essential features of "long-term" deprivation. Nor can one argue that an annual accounting period is a useful "compromise" between needs for short- and longer-run periods. Since heterogeneity is the essential empirical feature of both patterns of deprivation and program needs, it is crucial to have measures of *both* long- and short-run deprivation rather than a compromise that fails to capture the essential features of either.

Since the CPS does not (and, given memory problems, cannot) ask about poverty for any year prior to the calendar year just preceding the March interview, nor does it provide data on intrayear (for example, monthly) income dynamics, its annual accounting period is also ill-suited for describing trends in any of the key components of patterns of poverty and dependence: onset and duration of initial spells and spacing and length of second and subsequent spells. The absence of subannual or multiyear data also renders it incapable of describing events associated with the beginning or ending of spells. To be fair, we should note that the CPS was designed to be a labor-force survey and its annual income information has the status of a "supplement" that is administered in only one month (March) of the year.

The Survey of Income and Program Participation

The SIPP was begun largely in response to the limitations of the CPS in providing needed details on income dynamics and program participation. SIPP's panels have varied in size from thirteen thousand to twenty-one thousand five hundred households. The 1993 panel has twenty thousand households. SIPP's observation window is wider than that of the CPS and its thrice-a-year interviews provide data over a monthly accounting period. Panels begun between 1984 and 1995 were designed to run for two and a half years. Beginning in 1996, the census changed the sample design and will field nonoverlapping panels of about forty thousand households to be followed for a total of fifty-two months. In addition, the 1996 welfare reform legislation provides funds to the Census Bureau to conduct a special SIPP panel, the Survey of Program Dynamics, or SPD, to last for ten years. The SPD will make special efforts to collect data on the children in SIPP households. It will be designed as an extension of the SIPP panel begun in 1992 and 1993.

The core SIPP questionnaire, repeated every four months, asks detailed questions concerning employment, income, and participation in federal social-support programs. Much of the information is collected on a month-by-month basis. These questions are asked about all adults age fifteen and over in the household. Special modules covering personal history and data on school enrollment and financing are administered once or twice to each panel.

In addition, there are a number of special topical modules. Some have been asked of every panel to date; others have been fielded only once or twice. Topics include child care arrangements, child-support agreements, functional limitations and disability, utilization of health-care services, support for nonhousehold members, and others.

SIPP's features are better suited to the task of describing the dynamics of deprivation and dependence, but some problems remain. An examination of figure 12.1 shows that a fifty-two-month accounting period is much more likely to capture a mixture of short- and long-term recipients, although it is still a biased sampling of the "ever-on" population. Complete spells lasting more than fifty-two months will not be observed in their entirety in SIPP, nor will repeat spells that are spaced more than fifty-two months apart. A serious problem for longitudinal indicators of deprivation and dependence is that current plans for nonoverlapping samples in SIPP introduce a very unhelpful break in SIPP-based time-series on many potential dynamic social indicators. For example, it would be helpful to use data from adjacent years to calculate rates of transition out of and into poverty among children. Nonoverlapping samples between years t and t + 1 render it impossible to compute transition rates between those years.

On the plus side, however, the fifty-two-month panel period is sufficient to observe many transitions into and out of poverty and onto and off welfare rolls, as well as providing ancillary information needed to couple these transitions with events such as marriage/divorce and employment/job loss. Monthly data from the Survey of Income and Program Participation have been used to provide a number of interesting indicators of poverty and welfare incidence and transitions (U.S. Bureau of the Census 1991, 1992).

Welfare Caseload Statistics

Apart from recent SIPP-based reports on receipt of benefits from various transfer programs, the most comprehensive source of time-series information on "point-in-time" welfare samples is caseload data calculated from data provided by the states and presented periodically in the "Green Book" of the Committee on Ways and Means of the House of Representatives. For the AFDC program, for example, the *Green Book* (1993) provides useful information on: total spending on AFDC benefits; state benefit levels; number of child recipients; demographic characteristics of recipient families; past duration of receipt; and fraction of recipients with no reported income other than AFDC.

The 1996 Personal Responsibility and Work Opportunity Act requires states to submit monthly case record data on families who receive assistance under the AFDC-replacement Temporary Assistance for Needy Families (TANF) program. The required data include: the amount and type of assistance provided under TANF; the length of time on each type of assistance under TANF; work program participation; whether benefits were terminated due to sanctions, time limits, or other reasons; and participation in other federal programs. These requirements should provide state- and even county-level data on social assistance receipt that is roughly comparable to that provided as part of the old AFDC system.

Longer-Run Surveys

Although not used to report "official" statistics, the Panel Study of Income Dynamics (PSID) and National Longitudinal Survey of Youth (NLSY) have provided a wealth of longer-run intra- and intergenerational data on both deprivation and dependence. The PSID began with a representative sample of households in 1968 and provides annual data on income and, since 1983 for certain transfer incomes such as AFDC, monthly data on dependence for its sample households. By following children as they leave home and counting new births as part of its sample of individuals, the PSID has a mechanism for providing continuously representative household samples (except for immigration) as well as representative intergenerational data.

The National Longitudinal Survey was begun in 1979 with a nationally representative sample of fourteen- to twenty-one-year-olds. It has taken annual interviews with its sample since 1979 and conducted extensive assessments of the children of the mothers in the cohort every two years beginning in 1986. Interviews taken with parents of members of the original cohorts provide rich intergenerational information. Extensive cognitive and behavioral information on children born to women in the original cohorts has been gathered every two years since 1986. A new sample of adolescent cohorts will be drawn and interviewed in 1997.

RECOMMENDATIONS

Our discussion thus far points to the need for routinely reported indicators of deprivation and dependence that describe both short- and longer-run dynamic aspects of poverty and antipoverty programs. In particular, our conceptual discussion points to the need for time-series of indicators of:

- the number and characteristics of the "point-in-time" population of poor or dependent children or families with children;

- the number and characteristics of children experiencing first and subsequent transitions into and out of poverty or dependence and the events associated with these transitions;

- the number and characteristics of "long-term" poor or dependent children; and

- intergenerational correlations of poverty and welfare receipt.

Although fatally flawed by problems of data quality, CPS-based poverty indicators should serve as a model for how poverty indicators are processed and publicized. Compiled within six months of the completion of interviewing and reported at the same time each year, the CPS poverty indicators receive a great deal of publicity. It is crucial that all of the recommended indicators of short-run poverty or dependence be as timely and regular as the CPS poverty counts.

Furthermore, the methodology associated with the CPS poverty counts produces a reasonably consistent time-series of poverty data. This is essential, given the difficulty in understanding and explaining the effects of changes in the methodology used in compiling the statistics. Finally, timely release of the CPS microdata files enables researchers to explore the robustness of the "official" indicators to various changes in definition and to produce tabulations of the poverty data that are better suited for particular policy concerns. The desirability of all social indicators should be evaluated with an eye toward these characteristics.

We now turn to detailed recommendations regarding these indicators. Our discussion assumes that the basic designs of the Current Population Survey and Survey of Income and Program Participation remain the same, with SIPP maintaining its intended fifty-two-month duration. We further assume that the NLSY will continue with its current sample and start interviewing a new sample as planned. Finally, we assume that the PSID will continue with its evolutionary sample, but will start collecting data every other year in 1997.

Short-Run Indicators of Poverty

Average Monthly Poverty Rates and Characteristics of the Poor   These should be published annually, based on data from SIPP. The month is the most appropriate accounting period for measurement of short-run poverty, although it makes sense to average the monthly poverty rates over a calendar year to smooth out seasonal fluctuations. At least some indicators should be provided using the child as the unit of analysis and separately by the child's developmental stage. Some indicators should also take into account the suggestions for changes in the poverty measure made by the National Research Council. Although rates of poverty are most important, indicators showing the degree of poverty (the average gap between the incomes of the poor and the poverty line) should also be compiled. These average monthly rates should replace the CPS annual poverty rates as the principal source of short-run poverty estimates. For purposes of historical comparisons, it would be useful to continue the basic CPS time-series as well, although this should have a lower priority than furthering the timely release of the SIPP-based data.

Rates of Transitions into and out of Poverty   These should be published annually, based on monthly data from SIPP, with at least some indicators using children as the unit of analysis. Methodological work is needed to determine the optimal measurement of an entry into or exit from a spell of poverty (yearly poverty transitions are too long term, but monthly poverty transitions may be too short term—does a single month out of poverty constitute a true "exit" from poverty?) Time-series data on the gross flows into and out of poverty will be invaluable in understanding the net changes in the average monthly rates. It should be noted that the current SIPP plans for nonoverlapping panels will make it impossible to construct a continuous time-series of these indicators. Some indicators should also take into account the suggestions for changes in the poverty measure made by the National Research Council.

Events Associated with Transitions into and out of Poverty   These should be published annually, based on monthly data from SIPP, with at least some indicators using the child as the unit of analysis. These data should be coupled with the transition data listed above. It would be very useful to be able to track the marital, fertility, and employment events associated with transitions into and out of poverty—in the case of transitions into poverty: divorce/separation; the birth of a child to an unmarried woman; involuntary job loss; voluntary withdrawal from the labor force; cessation of transfer income payments. Welfare-related events such as sanctions and time limits are crucial as well. These events need not be defined to be mutually exclusive, since transitions may result from combinations of them. It should be noted that the current SIPP plans for non-overlapping panels will make it impossible to construct a continuous time-series of these indicators. Some indicators should also take into account the suggestions for changes in the poverty measure made by the National Research Council.

Income Changes Surrounding Important Demographic and Employment Events   These should be published annually, based on monthly data from SIPP, with at least some indicators using the child as the unit of analysis. Past work has shown dramatic differences for exhusbands, exwives, and children in income changes surrounding divorce or separation (Duncan and Hoffman 1985). These changes need to be tracked on a routine basis in order to monitor progress in child-support enforcement and other policies aimed at promoting an equitable burden following marital dissolution. Other candidate events include: welfare sanctions and time limits associated with the 1996 welfare reform legislation and waivers granted to states prior to 1996; job loss, with the attendant change in earned and family income and health insurance coverage; and welfare-to-work transitions, for which changes in total income and health insurance coverage are of greatest interest. The infrequency with which these events occur may require the pooling of several SIPP panels and less-than-annual reporting. It should be noted that current SIPP plans for nonoverlapping panels will make it impossible to construct a continuous time-series of this indicator.

Long-Run Indicators of Poverty

Distribution of Poverty Experiences over Multiyear Accounting-Period "Windows"   These should be published periodically, based on data from SIPP, with at least some indicators using the child as the unit of analysis. As argued by Gottschalk and Moffitt (1994) in the context of welfare receipt, a "total time in poverty" measure, when taken over a multiyear accounting period, provides a useful approximation of the distribution of short- and longer-run experiences depicted in figure 12.1. This should be taken once per SIPP panel, using as long a window as possible and compiled separately by developmental period. For a fifty-two-month panel, this indicator would take the form of a distribution of the total number of months out of fifty-two that a child's household income was below the poverty line. Multiyear poverty and dependence indicators should be checked against and extended to longer accounting periods (the entire period of childhood in the PSID) using data from the PSID and NLSY.

Intergenerational Indicators of Poverty

Intergenerational Poverty Correlations   Both the PSID (see Solon 1992) and NLSY (see Zimmerman 1992) can be used to compare the parental economic status of adolescents with the economic status of those same individuals one to two decades later when the adolescents are well into their early adult years. The design of the PSID now provides a substantial number of cohorts for whom intergenerational correlations can be calculated. Intergenerational correlations of poverty and earnings should be calculated and tracked periodically. An example of this would be the cross-classification of the years an individual spends poor during adolescence while living as a dependent against the years he or she spends poor as an adult.

Short-Run Indicators of Dependence

"Green-Book"-Type Indicators of Point-in-Time Welfare Receipt Caseload records should be used to provide point-in-time indicators such as number of child recipients, demographic characteristics of recipient families, and the fraction of recipients with no reported income other than AFDC. Virtually all of this information is available in SIPP, but for much smaller samples of recipients.

Rates of Transitions onto and off Major Social-Assistance Programs These should be published annually, based on monthly data from SIPP, with at least some indicators calculated using the child as the unit of analysis. As with poverty, methodological work is needed to determine the optimal measurement of the beginnings and endings of spells of social-assistance receipt. In contrast to the situation with poverty spells, there is some chance that the retrospective reports of social-assistance history can be used to classify transitions according to whether they are associated with first versus subsequent spells of receipt.

Events Associated with Transitions onto and off Major Social-Assistance Programs These should be published annually, based on monthly data from SIPP, with at least some indicators calculated using the child as the unit of analysis. These data should be coupled with the transition data listed above. As with poverty, it would be very useful to be able to track the marital, fertility, employment, and welfare-law sanction and time-limit events associated with transitions into and out of first and subsequent spells of social-assistance receipt.

Take-up Rates for Major Transfer Programs Affecting Children These should be published annually, based on monthly data from SIPP, with at least some indicators calculated using the child as the unit of analysis. Since SIPP was designed to provide almost all of the information needed to determine program eligibility, it can be used to monitor the fraction of children whose families qualify for various means-tested transfer programs but do not receive them.

The Percent of Income from Employment Versus Means-Tested Assistance These should be published annually, based on monthly data from the SIPP, with at least some indicators calculated using the child as the unit of analysis. This indicator will measure the degree of dependence by household characteristics. This measure would reflect the difference between households where means-tested assistance is the only source of income and those where assistance is a small supplement to earnings from paid employment.

Long-Run Indicators of Dependence

Distribution of Welfare-Receipt Experiences over a Multiyear Accounting-Period "Window"   These should be published periodically, based on data from SIPP, with at least some indicators using the child as the unit of analysis. As with poverty indicators, a "total time on welfare" measure, when taken over a multiyear accounting period, provides a useful approximation of the distribution of short- and longer-run experiences depicted in figure 12.1. Given the twenty-four-month limit on receipt of welfare in the absence of work mandated by the 1996 welfare reform legislation, it would be useful for compile information on months of welfare receipt coupled with no employment. This should be compiled once per SIPP panel, using as long a window as possible. Similar measures should also be calculated over the very long accounting periods of the PSID and NLSY.

Intergenerational Indicators of Dependence

As with intergenerational poverty indicators, the PSID and NLSY samples should be used to calculate a time-series of associations of transfer-program receipt between parents and children. An example of such associations are presented by Duncan, Hill, and Hoffman (1988), who tabulate, for a representative sample of females, the distribution of years between ages fourteen and sixteen in which parents received income from AFDC compared with the number of years between age twenty-one and twenty-three in which daughters themselves received AFDC.

Experimental Indicators

Associations Between Family Income and Child Outcomes   SIPP is experimenting with question modules focused on child development and may obtain periodic measurements of child health and cognitive development. It would be useful to track associations between household economic status measured between years one and four with children's outcomes measured at the end of the fourth year to see if income-outcome linkages were growing stronger or weaker over time.

The Fab Five

If forced to condense the above list to a handful of indicators, we would opt for the following:

- *Short-run children's poverty:* average monthly poverty rates for children, published annually, based on SIPP.
- *Longer-run children's poverty:* multiyear (fifty-two-month) distribution of time in poverty for children, published as often as possible, based on SIPP.

- *Short-run children's dependence:* point-in-time AFDC recipiency rates for children, published annually, based on caseload data.

- *The degree of dependence:* average monthly measures of the percent of family income from employment versus means-tested assistance, published annually, based on SIPP.

- *Longer-run children's dependence:* multiyear (fifty-two-month) distribution of time spent receiving AFDC income for children, published as often as possible, based on SIPP.

The work for this paper was supported in part by the National Institute for Child Health and Human Development as part of its Family and Child Well-Being Research Network. Many of the ideas for indicators based on data from the Survey of Income and Program Participation were developed while Duncan participated on the National Research Council's Panel to Evaluate the Survey of Income and Program Participation. Pat Ruggles and Connie Citro made extensive contributions to the social indicators portion of the Panel's work. This paper has benefited from helpful comments from Terry Adams, Rebecca Blank, Jeanne Brooks-Gunn, Brett Brown, Jason Cohen, Sheldon Danziger, Dorothy Duncan, Pamela Klebanov, Ann McCormick, and Kristin Moore and from the research assistance of Gretchen Caspary.

NOTES

1. For example, U.S. Bureau of the Census (1991, table D-3) reports an overall poverty rate in 1988 (13.0 percent) that is 30 percent higher using data from the Current Population Survey than the poverty rate (at 10.0 percent) calculated from the Survey of Income and Program Participation.

2. This estimate is from Bane and Ellwood and is based on annual data. Monthly data on AFDC (Pavetti 1994) and Food Stamp (Burstein 1993) receipt show even more exits and reentries.

3. Bane and Ellwood (1983) illustrate this point as follows: Suppose that a hospital has 100 beds, 99 of which contain very long-term patients. The 100th bed is used by short-term patients, each of whom stays in the hospital for only one day. Over the course of one year, there will be 464 patients in these beds—99 long-term patients and 365 short-term patients. Thus, the fraction of patients ever in the hospital over the course of the year who are short term is very high—79 percent (365/464). On the other hand, at any point during the year, 99 percent of all beds will house long-term patients. Thus, because the longer-term patients are much more likely to show up in a patient count at any point during the year, they dominate the hospital "caseload" at any point.

4. For example, Duncan, Hill, and Hoffman (1988) show that the majority (66 percent) of daughters from highly dependent parental families did not, when in their early twenties, share the fate of their parents. At the same time, however, the fraction of daughters from highly dependent homes who themselves become highly dependent (20 percent) was much greater than the fraction of daughters from nonrecipient families who become highly dependent (only 3 percent). Mary Corcoran reports similar patterns using unpublished PSID data on intergenerational poverty.

5. Mathiowetz (1994) provides evidence from a validation study that earnings cannot be recalled reliably for more than one calendar year, especially if earnings change substantially.

REFERENCES

Bane, M. J., and D. Ellwood. 1983. "The Dynamics of Dependence and the Routes to Self-Sufficiency." Final report to the U.S. Department of Health and Human Services. Cambridge, Mass.: Harvard University, Kennedy School of Government.

————. 1994. *Welfare Realities: From Rhetoric to Reform.* Cambridge, Mass.: Harvard University Press.

Burstein, N. R. 1993. "Dynamics of the Food Stamp Program as Reported in the Survey of Income and Program Participation." In *Current Perspectives on Food Stamp Program Participation.* Cambridge, Mass.: Abt Associates, Inc.

Carnegie Corporation. 1994. *Starting Points: Meeting the Needs of Our Youngest Children.* New York: Carnegie Corporation.

Children's Defense Fund. 1994. *Wasting America's Future: The Children's Defense Fund Report on the Costs of Child Poverty.* Boston, Mass.: Beacon Press.

Citro, C. F., and R. T. Michael, eds. 1995. *Panel on Poverty and Family Assistance: Concepts, Information Needs, and Measurement Methods.* Washington, D.C.: National Academy Press.

Committee on Ways and Means. 1993. *1993 Green Book: Background Material and Data on Programs Within the Jurisdiction of the Committee on Ways and Means.* Washington: U.S. Government Printing Office.

Duncan, G. J. 1984. *Years of Poverty, Years of Plenty.* Ann Arbor, Mich.: Institute for Social Research.

Duncan, G. J., and J. Brooks-Gunn, eds. 1997. *Consequences of Growing Up Poor.* New York: Russell Sage Foundation.

Duncan, G. J., M. S. Hill, and S. D. Hoffman. 1988. "Welfare Dependence Within and Across Generations." *Science* 239: 467–71.

Duncan, G. J., and S. Hoffman. 1985. "A Reconsideration of the Economic Consequences of Marital Dissolution." *Demography,* 22: 485–97.

Duncan, G. J., and W. Rodgers. 1991. "Has Children's Poverty Become More Persistent?" *American Sociological Review* 56: 538–50.

Duncan, G. J., and W. Yeung. 1995. "Extent and Consequences of Welfare Dependence," *Child and Youth Services Review* 17: 157–82.

Ellwood, D. 1986. "Targeting 'Would-Be' Long Term Recipients of AFDC." Report prepared for the Department of Health and Human Services. Princeton, N.J.: Mathematica Policy Research, Inc.

Gottschalk, P. 1994. "Is the Intergenerational Correlation in Welfare Participation across Generations Spurious?" Working paper. Chestnut Hill, Mass.: Economics Department, Boston College.

Gottschalk, P., and R. Moffitt. 1994. "Welfare Dependence: Concepts, Measures, and Trends" *American Economic Review* 84(2): 38–42.

Hill, M., and G. Duncan. 1985. "Conceptions of Longitudinal Households: Fertile or Futile?" *Journal of Economic and Social Measurement* 13(3–4): 361–75.

Huston, A. 1991. *Children in Poverty: Child Development and Public Policy.* Cambridge, England: Cambridge University Press.

Lewis, O. 1968. *La Vida, a Puerto Rican Family in the Culture of Poverty: San Juan and New York.* London, England: Panther Books.

Mathiowetz, N. 1994. "Autobiographical Memory and the Validity of Survey Data: Implications for the Design of the Panel Study of Income Dynamics." Working Paper. Ann Arbor, Mich.: Survey Research Center, University of Michigan.

Mayer, S. 1994. "Measuring Income, Employment and the Support of Children." Working Paper. Chicago: Harris School, University of Chicago.

————. 1997. *What Money Can't Buy: The Effect of Parental Income on Children's Outcomes.* Cambridge, Mass.: Harvard University Press.

Moynihan, D. P. 1991. "Social Justice in the Next Century." *America* 165(6): 13–137.

Pavetti, L. 1994. *Policies to Time-Limit AFDC Benefits: What Can We Learn from Welfare Dynamics?* Mimeo. Washington, D.C.: The Urban Institute.

Rupp, K., and C. G. Scott. 1995. "Length of Stay on the Supplemental Security Income Disability Program." *Social Security Bulletin* 58(1): 29–47.

Solon, G. 1992. "Intergenerational Income Mobility in the United States." *American Economic Review* 82(3): 393–408.

Smith, J. R., J. Brooks-Gunn, and P. K. Klebanov. Forthcoming. "Consequences of Living in Poverty for Young Children's Cognitive and Verbal Ability and Early School Achievement." In *Consequences of Growing Up Poor,* edited by G. J. Duncan and J. Brooks-Gunn. New York: Russell Sage Foundation.

U.S. Bureau of the Census. 1991. "Transitions in Income and Poverty Status: 1987–1988." *Current Population Reports,* series P-70, no. 24. Washington: U.S. Government Printing Office.

———. 1992. "Characteristics of Recipients and the Dynamics of Program Participation: 1987–1988." *Current Population Reports,* series P-70, no. 31. Washington: U.S. Government Printing Office.

———. 1993. "Poverty in the United States, 1992." *Current Population Reports,* series P-60-185, Washington: U.S. Government Printing Office.

U.S. Bureau of the Census Web Page. 1997. "Dynamics of Economic Well-Being: Program Participation, 1991 to 1993" [Online]. Available at http://www.census.gov/hhes/www/transfer.html. (May 27, 1997).

U.S. Department of Health and Human Services. 1996. "Indicators of Welfare Dependency and Well-Being: Interim Report to Congress." Washington: U.S. Department of Health and Human Services (October).

Yeung, W., J. Brooks-Gunn, G. Duncan, and J. Smith. 1996. "Does Parental Welfare Dependence Harm Children?" Mimeo. Northwestern University.

Zimmerman, D. 1992. "Regression Toward Mediocrity in Economic Stature." *American Economic Review* 82(3): 409–29.

13

Parental Employment and Children

Judith R. Smith, Jeanne Brooks-Gunn, and Aurora Jackson

NEGATIVE CHILD OUTCOMES have been linked to living in poverty or economic disadvantage (Brooks-Gunn and Duncan 1997; Duncan and Brooks-Gunn, forthcoming; Haveman and Wolfe 1995). Low birth weight, higher levels of infant mortality, stunting, malnutrition, poor scores on cognitive standardized tests, and higher levels of behavior problems and school dropout all are associated with living in poverty. Children's economic security is dependent on family income, parental employment, and government income transfers when family income and parental labor force participation are insufficient or nonexistent. In addition, the macro economy affects parent's earning capacities, which affects children's economic security.

Several models describe how parental income might affect children's life chances (see chapter 11, this volume). The investment model suggests that higher family income leads to greater child well-being via increased parental purchasing power to invest in food, housing, medical care, and education. An alternative model examines the indirect effects of economic deprivation on child well-being via increases in family stress, which diminish the parent's ability to provide stability, warmth, adequate attention, supervision, and cognitive stimulation to their children. A third model focuses on the effects on children of parent's norms and values. This theory suggests that children's success in the world is affected by their parent's norms and values, which are dependent on their type of employment, community, and position in the social hierarchy. Each of these three models assumes that greater economic resources will improve the well-being of children either directly or indirectly.

Although consensus exists regarding the links between increased family income on child well-being (Duncan, Yeung, Brooks-Gunn and Smith forthcoming; but see Mayer, 1997, for an alternative viewpoint), policy researchers disagree as to the effect of parental employment on child well-being, specifically maternal employment. While it has been implicitly accepted that fathers need to work in order to provide economic security for the family, this assumption has not held for women. Women's role has traditionally not been to provide their children with economic security, but with domestic security. Child care has traditionally been the woman's (unpaid) job. Traditionally, a mother was seen as doing a "good job" when she devoted her time to child and family responsibilities, rather than market work outside of the home. As women have increasingly entered the paid labor force, a key question has been whether or not the added income from her employment outweighs the cost to children and spouse of having both parents unavailable for full-time domestic home production.

Most women with young children are now employed outside of the house. The increase in women's labor force participation is associated with increased economic well-being of children. During the 1980s the significance of a woman's contribution to family income became critical in offsetting the declines in men's earnings. If not for the increased work effort of their mothers, families of children in the poorest income group (the bottom 20 percent of the income distribution) would have lost 7.2 percent of their income compared to the actual loss of 2.5 percent during the recessions of the 1980s. Longitudinal studies show the importance of a mother's earnings in providing income to raise her family's income to above the poverty threshold (Bane and Ellwood 1983; Danziger and Gottschalk 1990; McLanahan and Sandefur 1994). A critical issue is under what circumstances will the financial benefits of being a working mother also lead to improved emotional well-being for the mother, child, and/or the family.

Understanding the various aspects of family life that may be affected by increased maternal and paternal employment are important to any discussion on economic security, as increased parental employment is one mechanism by which children's economic security can be improved. Examining the dynamics of parental employment must also include the trade-offs made by working parents which might negatively affect child well-being. Parental employment reduces the amount of time mothers and fathers have available for supervision and leisure time with children. In addition, the quality of the child care selected by the family may be of much poorer quality than that which the mother or father could have provided if they did not have to work outside of the home. Indicators of child well-being must be able to account for whether or not the economic benefits accrued from employment offset any stress experienced by the child as a result of the parent's employment. We first review briefly the historical changes in mothers' workforce participation, keeping in mind the importance of age of the child and marital status of the mother in interpreting rates of labor force participation. Then, the effects of maternal employment on the child are considered. In the next section, the three contexts most centrally influenced by working are identified. They are the parent's job, the home, and the child care environment. The chapter concludes with a brief discussion of the relative importance of current changes in parents' employment on child well-being and a recommendation of the critical measures of parental employment for inclusion in future data collection efforts.

THE CHANGING WORK STATUS OF PARENTS

The large numbers of mothers in the labor force are redefining family life. Family role definitions, family division of time, child care arrangements, and a woman's experience in both the workplace and at home with her children all may be affected. Over 73 percent of all women with children ages six to seventeen are employed outside the home and over half of women with children under one year-old are working (U.S. Census, *Current Population Reports* 1996). Although the employment of women with children outside of the home necessitates reliance on nonparental child care, federal legislation and marketplace solutions do not adequately address this reality, leaving individual families to balance work and family without adequate support. While there have been some recent incremental changes in policies which affect working families, such as the Family Leave Bill of 1992, the 1990 Child Care and Development Block Grant, and significant increases in the Earned Income Tax Credit, a working mother in the United States is not yet assured of a paid parental leave, affordable quality child care, or a choice to work shorter hours to accommodate child-rearing responsibilities (Hyde 1991; Kamerman 1980; Kamerman and Kahn 1981, 1991, 1996). Additionally, the time limits mandated in Temporary Assistance for Needy Families (TANF) will limit the options available for poor mothers with young children to remain at home with their children, as well as increase the demand and the competition among the formerly welfare-dependent and the working poor for low-cost child care.

Lost in most debates about employment is the role of the father. What are the effects of paternal employment on family functioning and child well-being. We know very little. A father's employment has never been seen as a possible risk factor for child well-being, except in terms of job loss. Current demographic changes include relatively high rates of unemployment, underemployment, and job loss for some groups of fathers (young minority men, men with little education, men employed in low-wage jobs, as well as men losing jobs due to corporate downsizing) and the dramatic increase in divorce and never-married families. Consequently, we believe that the effects of a father's employment (or lack of employment and lack of contribution to family income) on child functioning and adolescents' perceptions of the world of work must be further studied.

Women's work outside of the home has challenged traditional ideas on sex roles and child care. With the development of a market economy and the move of production to outside of the family unit, women's status declined. The ideology of "true womanhood" and the science of "educated motherhood" emerged to define a woman's sphere within the home as "keeper of the hearth" and "heart" (Bernard 1981; Cott 1977; Ehrenreich and English 1978; de Mause 1974; Lopata, Miller, and Barnewolt 1984; Oakley 1974). In the 20th century, findings from psychological and psychoanalytic research have been used by some to justify a woman's role outside of the market place or as a part-time or poorly compensated employee.

Despite the ideological support for an at-home unemployed mother, women's labor force participation rate has grown almost continuously since the Industrial Revolution. Even in the preindustrial 19th century, women typically were not available for full-time child rearing, as they had to work many hours at home doing farm and domestic chores. Women's labor force participation rates did recede temporarily after World War II when women were pulled out of jobs they held during the war to create jobs for the returning soldiers (Bergmann 1986). The post–World War II period of economic growth and the baby boom led to a divergence from the trend of increasing women's employment. From 1950 to 1970, the modal family type was a two-parent family with an employed father and an unemployed mother/housewife available for full-time child care. Since 1970, this family type has become the exception. Figure 13.1 shows the change in the typical family, from the "traditional" family with only one earner (the husband) to dual-earner families.

Figure 13.1   Trends in Numbers of Dual– and Single–Wage Earner Families: The Changing Labor Force Patterns of Families, 1940 to 1988

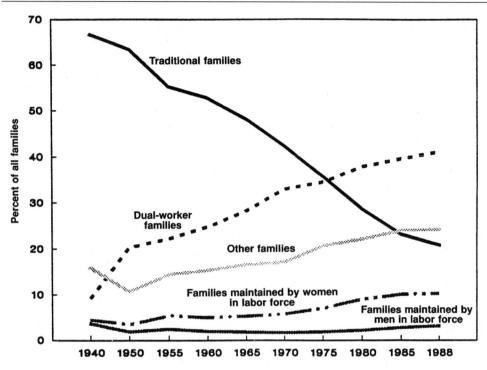

Source: *Monthly Labor Review*, March 1990, p. 18.

The rates of increased labor force participation vary among demographic groups. Poverty and the lack of support from a father or husband have consistently motivated nonwhite, immigrant, and low-income women to move into the labor force at higher rates than other women (Kessler-Harris 1982). Yet, the differential between white and nonwhite women's labor force participation, which was greater than 2:1 in 1900, is now almost even, with white women and black women with children under eighteen working respectively at rates of 73.5 and 73.7 percent (U.S. Census, *Current Population Reports* 1996).

Factors that have led to women's steadily increasing labor force participation rates are highly influenced by structural economic and technological changes in the society, and accompanying changes in mores and expectations. Some of these changes include: technological change and families' desire for new consumer products, introduction of labor-saving devices in the home, growth of "suitable" occupations for women (clerical and service jobs), women's remaining at their jobs after marriage and childbirth, and increasing wage rates which make staying out of the labor force a costly choice (Bergmann 1986; Oppenheimer 1979). Recessions and growing rates of unemployment and underemployment were partly responsible for the increased labor force participation rates of working married mothers since the mid-1970s.

Although the age of a mother's youngest child affects mother's participation rates, this has become less and less a constraining factor for married women. In fact, starting in the 1970s the greatest increases in labor force participation rates have been among married women with children under age one (see figure 13.2). Divorced women with children have had the highest labor force participation rates of mothers with children. Figure 13.3 shows that beginning in the mid-1980s the labor force participation rates of married women with children started to approach that of divorced women. Never-married mothers have the lowest labor force participation rates. Never-married mothers tend to be on average very young, unskilled women with no previous labor force participation history. Their lack of skills limits them to be eligible for only minimum wage jobs inadequate to support their families; many have had to rely on public assistance. Demographic factors such as increasing numbers of single-parent families, the lack of sufficient child support, and the low labor force participation of never-married single mothers have become a critical social policy problem because of the related poverty rates of these families.

Effects of Maternal Employment on the Child

The question posed by developmental researchers has been whether or not children are influenced by a mother's employment outside of the home. Most studies have begun by examining the direct effects of maternal employment on children. Studies have focused on effects on children in several age groups—infancy, preschool, and, to a lesser degree, middle-childhood and adolescence. Outcomes of interest include verbal performance, school achievement, behavior problems, so-

Figure 13.2   Labor Force Participation Rates of Women with Youngest Children, Birth to Age Three

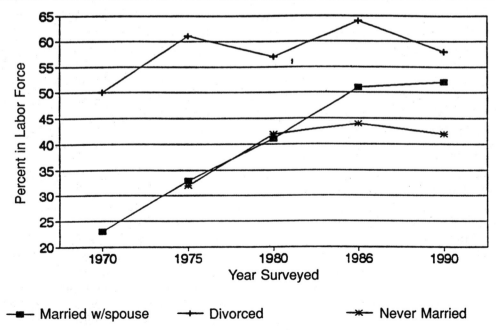

Source: Bureau of Labor Statistics, Bureau of the Census, *Current Population Survey.*

Figure 13.3   Labor Force Participation Rates of Women with Youngest Children, Birth to Age Six

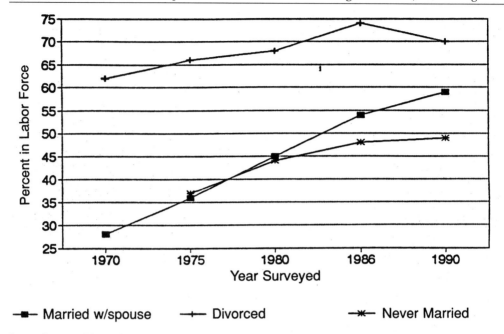

Source: Bureau of Labor Statistics, Bureau of the Census, *Current Population Survey*.

cial relationships (especially with the mother and peers). In adolescence, some researchers have investigated outcomes related to motivation and sex role identification. Various dimensions of the mother's work, beyond her absence from the home, are too infrequently studied—timing, intensity, work preference, continuity, and strain between work and parenting roles. Little attention has been paid to income and its link with other work-related dimensions.

Generally, maternal employment per se is not consistently associated with negative outcomes for school-aged children (Gottfried and Gottfried 1994). Indeed, maternal work seems to have benefits for adolescents (Hoffman 1979). The only overall negative effects have been reported for young children. At least four lines of research focus on the effects of maternal employment and the young child. The first research tradition involves relatively small samples which have shown that children who experienced out-of-home care had a strained mother-child relationship as measured by the Ainsworth Strange Situation Paradigm[1] and were less well adjusted—more aggressive with peers and less compliant to adult demands in their school-age years (Ainsworth 1964; Barton and Schwarz 1981; Belsky 1988; Erickson, Farber and Egeland 1982; Haskins, 1985; Schwartz, Strickland, and Krolick 1974; Schwarz 1983; Vaughn, Gove, and Egeland 1980). Several questions, however, have been raised about the validity of using the Strange Situation Paradigm when studying the effects of predictable separations due to employment. In addition to questions raised about the validity of the Strange Situation Paradigm, many of the smaller studies on maternal employment and effects on children are limited methodologically in several other ways:

employment is measured via a gross variable of "employed" or "not employed,"—without any indication of the number of hours the mother worked; samples are only generalizable to middle-class, two-parent, white households with school-age children; the mother's attitudes about her work are often overlooked; and they are cross-sectional rather than longitudinal in design.

A second line of research, which corrects some of the limitations listed above, is secondary analysis research done from national and larger scale studies, primarily the mother-child data of the National Longitudinal Study of Youth (NLSY). The NLSY data set is longitudinal with detailed information on the mother's work experience over each year in the child's life (Baker and Mott 1989; Chase-Lansdale, Mott, Brooks-Gunn, and Phillips 1991). One limitation of the data is that it includes no direct observation of the mother/child interaction. Instead there are child-performance outcome variables such as the child's verbal ability (Peabody Picture Vocabulary Test-Revised [PPVT-R], Dunn and Dunn 1981) or maternal reports of behavior problems. All researchers using the PPVT-R as the dependent variable, except for Desai, Michael, and Chase-Lansdale (1989), have found that a mother's hours of employment outside of the home in the first year of the child's life have a unique and negative effect, albeit relatively minor, on the child's verbal facility (Baydar and Brooks-Gunn 1991; Blau and Grossberg 1990; Parcel and Menaghan 1994; Smith 1994). In addition, full-time employment was found to have a stronger negative effect than part-time employment in the first year. (Baydar and Brooks-Gunn 1991; Smith 1994). However, no negative effects were found on the child outcomes for a mother's employment hours during the second or third years in the child's life.

A third approach has been to look at the child care arrangements of working mothers. Baydar and Brooks-Gunn (1991) and Smith (1994) using the NLSY mother-child data both found that type of care is an important explanatory variable in the maternal employment environment. Effects of child-care arrangements on the child's verbal facility (PPVT-R) vary with the gender and poverty status of the child.

The fourth approach of researchers has been to study how mother's employment is associated with children's views of gender relationships (Hoffman 1974, 1989; Moore and Hofferth 1979; Mortimer and Sorensen 1984). For girls and boys a working mother who contributes to the family's income provides a role model that is different from that of a nonemployed homemaker. A mother's employment may also change family relationships, with the father or the children assuming more responsibility for household chores and child care (Baruch and Barnett 1987; Darling-Fisher and Tiedje 1990; Gilbert 1985; Gottfried and Gottfried 1988, 1994; Hoffman 1989; Manke, Seery, McHale 1994; McHale and Crouter 1992; Pleck, Staines, and Lang 1980).

Research has also examined how a woman's employment can effect her own physical or psychological well-being, as well as her child's well-being. Theoretically, combining work with family roles has been associated with detrimental effects and beneficial effects. For example, Goode (1960) argued that the more roles people accumulate, the more likely they are to encounter incompatible expectations or excessive demands on their time and energy (role strain). The further assumption of this perspective is that role strain erodes psychological well-being. Others (Barnett and Marshall 1992; Baruch and Barnett 1987; Marks

1977; Sieber 1974) have challenged this view, arguing instead that multiple roles can enhance well-being by offering multiple opportunities for increased status, privileges, and self-esteem, particularly when people are committed to the roles they occupy. Studies concerned with the relationship between women's psychological well-being and paid employment have looked at the mediating variables of social support, marital status, type of job, number of children in the household, and preference for employment (Cleary and Mechanic 1983; Kessler and McRae 1982; Radloff 1975). Employment has been found to lead to negative consequences for some women who experience overload either due to heavy demands within the job or multiple role strain.

A mother's level of satisfaction with her role has been the most extensively studied mediator between maternal employment and child development. Many studies have confirmed that a mother's satisfaction with her role, whether she is employed or not, has positive effects on her children (Baruch and Barnett 1986; Farel 1980; Gove and Zeiss 1987; Hock 1980; Hoffman 1989; Ross, Mirowksky, and Huber 1983; Spitze 1988). In contrast, dissatisfaction with the maternal role is associated with negative effects on children—both in the school adjustment (Farel 1980; Woods 1972) and behavior problems (Barling, Fullager, and Marchl-Dingle 1986; Forehand, McCombs, and Brody 1987; Hock 1980; Lerner and Galambos 1985). The underlying hypothesis is that a woman's feelings of self-fulfillment influence her functioning as a mother and affect what is mediated to her child through her child-rearing practices. Improved self-esteem in the mother is hypothesized to lead to positive mood changes in the mother, more acceptance by the mother of her child, and more sensitive mothering.

Reviews of this evidence have concluded that although employed women in comparison with their nonemployed counterparts are in somewhat better mental health, maternal preferences with regard to employment are a significant factor in this relationship (Gove and Peterson 1980; Kamerman and Hayes, 1982; Spitze 1988). However, since this research is based largely on samples of middle-class, married, white women, little is known about the effects of early employment on the psychological well-being of poor, single, and minority mothers, or the processes linking their employment to developmental outcomes for their children. Jackson's recent (1992, 1993, 1994) studies of psychological well-being in a sample of single, employed, black mothers of preschoolers found that mothers who preferred their current employment status, while no less depressed, were lower in role strain than their employed counterparts who preferred to stay home. Marshall and Barnett (1991) found that there were clear gains for all women who combine work and family, but that the strains were particularly intense for working-class women because of their limited resources to help them with the double shift of combining work and family.

The type of job the mother performs has also been investigated as mediating between the mother's employment and her functioning at home with her children. Jobs which encourage autonomy and self-direction have been shown to affect the mother's intellectual flexibility and positively affect the mother-child interaction at home (Miller, Schooler, Kohn, and Miller 1979; Menaghan and Parcel 1990; Parcel and Menaghan 1994). The lack of opportunity for less educated women to acquire jobs that encourage autonomy and self-direction has ramifications for the mother's role satisfaction, as well as for the quality of the home learning environment she provides for her children (Parcel and Menaghan 1997).

Family and Community Resources:
A Framework for Studying Effects of Employment

Different frameworks have been proposed to explicate the links between the various contexts in which children reside and children's well-being. Developmentalists have favored models focusing on the interplay of various ecosystems (or contexts), on the contribution of risk and protective factors, and on the socialization practices of the family, school, and peer group (Bronfenbrenner 1979; Garmezy and Rutter 1983; Maccoby and Martin 1983; Bornstein 1995). More economically oriented frameworks have focused on resources which are available to children (Haveman and Wolfe 1994, 1995). And more sociologically focused frameworks often add social capital and networks to their equations (Coleman 1988). All of these frameworks have been used (to varying extents) in the investigation of the effects of parental employment, job loss, and unemployment upon children and adolescents. However, the data collected (and the types of sample used) vary somewhat across disciplines. Thus, we know a great deal about mother-child relationships around a year of age vis-à-vis maternal employment; however, information is based on a series of small-scale studies (forty to one hundred children) of primarily white middle-class families, with the exception of the Minnesota study (Belsky and Steinberg 1978 ; Clarke-Stewart 1989; Erickson, Sroufe, and Egeland 1985). Likewise, data on the links between income, single parenthood, and maternal employment are quite extensive for outcomes such as school achievement (Krein and Beller 1988; McLanahan 1985; McLanahan and Sandefur 1994). However, little is known about the associations between maternal employment and family processes as they influence children, or about how these associations might be affected by the age, health, or gender of the child; the age, education, or marital status of the mother and father; or the type and intensity of work performed.

We believe that more microanalytic and macroanalytic perspectives need to be integrated if we are to go beyond a mere description of parental employment patterns. To this end, a family and community resource framework is adapted here (see Brooks-Gunn, Brown, Duncan, and Moore 1995 for a more complete explication of this model, which is based on the work of Haveman and Wolfe 1994, and Coleman 1988). At least four categories of family resources are identified—income, time, human capital, and psychological capital resources. The last category includes many of the so-called process variables—parenting behavior, parental attitudes and beliefs, parental emotional health, and social support. Parental employment potentially may influence all four family resources, which in turn affect child outcomes. Thus, we expect that parental employment will have many more indirect than direct effects upon children. Understanding how families allocate resources within the family is critical to the specification of policies related to enhancing the well-being of children whose parents work.

Community resources include institutions such as schools and child care settings, as well as income, human capital, and social capital resources. Most studied in terms of maternal employment is the availability of schools and child care.

Also important are the social networks that help parents to find adequate child care, to lobby for more or better child care, and to locate jobs (or jobs with adequate benefit packages).

The intersection between family and community resources also needs to be specified (Brooks-Gunn 1995). This is especially true when considering maternal employment which is dependent on child care. Additionally, little work has considered the characteristics of the child that may influence the ways in which maternal employment and family or community resources interact. For example, some but not all work suggests that infant boys are more likely to be affected by maternal employment than girls (Belsky 1988; Chase-Lansdale and Owen 1987; Desai, Chase-Lansdale, and Michael 1989).

Family resources will be briefly discussed here vis-à-vis what is known about their links with employment and child outcome and their potential value as mediators or moderators of the association between parental employment and child outcome. The income brought into the family has the most obvious and potent effect on the quality of family life and child well-being (Brooks-Gunn and Duncan 1997; Smith, Brooks-Gunn, and Klebanov forthcoming). Research suggests that family income is one of the most important factors in the young child's environment and is related to less adequate prenatal care (Kalmuss and Fenelly 1990); low birth weight, and infant mortality (Starfield et al. 1991; Klerman 1991); lower scores on cognitive and verbal tests (Duncan, Brooks-Gunn, and Klebanov, 1994; McLoyd 1990); worse physical health (Miller and Korenman 1994; Korenman and Miller, forthcoming); lower levels of school readiness (Copple et al. 1993); and higher rates of adolescent high-risk behavior (Dryfoos 1991). Inadequate income, unemployment, or economic strain can affect children indirectly by influencing the parent's well-being which then affects their attitudes and the quality of the parent-child interaction (Crinic 1983; Conger, Yang, Lahey, and Krupp 1984; Conger, Ge, Elder, Lorenz, and Simons, 1994; Conger, Conger, and Elder, 1997; Elder 1988; Kohn 1969; McLoyd, Jayaratne, Ceballo, and Borquez 1994; Pascoe and Earp 1983; Tulkin and Kagan 1972). The stress associated with low income may severely limit the emotional energy mothers have to invest in parenting. Economic hardship has been shown to place women with children at high risk for depression (Aber, Brooks-Gunn, and Maynard 1995; Belle 1982, 1990; Hall, Williams, and Greenberg 1985; Pearlin and Johnson 1977). Maternal psychological distress, in turn, has been implicated as a mediator between economic hardship and child developmental outcomes through its effect on parenting (McLoyd 1990).

Time is a second important parental resource which is affected by a parent's employment situation. If both parents are employed outside of the home, a critical question is how this affects the quality and quantity of the time that the child gets to spend with the parents and other caregivers. Family activities can include sharing play and leisure time, eating together, doing housework, and educational activities like reading or watching a movie. Time-use diaries have been successfully used to describe how much time is spent by parents in child-oriented activities (Timmer, Eccles, and O'Brien 1985). However, no nationally representative database is currently available that includes time diaries of families with children.[2] Time spent with other caregivers can be educational and/or nurturing, or lacking in adequate stimulation or developmentally appropriate caregiving. A large body of research has documented the importance of quality of child care type on child well-being.

A secure emotional base for the developing toddler is thought to be a critical psychological resource. Developmental frameworks document the existence of stages in the young child's development as it occurs within the mother/child relationship (Bowlby 1969, 1973; Freud 1905; Erikson 1959; Piaget 1937; A. Freud 1944; Kohut 1971; Kernberg 1967; Greenspan 1981; Mahler, Pine, and Bergman 1975; Stern 1985). All of these schemas describe the emergence of a focused attachment to the mother (or primary caregiver) beginning during the second six months of the child's life which follows a developmental timetable. The documentation of phase-specific developmental achievements by the very young child within the relationship with the parent raises the question: Will these achievements be delayed or impaired if the mother is absent for some part of the day?

PARENTAL EMPLOYMENT IN THE CONTEXT OF WORK, HOME, AND CHILD CARE

To understand both the intersection of work and family and the possible effects on the family system, the multiple contexts in which parents and children operate must be identified (Bronfenbrenner 1986, 1989). The three most important are the work environment, the home environment, and the child care environment. Each context will be discussed separately. Measures of these three environments will be identified. In a later section, three data sets will be reviewed with an eye to their inclusion of each domain and specific measures within each domain.

Parental Employment in the Context of Work

Understanding the effect of a parent's employment situation needs documentation of data on several aspects of the parent's job. Data are needed on employment hours of both parents. Child well-being will be affected by the inputs of both parent's employment, as well as child care arrangements and time allocation in the family. We will focus first on the data needed on the mother's employment situation and then point out how the data needs would be similar or different for describing the father's situation.

Mother's Employment Situation   The mother's age at the birth of her first child, her prior employment experience, her educational achievement, and the number and age of other children all are associated with the likelihood and strength of her ability to contribute to the family's economic well-being. The employment experiences and educational level of women prior to childbirth are important indicators of the strengths of a woman's labor force attachment. Years of employment prior to childbirth and work status during pregnancy have been shown to be predictive of the timing or reentry into the labor force after childbirth as well as providing some data on mother's access to higher paying jobs, health insurance to cover prenatal care; childbirth and well-baby care; and disability insurance coverage for a paid, short-term maternity leave. Young women with no prior labor-force attachment, and a low level of educational attainment, are less likely to seek employment after childbirth and may remain out of the labor force for many years and therefore their children will be at greater risk for poverty under these circumstances (Bumpass and Sweet 1980; Leibowitz 1974).

Information needs to be collected in order to study the effects of a mother's employment on: length of time mother spent out of the labor force with her infant or toddler (if any), or age of child when mother began employment; intensity (number of hours worked each week) during each year of the child's life; marital status and number of other adults in the household; number of job changes the mother made over the year (stability); and proportion of family income provided by mother's income.

Longitudinal data are important to capture the timing and intensity of employment; the age of the child when a mother returns to or begins employment; how employment hours change (if they do) as children enter school or preschool; and whether work schedules include seasonal fluctuations. Some researchers have found that some dual-earner families become single-earner families during the summer (Crouter and McHale 1993). Gathering data on a workers' daily and yearly schedule may lead, however, to more variation than is interpretable. As many jobs include shift work, or seasonal fluctuations, a focus on the worker's feelings about her schedule, rather than detailed schedule information beyond total hours worked per week, may be most profitable (Presser 1989).

A second and obviously critical aspect that needs to be measured of a mother's employment situation is her salary. Knowing a mother's hourly wage is necessary to understand how much her hours outside of the home are providing economic benefits to the family. How much income is necessary to compensate for the possible stress the child might experience from coping with a mother's absence? Smith (1994) found that a mother's salary of twenty-three thousand dollars could offset the negative effects on the child's verbal facility from the mother's forty hours of employment per week in the first year. This implies that most low-skilled mothers working at a minimum wage job would not be able to earn a high enough salary to offset the negative effects of the mother's absence and that their children would be at higher risk for negative effects from early employment. Racial differences in wages affect children's economic status more than maternal employment per se (Eggebeen and Lichter 1991).

Data on access and availability to various packages of fringe benefits are critical for our understanding of how effective a job is in meeting family and individual needs. Employment benefits have been termed the "new property." Benefits accounted for 27 percent of employee compensation in 1989 compared to 17 percent in 1966. For those who work, pensions are a principal form of wealth, providing greater value for middle-aged Americans than the once prized family home or the automobile. Lack of benefits in the majority of jobs available to women who work in part-time employment increases the inequality between children in these families compared to those whose parents work at jobs that provide a full menu of benefits. With the increasing likelihood of marital disruption, a good job may become more central to economic security than family relationships (Drucker 1976; Reich 1964; Glendon 1981; Kamerman and Kahn 1988).

Information on workers' benefits should track whether the individual receives a pension, health insurance, paid vacation time, maternity or parenting leave, flexibility of work schedule, child care vouchers, or counseling services. The National Longitudinal Survey of Youth (NLSY), one of the few surveys to include questions about fringe benefits, recently was amended to include even more questions on the core benefits available to workers including dental insurance, training/education subsidies, profit-sharing, maternity/paternity leaves, flexible hours, employer-subsidized child care, and retirement benefits offered at the current job (Baker and Mott 1993; Brooks-Gunn, Brown, Duncan, and Moore 1995; Kamerman 1988).

Employment can offer not only the possibility of employer-provided benefits but also the government concomitants of employment—including social security, disability insurance, unemployment insurance, and Medicare. Social security coverage is a critical benefit of employment, yet most survey questionnaires do not differentiate whether a worker is being paid on or off the books (that is, whether the employee is eligible for social security). For those women not in the labor force, it is important to know if they and their children are covered by the father's benefit package or by statutory benefits such as Medicaid or Medicare.

Measures of the mother's working conditions in terms of the level of routinized or occupationally complex working conditions may be important. Some studies have shown that parents encourage the styles of behavior that are rewarded in their own line of work (Miller, Schooler, Kohn, and Miller 1979; Parcel and Menaghan 1990, 1994; Schooler 1987). Kohn's social structure and personality framework are applicable when studying the impact of a mother's employment conditions on her care of her children when she is with them. Occupational complexity and opportunities for self-direction and autonomy on the job are critical dimensions of parental working conditions that influence child-rearing values and behavior (Kohn 1969; Kohn and Schooler 1973, 1982; Parcel and Menaghan 1994). Parents in high-complexity occupations place less emphasis on direct parental control; instead, their parenting style promotes the child's internalization of parental norms. When internalization is successful, children use these internal standards to monitor their own behavior, reducing the frequency of "acting out" behavior and the necessity for parents to impose external control. All data sets that measure a mother's job by Census Bureau categories can be linked using the *Dictionary of Occupational Titles* to assess levels of occupational complexity (Parcel 1989).

Job satisfaction is affected by the physical environment, as well as by relations with supervisors and fellow workers. Opportunities for social contact can be particularly beneficial for single mothers with few other sources for social support; these can have possible crossover effects for their children (Parry 1986; Warr and Parry 1982; Repetti 1989). Rauh (1994) has shown the positive effect of job-linked social networks for pregnant women and mothers of young children. The physical environment of the workplace is another significant contributor to employee well-being. Working in physically dangerous or unhealthy conditions affects a workers' well-being. Salary, experience, and opportunities for promotion are critical facets of job satisfaction, particularly for women whose income is necessary for their families' well-being (Feldberg and Glenn 1979; Loscocco 1990; McKenry and Hamdorf 1985; Martin and Hanson 1985). More research is needed to understand what job satisfaction is really tapping. A survey of 250,000 working women completed by the Women's Bureau of the Department of Labor found that while 80 percent of the women reported that they loved their jobs, nearly half of them reported feeling that they were underpaid because they were women and under stress because they were managing both work and family (Lewin 1994).

With changing expectations for women to hold dual roles as workers outside of the home and homemakers, data is necessary to track women's satisfaction with their dual or single role. We need to know about a women's level of satisfaction in terms of being a worker and also her satisfaction in terms of facilitating relationships with her children and family. It would be informative to know whether an employed mother would prefer to be working less hours or not working at all, and to have a mother's report of the emotional and concrete help she receives from a spouse or other household members.

Father's Employment Situation   Research on the effects of a father's employment situation on child well-being is very limited. Several aspects of the father's work have been shown to be important, however. One focuses on the effects of job loss on the family and on children. Elder (1988) looked at the effects of father's unemployment during the Great Depression; and Conger et al. (1992, 1994, 1997) have looked at unemployment in Midwestern farm communities during the 1980s. Both studies found that potential job loss and unemployment are associated with instability, hostility, and inconsistent parenting on the part of father, and these sorts of behavior are linked to less optimal child and adolescent outcomes. Additionally, the fathers who were more unstable prior to job loss were most likely to show very high levels of negative parenting when a job crisis occurred (an accentuated effect); children in such families have the worst outcomes. Interestingly, maternal parenting behavior was not particularly predictive of child outcomes, and was less likely to be influenced by the job loss of the father. Whether or not similar links would be found in families where the mother is the primary wage earner is not well studied (McLoyd 1990).

Another line of research focuses on the complexity of the parent's occupation. Kohn's (1969) work found that fathers with jobs that encouraged self-direction, promoted independence in their children rather than conformity (Kohn and Schooler 1982; Schooler 1987). The father's salary is of obvious importance in determining family income and the socioeconomic status of the family and associated child well-being. Parcel and Menaghan (1994) are the only ones to date to investigate the effect of a father's work schedule (employment hours) on child outcomes. They found elevated behavior problems in children under three when fathers were working less than full-time. They suggest that "fathers' work schedules may be important pathways through which children absorb appropriate behavioral norms and develop verbal skills that serve as the foundation for future cognitive attainment" (p. 1003).

Parental Employment in the Context of the Home

There is a large body of research which connects children's home environments and their health and development (Bradley and Tedesco 1982; Bradley et al. 1988; Bradley et al. 1994; Clarke-Stewart 1973; Wachs and Gruen, 1982). Employment may affect the child's home environment in several ways. Increased income can allow the parents to buy more educational toys or books, which can increase the level of cognitive stimulation in the home. Employment can also increase the parents' cognitive functioning, which, in turn, will affect their interaction with the child. Working may also affect the mood of the parents when they are at home, thereby increasing or decreasing their emotional availability for interaction with the child. Finally, employment can affect the parents' resources to create a safe, well-ordered, and clean home environment.

Provision of Learning Experiences and Responsivity

A large number of researchers studying the relationship between the home environment and child development rely on the Home Observation Measure of the Environment (HOME) scale—a standardized measure of the environment which was originally developed to identify and describe the homes of infants and children who were at significant developmental risk (Bradley, Caldwell, Rock, Hamrick, and Harris 1988; Elardo and Bradley 1981). The full HOME scale taps *cognitive variables* including language stimulation, provision of a variety of learning experiences and materials, and encouragement of child achievement; *social variables* include the parents' responsiveness and warmth; and a measure of the *physical dimensions* of the home including cleanliness, safety, and amount of sensory input. Several researchers using the HOME scale have investigated how maternal employment and paternal employment influence the child's home environment. Several constructs in the HOME scale have been linked to child outcomes: maternal warmth and responsivity, variety of learning experiences, safety of the physical environment, father involvement, and the level of parental punitiveness (Bradley 1995; Bradley et al. 1994; Gottfried and Gottfried 1988; Smith, Brooks-Gunn, and Klebanov 1997). Menaghan and Parcel (1991) found that maternal working conditions influence the quality of a child's home environment. Those mothers who worked in occupations with more substantively complex work activities created home environments that were more cognitively enriched and more conducive to socioemotional development.

Time Allocation   Employment may affect the time availability of the mother and father for family activities and may limit leisure time. Mother's time in the labor force is often taken as a possible problematic indicator of time not available for parenting. The total number of parental hours available to children is dependent on how many parents are available in a family and how much they work outside the home. As more children are being raised in households with only one parent or in households where both parents are employed full-time, these households have fewer hours available for both child care and employment. Collection of data on the effect of dual-parent or single-parent working families on time allocation in family members' lives is much needed. The Michigan Time Use Studies successfully obtained detailed information on family members' time use (Juster and Stafford 1985). These time diaries were able to provide information on family processes by documenting the division of labor within the family and demonstrating the role of gender, marital status, educational attainment, and employment status on time allocation for household chores, leisure time, or television viewing. They found, for example, that single mothers spend more time in employment than married mothers, that employed mothers spend much less time on housework than nonemployed (single-earner) mothers, and that college-educated parents spend more time reading to their children than lesser educated parents (Timmer, Eccles, and O'Brien 1985).

Maternal education is often used as a measure of the likely quality of the mother's time with the child. We see the collection of time diaries as an extremely useful addition to a data collection effort. The new Child Development Supplement which will be added in 1997 to the Panel Study of Income Dynamics (PSID) will make a significant contribution to our knowledge on time allocation within families. It will include a time-use diary for children ages three to twelve. Children and/or their parents will be asked to account for all their activities on a particular day by describing what they did, where the activity took place, and who else was there with the child. This data will allow researchers to link variation in parental work schedules with children's daily lives.

While employment may bring in additional income to the family, it may also create "time poverty"—a deficit of social time for shared family activities, leisure time, or household chores. Juster and Stafford (1991) found that although women have been increasing their hours spent in the labor market and decreasing their time in home production, there has been a net increase in hours spent in leisure time. To study the changing use of time, we need detailed time diaries on how parents and children are dividing their time between employment, home production, leisure, and family interaction. Information is needed on: the amount and nature of time parents and other caretakers spend with children; the amount of time older children and adolescents spend in unsupervised activities; and the amount and nature of the household activities each member of the family is performing.

Smaller studies are doing innovative research tracking parental time allocation—in terms of its effects on monitoring of school-aged children's activities, and on the allocation of household chores between spouses and among children (McHale, Bartko, Crouter, and Perry-Jenkins 1990; Manke, Seery, and McHale 1994). For example, Manke et al. found that fathers in dual-earner families performed more housework than fathers in single-earner families and that girls did more housework than boys, with girls in some families substituting for their father's household tasks. In a research study which compares siblings within a large study of midwestern families, funded by National Institute of Child Health and Human Development (NICHD), Crouter and McHale will be able to track within family variation on time allocation and chore division, focusing on possible gender and temperament differences of the children.

Changing Gender Relations   Changing labor force participation rates of women affects women's and men's role definitions. Women's greater economic independence can influence children's images of what men and women do and can become. Rather than only investigate the effect of a mother's salary, some researchers instead look at the gap between a mother's and a father's income in dual-earner families. The hypothesis is that the gap between spouses' income can be predictive of marital equality in terms of the power that the lesser earner has in family decision making (McHale and Crouter 1992). How this might affect children's well-being is not known.

Parental Employment in the Context of Child Care

When a child's parents are both employed, alternative child care arrangements must be provided for. The quality of this care may have a direct effect on child well-being, as well as have a spillover effect on the parents' job satisfaction and "peace of mind." A critical question is whether the quality of the child care enhances or undermines the effects of parental employment on child well-being.

Longitudinal studies done in Sweden, where there is universal, high-quality affordable child care, found positive effects for early entry to substitute group care for cognitive and social development. No equivalent comprehensive longitudinal data exist on effects on children of different types of child care in the United States.[3] Descriptions of child care arrangements have demonstrated repeatedly that quality of care varies tremendously between and within states, depending on licensing and regulatory controls (Galinsky and Friedman 1993; Brayfield, Deich, and Hofferth 1993; Morgan 1987; Whitebook, Howes, and Phillips 1989). The most commonly used type of care for preschool children is unlicensed informal care by a relative or nonrelative (family day care). This popular form of care, however, is the least studied in terms of effects on child well-being. Smith (1994), using the NLSY mother-child data, found that there were strong negative effects on a child's verbal facility if the mother was employed and the child was cared for in informal relative care by a father, stepfather, or sibling. Galinsky and Friedman (1993) also found negative effects for young children if the care was provided by a relative in the relative's home. Much more information is needed about the informal and formal child care environments of preschool children, as well as the arrangements being made for school-aged children after dismissal from school (Brayfield, Deich, and Hofferth 1993; Hofferth 1995; Caughy, DiPietro, and Strobino 1994; Hayes, Palmer, and Zaslow 1990; Meyers 1993; Philips, Voran, Kiser, Howes, and Whitebrook 1994).

DATA COLLECTION EFFORTS

We have examined three large longitudinal data sets vis-à-vis the data collected on parental labor force participation and family resources. The data sets are the National Longitudinal Survey of Youth mother-child data, the Panel Study of Income Dynamics, and the Current Population Survey (see Brooks-Gunn, Brown, Duncan, and Moore 1995).

The National Longitudinal Survey of Youth mother-child data is a supplement to the annual NLSY survey begun in 1979 (Baker and Mott 1989). The original sample included over twelve thousand young men and women ages fourteen to twenty-one. The sample includes a special military subsample, as well as oversampling for blacks, Latinos, and poor whites. The data include rich, detailed information on the respondents' labor force participation for each week beginning in 1979. Parents are interviewed each year since 1979 about hours, salary, fringe benefits, and some job-satisfaction measures.

In 1986, child assessment measures were given to the children of those women who had become mothers (n = 2,918). Child assessment measures have continued on a biannual basis. The sample, however, is not nationally representative, as it only represents those women who gave birth in the early phase of their employment careers (Chase-Lansdale et al. 1991). By 1992 assessments had been obtained on the children of 70 percent of childbearing women. (Children of women in the youth cohort who delayed childbearing into their late thirties will be included when they give birth.)

The Panel Survey of Income Dynamics is a survey which has been conducted on an annual basis since 1968. In 1993, the survey involved some 7,900 households, with an oversampling of black and Latino families. A strength of the data set for studying the effects of parental employment is its extensive and detailed information on family material resources and the transfer of income on a monthly basis. A strong limitation of the data for studying the effects of parental employment on children is that there is only very limited child outcome measures for children before they turn sixteen-years-old. Yet one can trace the long-term effects of a parent's employment situation on adolescents or young adults (over age sixteen). However, in 1997, PSID collected information on birth to twelve-year-old children both from the parents and from the children themselves. This new data collection will provide data on time use and social support at the family, school, and neighborhood levels; as well as parental psychological resources and sibling characteristics. The new child supplement will allow for data collection on the links between a parent's employment situation and children's cognitive and behavioral development in a nationally representative sample of 3,167 children.

The Current Population Survey (CPS) is intended to provide estimates of employment, unemployment, and general characteristics of the labor force. Monthly labor force data is collected for the nation, eleven of the largest states, New York City, and Los Angeles. The total sample size is approximately 71,000 households. About 57,000 households are interviewed in the monthly survey. The data set is not intended to study the effects of employment on children, but demographic data have been collected on the children in the adult respondents' households beginning in 1979. One can get detailed estimates of the types of jobs that parents are holding, their hours, unemployment spells, fringe benefits, and more.

Table 13.1 lists child developmental outcomes which may be affected by the parent's employment situation. The NLSY is the only data set of the three with currently available data on the cognitive and socioemotional development of young children. Table 13.2 includes the domains of the parental and family envi-

Table 13.1   Child Developmental Outcome Measures

	NLSY	PSID	CPS
Cognitive development	x	x97	
Grade failure	x	x97	
Socioemotional development	x	x97	
Behavior problems	x	x97	
Attitude toward work	x****		
High school dropout	x****	x	x
Teenage birth		x	x

x Available every year of data collection
x97 Fielded in 1997
x**** in the 1994 data only for youth and teens

Table 13.2 Work Context

Mothers' Job Characteristics	NLSY	PSID	CPS
Employment in years prior to birth of child	x	x	
Employment hours during pregnancy	x	x	
Length of maternity/parenting leave	x	x	
Age of child when mother began (resumed) employment	x	x	x**
Hours of work each quarter of first year	x	x	x**
Hours of work each year of child's life	x	x	x**
Summer hours (if different than rest of year)	x		x**
Number of job changes each year	x	x	x**
Weeks of unemployment (looking for work)	x	x	x
Mother's satisfaction with schedule (subjective measure)			
Salary—hourly and yearly	x	x	x
Proportion of family income contributed			
Record of fringe benefits received	x	x*	
paid vacation, health and dental insurance, maternity leave, flexible schedule	x	x*	
Social security coverage on job			
Whether employee experienced downsizing		x	
Occupational complexity of job			
3-digit occupational code	x	x	x
Job satisfaction	x		
peer relations	x*		
income	x*		
physical safety and cleanliness	x*		
Preference for employment	x***		

Fathers' Job Characteristics	NLSY	PSID	CPS
Father's hours of work each year of child's life	x**	x	x**
Summer hours (if different)			x**
Number of job changes each year			x**
Weeks of unemployment (looking for work)	x**	x	x**
		x	
Father's satisfaction with schedule (subjective measure)		x	
Salary—hourly and yearly	x**	x	x**
	x*		
Record of fringe benefits received		x*	
paid vacation, health and dental insurance, maternity leave, flexible schedule		x*	
Social security coverage on job			
Does father pay child support			
Whether employee experienced downsizing		x	
Occupational complexity of job			
3-digit occupational code	x**	x*	x*
Job satisfaction			
peer relations			
income			
physical safety and cleanliness			

x Available every year of data collection
x* Only available in one or occasional years
x** Only data on individuals within the household. Data set is a household survey and individuals outside of the household cannot be traced
x*** For those who were unemployed only

ronment with the following categories: mothers' job characteristics, fathers' job characteristics, the home environment, and the child care environment. Several gaps in our current data collection efforts are apparent from tables 13.1 and 13.2. Child outcomes are only currently available in the NLSY, and this sample is only nationally representative of younger mothers and their children. (As discussed, the PSID is adding a Child Development Supplement in 1997, which will provide child outcomes on a nationally representative sample.) Second, job satisfaction measures for both mother and father are limited to a global measure collected for mothers each year and data collected on occasion about other domains. None of the three data sets allows for measurement of occupational complexity, but they all have census codes which can be merged with the *Dictionary of Occupational Titles* which can measure occupational complexity. Measurement of the home environment is primarily captured in the NLSY with the HOME scale. None of the data sets have time diaries, with the exception of the upcoming PSID data. Child care arrangements are most fully described in the NLSY and forthcoming PSID Child Supplement (see table 13.3). Parental resources for the mother are fairly well documented in all of the three data sets, with the NLSY also including a measure for material intelligence, self-esteem, and depression. The largest gap involves fathers' employment. Detailed parental data within the NLSY are only available if the father lives in the household and is married to the mother. We can know little about the effect of father's employment (or non-employment) on children from divorced or never-married families, with the exception of the forthcoming PSID Child Development Supplement.

CONCLUSION

Several significant demographic shifts may affect the well-being of children. First, labor force participation of women with children has increased dramatically—more women are entering and remaining in the labor force than ever before. The largest recent rise in labor force participation is among women with children under one year of age. These trends are necessitating changed family circumstances and time allocations. For married women, a two-earner family is now the norm, rather than the so-called traditional family of a male breadwinner and an at-home mother. Among the growing numbers of single-parent female-headed households who are also employed, there is the stress of managing employment schedules and child care arrangements without the support of a spouse. Second, for women, a job, rather than marriage, is the institution which promises economic security via the provision of fringe benefits that include health insurance, pensions, and social security coverage. Third, inequities between professional workers and less-skilled workers are increasing. While workers with higher schooling levels and more experience have been able to keep up with inflation, the real earnings of younger and less educated workers have fallen sharply. Fourth, poverty among children is increasing when parents are out of the labor force and dependent on public transfers, primarily TANF. Fifth, poor women with young children, who are out of the labor force and receiving TANF, are now expected to obtain employment. Women with preschool children and very young children (state requirements vary, from beginning at three months to two years of age) are now considered eligible for employment and must participate in training and employment programs. Sixth and finally, time limits have been imposed on welfare receipt and poor families will be ineligible for income support after five years of receipt.

Understanding the effect of maternal employment upon children is extremely limited, given that so few studies have included data on occupational complexity, benefits, flexibility of work hours, commuting time, and the stresses of balancing work and family for the mother, let alone the father. In addition, the research on parental employment and child well-being for the most part has ignored the experiences of low-income and minority families, who work in jobs that are low-paying, with few benefits, opportunities for promotion, or autonomy. Finally, research is needed to investigate the effects on child well-being of family income moving from just below the poverty threshold to just above the poverty threshold (Brooks-Gunn and Duncan 1997).

Our review of currently available data on parental employment leads to the following recommendations on measures of critical importance to be included in future data collection efforts:

- Child developmental outcome measures collected throughout infancy and childhood

- Mother's job characteristics should include: employment history prior to child-birth, length of maternity/parenting leave, hours of employment in each year of the child's life including summer hours and number of job changes, a subjective measure of mother's satisfaction with her employment schedule, mother's salary, fringe benefits, and social security coverage

- Father's job characteristics should include hours of work for each year of the child's life including summer hours and number of job changes and unemployment; length of parenting leave, a subjective measure of father's satisfaction with his employment schedule, father's salary, fringe benefits, social security coverage, and whether or not he pays child support

- For measures of the home environment, one question for both the mother and the father should be the amount of time spent with the child on a typical weekday and for noncustodial fathers the amount of time per week spent with the child

- All the child care questions listed in table 13.4 are of critical importance.

Table 13.3   Child Care Context

	NLSY	PSID	CPS
Longitudinal history of child care arrangements	x	x97	
Type of care			
center, family day care, relative at home, relative at other's home	x	x97	
Type of after school care	x	x97	
Ratio of adult to child	x*	x97	
Caregiver's training	x	x97	
Caregiver's educational background		x97	
If relative, preference for providing child care			

Table 13.3   *Continued*

	NLSY	PSID	CPS
Number of changes over year	x	x97	
Number of child care arrangements in a week	x	x97	

x Available every year of data collection
x97 Fielded in 1997
x* Only available in one or occasional years

Table 13.4   Home Context

Mother's Home Characteristics			
	NLSY	PSID	CPS
HOME scale	x	x97	
Amount of time spent with child on typical weekday between 7 A.M. and 9 P.M.	x97		
Time spent with child on typical weekend day		x97	
Time spent with child during summer			
Time spent on leisure time			
Time spent with spouse			
Time spent in housework per day		x	
Strain/gains of work to parenting			
Strain/gains of work to marriage			
Satisfaction with parenting		x97	
Sex role attitudes	x*		
Number of children in household	x	x	x

Father's Home Characteristics			
	NLSY	PSID	CPS
Amount of time spent with child on typical weekday between 7 A.M. and 9 P.M.		x97	
Time spent with child on typical weekend day		x97	
Time spent with child during summer			
Time spent on leisure time			
Time spent with spouse			
Time spent in housework per day		x	
If noncustodial parent, number of hours spent with child during typical week		x97	
Strain/gain of work to parenting			
Strain/gain of work to marriage			
Satisfaction with parenting		x97	
Sex role attitudes			
Number of children in the household		x	x

x Available every year of data collection
x97 Fielded in 1997
x* Only available in one or occasional years

We want to thank the Child and Family Well-Being Network of the National Institute for Child Health and Human Development family for their support of the writing of this paper.

NOTES

1. The Strange Situation Paradigm is a standardized laboratory experiment to assess the quality of the mother-child attachment through a procedure that studies the child's reaction to the mother's brief separation from the child. The experiment examines the child's interaction with an observer during mother's absence and the child's treatment of the mother on her return (Ainsworth 1964).

2. The forthcoming 1997 Panel Study of Income Dynamics Child Supplement does include a time diary for all children ages three to twelve.

3. The National Institute of Child Health and Human Development Study of Early Child Care is currently in the data collection stage. This study will make a significant contribution in providing detailed longitudinal data on the experience of children and their families in a variety of child care settings through the entry into kindergarten. The data will also include many key measurements of the parent's employment situation. This data, however, are not nationally representative and access to the data is restricted to the investigators (Friedman, Brooks-Gunn, Vandell, and Weinraub 1994; NICHD Early Child Care Study forthcoming).

4. The federal data that is now available include the 1990 National Child Care Survey (NCCS), the Profile of Child Care Settings, and data from the Current Population Survey. The NCCS provides a cross-sectional picture of the child care arrangements of children under age thirteen in a nationally representative sample of families (Hofferth, Brayfield, Deich, and Holcomb 1991). The Profile of Child Care Settings presents information on the supply of child care provided in public and private child care centers, nursery schools, and preschools, as well as regulated family day care homes (Kisker, Hofferth, Phillips, Farquhar 1991). The Current Population Survey (Household Survey) obtains data every other year on whether children three- and four-years of age are enrolled in a nursery or day care center with some educational component. CPS data indicate that preschool participation was low for poor children. Only 35 percent of poor three- and four-year-olds attend preschool. Participation rates are particularly low for children in immigrant families and children in rural households. In addition, only 29 percent of eligible three- and four-year-olds attend Head Start (General Accounting Office 1994).

REFERENCES

Aber, L., Brooks-Gunn, J. and R. Maynard. 1995. Effects of Welfare Reform on Teenage Parents and Their Children. *The Future of Children: Critical Issues for Children and Youth* 5: 53–71.

Ainsworth, M. 1964. Patterns of Attachment Behavior Shown by the Infant in Interaction with His Mother. *Merrill-Palmer Quarterly of Behavior and Development* 10: 51–58.

Baker, P., and F. Mott. 1989. *NLSY Handbook 1989: A Guide and Resource Document for the National Longitudinal Survey of Youth 1986 Child Data*. Columbus, Ohio: Center for Human Resource Research, The Ohio State University.

Bane, M. J., and D. Ellwood. 1994. *Welfare Realities*. Cambridge, Mass.: Harvard University Press.

———. 1983. "Slipping into and out of Poverty: The Dynamics of Spells." Working paper, no. 1199. Cambridge, Mass.: National Bureau of Economic Research.

Barling, J., C. Fullagar, and J. Marchl-Dingle. 1986. "Employment Commitment as a Moderator of the Maternal Employment Status/Child Behavior Relationship." *Journal of Occupational Behavior* 9: 113–22.

Barnett, R. C., and N. C. Marshall. 1992. "Worker and Mother Roles, Spillover Effects, and Psychological Distress." *Women and Health* 18(2): 9–14.

Baruch, G. K., and R. C. Barnett. 1987. "Role Quality and Psychological Well-Being." In *Spouse, Parent, Worker*, edited by F. Crosby. New Haven, Ct.: Yale University Press.

Baydar, N., and J. Brooks-Gunn. 1991. "Effects of Maternal Employment and Child-Care Arrangements in Infancy on Preschoolers' Cognitive and Behavioral Outcomes: Evidence from the Children of the National Longitudinal Study of Youth." *Developmental Psychology* 27: 918–31.

Belsky, J. 1988 "The 'Effects' of Infant Day Care Reconsidered." *Early Childhood Research Quarterly* 3: 227–35.

Belsky, J., and D. Eggebeen. 1991. "Early and Extensive Maternal Employment/Child Care and Four- to Six-Year Olds' Socioemotional Development: Children of the National Longitudinal Study of Youth." *Journal of Marriage and the Family* 53: 1083–99.

Belsky, J., and L. Steinberg. 1978. "The Effects of Day Care: A Critical Review." *Child Development* 49: 706–17.

Bergmann, B. 1986. *The Economic Emergence of Women.* New York: Basic Books.

Blau, F., and A. Grossberg. 1990. "Maternal Labor Supply and Children's Cognitive Development." Working Paper 3536. Washington, D.C.: National Bureau of Economic Research.

Bornstein, M. 1995. *Handbook of Parenting.* Hillsdale, N.J.: Erlbaum.

Bowlby, J. 1951. *Maternal Care and Mental Health.* Geneva, Switzerland: World Health Organization.

———. 1969. *Attachment.* New York: Basic Books.

Bradley, R., D. J. Mundfrom, L. Whiteside, P. H. Casey, and K. Barrett. 1994. "A Factor Analytic Study of the Infant-Toddler and Early Childhood Versions of the HOME Inventory Administered to White, Black, and Hispanic American Parents of Children Born Preterm." *Child Development* 65: 880–88.

Bradley, R., and L. Tedesco. 1982. "Environmental Correlates of Mental Retardation." In *The Psychology of the Abnormal Child*, edited by J. Lachenmeyer and M. Gibbs. New York: Gardner Press.

Bradley, R. H., B. M. Caldwell, S. L. Rock, K. E. Barnard, C. Gray, M. A. Hammond, S. Mitchell, L. Siegel, C. Ramey, A. W. Gottfriend, and D. L. Johnson. 1989. "Home Environment and Cognitive Development in the First Three Years of Life: A Collaborative Study Involving Six Sites and Three Ethnic Groups in North America." *Developmental Psychology* 25 (2): 217–35.

Bradley, R., B. Caldwell, S. Rock, H. Hamrick. and P. Harris. 1988. "Home Observation for Measurement of the Environment: Development of a Home Inventory for Use with Families Having Children Six to Ten Years Old." *Contemporary Educational Psychology* 13: 58–71.

Brayfield, A., S. G. Deich, and S. Hofferth. 1993. *Caring for Children in Low-Income Families: A Substudy of National Child Care Study, 1990.* Washington D.C.: Urban Institute Press.

Bronfenbrenner, U. 1979. "Contexts of Child Rearing: Problems and Prospects." *American Psychologist* 34: 844–50.

———. 1986. "Ecology of the Family as a Context for Human Development: Research Perspectives." *Developmental Psychology* 22: 723–42.

———. 1989. "Ecological Systems Theory." In *Six Theories of Child Development: Revised Formulations and Current Issues*, edited by R. Vasta. Greenwich, Ct.: JAI Press.

Brooks-Gunn, J. 1995. "Growing Up Poor: Context, Risk and Continuity in the Bronfenbrenner Tradition." In *Linking Lives and Contexts: Perspective on the Ecology of Human Development*, edited by P. Moen, G. H. Elder, and K. Lusher. Washington, D.C.: American Psychological Association Press.

Brooks-Gunn, J., B. Brown, G. J. Duncan, and K. A. Moore 1995. "Child Development in the Context of Family and Community Resources: An Agenda for National Data Collections." In *Integrating Federal Statistics on Children: Report of a Workshop*. Washington, D.C.: National Academy Press.

Brooks-Gunn, J., and G. J. Duncan. Forthcoming. "Growing Up Poor: Consequences for Children and Youth." *Futures of Children.*

Brooks-Gunn, J., P. K. Klebanov, and F. Liaw. 1994. "The Learning, Physical, and Emotional Environment of the Home in the Context of Poverty: The Infant Health and Development Program." *Children and Youth Services* 17 (1/2): 251–76.

Caughy, M. O. B., J. A. DiPietro, and D. M. Strobino. 1994. "Day-Care Participation as a Protective Factor in the Cognitive Development of Low-Income Children." *Child Development* 65: 457–71.

Chase-Lansdale, P. L., F. L. Mott, J. Brooks-Gunn, and D. Phillips. 1991. "Children of the National Longitudinal Study of Youth: A Unique Research Opportunity." *Developmental Psychology* 27(6): 918–31.

Chase-Lansdale, P. L., and M. T. Owen. 1987. "Maternal Employment in a Family Context: Effects on Infant-Mother and Infant-Father Attachments." *Child Development* 58: 1505–12.

Clarke-Stewart, K. A. 1989. "Day Care: Maligned or Malignant." *American Psychologist* 44: 266–73.

Cleary, P. D., and D. Mechanic. 1983. "Sex Differences in Psychological Distress among Married People." *Journal of Health and Social Behavior* 24: 111–21.

Coleman, J. 1988. Social Capital in the Creation of Human Capital. *American Journal of Sociology* 94: S95–S120.

Coleman, J. S. 1991. "Policy Perspectives: Parental Involvement in Education." Washington, D.C.: Office of Educational Research and Improvement: U.S. Department of Education.

Conger, R., K. Conger, and G. Elder. 1997. "Family Economic Hardship and Adolescent Adjustment: Mediating and Moderating Processes." In *Consequences of Growing Up Poor*, edited by G. J. Duncan and J. Brooks-Gunn. New York: Russell Sage Foundation.

Conger, R., K. Conger, G. Elder Jr., F. Lorenz, R. Simons, and L. Whitebeck. 1992. "A Family Process Model of Economic Hardship and Adjustment of Early Adolescent Boys." *Child Development* 63: 526–41.

Conger, R., X. Ge, G. Elder Jr., F. Lorenz, and R. Simons. 1994. "Economic Stress, Coercive Family Process, and Developmental Problems of Adolescents." *Child Development* 65 (2): 541–61.

Cott, N. 1977. *The Bonds of Motherhood*. New Haven: Yale University Press.

Crouter, A. C., and S. M. McHale. 1993. "Temporal Rhythms in Family Life: Seasonal Variation in Relation Between Parental Work and Family Processes." *Developmental Psychology* 29(2): 198–205.

Danziger, S., and P. Gottschalk. 1990. *How Have Families with Children Been Faring?* Discussion paper, no. 801–86. Madison: University of Wisconsin.

Darling-Fisher, C. S., and L. B. Tiedje. 1990. "The Impact of Maternal Employment Characteristics on Father's Participation in Child Care." *Family Relations* 39(1): 20–26.

DeMause, L. 1974. *The History of Childhood*. New York: Psychohistory Press.

Desai, S., L. Chase-Lansdale, and R. Michael. 1989. "Mother or Market?: Effects of Maternal Employment on Cognitive Development of Four-Year-Old Children." *Demography* 26: 545–61.

Dodge, K. A., G. S. Pettit, and J. E. Bates. 1994. "Socialization Mediators of the Relation between Socioeconomic Status and Child Conduct Problems." *Child Development* 65(2): 649–65.

Drucker, P. 1976. *The Unseen Revolution: How Pension Fund Socialism Came to America*. New York: Harper and Row.

Duncan, G. J. and J. Brooks-Gunn. 1997. *Consequences of Growing Up Poor*. New York: Russell Sage Foundation.

Duncan, G., J. Yeung, J. Brooks-Gunn, and J. Smith. Forthcoming. "Does Poverty Affect the Life Chances of Children? *American Sociological Review*.

Dunn, L. M., and L. M. Dunn. 1981. *Peabody Picture Vocabulary Test—Revised*. Circle Pines Min.: American Guidance Service.

Eggebeen, D., and D. Lichter. 1991. "Race, Family Structure, and Changing Poverty among American Children." *American Sociological Review* 56: 801–17.

Ehrenreich, B., and D. English. 1978. *For Her Own Good: 150 Years of Expert Advice to Women.* Garden City, N.Y.: Doubleday.

Elder, G. 1974. *Children of the Great Depression: Social Change in Life Experience.* Chicago: University of Chicago Press.

———. 1988. "Economic Stress in Lives: Developmental Perspectives." *Journal of Social Issues* 44: 25–45.

Elder, G., T. Nguyen, and A. Caspi. 1985. "Linking Family Hardship to Children's Lives." *Child Development* 56: 361–375.

Erickson, M., A. Sroufe, and B. Egeland. 1985. "The Relationship Between Quality of Attachment and Behavior Problems in Preschool Children in a High-Risk Sample." In *Growing Points in Attachment Theory and Research*, edited by I. Bretherton and E. Waters. *Monographs of the Society for Research in Child Development* 50(1–2, Serial no. 209): 147–166.

Farel, A. 1980. "Effects of Preferred Maternal Roles, Maternal Employment and Socio-Demographic status on School Adjustment and Competence." *Child Development.* 50: 1179–1186.

Forehand, R., A. McCombs, and G. Brody. 1987. "The Relationship Between Parental Depressive Mood States and Child Functioning." *Behavior Research and Therapy* 9: 1–20.

Friedman, S. L., J. Brooks-Gunn, D. Vandell, and M. Weinraub. 1994. "Effects of Child Care on Psychological Development: Issues and Future Directions for Research." *Pediatrics* 94 (6, Suppl.): 1069–1070.

Galinsky, E., J. T. Bond, and D. Friedman. 1993. "The Changing Workforce: Highlights of the National Study." Working paper. New York: Families and Work Institute.

Galinsky, E., and D. E. Friedman. 1993. *Education Before School: Investing in Quality Child Care.* New York: Scholastic Press.

Garmezy, N., and M. Rutter, eds. 1983. *Stress, Coping, and Development in Children.* New York: McGraw-Hill.

Gilbert, L. 1985. *Men in Dual-Career Families: Current Realities and Future Prospects.* Hillsdale, N.J.: Erlbaum.

Glendon, M. A. 1981. *The New Family and New Property.* Seattle, Wash.: Butterworths.

Goode, W. J. 1960. "A Theory of Role Strain." *American Sociological Review* 25: 483–96.

Gottfried, A. E., and A. W. Gottfried, eds. 1988. *Maternal Employment and Children's Development: Longitudinal Research.* New York: Plenum Press.

———. 1994. "Role of Maternal and Dual-Earner Employment Status in Children's Development." In *Redefining Families: Implications for Children's Development*, edited by A. E. Gottfried and A. W. Gottfried. New York: Plenum Press.

Gove, W., and C. Zeiss. 1987. "Multiple Roles and Happiness." In *Spouse, Parent, Worker*, edited by F. Crosby. New Haven: Yale University Press.

Gove, W. R., and C. Peterson. 1980. "Update of the Literature on Personal and Marital Adjustment: The Effect of Children and the Employment of Wives." *Marriage and Family Review* 3: 63–69.

Haskins, R. 1985. "Public School Aggression among Children with Varying Day-Care Experience." *Child Development* 56: 689–703.

Haveman, R., and B. Wolfe. 1994. *Succeeding Generations: On the Effects of Investments in Children.* New York: Russell Sage Foundation.

———. 1995. "On the Determinants of Children's Attainments: A Review of Methods and Findings." *Journal of Economic Literature* 33: 1824–78.

Hayes, C. D., J. L. Palmer, and M. J. Zaslow, eds., 1990. *Who Cares for America's Children? Child Care Policy for the 1990s.* Washington D.C.: National Academy Press.

Hock, E. 1980. "Working and Nonworking Mothers and Their Infants: A Comparative Study of

Maternal Care-Giving Characteristics and Infant Social Behavior." *Merrill Palmer Quarterly* 26: 79–101.

Hofferth, S. L. 1995. *Caring for Children at the Poverty Line.* Children and Youth Services Review 17: 61–90.

Hofferth, S. L., A. Brayfield, S. Deich, and P. Holcomb. 1991. *The National Child Care Survey 1990.* Washington, D.C.: The Urban Institute.

Hoffman, L.W. 1974. "Fear of Success in Males and Females: 1965 and 1971." *Journal of Consulting and Clinical Psychology* 42: 353–58.

———. 1979. "Maternal Employment: 1979." *American Psychologist* 34: 859–65.

———. 1989. "Effects of Maternal Employment in the Two-Parent Family." *American Psychologist* 44: 283–92.

Jackson, A. P. 1992. "Well-Being among Single, Black Employed Mothers." *Social Service Review* 66: 399–409.

———. 1993. "Black Single Working Mothers in Poverty: Preferences for Employment, Well-Being, and Perceptions of Preschool-Age Children." *Social Work* 38: 26–34.

———. 1994. "The Effects of Role Strain on Single, Working, Black Mothers' Perceptions of Their Young Children." *Social Work Research* 18: 36–40.

Juster, F. J., and F. Stafford, eds. 1985. *Time, Goods and Well-Being.* Ann Arbor, Mich.: University of Michigan.

Kamerman, S. B. 1980. *Parenting in an Unresponsive Society: Managing Work and Family Life.* New York: Free Press.

———. 1988. "Maternity and Parenting Benefits: An International Review." In *The Parental Leave Crisis: Toward a National Policy*, edited by E. Zigler and O. Frank. New Haven, Ct.: Yale University Press.

Kamerman, S. B., and C. D. Hayes, eds. 1982. *Families That Work: Children in a Changing World.* Washington, D.C.: National Academy Press.

Kamerman, S. B., and A. Kahn. 1981. *Child Care, Family Benefits and Working Parents.* New York: Columbia University Press.

———. 1988. *Mothers Alone: Strategies for a Time of Change.* Dover, Mass.: Auburn House.

———. 1991. *Child Care, Parental Leave, and the Under 3's.* New York: Auburn House.

———. 1996. *Starting Right.* New York: Columbia University Press.

Kessler, R., and J. McRae. 1982. "The Effects of Wives' Employment on the Mental Health of Married Men and Women." *American Sociological Review* 47: 216–27.

Kessler-Harris, A. 1982. *Out to Work: A History of Wage-Earning Women in the United States.* Oxford, England: Oxford University.

Kisker, E., S. Hofferth, D. Phillips, and E. Faruhar. 1991. *A Profile of Child Care Settings: Early Education and Care in 1990.* Washington: U.S. Government Printing Office.

Kohn, M. 1969. *Class and Conformity: A Study in Values.* Chicago: University of Chicago Press.

Kohn, M., and C. Schooler. 1973. "Occupational Experience and Psychological Functioning: An Assessment of Reciprocal Effects." *American Sociological Review* 38: 97–118.

———. 1982. "Job Conditions and Personality: A Longitudinal Assessment of Their Reciprocal Effects." *American Journal of Sociology* 87: 1257–86.

Korenman, S., and J. Miller. 1997. Long Term Poverty and Physical Health in the National Longitudinal Study of Youth. In *Growing Up Poor*, edited by G. Duncan and J. Brooks-Gunn, New York: Russell Sage Foundation.

Krein, S., and A. Beller. 1988. "Educational Attainment of Children from Single-Parent Families: Differences Between Exposure, Gender and Race." *Demography* 25: 221–34.

Leibowitz, A. 1974. "Education and Home Production." *American Economic Review* 64: 243–50.

Lerner, J., and N. Galambos. 1985. "Maternal Role Satisfaction, Mother-Child Interaction, and Child Temperament: A Process Model." *Developmental Psychology* 21: 1157–64.

Lewin, T. 1994. "Working Women Say Bias Persists." *The New York Times*, Oct. 15, 1994, B1.

Lopata, H., C. Miller, and D. Barnewolt. 1984. *City Women: Work, Jobs, Occupations Careers.* New York: Praeger.

Maccoby, E. E., and J. A. Martin. 1983. "Socialization in the Context of the Family: Parent-Child Interaction." In *Handbook of Child Psychology*, edited by P. H. Mussen and E. M. Hetherington. New York: John Wiley and Sons.

Manke, B., B. L. Seery, and S. M. McHale. 1994. "The Three Corners of Domestic Labor: Mothers', Fathers', and Children's Weekday and Weekend Housework." *Journal of Marriage and the Family* 56(3): 657–68.

Marks, S. R. 1977. "Multiple Roles and Role Strain: Some Notes on Human Energy, Time, and Commitment." *American Sociological Review* 42: 921–36.

Marshall, N., and R. Barnett. 1991. "Race, Class and Multiple Role Strains and Gains Among Women Employed in the Service Sector." *Women and Health* 17(4): 1–19.

Mayer, S. 1997. *Does More Money Buy Better Children?: The True Relationship Between Parental Income and Children's Chances.* Cambridge, Mass.: Harvard University Press.

McHale, S., W. Bartko, A. Crouter, and M. Perry-Jenkins. 1990. "Children's Housework and Psychosocial Functioning: The Mediating Effects of Parents' Sex Role Behaviors and Attitudes." *Child Development* 61: 1413–26.

McHale, S. M., and A. C. Crouter. 1992. "You Can't Always Get What You Want: Incongruence Between Sex-Role Attitudes and Family Work Roles and Its Implications for Marriage." *Journal of Marriage and the Family* 54: 537–47.

McLanahan, S., and G. Sandefur. 1994. *Growing Up with a Single Parent: What Hurts, What Helps.* Cambridge, Mass.: Harvard University Press.

McLanahan, S. 1985. "Family Structure and the Reproduction of Poverty." *American Journal Of Sociology* 90: 873–901.

McLoyd, V. C. 1990. "The Impact of Economic Hardship on Black Families and Children: Psychological Distress, Parenting, and Socioemotional Development." *Child Development* 61: 311–46.

McLoyd, V. C., T. E. Jayaratne, R. Ceballo, and J. Borquez. 1994. "Unemployment and Work Interruption among African American Single Mothers: Effects on Parenting and Adolescent Socioemotional Functioning." *Child Development* 65(2): 562–89.

Menaghan, E., and T. Parcel. 1991. "Determining Children's Home Environments: The Impact of Maternal Characteristics and Current Occupational and Family Conditions." *Journal of Marriage and the Family* 53: 417–31.

Meyers, M. K. 1993. "Child Care in JOBS Employment and Training Programs: What Difference Does Quality Make?" *Journal of Marriage and the Family* 55: 767–83.

Miller, J., C. Schooler, M. Kohn, and K. Miller. 1979. "Women and Work: The Psychological Effects of Occupational Conditions." *American Journal of Sociology* 85: 66–94.

Moen, P., and E. Dempster-McClain. 1987. "Employed Parents: Role Strain, Work Time and Preferences for Less." *Journal of Marriage and the Family* 49: 579–90.

Moore, K., and S. Hofferth. 1979. "Effects of Women's Employment on Marriage." *Marriage and Family Review* 2: 27–36.

Morgan, G. 1987. *The National State of Child Care Regulation.* Watertown, Mass.: Work/Family Directions.

Mortimer, J. T., and G. Sorenson. 1984. "Men, Women, Work, and Family." In *Women in the Workplace*, edited by K. M. Borman, D. Quarm, and S. Gideonese, Norwood, N.J.: Ablex.

Oakley, A. 1974. *Women's Work: A History of the Housewife.* New York: Pantheon Books.

Oppenheimer, V. 1979. *The Female Labor Force in the United States: Demographic and Economic Factors Governing Its Growth and Changing Composition.* Westport, Conn.: Greenwood Press.

Parcel, T., and E. Menaghan. 1994. "Early Parental Work, Family Social Capital, and Early Childhood Outcomes." *American Journal of Sociology* 99: 972–1009.

————. 1997. "Effects of Low-Wage Employment on Family Well-Being." *The Future of Children* 17: 122–27.

Parcel, T. 1989. "Comparable Worth, Labor Markets and Earnings." In *Pay Equity: Empirical Inquiries,* edited by R. Michael, H. Hartmann, and B. O'Farrell, Washington, D.C.: National Academy Press.

Parke, R. D. 1982. "The Father-Infant Relationship: A Family Perspective." In *Women: A Developmental Perspective,* edited by P. Berman. Bethesda, Md.: U.S. Department of Health and Human Services.

Parke, R. D. 1995. "Fathers and Families. In *Handbook of Parenting, Vol. 2.,* edited by M. Bornstein. N.J.: Lawrence Erlbaum.

Parry, G. 1986. "Paid Employment, Life Events, Social Support, and Mental Health in Working-class Mothers." *Journal of Health and Social Behavior* 27: 193–208.

Phillips, D., M. Voran, E. Kiser, C. Howes, and M. Whitebook. 1994. "Child Care for Children in Poverty: Opportunity or Inequity?" *Child Development* 65: 472–92.

Piotrkowski, C., and M. Katz. 1982. "Indirect Socialization of Children: The Effects of Mothers' Jobs on Academic Behaviors." *Child Development* 53: 1520–29.

Pleck, J. H., G. L. Staines, and L. Lang. 1980. "Conflicts Between Work and Family Life." *Monthly Labor Review* 103: 29–31.

Presser, H. 1989 "Can We Make Time For Children? The Economy, Work Schedules, and Child Care." *Demography* 26: 524–41.

Radloff, L. 1977. "Sex Differences in Depression: The Effects of Occupational and Marital Status." *Sex Roles* 1: 249–65.

Rauh, V. 1994. "Employment as Social Capital for Pregnant Women." Paper presented at the 122nd Annual Meeting of American Public Health Association, Washington, D.C. (Oct. 1994).

Reich, C. 1964. "The New Property." *Yale Law Journal* 74 (April): 1245–57.

Repetti, R. 1987. "Linkages Between Work and Family Roles." In *Family Processes and Problems: Social Psychological Aspects,* edited by S. Oskamp. Newbury Park, N.J.: Sage Publications.

Ross, C., J. Miroskwy, and J. Huber. 1983. "Dividing Work, Sharing Work and In-Between: Marriage Patterns and Depression." *American Sociological Review* 48: 809–23.

Schwartz, J. C., R. G. Strickland, and G. Krolick. 1974. "Infant Day Care: Behavioral Effects at Preschool Age." *Developmental Psychology* 54: 502–6.

Schwartz, P. 1983. "Length of Day-Care Attendance and Attachment Behavior in Eighteen-Month-Old Infants." *Child Development* 54: 1073–78.

Sieber, S. D. 1974. "Toward a Theory of Role Accumulation." *American Sociological Review* 39: 567–78.

Smith, J., and J. Brooks-Gunn. 1997; forthcoming. Correlates and Consequences of Harsh Discipline for Young Children. *Journal of the Archives of Pediatrics and Adolescence.*

Smith, J., J. Brooks-Gunn, and P. K. Klebanov. 1997. "Consequences of Living in Poverty for Young Children's Cognitive and Verbal Ability and Early School Achievement. In *Consequences of Growing up Poor,* edited by G. J. Duncan and J. Brooks-Gunn. New York: Russell Sage Foundation.

Smith, J. 1994. "Maternal Employment and the Young Child." Ph.D. diss., Columbia University, New York.

Spitze, G. 1988. "Women's Employment and Family Relations: A Review." *Journal of Marriage and the Family* 50: 595–618.

Staines, G. 1980. "Spillover Versus Compensation: A Review of the Literature on the Relationship Between Work and Nonwork." *Human Relations* 33: 111–29.

Starfield, B., S. Shapiro, J. Weiss, K. Y. Liang, K. Ra, D. Paige, and X. Wong. 1991. "Role of Family Income and Low Birth Weight." *American Journal of Epidemiology* 134(10): 1167–74.

Timmer, S., J. Eccles, and K. O'Brien. 1985. "How Children Use Time." In *Time, Goods and Well-Being*, edited by F. J. Juster and F. Stafford. Ann Arbor, Mich.: University of Michigan Press.

U.S. Bureau of Labor Statistics. 1990, March. *Monthly Labor Review*. Washington: Government Printing Office.

Vaughn, B., F. Gove, and B. Egeland. 1980. "The Relationship Between Out-of-Home Care and the Quality of Infant-Mother Attachment in an Economically Disadvantaged Population." *Child Development* 51: 1203–14.

Wachs, T. D., and G. Gruen. 1982. *Early Experience and Human Development*. New York: Plenum.

Warr, P., and G. Parry. 1982. "Paid Employment and Women's Psychological Well-Being." *Psychological Bulletin* 91: 498–516.

Whitebook, M., C. Howes, and D. Philips. 1989. *Who Cares? Child Care Teachers and the Quality of Care in America., Final Report of the National Child Care Staffing Study*. Oakland, Calif.: Child Care Employee Project.

Woods, M. 1972. "The Unsupervised Child of the Working Mother." *Developmental Psychology* 6: 14–25.

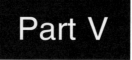

Part V

Population, Family, Neighborhood

Demographic Change and the Population of Children: Race/Ethnicity, Immigration, and Family Size

Dennis P. Hogan and David J. Eggebeen

THE PURPOSE OF this chapter is to evaluate the status of our understanding of three important features of the population of children: race/ethnicity, immigration, and family size. Previous treatment of these indicators has been uneven, with no standard approach or measures. Family size changes and their implications for children, as well as race/ethnic variations in child living arrangements and the experience of poverty have received the most attention. In contrast, immigration has been virtually ignored (see Jensen 1994 for an exception). For example, the absence of information on Hispanic origins until recent censuses, and subsequent variations in its measurement, restricted Hernandez to black/white comparisons for all except the most recent decade. The waves of immigration of white ethnic groups that transformed the population of American children during the first half of this century, and the more recent immigration waves of nonwhites that have been a driving force in demographic change since the mid-1960s, are largely ignored. Are these neglected aspects of the family origins of children important? Do they alter or modify the consequences of family structure and family socioeconomic resources? These are issues that we will address.

We will also look at measures of family size. This is a potentially important measure of child well-being while growing up, potentially affecting socialization patterns, parent-child interactions, and access to resources. Declines in the average number of children and changing family structures over the past forty years have undoubtedly altered the family sizes of children and, possibly, their well-being.

This volume on the indicators of children's well-being offers a fresh opportunity to reach a collective agreement about the best social indicators of child well-being. Armed with such a consensus it may be feasible to significantly improve our knowledge of the complex life course of children, viewed in the cultural and social structural contexts to which they and their families are assigned. This is even more important for certain states and regions of the nation in which there is great diversity in the race/ethnic and immigration experiences of children. We will argue that such an approach can significantly improve the reporting on children's well being, and that modest modifications in usual procedures for the collection and production of data on children will prove particularly helpful.

We will deal with each of these features (race/ethnicity, immigration, and family size) in turn. After discussing why knowledge of a feature is important, we plan to describe how it is currently measured in the U.S. Census of Population, paying particular attention to the relevance of these measures for understanding the experience of children. We will briefly, and somewhat superficially, describe the population of children for the indicator using Public Use Microdata (PUMS) files of the 1990 Census of Population. Our assessment of each of these features will conclude with a discussion of how they can best be defined using currently available procedures and instruments of data collection.

RACE AND ETHNICITY
Rationale

Race and ethnicity are not variables that *directly* measure child well-being. Few if any analysts would claim that, controlling for socioeconomic resources and socialization environment (family structure and size), children of one race have inferior well-being compared to children of another race, per se. Rather, race and ethnicity are important because they: index average levels of socioeconomic resources in families and modal forms of family structure, both of which are direct measures of the well-being of children; measure the access of the families to opportunities for achievement (labor markets, advanced education); and are associated with the concentration of families in neighborhoods that define the social structures and cultural experiences of children outside of their families. Race and ethnicity thus are used in studies of child well-being as variables that classify children into types that have distinct outcomes on measures of well-being. Such use is one way in which groups of children "at risk" may be defined. But race and ethnic information may also serve as control variables that define distinct population subgroups. This is done when looking at the association of other factors with child well-being, as, for example, with the effects of single-parent family structure on family income.

Measurement

For the past half-century most demographic data collection and research has viewed a person's race and/or ethnicity as a matter of self-identification. While members of the society may ascribe race or ethnic identity to a person with whom they interact, and modify their actions accordingly, researchers see this as secondary to self-identification. One reason for this is the virtual impossibility of defining race and ethnicity precisely in a multicultural society such as ours, in which intermarriage and ethnic mixing are commonplace. Another is that race and ethnicity are seen as cultural concepts of considerable importance to person's definition of identity and community. Typically this self-identification is communicated to the larger society and used by members of that society to classify persons in the metric of social relations. But as a subjective concept that may be represented differently in various settings, ethnicity is not always reported consistently across different contexts even when the informant is the same person (U.S. Bureau of the Census 1974). This problem is exacerbated across different interview contexts.

This situation is even more confusing in the case of children. In situations in which parents and children live together, the race and ethnicity of each member of the family can be ascertained. In many cases, there is agreement and the ethnicity of the child likewise can be assigned. But in cases of different race or ethnicity of the father and mother or ethnic difference between the head of the household and other adults in the household the situation is less well defined. In such cases a procedure may be developed for determining the race and ethnic origins of children from data on adults in their family. But the logic of an analysis using *subjective parental* race and ethnic self-identification information to *objectively* classify children based on their origins is not clear.

We believe a preferable strategy is to obtain "self-identified" (actually, in the case of children, family-identified) race and ethnic origin information for each child. In this way, each family (or its representative respondent) can indicate the race and ethnic identification with which the child is being raised, reflecting the way in which the child is presented to society (for example, in the child's neighborhood, school).

This procedure has the additional advantage of permitting similar rules of classification for children whose parents are not both coresident and whose race and ethnic origins are partly unknown. We thus are in agreement with Rogers (1989) that race and ethnicity of children should be determined on the basis of identification within the family of socialization. Our suggested procedure, however, is based on a family informant's responses about the child (making it a purely subjective measure), rather than on the automatic assignment of race and ethnicity of the coresident mother.

We note that while this recommendation is currently the procedure followed by the decennial census, it typically is not the practice in studies of children that are not household-based. For example, birth certificates typically collect ethnicity of the mother, but not always of the father, and not of the infant. Infant death certificates provide the race or ethnicity of the child as reported by a "knowledgeable" informant (possibly a family member, but possibly a physician, coroner, or funeral director). Mothers more often provide birth certificate data whereas fathers more often are informants for the death certificate. Norris and Shipley (1971) report that in California from 1965 to 1967 as many as 17 percent of Chinese and 43 percent of Japanese infants were given discrepant race assignments at birth and at death.

Ideally, we believe that whenever possible data collection instruments for children should directly collect information on the race and ethnicity of children. This can be readily done with census questions, but these may be usefully modified (Entwisle and Astone 1994). Under their recommended procedure, Latino ancestry is ascertained first. For those reporting Latino origins, Mexican, Puerto Rican, and Cuban nativity is then determined. All children are then classified according to whether they are white, African American, American Indian, Asian and Pacific Islander, or other (specified). This collection procedure has the advantage of keeping Hispanic origins and race as separate concepts, while allowing investigators readily to classify children into mutually exclusive and exhaustive categories that combine race and ethnicity (as we suggest in this essay).

We have argued that race and ethnicity in the United States are socially and culturally determined rather than biologically or genetically defined. Accordingly, the questions used to elicit racial identification and the measures constructed from this information have varied over time and reflect the size and impact of any given minority at that time. Membership in the "majority" population also changes over time as groups once regarded as inferior gain in social standing and are held at less social distance. (For example, three ethnic groups who are today usually included as part of the white majority are Italians, Irish, and Jews. These groups would not have been so regarded in the early part of this century.) In other cases (such as Native Americans), self-identification with an ethnic identity has grown and waned with ethnic consciousness and sentiment. Throughout our national history, however, selected race and ethnic groups have merited attention; analysts cannot afford to ignore such defining constructs in the fabric of American life when they study children. This is apparent in the examinations of the well-being of American children of different race and ethnic origins in 1990.

Application and Evaluation

The 1990 Census of the United States uses a series of questions about race and national origin to define all persons as black, Native American (American Indian), Asian and Pacific Islander, and white. In some published tabulations the "other" races are not shown separately, but are included in the figures for the total population (due to sample size considerations).

Hispanic origin information is gotten from all respondents so that both blacks and whites can be further classified as Hispanic origin or not. In its tabulations the Census Bureau typically shows data for whites, blacks, and others (Native Americans, Asian and Pacific Islanders), with data for Hispanics (both white and black) tabulated separately. With this approach, the race and ethnic identification of the population is not defined in a mutually exclusive and exhaustive categorization. One argument in its favor is that it does tap American reality—many Puerto Ricans and Cubans are self-identified as being both black and Hispanic. This solution seems acceptable when doing cross-tabulations of census data and does not lead to analytic error. But this solution is not succinct, effectively doubling the number of tabulations needed. Another possibility would be to subdivide the black and white categories according to Latino origins. But this also is costly for analytic clarity since it produces a new category (black Latinos) with very few children in that category. One 1984 study, for example, found that only 2 percent of Mexican American births, 7 percent of Puerto Rican births, and 12 percent of Central and South American births in the United States were black (National Center for Health Statistics 1987:10, as reported in Rogers 1989).

We believe that it may be useful to retain the race and Latino ancestry variables as separate constructs in local or regional studies of populations in which Latinos are predominantly of Puerto Rican or Central and South American origins, but that there is little analytic advantage associated with this distinction for the Latino population as a whole, and for areas in which Mexican Americans predominate. We therefore advocate that for most studies of children the population first be defined as either black or nonblack, followed by a categorization of the nonblacks into those of Hispanic and non-Hispanic origin. This recommended procedure thus gives emphasis to the black/white racial line which has always assumed primary importance in the nation's history. Blacks of Hispanic origin are, if anything, typically even more disadvantaged than non-Hispanic blacks, suffering both from their minority racial identification, language differences, and predominant migrant origins. To the extent that race and ethnic identification are measures of socioeconomic resources and access to achievement opportunities, this is a reasonable classification for analysts to use. It also preserves a distinct Latino category of nonblack children for this rapidly growing minority.

A study of children using 1990 census data shows that it is useful to distinguish whether children are non-Hispanic white, black, Hispanic (Latino), Asian and Pacific Islander, or American Indian (Hogan and Lichter 1994). For example, 81 percent of white and 84 percent of Asian children live with both parents, compared to 64 percent of Latinos, 56 percent of American Indians, and 37 percent of blacks. Poverty rates are 11 percent for whites, 17 percent of Asians, 31 percent of Latinos, and 39 percent of American Indians and blacks. These poverty rates are more greatly affected by family structure for some of the groups than for others—standardized for family structure, the poverty rate is 11 percent for whites, 18 percent for Asians, 27 percent for Latinos, 22 percent for blacks and 31 percent for American Indians. By distinguishing these five race/ethnic groups it thus can be seen that family structure plays a key role in the high poverty levels of black children, but is of much less importance for Latinos and American Indians. For these other groups, immigrant status, education, and access to economic opportunities are of the utmost importance.

Further analysis demonstrates how family structure and labor supply decisions distinguish children in these race and ethnic groups (Hogan and Lichter 1994). Between one-fifth and one-quarter of children who are white, Latino, and Asian live in two-parent families in which only the father works full-time; only 7 percent of black children live in this type of traditional family environment. Asians (36 percent) and whites (27 percent) most often live in families in which both parents are present and working full-time. For black children, life in a mother-headed family in which the mother does not work or works full-time are equally typical experiences.

Specialists in ethnic studies often argue that it is extremely important to distinguish national origins among the various Hispanic groups and among Asian and Pacific Islanders. Indeed, Hogan and Lichter (1994) find substantial variations in family structure and economic well-being of Puerto Rican, Cuban, Mexican American, and other Hispanic children. For example, almost one-third of Mexican-origin children and 40 percent of Puerto Rican children are poor, compared to only 14 percent of Cuban children. The poverty rate of Puerto Rican children would decline to 25 percent if Puerto Rican children had living arrangements like those of whites, but living arrangements were much less important in explaining the poverty of Mexican- and Cuban-ancestry children. The inferior well-being of Puerto Rican children compared to those in other Latino groups appears to be more a function of their distinct family structure differences than anything else (such as geographic concentration, cultural differences, linguistic isolation). This finding is consistent with studies of family support to the elderly among these groups (Himes et al. 1996).

Other tabulations of the 1990 census suggest that systematic differences by national origin group among the Asians are tied mainly to migration experiences.

Third- or later-generation Asian children differ little in family structure and poverty by whether they are of Chinese or Japanese origin, and have experiences more like those of native whites. More recent Asian immigrant groups are disadvantaged by linguistic isolation, nontransferrable human capital skills, and family separation. But the national origin groups do not show distinct systematic differences in the well-being of children, taking these features of the immigrant experience into account. Indeed, research shows that there are few differences among these Asian immigrant groups in support to elderly family members, once these other distinguishing features of their immigrant experience are taken into account (Himes et al. 1996).

Recommendations

Based on these findings, we believe it is useful to distinguish a minimum of five race and ethnic groups in studies of child well-being—non-Hispanic white, black, Latino (nonblack), Asian and Pacific Islander, and American Indian. We strongly urge the use of these categories of race and ethnic identification whenever possible to obtain reasonably complete information on ethnic identity and opportunity.

Such a breakdown is appropriate when analyzing current census data on children. But changes over time in race and ethnicity identification information, and changes in the salience of different ethnic identities over time, often render such detailed categories impossible or useless for historical comparisons. In the case of historical work, a distinction between blacks and nonblacks, with attention to Hispanics in recent decades, has been the preferred strategy (Hernandez 1983) for studies focusing on the experiences of the national population of children.

But apart from census studies, even the largest surveys (such as the Current Population Survey) typically lack the sample designs (primary sampling units with concentrations of race and ethnic minorities) and overall sample sizes to represent Asian and Pacific Islander children and American Indian children separately. Resultant sample files made available to investigators have far too few cases to represent adequately the different Asian-origin groups, and usually are too small to represent any Latino groups individually (except Mexican Americans in the case of an oversample). This is true of such frequently used data sources as the National Longitudinal Survey of Youth, the associated Mother/Child Files, and the National Survey of Families and Households.

In this situation constrained by practical considerations, we recommend using a threefold race and ethnic classification for children: nonblack non-Hispanics, nonblack Hispanics, and blacks. With this classification, all children who are identified by their family member as black—whether Hispanic or non-Hispanic—are classified as black. American Indians and Asians and Pacific Islanders are classified with whites in the nonblack non-Hispanic group. We believe this procedure is acceptable if not desirable. The small numbers of American Indians and Asians and Pacific Islanders have little impact on the white category when included there; the advantage of the procedure is that it permits all children to be assigned a race and ethnic identity rather than being dropped from study. The disadvantage is that in this case it is more a nonidentity—nonblack non-Hispanic—than a socially meaningful identity.

An alternative solution is to include only whites in the first category, excluding American Indians and Asians and Pacific Islanders from any of the identified groups. With this solution all children, including these two rarer groups, are included in the total and each category is a more accurate reflection of social identity. The drawback here is that the parts do not add to the whole.

We produced tabulations from the 1990 census to illustrate the application of these alternative race and ethnic identifications of American children. These tabulations were done for the entire United States and separately for four states (California, Florida, Minnesota, and Pennsylvania) with widely differing race and ethnic compositions. Just under three-quarters of American children are nonblack non-Hispanic in 1990. This proportion varies greatly across the selected states from a high of 95 percent in Minnesota to a low of 57 percent in California. Most children in the United States are either white non-Hispanic, black (15 percent), or Hispanic (12 percent); fewer than 3 percent are Asian and Pacific Islander and less than 1 percent are American Indian. For the nation, we believe that a three-category classification of race and ethnicity (nonblack non-Hispanic, nonblack Hispanic, and black) is quite adequate to index average levels of socioeconomic resources in families and modal forms of family structure; measure the access of the families to opportunities for achievement; and indicate the concentration of families in neighborhoods which define the social structures and cultural experiences of children outside of their families.

However, these tabulations also illustrate the importance of using the more detailed five-category scheme (that separates out Asian and Pacific Islanders and American Indians) for particular states. The unique situation of Asian children in California, for example, would be obscured without a more elaborate classification of race and ethnic identity. Asians constitute 9.9 percent of all children in California, while blacks make up only 7.8 percent of children in that state. One-third of all children in California are Hispanic, highlighting the importance of this group in California's recent population history.[1]

IMMIGRATION

Rationale

Children who are themselves immigrant or descendants of immigrant parents typically have distinctly different social origins than other American children, both minority and majority. Besides distinct ethnic origins, minority children often grow up in homes with more complex family structures, with inferior or nonconvertible socioeconomic resources, and with linguistic or geographic isolation from the nonimmigrant white majority. The families of children living in ethnic enclaves may even lack access to the full labor markets of the communities, while having privileged access to labor markets serving the local immigrant population.

For these reasons we anticipate that the immigrant experiences of children are important to distinguish in studies of child well-being. But the immigration status of children and their parents has been notably absent in prior studies of children. This is true even though great attention has been devoted to the experiences of immigrant adults. For example, in his census monograph on American children, Hernandez (1993) makes only passing reference to the impact of immigration on the population history of the twentieth-century United States and ignores differences between children of immigrants and those of native origins. In their otherwise comprehensive study of immigrants in the United States, Jasso and Rosenzweig largely ignore the experiences of children in immigrant families, except for a brief treatment of their school enrollment. Yet as Jensen and Chitose (1994) have argued, such an investigation would be a natural extension of Lieberson's (1980) research on the progress of turn-of-the-century immigrants and the work of Portes and Zhou (1993) on the political economy of immigrant families.

We thus have reason to believe that immigrant status may be an important factor differentiating the life chances of American children. Recent increases in immigration, especially the shift to migration based on family reunification preferences (Jasso and Rosenzweig 1990), mean that an increasing percentage of children are either foreign-born or live with foreign-born parents. By 1990, 14.7 percent of American children were either foreign-born or the child of a foreign-born coresident parent (Jensen and Chitose 1994). Yet few studies, even comprehensive census-based monographs focused on children and on immigration, have attended to this issue. What we try to determine here is whether this neglects an important aspect of American child well-being, or whether immigration status can continue to remain ignored.

Measurement

The first matter to be discussed is how immigration status is, and should be, measured for children. The 1980 census monograph on immigration (Jasso and Rosenzweig 1990) provides an excellent reference work on the measurement of immigration and the analysis of the immigrant experience. For all of the twentieth century the decennial census has collected information on country of birth, and most censuses have asked about year of entry to the United States for those who were foreign-born. Until recently the census also identified whether parents were foreign-born and, typically, their country of birth. But this information on nativity was last collected in a comprehensive fashion in the 1970 census. For adults, therefore, current census procedures do not permit identification of nativity status.

The situation is different for children who coreside with their parents, since the census collects country of birth for all persons in the household. Studies of immigration on the well-being of children thus can still make use of a nativity distinction (foreign-born, native-born of a foreign-born parent, or native-born of native parents) as long as the investigator is willing to restrict study to children who coreside with parents. For children who coreside with only one parent, nativity still can be defined based on the coresident parent. Insofar as it is the distinct family environment of immigrants that is thought to influence child well-being, these restrictions and limitations in defining nativity status are not problematic. Another advantage of a focus on the nativity of children is the comparability of this measure over extended periods of time.

The censuses of this century have made repeated but varied attempts to assess the integration of immigrants into the national population. Sometimes the focus has been on the timing of entry and length of time in the United States, and on whether the immigrant is a naturalized citizen. Other times the census has collected data on language—either mother tongue, English-language ability, or language spoken at home—as an indicator of acculturation and isolation from the larger society. The variations in these questions over time hinder the analysis of trends.

But these measures are inferior to immigration status for studies of children. Participation in the census and completion of its long-form questionnaire is itself partly dependent on language ability. A scale of English-language ability is also far more subjective a categorical report of nativity, and is probably subject to much greater variability across potential respondents within the household. For some immigrants, the ability to speak English is an indicator of socioeconomic status in the country of origin more than it is a measure of isolation after migration. As Jensen and Chitose (1994) have argued, language facility may be more important for some immigrant groups than for others. Those who have established immigrant communities that constitute ethnic enclaves (community and labor market) may actually benefit from greater retention and use of mother tongue. For these reasons, we recommend the use of nativity over alternative measures of the immigrant experience of children.

Application and Evaluation

Does nativity matter? Jensen and Chitose (1994) have provided a comprehensive description of children who are foreign-born or native-born of foreign-born parent(s) (which we will refer to as "immigrant" children) compared with children who are native-born of native-born parents (whom we call "natives"). Their analysis uses 1990 census data for children who coreside with a parent who is household head or the spouse of the head. They find that, on average, immigrant-origin children have households that are of larger size (5.2 versus 4.4 for the natives), due only in part to a larger number of related children (2.7 versus 2.2). Immigrant children more often grow up in families in which the head of household is male and married, compared to native children. They live in housing units that are smaller and more crowded.

The immigrants on average experience inferior economic circumstances—22 percent of immigrant children compared to 17 percent of native children are in poverty. But poverty among the immigrant children appears to be a transient situation—native-born children whose parents arrived in the U.S. prior to 1975 (five years or more before the census) have poverty levels lower than the native-born. In contrast, over one-third of recent immigrant children are in poverty.

For some immigrant children, however, the household head lacks educational credentials to ensure occupational success in the overall labor market (one-quarter live in households where the head has eight years or less of schooling compared to only 3 percent of native children). Additionally, many of the immigrant children grow up in houses that are linguistically isolated (a household in which no one over fourteen speaks only English or English as a second language "very well"). Fewer than 1 percent of the native children live in linguistically isolated households, compared to 41 percent of the foreign-born children and 21 percent of the native-born children of foreign-born parents. Spanish is the most common language spoken among the linguistically isolated, accounting for almost half of the children in those families.

These circumstances force more reliance on multiple workers and multiple jobs and on jobs in ethnic enclaves to escape poverty. These differences are even greater when foreign-born children are compared to native-born children of native parents.

Thus, a variable measuring the immigrant origins of children indexes average levels of socioeconomic resources in families and modal forms of family structure, both of which are direct measures of the well-being of children; measures the access of the families to opportunities for achievement (labor markets, advanced education); indicates membership in a family with cultural attitudes, values, and family relations that may differ from those of the majority; and is associated with the concentration of families in neighborhoods that define the social structures and the cultural experiences of children outside of their families. As such, immigrant status is a useful distinction to make in national studies of the well-being of children in which there are sufficient numbers of immigrant children for analysis.

However, the origin characteristics and national origins of immigrant children vary greatly (in large part as a consequence of changing U.S. immigration policies), and show pronounced change over time (Jasso and Rosenzweig 1990). In 1990, 31 percent of first- and second-generation immigrant children were of Mexican origin and 34 percent were of Asian origin (using race and ethnic information for their household head; Jensen and Chitose 1994). However, looking just at the foreign-born children, 56 percent were of Asian origin.

These immigrant children are not distributed evenly among the states, concentrating in states with major metropolitan areas (California, Connecticut, New Jersey, New York, and Illinois) and in some states with closer proximity to Latin America (Arizona, California, and Texas). Indeed, just four states (California, New York, Texas, and Florida) account for 63 percent of first- and second-generation immigrant children (compared with 25 percent of the native children). California, as home to both many Mexican and Asian immigrants, is one state for which it is particularly important to consider the immigration status of children—34 percent of all first- and second-generation immigrant children live in California. Thirty-eight percent of all children in California are either foreign-born or native-born to foreign-born parents (calculated from data in Jensen and Chitose 1994, table 1 and p. 4).

Recommendations

We conclude that studies of child well-being at the national level would benefit from identifying the immigrant status of children. While a measure that distinguishes foreign-born, native-born of foreign-born parent(s), and native-born of native parents is conceptually ideal, a simple distinction between immigrant children (foreign born or native-born, of foreign-born parents) and natives is adequate, given that the families' characteristics depend mostly on the parents' immigration status. In some states and major urban areas, most notably California, an adequate analysis of the well-being of children is not possible without consideration of immigrant status.

These recommendations ignore the extent to which immigrant status will differentiate children already considered separately by race and ethnicity. Seventy-nine percent of immigrant children would already fall into either the Asian and Pacific Islander (34 percent) or Hispanic (45 percent) race/ethnic classification we have recommended. Conversely, fully 91 percent of the Asian and Pacific Island–origin children are either first- or second-generation, as are 55 percent of the Hispanic children. There thus is not great overall analytic gain from considering both immigration status and race/ethnic origins in studies of the well-being of American children. However, such a distinction is of much greater importance in analyses of the impact of national immigration policies on the well-being of children. This is especially the case for the study of children in California, where it is essential that studies of children consider immigrant status as well as race and ethnicity.

FAMILY SIZE

Rationale

Population size is a central concern of demographers. Because of this, analysis of the components of population growth—fertility, mortality, and migration—form the intellectual core of what demographers do. Of these three components, the preponderance of attention has been given to fertility, in no small part because it is the most amenable of the three to intervention. Historically, much of this attention has been on the causal mechanisms involved in the timing and number of children born, as well as the consequences of fertility shifts for adults, families, and societies. Less appreciated, at least until recently, is that as women have changed the timing and number of children they bore, the sibling experience of children across successive cohorts has inevitably changed as well (Blake 1989; Eggebeen 1992).

That family size matters for children's well-being has been amply demonstrated by the work of Blake (1989). Drawing on a broad array of nationally representative data sets, she assembles overwhelming evidence that the number of siblings negatively effects cognitive development, some aspects of social development, and, most significantly, educational attainment. There are several possible reasons for these relationships. Blake, for example, suggests a "dilution model" of parental inputs. Quite simply, the more children, the more parental resources are divided and hence, the lower the quality of the output (Blake 1981, 1989).

Others point to the theoretical importance of group size on the possible interaction patterns of members of a small group. Thus, small group theory, when applied to family units, implies that parenting styles are probably quite different in large and small families. Specifically, a greater number of children increases the likelihood of parental frustrations in dealing with the complexities of individual personalities and needs, the variety of role definitions, and the day-to-day demands and pressures of family life. Such frustrations and pressures may lead to more punitive, authoritarian parenting styles. Indeed, tests for differences in parenting styles by family size are generally supportive of these notions, finding that behavioral control, methods of rule implementation, and affection patterns all vary in families by the number of children (Elder and Bowerman 1963; Nye, Carlson, and Garrett 1970; Peterson and Kuntz 1975; Scheck and Emerick

1976; Kidwell 1981, 1982). In any case, both explanations agree that having a large number of siblings is a disadvantage for a child.

Measurement

Because the census collects information about all the occupants of households and how they are related to the household head, the family sizes of children constitute the data of choice. In addition, the census has collected this information on household occupants in a fairly standard way for some time, thus making comparisons over time relatively easy to do.

There are two ways of determining family size in census data. The first is to use the question asked of women (or, in this case, the mother of the child) on the number of children ever born. The major advantage in using this question is that it better approximates the experiences of siblings over the course of childhood than questions which focus on current living arrangements. But assessments of the number of siblings currently living with a child underestimate the experience of siblings over the course of childhood (Hernandez 1993, table 2.3). For example, the median number of siblings aged 0 to 17 for children in 1980 was 1.8, but the median number of children ever born to mothers of those children was 2.26.

The problem with using this "children ever born" measure of family size is that the number of children ever born to a child's mother is not necessarily the number of siblings they have experienced in childhood (because of not having coresidence or death). In particular, last-borns also may have had little, if any, exposure to older siblings, who in some cases may be out of the home for much of the last-born's childhood.[2] Since the question is asked only of women, we cannot determine the sibling experience of children living with their fathers but not their mothers (4.8 percent of all children in the 1990 census (Eggebeen, Manning, and Snyder 1996). Also, the sibling experience of children with a stepmother is inaccurately represented, since she reports her fertility history, not that of the biological mother of the child.

The second way to determine the family sizes of children is to count up the number of siblings of the child currently living in the household. A major advantage is that it can be obtained for all children living in households. This avoids some of the problems with using maternal report of children ever born outlined above (inaccuracies for children with stepmothers and children in father-only families). It also focuses attention on the immediate situation of children (with whom are they currently sharing parental and familial resources). This is more relevant both as a measure of small-group dynamics and resource dilution. However, because it is a cross-sectional snapshot, this measure does not do very well at indicating the life course experience of a child.

Most studies have used some form of the number of children or number of coresident siblings to indicate the family size situation of children. What this misses is a key link between family size and the well-being of children: the number of parents or adult caretakers of the child and their siblings. That is, not only are the resources available to a child determined by the number of siblings with which a child has to compete, but also by the number of caretakers dispensing those resources. This distinction is especially important when considering the situations of minority children, who are more likely than white children to live in extended or complex households (Hernandez 1993). Such consideration improves the specification of the resource-dilution model, but is not useful as a measure of interaction complexity (which depends on actual size).

A useful way to take into account both of these factors is to calculate ratios of children to parents or adults in the home. There are both potential advantages and drawbacks to using ratios as proxies of potential resources available to children. First, we are assuming that having more adults in the home is advantageous to the child. While most of the time this is a reasonable assumption, it could very well be that in some cases additional adults (such as a dependent elderly grandparent) *compete* with the child for the parent's attention. This possibility has not been addressed in the literature, unfortunately. Where the consequences of additional adults in the household have been analyzed, the focus has been on their economic consequences. That is, these additional adults in the household are portrayed as part of an adaptive strategy, used to cope with poverty by providing additional income or freeing the mother to enter the labor force (Tienda and Angel 1982, 1985).

A second assumption that is made in using these ratios is that all adults in the home are of equal value when it comes to imparting resources to children. This assumption may seem especially heroic when the additional adult is a nonrelative like a roomer or boarder. In most cases, however, the additional adult is some sort of relative (grandparent or aunt/uncle) for whom it is reasonable to assume they provide something for the benefit of the child. More problematic are cohabitating partners. The 1990 census is the first census to explicitly ask about persons who are not related to the householder but "have a close personal relationship with the householder." A not insignificant proportion of children (3.5 percent) were living with a parent who was cohabitating at the time of the 1990 census (Manning and Lichter 1996). Unfortunately, whether or under what conditions cohabitating adults are in fact parents or function as surrogate parents is unknown.

Despite these drawbacks, child/adult ratios offer some distinct advantages. By taking into account both the number of potential givers of resources as well as the potential number of competitors for resources, child/adult ratios more accurately approximate parental resources available to the child than simple counts of the number of children ever born or number of siblings. These ratios also require very few pieces of information (just the number of children and adults or parents in the household), making historical comparisons easy. Finally, it is fairly easy to vary assumptions about resource-sharing within households by calculating ratios based on parents only or on related family members only, instead of on all children relative to all adults in the household.

Application and Evaluation

Based on calculations from the 1990 census, we provide in table 14.1 some examples of the distributions of children by family size. Nationally, less than one-quarter of dependent children live in households where they are the only child; that is, households in which they have no competitors for adult or parental attention. However, living with large numbers of siblings also has become quite rare: only about 5 percent of children live in households of five or more children.

Table 14.1   Family Sizes of Children

| | Total | Race | | | State | | | |
		White	Black	Hispanic	Calif.	Fla.	Minn.	Pa.
Number of related children <18								
1	22.5	23.6	21.8	16.9	20.6	25.9	18.7	23.9
2	39.3	42.1	32.2	31.0	36.5	39.2	38.5	41.1
3	23.8	23.2	24.1	26.8	23.9	27.6	28.4	23.8
4	9.1	7.6	12.6	14.5	10.9	8.1	9.9	7.9
5	3.2	2.3	5.2	5.9	4.4	2.9	3.1	2.1
6	1.2	0.7	2.4	2.8	2.0	0.8	0.8	0.7
7+	0.8	0.5	1.7	2.0	1.7	0.6	0.5	0.6
Average number of related children	2.39	2.27	2.62	2.80	2.56	2.28	2.45	2.28
Ratios								
All families								
Kids/all adults	1.25	1.17	1.57	1.35	1.23	1.21	1.31	1.19
Kids/parents	1.47	1.31	2.06	1.80	1.58	1.45	1.43	1.38
Two-parent families								
Kids/all adults	1.10	1.09	1.11	1.17	1.11	1.03	1.19	1.08
Kids/parents	1.20	1.16	1.27	1.42	1.30	1.13	1.24	1.15
Single-parent families								
Kids/all adults	1.83	1.67	2.01	1.94	1.74	1.82	1.99	1.73
Kids/parents	2.42	2.08	2.72	2.77	2.50	2.37	2.37	2.28

Source: 1990 Public Use Microdata files of the 1990 U.S. Census of Population.

While the mean number of children in the household is 2.39, the average child per adult is considerably lower (1.25). However, this ratio is quite sensitive to various assumptions. For example, if one assumes that only parents make significant contributions to child well-being, the ratio of children per parent is about 18 percent higher than the child/adult ratio.

Even more significant, however, are assumptions about single- versus two-parent families. To wit, if one assumes that two parents offer a number of intangible benefits to children beyond reducing the child/adult ratio (for example, that a ratio of four children to two parents is "better" than a ratio of two children to one parent), then one may want to calculate separate ratios by the number of parents. Child/adult and child/parent ratios are considerably lower for children in two-parent families. Children in single-parent families are more likely than children in two-parent families to have other adults present in the household from which they can potentially draw resources. However, these other adults do not offset the disadvantage to these children of having only one parent. The ratio of children to all adults is 1.83 in single-parent homes (about 52 percent higher), compared to a ratio of children to parents of 1.2 for children in two-parent families.

We also examined race/ethnic and selected state differences in these measures of adult/child ratios. We do not go into the specific differences here other than to note that national totals obscure significant subgroup diversity in children's family experiences (the data are provided in table 14.1). For example, white children retain considerable advantage over minority children in the number of sib-lings and in the ratios. There is moderate diversity across states as well; some-thing often overlooked in more typically used national level data. Interestingly, these state differences in ratios do not appear to be associated with large minority populations. Minnesota, for example, which is 95.1 percent white, has the high-est child/adult ratio (1.31) and the highest child/adult ratio among children in two-parent families (1.19) of the four states portrayed.

Recommendations

It is clear from the studies reviewed in this chapter that family size is an impor-tant determinant of children's well-being. We recommend measuring family size in two ways.

The first is a simple count of the number of dependent (under age eighteen) children living in the household. This indicator is readily available in most data sets, and, of course, is already commonly used. To the degree that children's well-being is conditioned by the different group dynamics that operate in large fami-lies versus small families, it is imperative to take number of siblings into account.

Adult/child or parent/child ratios are recommended as a second indicator. It is important to use ratios because these indicators more precisely measure resource dilution, which also is a threat to the well-being of children. Unfortunately, it is not clear under what conditions one should use child/parent ratios instead of child/adult ratios as an indicator of available resources. Until more is known about the role other adults play in the lives of children living in complex house-holds, researchers should be wary about making assumptions that the presence of each coresident adult equally benefits the child.

CONCLUSIONS

Our concern in this paper has been the measurement of three fairly neglected components of the population of children: race/ethnicity, immigration, and fam-ily size. Aside from the specific recommendations discussed above, we conclude by noting that none of the recommendations we make involve radical restructur-ing of our data collection enterprises or the ways researchers have commonly used these indicators. This is good. It implies that we can have reasonable confi-dence in what we have learned from past research using conventional practices. It also means that with appropriate sensitivity to the historical boundedness and theoretical assumptions underlying the indicators, researchers can early on incor-porate most of the above suggestions into their assessment of children's well-being.

Support for this research was provided by core funding (P30 HD28263-01) from the National Institute of Child Health and Human Development to the Population Research Institute, Pennsylvania State University. We thank Wendy Manning for graciously providing us with access to child files she created from the 1990 census and Kristen Robinson for computer tabulations. The related research of our colleagues Leif Jensen and Dan Lichter also was very helpful for this chapter.

NOTES

1. While an argument might be made for distinguishing national origin groups among the Hispanics, the geographic concentrations of particular national origin Latino groups in certain cities and states renders such a distinction unnecessary for most purposes.

2. To be sure, this does not mean that they stop being potential competitors for parental resources, as there is a growing recognition that parental help and support to independent living adult children characterizes a significant minority of American families (Hogan, Eggebeen, and Clogg 1993).

REFERENCES

Bane, M. J. 1976. "Marital Disruption and the Lives of Children." *Journal of Social Issues* 32: 103–17.

Bernert, E. H. 1958. *America's Children*. New York: John Wiley and Sons.

Blake, J. 1981. "Family Size and the Quality of Children." *Demography* 18: 421–42.

———. 1989. *Family Size and Achievement*. Berkeley, Calif.: University of California Press.

Bumpass, L. L. 1984a. "Children and Marital Disruption: A Replication and Update." *Demography* 21: 71–82.

———. 1984b. "Some Characteristics of Children's Second Families." *American Journal of Sociology* 90: 608–23.

Bumpass, L. L., and R. Rindfuss. 1979. "Children's Experience of Marital Disruption." *American Journal of Sociology* 85: 49–65.

Duncan, G. J., and W. Rodgers. 1991. "Has Children's Poverty Become More Persistent?" *American Sociological Review* 56: 538–50.

Eggebeen, D. J. 1988. "Determinants of Maternal Employment for White Preschool Children: 1960–1980." *Journal of Marriage and the Family* 50: 149–59.

———. 1992. "Changes in Sibling Configurations for American Preschool Children." *Social Biology* 39: 27–44.

Eggebeen, D. J., and D. T. Lichter. 1991. "Race, Family Structure, and Changing Poverty Among American Children." *American Sociological Review* 56: 801–17.

Eggebeen, D. J., T. R. Snyder, and W. D. Manning. 1996. "Children in Single Father Families in Demographic Perspective." *Journal of Family Issues* 17: 441–65.

Elder, G., and C. E. Bowerman. 1963. "Family Structure and Child Rearing Patterns: The Effect of Family Size and Sex Composition." *American Sociological Review* 28: 891–905.

Entwisle, D. R., and N. M. Astone. 1994. "Some Practical Guidelines for Measuring Youth's Race/Ethnicity and Socioeconomic Status." *Child Development* 65: 152–40.

Furstenberg, F., Jr., C. W. Nord, J. L. Peterson, and N. Zill. 1983. "The Life Course of Children of Divorce: Marital Disruption and Parental Contact." *American Sociological Review* 48: 656–68.

Glick, P. 1976. "Living Arrangements of Children and Young Adults." *Journal of Comparative Family Studies* 7: 321–33.

———. 1979. "Marrying, Divorcing, and Living Together in the United States Today." *Population Bulletin* 32: 5.

Hernandez, D. J. 1993. *America's Children, Resources from Family, Government, and the Economy*. New York: Russell Sage Foundation.

Hines, C. L., D. P. Hogan, and D. J. Eggebeen. 1996. "Living Arrangements of Minority Elders." *Journal of Gerontology* 51(1): S42–S48.

Hofferth, S. 1985. "Updating Children's Life Course." *Journal of Marriage and the Family* 47: 93–116.

Hogan, D. P., D. J. Eggebeen, and C. C. Clogg. 1993. "The Structure of Intergenerational Exchanges in American Families." *American Journal of Sociology* 98: 1428–58.

Hogan, D. P., and D. T. Lichter. 1994. "Children and Youth: Living Arrangements and Welfare." In *State of the Union, vol. 2*, edited by R. Farley. New York: Russell Sage Foundation.

Jasso, G., and M. R. Rosenzweig. 1990. *The New Chosen People: Immigrants in the United States.* New York: Russell Sage Foundation.

Jensen, L., and Y. Chitose. 1994. "Today's Second Generation: Evidence from the 1990 U.S. Census." *International Migration Review* 28: 714–35.

Kidwell, J. S. 1981. "Number of Siblings, Sibling Spacing, Sex, and Birth Order: Their Effects on Perceived Parent-Adolescent Relationships." *Journal of Marriage and the Family* 43: 315–32.

———. 1982. "The Neglected Birth Order: Middleborns." *Journal of Marriage and the Family* 44: 225–35.

Lowry, I. S. 1980. *The Science and Politics of Ethnic Enumeration.* Working Paper, P-6435. Santa Monica, Calif.: The RAND Corporation.

Manning, W. D., and D. T. Lichter. 1996. "Parental Cohabitation and Children's Economic Well-Being." *Journal of Marriage and the Family* 58: 998–1010.

Norris, F. D., and P. W. Shipley. 1971. "A Closer Look at Race Differentials in California's Infant Mortality, 1965–67." *HSMHA Health Report* 86: 810–14.

Nye, F. I., J. Carlson, and G. Garrett. 1970. "Family Size, Interaction, Affect and Stress." *Journal of Marriage and the Family* 32: 216–26.

Peterson, E. T., and P. R. Kunz. 1975. "Parental Control Over Adolescents According to Family Size." *Adolescence* 10: 419–27.

Portes, A., and M. Zhou. 1993. "The New Second Generation: Segmented Assimilation and Its Variants." *The Annals* 530: 74–96.

Rogers, R. G. 1989. "Ethnic Differences in Infant Mortality: Fact or Artifact?" *Social Science Quarterly* 70: 642–49.

Scheck, D. C., and R. Emerick. 1976. "The Young Male Adolescent's Perception of Early Child-Rearing Behavior: The Differential Effects of Socioeconomic Status and Family Size." *Sociometry* 39: 39–52.

Sweet, J. 1974. "The Living Arrangements of Children." Working Paper, 74–28. Madison, Wisc.: Center for Demography and Ecology, University of Wisconsin–Madison.

Tienda, M., and R. Angel. 1982. "Determinants of Extended Household Structure: Cultural Patterns or Economic Need?" *American Journal of Sociology* 87: 1360–83.

———. 1985. "Household Structure and Labor Force Participation of Black, Hispanic, and White Mothers." *Demography* 22: 381–94.

U.S. Bureau of the Census. 1974. "Consistency of Reporting of Ethnic Origin in the Current Population Survey." Technical paper, no. 31. Washington: U.S. Government Printing Office.

15

Family Structure, Stability, and the
Well-Being of Children

Gary D. Sandefur and Jane Mosley

THE SOCIAL DEMOGRAPHY of the American family has been one of the central foci in domestic population research for some time. The interest and importance of this issue is reflected in the annual publication of two current Census Bureau population reports—"Household and Family Characteristics" and "Marital Status and Living Arrangements"—as well as the reproduction of material from these reports in the annual *Statistical Abstracts* and the *Green Book*. Further, the U.S. Bureau of the Census publishes pages and pages of tables on marital status, family structure, and living arrangements based on data from each decennial census. In addition to the census and annual Current Population Surveys, the federal government sponsors a number of other data collection efforts including the Survey of Income and Program Participation (SIPP) and the National Survey of Families and Households (NSFH) that accumulate more detailed data on family structure and the stability in families over time.

The interest in these issues is fueled by scientific and intellectual curiosity, but also by the knowledge that family structure and stability are related to how well families are functioning and to the extent to which they provide a nurturing situation for the children in these families. As Zill and Nord (1994) point out, "Among the functions families are expected to fulfill are: providing for the basic physical needs of their members, including food, clothing, and shelter; teaching children right from wrong, to respect the rights of others, and to value other societal institutions; and monitoring and supervising children in their daily activities to protect them from harm and to ensure that they behave according to the rules of society." Scholars and policymakers are interested in family structure and stability because they believe that these affect the ability of families to fulfill these key functions, and thus affect the well-being of children.

The major goals of this chapter are to review existing local, state, and national data on indicators of family structure and stability, to examine briefly the research on the effects of family structure and stability on child, adolescent, and early adult well-being, and to suggest ways in which we might improve the quality and usefulness of our indicators. The major themes of the paper are: family structure and stability are not *direct* indicators of child well-being, but they are associated with many of these indicators; we need to rethink the way in which we measure family structure and stability to take into account the many types of families in our society; and the study of family instability needs to pay more attention to related issues such as child abuse and neglect and foster care placements.

What Do We Mean by Family Structure and Family Stability?

There is no "official" definition of family structure in social demography, but, when most social scientists use this term, they are generally referring to the marital status of the parents. A common convention in many reports on family structure is to distinguish between two-parent and single-parent families. Some reports and studies distinguish among types of single-parent families. Some studies, for example, identify single-parent families headed by men and by women, and distinguish among those created by out-of-wedlock childbearing, separation, divorce, or the death of one of the parents. Less common but still possible with the Public Use Microdata Samples from the decennial censuses and current population surveys is the identification of extended families with grandparents and other adult relatives in the same household. Although these data do not permit the assessment of extended family relationships involving individuals who do not reside together, ethnographers have attempted to examine these aspects of family structure.

Family stability is generally defined in terms of changes in the marital status of the parents. Most often, when social scientists discuss family stability, they are referring to divorce or separation. Other types of family stability events include marriage for previously never married parents, remarriage for divorced individuals, and changes in extended family residential patterns and relationships. The availability of prospective or retrospective family residential histories in data sets such as the NSFH, the National Longitudinal Survey of Youth-1979 cohort (NLSY), and the Panel Study of Income Dynamics (PSID) has allowed researchers to examine the stability of family structure over time, at least at the national level.

We know less about some of the other dimensions of family stability. We now have, for example, valid and reliable scales of family violence, conflict, and home environment (Daro 1994; National Research Council 1993). Some national surveys have included some of these scales, but in general, they have been used most often with local and not necessarily representative samples. Other areas where data collection is clearly inadequate, but where there are signs of improvement, are the three major types of child abuse (emotional, physical, and sexual), child neglect, and experiences with foster care (Courtney and Collins 1994; Daro 1992; Goerge, Wulczyn, and Harden 1994; Green Book 1993; National Research Council 1993).

Plan of Attack We begin by briefly reviewing what we know about the effects of family structure and family stability on child well-being. To do this, we borrow extensively from McLanahan and Sandefur (1994), and also draw from recent reviews by Hernandez (1986; 1993) and Seltzer (1994). Second, we discuss widely used indicators of family structure and stability and examine how these indicators are collected and published at the local, state, and federal level. Finally, we recommend some changes in the data that we collect to report on family structure and stability.

A BRIEF REVIEW OF RESEARCH ON THE RELATIONSHIP BETWEEN FAMILY STRUCTURE AND STABILITY AND DIRECT INDICATORS OF CHILD WELL-BEING

Why It Is Important to Measure Family Structure and Stability

We would not be concerned with family structure and stability in a volume on child indicators unless there were some scholarly support for a connection between family structure and stability and the well-being of children. Many of us who study family structure and stability and its effects on children, adolescents, and young adults emphasize the fact that family structure is *not* a direct indicator of how well children are doing. That is, most of us would not say that a child in a two-parent family is necessarily doing better than a child in a one-parent family. Many of us, however, believe that family structure does affect child well-being and that it does so through its influence on family functioning.

Our discussion of the association between family structure and child well-being draws heavily from McLanahan and Sandefur (1994). We argue that children benefit from their parents and other family members in many ways, including benefiting from intellectual stimulation and from knowing that working hard and getting a good education will pay off in the future. Knowing this is facilitated by having a close relationship with a parent who is committed to helping his or her children and who is able to supervise their activities. Further, parents in our society bear primary responsibility for making sure that their children's needs are met. Parents determine how much money is devoted to the development of children, and they provide guidance and supervision. They also provide connections to other adults in the community, schools, and labor market that are crucial for the development of children and for the opportunities available to children at different points in their lives. When one parent is forced or voluntarily chooses to do this alone, these processes and connections are often weakened. This occurs primarily through a loss of *economic*, *parental*, and *community* resources.

Information from the census, CPS, and other data clearly shows that one-parent families have considerably fewer *economic* resources than two-parent families. In 1992, approximately 45 percent of families with children headed by single mothers had incomes below the poverty line, as compared with 8.4 percent of families with children headed by two parents (U.S. Bureau of the Census 1993). Not all of the difference in income is due to the consequences of divorce or a decision to bear a child out of wedlock. But our research and that of other social scientists clearly has shown that divorce and out-of-wedlock childbearing substantially do reduce the income of custodial parents, relative to what it would be if they were married. A number of factors create this situation. Among them is that many noncustodial fathers do not pay adequate child support.

The absence of a parent also leads to lower access to *parental resources*. Fathers who live in separate households see their children less often. Interacting with a former spouse and maintaining a relationship with a child who lives in another household can be very difficult and painful. Many fathers respond by reducing the amount of time that they spend with their children or disengaging completely (Wallerstein and Kelly 1980). Family disruption also alters the mother-child relationship. Most single mothers are forced to fill multiple roles simultaneously, without adequate support. Some experience high levels of stress and become anxious and depressed (McLoyd and Wilson 1991; McLeod and Shanahan 1993; Hetherington, Cox, and Cox 1978). This can lead to inconsistent and ineffective parenting.

In families where the mother remarries or cohabits with an adult male, the quality of parenting is still likely to be lower than in families with two biological parents. From the child's point of view, having a new adult move into the household creates another disruption. Rather than assisting with the responsibilities of parenting, stepfathers sometimes compete with the child for the mother's time, adding to the mother's and the child's level of stress.

Finally, residing in a one-parent family can lower access to *community resources*. This occurs partially through income; that is, families with more income can afford to live in communities with better facilities such as day care centers, schools, parks, and community centers. Another reason for the connection between family structure and community resources is the higher residential and geographical mobility of children with divorced and separated parents relative to those with two parents (McLanahan, 1983; Haveman, Wolfe, and Spaulding 1991; Speare and Goldsheider 1987). When parents and children live in a community for a long time, they develop close ties that provide emotional support as well as information about the broader community. When a family moves from town to town or from neighborhood to neighborhood, these ties are undermined and often destroyed.

In our view, then, family structure affects the economic resources of children, the parental resources available to them, and the community resources to which they have access. These in turn affect direct measures of child and later adult well-being, such as social and emotional adjustment, educational attainment, family formation, and labor force participation. As Hernandez (1993) points out, children who live with one parent or with a parent and stepparent suffer disadvantages relative to those in intact families in terms of economic circumstances, psychological functioning, behavior problems, education, and health.

The Effects of Family Structure on Social and Emotional Adjustment

Much of what we know about the effects of family structure on the social and emotional well-being of children comes from studies of the aftermath of divorce. We know less about the effects on social and emotional well-being of growing up in a family unit created by out-of-wedlock childbearing. As Seltzer (1994) points out, we should think of divorce as one among several possible risk factors for social and emotional maladjustment: "Some children show no ill effects. As in medical research on risk factors in illness, studies about the effects of divorce are useful for predicting differences between categories of people but cannot address directly whether a specific individual will be harmed by divorce."

Three aspects of parental resources that are critical in the social and emotional development and adjustment of children are often involved in divorces. First, the conflict between the mother and father itself affects the social and emotional well-being of the children. In fact, research has shown that children who live in two-parent families characterized by high conflict between the mother and father experience similar adjustment problems to children who live in single-parent families (Hanson 1993; Peterson and Zill 1986). Conflict between parents often continues after divorce and continues to affect the children.

Second, children generally feel a huge sense of loss following a divorce (Wallerstein and Kelly 1980). They become very concerned about who will provide their care.

Third, the parenting style of the custodial parent, generally the mother, is altered by divorce, especially in the short run. The parenting practices of the custodial mother are more erratic during the first couple of years following a divorce (Hetherington et al. 1982).

Divorce, then, through its association with conflict, its effects on children's perceptions of the stability of their lives, and its effects on the parenting style of the mother, leads to short-term anxiety, depression, and disruptive behavior in children (Chase-Lansdale and Hetherington 1990). Although the research is clearer and more compelling regarding the short-run effects, Zill et al. (1993) found some evidence that these effects persist over the childhood of individuals. Further, there is evidence that multiple transitions, such as remarriage and subsequent divorces, can create even more harm (Amato and Booth 1991; Furstenberg and Seltzer 1986).

The Effects of Family Structure on Educational Attainment

We again will rely heavily on McLanahan and Sandefur (1994) for our discussion of the effects of family structure on educational attainment, family formation, and labor force participation. We compare outcomes for two-parent and one-parent families, where the group of one-parent families includes families with stepparents, and in which the differences are adjusted for race, sex, mother's education, father's education, number of siblings, and place of residence. We note the extent to which some of these differences are due to income, parental resources, and community resources.

Family structure and instability affect educational attainment through their effects on income, parental resources, and community resources. Income affects the quality of schools that children attend through its effect on the neighborhoods in which people can live and the ability of parents to send their children to private schools. Income also affects whether or not parents can afford to pay for lessons after school and whether they can take their children on trips or send them to camps during the summer.

The lower amount of parental time available to children in single-parent families also affects school achievement. Nonresident parents generally are not involved in the day-to-day rituals of homework and studying for tests, and the resident parent may be so busy with the other tasks of managing a job and household that she does not have as much time as she would like to spend with her children.

Residential mobility may also be associated with the relationship between family structure and educational attainment. Families that have lived in neighborhoods for fairly short periods of time are less familiar with the after-school resources and activities than families that have been longer-term residents. The loss of economic resources, parental resources, and community resources may lead children to invest less in themselves by reducing their motivation or expectations.

One major indicator of educational attainment is high school graduation. Only 15 percent of young adults fail to graduate from high school by the time they reach adulthood (U.S. Bureau of the Census 1991). McLanahan and Sandefur's results showed that among those in the National Longitudinal Survey of Youth, 13 percent of children from two-parent families dropped out of high school while 29 percent of children from one-parent families dropped out of high school. The results were similar in analyses with data from the Panel Study of Income Dynamics, the High School and Beyond Survey, and the National Survey of Families and Households.

Additional analyses with the High School and Beyond Study showed that children from one-parent families had significantly lower achievement test scores, college expectations, grade-point averages, and school attendance. Further, results show that among high school graduates, those from one-parent families are less likely to attend college than those from two-parent families. And among those who attend college, those from one-parent families are less likely to graduate than those from two-parent families. The differences in college attendance and college graduation are smaller than the differences in high school graduation.

When we include measures of income and income loss in the analysis, McLanahan and Sandefur find that income accounts for about one-half of the difference in the rates of dropping out of high school and also many of the other indicators of educational attainment. Although the effects of parental resources and community resources are not as powerful as those of income, they also account for a substantial proportion of the association between family structure and educational attainment.

The Effects of Family Structure and Stability on Family Formation

Family structure can affect early family formation in two ways. First, residing in a single-parent family lowers family income, which reduces a young woman's expectations that she will be able to continue with her education beyond high school. If young women perceive that they have few opportunities for education or interesting careers, the incentives to delay childbearing are not very strong. In these cases, early marriage and/or early childbearing are not seen as the detrimental events that they might otherwise be.

Second, residing in a single-parent family lowers parental resources and community resources. This means that the resident mother may be less able to monitor and constrain her children's behavior than are two parents. This leads to increased opportunities for the children to engage in irresponsible sexual activity, where "irresponsible" refers to unprotected sexual intercourse and the failure to financially support a child once it is born.

McLanahan and Sandefur compared the rates of teen out-of-wedlock childbearing and teen marital childbearing from women from one-parent and two-parent families using data from the NLSY, PSID, HSB, and NSFH. Again, we adjusted these differences for race, sex, mother's education, father's education, number of siblings, and place of residence. The results from the NLSY reflect what we found in the other data sets. Among women from two-parent families,

5 percent had a teen marital birth and 6 percent had a teen out-of-wedlock birth; among women from one-parent families, 14 percent had a teen marital birth and 13 percent had a teen out-of-wedlock birth. In sum, women from one-parent families are more likely to have a teen birth, and more likely to have a teen birth out-of-wedlock. Although men are much less likely to become teen fathers than women are to become teen mothers, living in a one-parent family increased the likelihood of becoming a teenage father according to analyses using data from the NLSY, PSID, and NSFH, but not from the HSB. Again, a good deal of these differences can be accounted for by differences in income, parental resources, and community resources.

Labor Force Participation

One would expect family structure to affect labor force participation partially through its effects on education—that is, individuals from one-parent families achieve lower levels of education and thus will be less successful in the labor market. But, there are also other ways in which family structure can affect labor force participation. Many jobs are found through networks and local connections. The presence of two parents means that the child can rely on two people to provide connections, two people to provide advice on how to seek a job, and two people to consult with during the process of looking for a job. Children in one-parent households may have only one working parent with whom to consult, and this parent may have very little time to be concerned with the employment of her child. In some cases, children in single-parent families have no working parents with whom to consult.

The lack of community resources also weakens children's connection to the labor force. Children who live in very poor communities where many adults are jobless and on welfare have less information about how to find a job than children who live in prosperous communities. Children whose families have moved several times will have fewer contacts in their current neighborhood to use in searching for a job than children who have lived in one neighborhood for much of their childhood.

To examine the effects of family structure, family stability, income, parental resources, and community resources on labor force participation, McLanahan and Sandefur used idleness, defined as not being in school and not working, as the outcome measure. Our results showed that young men from one-parent families were about 1.5 times as likely to be idle as young men from two-parent families in each of the four data sets (NLSY, PSID, HSB, and NSFH) that we used. This was true whether we looked at all young men or just at those who had completed high school. Further, evidence from the NLSY suggests that even between ages twenty-three and twenty-six, young men from disrupted families are more likely to be idle than are young men from two-parent families. As with educational attainment and early family formation, a good deal of these differences are due to income, parental resources, and community resources.

Summary   In sum, a good deal of evidence suggests that family structure and stability are associated with direct indicators of child and later adult well-being such as social and emotional adjustment, educational outcomes, family formation, and labor force participation. These associations occur through the impact of family structure and stability on family functioning. Consequently, our understanding of the well-being of children in our society is enhanced by our knowledge of the types of families in which they live and the stability of their family lives during childhood.

MEASURES OF FAMILY STRUCTURE AND STABILITY
Family Structure in the Household of Residence

The census and the Current Population Surveys are the most widely used sources of information on family structure in the household of residence. In the census and the Current Population Surveys, what we know about family structure is based on questions about marital status (married—spouse present, married—spouse absent, widowed, divorced, separated, never married) and relationship to the householder or reference person. Using these data, one can identify children who are living with a married couple, a married adult whose spouse is absent, or a single adult who is widowed, divorced, separated, or never married. A researcher can also determine if the child is a natural/adopted child, stepchild, grandchild, brother/sister, other relative, foster child, partner/roommate, or nonrelative of the householder.

If there are two unmarried adults in the household, one can use the relationship to the reference person to determine if the other adult is a parent, brother/sister, other relative of the reference person, nonrelative, or partner/roommate of the reference person. In the 1990 census, and, beginning in 1995, the March Current Population Survey, the question on relationship to the reference person permits one to identify individuals who are cohabiting with the reference person rather than inferring this from the partner/roommate response.

Although these pieces of data permit the identification of several alternative family types, some types of families in which researchers and policymakers are particularly interested cannot be identified. First, we cannot identify children who are living with two biological parents not married to one another. We can determine if a child is living with one biological parent who is cohabiting or partnering with another adult, but we do not know if the other adult is also a biological parent. Since this is an increasingly common, though still relatively rare, situation in American society, we could benefit from having such information.

Second, we cannot always distinguish between children who are residing with two biological/adoptive parents and one biological and one stepparent. We can do this if the stepparent is the reference person. But, if the biological parent is the reference person and the stepparent is not, the data in the census and the Current Population Survey do not permit us to determine that a stepparent is in the household. Again, this is an increasingly common family arrangement in our society, and one that has consequences for children, so we could probably benefit from having such information available from the census and CPS data.

Other data sets allow us to identify children who are living with one biological parent and one stepparent. Sandefur, McLanahan, and Wojtkiewicz (1992) found that in the National Longitudinal Survey of Youth, 5 percent of the respondents aged fourteen to seventeen resided with a stepparent throughout the period in their lives from age fourteen to seventeen. The percentage who are residing with a parent and stepparent at a particular point in time would be even higher. The High School and Beyond Survey, the National Survey of Families and Household, and the Panel Study of Income Dynamics all permit researchers to identify individuals who reside with a parent and stepparent.

Family Structure Outside the Household of Residence

A number of researchers over the years have argued that extended families, most generally defined as multigenerational families, play important roles in the lives of some children. The Current Population Surveys and the 1990 census permit the identification of households in which some grandparents or other adult relatives reside. The data allow us, for example, to determine if a child is residing with a grandparent who is the householder, or if the child is residing in a household in which a parent or other adult relative of the householder is present. Information from the 1993 March Current Population Survey shows that 5 percent of the children under eighteen in the United States were living in the home of their grandparents. Approximately 1.5 percent of children under eighteen were living with a grandparent with no parent present in the household. The percentage who reside in the home of a grandparent varies with race and ethnicity: 12 percent of black children, 6 percent of Hispanic children, and 4 percent of white children resided in the home of their grandparents (Saluter 1994).

The census and the CPS do not allow us to examine the structure of relationships with parents, grandparents, or other adult relatives who do not reside in the household. Ethnographers and other researchers have argued for some time that such relationships are an important aspect of family structure, and that data from the census and CPS provide a somewhat misleading picture of family structure.

Given the mobility of the American population, relationships with grandparents and other adult relatives outside the household may be less common now than they were several years ago. That is, children may be less likely now than thirty years ago to live in places where regular contact with such relatives is a regular occurrence. This is an empirical question, of course, but one on which we have very little systematic information.

One important type of relationship that goes beyond the household of residence is, however, probably more important now than several years ago—the relationship with a noncustodial parent. Data from the Child Supplement of the National Longitudinal Survey of Youth, the National Survey of Families and Households, and other sources suggest that some children have regular contact with a noncustodial parent. The structure of these relationships is in some ways shaped by the legal custody arrangements that accompany divorce, but children may also have relationships with a noncustodial parent who was never married to the custodial parent.

Relationships with adult relatives outside the household are very complex, and it is too much to expect the census and the CPS to capture all of the qualities of these relationships. A legitimate issue to pose is whether it is worthwhile to ask some basic questions in the census and the CPS about relationships with relatives outside the household. Such questions might explore legal custody arrangements for noncustodial parents, the proximity of noncustodial parents and other adult relatives, and the amount of time that children spend with these individuals. These questions would complement the existing information on living arrangements.

Family Stability

Several national data sets that are used to study children now include information on family stability during childhood. This information is sometimes prospective (the Panel Study of Income Dynamics and the Survey of Income and Program Participation) and sometimes retrospective (the National Survey of Families and Households and the National Longitudinal Survey of Youth).

In order to collect prospective information on family stability, one must follow children from birth through their childhood to the time when they leave home to establish their own households. The Panel Study of Income Dynamics allows us to do this because it has followed the same families and their offspring since 1968. Each year the PSID asks a series of questions that allows researchers to determine with whom children are residing. Researchers can compare this information across years to determine whether the living arrangements of children have changed, how often these arrangements have changed, and how many years children have resided in various kinds of living arrangements. Since the data are based on with whom one is living at the time of the survey, changes that occur during the year between surveys are not necessarily observed. If one parent leaves the household after one data collection point, but returns before the next data collection point, the PSID would not record this as a change in living arrangements.

An advantage of the prospective data in the Survey of Income and Program Participation is that it does record changes during a year. The disadvantage of the SIPP is that the children are observed for a much shorter period of time than during the PSID, so one cannot track family stability and instability throughout childhood.

Both the National Survey of Family and Households and the National Longitudinal Survey of Youth collect retrospective data on living arrangements at specific ages. These data are obtained by asking people to specify with whom they were residing at birth and then ages one through nineteen. Wojtkiewicz (1992) used the data from the National Survey of Families and Households to explore the nature of changes in family structure during childhood. He reported that "The general pattern is that children start out at birth in either mother-only or mother/father families. As the cohort ages, the percentage in mother-only and in mother/stepfather families increases, while the percentage in mother/father families decreases. The percentages living with father only or with father and stepmother are not large at any age. Among non-Hispanic whites, living only with grandparents or other relatives is not common. Among blacks, however, a noticeable percentage of children live only with grandparents."

The work of Wojtkiewicz and others has provided us with a much more complete picture of family instability than we previously had from data on family structure at particular ages or particular points in time. We do not yet know, however, what aspects of family instability we are missing by using only yearly data to determine with whom children are residing.

Measurement of family instability during a year is especially important if one is interested in examining experiences with foster care. Although being in foster care is a relatively rare experience in American society, the percentage of children in foster care continues to increase. Further, experience in foster care is an indicator of extreme family instability. In 1992, 1.4 percent of children in New York, .9 percent of children in California, 1 percent of children in Illinois, .5 percent of children in Michigan, and .2 percent of children in Texas were in some form of foster care placement at any given point during the year (Goerge, Wulczyn, and Harden 1994). During the 1988–1992 period, the average duration for a first placement in foster care ranged from 9.2 months in Texas to 30.1 months in Illinois (Goerge, Wulczyn, and Harden 1994). One may miss a number of foster care placements if one is relying solely on annual data on living arrangements.

Child Abuse and Neglect

Indicators of extreme family instability other than foster care include child abuse and neglect. Few national data collection efforts include questions on child abuse and neglect. In the case of the census, the CPS the SIPP, and the PSID, it would be inappropriate to ask a householder if he/she or any other adult in the household has abused or neglected a child. It would also be difficult to ask a youth residing with a parent in the NLSY, HSB, or NSFH if he/she had experienced abuse or neglect.

The incidence of child abuse and neglect appears to be increasing in American society (Panel on Research on Child Abuse and Neglect [NCCAN] 1993). A National Academy of Sciences Panel reported that "From 1976, when the first national figures for child maltreatment were generated to 1990, the most recent year covered by the National Child Abuse and Neglect Data System, reports of maltreatment have grown from 416,033 per year (affecting 669,000 children) to 1,700,000 per year (affecting 2,712,917 children)" (Panel on Research on Child Abuse and Neglect 1981, 1988, 1992). The Panel notes, however, that the meaning of this increase is not completely clear because of the limitations of the data and likely increases in the reporting of incidents.

One might question whether a consideration of abuse and neglect has a place in assessing family structure and stability. Abuse and neglect are indicators of the functioning of families and are associated with family structure and stability, but are they really measures of family structure and stability? Our view is that even if one considers child abuse and neglect to be measures of family functioning as opposed to measures of family instability, one cannot understand family structure and stability without understanding the role of child abuse and neglect in American society.

Research on child abuse and neglect has arrived at a convention of distinguishing among four distinct phenomena: sexual abuse; physical abuse; emotional maltreatment; and neglect (Panel on Research on Child Abuse and Neglect 1993). Although researchers generally agree that the incidence and prevalence of these has increased over time, we have relatively poor information on their actual occurrence in our society. There are many problems to be overcome in order to get better information, but a number of suggestions for improvement exist in the literature.

One can also ask whether existing national data collection efforts on children and families can pose worthwhile questions about these phenomena. The National Academy Panel on Research on Child Abuse and Neglect summarizes some of the results of studies of self-reported sexual abuse. The recent "sex" survey carried out by the National Opinion Research Center apparently asked a retrospective question about sexual abuse as a child and found that responses to this question were associated with adult sexual behavior. Straus and Gelles (1986) report the results of asking questions in two nationally representative surveys about physical abuse and verbal forms of emotional maltreatments. These questions are part of the Conflict Tactics Scale, a scale with known desirable statistical properties. There are, then, developed questions and scales that appear to allow us to examine these issues in national surveys.

Major Regularly Published Reports on Family Structure and Stability

Part of the charge of this chapter is to review reports on family structure and stability. We address this by briefly discussing the Current Population Reports and two recent examples of reports by nongovernmental organizations.

The U.S. Bureau of the Census currently publishes each year two major reports on family structure. These are both based on the March Current Population Survey. One is entitled "Marital Status and Living Arrangements" and the other is entitled "Household and Family Characteristics." In addition, the Bureau periodically publishes special reports using data from the Current Population Surveys, the decennial census, or the Survey of Income and Program Participation. The two regularly published reports are among the most widely used documents published by the federal government.

The major difference between the two annual publications is that "Marital Status and Living Arrangements" uses people as the major unit of analysis, while "Household and Family Characteristics" uses households or families as the major units of analysis. For the purposes of assessing the family structure of children in our society, "Marital Status and Living Arrangements" is most useful since it provides information on living arrangements in March of the reference year for children in general and children in different social groups (race and ethnic groups, age groups, and gender). "Household and Family Characteristics," however, provides important supplemental information since one can use the tables in it to examine the characteristics of families with children.

We have noted what we consider to be the major weaknesses of these reports above, namely, the lack of information on stepparents, cohabiting biological parents, and relationships with noncustodial parents. Given the importance of these reports to the research and policy communities, we need to give serious thought to efforts to overcome these shortcomings. In addition, at some point the CPS will have to modify its sample to include a larger sample of, and these reports will have to provide information on, the Asian population in our society. It is probably too much to hope that the CPS would permit collection of, and these reports would some day include, data on the American Indian population. Until changes are made, researchers and the policy community will have to rely on reports from the decennial census for data on Asians and American Indians, as well as on specific ethnic groups within the broad Hispanic and Asian categories.

One cannot expect the Census Bureau to report each year on family structure at the local and state level, but the Bureau does produce such reports from each decennial census. It is possible, however, to use the data from the Current Population Surveys to produce estimates of types of family structure at the state level each year. A number of nongovernmental organizations over the years have used census or CPS tables or Public Use Samples to prepare their own reports on local areas or states. These include the National Center for Children in Poverty, and the Children's Defense Fund, as well as the Anne E. Casey Foundation, one of the sponsors of the work that has gone into this volume.

The *Kids Count Data Book: State Profiles of Child Well-Being*, uses the 1983 through 1993 March Current Population Surveys to estimate the percentage of children who are in single-parent families in each state in 1985 through 1991. This is accomplished by computing five-year averages for each state. The report indicates considerable variation across states in the percentage of children who live in single-parent families. For example, 25 percent of children in the United States lived in single-parent families in 1991, but the range was from 14.4 percent in North Dakota to 57 percent in the District of Columbia (*Kids Count Data Book* 1994). This illustrates the diversity in family structure across the country, but as the authors acknowledge, this disguises racial, ethnic, and local diversity in family structure within the states. Still, it is a model for what one can do with the data from the Current Population Surveys.

RECOMMENDATIONS FOR IMPROVING OUR INDICATORS OF FAMILY STRUCTURE AND STABILITY

A few important assumptions bear repeating: family structure and stability are not *direct* indicators of child well-being. They are, however, associated with many, if not all, of these direct indicators. Further, our understanding of how children are doing in our society is not complete without a good picture of family structure and stability. Given these assertions or assumptions, the research and policy communities could benefit from modifying the way in which we measure family structure and stability.

Modify the Way in Which Family Structure Is Measured in the Census and the Current Population Surveys

The nature of the American family and the prevalence of different types of families have changed dramatically during the past several years, and the decennial censuses and the Current Population Surveys need to change to reflect this. First, the data should allow researchers to identify individuals who reside with one biological parent and one stepparent. This is becoming an increasingly common family arrangement in American society, and research suggests that residing with a stepparent and parent is a much different situation than residing with two biological parents (McLanahan and Sandefur 1994; Sandefur, McLanahan, and Wojtkiewicz 1992).

Second, the data should allow researchers to identify families in which the child is residing with two cohabiting biological parents. Again, research suggests that this is an increasingly common experience for children. As of yet, we know little about the association of this type of family structure with various child outcomes.

Third, the data should provide some information on one critical aspect of family structure outside the household of residence, and that is the relationship with the noncustodial parent. Residing with one parent has become increasingly common in our society, and research suggests that the relationship with the non-custodial parent may be an important factor in the social and emotional development of children. Yet, we know very little about the nature of these relationships. The Bureau of the Census should explore asking two basic questions: one question on the geographical proximity of the noncustodial parent and a second question on the frequency of contact with the noncustodial parent.

Collect Monthly Family Residential Histories in National Surveys of Families, Children, and Youth

The availability of prospective family residential histories in the Panel Study of Income Dynamics and retrospective family residential histories in the National Longitudinal Survey of Youth and the National Survey of Families and House-holds has permitted us to begin to explore the consequences of family instability for children during their childhood and later in their lives. These histories, how-ever, miss some short-term changes in living arrangements that might be critical factors in the social and emotional development and adjustment of children. The incidence of living with grandparents or other adult relatives, for example, may be much higher than we currently observe in the CPS or in data based on yearly histories. A family characterized by a high degree of conflict or other problems may send its children to live with other relatives for fairly short periods of time even though the yearly data may record no or only one or two disruptions during the lifetime of the child. These short-term disruptions may be strongly associated with the social and emotional adjustment of children, and with other outcomes later in their lives. Further, monthly residential histories would permit us to observe the residential patterns of children who spend part of the year with their mothers and part of the year with their fathers.

One obvious problem with this change is that it would be more time-consuming and costly than the current yearly residential histories. Many surveys, how-ever, currently ask monthly questions on school enrollment and employment. A careful analysis of family instability may be as important as a careful analysis of their school enrollment in understanding their lives.

Improve the Information That Is Available on Experiences with Foster Care, Both in National Surveys and Through Administrative Data

The March Current Population Survey currently asks questions that allow us to identify children who are residing with foster parents if those foster parents are the householder or reference person. Also, the National Longitudinal Survey of Youth and other data sets allow one to identify people who have lived with a foster parent for most of the year at a particular age. Since many placements in

foster care last less than a year, monthly residential histories, such as those discussed earlier will yield better national estimates of experiences with foster care
during childhood.

Research using the Multistate Foster Care Data Archive illustrates that administrative data, collected with the needs of the policy and research communities in mind, can be useful in understanding the incidence and prevalence of
foster care experiences and the consequences of these for children (Goerge,
Wulczyn, and Harden 1994). This Archive now includes longitudinal data from
California, Illinois, Michigan, New York, and Texas. Efforts are underway to
expand the Archive to include other states. Data from projects such as the Multistate Foster Care Data Archive, combined with better data on foster care from
representative national samples of children and families, will make it possible for
us to understand the extent, nature, and consequences of the experience of foster
care.

Improve Our Understanding of Child Abuse and Neglect Through Including Questions in National Surveys on Families and Children, and Through Improving the Quality of Administrative Data

Improving our understanding of child abuse and neglect will be enhanced by
consistency in definitions of child abuse and neglect across local areas and in
developing national standards for reporting that are used consistently in all localities (Daro 1992). In addition, scales that tap the potential or actual occurrence of child abuse and neglect can be included in national surveys of families
and children. The National Academy of Sciences Panel on Research on Child
Abuse and Neglect points out that, unfortunately, "Research on child abuse and
neglect has been severely hampered by the lack of instruments to measure the
phenomena. Relatively few instruments have reported reliability and validity"
(1993). Further, those instruments with known reliability and validity generally
include many items, making it very expensive to include them in national surveys.

Nonetheless, we should give some thought to trying to include some of these
instruments in some of our national surveys of children and families. These instruments include the Conflict Tactics Scale (Straus and Gelles 1986) and the
Child Abuse Potential Inventory (Milner and Wimberly 1979) for assessing the
current family situation, and the Childhood History Questionnaire (Milner,
Robertson, and Rogers 1990) for examining retrospective information on experiences during the respondent's childhood.

Reports on Family Structure and Stability

This is a very brief set of recommendations. First, the U.S. Bureau of the Census
should continue to issue its two major yearly reports on family structure. The
reports should include information on parent/stepparent families, cohabiting biological parents, and contact with nonresident parents. Second, reports such as
Kids Count should be issued each year to provide information on family structure
at the state level. Third, we need to report more systematically on child abuse
and neglect and placements in foster care.

BEST INDICATORS OF FAMILY STRUCTURE
FOR CHILD WELL-BEING

Since we have focused exclusively on family structure and its relationship to child well-being, we now take a slightly different turn than some of the other chapters. Instead of discussing what we feel are the most important *overall* indicators of child well-being, we instead note what we feel are the most important components of child well-being in the context of family structure.

As we mentioned earlier, trends in the percentage of children in single-parent families have large scale implications for children's well-being. All else being equal, children living with single parents fare worse than those in two-parent families on a number of outcomes. We also believe more attention should be paid to variation in single-parent families. For example, consequences may well be different for children living with a divorced parent than children living with a never-married parent.

Related to the percentage of children in single-parent families is the idea that the presence of adults in a home has important ramifications for children. Additional adults could be in a household due to remarriage, cohabitation, or through the presence of extended kin. In some instances, particularly with extended kin, these other adults may provide an important addition to the social support system. Other situations, however, such as where a stepparent or partner is present, may cause adjustment difficulties for children.

A third issue to be cognizant of is the child's relationship with the noncustodial parent. Research has shown that a great deal of variation exists for children regarding contact with the noncustodial parent (Seltzer 1994).

SUMMARY AND CONCLUSIONS

Some observers have suggested that the decline in family values and the breakup of the American family are among the major causes of other problems in American society, but the existing evidence does not suggest that this is the case. Family structure and stability, child abuse and neglect, and foster care placements increase the risk of some adverse outcomes and decrease the probability of some positive outcomes for children during childhood and later as adults. If we are to understand the condition of children in our society, we must understand their family living arrangements and changes in these family living arrangements over time.

In order to do this, we need to make some changes in the data collected by the decennial censuses and the March Current Population Surveys. These changes are needed to take into account the transformation of the American family during the past several years. Residing with cohabiting, but unmarried, biological parents or with a parent and stepparent have become increasingly common experiences in our society. Data that do not allow us to identify these types of living arrangements are misleading. Further, these regularly collected national data should contain information on the relationships between children and nonresidential parents. The amount of contact that children in single-parent families have with their nonresident parent varies widely, and research suggests variations in this contact may be associated with variations in direct indicators of child well-being.

We need to use some of our national surveys of families and children to look more carefully at family instability, foster care placements, and child abuse and neglect. Better information on family instability and foster care placement can be obtained by using prospective and retrospective *monthly* as opposed to *yearly* recording. We already collect monthly information on employment and schooling in many national data sets, and these efforts can serve as models for our efforts to collect monthly family residential histories. We should also investigate the possibility of including existing scales on family conflict and child abuse and neglect in national data collection efforts.

REFERENCES

Amato, P. R., and A. Booth. 1991. "The Consequences of Parental Divorce and Marital Unhappiness for Adult Well-Being." *Social Forces* 68: 895–914.

Chase-Lansdale, P. L., and E. Mavis Hetherington. 1990. "The Impact of Divorce on Life-Span Development: Short and Long-Term Effects." In *Life Span Development and Behavior*, edited by P. B. Baltes, D. L. Featherman, and R. M. Lerner. Hillsdale, N.J.: Erlbaum.

Committee on Ways and Means, U.S. House of Representatives. 1993. *Green Book*. Washington: U.S. Government Printing Office.

Courtney, Mark E., and Raymond C. Collins. 1994. "New Challenges and Opportunities in Child Welfare Outcomes and Information Technologies." *Child Welfare* 73(5): 359–78.

Daro, Deborah. 1992. "Building a National Child Welfare Data Base: Utilizing a Variety of Sources." *Protecting Children* 8(3): 4–6, 24–25.

———. 1994. "Health Families America: A Guide for Evaluating Healthy Families America Efforts." Chicago: National Committee to Prevent Child Abuse.

Furstenberg, Frank F., Jr., and Judith A. Seltzer. 1986. "Divorce and Child Development." In *Sociological Studies in Child Development*, edited by Patricia A. Adler and Peter Adler. Greenwich, Conn.: JAI Press.

Goerge, Robert M., Fred H. Wulczyn, and Allen W. Harden. 1994. "A Report from the Multistate Foster Care Data Archive: Foster Care Dynamics, 1983–1992." Chicago: The Chapin Hall Center for Children, the University of Chicago.

Hanson, Tom L. 1993. *Family Structure, Parental Conflict, and Child Well-Being*. Ph.D. diss. University of Wisconsin–Madison.

Haveman, Robert, Barbara Wolfe, and James Spaulding. 1991. "Childhood Events and Circumstances Influencing High School Completion." *Demography* 28: 133–58.

Hernandez, Donald J. 1986. "Childhood in Sociodemographic Perspective." *Annual Review of Sociology* 12: 159–80.

———. 1993. *America's Children: Resources from Family, Government, and the Economy*. New York: Russell Sage Foundation.

Hetherington, Mavis, Martha Cox, and Roger Cox. 1978. "The Aftermath of Divorce." In *Mother-Child, Father-Child Relations*, edited by Joseph H. Stephens and Marilyn Matthews. Washington, D.C.: National Association for the Education of Young Children Press.

———. 1982. "Effects of Divorce on Parents and Children." In *Non-traditional Families: Parenting and Child Development*, edited by M. E. Lamb. Hillsdale, N.J.: Erlbaum.

Kids Count Data Book. 1994. Baltimore, Md.: The Annie E. Casey Foundation.

McLanahan, Sara. 1983. "Family Structure and Stress: A Longitudinal Comparison of Male and Female-Headed Families." *Journal of Marriage and the Family* 45: 347–57.

McLanahan, Sara, and Gary Sandefur. 1994. *Growing Up with a Single Parent: What Hurts, What Helps*. Cambridge, Mass.: Harvard University Press.

McLeod, Jane D., and Michael J. Shanahan. 1993. "Poverty, Parenting, and Children's Mental Health." *American Sociological Review* 58: 351–66.

McLoyd, Vonnie C., and Leon Wilson. 1993. "The Strain of Living Poor: Parenting, Social Support, and Child Mental Health." In *Children in Poverty: Child Development and Public Policy*, edited by Aletha C. Huston. New York: Cambridge University Press.

Milner, J. S., and R. C. Wimberly. 1979. "An Inventory for the Identification of Child Abusers." *Journal of Clinical Psychology* 35: 95–100.

Milner, J. S., K. R. Robertson, and D. L. Rogers. 1990. "Childhood History of Abuse and Adult Child Abuse Potential." *Journal of Family Violence* 5: 15–34.

National Center for Child Abuse and Neglect. 1981. "National Study of the Incidence of Child Abuse and Neglect." Washington, D.C.: U.S. Department of Health and Human Services.

———. 1988. "Study Findings: Study of National Incidence and Prevalence of Child Abuse and Neglect." Washington, D.C.: U.S. Department of Health and Human Services.

———. 1992. "National Child Abuse and Neglect Data System, Working Paper I, 1990 Summary Data Component." Washington, D.C.: U.S. Department of Health and Human Services.

Panel on Research on Child Abuse and Neglect. 1993. *Understanding Child Abuse and Neglect*. Washington, D.C.: National Academy Press.

Peterson, J. L., and Nicholas Zill. 1986. "Marital Disruption and Behavior Problems in Children." *Journal of Marriage and the Family* 48: 295–307.

Saluter, Arlene F. 1994. "Marital Status and Living Arrangements: March 1993." U.S. Bureau of the Census, *Current Population Reports*, series P-20, no. 478. Washington: U.S. Government Printing Office.

Sandefur, Gary D., Sara McLanahan, and Roger Wojtkiewicz. 1992. "The Effects of Parental Marital Status During Adolescence on High School Graduation." *Social Forces* 71: 103–22.

Seltzer, Judith A. 1994. "Consequences of Marital Disruption for Children." *Annual Review of Sociology* 20: 235–66.

Speare, Alden, Jr., and Frances K. Goldscheider. 1987. "Effects of Marital Status Change on Residential Mobility." *Journal of Marriage and the Family* 49: 455–64.

Straus, M. A., and R. J. Gelles. 1986. "Societal Change in Family Violence from 1975 to 1985 as Revealed by Two National Surveys." *Journal of Marriage and the Family* 48: 465–79.

U.S. Bureau of the Census. 1993. "Poverty in the United States, 1992." *Current Population Reports*, series P-60, no. 188. Washington: U.S. Government Printing Office.

———. 1991. *Statistical Abstracts of the United States*. Washington: U.S. Government Printing Office.

Wallerstein, Judith S., and Joan B. Kelly. 1980. *Surviving the Breakup: How Children and Parents Cope with Divorce*. New York: Basic Books.

Wojtkiewicz, Roger. 1992. "Diversity in Experiences of Parental Structure during Childhood and Adolescence." *Demography* 29: 59–68.

Zill, Nicholas, D. R. Morrison, and M. J. Coiro. 1993. "Long-term Effects of Parental Divorce on Parent-Child Relationships, Adjustment, and Achievement in Young Adulthood." *Journal of Family Psychology* 7: 91–103.

Zill, Nicholas, and Christine Winquist Nord. 1994. *Running in Place: How American Families Are Faring in a Changing Economy and an Individualistic Society*. Washington, D.C.: Child Trends, Inc.

16

The Influence of Neighborhoods on Children's Development: A Theoretical Perspective and a Research Agenda

Frank F. Furstenberg, Jr., and Mary Elizabeth Hughes

THE INFLUENCE OF neighborhoods on children's development recently has become a hot topic among researchers in the social sciences, largely due to the issues raised in Wilson's seminal book, *The Truly Disadvantaged* (1987). Wilson's thesis about the devastating impact of economic stagnation and urban disintegration put poverty research back on the social science agenda. A good deal of this renewed interest in poverty has identified the neighborhood as a critical element in the reproduction of social disadvantage, echoing themes emphasized earlier in this century by Chicago School sociologists (for instance, Park and Burgess 1924; Shaw and McKay 1942; Tannenbaum 1938; Thrasher 1927). Whether and by what means the characteristics of communities influence children's well-being is not only of theoretical interest to social scientists; these questions are also immensely important to those formulating public policies addressing social inequality (Jencks and Peterson 1991; Lynn and McGeary 1990).

A few years ago, Jencks and Mayer (1990) surveyed the literature on the social consequences of growing up in a poor neighborhood. Into the late 1980s, they could locate only a handful of studies that met their methodological standards for providing reliable, quantitative evidence on the impact of neighborhoods on children's life chances. Moreover, virtually none of the studies in their review examined *how* neighborhoods affect children's lives—that is, explored the processes by which communities shape children's development. Noting several alternative explanations of how neighborhoods could influence children's chances, Jencks and Mayer lamented the tendency of researchers to rely on a "black box" model of neighborhood effects.

It is no exaggeration to state that more studies have been completed in the past few years on the relationship of neighborhood characteristics to children's life chances than were included in the entire Jencks and Mayer review. However, though researchers have shown no lack of interest in neighborhood research, when considered as a whole the results of this new crop of studies are inconclusive (see Gephart [1994] for a recent review). Furthermore, a disappointing amount of attention has been devoted to opening the black box containing the processes by which neighborhoods influence children's lives. A skeptical reader might easily conclude on the basis of the available research that neighborhoods matter rather little, if they matter at all. Yet even the skeptic would likely agree that it is much too soon to draw any conclusions about the importance of neighborhood influences on children's development.

In this chapter we assess the state of neighborhood research and suggest research strategies for furthering our understanding of the influence of neighborhoods on children's well-being. We begin by discussing the challenge of showing that development is intrinsically linked to features of the spatial context in which children grow up, identifying several theoretical orientations that suggest causal linkages between features of communities and children's well-being. We emphasize the need for a cross-disciplinary approach, as the influence of neighborhoods on children is at the intersection of several disciplines. We briefly review existing research and discuss its limitations. We argue that in many respects existing data are not well suited to test theories of neighborhood effects, therefore further progress in understanding their magnitude and mechanisms will require original data collection. In the third section of the chapter, we outline a set of issues critical to designing research on neighborhood effects. In the fourth section, we discuss approaches to measuring neighborhood, family, and individual characteristics in order to test different explanations of community influences on children's developmental trajectories. We conclude by summarizing the implications of our comments for those interested in initiating research projects concerning neighborhood effects.

THEORETICAL ORIENTATIONS ON NEIGHBORHOODS AND CHILD DEVELOPMENT

In their review, Jencks and Mayer (1990) classified into four broad models the potential mechanisms by which neighborhoods may influence children's experience. The first class, epidemic models, emphasizes the normative system that develops in enclosed communities of like-minded individuals (Case and Katz 1991; Crane 1991). Residents of a confined geographical space are likely to share the same attitudes, beliefs, and behavior and hence to adopt and adhere to common ways of doing things. These subcultural practices develop from what criminologist Edwin Sutherland referred to as the "differential association" that typically occurs among neighbors and friends or within local collectivities (Sutherland 1937). The more exclusively people interact with members in segregated social milieus the more alike will be their beliefs and behavior.

The epidemic model postulates the social contagion of norms or prescribed practices transmitted primarily by peers. It is distinguished from a second source of neighborhood influence which Jencks and Mayer referred to as collective socialization. The essential feature of this explanation, according to Jencks and Mayer, is the role of community adults—not just a child's parents—in promoting certain types of behavior to children. Socially-approved-of behavior is reproduced by the presence of role models and mechanisms of social control employed by adults, thereby discouraging alternative forms of behavior. This explanation also has a long and honored tradition in criminological research (see, for example, Cohen 1955 and Matza 1964).

The presence of institutional resources in the form of schools, police protection, strong neighborhood organization, and community services provides a third model of community influence on children. Jencks and Mayer argue that the benevolent intrusion of agents into the community is a potential source of influence distinguishing good and bad neighborhoods. The availability of these resources both promotes opportunity and prevents problem behavior (Cloward and Ohlin 1960).

All three of these models predict that disadvantaged children will do better when they reside in affluent neighborhoods where presumably they have access to conforming peers, successful adult models, and abundant resources. The fourth model outlined by Jencks and Mayer suggests that the proximity of well-off neighbors may have the perverse effect of creating further problems among the less advantaged. If children perceive that they are at a disadvantage relative to their peers, this may diminish their motivation to conform. Alternative cultures may arise that sanction deviant behaviors. Competition for scarce resources may also limit the chances of the less advantaged with respect to the more advantaged. Finally, poor children could be at a comparative disadvantage in neighborhoods where they are in the minority if they are subject to negative labeling by their more affluent peers (Lemert 1951; Clinard 1964).

The processes that Jencks and Mayer identify need not be viewed as discrete or alternative mechanisms of neighborhood influence. Rather, they could be complementary processes. Theoretical orientations within sociology that posit links between children's well-being and characteristics of the spatial communities in which they grow up typically include several of these mechanisms.

One such theoretical orientation is social disorganization theory, which originated with the insights of Shaw and McKay (1942) and has since been elaborated by others (Bursik 1988; Kornhauser 1978; Sampson and Groves 1989). Shaw and McKay's interest was in explaining the existence and persistence of ecological patterns in rates of delinquency and crime. Based on their empirical finding that areas with high rates of deviant behavior were also characterized by low economic status, ethnic heterogeneity, and high population turnover, they argued that these conditions led to social disorganization, which in turn led to deviant behavior among individuals. The level of social organization in the community, or the degree to which residents are able to realize common goals and exercise social control, is seen as a reflection of both systems of social relationships within the community and the content and consensus of values. The structural aspects of communities identified by Shaw and McKay are expected either to promote or to inhibit social organization along these dimensions. The likelihood of deviant behavior among individuals is higher where the community is relatively disorganized, a view that encompasses several of the mechanisms we have discussed. Shaw and McKay's empirical findings have been confirmed in more recent work, which also has demonstrated other ecological correlates of high rates of deviance. However, detailing and testing the intervening mechanisms remains an important topic for future research (Elliott et al. 1994; Sampson 1992).

Wilson's (1987, 1991) argument regarding the causes and consequences of concentrated poverty is another comprehensive theory of the influence of communities on individuals. Wilson built upon important ingredients of the Chicago School tradition regarding ecological patterns within urban areas to explain how disadvantage may be socially reproduced from one generation to the next. Differentiating his theory from alternative explanations that either rely exclusively on cultural or structural conditions, Wilson instead argued that persistent poverty is created and sustained by a unique amalgamation of economic, social, and cultural elements that are fused together creating specialized local environments. Macroeconomic conditions have reduced the demand for unskilled labor and limited the chances of those less equipped by education and background to compete for scarce jobs. Institutional resources within poverty neighborhoods have declined with the exit of middle-class residents seeking more desirable locations and the limited commitment of government to sustain inner-city institutions. Declining rates of marital stability due to the lack of marriageable males has decreased the availability of role models within the family. These forces have in turn permitted the spread of ghetto-specific cultural beliefs that undermine commitment to conventional norms. Children raised in these areas of concentrated poverty are therefore isolated from the conventional values and networks that would support their mainstream development.

While not specifically focusing on the influence of neighborhoods, Coleman's (1988) concept of social capital does suggest the potential importance of local communities in shaping children's life courses. Coleman uses the term "social capital" to refer to social relationships that serve as resources for individuals to draw upon in implementing their goals. He identifies three forms of social capital: norms, reciprocal obligations, and opportunities for sharing information. The neighborhood is clearly a potentially important reservoir of social capital (Furstenberg 1993). Sampson (1992) has argued that the concept of social capital dovetails with social disorganization theory in that the lack of social capital is one of the distinguishing features of individuals in socially disorganized communities. The presence or absence of social capital—or at least social capital that is useful in achieving mainstream goals—in a community is thus a further link between the structure of communities and the development of children.

Social disorganization theory, Wilson's theory on the impact of concentrated poverty and social isolation, and Coleman's concept of social capital may be conceived as overlapping, rather than competing explanations. They each hypothesize links between the socioeconomic composition of communities—ethnic diversity, poverty rates, residential stability—and the development of children via intervening social processes such as those outlined by Jencks and Mayer. The differences among them are largely differences of emphasis in the particular compositional features considered important and the roles of various intervening mechanisms. But they are each based on a causal framework that considers the socioeconomic composition of communities the ultimate source of community influences.

While these explanations share the view that the characteristics of the local community are a potent influence on individual experience, they place relatively little emphasis on the developing child or even the family dynamics that may contribute to children's acquisition of values, skills, and practices. They focus instead on how the community context influences the developing child, more or less assuming uniformity in the response of families and children to their immediate environments. Dennis Wrong once referred to this sociological vision as "the oversocialized view of man" (Wrong 1961).

A contrasting, but complementary, approach to community influences is taken by psychologists. Within social psychology, an important tradition of research exists that has attempted to connect community influences to the developing child. First established by Lewin (1951), applied and elaborated by Barker (1968) to the study of children, and further developed recently by Urie Bronfenbrenner and his students, environmental or contextual psychology examines the ways that parents and children organize, adapt to, and shape their immediate environments (Bronfenbrenner 1979, 1986; Garbarino 1992; Steinberg 1990). Psychologists have studied context as a socially constructed system of external influences that is mediated by the minds of individuals. This is not to say that environments are merely epiphenomenal—a perspective that invites considerable opposition in some sociological quarters—but, whatever influences local environments have on children must be seen as a product of how these environments are perceived and interpreted by parents and children (Medrich, Roizen, Rubin, and Buckley 1982). In this respect, the neighborhood is very much like the family itself, which, as psychologists have demonstrated, is a context where different members live in different, albeit overlapping, psychological worlds (Dunn and Plomin 1990).

This perspective adds a further dimension to the complexity of investigating contextual influences, for it implies that in the course of growing up children encounter and respond to a changing set of environments that both affect and are affected by the child's experiences. A feature of socialization within any culture is that environments are socially arranged—more or less deliberately—for children's acquisition of knowledge and skills. However, especially in the adolescent years, children may be granted considerable discretion to select environments even though their elders may maintain considerable indirect control of their options. This observation closely parallels sociological and anthropological perspectives examining how social niches are both organized, discovered, and cultivated by parents and children during childhood (Thorne 1993; Fine 1987). These processes proceed in tandem with the children's acquisition of knowledge, beliefs, and competencies that shape their future prospects and personal well-being.

If we apply this perspective to neighborhoods, it is obvious that community influences represent a subtle and changing blend of social and individual processes. Parents, to the extent possible, locate and select desirable environments for their children, channeling their access to favorable settings or at least segregating them from undesirable locales (Furstenberg, 1993). The parents' abilities to do so depend on their material, social, and personal resources as well as on their skill at gaining compliance from their children (Walker and Furstenberg 1994). Their success at implementation is also affected by characteristics of their children that make them more or less receptive to adult or peer influences. Like their parents, children actively participate in organizing their environments. Furthermore, they change in their capacity to do so as they get older and respond differently to past experiences and present circumstances.

Encounters with neighborhoods are not only shaped by parenting processes and children's experiences, but also by gender, class, and ethnicity. Like age, the child's gender is likely to result in sharply divergent experiences which modify the impact of neighborhoods on development. Girls typically are granted less autonomy and are subject to greater domestic control. Especially in low-income areas, boys often have more access to street life, and at younger ages. Thus, neighborhood influences may operate differently for different age groups by gender.

A great deal of evidence testifies to the way that social-class differences mark the character of neighborhood organization and culture (Baumgartner 1988; Gans 1962; Kornblum 1974). How these features of local environments influence the developmental process has been the study of numerous ethnographic studies. It is less clear from the abundant literature on class and community to what extent neighborhoods are simply a product of class composition or take on an emergent character due to the density of particular social class groupings. Even less is known about how ethnicity alters class cultures in ways that create distinctive environments that may shape the course of children's development.

It is not only children and their families who interpret characteristics of neighborhoods. A child's residence might also affect how they are perceived by others who may influence their success, such as teachers or employers. Neighborhoods might reify or concretize race and class distinctions both internally through socialization and externally through labeling. Thus, the meaning of neighborhood distinctions may be experienced by children only as they begin to recognize their place in the social order.

Recognizing that parents and children are not passive recipients of neighborhood influence, but interact with their environments, also focuses attention on the manner in which parents and children *create* their environment. For instance, residential mobility is a key means by which parents choose the environment experienced by their children. Because of changes in residence, a child may be exposed to a variety of different neighborhoods while growing up. The impact of a particular community on a child will likely depend on the child's duration of exposure to the characteristics of that community, the ages at which it occurs, and, perhaps, the types of neighborhoods that precede and follow it. Even more important, residential mobility is also an important strategy that parents can and do use to select suitable environments for their children. Neighborhoods with particular constellations of characteristics—including child outcomes—may be created by family mobility rather than the effects of emergent properties of neighborhoods on children. In this perspective, the relationship between neighborhoods and children's outcomes is the opposite of that assumed by these mechanisms.

However, spatial communities are not merely created by the residential stability or mobility of families. Any theory of neighborhood influence assumes some degree of social interaction among members of the neighborhood. However, the quantity and quality of social interaction within a neighborhood are the result of investments in social relationships by those living in the neighborhood. Given limited resources, parents may choose not to invest in community building. Parents—especially women, who are the traditional community builders—may simply be too busy with the demands of jobs and family care to devote themselves to nurturing relationships with community members (Walker and Furstenberg 1994). Residential mobility may reduce attachment to the local community and the perceived incentive to invest in social relationships. Finally, parents may devote their attention to alternative communities, which may then become more relevant to their children's chances than the local community. Particularly important in this regard may be schools, churches, and parents' networks of kin and friends outside the neighborhood. Children themselves, especially as they grow older, may relate to alternative reference groups, such as school communities or peer groups. The extent to which these alternative groups replace neighborhoods as communities of reference depends on the extent to which they are separate or overlapping social worlds.

The ability of families in choosing their residential communities and their networks of interaction suggests that understanding the manner in which communities are formed is essential to understanding the influence of neighborhoods on children's outcomes. Recognizing whether and by what means parents can and do select their neighborhoods of residence to maximize their children's well-being is central to comprehending the effect of spatial communities on children's development (Tienda 1991). Likewise, the ways in which parents trade off investments in the local community with investments in other resources such as income or alternative communities is a key aspect of the relationship of neighborhoods to children's well-being.

Given these considerations, demonstrating the "effect of neighborhoods" on children's experiences may be a far more daunting challenge than many researchers believe. If we are to demonstrate that the content and process of socialization is altered by conditions in local environments, then we must be prepared to show exactly how conditions within neighborhoods influence normative expectations, social control, links to opportunities, and exposure to dangers and how these influences vary by the child's age, gender, class, and ethnicity. Moreover, we need to be aware of the ways in which local differences will be mediated by parents and other important figures in the child's life who interpret and respond to these conditions, and how the children themselves define the environment and react to those who mediate it. Any explication of neighborhood effects must also take account of the children's changing exposure to and construction of their environments as they grow older, implying a need to consider the developmental trajectories of children, rather than statuses at a single point in time. Finally, understanding of neighborhood effects must be based on an appreciation of the ways in which parents and children create their communities, through mobility and through investment in social relationships.

If neighborhoods are a significant factor in children's development, different trajectories of development should emerge in different contexts, depending on the child's characteristics and his or her experience with and exposure to the positive and negative features of local environments. When we are able to demonstrate this pattern, then and only then do we begin to approach a convincing case for the influence of neighborhoods on development.

ASSESSING EXISTING RESEARCH ON NEIGHBORHOODS AND CHILDREN

Empirical research on the links between neighborhood characteristics and children's development has made limited progress on the broad agenda we have described. In part this reflects the newness of interest in neighborhood effects; despite a spate of new analyses, a critical mass of scholarship has yet to accumulate. For instance, most existing analyses of neighborhood effects focus on the adolescent, rather than the childhood, years (Gephart 1994). The relative new-ness of the endeavor also has led to conceptual gaps as researchers grapple with formulating questions, especially in light of the cross-disciplinary connections which both enrich and complicate approaches to research (Cook et al. 1994; Elliott et al. 1994; Tienda 1991). However, the primary impediment to progress in understanding the effects of neighborhoods on children continues to be the lack of data sources that contain information on neighborhoods, families, and children. Until recently, there were no studies explicitly designed to answer ques-tions of neighborhood influence on parents and children (Jessor 1993). Thus quantitative researchers perforce have had to rely on secondary analysis of exist-ing sources of data which are not well suited to address these questions. While some existing qualitative and ethnographic studies of neighborhoods speak more directly to some of the issues that we have touched upon, this research is usually not designed to contrast the experiences of children living in different commu-nities.

Typically, quantitative research on neighborhood effects has used existing ad-ministrative areas, usually census tracts, to represent neighborhoods. One strategy has been to link individual records from a survey with sociodemographic charac-teristics of the census tract in which the individual resides. Individual statuses are then modeled as a function of both census tract characteristics and individual and family characteristics (for example, Aber et al. 1993; Brooks-Gunn, Duncan, Klebanov, and Sealand 1993; Clark and Wolf 1992; Duncan, Brooks-Gunn, and Klebanov 1994; Hogan and Kitagawa 1985). Another approach has related ag-gregated data on children's outcomes to census tract characteristics (for example, Aber et al. 1992; Coulton and Pandey 1992; Garbarino and Sherman 1980; Sampson and Groves 1989; Simcha-Fagin and Schwartz 1986).

When considered as a whole, the research utilizing these approaches has pro-duced mixed results. Some analyses have shown correlations between census characteristics and outcomes, while in others the associations have been weak or nonexistent. Interpreting the findings is complicated by differences in the neigh-borhood characteristics employed in different studies, as well as variations in the number and type of individual and family control variables, or in the case of aggregate-level studies, the absence of individual controls. It is difficult to argue based on existing evidence that children living in neighborhoods with particular sociodemographic profiles differ in obvious ways, even controlling for individual characteristics. Thus despite the intensity of interest in neighborhood influences, the conclusion that Jencks and Mayer reached several years ago remains: quan-titative research has not demonstrated a convincing association between neigh-borhoods and children's development, much less established the causal pathways between characteristics of neighborhoods and child development (see Gephart 1994 for a comprehensive review of recent research).

Even if the results of these types of studies were to converge to a consistent pattern of associations, they would be of limited utility in understanding the complex pathways of influence among neighborhoods, families, and children. No matter how well executed, studies such as these can only demonstrate an associa-tion at a point in time between sociodemographic characteristics of neighbor-hoods and children's statuses. That is, they do not open the black box containing the causal directions between neighborhood conditions and children's lives. The inclusion of only neighborhood sociodemographic information not only obscures intervening mechanisms between neighborhoods and individuals, it also obscures the relationships among neighborhood characteristics. Both of these restrictions impede the evaluation of competing theories of neighborhood effects. The use of cross-sectional data does not permit dynamic analyses of neighborhoods and children. It is thus virtually impossible to assess theories of neighborhood effects against theories that argue that observed differences in outcomes across neighborhoods are due to differential selection into neighborhoods (Tienda 1991).

Ethnographers have taken quite a different tack from quantitative researchers in their efforts to demonstrate connections between neighborhood conditions and children's development. With relatively few exceptions, they have adopted a case example approach, examining in detail how the social organization of a particular community orders family life, socialization practices, and child outcomes. Mostly, they have relied on a time-honored anthropological practice of providing vivid evidence suggesting differences (or sometimes similarities) between them and us. Comparisons are often implicit and explanations rely more on assembling configurations of interrelated practices and their meanings (exceptions are Sullivan 1989 and Burton, Obeidallah, and Allison 1996).

Much of what we know or at least suspect we know comes from the persuasive accounts of urban sociologists and anthropologists (for example, Anderson 1990; Burton 1990; Hannerz 1969; Rainwater 1970; Stack 1974; Williams and Kornblum 1994). In an impressive meta-review of a large body of qualitative research on poor and near-poor neighborhoods, Jarrett (1992) attempted to identify how the availability and quality of institutional resources, particular mechanisms of social control, and the social climate support conventional behavior or tolerate departures from mainstream norms. Her findings suggested that family processes and socialization practices may indeed differ across communities depending on their economic status and racial composition.

In summary, while there is no lack of real-world motivation and theoretical speculation for exploring the effects of neighborhoods on children's development, the existing body of empirical work provides little evidence for or against the effects of neighborhoods—especially in the childhood years. Recent quantitative research on the links between neighborhoods and development has not demonstrated convincing associations between neighborhoods and development, much less addressed the particular pathways of influence by which neighborhoods influence children and youth. Ethnographic research, while providing tantalizing suggestions of community dynamics, lacks the generalizability to provide solid evidence.

Some progress in understanding the influence of neighborhoods on children may be made by continuing to link existing surveys with administrative data, especially if this work exploits the longitudinal aspects of surveys. While these models will not untangle the processes by which neighborhoods influence children's development, they may be considered a logical starting point for assessing the impact of neighborhoods on children's outcomes. Determining whether associations exist between neighborhoods of various types and children's statuses will demonstrate whether there is anything to be explained by more detailed models that do open the black box. These associative models will be most helpful when processual theories are used to guide the characterization of neighborhoods and model-building. It is also important that studies estimate models both with and without available processual variables. The failure of existing research to find a consistent pattern of associations is due in part to differences across studies in the extent to which variables measuring mediating processes are included.

However, real progress in understanding the relationships among neighborhoods, families, and children will require initiating research explicitly designed to address these questions (Furstenberg 1992; Jessor 1993). In the remainder of the chapter we outline issues of design and measurement that we believe researchers need to consider in planning primary research in this area. As the most powerful tools for disentangling the effects of neighborhoods on individuals are not statistical, but conceptual, we emphasize the importance of grounding both design and measurement in theoretical orientations.

ISSUES IN DESIGNING RESEARCH TO TEST FOR NEIGHBORHOOD INFLUENCES

In this section, we discuss five issues that we believe are important in planning data collection that addresses the relationship between neighborhoods and children's development. We later suggest specific research strategies that employ various combinations of these desired elements.

Multilevel Designs

The first consideration in designing neighborhood research is the need for studies to be *multilevel*; that is, to include and analyze data on both neighborhoods and individual children within these neighborhoods. In addition, as family management strategies may be an important link between communities and children, data on family processes should be collected as well (Furstenberg 1993; Sampson 1992). In this framework, children may be perceived as nested within families and families within neighborhoods.

With this approach, the structure of the data mimics the structure of the general theoretical proposition that properties of communities affect families and children, enabling both logical tests of the proposition and assessments of competing explanations (Smith 1989). The central question in neighborhood research is whether families and individuals with similar characteristics behave differently in distinct environments (Jencks and Mayer 1990). In the absence of true experiments assigning individuals to neighborhoods at random, research designs must approximate the experimental design by comparing similar individuals living in different areas. Detailed individual- and family-level information is necessary to statistically examine similarities and differences in individuals across neighborhoods, while neighborhood-level information is necessary to describe the properties of neighborhoods that account for any observed spatial differences. In fact, this is only a poor approximation of an experiment. But continuing evidence that families and individuals respond in patterned ways to different contexts establishes plausible evidence of neighborhood effects.

Clearly, researchers are aware of the utility of multilevel analyses, as the existing research linking census tract characteristics to individual data attests. We discuss this approach here to underscore the need to undertake projects that are explicitly designed to collect data at multiple levels.

Specification of Neighborhoods

A second consideration in designing neighborhood research is the manner in which the relevant geographic community is defined. As indicated above, most of the recent research on the effects of neighborhoods on development has used census tracts as a proxy for neighborhoods, an approach dictated by cost and convenience rather than by empirical evidence that tracts represent neighborhoods. While census tracts may be a convenient starting point for measuring neighborhood differences, researchers must consider other ways of sampling communities that take into account local definitions of neighborhoods that may either be more or less geographically circumscribed. Census tracks clearly capture some important elements of geographical and social space, but they may not depict the neighborhood as it is experienced by residents, who may relate to smaller areas within census tracts or areas that fall outside the boundaries (Elliott et al. 1994).

However, delineating geographic neighborhoods is difficult, because the concept of neighborhood is not precise (Chaskin 1994). There is growing evidence that residents in close geographical proximity often do not agree on the boundaries of their neighborhood. In research undertaken by the MacArthur Network on Adolescents at Risk, very different levels of agreement among residents about the size of their "neighborhood" have been discovered. There is also evidence of large differences within census tracts on definitions of the neighborhood (Elliott et al. 1994; Furstenberg et al. forthcoming; Cook et al. 1994). Furthermore, adults and youth—even adults and youth in the same household—do not necessarily share the same definition of the neighborhoods. Geographical neighborhoods are not highly relevant entities for many parents, as their ties extend beyond their neighborhood (Medrich, Roizen, Rubin, and Buckley 1982; Wynn, Richman, Rubenstein, and Littell 1988). Important social institutions are often located beyond the confines of the neighborhood—however defined—implying that many residents are weakly attached to the areas where they reside (Walker and Furstenberg 1994). "Family" neighborhood is a highly malleable concept full of personal meaning but often idiosyncratic and not invariably consequential for behavior. An added complication is that neighborhoods, however defined, are themselves nested in broader communities. Especially as children grow older, their behavior may reflect the influence of local labor market conditions or public policy mandates that apply to larger geographical areas.

While we offer no simple solutions to these difficult issues, we believe recognition of the ambiguity of neighborhood boundaries has several implications for designing research. First, it may be valuable for researchers planning primary data collection to do a small-scale preliminary investigation of the definitions of neighborhood that are relevant to their area of examination. Second, including several overlapping definitions of neighborhood in one study would enable comparison of relationships under different definitions (for example, Brooks-Gunn, et al. 1993). Third, by querying neighborhood residents about their social ties outside their residential communities, it may be possible to test the extent to which individuals within communities are relatively isolated from competing reference groups that influence them and their children. Finally, researchers should be sensitive to the idea that we may not find neighborhood effects—precisely because internal definitions of sociospatial communities are so variable across individuals. These considerations are all the more important as it is likely that even new data collection efforts will have to rely on administrative boundaries, at least to some extent. Building in one or two of the first two features may permit testing the fourth possibility.

Sampling Strategies

As we have argued, data collection will be most useful when it is conducted in a multilevel framework. However, it is important that the data include both a sufficient number of neighborhoods and a sufficient number of families and children within each neighborhood to support adequate statistical tests of hypotheses. This implies a strategy whereby neighborhoods are sampled first and then families and individuals sampled within neighborhoods in a manner that yields approximately equivalent numbers of families and individuals per neighborhood.

To test hypotheses about the influence of neighborhood characteristics on children, it is necessary to perform a statistical comparison of children with similar personal characteristics across neighborhoods. Since neighborhood characteristics tend to cluster together, it is impossible to disentangle the effects of particular mechanisms of influence on children without large samples of both neighborhoods and children. Moreover, as we noted earlier, it is also of interest to examine the interaction of neighborhood characteristics and family processes as they influence children, further raising the sample-size demands.

Comprehensive samples of neighborhoods would also provide an opportunity for a baseline description of how much variability there actually is in neighborhood conditions (Cook et al. 1994). Similarly, much of the interest in neighborhood effects has come out of the interest in poverty, yet it is as important to ascertain whether effects of neighborhoods exist for affluent neighborhoods as well. In particular, nonlinearities or threshold levels in the effects of neighborhoods on children are important from a policy perspective (Crane 1991; Jencks and Mayer 1990). Finally, dense samples of families and individuals within neighborhoods would enable researchers to generate reliable measures of neighborhood characteristics by aggregating individual responses (Cook et al. 1994).

Longitudinal Approaches

As we noted above, all of the published research on the relationship of neighborhoods to children's development has employed cross-sectional data, limiting the casual inferences that may be drawn from the analyses. Longitudinal designs are called for in which neighborhoods and individuals are followed over time—either in separate studies or, ideally, within the same study.

Neighborhood research on children thus far has tended to view neighborhoods as relatively static entities. However, neighborhoods also have developmental trajectories, and the rate and manner in which a particular neighborhood is changing may have important implications for child development. Neighborhood change might be a particularly salient force if the change is rapid and dramatic, such as gentrification or an influx of immigrants. The Chicago School tradition of research explicitly considered the influence of transitional neighborhoods on the life chances of children. To our knowledge, no recent study has mapped how changes in neighborhoods relate to the changing circumstances of children, though this notion is central to Wilson's theory of neighborhood influence (Tienda 1991). In general, attention to the research traditions on community organization and change would help inform current research on the influences of neighborhoods on children (for example, Sampson and Morenoff 1994).

At the individual level, the need for longitudinal data follows directly from our emphasis on children's development. Demonstrating neighborhood influences, we have argued, requires demonstrating the processes in the immediate milieu that affect the cumulative experience of children as they develop over time. Thus, we must attend to the slope of life course trajectories, not simply to the level of outcomes or statuses at a point in time. Such a strategy requires tracking the same individuals using repeated measures of different domains of development as they encounter distinctive neighborhood environments over time. Furthermore, one of the strongest ways of demonstrating neighborhood influence on children's development would be to link the length of *exposure* to neighborhood conditions to specific paths of development (Tienda 1991). Longitudinal research would permit analyzing neighborhood effects by duration of exposure.

Perhaps most importantly, longitudinal research on both neighborhoods and individuals would illuminate the causal relationships among neighborhood change, family management processes, and children's well-being. A principal ingredient of several of the sociological theories relating neighborhoods to children's life chances is the stability of the neighborhood. This is most notable in social disorganization theory, in which residential instability is one of the main structural correlates of high delinquency rates. However, it is unclear from this association just which way the causal arrow points. For instance, the principal competing explanation for any net differences observed among individuals in separate neighborhoods is nonrandom selection into neighborhoods. That is, observed differences in behavior across neighborhoods are argued to be due to the presence in separate neighborhoods of individuals with distinct, but unobserved, characteristics. The differential pattern of residence is due to the dynamics of residential mobility, as the qualities of neighborhoods attract or expel migrants with particular characteristics. However, residential mobility is also one strategy that parents might employ to obtain the environment they desire for their children. Thus there is a complex relationship between the stability and characteristics of neighborhoods and local migration, a relationship that is at least partially mediated by processes of family management. Sorting out this tangle requires longitudinal data that trace family management and mobility within the context of changing communities.

Combining Quantitative and Qualitative Approaches

As we reported earlier, most ethnographic studies have focused on documenting the influence of single communities. We believe that there is a much larger role for qualitative researchers to carry out their studies both across place and over time. Indeed, we share the view of a growing number of urban ethnographers that fieldwork can be embedded into research designs that include both systemic surveys and observations. Many researchers currently use fieldwork for hypothesis generation rather than hypothesis testing, a condescension to the potential of qualitative methods to detect and document processes that are not easily captured by survey procedures. We have at least as much hope that qualitative methods will illuminate neighborhood effects as quantitative methods, but we believe that studies employing both procedures in tandem have the greatest possibility of collecting convincing evidence of how neighborhood influences affect human development.

MEASURING CONCEPTS RELEVANT TO NEIGHBORHOOD RESEARCH

In the preceding section we sketched elements of research design that are important for researchers in exploring potential neighborhood influences on child development. This section takes up how to conceptualize and measure relevant features of large communities, neighborhoods, families, and children. We devote most of our attention to issues in measuring neighborhood conditions and processes, as these are both critical to neighborhood research and conceptually underdeveloped. We include a short discussion of broad opportunity structures as a reminder that neighborhoods, families, and children are embedded in economic markets and local cultures that affect children's life chances. Family and child measures are routinely collected in other research; therefore we discuss only aspects that seem to us unique to the study of neighborhoods.

Measuring Broader Opportunities and Constraints

While the focus of this chapter is the impact of neighborhood conditions on children, neighborhoods are themselves embedded in broader geographic communities whose properties also shape behavior. These include labor, marriage, and housing markets, levels of welfare benefits, structure of property taxes, and other conditions that constrain or promote local attitudes and practices. As children grow older, these conditions begin to permeate their perceptions of opportunities and shape their adaptations and decision strategies. The qualities of the broader environment may also condition the influence of neighborhood characteristics (Case and Katz 1991). This level of community, while not as indistinct as the neighborhood, is also difficult to circumscribe. However, here we conceptualize it as the metropolitan area or, in nonmetropolitan areas, the county.

A variety of data characterizing the demographic composition, economic climate, housing context, and health and educational resources for metropolitan areas and counties is available from the Bureau of the Census (for example, U.S. Bureau of the Census 1991). Other information may be more difficult to assemble, especially if the aim is to build a data set that includes all areas in the United States. Thus building a data set that includes all theoretically relevant aspects of metropolitan or county contexts is a potentially arduous task. If the aim is to characterize a specific area or county, recourse can be made to local administrative records and sources to obtain not only a characterization of the context at a point in time, but its recent history as well (for example, Coulton and Pandey 1992).

Measuring Neighborhood Conditions, Processes, and Trajectories

The complete evaluation of neighborhood influences on children would require obtaining direct measures of all the community characteristics relevant to how theories explain the influence of neighborhoods on the developing child. For instance, social disorganization theory posits a causal chain from the socio-demographic composition of the neighborhood, through the social organization of the neighborhood, to children's outcomes. Testing the theory requires measuring both neighborhood sociodemographic composition and the neighborhood social processes hypothesized to mediate its effects on children's behavior. However, researchers are only beginning to include direct measures of these social processes in tests of social disorganization theory (for example, Sampson and Groves 1989; Simcha-Fagin and Schwartz 1986). Including all dimensions of neighborhoods hypothesized to have effects on child development not only enables more complete tests of theories; it also illuminates the causal structure among neighborhood-level variables, suggesting which aspects of neighborhoods are potential targets for policy manipulation.

Collecting direct measures of neighborhood conditions, processes, and trajectories involves careful consideration of the attributes of communities considered central to various theories of neighborhood influence. We specify and discuss four broad dimensions of neighborhood conditions that arise in theories of neighborhood influence. These dimensions of neighborhoods are likely to be highly interrelated. Indeed, any strong neighborhood effects are likely to occur when neighborhood conditions are favorable on many dimensions. While we have discussed the difficulty of defining neighborhoods in geographic terms, here we sidestep this thorny question and assume that the relevant unit is known. However, it must be recognized that measuring the neighborhood and measuring the properties of the neighborhood must actually occur together.

Characterizing neighborhoods requires not only greater conceptual specification; more precision in how these constructs are measured is also needed. Developing techniques to measure the properties of neighborhoods adequately is an important area for future work (Cook et al. 1994). Reference to existing literatures in overlapping areas, for instance, community psychology and urban sociology, would be helpful both for developing community concepts and the techniques to measure them (for instance, Shinn 1988). Careful attention to meaning and measurement is especially important in light of the methodological constraints inherent in identifying social effects (Manski 1993).

Neighborhood Infrastructure   At the neighborhood level, local infrastructure provides the physical reality in which social life and individual development occurs. Features such as the types and quality of housing, the use and arrangement of space, and the level of deterioration are fixed over short periods of time and thus provide boundaries of community development and change. Physical characteristics may also represent important constraints to social relationships (Williams and Kornblum 1994). For instance, an area composed mainly of rental apartments may have a very different character than one composed of owner-occupied single-family row houses. This may be due to the attributes of the people who choose to live in each area, the levels of residential mobility, the ways in which the arrangement of space fosters or inhibits social exchange, or a combination of all three. In this manner, infrastructure may be the ultimate cause of neighborhood influences on children or, alternatively, the selection of certain families into certain neighborhoods. If this is indeed the case, policy might then be fruitfully focused on changing infrastructure.

Data on infrastructure may be the simplest neighborhood-level information to assemble. In situations where tracts or other census designations are used to approximate neighborhoods, some information may be obtained from the Census of Housing, which contains extensive information on housing infrastructure. To supplement this data, or in cases where census definitions are not used, field-workers can directly record the physical features of neighborhoods, supplementing their observations with detailed maps and data available from local administrative sources, such as zoning boundaries and conditions of streets. Developing specific indicators would be relatively straightforward, as the concepts are concrete. For example, measures could include the percentage of various types of buildings—row homes, apartments, detached houses; the presence of open spaces such as parks or vacant lots; the presence of graffiti and vandalism; the presence of vacant and boarded-up buildings; the distance of detached houses from each other; and even architectural details such as whether homes have porches or stoops. Combined indices may be constructed that gauge the potential for social exchange in a given combination of infrastructure.

Neighborhood Demographic Composition   As we have discussed, sociodemographic composition has been utilized by virtually all recent census tract–based studies as a general indicator of neighborhood conditions. While we have emphasized the limits of this approach, our comments should not be interpreted as an argument to leave demographic characteristics out of neighborhood analysis. In fact, as central components of several theoretical stances, they should be included. Under the rubric demographic we include several attributes of the neighborhood population: age, household structure, racial composition, educational level, income level, and mobility status. Each of these characteristics represents an aspect of the local population that may have an effect on children's well-being. For instance, a neighborhood in which the local population is highly educated may provide role models for educational attainment, increasing children's attachment to school. A neighborhood with a high concentration of well-off individuals may be better able to mobilize political resources in order to defeat legislation or policy that may threaten the safety or integrity of the neighborhood. Each of these effects is the result of the demographic structure, in contrast to an effect of another type of characteristic for which demographic structure is a proxy.

Obviously, studies using census tract or other census units to circumscribe neighborhoods will have the resources of the population census with its myriad items describing local populations. To the extent that other definitions of neighborhoods are used, obtaining data about demographic composition may be more difficult. Responses from surveys of families and individuals may be aggregated, but if the sampling frame includes only households with children, the results may be seriously distorted. Basic aspects of population structure may be calculated using small-area methods for demographic estimation (for example, Myers and Doyle 1990). However, this technique relies on precise information about housing composition within the area, which may not be readily available. Furthermore, utilizing this approach then confounds demographic composition with housing infrastructure. Another, but difficult, possibility is a neighborhood census.

Neighborhood Institutions　　The importance of local institutions is also highlighted in theories of neighborhood effects. Wilson (1987, 1991) assigns an important role to the absence of middle-class-sponsored institutions in isolating the underclass. Jencks and Mayer (1990) cite institutional resources as mechanisms of socialization and social control. Neither one of these theorists specifies exactly what types of institutions may be most important to children's development. Here we distinguish two types of institutions. One represents commitment and attention from outside the neighborhood, and to some extent may link the neighborhood to the broader community. Examples of these types of institutional resources include: police protection, social welfare agencies, public health clinics, libraries, and the advocacy of local politicians. The second type of institution is indigenous to the community: local businesses, churches, community centers. Of course, especially important are any institutions who specifically target children and/or their parents.

In order to assess the salience of institutions for the development of children, it would be helpful to collect two sorts of data: an objective inventory of all agencies with a presence in the neighborhood and parents' and children's perceptions and actual use of these institutional resources (Wynn, Richman, Rubenstein, and Littell 1988). Objective presence may not matter so much as the residents' knowledge and opinion of the relevance of the institutions to their lives. For instance, knowing about the presence of a community center may not be illuminating unless the researcher also knows that residents consider it viable only for a particular ethnic group.

There are no data sources we know of that provide inventories of institutions across various neighborhoods no matter how defined. Therefore, considering the presence of institutions requires original data collection. Listings of neighborhood institutions can be collected by fieldworkers by the combination of observation and recourse to the administrative sources we have suggested for measuring infrastructure. In the case of institutions, however, interviews with local informants and leaders of institutions will be important to determine the institution's mission and actual presence in the community. Residents' knowledge of the existence of and participation in institutions can be obtained by survey procedures (Cook et al. 1994). If the survey follows the institutional inventory, it will be possible to ask respondents about particular institutions specifically.

Indicators might include the presence of specific types of institutions or a summary measure indicating the general level of institutional resources in the community. The specific institutional measure would be important to use if the institution were directly related to an outcome of interest—for instance, a family-planning clinic when studying school-age childbearing—or was directly aimed at parenting processes. Both the general and specific indicators could be discounted or inflated by data on residents' perceptions. Alternatively, aggregated measures of individual responses on awareness, use, and opinions of institutions could be used independently.

Neighborhood Social Organization   While many of the theories discussed above refer to physical, demographic, or institutional properties of neighborhoods, it is the qualities of the social environment that are the proximate determinants of child development. Each of the three dimensions of neighborhood life discussed here indirectly affects children's development via its effects on social relationships within the neighborhood. The mechanisms that Jencks and Mayer (1990) refer to are essentially *social* processes by which the content and qualities of social interaction shape the behavior of individuals. Thus measurement of concepts related to neighborhood social organization is central to advancing research on the influence of neighborhoods on children.

Along with Sampson (1992), we argue that the importance of neighborhood social organization is its role in generating social capital for individuals. Characteristic patterns of social organization in neighborhoods either facilitate or inhibit the creation of neighborhood-based social capital, which in turn affects family management and children's well-being. Coleman (1988) elaborated three forms of social capital: shared norms, reciprocal obligations, and information channels. To the extent that parents and children possess social capital in the neighborhood, the neighborhood may be more or less of an influence on their lives.

In varying degrees, neighborhoods are normative communities representing common values that are reinforced by social control. The extent to which adults and youth in the neighborhood subscribe to and promote mainstream norms is a component of several theories suggesting neighborhood effects. Networks of reciprocal obligation and exchange are particularly important to child development when they exhibit intergenerational closure, which occurs when parents of children who are friends are themselves friends. The existence of informal networks of association in the neighborhood ensures that children are monitored by adults other than their parents, facilitating collective socialization. Dense social networks within the community may also connect children to opportunities for modeling, mentoring, and sponsorship. The opportunity for information acquired in social relationships is also an important aspect of neighborhood-based social capital. The density of child contacts with adults that can offer social guidance and support is an important aspect of the child's position in the opportunity structure. This is especially the case if these adults can inform children of opportunities outside the neighborhood.

We recognize that the existence of norms, networks, and information need not imply a prosocial or conventional orientation (Sutherland 1939; Cloward and Ohlin 1960; Sullivan 1989). Neighborhoods can provide normative support to disengage from conventional behavior, mentoring for criminal roles, and opportunity structures for illicit activities. Thus, studies of neighborhood influence should measure the availability of social support for underground activities or tolerance for behavior outside the mainstream.

While social organization is the most critical element in most theories of neighborhood effects, it is also the most elusive to measure. In order to gauge the extent to which the neighborhood facilitates the formation of social capital among individuals, we need to measure the extent to which the neighborhood is a normative community, the extent to which there are informal networks in the community (and the density and closure of these networks), and the opportunities for information that exist in social relationships within the neighborhood.

Information on the social organization of neighborhoods can be gathered in either structured or qualitative interviews with individuals. In fact, a scenario in which qualitative and quantitative interviews are employed, not as alternatives or in sequence, but in a series of feedback loops, would likely yield the most optimal measures of neighborhood social fabric. Utilizing individual reports, multivariate scales could be built that summarize aspects of neighborhood social organization (for example, Cook et al. 1994). However, individual evaluations of neighborhood social organization tend to be distorted, as respondents apply internal, non-standardized yardsticks in their responses to an interviewer's questions. Assessment of neighborhood social processes by outside observers would help to correct for the difficulty that individuals have in standardizing their perception of their local environment.

Measuring Properties of the Family System

It is beyond the scope of this chapter to discuss in any detail the dimensions of family systems that are relevant to the developing child. However, we would like to emphasize three aspects of family life that are of central importance to assessing the effects of neighborhoods on children and should therefore be included in any data collection efforts.

First, it is of central importance that information on residential mobility be collected, including length of time in the neighborhood, reasons for moving, and, when possible, characteristics of the previous neighborhood. In cross-sectional studies this information can be collected in a retrospective residence history; in longitudinal studies it may be collected prospectively. Second, we cannot ignore the importance of how parents relate to their local environments, how they draw upon resources in their communities, and how they manage and shape the child's milieu. Of particular importance is the degree to which parents possess neighborhood-based social capital. The neighborhood may present a favorable environment for the generation of social capital, but individual parents may or may not exploit these resources. We know relatively little about how neighborhoods influence the creation and management of social capital.

Finally, parents' ability to create and sustain a normative system in the household and generate reciprocal obligations with their children can be thought of as a form of family-based social capital. Simply put, parents who invest in their children by establishing and maintaining expectations and obligations are likely to gain a greater degree of compliance or adherence to their values. Family-based social capital has features similar to the capital that inheres in community ties. Consequently, we want to measure shared norms within the family, social-connectedness of family members as indicated by the strength and salience of bonds, and the sense of reciprocal obligations.

Measuring Children's Development

We also will not discuss what measures of child development might be included in neighborhood studies, as there is ample information on this issue available elsewhere. However, we would like to emphasize two features of children' lives that we think are of particular importance in assessing neighborhood effects. First, it would be helpful to measure children's acquisition of social capital during childhood—for example, children's contacts, identification of and respect for adults within the neighborhood, and involvement in and service to community institutions. Such measures provide an indication of the extent to which children are increasingly bonded to and regulated by norms outside the family and their ability to call upon support and sponsorship by figures other than parents. Second, many of our surveys collect data on aspirations and attainment. Yet, we know relatively little about children's changing knowledge of and competency with the social world. For example, little is known about what children believe is required to go to college, what employers look for when they are hiring, how to obtain medical information (for example, for getting an abortion), and the like. Such information is an important indicator of children's position in the opportunity structure.

CONCLUSION

We have argued that progress in understanding the influences of neighborhoods on children's development will require designing primary research aimed explicitly at addressing the complex questions generated by current theoretical orientations. To this end, we outlined issues of both design and measurement that we deemed important in planning such research. However, we recognize that it is impossible, and probably not desirable, to combine all the elements we suggest in a single study. Throughout our review, we have ignored the very real constraints of cost, time, and manageability. In this section we propose several types of projects that combine various features of these desiderata. While these proposals certainly do not exhaust the possibilities, they suggest potential ways in which the elements we have discussed may be implemented practically.

While we have been critical of approaches that combine demographic information about census tracts with survey data, we recognize that this strategy is often the best available. We believe these approaches could be elaborated fruitfully in two ways. First the longitudinal nature of many of the surveys can be exploited more fully. This strategy is likely to be most informative when the study contains both census tract data over time and repeated measures of development. This conjunction of information makes it possible to calculate exposure intervals to varying contexts as well as the examination of cases that migrate across contexts. The relatively low cost of augmenting existing longitudinal data sets makes this a promising strategy for several large-scale longitudinal surveys containing developmental outcomes, for instance, the Panel Study of Income Dynamics, the National Longitudinal Survey of Youth, and the National Survey of Families and Households.

A second strategy that builds on the tract-survey combination approach is to add additional tract-level information to the data set, such as information on infrastructure or institutions that may be available from administrative sources. We recognize that this may well be impossible with the national data sets that include a large number of census tracts; this strategy may be most feasible with locally concentrated samples. If such is the case, direct observation could be used to supplement data from administrative sources. To the extent that the data sets are also densely sampled within areas, individually based measures may also be constructed. A distinct advantage of including other measures of census tract characteristics is that it permits investigators some way of testing of how demographic profiles are related to theoretically relevant features of local milieus. Again, this is a budget strategy to approaching our ideal design.

As we have argued, new data collection aimed at disentangling the influences of neighborhoods must be multilevel and must sample at the neighborhood level first, as the unit of comparison is fundamentally the neighborhood. Elements on which more compromise is possible include the definition of neighborhood employed, whether the study is longitudinal, and the extent to which quantitative and qualitative work are combined.

A broad program of research undertaken by the MacArthur Foundation Research Network on Successful Adolescent Development Among Youth in High-Risk Settings has sponsored a series of studies that have adopted this strategy. In a number of different sites, the influence of neighborhood is being assessed by following dense samples of families and youth, each of which represent a number of neighborhoods or communities with contrasting social characteristics. Several of these studies are carefully assessing the individual and added influence of families, schools, peers, and neighborhoods.[1]

Studying neighborhoods within a single area not only has the advantage of lower costs and ease of management; such a strategy also has the theoretically attractive property of holding broader opportunity structures constant. This type of study could include all or some of the following elements: a survey of *neighborhoods* that characterizes all neighborhoods in the city and that may or may not contain a component aimed at determining the boundaries of neighborhoods; dense sampling in enough neighborhoods to provide data for quantitative analysis; and selecting a subset of these neighborhoods for extensive ethnographic comparison to add depth and richness to the statistical comparisons. The study could be extended to be longitudinal by tracing individuals and neighborhoods over time. Finally, a comparative dimension could be added if similar studies were being conducted in other cities. A second broad category of project would incorporate national samples of neighborhoods, selected either strategically or probabilistically. These studies would resemble the efforts of a series of Russell Sage Foundation–funded studies that are examining the influence of macroeconomic conditions on family life and the marital and economic transitions of young adults. The potential components would be essentially similar to those suggested for city-based studies.

Finally, too little research on neighborhood effects has capitalized on planned and natural experiments. The Gautreaux study stands as a major exception, where Rosenbaum and his colleagues examined the effects of random assignment to geographical mobility among low-income families in Chicago (Rosenbaum and Popkin 1992). Evaluation of different types of housing policies on families and children provides an attractive site for examining neighborhood effects on low-income families. Studies of communities in rapid transition also afford an opportunity to examine how families react to community change and how different cohorts of children may fare over time in different environmental conditions. Careful inspection of housing projects that undergo change may also provide another avenue to looking at the mechanisms that affect the course of children's development. Of course, these strategies require a timely awareness of local conditions and the cooperation of local players.

Because we have identified concepts that need to be measured, rather than evaluating established measures, we are less able to recommend a set of specific measures for priority in data collection. However, we can identify which concepts we believe are the most essential to measure. By far the most critical concept for which to develop measures is neighborhood social organization. Overlapping with this, and also of high priority, is measuring how parents and children interact within neighborhoods, including information on residential mobility. These concepts are at the heart of all the various theoretical formulations. Efforts to improve the way they are measured—even on surveys not particularly focused on neighborhood influences—should have a high payoff in differentiating competing explanations.

In closing, we note that Jencks and Mayer (1990) argued powerfully that understanding neighborhood influences on children would require a long-term commitment from both the research and funding communities. Their argument remains true today, with the added urgency that we are exhausting the possibilities of existing data without advancing our understanding of how neighborhoods influence the development of children. Significant progress in combining the rich insights of sociological and psychological theories of whether and how neighborhoods shape the course of development requires a greater commitment to designing and executing more innovative investigations. This process will be neither easy nor inexpensive, but the potential rewards to researchers and policy-makers justify a bolder approach.

The authors acknowledge the helpful comments of Greg Duncan, Donald Hernandez, Christopher Jencks, Susan Mayer, Ronald Mincy, and Karen Walker and the ongoing advice of Julien Teitler and Lynne Geitz. This research was supported in part by the MacArthur Foundation Research Network on Successful Adolescent Development Among Youth in High-Risk Settings. The paper reflects many ideas gained in collaborative research and discussions with committee members including Albert Bandura, James Comer, Tom Cook, Jacquelynne Eccles, Glen Elder, Del Elliott, Norman Garmezy, Robert Haggerty, Beatrix Hamburg, Dick Jessor, Arnold Sameroff, Marta Tienda, and Bill Wilson.

NOTES

1. Furstenberg, Cook, Eccles, Elder, and Samaroff have been conducting a comparison of urban neighborhoods in Philadelphia. In separate studies, Cook and colleagues and Eccles, Sameroff, and colleagues are studying the influence of neighborhoods, schools, families, and peer groups on youth in Prince Georges County, Maryland. Elliot, Wilson, and colleagues are examining neighborhood influences in Denver and Chicago. Finally, Elder and colleagues (Conger and Elder 1994) have been looking at community influences in rural Iowa.

REFERENCES

Aber, J. Lawrence, Robin Garfinkel, Christina Mitchell, La Rue Allen, and Edward Seidman. 1992. "Indices of Neighborhood Distress: Their Association with Adolescent Mental Health and School Achievement." Paper prepared for the conference at the University of Michigan, Ann Arbor, on *The Urban Underclass: Perspectives from the Social Sciences,* Ann Arbor, Mich. (June 1992).

Aber, J. Lawrence, Edward Seidman, La Rue Allen, Christina Mitchell, and Robin Garfinkel. 1993. "Poverty-Related Risks and the Psychological Adaptation of Urban Youth: Testing Mediational Models." Unpublished manuscript.

Anderson, Elijah. 1990. *Street Wise: Race, Class, and Change in an Urban Community.* Chicago: University of Chicago Press.

Barker, Roger G. 1968. *Ecological Psychology.* Stanford, Calif.: Stanford University Press.

Baumgartner, M. P. 1988. *The Moral Order of the Suburb.* New York: Oxford University Press.

Bronfenbrenner, Urie. 1979. *The Ecology of Human Development: Experiments by Nature and Design.* Cambridge, Mass.: Harvard University Press.

———. 1986. "Ecology of Family as a Context for Human Development." *Developmental Psychology* 22(6): 732–42.

Brooks-Gunn, Jeanne, Greg J. Duncan, Pamela Kato Klebanov, and Naomi Sealand. 1993. "Do Neighborhoods Influence Child and Adolescent Development?" *American Journal of Sociology* 99(2): 353–95.

Bursik, Robert J., Jr. 1988. "Social Disorganization and Theories of Crime and Delinquency: Problems and Prospects." *Criminology* 26: 519–52.

Burton, Linda M. 1990. "Teenage Childbearing as an Alternative Life-Course Strategy in Multigenerational Black Families." *Human Nature* 1: 123–43.

Burton, Linda M., Dawn A. Obeidallah, and Kevin Allison. 1996. "Ethnographic Perspectives on Social Context and Adolescent Development among Inner-City African American Teens." In *Ethnography and Human Development: Context and Meaning in Social Inquiry,* edited by Richard Jessor, Anne Colby, and Richard A. Shweder. Chicago: University of Chicago Press.

Case, Anne C., and Lawrence F. Katz. 1991. "The Company You Keep: The Effects of Family and Neighborhood on Disadvantaged Youths." Working Paper 3705. Washington, D.C.: National Bureau of Economic Research.

Chaskin, Robert J. 1994. "Defining Neighborhood." Paper prepared for the Neighborhood Mapping Project of the Annie E. Casey Foundation.

Clark, Rebecca L., and Douglas A. Wolf. 1992. "Do Neighborhoods Matter? Dropping Out Among Teenage Boys." Paper presented at the annual meeting of the Population Association of America, Denver, Colorado (April 30–May 3, 1992).

Clinard, Marshall B. ed. 1964. *Anomie and Deviant Behavior: A Discussion and Critique.* Glencoe, Ill.: The Free Press.

Cloward, Richard A., and Lloyd E. Ohlin. 1960. *Delinquency and Opportunity: A Theory of Delinquent Gangs.* Glencoe, Ill.: The Free Press.

Cohen, Albert Kircidel. 1955. *Delinquent Boys.* Glencoe, Ill.: The Free Press.

Coleman, James S. 1988. "Social Capital in the Creation of Human Capital." *American Journal of Sociology* 9: S95–S120.

Conger, Rand D., and Glen H. Elder, Jr., in collaboration with Frederick O. Lorenz, Ronald L. Simons, and Lee B. Whitbeck. 1994. *Families in Troubled Times: Adapting to Change in Rural America.* New York: Aldine de Gruyter.

Cook, Thomas D., Frank F. Furstenberg, Jr., Jeong-Ran Kim, Julien O. Teitler, Lynne M. Geitz, Jacquelynne Eccles, Glen H. Elder, Jr., and Arnold Sameroff. 1994. "Neighborhood Differences in Resources for Promoting the Positive Development of Adolescents: The Roles of Financial, Human, Social, Cultural and Psychological Capital." Manuscript in preparation.

Coulton, Claudia J., and Shanta Pandey. 1992. "Geographic Concentration of Poverty and Risk to Children in Urban Neighborhoods." *American Behavioral Scientist* 35(3): 238–57.

Crane, Jonathan. 1991. "The Epidemic Theory of Ghettos and Neighborhood Effects on Dropping Out and Teenage Childbearing." *American Journal of Sociology* 96(5): 1226–59.

Duncan, Greg J., Jeanne Brooks-Gunn, and Pamela Kato Klebanov. 1994. "Economic Deprivation and Early Childhood Development." *Child Development* 65(2): 296–318.

Dunn, Judy, and Robert Plomin. 1990. *Separate Lives: Why Siblings Are So Different.* New York: Basic Books.

Elliot, Delbert S., and David Huizinga. 1990. "The Mediating Effects of Social Structure in High-Risk Neighborhoods." Paper presented at the annual meetings of the American Sociological Association, Washington, D.C. (Aug. 11, 1990).

Elliott, Delbert S., William Julius Wilson, David Huizinga, Robert Sampson, Amanda Elliott, and Bruce Rankin. 1995. "The Effects of Neighborhood Disadvantage on Adolescent Development." Paper in progress.

Fine, Gary Alan. 1987. *With the Boys.* Chicago: The University of Chicago Press.

Furstenberg, Frank F., Jr. 1992. "Adapting to Difficult Environments: Neighborhood Characteristics and Family Strategies." Paper presented at the annual meeting of the Society for Research on Adolescents (March 19, 1992).

———. 1993. "How Families Manage Risk and Opportunity in Dangerous Neighborhoods." In *Sociology and the Public Agenda,* edited by William J. Wilson. Newbury Park, Calif.: Sage Publications.

Furstenberg, Frank F., Jr., Thomas D. Cook, Jacquelynne Eccles, Glen H. Elder, Jr., and Arnold Sameroff. 1996. *Managing to Make It: Urban Families in High-Risk Neighborhoods.* Manuscript in progress.

Gans, Herbert J. 1962. *The Urban Villagers.* New York: The Free Press.

Garbarino, James. 1992. *Children and Families in the Social Environment,* 2d ed. New York: Aldine De Gruyter.

Garbarino, James, and Deborah Sherman. 1980. "High-Risk Neighborhoods and High-Risk Families: The Human Ecology of Child Maltreatment." *Child Development* 51: 188–98.

Gephart, Martha A. 1997. "Neighborhoods and Communities as Contexts for Development." In *Neighborhood Poverty,* vol. 1, edited by Jeanne Brooks-Gunn, Greg J. Duncan, and J. Lawrence Aber. New York: Russell Sage Foundation.

Hannerz, Ulf. 1969. *Soulside: Inquiries into Ghetto Culture and Community.* New York: Columbia University Press.

Hogan, David P., and Evelyn M. Kitagawa. 1985. "The Impact of Social Status, Family Structure, and Neighborhood on the Fertility of Black Adolescents." *American Journal of Sociology* 9: 825–55.

Jarrett, Robin L. 1992. *A Comparative Examination of Socialization Patterns Among Low-Income African-Americans, Chicanos, Puerto Ricans, and Whites: A Review of the Ethnographic Literature.* Evanston, Ill.: Northwestern University, Center for Urban Affairs and Policy Research.

Jencks, Christopher, and Susan Mayer. 1990. "The Social Consequences of Growing Up in a Poor Neighborhood." In *Inner-City Poverty in the United States,* edited by Laurence E. Lynn and Michael G. H. McGeary. Washington, D.C.: National Academy Press.

Jencks, Christopher, and Paul E. Peterson, eds. 1991. *The Urban Underclass.* Washington, D.C.: The Brookings Institution.

Jessor, Richard. 1993. "Successful Adolescent Development Among Youth in High-Risk Settings." *American Psychologist* 48(2): 117–26.

Kornblum, William. 1974. *Blue Collar Community.* Chicago: University of Chicago Press.

Kornhauser, Ruth. 1978. *Social Sources of Delinquency.* Chicago: University of Chicago Press.

Lemert, Edwin M. 1951. *Social Pathology: A Systematic Approach to the Theory of Sociopathic Behavior*. New York: McGraw-Hill Book Company, Inc.

Lewin, Kurt. 1951. *Field Theory in Social Science*. New York: Harper & Row.

Lynn, Laurence E., and Michael G. H. McGeary, eds. 1990. *Inner-City Poverty in the United States*. Washington, D.C.: National Academy Press.

Manski, Charles F. 1993. "Identification Problems in the Social Sciences." *Sociological Methodology* 23: 1–56.

Matza, David. 1964. *Delinquency and Drift*. New York: John Wiley and Sons, Inc.

Medrich, Elliott A., Judith Roizen, Victor Rubin, and Stuart Buckley. 1982. *The Serious Business of Growing Up*. Berkeley, Calif.: University of California Press.

Myers, Dowell, and Alan Doyle. 1990. "Age-Specific Population-Per-Household Ratios: Linking Population Age Structure with Housing Characteristics." In *Housing Demography: Linking Demographic Structure and Housing Markets*, edited by Dowell Myers. Madison, Wisc.: University of Wisconsin Press.

Park, Robert E., and Ernest W. Burgess. 1924. *Introduction to the Science of Sociology*. Chicago: University of Chicago Press.

Rainwater, Lee. 1970. *Behind Ghetto Walls*. Chicago: Aldine Publishing Co.

Rosenbaum, James E., and Susan J. Popkin. 1992. The Gautreaux Program: An Experiment in Racial and Economic Integration. *The Center Report: Current Policy Issues* 2(1).

Sampson, Robert J. 1992. "Family Management and Child Development: Insights from Social Disorganization Theory." In *Advances in Criminological Theory*, vol. 3, edited by J. McCord. New Brunswick: Transaction Books.

Sampson, Robert J., and W. Byron Groves. 1989. "Community Structure and Crime: Testing Social-Disorganization Theory." *American Journal of Sociology* 94(4): 774–802.

Sampson, Robert J., and J. D. Morenoff. 1994. "Ecological Perspectives on the Neighborhood Context of Poverty and Social Organization: Past and Present." Unpublished manuscript.

Shaw, Clifford, and Henry D. McKay. 1942. *Juvenile Delinquency and Urban Areas*. Chicago: University of Chicago Press.

Shinn, Marybeth. 1988. "Mixing and Matching: Levels of Conceptualization, Measurement, and Statistical Analysis in Community Research." Paper presented at De Paul University at the conference on Researching Community Psychology: Integrating Theories and Methodologies, Chicago, Ill. (September 1988).

Simcha-Fagan, Ora, and Joseph E. Schwartz. 1986. "Neighborhood and Delinquency: An Assessment of Contextual Effects." *Criminology* 24: 667–704.

Smith, Herbert L. 1989. "Integrating Theory and Research on the Institutional Determinants of Fertility." *Demography* 26(2): 171–84.

Stack, Carol B. 1974. *All Our Kin*. New York: Harper & Row.

Steinberg, Lawrence. 1990. "Autonomy, Conflict, and Harmony in the Family Relationships." In *At the Threshold: The Developing Adolescent*, edited by S. Shirley Feldman and Glen R. Elliott. Cambridge, Mass.: Harvard University Press.

Sullivan, Mercer. 1989. *Getting Paid: Youth Crime and Work in the Inner City*. Ithaca, N.Y.: Cornell University Press.

Sutherland, Edwin Hardin. 1937. *The Professional Thief: By a Professional Thief*. Chicago: The University of Chicago Press.

———. 1939. *Principles of Criminology*. New York: Lippincott.

Tannenbaum, Frank. 1938. *Crime and Community*. New York: Columbia University Press.

Thorne, Barrie. 1993. *Gender Play: Girls and Boys in School*. New Brunswick, N.J.: Rutgers University Press.

Thrasher, Frederic M. 1927. *The Gang*. Chicago: University of Chicago Press.

Tienda, Marta. 1991. "Poor People in Poor Places: Deciphering Neighborhood Effects on Poverty Outcomes." In *Macro-micro Links in Sociology,* edited by Joan Huber. Newbury Park, Calif.: Sage Publications.

U.S. Bureau of the Census. 1991. *State and Metropolitan Area Date Book.* Washington: U.S. Government Printing Office.

Walker, Karen, and Frank F. Furstenberg, Jr. 1994. "Neighborhood Settings and Parenting Strategies." Paper presented at the annual meetings of the American Sociological Association, Los Angeles, Calif. (Aug. 4–7 1994).

Williams, Terry, and William Kornblum. 1994. *The Uptown Kids: Struggle and Hope in the Project.* New York: Putnam.

Wilson, William Julius. 1987. *The Truly Disadvantaged: The Inner-City, the Underclass, and Public Policy.* Chicago: University of Chicago Press.

———. 1991. "Public Policy Research and 'The Truly Disadvantaged.'" In *The Urban Underclass,* edited by Christopher Jencks and Paul E. Peterson. Washington, D.C.: The Brookings Institution.

Wrong, Dennis. 1961. "The Oversocialized Conception of Man in Modern Society." *American Sociological Review* 26: 183–93.

Wynn, Joan, Harold Richman, Robert A. Rubenstein, and Julia Littell. 1988. *Communities and Adolescents: An Exploration of Reciprocal Supports.* Washington, D.C.: Youth and America's Future, William T. Grant Foundation, Commission on Work, Family and Citizenship.

Potential and Problems in Developing Community-Level Indicators of Children's Well-Being

Claudia J. Coulton

CHILDREN AND THEIR families live within local communities and these are important units for assessing child well-being. It is indeed at the level of the local community that many of the processes that affect children transpire. Children interact with neighbors; participate in local institutions; receive social, health and educational services; develop a sense of safety and belonging; form a vision of their opportunities; know what is expected of them and what they can expect from others. Parents' implicit understanding of the importance of local community is reflected in the serious thought that many of them give to their residential choices. Yet the locational options of a significant number of families are constrained by racism, low income, insufficient information, or public policy. Understanding the variation in child well-being across local communities is thus a crucial component of policy analysis, program planning, and service delivery.

Developing indicators of child well-being at the local community level, however, poses numerous conceptual, methodological, and practical challenges. These challenges, as well as the important benefits of undertaking this level of measurement, are the focus of this chapter.

LOCAL COMMUNITIES AS UNITS OF ANALYSIS

Although the term "community" is a social rather than a geographic unit, the discussion in this chapter will be limited to local communities that are bounded spatially. Such communities can serve as units for the measurement of child well-being. The local community of interest is typically the neighborhood, although for some purposes it is a political jurisdiction such as a ward or town, or a service delivery zone such as a school or health district.

Neighborhood boundaries are often difficult to draw because there is little consensus about what constitutes a neighborhood. Social scientists hold varying perspectives on the degree to which the term implies homogeneity, social interaction, and place identity on the part of the residents (White 1987). Most definitions of neighborhood imply a degree of social cohesion that results from shared institutions and space, but it is also widely accepted that neighborhoods differ in their levels of community social organization and integration (Lyon 1987). Further, it seems that the neighborhoods that are least cohesive and organized may be the poorest community environments for rearing children (Coulton et al. 1995; Garbarino and Sherman 1980; Sampson 1992).

Despite the definitional ambiguities of neighborhood or other meaningful localities, local community indicators typically require geographic boundaries. These boundaries may be phenomenological, interactional, statistical, or political.

At the phenomenological level, each resident has a sense of the boundaries that are personally meaningful. These vary even for the same individual depending upon the context (Galster 1986). However, under some circumstances it is possible to use the consensus of residents as the basis for drawing geographic boundaries for neighborhoods. In our research on Cleveland's neighborhoods we have found some areas where there is considerable agreement among neighbors on the boundaries of their neighborhood, while in other locales neighborhood boundaries seem virtually idiosyncratic. Consensus seems to be greater in areas with higher levels of community identity and attachment (Korbin and Coulton 1994). Where adequate consensus exists, the residents' perceived boundaries can be used to form units for the development of indicators. However, this consensus may change over time, making consensual boundaries problematic for tracking changes in communities over time.

A second approach to generating community area boundaries is to use the patterns of social interaction of residents. This involves a process of "mapping locally-based social interaction onto a spatial grid" (Entwisle 1991). Friendship patterns and daily activities both have been used as methods of tieing interaction patterns to spatial locations.

Statistical definitions of local community areas are a third approach. Census tracts have been most widely used to date in local indicator development even though concerns have been raised about the degree to which these units resemble the space that is meaningful to residents (Tienda 1991). Nevertheless, census tracts have proven quite useful for local planning and research on neighborhoods (White 1987; Kasarda 1993; Galster and Mincey 1993; Pandey and Coulton 1994). Block groups have also served as proxies for neighborhoods in some studies (Taylor et al. 1984).

There is also a tradition in cities such as Chicago, Cleveland, Philadelphia and elsewhere for designated neighborhoods to be used for planning purposes. Such local designations have been supported by the Census Bureau. Unlike census tracts, these designated neighborhoods can vary considerably in size but take into account local sentiments on natural boundaries. Although designated neighborhoods do not always match resident perceptions, they have been used successfully in research (Galster and Hesser 1982).

Political units such as wards, districts, and towns are a fourth approach to defining community areas. But they seldom can be equated to neighborhoods and they lack a social meaning. Nevertheless, when community indicators are used for planning or evaluation, political units may be appropriate for analysis.

Choosing a set of geographic boundaries for community indicators depends upon several considerations. First, it is important that the unit be constant over time so that trends can be tracked. Second, it must be possible to allocate available data to the unit of analysis that is chosen. Third, the choice of units should be appropriate given the assumptions and purposes underlying the set of indicators. In this regard, varying conceptual perspectives on community indicators are discussed in the next section.

In the remainder of this chapter I will use the term "community area" to refer to the unit of geography that has been chosen, be it a census tract, neighborhood, or town. I will use the term "community indicator" to refer to measures that are made on these units of geography.

PERSPECTIVES ON COMMUNITY-LEVEL MEASUREMENT

Two quite different perspectives can be taken on community indicators for families and children. One I will label *outcome orientation*, the other *contextual orientation*. The *outcome orientation* views community areas as valuable units for measuring the status of children against various social, health, and developmental outcomes. Comparing the status of children across community areas can reveal inequalities that suggest levels of need and indicate where resources should be targeted. These comparisons also can point to differences in program effectiveness or practices across community areas. These are the purposes for which community indicators are often obtained and outcomes do indeed vary considerably across community areas within counties or metropolitan areas (Coulton and Pandey 1992).

This *outcome orientation* makes few assumptions about the relationships between community areas and their families and children. The outcome measures represent the status of a population of children who live in specified local areas. The ways in which the local communities themselves affect these outcomes remain unspecified.

An alternative view of communities, though, is to measure them as environments for families and children. This *contextual orientation* is based on the assumption, for which there is some empirical support, that community areas (for example, neighborhoods) can affect children and their families positively or negatively. Some of these effects are reflected in higher or lower rates of health and social and developmental outcomes. But from this perspective it is the community structure and processes that are the relevant focus of measurement.

The *contextual orientation* makes some strong assumptions about how communities affect families and children. I have reviewed the several extant lines of research on the effects of neighborhoods on families and children in another work (Coulton 1994), but I will summarize them here. For convenience, this summary discusses the research under four broad headings that are not mutually exclusive: compositional effects, community context of effective parenting, effects of stressful neighborhood environments, and community social organization.

First, recent interest in extreme poverty neighborhoods has spawned a series of studies designed to determine whether neighborhood socioeconomic composition affects life chances of children over and above family background factors. Although not adopting any uniform theoretical perspective, these studies can be loosely classified as subscribing to a model of socialization processes within neighborhoods through adult, peer, or institutional influences (Jencks and Mayer 1990). Research on the socioeconomic composition of communities reveals that having sufficient affluent families in a neighborhood promotes school achievement, cognitive development, and the avoidance of teen childbearing (Brooks-

Gunn et al. 1993; Clark 1992; Crane 1991; Duncan 1993). The positive effects of middle-class and affluent neighbors has been found by these studies to be more important as a context for children than the negative effects of having poor neighbors.

Second, the community context for parenting has been explored in several important studies. These studies shed light on how social networks, resources, local institutions, and environmental stressors shape parenting style. Parents adapt to dangerous and depleted environments by restricting their children's activities and isolating themselves from the surrounding area (Furstenberg 1993). These adaptations, while understandable and necessary for safety, may not promote academic achievement and future economic success. Also, individual parents who adopt effective child-rearing styles will not be as successful when they are surrounded by less effective parents. The distribution of effective parents differs across types of communities (Steinberg et al. 1992; Steinberg and Darling 1994).

Third, the negative effects on families and children of stressful conditions in poor, urban environments have been explored in many studies. Getting most attention in recent years has been the negative impact of chronic exposure to violence in the community (Martinez and Richters 1993; Garbarino et al. 1992; Zapata et al. 1992). Daily hassles, though less dramatic, have been found to be a significant cause of parental distress in poor neighborhoods, too (Caspi et al. 1987; Garbarino and Sherman 1980). Considerable work on how resourceful parents adapt to these stressful conditions is contained in this line of research as well. Kinship networks and neighbors are used quite effectively by some parents (Lee et al. 1991; McAdoo 1986). For others, network relationships can actually be a further source of strain (Riley and Eckenrode, 1986).

Fourth, community social organization is proving to be a useful framework for understanding the relationship between macro-structural change and the experience of families and children within neighborhoods (Sampson 1992). As neighborhoods decline economically, experience population turnover, and contain large numbers of children in female-headed families, the community's internal control is diminished. Studies of crime and delinquency, in particular, support the contention that this occurs through the effects of the macro-structure on processes within the community such as friendship networks, institutional participation, normative consensus, and monitoring of the environment (Bursik and Grasmick 1993; Sampson and Groves 1989; Sampson 1991). Dimensions of community structure such as economic resources, residential mobility, family structure and age distribution of the population have been linked to varied childhood outcomes including child maltreatment, delinquency, teen childbearing, and low birth weight rates (Coulton et al. 1995).

Regardless of whether an *outcome orientation* or *contextual orientation* is chosen, caution must be exercised in interpreting differences among communities. Community selection processes are complex and difficult to isolate but can be important explanations for variation among local areas (Tienda 1991). On the one hand, self-selection of families into particular communities and forced selection of communities by families due to discrimination, affordability, or public policy may be responsible for variation in outcomes or community context. On the other hand, preexisting differences in social, economic, and institutional structures and processes can affect children within communities regardless of the selection processes that led to their presence in a particular community in the first place.

Even with these caveats in mind, community area boundaries need to be consistent with the orientation that is chosen. The *outcome* and *contextual orientation* also call for somewhat different types of indicators to represent the well-being of children in communities. Examples of such indicators are provided in the next section.

COMMUNITY INDICATORS OF CHILDREN'S WELL-BEING

Community indicators are measures of child and family well-being tied to local community areas. Indicators that reflect an *outcome orientation* include social, health, and developmental outcomes for the population living in local areas. Indicators that reflect a contextual orientation include measures of the community structure and process that are believed to affect children and family life.

Neighborhoods and other community areas can change rapidly. Thus, community indicators from either orientation should be calculated and available annually or biannually.

Outcome Indicators

Outcome indicators that are useful at the community level include many of those that have been proposed for use at the national and state level. I will not repeat the conceptual justification for their use since this is covered in other chapters in this volume. However, data sources and availability differ at the community level, placing limitations on what is practical. In particular, large-scale surveys seldom have sufficient sample size to make estimates for small areas. Furthermore, the base rates of some outcomes useful at the state or national level will be too low to allow valid measurement at the local community area level.

Table 17.1 offers a list of indicators that we have used in Cleveland's neighborhoods and the surrounding metropolitan area as an illustration of what is currently possible. This is not an exhaustive list. The indicators are organized according to the general categories suggested by Zill (1991). Our system in Cleveland allows calculation of the indicators for block groups, census tracts, neighborhoods officially designated as planning areas, or any other subareas of the county that can be aggregated from block groups, such as areas defined by residents or neighborhood leaders. This type of flexibility is highly desirable in local indicator work.

Measures of health and safety of children are the types of outcomes most readily available at the local level. Local health departments, hospitals, police jurisdictions, child welfare agencies, and coroners all are potential collaborators for developing indicators in this area. Infant death rates and low birth weight rates and other measures of infant and child health can be calculated from birth and death certificates which are readily available and can be geocoded for aggregation into small areas. Rates from year to year are quite unstable in small areas; three-year averages are preferred.

Child maltreatment rates can be calculated from official reports and are rea-

Table 17.1   Examples of Community Outcome Indicators for Children Available in the Cleveland Metropolitan Area

Indicator	Measure	Data Sources
Health and safety		
Infant death rate	Infant deaths/live births	Vital Registrar
Low birth weight rate	Births < 2500 grams/live births	Vital Registrar
Child maltreatment report rate	Reports of abuse or neglect/population < 18	County Children's Services
Trauma rate[a]	Children's injuries/population < 18	Hospital Emergency Rooms
Child homicide rate	Child homicides/population < 18	County Coroner
Child suicide rate	Child suicides/population < 18	County Coroner
Social behavior		
Teen childbearing rate	Births to teens/females 12–17	Vital Registrar
Delinquency rate	Delinquent filings/population 10–17	County Juvenile Court
Teen drug violation arrest rate	Drug arrests of teens/population 12–17	Municipal Police Departments
Cognitive development and achievement		
High school graduation rate	Persons graduating/persons entering 9th grade	Board of Education
Performance in math and reading	Mean performance score	Board of Education
Youth employment rate	Employed persons 16–25/persons 16–25	U.S. Census, STF-4
Economic well-being		
Family poverty rate	Poor families/total families	U.S. Census, STF-3
Child poverty rate	Children in poor families/children in families	U.S. Census, STF-3
Child public assistance rate	Public assistance recipients < 18/population < 18	County Entitlement Services

[a]Planning and development of this data source is currently under way.

sonably comparable in terms of definitions and criteria within one agency jurisdiction. However, over- and underreporting biases may differ across community
areas and must be assessed carefully (see the section in this chapter on reporting
bias).

Trauma rates can be calculated for children if trauma registries exist in the
emergency departments of most major hospitals serving the communities of interest. We are currently in the planning stages for such a registry system for
Cleveland. The trauma events will be geocoded using the home address of the
patient and aggregated by age to yield rates for children. A seriousness threshold
for inclusion in this indicator will need to be developed.

Child homicide rates and suicide rates as well as gun-related deaths for community areas can be calculated from the coroner's data. Because these are rare
events, multiple years need to be averaged and rather large community areas
must be used for analysis.

Measures of what Zill (1991) labels moral and social development and emotional development are more difficult to obtain at the local level without resort-
ing to impractical neighborhood surveys. One useful measure, though, is the teen
childbearing rate, which is based on births to teens per one thousand females
ages twelve to seventeen.

The delinquency rate is another possible indicator of moral and social development and is derived from court records which are classified as to level of
offense and age of offender and then geocoded. Delinquency filings are counted
per one thousand males and females ages ten to seventeen. Further refinements
of this indicator can include separate rates for males and females, separate rates
for violent offenses and direct age standardization.

Teen drug violation arrest rates are also available and can be calculated from
arrest records of the police departments. Caution must be exercised when comparing these rates across police precincts or municipalities because police practices may differ. While these rates do suggest the communities in which drug
activities result in youth interacting with the criminal justice system, they cannot
be used as valid measures of drug abuse or involvement in drug use or sales as a
whole.

Measures of cognitive development and academic achievement can be developed for communities in collaboration with local school systems. High school
graduation rates require student-level data from the schools geocoded so students
can be assigned to neighborhoods. If multiple years of data files are available,
counts of students entering the ninth grade in each community area are divided
into counts of students graduating four years later. Student performance is measured as the mean score achieved by students at selected grade levels on standardized achievement tests.

These school-based measures are more practical in neighborhoods where most
of the children attend public schools. We have found some neighborhoods in
Cleveland, though, with fewer than 50 percent of the children enrolled in public
schools. A valid school completion indicator for these areas would require obtaining student data with home addresses from more than thirty private and
parochial schools, all of whom have differing methods of data collection and
storage. This task has been impractical thus far.

Youth employment can also be considered an indicator of achievement. It uses the decennial census to calculate the labor force status of young men and women, sixteen to twenty-five, who are not in school. Unfortunately, we have not yet found a measure of youth employment at the community level that is available more frequently than each decade. However, the use of the state reporting system related to unemployment compensation is being explored.

The economic status of families, a final category suggested by Zill (1991), is available at the community level from the decennial census. The family poverty rate, child poverty rate, and family median income can all be calculated easily. However, we know that the actual economic status of families in a neighborhood can change rapidly during a decade. Therefore, we are developing a model for estimating these rates in each subsequent year using variables derived from AFDC and Food Stamp recipients in each community area. Our previous experience in estimating overall poverty rates for census tracts between 1980 and 1990 showed fairly high accuracy. Public assistance counts for various programs were benchmarked to census counts of poor persons and the model was used as an estimator in intercensal years.

Child public assistance rate is an additional indicator of the economic status of families which is available yearly. Public assistance families typically have income that is well below the poverty threshold. This indicator reflects, therefore, the children with the most extreme economic deprivation. It can be calculated using the monthly average caseload of children receiving public assistance in each community area divided by the number of children living in the area. The monthly public assistance case files are geocoded and counts are produced for the desired units of geography.

Contextual Indicators

The search for practical measures of community environments has an extended history (Rossi 1970). However, the identification of indicators of community context that may be important factors in the well-being of children requires either scientific research or a set of assumptions that link aspects of community structure and process to effects on families and children. Unfortunately, research that pinpoints those aspects of community that affect children and families has yet to yield definitive connections. Nevertheless, the research described in the section on perspectives can be used to suggest a set of indicators of community context that are worthy of experimentation.

Table 17.2 presents a set of indicators of community context for children which we have been exploring in Cleveland's neighborhoods. At the aggregate level, they have been linked to rates of child maltreatment, teen childbearing, low birth weight, and delinquency (Coulton et al. 1995). Ethnographies conducted in selected neighborhoods representing varying levels of risk for children generally confirm that these factors coincide with residents' perceptions of the neighborhood as "good or bad places for raising children" (Korbin and Coulton 1994). The data sources for these contextual indicators are much more limited at the community level than they are for the outcome types of indicators. Since many come from the decennial census they only are available at ten-year intervals.

The economic status of neighbors is suggested as an important contextual indicator for the well-being of children both in compositional research and com-

Table 17.2 Examples of Indicators of Community Context for Children Used in Cleveland Metropolitan Areas

Indicator	Measure	Data Sources
Socioeconomic composition		
Middle-class neighbors	% families with income $35,000	U.S. Census, STF-3
Affluent neighbors	% families with income $50,000	U.S. Census, STF-3
Managerial and professional workers	% managerial and professional workers	U.S. Census, STF-3
Poverty rate	% persons below poverty threshold	U.S. Census, STF-3
Poverty estimates	Estimate of % persons below poverty threshold	Estimates using public assistance counts
Age and family structure		
Female-headed families with children	% families with children headed by female	U.S. Census, STF-1
Nonmarital birth rate	% births to unmarried mothers	Vital Registrar
Elderly population	% population 65	U.S. Census, STF-1
Male/female ratio	Adult males (21–64)/adult females (21–64)	U.S. Census, STF-1
Child/adult ratio	Population 0–12/population 21 +	U.S. Census, STF-1
Residential mobility		
Population gain or loss	1990 population-1980 population	U.S. Census, STF-1
Movers in < 5 years	% who moved between 85–90	U.S. Census, STF-3
Residential tenure < 10 years	% in current residence < 10 years	U.S. Census, STF-3
Environmental stress		
Vacant and boarded houses	% housing units vacant or boarded	Municipal housing departments
Housing code violations	% units substandard	Municipal housing departments
Personal crime	FBI index crimes against persons/1,000 population	Municipal police departments
Drug arrests	Drug arrests/1,000 population	Municipal police departments
Support for effective parenting		
School locations	% children attending school < 15 minute drive	Board of Education
Recreational opportunities	Parkland and recreational areas/square mile	Recreation and Park Departments
Community participation	% parents attending school conferences	Board of Education

munity social organization research. The compositional research, though, emphasizes that measurement needs to reflect not only overall economic status such as median income or poverty rate but must also include an indicator of the presence of middle-class or affluent neighbors (Brooks-Gunn et al. 1993; Clark 1992; Crane 1991; Duncan 1993).

The importance of the age and family structure of a community is also implicated as an important factor in the well-being of children. Specifically, community areas with a higher percentage of elderly persons, a more equal ratio of men to women, a greater percentage of two-parent families, and a more favorable adult/child ratio are found to correlate with lower rates of poor outcomes and to be perceived by residents as promoting a better environment for children (Coulton et al. 1995; Korbin and Coulton 1994).

Several indicators of residential mobility are deemed important because population turnover has been repeatedly connected to aspects of community process (Freudenburg 1986). Most important as a context for children is the negative effect of residential mobility on parent-to-parent networks and support for institutions serving children.

Indicators of environmental stress are potentially useful because they may directly affect parents' ability to protect and nurture their children and because of the negative effects of these factors on community social organization. Substandard and abandoned housing is associated with growing disorder and fear of crime (Skogan 1990). High levels of personal crime and drug selling are seen by residents as a source of anxiety and distraction that affects their parenting (Furstenberg 1993; Korbin and Coulton 1994).

On the positive side, some contextual supports for effective parenting are also suggested. Parental involvement with social institutions, neighbor-to-neighbor relations, and community resources for families are but a few of the important features of community that seem important (Zill and Nord 1994; Garbarino and Sherman 1980). Unfortunately, few data sources are readily available for measuring resources at the local community level. Community resources for children have been studied in national and local surveys, but surveys are seldom practical for local indicators. New sources of data need to be developed to measure these aspects of community context.

METHODOLOGICAL CONSIDERATIONS FOR COMMUNITY-LEVEL INDICATORS
Assignment of Geographical Location

There are numerous methodological problems pertinent to making measurements of child and family well-being for small geographic areas such as communities. Because definitions of community areas typically have some geographic boundaries, data used for community indicators must be suitable for assignment to geographic units. Administrative agency data, which is often the preferred source for local community indicators, must be obtained with the street addresses intact. The addresses can be geocoded using the TIGER files and aggregated to the desired geographic boundaries (block groups, census tracts, resident-defined neighborhoods, wards, catchment areas, school zones, and so on).[1]

In our experience, agencies differ considerably in the accuracy and validity of their addresses for this purpose. Problems include the timeliness of the address, whether it is verified or not, and administrative conventions that can be misleading. For example, some agencies overwrite addresses when there is a move so the address is the most current one. This may differ from the address at which an event of interest occurred, such as an arrest or a child-abuse incident. Also, the address given may not be a home address, which is usually the one desired for community analysis, but an office or agency where a service was delivered. Finally, when the address is obtained by the agency for informational rather than service delivery purposes, accuracy may be low and a substantial number of addresses may not be codable without considerable effort expended on the correction of errors.

Finally, for some indicators, there may be ambiguity as to which geographic area to assign a case. For example, infant deaths are ordinarily assigned to the community area in which the death occurred. However, since infant death is highly related to conditions in the prenatal period, it may be more useful to assign the death to the community area in which the birth occurred.

Small-Area Limitations

The geographic units for community indicators are typically fairly small. Block groups vary considerably in their population size but may have anywhere from just a few to hundreds of housing units. While census tracts have an average population of four thousand, many are quite a bit smaller especially in central cities that have been losing population. Designated neighborhoods can be of any size depending on the methodology used for drawing the boundaries. This small geography poses several limitations.

The first is the unavailability of survey data. There are no national surveys with sample sizes adequate to provide valid estimates for small areas such as neighborhoods and census tracts. Even statewide or metropolitan-wide surveys are seldom adequate for these purposes. Only the decennial census in which 15 percent of the households complete the long-form provides some estimates of family structure and economic status that can be used for small geographic areas. The Public Use Microdata (PUMS) 5 percent sample from the census can be used to make estimates at the subcity level, but these areas of one hundred thousand minimum population seldom correspond to any meaningful definition of community area.

Surveys are periodically undertaken locally which are capable of generating measures of child and family well-being for small, geographically defined communities. However, it is seldom feasible to draw adequate size samples for all neighborhoods in a region when a multistage sampling method to be used. Thus, these surveys do not provide measures for all community areas but only for a sample, selected randomly or otherwise. Furthermore, these expensive surveys are seldom repeated. Thus they do not yield measures over time, which is desirable for indicators.

Low base rates is a second problem with small-area analysis. Outcomes of significant interest such as childhood deaths from trauma can show extreme variation in rates because they are rare. Since aggregating geography to achieve sufficient population size would often negate the purpose of community area analysis, multiyear averages must be used to obtain a stable trend. The disadvantage, of course, is that important changes in conditions may be obscured in the short run.

A third problem is the fact that meaningful geographic units often have *markedly unequal population sizes.* The stability or reliability of an indicator will be better in larger areas than in smaller areas. An extreme rate in a smaller area must be viewed with considerable caution. For some purposes, such as statistical modeling, the geographic units can be weighted for their population size, but such weighting typically does not make sense when the indicators are being used for local planning or policy purposes.

Reporting Bias and Error

Although error and bias must be considered in all work on indicators, there are two problems that are particularly troubling at the local community level. First, because local community indicators rely so heavily on administrative agency data they are beset by the reporting bias and error in those data sources. The nature of these problems are likely to vary from one indicator to another. Birth and death certificates, for example, are known to be quite complete. However, causes of death on death certificates or information about the mother's health contained in birth certificates are prone to error. These errors differ depending upon the hospitals and physicians involved in their completion. Thus, the degree of error will differ across community areas.

Reports of criminal or deviant acts are subject to the most severe and troubling sorts of bias. Police reports and court records are known to underestimate the true levels of criminal and violent events (O'Brien 1985). More important, they are also biased by differences that may exist across jurisdictions in victims' or observers' tendencies to report (Sampson 1985) and government officials' tendency to file reports and take action (Sherman 1989; O'Toole et al. 1983). Unfortunately, the direction of the bias in each of the community areas cannot be known, but it can account for some part of the observed differences.

The problem of errors and bias in administrative records requires careful investigation in each instance. Few generalizations can be made across regions. Generally, though, errors will be fewer when the data element used serves a mandated function or vital purpose of the agency. Information gathered by the agency only for descriptive purposes often can be misleading due to large amounts of missing data or coding errors. Reporting bias is particularly troubling when the direction of the bias is not the same in all community areas.

It is desirable, therefore, that efforts be made to validate widely used indicators based on administrative records against other data sources. Specially designed community surveys can be useful for establishing the validity of indicators derived from administrative agencies or other sources. For example, Jill Korbin and I have a study in the planning stage that will use a survey instrument to measure aspects of child abuse and neglect. The survey will be conducted in a random sample of neighborhoods whose rates of child abuse and neglect have been calculated based on official reports to the county authorities. These two sources of data can be compared to illuminate the issue of reporting bias and error in both the survey and administrative agencies.

Another example of validating administrative data against another source are the infant mortality reviews that are being carried out as a part of Cleveland's Healthy Start Program and are being performed in other Healthy Start cities. In Cleveland, the infant mortality review has revealed variation across hospitals and physicians in classifying causes of death and in deciding what is a live birth. When corrected, the quality of this source of administrative data will be improved.

An additional issue that is pertinent to local community indicators is the amount of undercounting and missing data. This problem has received considerable attention with respect to the decennial census. Most troubling for community indicators is that the amount of undercounting and missing data are not uniform across community areas. Census counts are more likely to be undercounts when they pertain to young men and minorities in central city neighborhoods, for example. Furthermore, the amount of missing data that the census bureau imputes is greater in low-income, minority neighborhoods leading to differential reliability of census indicators (White 1987). Adjusting for the estimated undercount in some neighborhoods may be necessary, but it also introduces another source of error since the true undercount cannot be known in each location.

Small-Area Population Estimates

Community indicators are often reported as rates in which the areas' population is used as the denominator. Rates may be reported per hundred, one thousand, or one hundred thousand persons. Unfortunately, population estimates are not universally available at the block group or census tract level between censuses, so rates in intercensal years will be less valid. While established methods of population estimation are used at state and county levels, their application to areas as small as block groups, census tracts, or neighborhoods has not been widespread (Heeringa 1982).

Nevertheless, the sources of data needed to perform these population estimates generally can be obtained for community areas through geocoding. The housing unit method of population estimates, for instance, can use building and demolition permits, utility hookups and disconnections, or county assessor tax records to update housing unit counts after a census. The component-cohort method relies on birth and death certificates. While estimating small-sized areas results in greater error, there is evidence that useful estimates are possible (Smith and Cody 1994).

The ability to develop indicators for community areas would be greatly enhanced if the Census Bureau were to assist local communities in efforts to estimate small-area population. Federal involvement could bring uniformity across metropolitan areas in the methodologies that are used and allow the development of data sources that are national rather than local. For example, the address registries of the postal service have a level of national standardization that local utility companies, housing departments, and county assessors do not. If such a registry could be linked with census geography, significant intermetropolitan sources of variation could be reduced.

Standardization

Community-level indicators are applied to areas of widely differing demographic makeup. In some instances, therefore, it may be useful to apply age or gender standardization. Small geographic areas often display marked variability in age and gender distribution. Some childhood indicators are sensitive to the particular age distribution that is present in the community. For example, teen births are concentrated in older teens and occur with less frequency in younger teens. Therefore, if two communities have a similar number of teens but the teens in one community tend to be older, the community with older teens would be expected to have a higher teen birth rate. Age standardization can compensate for differing age distributions and is probably worth the extra computational steps when children's ages put them at greater or lesser risk for particular outcomes.

There are also indicators that may be sensitive to gender distribution in the community. For example, delinquent behavior is known to be more frequent among boys. Gender-specific rates should be calculated for these types of indicators.

Other forms of statistical adjustment have been suggested for indicators, such as adjusting outcome indicators for the economic status or ethnicity of the population (Zill 1991). In general, risk adjustment would not seem to be justified in community-level analyses. Such adjustment would obscure important ways in which communities that are more affluent differ from those that are lower income or ways in which some communities may be favored over others in resource distribution.

An exception to this general discouragement of risk adjustment would be the situation where community indicators are being used for program evaluation. Known risk factors for a particular outcome which are not amenable to the effects of the intervention would be suitable factors to use in adjustment. For example, mother's age, ethnicity, and educational attainment are known risk factors for infant mortality. Community area rates of infant mortality could be adjusted for these factors in an evaluation of an infant mortality prevention program.

ANALYSIS AND INTERPRETATION OF COMMUNITY-LEVEL INDICATORS

The analysis of community indicators can take several forms. First, each community or area can be examined over time to determine the amount and direction of change in each indicator. When areas are small, multiyear averages must be used and a fairly long time trend is needed to detect significant variation. Nevertheless, for practical purposes neighborhood residents and organizations are often interested in monitoring these types of trends.

Second, community areas can be compared with one another cross-sectionally on each indicator. Areas can be ranked on selected indicators and maps can be used to determine the location of communities that are relatively high and relatively low on the various indicators. Cross-sectional analyses of this type are often useful for planning purposes such as choosing locations for programs or deciding where to target resources. Also, they allow areas that are performing poorly to identify areas that are performing better and seek their advice and assistance for improvement. These cross-sectional comparisons must be made cautiously, though, due to differences in reporting biases and an expected amount of random variation at any given period in time.

Third, community areas can be grouped according to their similarities on a set of indicators. Such clusters can aid community leaders in recognizing the inter-relationships among several aspects of children's well-being. The recognition that several troubling outcomes or conditions are concentrated in a few areas can lead to greater collaboration and service integration. Maps that allow overlaying of several indicators can be powerful visual aids in this process and promote com-munity approaches to problem-solving.

Fourth, panel studies of change in multiple indicators across multiple commu-nity areas are possible (Pandey and Coulton 1994). Such analyses can suggest the degree to which change in an indicator leads or lags change in other indicators. This knowledge can allow communities to anticipate improvement or deteriora-tion and react accordingly.

Finally, indices that capture the metropolitan-wide distribution of community indicators are quite useful. For example, an important concern today is that poor children and their families are often isolated from the rest of the population in inner-city enclaves and this concentration of families at risk is particularly detri-mental (Wilson 1987). A commonly used method of determining this level of concentration is to establish a threshold that is considered detrimental. With respect to poverty, census tracts with poverty rates of 40 percent or more are considered extreme poverty areas (Kasarda 1993). A resulting index of concentra-tion pertinent to child well-being is the percentage of all children in a county or metropolitan area who live in these extreme poverty neighborhoods.

Another method of determining the local distribution of child well-being is to calculate an index of dissimilarity (D) (Lieberson 1980) for selected child out-comes. For example, the degree to which low birth weight babies are segregated from babies whose weights are in the normal range could be calculated for a metropolitan area. The D index varies from 0 to 1 and represents the proportion of those babies who would have to be moved to achieve an even distribution of low birth weight babies throughout the metropolitan area. It reveals the amount of segregation of childhood outcomes within the metropolitan area.

COMMUNITY INVOLVEMENT AND DISSEMINATION OF INDICATORS

Perhaps more than at any other level, the development of community indicators requires the involvement of local residents and leaders. They need to be involved in designating the appropriate geographic units to be studied as well as setting priorities regarding the types of indicators to be sought. Because of the demands of data cleaning and geocoding, the generation of community indicators can be quite expensive and the community needs to influence the choices that are made.

Community residents and leaders also play an important role in interpreting trends and patterns that are observed in the indicators. They are aware of changes that are occurring in their communities that may account for the findings. They are also the vehicle for converting the information that indicators provide into action.

Since local and state administrative agencies are the source of much community indicator data, their involvement is essential, too. Collaborative relationships need to be established so that the agency as well as the community can benefit from the information that is generated. Data preparation may be burdensome for the agency and there are often serious concerns about the protection of confidentiality, especially since addresses are needed for geocoding. These barriers can be overcome when all parties see the benefit of producing the information.

Getting community-level indicators into the hands of the public in a useful format is not a trivial problem, though. Because there are so many units of geography of potential interest, the indicators need to be part of a system that can be quickly and easily manipulated, preferably by users as well as analysts. Taking Cleveland and its suburbs as an example, there are 1,535 block groups, 495 census tracts, 35 city neighborhoods, and 58 suburban municipalities. Indicators for each of these units need to be readily available.

To accommodate these hierarchically structured units of geography and over eighty indicators for a thirteen-year period, we have created an interactive information system that is available to community-based organizations (Chow and Coulton 1996). Using the system that we have named Cleveland Area Network for Data and Organizing (CANDO), users can generate their own geography and trend analyses for indicators of their choice. We also produce a hard-copy report of selected indicators each year for one unit of geography, the thirty-five Cleveland neighborhoods.

A NATIONAL SYSTEM OF COMMUNITY INDICATORS

Recent advances in geographic information systems and computing networks have allowed many metropolitan areas to begin generating community area indicators. Several cities such as Cleveland, Providence, Atlanta, Chicago, Boston, Denver, and Oakland, to name a few, are moving toward systems that create, store, and analyze relatively comprehensive sets of indicators for small geographic areas. They use a combination of census and administrative agency data and occasionally special-purpose surveys and other unique data sources.

Local efforts such as these can contribute to a greater national understanding of the well-being of children in communities if they become linked together. Such linking requires considerable effort, however. A number of issues need to be addressed.

First, definitions of communities and neighborhoods need to be refined. Criteria need to be established for setting boundaries that are practical, meaningful, and comparable across cities. Perhaps several different methods of aggregation will be required depending upon whether the focus is on outcomes or community context, for example.

Second, a uniform set of indicators must be defined for collection in multiple metropolitan areas. The list should be of manageable size but also capture most of the types of outcomes that are important. Some of the indicators selected should measure context as well so that variance in outcomes can be examined as a function of differences in context across metropolitan areas.

Third, administrative records from various jurisdictions must be studied to determine comparability. State and local authorities will differ in reporting requirements, classification systems, and patterns of error and bias in their records. Methods of standardizing information across jurisdictions will be essential.

Finally, a common approach to estimating population at the block group or census tract level in intercensal years will be required. The method used will need to be equally valid in all regions to make the community indicators comparable. A single national data source would facilitate this, although common local data sources should also be tested.

Comparable community indicators that are provided by many states and metropolitan areas should eventually be able to inform policy debates. Many federal programs are passed through to the local level for implementation, but the outcomes currently are not available for the small areas for which the programs have been targeted. This gap could be filled by a national system of community indicators. Without community indicators, little can be known nationally about the local context in which children live and toward which national policy is directed.

CONCLUSIONS AND RECOMMENDATIONS

The ecological context of childhood includes the community as an essential feature. Indicators of children's well-being should be available for community areas, even though the mechanisms through which children are affected are only beginning to be understood. Both outcome and contextual measures are desirable, but at a minimum, communities should collect the outcome indicators in table 17.1. These are essential for local planning and evaluation and should be produced yearly in most instances. Community indicators also can contribute to a national understanding of children's well-being within their residential locales.

Since administrative records are often relied upon, local agencies should be encouraged to examine their databases as potential sources for valid community information. Adding geocoding capacity to agency systems can reduce error and overcome problems of confidentiality involved with releasing actual addresses. State- and national-level reporting standards should be developed for administrative records so that indicators based on administrative data can become more reliable and comparable.

Consideration should also be given to designing surveys that will allow measurement at the community area level. Although surveys may be impractical for ongoing measurement, survey findings are useful for validating indicators based on other sources of data. Sampling designs in most existing surveys have insufficient respondents from any community area to allow aggregate measures of community characteristics. However, multistage samples in which households are sampled within block groups or census tracts may be adapted for this purpose and this strategy should be encouraged.

Most community indicators must be adjusted for population size. The lack of population estimates between censuses for block groups or census tracts now limit the validity and comparability of community indicators. Federal leadership is required in this area along with local community involvement. The diversity of methods and data sources that are now being used limit comparability from one state or metropolitan area to another. National data sources such as postal address files would have considerably less variability than current local sources and these methodologies should be tested.

National standards for community indicators are worthy of experimentation. This effort must be led by local communities with experience in developing their own systems of indicators. Communities would not be expected to limit their own interests to areas covered by the national standards. Yet, a national system could guarantee a minimum base of information that would be widely available. Experimentation of this sort should also move the field toward an emerging consensus regarding definitions of community and its important dimensions for child well-being.

Finally, community indicator development must be informed by research to address the complex question of how communities affect families and children. The negative and positive childhood outcomes that are now of significant policy focus are certainly fostered or prevented to some degree by resources and processes within the community. However, thus far, the scientific literature contains considerable ambiguity regarding the strength and direction of these forces. To reduce this ambiguity, it is particularly important that researchers move beyond static models of neighborhood effects toward models that are dynamic and reciprocal. A mix of quantitative and qualitative methods is needed to uncover these processes and reveal how and why communities change and influence the resident families and children. Community indicators can be refined as this understanding unfolds.

NOTE

1. The TIGER files are computer files that link addresses to map coordinates. They are prepared by the Census Bureau.

REFERENCES

Brooks-Gunn, J., G. J. Duncan, P. K. Klebanov, and N. Sealand. 1993. "Do Neighborhoods Influence Child and Adolescent Development?" *American Journal of Sociology* 99: 353–95.

Bursik, R. J., and H. G. Grasmick. 1993. *Neighborhoods and Crime.* New York: Lexington Books.

Caspi, A., N. Bolger, and J. E. Eckenrode. 1987. "Linking Person and Context in the Daily Stress Process." *Journal of Personality and Social Psychology* 52: 184–95.

Chow, J., C. J. Coulton. 1996. "Strategic Use of a Community Database for Planning and Practice." *Computers in Human Services* 13: 57–72.

Clark, R. 1992. *Neighborhood Effects on Dropping Out of School among Teenage Boys.* Washington, DC.: The Urban Institute.

Coulton, C. 1996. "Effects of Neighborhoods in Large Cities on Families and Children: Implications for Services." In *Children and Their Families in Big Cities,* edited by A. Kahn and S. Kammerman. New York: Cross National Studies Research Program.

Coulton, C., J. Korbin, J. Chow, and M. Su. 1995. Community Level Factors and Child Maltreatment Rates. *Child Development* 66: 1262–76.

Coulton, C. J., and S. Pandey. 1992. "Geographic Concentration of Poverty and Risk to Children in Urban Neighborhoods." *American Behavioral Scientist* 35: 238–57.

Crane, J. 1991. "Effects of Neighborhoods on Dropping Out of School and Teenage Childbearing." In *The Urban Underclass,* edited by C. Jencks and P. E. Peterson. Washington, D.C.: The Brookings Institution.

Duncan, G. J. 1993. *Families and Neighbors as Sources of Disadvantage in the Schooling Decisions of White and Black Adolescents.* Ann Arbor, Mich.: University of Michigan Press.

Entwisle, B. 1991. "Micro-Macro Theoretical Linkages in Social Demography: A Commentary." In *Macro-Micro Linkages in Sociology,* edited by J. Huber. Newbury Park, Calif.: Sage.

Freudenburg, W. R. 1986. The Density of Acquaintanceship: An Overlooked Variable in Community Research. *American Journal of Sociology* 92: 27–63.

Furstenberg, F. F. 1993. How Families Manage Risk and Opportunity in Dangerous Neighborhoods. In *Sociology and the Public Agenda,* edited by W. J. Wilson. Newbury Park, Calif.: Sage Publications.

Galster, G. C. 1986. "What Is Neighborhood? An Externality-Space Approach." *International Journal of Urban and Regional Research* 10: 243–61.

Galster, G. C., and G. W. Hesser. 1982. The Social Neighborhood: An Unspecified Factor in Homeowner Maintenance? *Urban Affairs Quarterly* 18: 235–54.

Galster, G. C., and R. B. Mincey. 1993. "Understanding the Changing Fortunes of Metropolitan Neighborhoods: 1980 to 1990." *Housing Policy Debate* 4: 303–48.

Garbarino, J., N. Dubrow, K. Kostelny, and C. Pardo. 1992. *Children in Danger.* San Francisco: Jossey Bass.

Garbarino, J., and D. Sherman. 1980. "High-Risk Neighborhoods and High-Risk Families: The Human Ecology of Child Maltreatment." *Child Development* 51: 188–98.

Heeringa, S. G. 1982. "Statistical Models for Small Area Estimation." *Readings in Population Research Methodology* 5: 126–32.

Jencks, C., and S. E. Mayer. 1990. "The Social Consequences of Growing Up in a Poor Neighborhood." In *Inner-City Poverty in the United States,* edited by L. E. Lynn and M. G. H. McGeary. Washington, D.C.: National Academy Press.

Kasarda, J. 1993. "Inner-City Concentrated Poverty and Neighborhood Distress: 1970 to 1990." *Housing Policy Debate* 4: 253–302.

Korbin, J. E., and C. J. Coulton. 1994. Final Report: *Neighborhood Impact on Child Abuse and Neglect.* Washington, D.C.: National Center for Child Abuse and Neglect.

Lee, B. A., K. E. Campbell, and O. Miller. 1991. "Racial Differences in Urban Neighboring." *Sociological Forum* 6: 525–50.

Lieberson, S. 1980. *A Piece of the Pie: Blacks and White Immigrants since 1880.* Berkeley, Calif.: University of California Press.

Lyon, L. 1987. *The Community in Urban Society.* Chicago: Dorsey Press.

Martinez, J. E., and P. Richters. 1993. "The National Institutes of Mental Health Community Violence Project: Children's Distress Symptoms Associated with Violence Exposure." *Psychiatry* 56: 22–35.

McAdoo, H. P. 1986. "Strategies Used by Black Single Mothers against Stress." *Review of Black Political Economy* 14: 153–66.

O'Brien, R. M. 1985. *Crime and Victimization Data.* Newbury Park, Calif.: Sage Publications.

O'Toole, R., P. Turbett, and C. Nalpeka. 1983. "Theories, Professional Knowledge, and Diagnosis of Child Abuse." In *The Dark Side of Families: Current Family Violence Research,* edited by D. Finkelhor, R. Gelles, G. Hotaling, and M. Strauss. Newbury Park, Calif.: Sage Publications.

Pandey, S., and C. J. Coulton. 1994. "Unraveling Neighborhood Change Using Two-Wave Panel Analysis: A Case Study of Cleveland in the 80s." *Social Work Research* 18: 83–96.

Riley, D., and J. Eckenrode. 1986. "Social Ties: Subgroup Differences in Costs and Benefits." *Journal of Personality and Social Psychology* 51: 770–78.

Rossi, P. 1970. *Community Social Indicators.* Baltimore, Md.: Johns Hopkins University Press.

Sampson, R. J. 1985. "Neighborhood and Crime: The Structural Determinants of Personal Victimization." *Journal of Research in Crime and Delinquency* 22: 7–40.

————. 1991. "Linking the Micro- and Macro-Level Dimensions of Community Social Organization." *Social Forces* 70: 43–64.

————. 1992. "Family Management and Child Development: Insights from Social Disorganization Theory." *Advances in Criminological Theory* 3: 63–93.

Sampson, R. J., and W. B. Groves. 1989. "Community Structure and Crime: Testing Social-Disorganization Theory." *American Journal of Sociology* 94: 775–802.

Sherman, L. 1989. "Hot Spots of Predatory Crime: Routine Activities and the Criminology of Place." *Criminology* 27: 27–56.

Skogan, W. G. 1990. *Disorder and Decline*. Berkeley, Calif.: University of California Press.

Smith, S. K., and S. Cody. 1994. "Evaluating the Housing Unit Method." *APA Journal* 60: 209–21.

Steinberg, L., and N. Darling. 1994. The Broader Context of Social Influence in Adolescence. In *Adolescence in Context*, edited by R. Silbereisen and E. Todt. New York: Springer.

Steinberg, L., S. D. Lamborn, S. M. Dornbush, and N. Darling. 1992. "Impact of Parenting Practices on Adolescent Achievement: Authoritative Parenting, School Involvement and Encouragement to Succeed." *Child Development* 63: 1266–81.

Taylor, R. B., S. D. Gottfredson, and S. Brower. 1984. "Block Crime and Fear: Defensible Space, Local Social Ties, and Territorial Functioning." *Journal of Research in Crime and Delinquency* 21: 303–31.

Tienda, M. 1991. "Poor People and Poor Places: Deciphering Neighborhood Effects on Poverty Outcomes." In *Macro-Micro Linkages in Sociology*, edited by J. Huber. Newbury Park, Calif.: Sage.

White, M. 1987. *American Neighborhoods and Residential Differentiation*. New York: Russell Sage Foundation.

Wilson, W. J. 1987. *The Truly Disadvantaged: The Inner City, the Underclass, and Public Policy*. Chicago: The University of Chicago Press.

Zapata, B. C., A. Rebolledo, E. Atalah, B. Newman, and M. C. King. 1992. "The Influence of Social and Political Violence on the Risk of Pregnancy Complications." *American Journal of Public Health* 82: 685–90.

Zill, N. 1991. *Improving* Kids Count: *Review of an Annual Data Book on the Condition of Children in the Fifty States of the U.S.* Washington, D.C.: Child Trends.

Zill, N., and C. W. Nord. 1994. *Running in Place: How American Families are Faring in a Changing Economy and Individualistic Society*. Washington, D.C.: Child Trends.

Part VI

Social Development and Problem Behavior

18

Indicators of Positive Development in Early Childhood: Improving Concepts and Measures

J. Lawrence Aber and Stephanie M. Jones

ACCORDING TO TAKANISHI and her colleagues (see Chapter 20, this volume), research on adolescent development has yielded more concepts and measures describing maladaptation and problematic development than those describing adaptation and positive development. While not as extreme, much the same can be said of research on early childhood development. But for reasons put forward by Moore (Chapter 2, this volume) and Brooks-Gunn, Brown, Duncan, and Moore (1994), designers of systems of childhood indicators should balance their emphasis between measures of positive development and measures of problematic development.

There are good conceptual and policy reasons to create an indicator system that includes measures of both positive and negative development and status. The main conceptual reason is that not all things that sound unidimensional are unidimensional. Take for example, children's expression of emotion. Measures of positive affect and measures of negative affect are empirically independent if rated separately (rather than being forced onto a single continuum from positive to negative). Children rated as high in both positive and negative affect have very different developmental histories and future life chances than children rated as high on negative affect only (Belsky, Hsieh, and Crnic 1996). Similarly, authoritative and authoritarian parenting styles can be forced onto a single dimension or rated independently. When rated independently, the combination of high authoritative and high authoritarian parenting has a very different effect on the cognitive development of low-income preschoolers than the combination of high authoritative and low authoritarian parenting (Morris, Aber, and Brooks-Gunn forthcoming). In short, the positive is not always the opposite of the negative. Thus, concepts and measures of positive development should be and can be developed in their own right.

The main policy reason for separately conceptualizing and measuring features of positive development is that program or policy efforts targeted at reducing negative outcomes are not the same as efforts targeted at increasing positive outcomes. Early childhood programs may reduce the number of I.Q.'s below 70 and/or raise the number above 115. They may reduce the expression of behavior problems and/or enhance children's mental health. They may reduce school failure and/or increase school success. To the extent that indicators of positive development are conceptually and empirically distinct from indicators of negative development, they offer a whole new perspective on the full range of program and policy issues for which we are developing indicator systems.

In this chapter, we focus on indicators of positive development in early childhood. Further, they are "indicators that pertain directly to child outcomes and children's well-being" rather than "indicators of institutional or jurisdictional performance." We have construed early childhood to cover the periods from infancy to late childhood, roughly ages birth to ten years, and to explicitly end before preadolescence/early adolescence. We address the state of indicators; the prospects for improved indicators by the end of the decade; and the steps, data sources, and methods required to obtain better indicators. Because the number of feasible, well-validated indicators of positive development in early childhood that meet Moore's (Chapter 2, this volume) criteria for indicators are few, and because the few that exist are described and analyzed in Brooks-Gunn et al. (1994) and Love (Chapter 19, this volume), we only briefly will discuss the current status of indicators. Rather, we focus on the concepts and methods which we believe are necessary to improve prospects for better indicators of positive development in early childhood. As has been emphasized by several other authors (Brooks-Gunn et al. 1994; Takanishi, Mortimer, and McGourthy this volume), in light of scarce resources, tough trade-off decisions will have to be made about how to invest our "indicator" dollars.

In individual evaluations and surveys, the trade-off which designers make nearly always involves a conservative bias in favor of already established measures of proven feasibility, reliability, and validity. We interpret the compilation of this volume on indicators of children's well-being, as well as several other national and international efforts (Ben-Arieh 1997), to indicate that we are becoming aware of some of the costs of this conservatism in reducing the ultimate power and value of future indicators of child well-being. Thus, it is to the future that we will be looking in these comments.

CURRENT STATUS OF INDICATORS OF POSITIVE DEVELOPMENT IN EARLY CHILDHOOD

We are interested in creating social indicators for a variety of purposes. These include: raising public awareness of, concern with, or attention to issues of children's well-being (consciousness-raising); monitoring and tracking the well-being of children in specifically defined political jurisdictions to promote action at the levels of cities and towns, states, regions, and the nation (social forecasting); and for use in academic and policy research to test explanatory models of the influence of economic, social, and program/policy factors on children's development (causal modeling). It is ideal when indicators can well serve consciousness-raising, social forecasting, and causal modeling purposes all at once, but there is certainly no guarantee that they will. Indeed, some measures most effective for consciousness-raising purposes may be highly ineffective for use in causal modeling, and vice versa.

The best examples to date of indicators bred for consciousness-raising (and to some extent, social forecasting) purposes are measures developed for *Kids Count* (1994) or similar efforts. Unfortunately, they focus nearly exclusively on indicators of negative status or problematic development. The death rate for children ages one to fourteen, the juvenile violent crime arrest rate and the percentage of children in poverty are examples of the indicators used by *Kids Count* to assess children's well-being. Childhood indicators bred for academic and policy research (and to some extent social forecasting) are much more likely to include measures of positive development. Examples of data sets with some indicators of positive development (that meet Moore's criteria of "indicators") include: the National Longitudinal Survey of Youth–Mother/Child Data (NLSY–M/C); the National Survey of Children (NSC); the National Health Interview Survey–Child Health Supplement (NHIS–CHS) (1988); and the National Survey of Families and Households (NSFH). Brooks-Gunn et al. (1994) describe and compare/contrast these and several other data sets and present numerous recommendations to improve the quality of indicators for use in policy research. The NLSY–M/C, NSC, and NSFH collected a broad array of age-appropriate child outcome measures in the domains of physical, cognitive, and social-emotional development. These domains were assessed using different information sources for different surveys (NLSY: mother interviews and in-home child assessment; NSC: interviews with parents, teachers, and children; NSFH: interviews with parents only).

As we will argue in this chapter, indicators should (nearly) always include children, not just their parents, as an important data source. Many of the ideas we outline below about how to develop improved indicators of children's well-being involve how to elicit and record responses from the children themselves. It is critical to give children a more direct voice in assessing their well-being. In addition, we will also argue that we should move beyond age-appropriate measures to the identification and creation of *stage-salient* measures to include in our tool kits of key indicators.

Data sets and measures developed for consciousness-raising (like the *Kids Count* data sets) are able to be collected longitudinally, can achieve considerable geographic specificity, but focus on negative outcomes to the exclusion of positive outcomes. Data sets and measures developed for testing causal models are too often cross-sectional or restricted to a very few longitudinal waves, cannot be reported at the level of political jurisdictions, but more often include measures of positive development. What is needed is to combine the longitudinal feasibility and geographic specificity of consciousness-raising measures with the emphasis on positive development and age-sensitivity of causal modeling measures. Most important, we need to go beyond the few standard measures of cognitive development (for example, the PPVT) and behavior problems (the Behavior Problem Index) to measures/indicators that operationalize the concept of positive development in a richer, more powerful, and useful way. But in order to measure positive development, especially in early childhood, we first have to decide what it is.

PROSPECTS FOR IMPROVED INDICATORS OF POSITIVE DEVELOPMENT IN EARLY CHILDHOOD

As Moore (chapter 2, this volume) points out, current approaches to the use of childhood indicators rarely assess positive behavior and development. We believe that there are two major reasons for the paucity of indicators of positive development in early childhood. First, like Moore, we believe there is little agreement over or discussion of the behavior and characteristics that define positive development. "Americans may agree that the absence of serious problems . . . is a component of positive development; but presumably there is 'something more' than the simple absence of problems" (Moore, this volume). Future prospects for better indicators of positive development depend heavily on our ability to conceptualize positive development. The conceptualization of positive development in the early childhood years is the main focus of this section of this chapter.

A second reason for the paucity of indicators of positive development is the continuing gap between developmental theories and methods, on the one hand, and sociological/economic theories and methods, especially survey methods, on the other—and this despite the efforts of many in this volume. This issue of theoretical rapprochements and methodological innovations will be the focus of a later section of the chapter.

While there has been little discussion of the concept of positive development in society more generally or in the social indicators field more specifically, discussions have begun in the fields of both child and youth policy (Zigler and Trickett 1978; Pittman and Cahill 1992; Hamburg 1990) and child and adolescent development (Sroufe 1983; Connell, Aber, and Walker 1995). Several theorists argue that childhood development is characterized by rapid growth and change in basic physical, cognitive, behavioral, and social-emotional capacities. Growth in these capacities requires and permits the reorganization and reintegration of these developing systems of capacities. One way to theoretically capture the orderly nature of these reorganizations of developing systems is with the concept of "stage-salient developmental tasks." Stage-salient developmental tasks are those newly emergent tasks which children must face (in particular social/cultural contexts) using their most recently developed capacities and which are critical to children's immediate and long-term adaptation. They represent the cutting edge of development where individual differences in the quality of adaptation and development are easily discerned. If individual differences in mastering stage-salient tasks are easily discerned, this has implications for the creation of indicators of positive development.

Perhaps the most widely influential early theory of stage-salient tasks was described by Erik Erikson when he presented his theory of eight major stages of psychosocial development over the life span in *Childhood and Society* (1950). Over the last twenty years, a number of developmentalists have built upon this idea and created a theory of stage-salient developmental tasks of early childhood that they began to operationalize through various measurement and assessment procedures (Sroufe 1983). These theoretical and methodological developments have led to success in describing and explaining continuity in adaptation/maladaptation in early development.

On the basis of these developments and successes, one potentially useful way to conceive of positive development is as children's success in negotiating this series of stage-salient developmental tasks. In table 18.1, we present a set of stage-salient tasks of early childhood, slightly modified from a similar set described by Sroufe (1983). After briefly describing the tasks and current ways of operationalizing them, we will discuss some of the benefits and costs of conceptualizing "positive development" in this way for the field of childhood indicators.

Table 18.1   Conceptualizing Positive Development as a Series of Stage-Salient Developmental Tasks to Be Negotiated

Transition Between Stages	Age Range	Developmental Task
Infancy/toddlerhood	0–3	Develop trusting relationships with primary caregivers and a sense of basic security.
Toddlerhood/preschool	2–5	Become actively curious, deeply explorative and inquisitive.
Preschool/early school age	4–7	Develop the ability to self-regulate thoughts, behavior, and emotions and to flexibly adjust the level of regulation/control to the demand and opportunities of different and changing contexts.
Early school age/middle childhood	6–9	Develop the skills to negotiate conflicts and solve interpersonal problems in nonaggressive ways.
Middle to late childhood	8–11	Consolidate a sense of self as competent and efficacious, in both social and academic spheres of life.

Stage-Salient Developmental Tasks of Early Childhood

This chapter is not the appropriate forum for a full explanation of the concept of stage-salient developmental tasks (see Sroufe 1979 for a full explanation). But since we are arguing that future prospects for improved measures of positive development in early childhood depend so heavily on this conceptualization, we must describe the general idea and some key tasks in more detail so that the logic of the argument is available for review.

The basic idea behind table 18.1 is that there is a hierarchy or set of priorities to the tasks of early childhood. Because humans are born in such a helpless state and depend on their relationships with their primary caregivers for protection, sustenance, emotional support, and cognitive stimulation, the most important task of infancy is develop a strong and trusting relationship with a finite set of primary caregivers. Only after infants develop a secure attachment to their primary caregivers are they optimally prepared to use those primary relationships as a secure base to go out and actively explore and learn about the world. According to this framework, developing an active curiosity, a skill at exploring the interpersonal and object worlds, and balancing exploration with maintaining a sense of security are the key tasks of toddlerhood.

As children's cognitive and metacognitive skills mature, they begin to exercise (and adults begin to expect them to exercise) more self-regulation of thought, behavior, and emotion. Developing self-control and the flexibility to adjust the level of self-control to the demands and opportunities of different and changing contexts is the key stage-salient task of the preschool years.

A certain capacity for self-regulation is necessary before children can begin to develop more advanced skills in negotiating interpersonal conflicts and in solving social problems, especially with peers (who are less skilled), rather than adults (who on average are more skilled), in nonaggressive ways. The development of interpersonal negotiation strategies and social problem-solving skills, especially in highly conflictual situations with peers, represents the cutting edge of social-emotional development in the early school-age years.

Finally, in middle to late childhood, building on the significant cognitive and social-emotional advances of early childhood, children begin to consolidate a sense of self. Individual differences in perception of self as competent and efficacious become more pronounced and increasingly predict behavior in both the social and academic spheres of life.

At present, each of these constructs can be measured quite effectively using labor-intensive "high-fidelity" methods in both laboratory and field conditions. Table 18.2 briefly reviews methods currently used by developmentalists to assess these constructs from infancy to early childhood. But with one or two important exceptions, these constructs are not yet able to be assessed using large-scale survey assessment techniques. This is the second major limit to improving indicators of positive development. (We will address this limit later in this chapter.)

Several other points are important to make regarding this way of conceptualizing positive development. First, stage-salient tasks do not mean stage-specific tasks. These tasks are not important at only one stage of development. On the contrary, most of them are life-course developmental issues. Each has precursers in earlier stages of development before it becomes especially salient. For example, before the preschool years in which self-regulation becomes salient, developmental precursers to self-regulation emerge in infancy (homeostatic regulation) and toddlerhood (elementary self-control) (see Kopp 1982 for a full description of the development of self-regulation). Each also remains an important feature of psychosocial functioning throughout the rest of the life course. Issues of trust/security and nonaggressive negotiation of conflict affect the quality of adaptation

Table 18.2   Current Methods Available to Assess Children's Success in Negotiating Stage-Salient Tasks

Age	Construct	Method	References
0–3	Security	Strange situation (lab)	Ainsworth et al. 1978
		Home-based Q-sort (parent rating)	Waters and Deane 1985
		Center-based Q-sort (caregiver rating)	Aber and Baker 1990
2–5	Curiosity	Curiosity Box	Arend, Gove, and Sroufe 1979
4–7	Self-regulation	Waiting game (lab)	Mischel et al. 1983, 1989
		California Q-sort (parent or caregiver rating)	Block and Block 1969, 1980
6–9	Interpersonal negotiation and problem-solving skills	Attributional bias scale (child assess)	Dodge and Frame 1982
		Social problem-solving measure (child assess)	Lochman and Dodge 1994
8–11	Self-efficacy/competence	PCCS (child assess)	Harter 1983, 1985

throughout life and may rise and fall in importance at various other points in the life course. What is meant by stage-salience is that this task becomes of overriding importance to the quality of adaptation for the first time at about this stage of development. That is what we mean by referring to stage-salient tasks as the cutting edge of development. And that is why, for an indicator system which wants to include measures of positive development, the concept offers some power. At that stage, an assessment of children in that domain is likely to be the clearest window into the quality of their adaptation. In addition, measures of the quality of adaptation to earlier stage-salient tasks are the best predictors of quality of adaptation to later stage-salient tasks (Sroufe 1979).

Second, this conceptualization of positive development emphasizes social-emotional development. There are both practical and theoretical reasons why we have chosen to do so. Practically, there are better measures that are usable in large-scale surveys for cognitive and physical development than for social-emotional development. Consequently, measures of cognitive and physical development have been employed more broadly in social indicator systems to date. Therefore, as a practical matter, we decided to focus on measures of positive social-emotional development in the hope of making a stronger case for their inclusion, and thus stimulating the work it will take to make good measures of social-emotional development available for large-scale indicator systems. We are not arguing that a full conceptualization of positive development should not include measures of cognitive and physical development. They should. (See Love, Aber, Brooks-Gunn 1994 for a similar argument about the difficulty of measuring social-emotional features of school readiness compared to cognitive development or physical health features.)

Theoretically we believe there is mounting evidence that supports a long-standing philosophy of early education that emphasizes the primacy of the social-emotional bases of later learning. For example, in a growing number of studies, measures of social-emotional development at earlier stages are better than earlier measures of cognitive development for predicting cognitive development and academic achievement at later stages (Alexander, Entwisle, and Dauber 1993; Entwisle and Alexander 1993).

Third, in this conceptualization of positive development, we have emphasized the abilities of the child, not the *contexts* of *inputs* to or *outcomes* of development. A comprehensive framework for understanding positive development will include concepts and measures of each of these features as well. (See Brooks-Gunn et al. 1994 for a discussion of this larger framework.) The ability to negotiate stage-salient tasks that we have described as at the heart of positive development is the dynamic feature of development that links inputs into development (like the quality of parenting, the quality of child care, the influence of peers) with policy-relevant outcomes (such as school-readiness, academic achievement, the development of severe behavioral and mental health problems). Therefore, contexts, inputs, and outcomes need to be conceptualized in stage-salient terms as well.

Specifically, there is a clear shift in the salience of certain developmental contexts as children move from one developmental stage to another. For example, primary caregivers are especially important earlier in development. They always remain important, but secondary caregivers (teachers and peers) become increasingly important later in development. Similarly, at the most general level, the quality of parenting is a crucially important input into development throughout childhood, but different features of parenting shift in salience over time. In infancy, the sensitivity of the parent in reading the baby's cues and the parent's contingent responsiveness to those cues are critical inputs into the stage-salient task of developing a secure relationship with the primary caretaker. Later, the parents' ability to help their toddler and preschooler cope with frustration during a difficult problem-solving task and derive a sense of mastery in coping with frustrating tasks are stage-salient parental inputs into the development of self-regulation. The implications of the concept of stage-salient tasks for conceptualizing and measuring contexts, inputs, and outcomes in an indicator system are important to work through. To my mind, what we have to decide is whether the potential coherence and power that adapting this developmental perspective on indicators provides can be achieved practically through the development of good measures capable of being used in large, field-based surveys, and is worth the added complexity that this perspective undoubtedly brings to the task of designing indicator systems. We will turn to these issues in the last section of this chapter.

Costs and Benefits of Conceptualizing "Positive Development in Early Childhood" as Success in Negotiating Stage-Salient Tasks

As we have suggested, the major costs for an indicator system of conceptualizing "positive development" in the manner described above are: the added complexity it brings to measurement and sampling; and the delay in including measures of positive development immediately, since there are few measures that are field-ready and can be pulled off the shelf. (This of course assumes that if we make the effort to develop survey-use measures of success in negotiating those stage-salient tasks, we will succeed. For reasons described later, we believe we will.) We believe the long-term benefits outweigh these short-term costs.

We will not pretend that the stage-salient tasks we have outlined are universal. Indeed, they are likely to be somewhat culture- and context-specific, at least in their details. But we assert that in the modern United States they have broad if not universal appeal and relevance. (Certainly, they have evidence supporting their predictive validity in forecasting later adaptation for samples of both African American and white children from both low-income and moderate-income families.)

We believe that if over the first five years of life, a child develops a sense of trust and security, curiosity and exploration skills, self-regulation and flexibility, then most parents would say "my child is developing positively" and most teachers would say "that child is ready for school." Similarly, if a child over the first five years of formal schooling (in addition to learning how to read, write, and think), develops skills to negotiate conflicts in nonaggressive ways and a realistic sense of self as competent and efficacious in both the social-emotional and cognitive-academic spheres of life, once again most parents would say "my child is developing positively" and most teachers would say "that child is ready for middle school/junior high school." In short, we are asserting the face validity of this conceptualization of positive development for parents and teachers. But we do not have to guess at this. We believe the face validity of criteria for positive development by parents and teachers is fundamental to the acceptance of these indicators, both by the public and by the policymakers who will use these indicators in making important decisions about resource deployment and the like. Consequently, we strongly recommend that studies of the parent and teacher beliefs and perceptions about criteria for positive development be conducted as part of the further development of indicators of positive development.

There are several other important advantages to this approach to conceptualizing and measuring positive development in early childhood. First and most important, it is built on twenty years of theory development and empirical research in child development (Ainsworth, Blehar, Waters, and Wall 1978; Arend, Gove, and Sroufe 1979; Sroufe 1979, 1983; Dodge 1980, 1986; Mischel and Mischel 1983; Mischel, Shoda, and Rodriguez 1989; Harter 1983, 1985). We understand the nature of those phenomena better than we did ten and twenty years ago; each of these phenomena is still the object of intensive scientific investigation, so theory and measurement will continue to advance; there is a growing cadre of young scientists working on these issues and interested in social policy toward children and families who are technically prepared to help make the methodological advances we will describe in the next section. For all those reasons, they seem like good concepts on which to focus intensive measure development work for use as indicators as defined by Moore (this volume).

Second, measures of these concepts permit us to monitor and examine children's development over critical program- and policy-relevant transitions as defined by Brooks-Gunn et al. (1994). Because of the rapid secular change in population, Brooks-Gunn et al. argue for short-term cross-sequential designs in policy-relevant research on child development. As we read their recommendations, they are arguing for launching multiple cohort studies that overlap every five to ten years. The framework and measurement described here enable policy researchers to focus on key processes that are believed to index the quality of adaptation over relatively short periods of time, that is, over the transition from one developmental stage to the next. It is important to note that because of the stage-salience of particular contexts, this framework has potentially greater policy relevance. The transition from toddlerhood to the preschool years increasingly involves the transition from less formal child care to more formal preschool education. And the transition from the preschool to the early school-age years involves the transition to formal elementary education. Variation in the quality of inputs from each of these contexts and how such variations effect development are the key policy- and program-relevant questions for which many policy researchers and policymakers want to use indicator systems. In our opinion, these uses are facilitated by the perspective on positive development adopted in this chapter.

A third and final advantage to this approach to conceptualizing and measuring positive development is that it helps tell a story to the public and to policymakers about what is important in development. While we may or may not want teachers to teach to the test, we certainly want policymakers and program developers/mangers to program to the indicators of positive development. Because of the causal links that scientific research is establishing between those measures of early adaptation and children's future life chances, it is likely that if programs and policies cause these indicators of positive development to improve, then this will forecast other improvements in indicators of policy-relevant outcomes.

This conceptualization of "positive development" is not offered as the final word but rather as a starting point for discussion among those interested in improving childhood social indicators. No doubt it will benefit from considerable debate, which will result in important modifications.

RECOMMENDATIONS FOR METHODS TO IMPROVE INDICATORS OF POSITIVE DEVELOPMENT IN EARLY CHILDHOOD

In this last section, we will address the methodological issues of how we can proceed to improve indicators of positive development in early childhood. As we indicated, an advantage to basing our conceptualization of positive development on these constructs is that they have already been successfully operationalized using labor-intensive, high-fidelity laboratory procedures. As we have learned more about the nature of these phenomena and as new investigators have begun to wish to use measures of these constructs in large-scale fidelity studies, a productive pressure is mounting to translate laboratory-based measures of key constructs in child development into survey-usable measures.

One example will help illustrate this point. In the early and mid-1980s, Dodge and his colleagues conducted very fruitful research on the developmental processes underlying individual differences in children's aggressive transactions with peers. They hypothesized that processes such as how children interpret the intentions of peers in ambiguous situations (attributions of hostile versus non-hostile intent) and children's social problem-solving skills (competent/prosocial versus incompetent/aggressive) explained why some children responded to provocations by peers in an extremely aggressive manner and some did not (Dodge 1980, 1986). To test these hypotheses derived from their social information processing theory of the development of aggression, they developed several intensive lab-based procedures for the assessment of children's attributions of hostile intent and social problem-solving skills. These procedures involved presenting children with videotaped recordings of peer interactions and expertly probing them on how they interpreted the intentions of the children in the tapes (hostile versus nonhostile) and their behavioral response if they were in the interaction. Children's responses further required expert coding. But these yielded impressive results in support of their hypotheses.

Such labor-intensive procedures are feasible in small-sample basic research studies but are prohibitively costly in time and money in large-sample field research studies. But the utility of the theory and constructs is potentially so high that when large-scale evaluations of intervention projects began to be designed, investigators began the process of trying to develop survey-type formats for assessing those constructs. Thus in order to evaluate an intervention designed to prevent conduct disorder, Dodge and his colleagues have developed and/or adapted field survey–type measures of the same constructs (Dodge and Frame 1982). Similarly, in designing an evaluation of a large-scale violence-prevention initiative in New York City, we and our colleagues at the National Center for Children in Poverty have further adapted the Fast Track survey measures of children's hostile attributional bias and their skills at resolving interpersonal conflicts (Aber, Brown, Chaudry, Jones, and Samples 1996). Data on approximately 7,500 children in grades one through six from our violence-prevention evaluation indicate that it is possible to develop survey-type measures of the same construct with only slightly less reliability and sensitivity than the laboratory-based measures but with greatly enhanced feasibility for use in large-scale field studies.

Not all efforts to adapt survey measures from laboratory measures of the same construct have been as successful as this example. Efforts to develop good survey-type measures of developmental processes for use in studies like Children of the NLSY have met with mixed results. Similarly, our attempts to adapt laboratory measures of parenting processes for use in large-scale evaluation of social programs have also met with mixed results (Aber, Berlin, Brooks-Gunn, and Carcagno 1994). Nonetheless, the experience with the Dodge measures extend the hope that careful work can yield better measures of critical constructs. We now turn to a set of concrete recommendations about how to learn from selected efforts at translating good laboratory measures into good survey measures to improve indicators of positive development.

First, accept the challenge of continuing to find ways to elicit information directly from children. They are the most important data source of information on how they are negotiating stage-salient tasks. Multiple sources of data for these constructs are ideal, but any system is incomplete without direct assessment of children. If we accept this challenge and do not try to get this information in a less valid way, necessity may become the mother of invention (as it has in the Dodge work).

Second, make the methods to elicit information from the children interesting, compelling, relevant, and understandable. Do not survey children as if they are little adults. Build on the growing body of practice wisdom on how to engage children in assessments. Besides Dodge's use of compelling videotapes as stimuli, other methods are proliferating—for instance, the use of blue and yellow puppets who make contrasting statements, so that children decide which puppet they most resemble (Eder and Mangelsdorf 1990).

Third, to make methods more compelling and accessible, make creative use of increasingly inexpensive and powerful modern technologies in field research—such as small, handheld VCRs (to present stimuli) and small laptop computers (both to present questions and record responses).

Fourth, plan to spend more time assessing children than adults; similarly, plan to spend more time training field researchers to work with children than with adults. The time increases only by a factor of two or three per unit of information. Resist the temptation to become more efficient by asking adults what you should be asking children.

Fifth, use multiple methods to improve how we ask questions. Contextualize judgments we ask children and parents to make by asking them "if, then" statements. Questions that take the form "If provoked, I get angry: 1) never, 2) sometimes, 3) often, 4) always" are much more likely to yield highly predictive responses than questions that do not properly contextualize the judgment (Mischel and Shoda forthcoming). Simplify response judgments that need to be made by children. Rather than ask them to rate something on a four-point scale, use two dichotomous judgments. For example:

"Some children are happy"   "Some children are sad"

"Are you more like the happy children or more like the sad children? Are you like the X child or only sort of like the X child?" Consider teaching children the skills they need to respond to you as part of the assessments. For example, for children who cannot read but can recognize forms, "This says YES; this says

NO. Now circle YES or NO." Consider using response formats that do not require that children know how to read. For example:

		X
		X
	X	X
	X	X
X	X	X
X	X	X
a little	some	a lot

Combined with powerful theory, and a history of good labor-intensive empirical work on constructs of interest, these recommendations have the potential of helping us to develop improved indicators of positive development for use in consciousness-raising, social forecasting, and causal modeling. It is time to make a serious investment in nurturing such measures if our interest in tracking positive development as well as problematic development in the emergent field of childhood social indicators is to move from rhetoric to reality.

CONCLUSION

In this chapter, we have argued that indicators of positive development in early childhood need to balance the current emphasis on indicators of problematic development. Further, we have argued that the major drawback to strengthening indicators of positive development is the lack of a shared conception of positive development that is rooted in good theory; supported by empirical evidence; face-valid with parents, teachers, and policymakers; and able to be operationalized not just in the laboratory using labor-intensive, high-fidelity techniques but also in the field using creative adaptations of survey techniques. We proposed "success in negotiating a finite series of stage-salient developmental tasks" as meeting these criteria since it is currently strongly rooted in good theory and has received empirical support in numerous small sample studies, and it has the potential of being perceived as face-valid by parents, teachers, and policymakers and could be operationalized using survey research techniques. The future of this feature of the larger effort at developing better indicators of child well-being hinges on investments in creative measure development and validation work.

We do not want to slow the train. We do want to encourage us to identify the very best measures of positive development in early childhood currently available. But we also want us to face up to the important tasks of concept and measure development if we really want a better child well-being indicator system in the next ten years.

REFERENCES

Aber, J. L., and A. Baker. 1990. "Security of Attachment in Toddlerhood: Modifying Assessment Procedures for Joint Clinical and Research Purposes. In *Attachment in the Preschool Years*, edited by M. Greenberg, D. Cicchetti, and M. Cummings. Chicago: University of Chicago Press.

Aber, J. L., L. Berlin, J. Brooks-Gunn, and G. Carcagno. 1994. "The 'Interactions and Developmental Processes' Study of the Teenage Parent Demonstration Project: Final Report." Working Paper. Princeton, N.J.: Mathematica Policy Research.

Aber, J. L., J. Brown, N. Chaudry, S. Jones, and F. Samples. 1996. "The Evaluations of the Resolving Conflict Creatively Program: An Overview. *Journal of Preventive Medicine*, 12(5) suppl.: 82–90.

Ainsworth, M., M. C. Blehar, E. Waters, and S. Wall. 1978. *Patterns of Attachment: A Psychological Study of the Strange Situation*. Hillsdale, N.J.: Erlbaum.

Alexander, K., D. Entwisle, and S. Dauber. 1993. "First-Grade Classroom Behavior: Its Short- and Long-term Consequences for School Performance." *Child Development* 64(3): 801–14.

Arend, R., F. Gove, and L. A. Sroufe. 1979. Continuity of Individual Adaptation from Infancy to Kindergarten: A Predictive Study of Ego-Resiliency and Curiosity in Preschoolers. *Child Development* 50: 950–59.

Belsky, J., K. Hsieh, and K. Crnic. 1996. "Infant Positive and Negative Emotionality: One Dimension or Two." *Developmental Psychology* 32: 289–98.

Ben-Arieh, Asher, and Helmut Wintersberger, eds. 1997 "Monitoring and Measuring the State of Children—Beyond Survival" EUROSOCIAL Report 62. Vienna, Austria: European Centre for Social Welfare Policy and Research.

Block, J. H., and J. Block. 1969. *The California Child Q-set*. Department of Psychology, University of California Berkeley. Unpublished manuscript.

———. 1980. The Role of Ego Control and Ego Resiliency in the Organization of Behavior. In *Minnesota Symposium on Child Psychology*, edited by W.A. Collins. 13: 39–101. Hillsdale, N.J.: Erlbaum.

Brooks-Gunn, J., B. Brown, G. J. Duncan, and K. Moore. 1994. "Child Development in the Context of Family and Community Resources: An Agenda for National Data Collections." Paper prepared for workshop, "Integrating Federal Statistics on Children," organized by the National Research Council's Committee on National Statistics and the Board on Children and Families, Washington, D.C. (March 31–April 1, 1994).

Center for the Study of Social Policy. 1994. *Kids Count Data Book: State Profiles of Child Well-Being*. Washington, D.C.: Annie E. Casey Foundation.

Connell, J. P., J. L. Aber, and G. Walker. 1995. "How Do Urban Communities Affect Youth?: Using Social Science Research to Inform the Design and Evaluation of Comprehensive Community Initiatives." In *New Approaches to Evaluating Comprehensive Community Initiatives*, edited by J. P. Connell, A. Kubisch, L. Schorr, and C. Weiss. Queenstown, Md.: The Aspen Institute.

Dodge, K. A. 1980. "Social Cognition and Children's Aggressive Behavior." *Child Development* 51: 162–70.

Dodge, K. A. 1986. "A Social Information-Processing Model of Social Competence in Children." In *Minnesota Symposium on Child Psychology*, edited by M. Perlmutter. Hillsdale, N.J.: Erlbaum.

Dodge, K. S., and C. L. Frame. 1982. "Social Cognitive Biases and Deficits in Aggressive Boys." *Child Development* 53: 620–35.

Eder, R., and S. C. Mangelsdorf. 1990. The Emotional Basis of Early Personality Development: Implications for the Emergent Self-Concept. In *Handbook of Personality Psychology*, edited by S. Briggs, R. Hogan, and W. Jones. Orlando, Fla.: Academic Press.

Entwisle, D., and K. Alexander. 1993. "Entry into School: The Beginning School iTransition and Educational Stratification in the United States." *Annual Review of Sociology* 19: 401–23.

Erikson, E. 1950. *Childhood and Society*. New York: W. W. Norton.

Hamburg, B. A. 1990. "Life Skills Training: Preventive Interventions for Young Adolescents." Working Paper. Washington, D.C.: Carnegie Council on Adolescent Development.

Harter, S. 1983. "Competence as a Dimension of Self-Evaluation: Toward a Comprehensive Model of Self-Worth." In *The Development of the Self*, edited by R. Leahy. New York: Academic Press.

———. 1985. "Self-Perception Profile for Children." University of Denver, Denver, Colorado. Unpublished Manuscript.

Kopp, C. B. 1982. "Antecedents of Self-Regulation: A Developmental Perspective." *Developmental Psychology* 18(2): 199–214.

Lochman, J. E., and K. A. Dodge. 1994. "Social Cognition Processes or Severely Violent, Moderately Aggressive and Non Aggressive Boys." *Journal of Consulting and Clinical Psychology* 62: 366–74.

Love, J., J. L. Aber, and J. Brooks-Gunn. 1994. "Strategies for Assessing Community Progress Toward Achieving the First National Education goal." Princeton, N.J.: Mathematica Policy Research.

Mischel, W., and H. N. Mischel. 1983. Development of Children's Knowledge of Self-Control Strategies. *Child Development* 54: 603–19.

Mischel, W., Y. Shoda, and M. Rodriguez. 1989. "Delay of Gratification in Children." *Science* 244: 933–38.

Mischel, W., and Y. Shoda. In press. "A Cognitive-Affective System Theory of Personality: Reconceptualizing the Invariances in Personality and the Role of Situations." *Psychological Review*.

Morris, P., J. L. Aber, and J. Brooks-Gunn. Forthcoming. "Contributions of Parenting Styles to the Cognitive School Readiness of Poor, African American Preschool Children." Unpublished manuscript under review.

Pittman, K., and M. Cahill. 1992. "Youth and Caring: The Role of Youth Programs in the Development of Caring." Commissioned paper for the Lilly Endowment research grant projects on youth and caring. Presented at the Youth and Caring Conference, Miami, Fla. (February 26 and 27, 1992).

Sroufe, A. 1979. "The Coherence of Individual Development: Early Care, Attachment and Subsequent Developmental Issues." *American Psychologist* 34: 194–210.

———. 1983. "Infant-Caregiver Attachment and Patterns of Adaptation in the Preschool: The Roots of Maladaptation and Competence." In *Minnesota Symposium on Child Psychology*, edited by M. Perlmutter 16: 41–83. Hillsdale, N.J.: Erlbaum.

Waters, E., and K. Deane. 1985 "Defining and Assessing Individual Differences in Attachment Relationships: Q-Methodology and the Organization of Behavior in Infancy and Early Childhood. *Monographs for the Society for Research in Child Development* 50: 41–65.

Zigler, E., and P. Trickett. 1978. "IQ, Social Competence, and Evaluation of Early Childhood Intervention Programs." *American Psychologist* 38(9): 789–98.

19

Indicators of Problem Behavior and Problems in Early Childhood

John M. Love

IN ONE BRIEF seven-year span, between 1981 and 1988, the proportion of young people receiving treatment for emotional or behavioral problems increased by more than 50 percent (Zill and Schoenborn 1990). The implications of this rise for our families, schools, and communities lead to increasing concerns with problem behavior and other problems exhibited by America's children. Unfortunately, what we know about these aspects of children's well-being is inconsistent and incomplete. As this chapter shows, our understanding of children's problem behavior and problems from a national perspective is limited by the nature of the questions asked in national surveys, the sampling and timing of the surveys, and our ability to interpret data from varied contexts. This chapter summarizes the state of the indicators of problem behavior and problems in early childhood, evaluates their limitations, suggests ways to improve measurements, and discusses future use of an improved set of indicators.

This chapter is purposely limited in scope. It is limited to concerns about young children from birth to preadolescence (although, in practical terms, we know most about indicators for children at the lower end of that age range). My review of indicators is also limited to the five major national surveys that currently collect or recently have collected information on problems in early childhood and behavior problems of young children. Other research on problems is mentioned primarily to show the importance of particular problems and to justify the use of particular indicators on a national level. Unfortunately, I have found little information on statewide indicators of problems and problem behavior, other than the broad major problem indicators included in the annual *Kids Count* data books: percent of low birth weight babies, infant mortality rate, child death rate, percent of children in poverty, and percent in single-parent families (Annie E. Casey Foundation 1994).[1]

The scope of problem behavior and other problems in young children is potentially enormous. The literature review presented here is highly selective and is not intended to be comprehensive at this stage. I use the shorthand term "problems" to refer to both behavioral problems (such as aggressiveness or withdrawn behavior) and other kinds of problems (such as emotional or cognitive disabilities).

Two major problems facing today's young people are violence and drugs. Both are sensitive issues and are not asked about in the major surveys of young children reviewed here. To accurately learn about the use of illegal substances requires very specialized skill in question design and interviewing. Perhaps for that reason questions on this topic have not been included in these surveys. It is also true, fortunately, that drug abuse is not a large problem with children under the age of eleven (although the problem appears to be increasing among preadolescents). Violence is something that happens to children with high and increasing frequency. In 1993, public social service and child protective agencies received about three million reports of abuse and/or neglect (American Humane Association 1994), three times the number reported in 1980. More than one-third of the reports were substantiated. Other forms of violence, as well as increases in homelessness, hunger, and poverty, all qualify as serious problems in early childhood (Children's Defense Fund 1994). Growing up in a single-parent family, especially when combined with poverty, teenage parenting, and other problems, may constitute an early childhood problem that warrants our attention beyond the overall rates documented in *Kids Count*. These problems—along with problems of physical health that are dealt with by other authors—are beyond the scope of this chapter. I focus here on problems that are reflected in the behavior or development of children.

IDENTIFYING THE MOST IMPORTANT INDICATORS OF PROBLEM BEHAVIOR AND PROBLEMS IN EARLY CHILDHOOD

For a volume on children's well-being, one could ask why essays that focus on "problems" are included. One answer may be that the sorts of behavior representing the flip side of well-being are relatively easy to define and measure. A more meaningful response, however, is that problems are attention-getting—the public, politicians, and policymakers readily respond to "report cards" of well-being if they include alarming rates of problems that directly affect the public or public institutions, such as schools and courts. Furthermore, problems often have clear costs associated with them. An argument can be made that actions to eliminate or reduce the problems are warranted because of the cost savings to society—and this can be done without appealing to the more nebulous benefits of "improving indicators of positive well-being." The benefits of reducing problems are clearly positive outcomes for the children, their families, and society.

There are several systematic ways to think about why a system of indicators of children's well-being should include measures of problems, or the negative side of well-being, and which indicators are the most important to measure. There are at least four considerations. It would be important to measure problems if:

1. The prevalence of the problem (or an increase in its prevalence), in and of itself, raises concerns among policymakers and practitioners working with children and families in the areas of education and social programs. (For example, the prevalence of aggressive behavior among five-year-olds may alert schools to the need to modify programs or prepare teachers to help the children adjust to the social and academic demands of kindergarten.)

2. The problems reflect (or are markers of) the experiences of children and the circumstances in which they live. (For example, anxiety and depression may

tell us something about the emotional support available in children's families or about the stresses families face.)

3. The problems help us understand a broader range of children's well-being. (For example, the prevalence of disabilities may inform us about children's school performance, or emotional problems may be associated with children's social competence with their peers.)

4. The persistence, incidence, or prevalence of problems allow us to predict important events later in children's lives. (For example, dropping out of school, drug abuse, crime, suicide, and intrafamily violence may be foreshadowed by high rates of behavior problems earlier in life.)

Research with young children provides an important backdrop to considerations of state-level or national indicators. I next review evidence related to these four considerations. Although many of the studies reviewed are based on relatively small samples, it is the emerging pattern of relationships that is important for guiding directions for indicator development.

The Prevalence of Behavior Problems Raises Concerns

The prevalence of developmental delays, learning disabilities, emotional and behavioral problems, and various combinations of problems led Zill and Schoenborn (1990) to conclude that these are "among the most prevalent chronic conditions of childhood and adolescence," with nearly 20 percent of three- to seventeen-year-olds having one or more of these conditions (that is, about 10.7 million youngsters). Furthermore, Zill and Schoenborn expressed concern that these figures may, in fact, underestimate the true prevalence, due to parents confusing or not recognizing the terminology used. On the basis of analysis of data from the National Health Interview Survey, Child Health Supplement (NHIS-CHS) conducted in 1988, Zill and Schoenborn reported the following percentages of children and youth, three to seventeen years of age, having:

- delays in growth or development (4.0 percent);
- learning disabilities (6.5 percent);
- significant emotional or behavioral problems (13.4 percent); and who have
- ever received treatment or counseling for these conditions (2 percent for developmental delays, 5 percent for learning disabilities, and over 10 percent for emotional or behavioral problems).

In the broadest terms, there is support for these percentages in a recent review by Benasich et al. (1994). They present evidence from smaller-scale surveys to show that between 15 and 18 percent of children have mild to moderate behavior problems (for example, Links 1983), with perhaps an additional 7 to 10 percent having moderate to severe problems. "Thus, about one-quarter of all children may be identified as having some form of behavior problems" (Benasich et al. 1994).

Behavior problems are also important in our society because their presence in children affects the way the children are judged by important adults in their lives.

For example, in its survey of kindergarten teachers about school readiness, the Carnegie Foundation for the Advancement of Teaching found that 43 percent of the teachers considered lack of emotional maturity as a serious problem for those children who entered school not ready to learn (Boyer 1991).

Behavior Problems Reflect Children's Life Circumstances

There is considerable evidence that the prevalence of behavior problems in young children is a direct function of the quality of children's family life and their experience in early care and education programs. Hagekull and Bohlin (1993), for example, reported that externalizing (aggressive) behavior in four-year-olds (measured on the Behar and Stringfield Preschool Behavior Questionnaire) was less frequent when the children lived in home environments of higher quality, as measured by the Home Observation for Measurement of the Environment (HOME) instrument, but was not related to the quality of the children's child care environments. Internalizing (withdrawn) behavior problems declined and positive behavior increased as a function of both higher-quality home and child care environments. In general, higher-quality environments contributed to fewer problems and more positive types of behavior. Caruso and Corsini examined behavior problems in a random sample of two-year-old children enrolled in child care programs in four Connecticut communities. Using the Child Behavior Checklist (CBCL) developed by Achenbach et al. (1987), Caruso and Corsini found scores on externalizing and internalizing problems that were lower (more favorable) than the norms developed by Achenbach. This finding is perhaps attributable to the higher socioeconomic status of the population sampled in Connecticut. Problem behaviors were not associated with any of the child care variables studied (including number of different arrangements and the child/staff ratio).

Using data from the 1986 mother and child supplements to the National Longitudinal Survey of Youth (NLSY), Parcel and Menaghan (1994) found that behavior problems measured by the Behavior Problems Index (BPI) were fewer when mothers of four- to six-year-old children had a stronger locus of control and provided stronger home environments. Furthermore, an unstable marriage during the child's first three years was associated with more behavior problems; problems were fewer when the child's mother was currently married. Maternal depression and stressful life events also are often associated with increases in child behavior problems (Fergusson et al. 1985). This appears to be true whether the mother or the child's teacher is completing the ratings (Benasich et al. 1994).

Luster and McAdoo (1994) analyzed NLSY data on African American children between six and nine years of age. They found scores on the BPI to reflect children's exposure to an accumulation of risks. They analyzed "risks" that included lower levels of maternal education and intelligence, low maternal self-esteem, poverty, large family, and less-supportive home environments. African American children with five or more risk indicators present were three times as likely to be at the extreme end of the antisocial dimension of the BPI than children with no risk factors.

Some studies find social class differences in the incidence of behavior problems, with children of lower socioeconomic status exhibiting higher problem scores, although such differences may be more likely to appear as children get older (Benasich et al. 1994). Gender differences also appear in the literature, with boys showing higher rates than girls, although not all studies find this difference (Caruso and Corsini 1994). These two findings raise questions about the generalizability of ratings across various subgroups, a point I return to later in the chapter.

The prevalence of behavior problems also reflects the earlier experiences of children. A very recent study found that the school-age behavior of children shows the deleterious effects of extremely low birth weight (ELBW), that is, less than 750 grams. Hack et al. (1994) found that, compared with children born at full term, the ELBW children had significantly more behavioral and attention problems, and poorer social skills and adaptive behavior, at six to seven years of age.

Behavior Problems Help Us Understand
Other Aspects of Child Well-Being

Children with aggressive behavior problems are likely to have persistent problems with school achievement. Such children consistently demonstrate delayed language development (Stevenson and Richman 1978). A study of British three-year-olds found that children with language delays exhibited behavior problems four times greater than those of nondelayed children (Richman 1977). Studies of older children with delayed language development find similar linkages with problem behavior, including later juvenile delinquency (Benasich et al. 1994; Earls 1987; Furstenberg et al. 1987; and Robins 1966). Denham and Burger (1991) found that preschool teachers' ratings of young children's affective and behavioral social-emotional competence, especially anger and sadness, were associated with social-emotional competence as rated by the teachers. Maladaptive behavior in preschool children has been related to earlier problems in forming attachments (Egeland et al. 1990; and Erickson et al. 1985).

Behavior Problems Predict Later Outcomes for Children

Cooper and Farran (1988) studied two classes of behavior problems: interpersonal skills, including physical and verbal aggressiveness and disruptiveness; and work-related skills, such as disorganization, dependence, distractibility, and noncompliance with directions. Having low interpersonal skills and low work-related skills constituted significant risks for placement in special education and retention in grade (two aspects of "maladjustment" in this study), but problem behaviors associated with classroom work were far more important in predicting maladjustment than were interpersonal skills.

Behavior problems identified at one age may be predictive of problems (or the absence of problems) later in life (Fagot 1984). Using data from the New York Longitudinal Study, Cameron (1978) found that scores on a measure of temperament in the first year of life predicted mild (but not more severe) behavioral problems later. In a longitudinal study of 190 at-risk children, Sroufe and Egeland (1989) found an especially strong link between aggressiveness in preschool youngsters and later problem behavior.

Children who display behavior problems in the early grades have poorer achievement outcomes later on (McKinney and Speece 1986). On the other hand, preschool children who are depressed, anxious, or withdrawn are at risk of a difficult adjustment to school (Brooks-Gunn and Petersen 1991; Gjerde and Block 1991; Petersen et al. 1993; and Rutter et al. 1986).

Which Indicators Are Most Important?

The research just reviewed does not provide clear empirical evidence for identifying the most important indicators. Rather, each study suggests some reason for valuing information on the particular problems or sorts of behavior on which the study focused. The choice of indicators is ultimately a judgment call, and a political judgment at that. The choice should be based on which indicators policymakers believe provide the most useful information for program planning and resource allocation. I have suggested that the decision on the most important indicators may be guided by concerns raised by the problem's prevalence and the knowledge that data on the problems may help us understand children's life circumstances or other aspects of their well-being, or predict later outcomes. Research on problems in early childhood suggests that the dimensions of the problems—or the measurement constructs—fall into six categories: emotional well-being; behavior problems; school-related problems; problems with the law; developmental delays and disabilities; and problems associated with child-rearing.

In my judgment, the most important indicators fall in three areas: behavior problems; school-related problems; and developmental delays and disabilities. Emotional well-being is an important problem area, but its measurement is more difficult (as discussed in this chapter in connection with specific surveys). For the purposes of community, state, or national indicators, reports from existing data systems can more efficiently indicate problems with the law. Problems associated with child-rearing—such as running away from home or being difficult to raise—are interesting to know about, but should have lower priority for investing measurement resources, at least on a national scale.

WHICH INDICATORS ARE NOW MEASURED AND HOW WELL ARE THEY MEASURED?

A review of the major national surveys provides additional perspective on these priorities. After discussing which indicators are currently measured, I turn to an analysis of how well they are measured.

What Is Currently Measured?

Five major surveys have measured problem behavior and problems of young children in some way:

1. National Household Education Survey (NHES);
2. National Survey of Children (NSC);
3. National Longitudinal Survey of Youth: Mother/Child Data (NLSY-M/C);
4. National Survey of Families and Households (NSFH); and
5. National Health Interview Survey–Child Health Supplement (NHIS-CHS).

Two of these surveys—NSC and NSFH—have no current plans for further data collections. Their contents may be of interest, however, in providing historical comparisons with future surveys.[2] Table 19.1 summarizes the relative emphasis that the five surveys place on key dimensions of early childhood problems and problem behavior. Table 19.2 provides detail on the variables included in these surveys. As might be expected, in contrast with the research literature, the surveys focus on narrower bands of behavior and problems. Even so, the three ongoing surveys offer rich sources of data, with differing emphases but with considerable collective breadth.

The single richest source of data is NHIS-CHS. It has extensive questions on emotional well-being that include the age at which the parent first noticed an emotional or behavioral problem, whether treatment has been obtained, and how disruptive the problem has been for the child's schooling. NHIS-CHS includes a thirty-two-item version of the BPI, with the standard twenty-eight items administered when the focal child is between the ages of five and twelve. It includes more questions than NHES:95 on the school-related problems of grade repetition or retention, the school contacting the parent about child problems, and suspensions or expulsions, perhaps because the NHIS-CHS sample encompasses an older group of children.[3]

NLSY-M/C is a major source of national data on children's development and achievement in areas relevant to school success, but contains relatively little in the problem behavior areas. It includes a temperament scale, with a few items that could be analyzed independently as problem indicators. It also includes the complete BPI and reports the usual six subscale scores (see table 19.2). NLSY-M/C contains no questions related to problems associated with school or developmental disabilities.

NHES:95 is the only national survey that puts a heavy emphasis on documenting whether five- to seven-year-old children have experienced developmental delays and specific learning disabilities—such as mental retardation and speech impairment—or serious emotional disturbance. It documents the nature of these disabilities, whether the child is receiving services for them, and, if so, who provides the services. The survey also contains a number of questions relating to grade retention (kindergarten to grade three) and whether school has contacted a parent about problems with the child's schoolwork or behavior. The emphasis of NHES:95, fielded in spring 1995, was to be somewhat different in its 1996 edition (under development at the time of this writing).

Table 19.1   Relative Emphasis Five Surveys Give to Six Areas of Problems in Early Childhood

Area	NHES:95	NSC	NLSY-M/C	NSFH	NHIS-CHS
Emotional well-being	0	x	x	x	X
Behavior problems	0	x	X	x	X
School-related problems	X	X	0	X	X
Problems with the law	0	x	0	x	0
Developmental delays and disabilities	X	0	0	0	x
Child-rearing problems	0	x	0	x	0

Note: Key to symbols: 0 = no questions related to the area; x = some questions; X = major emphasis among survey questions.

Table 19.2   Early Childhood Problem Variables Included in Major Surveys

	National Household Education Survey: 1995	National Survey of Children	National Longitudinal Survey of Youth: Mother/Child Data	National Survey of Families and Households	National Health Interview Survey: Child Health Supplement
Year begun	1991	1976	1986	1987–1988	1981
Sample sizes and children's ages	1993: 4,423 parents of preschoolers; 2,126 parents of kindergartners, 4,277 parents of primary school children; 62 parents of home-school children	1976: 2,301; 7–11 years of age (Later years followed up with children when they were adolescents and young adults)	1986: 4,971; 0–18 years of age; 1988: More than 6,000, 95 percent less than 10 years of age	7,926; age 5 and older	15,416; birth to 17 years of age
Collection frequency	1991, 1993, and then annual, with rotating topical focus	1976, 1981, 1987	Biennial	1987–1988; 1992–1993	Annual NHIS, but child supplement added in 1981 and 1988
Survey type	Telephone interviews	1976: In-person and self-administered	In-person interviews	In-person interviews; Self-administered survey	In-person interviews
Respondents	Parents of children ages 3 through 7 years	Children; Parent most knowledgeable about child, constituting national stratified probability sample; Self-administered teacher questionnaires	Women respondents of National Longitudinal Survey of Work Experience of Youth Adult	Adult's spouse/partner; Focal children 5 years of age or older	Most knowledgeable adult; 1 child, 0–17 years of age
Design	Cross-sectional	Longitudinal	Longitudinal	Cross-sectional	Cross-sectional
Next collection planned	Spring 1995	None planned	1995	Perhaps 1996 or 1997	1996

				Behavior Problems Index (32 items)
Emotional well-being indicators Rating scales	Child feels lonely? Fights or argues with brothers/sisters? Scale similar to BPI: - Shyness - Antisocial behavior - Hyperactivity	Temperament scales: 0–23 months: - Irritability Difficulty (composite) - Negative hedonic tone - Fearfulness 24–83 months: - Insecure attachment Behavior Problems Index (32 items) - Total score, plus: - Antisocial - Anxious/depressed - Headstrong - Hyperactive - Dependent - Peer conflict	Age 4 and under Statements rated often, sometimes, or not true: - Is fussy or irritable - Loses temper easily - Is fearful or anxious - Bullies, or is cruel or mean to others Ages 5–11: All of above except "fussy or irritable" plus: - Is unhappy, sad, or depressed	
Experienced problems/received treatment				Ever had an emotional or behavior problem for 3 months or more? (Y/N) - Age first noticed - Ever received treatment or counseling? - Had treatment or counseling in last 12 months? - No. times talked to doctor, psychologist, or counselor (*Table continues on p. 418.*)

Table 19.2 Continued

	National Household Education Survey: 1995	National Survey of Children	National Longitudinal Survey of Youth: Mother/Child Data	National Survey of Families and Households	National Health Interview Survey: Child Health Supplement
					about problem in past 12 months - In past 12 months did problem cause child to miss time from school? - How many days in last 12 months? - Did problem require special classes, school, or special help in past 12 months? - Take any medicine in past 12 months for problem?
Professional help				Seen doctor or therapist about any emotional or behavior problem? (Y/N) - Age of last occurrence	Ever seen psychiatrist, psychologist, doctor, or counselor about any emotional, mental, or behavior problem? (Y/N) - Last time (more or less than 12 months ago) In past 12 months, felt, or anyone suggested, that child

			needed help for any emotional, mental, or behavioral problem? (Y/N) Grade repetition for any reason? (Y/N) - Why? Anyone from school ask you to come talk about problems child having? (Y/N) - How long since last time? Ever suspended, excluded, expelled? (Y/N) - How many times? - How long since last time? - For health, behavior, or other reasons?
School-related problems	Attend 1 or 2 years of kindergarten? (Y/N) Repeat any grade, 1–3? (Y/N) - Which grades? Teacher or school contacted you about behavior problem? (Y/N) Teacher or school contacted you about problems with schoolwork? (Y/N)	Suspended or expelled? Class standing below middle, near bottom? Repeated a grade first time between 1976 and 1981? - Ever repeated? Parent received note about behavior or discipline problem in school? One or two grades behind in 1976?	Repeat grade? (Y/N) - Which grades? Meet with teacher or principal because of behavior problem? (Y/N) - How many times? Suspension or expulsion? (Y/N) - More than once? (Y/N) - Age of last occurrence	
Law enforcement		Stolen things more than twice?	Ever been in trouble with police? (Y/N) - More than once? (Y/N) - Age of last occurrence	
Child-rearing problems		How much trouble was child to raise? Ever ran away? - Once? - Two or more times?	Difficult to raise? (Y/N) Run away from home for 1 or more nights? (Y/N)	

(Table continues on p. 420.)

Table 19.2 *Continued*

	National Household Education Survey: 1995	National Survey of Children	National Longitudinal Survey of Youth: Mother/Child Data	National Survey of Families and Households	National Health Interview Survey: Child Health Supplement
Disabilities or developmental delays	Doctor or health professional told you child has developmental delay? (Y/N) Checklist of disabilities: - Specific learning disability - Mental retardation - Speech impairment - Serious emotional disturbance Does disability affect ability to learn? (Y/N) Receiving services for disability from: - School - Health or social service agency - Doctor or clinic			- More than once? (Y/N) - Age of last occurrence - How long gone?	Ever had delay in growth or development? (Y/N) Ever had a learning disability? (Y/N)

Note: Empty cells indicate that the survey did not include items on that variable.

How Good Are Our Indicators?

Moore (1994) has suggested eleven criteria for judging the adequacy of indicators of child well-being. I briefly examine the measures on these surveys in light of these criteria. Moore's first two criteria—comprehensive coverage and positive outcomes—are appropriate for evaluating the total set of indicators. Clearly, indicators of problems are neither comprehensive nor positive. When combined with other indicators considered by the authors of other chapters, however, they make important contributions toward a comprehensive set of indicators and allow for assessing both positive and negative aspects of children's development and behavior.

Clear and Comprehensible   The public can easily understand the problem behavior included in NHES:95, NLSY-M/C, and NHIS-CH. Even citizens who do not have school-age children can relate to the concreteness of the school-related problems of repeating grades or being suspended. The general public can also understand the specific disabilities listed on the NHES:95, although there is some danger that terms like "serious emotional disturbance" and "mental retardation" mean different things to different people. In fact, Zill and Schoenborn (1990) note that parents responding to the NHIS-CHS may have used the term "learning disability" more broadly than its technical definition.

Common Interpretation   The behavior problems that are most directly grounded in behavioral terms are most likely to have the same meaning across diverse populations or subgroups of the United States population. For example, the question, "Has anyone from (child's) school asked you to come talk about problems (child) is having?" is very likely to refer to the same events, whether the responding parent is young or old, African American or white, Northeasterner or Southerner. Indicators based on rating scales are more problematic. The individual items require subjective judgment. A parent's tolerance for an active child is likely to influence whether she or he decides that the child "often" or "sometimes" is "restless or overly active, cannot sit still" (BPI, Item 19; NHIS-CHS 1988). In the case of the BPI, the scales have been widely used, have been tested with many diverse populations, and are interpreted only as scales (for example, "hyperactive") and not as individual items. Unless items have been well tested, it is best to avoid subjective judgments in our indicators.

Some rating scales are not as psychometrically strong as the BPI. The temperament subscales on NLSY-M/C, for example, have few items each and, in some cases, low internal consistency (Mott and Quinlan 1991). Thus, not only do the items suffer from possible differential interpretation, the scale scores themselves are not adequately stable for providing the kinds of indicators that will be robust across subpopulations.

Another concern is the term "developmental delay," used in the NHES:95. School personnel and early intervention specialists use a variety of terms in referring to the various "delays" that children with special needs experience. Furthermore, specialists may use different language when talking with parents than they use with their colleagues. Thus, in their attempts to make a diagnosis understandable to a parent, the professional may avoid technical terms that would otherwise provide consistency. Research is needed to determine whether parents with diverse backgrounds will interpret the questions in the same way, and, if not, how the wording can be modified to obtain consistency.

Consistency over Time   Once there is common meaning across varied subgroups, it is important for that meaning to remain constant over time. Among the problems investigated in these surveys, the descriptions of disabilities have terminology that is most likely to change. Terms for various categories of disability have changed over the past decades. To use another example from Zill and Schoenborn (1994), the term "mentally retarded" used in the 1981 NHIS-CHS produced only a few positive responses, perhaps because of perceived stigma. The terms "developmental delay" and "learning disability" were substituted in 1988, and response rates increased.

Consistency should be considered in the context of both longitudinal and cross-sectional data collections. Because the nature of behavior problems changes as children develop, the same items cannot be used at every age level. In longitudinal designs, this means that observed differences between one collection time and another should not automatically be judged as a developmental change, but interpreted in light of changes in items or dimensions of behavior problems. In cross-sectional designs, care must be exercised in interpreting differences in the seriousness or prevalence of particular problems for, say, ten-year-olds compared with four-year-olds.

Forward-Looking   Moore suggests that our indicators should anticipate the future so that current surveys can provide baseline data for charting trends. The nature of the particular behavior problems measured by a standard scale such as the BPI is not likely to become any less important over time. Similarly, as long as the governors and chief state school officers are concerned with the national education goals, school-related problems like those tapped on NHES:95 will capture the public's interest. For poverty, violence, substance abuse, and similar problems, the annual statistics presented by *Kids Count* and the Children's Defense Fund provide evidence of trends that more detailed national surveys can chart.

Rigorous Methods   A persistent concern about measures of children's behavior problems and other problems is that the information typically is provided by an adult who is presumably knowledgeable about the child. These judgmental ratings have been subjected to some scrutiny in the research literature, and there is considerable evidence that the kinds of questions and scales incorporated in NHES:95, NLSY:M/C, and NHIS:CH provide robust indicators. In addition to the reliability and validity studies done in the context of the surveys themselves, researchers have shown that, in general, different adults can agree on their independent ratings of problem behavior (such as those made with the BPI). For example, Richters and Pellegrini (1989) found that mothers' and teachers' ratings of problem behavior gave similar pictures—at least to the extent one might expect, given that parents and teachers see the children in different contexts. Another indication of rigor (validity) is the extent to which scores on the scales are related to other events or behavior in understandable ways. Zill (1990) has shown that BPI scores of NHIS-CHS children distinguished those who had received psychological help during the past year from those who had not.

All of the surveys reviewed have established rigorous data collection methods. We can be reasonably sure that the procedures are consistent across different time points of the same survey. I do not know, however, the extent to which those responsible for administering NHES:95, for example, have adopted the same procedures for training field staff as used by NHIS-CHS.

Geographically Detailed   The surveys reviewed here provide indicators only at the national level. I have not found any state-level surveys obtaining these same data. For community-level indicators, it would be relatively straightforward to administer a small-scale survey, depending on the size of the community. I do not know the extent to which this is being done, but Thornton and Love (1994) describe a set of procedures that could be adopted by community agencies interested in measuring child and family well-being. Questions could be taken from NHES:95, NLSY-M/C, or NHIS-CHS to create parallel instruments that the staff of local agencies could administer with relatively little training.

Cost-Efficient   The rating scales and questions on young children's problems are straightforward and inexpensive to collect. The most commonly used scale, the BPI, is so widely used it now essentially can be considered a benchmark for other measures. Furthermore, the indicators included on these surveys are generally sound and can be continued into the future with no additional development costs.

Reflective of Social Goals   For young children entering kindergarten, the incidence of behavior problems can provide measures of our country's progress toward achieving the first national education goal that all children will start school "ready to learn." One of the major dimensions of readiness defined by the Goal 1 Technical Planning Group (Kagan et al. 1995) is social-emotional development. Within that dimension, decreased aggression, anxiety, and depression are reasonable constructs to assess (Love et al. 1994). For school-age children, grade repetitions, suspensions, and expulsions are reasonable indicators for the social goal of quality education for all children.

Adjusted for Demographic Trends   If indicators of children's problems and problem behavior allow a common interpretation in various population subgroups, there should be no need to adjust for changes in the national population composition over time. Further research is needed before we can know whether this is an issue for the indicators discussed here.

An Additional Consideration   It may be valuable to add another criterion to Moore's list. There is considerable evidence that context is critical for interpreting problem behavior. Although there is some stability over time and across situations in such behavior patterns as aggression and depression, there is also considerable variation. Some children may be more aggressive in the streets of their neighborhood than in the classroom; some are more withdrawn with adults than with peers; some argue with their siblings but cooperate with their teachers. A system of indicators will be more useful for understanding problems in early childhood if it includes extensive data on the contexts in which the sorts of behavior occur. The surveys reviewed here differ widely on this dimension. Both NLSY-M/C and NHIS-CHS contain a wide range of data on the children and their families, in addition to the problem-oriented variables listed in table 19.2. The longitudinal nature of the NLSY-M/C data create time-sensitive contextual variables that can greatly enrich interpretations of early childhood problems.

HOW CAN CURRENT MEASURES BE IMPROVED AND NEW MEASURES PRODUCED DURING THE NEXT DECADE?

The NHES could be strengthened by adding a module on behavior problems. At relatively little expense, the BPI items could be added. This would permit analysis of relationships between these important child characteristics and the school-related problems that NHES currently measures. This might help us understand, for example, why some children experience problems in school, and whether there is a relationship between patterns of such characteristics as aggression or antisocial behavior and problems with teachers, expulsions or suspensions, and even repeating grades. NHES could be further strengthened by creating a longitudinal component. If a subsample could be followed up in succeeding years, we could assess relationships between the incidence of behavior problems in preschool, for example, and school problems that appear in second grade.

The NLSY-M/C is an extremely rich data source for information on children's development. Because of this chapter's focus, the extensive data on children's achievement and positive developmental indicators have not been reviewed. Researchers can use these rich data in combination with NLSY-M/C's longitudinal design to address an extremely wide range of important questions about children and families (Zill and Daly 1993). Yet NLSY-M/C collects no parent reports of children's school-related problems, such as the NHES:95 items on grade repetitions, school-parent contacts about problems, or disabilities and developmental delays. Adding these questions to NLSY-M/C would greatly expand researchers' ability to investigate relationships between problems and positive aspects of child development.

The National Center for Education Statistics, which conducts NHES, has launched a major new longitudinal study, the Early Childhood Longitudinal Study (ECLS). A nationally representative sample of approximately twenty-four thousand kindergarten children will be selected in fall 1998 and followed through about fifth grade.[4] Researchers will conduct direct assessments of children, interview their parents and teachers, and obtain data from school records. Given the importance of problems in early childhood and their potential influence on children's school performance, ECLS could provide an excellent vehicle for learning more about these influences.

PRELIMINARY CONCLUSIONS

This review has been too narrowly focused to provide a complete analysis of measures of problems in early childhood. Nevertheless, it is clear that the major national surveys collectively provide a rich source of data that researchers can use to study the negative side of children's well-being. At the same time, there are limitations. These surveys provide only limited understanding of young children's problem behavior and problems for several reasons.

Comparability across surveys is incomplete. Except for the standard BPI and questions on school-related problems that are highly comparable, different aspects of emotional well-being are assessed. For example, only one survey obtains any detailed information on treatment that children may have received for emotional or behavior problems.

All of the surveys ask parents (overwhelmingly the mother) about their children's problems. Aside from that commonality, the surveys have different sampling methods and different sample sizes, and obtain information about children of different ages. NLSY-M/C and NHIS-CHS cover the span from birth to seventeen or eighteen years of age; NHES:95 and NSC span four-year periods that do not overlap. The former begins at age three, the latter at age seven.

Contextual information—or data on other aspects of the children's development or their families—is highly variable. NHIS-CHS and NLSY-M/C have the most extensive background and contextual data, NHES probably the least. The issue of contextual information should be examined more closely in the process of recommending improvements in national data on children's well-being.

NOTES

1. The other five *Kids Count* indicators pertain to adolescence: births to single teens, juvenile violent crime arrests, high school graduation rate, percent of teens not in school or labor force, and teen violent death rate.

2. There is a possibility that NSFH will be resurrected for another round of data collection in the near future.

3. NHIS also planned to field a survey of children with disabilities in 1994–1995 that is not included in this review.

4. The study completed the field-test phase in 1996–1997. The study team was led by National Opinion Research Center, which had a number of subcontractors working with it, including Child Trends, University of Chicago, University of Michigan, Michigan State University, Educational Testing Service, and Mathematica Policy Research. Jerry West is the NCES project officer.

REFERENCES

Achenbach, T. M., C. S. Edelbrock, and C. T. Howell. 1992. "Empirically Based Assessment of the Behavioral/Emotional Problems of Two- to Three-Year-Old Children." *Rutgers University. Unpublished manuscript.*

American Humane Association. 1994. *Child Abuse and Neglect Data.* Fact Sheet 1. Englewood, Colo.: American Humane Association, Children's Division (April).

Annie E. Casey Foundation. 1994. *1994 Kids Count Data Book: State Profiles of Child Well-Being.* Baltimore, Md.: Annie E. Casey Foundation.

Benasich, April Ann, Jeanne Brooks-Gunn, and Marie C. McCormick. 1994. "Behavioral Problems in the Two- to Five-Year-Old: Measurement and Prognostic Ability." *Journal of Developmental and Behavioral Pediatrics.*

Boyer, Ernest L. 1991. *Ready to Learn: A Mandate for the Nation*. The Carnegie Foundation for the Advancement of Teaching. Lawrenceville, N.J.: Princeton University Press.

Brooks-Gunn, Jeanne, and A. C. Petersen. 1991. "Studying the Emergence of Depression and Depressive Symptoms During Adolescence." *Journal of Youth and Adolescence*: 115–19.

Cameron, James R. 1978. "Parental Treatment, Children's Temperament, and the Risk of Childhood Behavioral Problems: 2. Initial Temperament, Parental Attitudes, and the Incidence and Form of Behavioral Problems." *American Journal of Orthopsychiatry* 48: 140–47.

Caruso, Grace-Ann L., and David A. Corsini. 1994. "The Prevalence of Behavior Problems Among Toddlers in Child Care." *Early Education and Development* 5: 27–40.

Children's Defense Fund. 1994. *The State of America's Children: Yearbook 1994*. Washington, D.C.: Children's Defense Fund.

Cooper, David H., and Dale C. Farran. 1988. "Behavioral Risk Factors in Kindergarten." *Early Childhood Research Quarterly* 3: 1–19.

Denham, Susanne A., and Christine Burger. 1991. "Observational Validation of Ratings of Preschoolers' Social Competence and Behavior Problems." *Child Study Journal* 21(3): 185–202.

Earls, F. 1987. "Temperament and Home Environment Characteristics as Causal Factors in the Early Development of Childhood Psychopathology." *Journal of the American Academy of Child Adolescent Psychiatry* 26: 491–98.

Egeland, B., M. Kalkoske, N. Gottesman, and M. F. Erickson. 1990. "Preschool Behavior Problems: Stability and Factors Accounting for Change." *Journal of Child Psychology and Psychiatry* 31: 891–909.

Erickson, M. F., Sroufe, and B. Egeland. 1985. "The Relationship Between Quality of Attachment and Behavior Problems in Preschool in a High-Risk Sample. Growing Points in Attachment Through Research," edited by I. Bretherton and E. Waters. *Monographs of the Society for Research in Child Development* 50 (1–2, serial no. 209): 147–66.

Fagot, Beverly I. 1984. "The Consequences of Problem Behavior in Toddler Children." *Journal of Abnormal Child Psychology* 12: 385–96.

Fergusson, E. M., B. A. Hons, L. J. Horwood, et al. 1985. "Family Life Events, Maternal Depression, and Maternal and Teacher Descriptions of Child Behavior." *Pediatrics* 75: 30–35.

Furstenberg, Frank F., Jr., Jeanne Brooks-Gunn, and S. Philip Mason. 1987. *Adolescent Mothers in Later Life*. New York: Cambridge University Press.

Gjerde, P. F., and J. Block. 1991. "Preadolescent Antecedents of Depressive Symptomatology at Age Eighteen: A Prospective Study." *Journal of Youth and Adolescents* 20: 217–32.

Hack, Maureen, H. Gerry Taylor, Nancy Klein, Robert Eiben, Christopher Schatschneider, and Nori Mercuri-Minich. 1994. "School-Age Outcomes in Children with Birth Weights Under 750g." *New England Journal of Medicine* 331: 753–59.

Hagekull, Berit, and Gunilla Bohlin. 1993. "Quality of Care and Problem Behaviors in Early Childhood." Paper presented at the Biennial Meeting of the Society for Research in Child Development. New Orleans, La. (March 25–28, 1993).

Kagan, Sharon Lynn, Evelyn K. Moore, and Sue Bredekamp, eds. 1995. "Reconsidering Children's Early Development and Learning: Toward Common Views and Vocabulary." Washington, D.C.: National Education Goals Panel.

Links, P.S. 1983. "Community Surveys of the Prevalence of Childhood Psychiatric Disorders: A Review." *Child Development* 54: 531–48.

Love, John M., J. Lawrence Aber, and Jeanne Brooks-Gunn. 1994. "Strategies for Assessing Community Progress Toward Achieving the First National Education Goal." Princeton, N.J.: Mathematica Policy Research, Inc.

Luster, Tom, and Harriette Pipes McAdoo. 1994. "Factors Related to the Achievement and Adjustment of Young African American Children." *Child Development* 65: 1080–94.

McKinney, James D., and Deborah L. Speece. 1986. "Academic Consequences and Longitudinal

Stability of Behavioral Subtypes of Learning Disabled Children." *Journal of Educational Psychology* 78: 365–72.

Moore, Kristin Anderson. 1994. "Criteria for Indicators of Child Well-being." Working paper. Washington, D.C.: Child Trends, Inc.

Mott, Frank L., and Stephen V. Quinlan. 1991. *Children of the NLSY: 1988 Tabulations and Summary Discussion.* Columbus, Ohio: Center for Human Resource Research, Ohio State University.

Parcel, Toby L., and Elizabeth G. Menaghan. 1994. "Early Parental Work, Family Social Capital, and Early Childhood Outcomes." *American Journal of Sociology* 99: 972–1009.

Petersen, A. C., B. Compas, J. Brooks-Gunn, M. Stemmler, S. Ely, and K. Grant. 1993. "Depression in Adolescence." *American Psychologist* 48: 155–68.

Richman, N. 1977. "Is a Behavior Checklist for Preschool Children Useful? In *Epidemiological Approaches in Child Psychiatry*, edited by P. J. Graham. London, England: Academic Press.

Richters, J., and D. Pellegrini. 1989. "Depressed Mothers' Judgments About Their Children: An Examination of the Depression-Distortion Hypothesis." *Child Development* 60: 1068–75.

Robins, Lee N. 1966. *Deviant Children Grown Up. A Sociological and Psychiatric Study of Sociopathic Personality.* Baltimore, Md.: Williams and Wilkins.

Rutter, M., C. E. Izard, and P. B. Read, Eds. 1986. *Depression in Young People: Developmental and Clinical Perspectives.* New York: The Guilford Press.

Sroufe, L. Alan, and Byron Egeland. 1989. "Early Predictors of Psychopathology and Competence in Children." Paper presented at the Biennial Meeting of the Society for Research in Child Development. Kansas City, Mo. (April 27–30, 1989).

Stevenson, J., and N. Richman. 1978. "Behavior, Language, and Development in Three-Year-Old Children." *Journal of Autism and Childhood Schizophrenia* 8: 299–313.

Thornton, Craig V., and John M. Love. 1994. "Comprehensive Strategies for Assessing the Outcomes of Community-Wide Efforts to Support Children and Families." Paper presented at the national conference of the Family Resource Coalition. Chicago, Ill. (May 5, 1994).

Zill, Nicholas, and Margaret Daly, eds. 1993. *Researching the Family: A Guide to Survey and Statistical Data on U.S. Families.* Washington, D.C.: Child Trends, Inc.

Zill, Nicholas, and Charlotte A. Schoenborn. 1990. "Developmental, Learning, and Emotional Problems: Health of Our Nation's Children, United States, 1988." *Advance Data from Vital and Health Statistics*, no. 190. Hyattsville, Md.: National Center for Health Statistics.

20

Positive Indicators of Adolescent Development: Redressing the Negative Image of American Adolescents

Ruby Takanishi, Allyn M. Mortimer,
and Timothy J. McGourthy

PREVAILING IMAGES OF American adolescents have clearly shaped decisions about which indicators of adolescent status are systematically collected. No good word or label that denotes the second decade of life in a positive vein currently exists. The word "adolescent" is almost always used in popular discourse to describe immature, irresponsible, and undesirable behavior of individuals, regardless of their age.

The rarity of positive indicators of adolescent development is easily demonstrated. A cursory look at national reports of indicators of adolescent health and education reveals the predominance of negative outcomes (Center for the Study of Social Policy 1993; Hechinger 1992; Gans, Blyth, Elster, and Gaveras 1990). Adolescent indicators represent a preoccupation with social problems, including teenage pregnancy, substance abuse, juvenile delinquency, school dropout, violence, and youth unemployment. While positive indicators of development during adolescence do exist, they remain neglected or overshadowed.

Researchers have contributed to the emergence of more positive images of adolescents in recent years. This view of adolescent development is based on studies involving nonclinical or nontroubled adolescents (Feldman and Elliott, 1990). A major statement reflecting a developmental perspective on early adolescence (ages ten to fourteen) was articulated in the Carnegie Council on Adolescent Development's report *Turning Points: Preparing American Youth for the 21st Century*, which identified desirable strengths and capacities of young adolescents (Task Force on Education of Young Adolescents 1989). Since that report, a youth development perspective has emerged (Pittman and Wright 1991). This perspective has contributed to the importance of understanding adolescents' perceptions and views, especially in research about their health (Millstein 1993), and to a shift from a deficit view of adolescents as problems to adolescents as resources in program development and implementation (Task Force on Youth Development and Community Programs 1992).

Two caveats cannot be avoided in an effort to identify positive indicators: the inevitability and the necessity of value judgments, in this case, identifying what is positive and hence desirable; and the recognition that what is considered problematic or desirable is socially constructed within a cultural and historical context (Schlossman and Cairns 1993). With these two caveats made explicit, this chapter views the adolescent years as a critical transition period in the preparation for adult life (Hamburg 1989).

The status of positive indicators of adolescent development is underdeveloped at this time. The focus on the negative aspects of adolescent development has contributed to the neglect of the research base and measurement requirements regarding positive indicators. The prospects for improved indicators can be enhanced by the support of fundamental research into some of these indicators, both in terms of their responsible measurement and the factors that contribute to observed outcomes.

Research on contributing factors is critical, given the current interest in the linkage of indicators with pressures for public accountability, that is, concern about outcomes. It is likely that for important indicators, such as educational achievement, both public institutions, such as schools, and private entities, such as families, contribute to measured outcomes. Based on the fact that multiple factors affect a given outcome, the allocation of public responsibility for educational achievement is not straightforward and often becomes highly politicized.

Furthermore, the availability of funds for research support and for the collection of indicator data by public agencies is limited. Difficult choices must be made. Public agencies already collect indicator data, and alterations in their collection practices will not be simple. Hence, careful consideration must be given to selecting those indicators that are scientifically defensible, publicly meaningful and useful, relatively inexpensive to collect, and limited in number. Moore's (1994) criteria are helpful in this regard, but the challenges of organizational change required for a more current, defensible indicator system at the federal, state, and local levels remain formidable and are not solely driven by scientific considerations. Such change will require the elimination of some existing indicators, the clustering of some indicators based on research, and the addition of new ones.

SELECTED INDICATORS OF POSITIVE ADOLESCENT DEVELOPMENT: AN OVERVIEW

Csikszentmihalyi and Larson (1984) have made the case that an adolescent's successful transition to adulthood is marked by learning to assume adult roles. Thus, our primary criterion for positive indicators of adolescent development is the attainment of social competency for adult roles and responsibilities. This includes being an educated and productive worker in a global economy; an individual with the knowledge and skills to maintain a healthy lifestyle; a caring family member, whether choosing to be a parent or part of a broader kinship group; and an active participant as a citizen in a democratic, multiethnic society.

In an ideal world with no limits on resources allocated to the production and collection of indicators, other positive indicators might be collected, such as attachment to parents during adolescence or involvement in household maintenance. However, we argue that indicators used for social purposes and supported by public funds should be tied to the desired goals of a society. Throughout this chapter, we attempt to attend to the necessity of making hard choices in the selection of indicators of positive adolescent development.

The following overview of selected indicators of positive adolescent development is provided both to describe the possibilities and to identify the current status of their measurement and future prospects. This overview is the basis from which the selection of four indicators will be made of high priority for further development. Candidates for indicators can be roughly assigned to one of three categories: *education and work; health-enhancing behavior; and preparation for adult roles.*

Indicators of Education and Work

Several indicators of adolescent development in the education and work area are addressed by other chapters in this volume. These are *graduation from high school, including literacy* (Hauser 1994); *critical thinking and problem-solving skills that enable participation in a high-technology, global economy* (Koretz 1994); and *postsecondary educational aspirations and expectations* (Kane 1994). To these, we would add *perception of opportunity regarding future adult social and economic status* as an indicator in the education and work category. It appears that the education indicators of positive adolescent outcomes (educational achievement, aspirations for postsecondary education, attainment of college education) are the best developed by the Moore criteria and most widely used and recognized at the present time.

However, as Hauser (1994) notes, the collection of indicators on high school dropout is often unreliable, misleading, and requires improvement. Kane (1994) makes the very critical point that in modern economies, completion of a high school education is not sufficient for a decent standard of living. For example, the average gap in lifetime earnings between a high school graduate and dropout is two hundred thousand dollars, while the gap for a college-educated and noncollege-educated person is one million dollars (U.S. Bureau of the Census 1994). Hence, a good case can be made to support Kane's recommendations that monitoring postsecondary education by gender and economic background should be improved immediately, and that resources might be shifted from indicators of high school completion to the postsecondary area.

An adolescent's *perception of opportunity* regarding future adult social and economic status, and the expectation that she/he will attain that status, constitute critical indicators of adolescent development and require further study. The U.S. Department of Education currently collects data on educational aspirations, which are one component of perception of the future. Perception of opportunity, however, is not limited to educational goals, but also includes what an individual thinks she/he will be in adult life and what the opportunities are to attain these goals (Wilson 1993; Elliott 1993; Wilson 1987). The research work on "possible selves" is very promising as a basis for developing an indicator of perception of future work roles (Cross and Markus 1994; Oyserman and Markus 1993; Oyserman 1993; Oyserman and Saltz 1993; Markus and Kitayama 1991; Oyserman and Markus 1990a, 1990b). These perceptions contribute to adolescents' decisions to become involved in learning and education, especially in the high school and postsecondary levels (Kane 1994). These perceptions are linked to social indicators such as educational achievement and involvement in postsecondary education.

Indicators of Health-Enhancing Behavior

Indicators of adolescent health status have typically focused on mortality and morbidity (Elster 1994). A review of the adolescent objectives for Healthy People 2000 reveals no positive indicators of adolescent health. In recent years, however, an interest in health promotion during the second decade of life has stimulated discussions about positive indicators of adolescent health (Millstein, Petersen, and Nightingale 1993). However, the state of the art regarding positive indicators of adolescent health has not kept pace with these recent developments in adolescent health promotion.

Positive indicators of adolescent health, including a *cluster of health-enhancing types of behavior and attitudes that promote lifelong healthy practices, including positive mental health outcomes* are, in comparison to the education indicators, under-developed. Elliott (1993) has proposed that there is a cluster of health-enhancing types of behavior that contribute to sound development during adolescence and throughout the life span. Drawing on the research on clusters of health-compromising behavior during adolescence, he puts forward the notion of healthy lifestyles as distinctive modes of living, defined by a pattern of behavior occurring with some consistency over time.

Evidence for health-enhancing lifestyles during adolescence is rather limited, partially due to the dominant focus on problems or poor outcomes. There is evidence for a cluster of health-enhancing behavior that includes exercise, adequate sleep, the use of safety belts, a healthy diet, seeking appropriate medical treatment, preventive physical examinations, and dental hygiene (Elliott 1993; Hansell and Mechanic 1990). Evidence for the clustering of health-compromising lifestyles, including substance abuse and delinquent behavior, is relatively strong (Merrill 1994; Dryfoos 1990; Fagan, Cheng, and Weis 1990; Elliott and Morse 1989; Donovan and Jessor 1985).

The following are potential indicators of positive adolescent health that are currently being collected on a national level and that could be employed in studies to test Elliott's idea of a cluster of health-enhancing sorts of behavior during adolescence:

Exercise and Fitness, Including Participation in Sports   The U.S. Public Health Service, in issuing its objectives for the year 2000, acknowledges the need to increase by at "least 50 percent the proportion of children and adolescents in first through twelfth grade who participate in daily school physical education" (U.S. Department of Health and Human Services 1991). The benefits of proper diet and physical activity may be particularly important during adolescence, both as a preventive measure in promoting sound development during the adolescent years and in discouraging specific diseases later in life (Sallis 1993).

National data on selected health-risk types of behavior, including information on physical fitness and healthy eating, are collected by federal agencies and by industry organizations, such as the National Sporting Goods Association, which conducts an annual survey of sports participation that includes young adolescents.

The Youth Risk Behavior Surveillance System (YRBSS), developed by the U.S. Centers for Disease Control and Prevention, is a major federal effort to measure health-risk behavior among adolescents throughout the United States, including adolescents who attend school. This system has three complementary components: national school-based surveys (collected biennially during odd-numbered years throughout the decade), state and local school-based surveys (conducted biennially during odd-numbered years throughout the decade), and a national household-based survey. In 1992, CDC and the U.S. Bureau of the Census incorporated a Youth Risk Behavior Supplement in the National Health Interview Survey and were thus able to obtain data from youth attending school and those not attending school—for example, dropouts. Also participating in the survey were college-aged youth, including those who had not finished high school, those who had completed high school but were not attending college, and those attending college (Kolbe, Kann, and Collins 1993). Youth Risk Behavior Surveillance System data are used to improve health and education policies and programs for youth nationwide.

Use of Seat Belts   Data are collected by Youth Risk Behavior Survey. Persons aged twelve to thirteen years were significantly less likely than those aged eighteen to twenty-one years to have reported "always" using safety belts when riding as a passenger in a car or truck.

Dental Hygiene   Adolescence is a pivotal period for dental and oral health, including prevention of dental caries, periodontal disease, and malocclusion (Albino and Lawrence 1993). National survey data on dental health problems of adolescents are collected by the National Institute of Dental Research, and through other surveys by the U.S. Department of Health and Human Services, including the National Health Interview Survey. These national surveys have yielded limited information about subgroups of the population (U.S. Congress 1991a, 1991b).

Healthy Diet   The U.S. Department of Health and Human Services collects data related to adolescent nutrition through various surveys, including the Youth Risk Behavior Survey, the National Health and Nutrition Examination Survey (NHANES), the Hispanic HANES, and the National Health Interview Survey. The U.S. Department of Agriculture collects data through its Nationwide Food Consumption Survey, the Diet and Health Knowledge Survey, National Evaluation of School Nutrition Programs, and the Continuing Survey of Food Intakes by Individuals, which is one component of the National Nutritional Monitoring System (U.S. Congress 1991a, 1991b).

Positive Mental Health   Compas (1993) has synthesized the research on the positive mental health outcomes of adolescents and has proposed a multiaxial framework. Based on this framework,

> Positive mental health during adolescence is defined as *a process characterized by development toward optimal current and future functioning in the capacity and motivation to cope with stress and to involve the self in personally meaningful instrumental activities and/or interpersonal relationships. Optimal*

functioning is relative and depends on the goals and values of the interested parties, appropriate developmental norms, and one's sociocultural group.[1]

Significantly for the potential of mental health as an indicator, Compas argues that the construct of positive mental health cannot be characterized by a single profile.

The development of an indicator for good mental health among adolescents would be highly desirable, given its potential linkage with other specific indicators of the health status of adolescents and the linkage of these indicators with educational achievement. Furthermore, assessments of adolescents reveal that mental health issues (reports of loneliness and depression, concerns about domestic violence and abuse) lead their list of health care needs (Millstein 1993).

Indicators of Preparation for Adult Roles

Another positive indicator of adolescent development is that older adolescents demonstrate preparedness for roles assumed as adults. The ability to be a caring friend and family member, and the ability to function productively as a member of the larger society are important, including the *capacity to be a responsible parent and citizen.* To understand the changing role adolescents assume in both the family and society, we focus on preparation of the adolescent for parenthood and for citizenship as two critical indicators.

Responsible Parenthood

Whether mother or father to a child, caregiver of a young child, or even an adult who has little or no contact with children, an important capacity is to be able to act in a parental role. Components of responsible parenthood, as identified by the Task Force on Meeting the Needs of Young Children (1994), include being knowledgeable about infant, child, and adolescent development, developing skills to support children and adolescents with developmentally appropriate guidance, knowledge of and access to family planning services and contraceptive methods, and having the motivation to be a good parent. Responsible parenthood represents a relatively new set of outcomes for the indicator field and requires further discussion regarding whether, using public funds, the United States wishes to invest in preparing youth for parenthood and in subsequently monitoring the outcomes of this preparation.

Adolescents acknowledge their need for information, skills, and support to become effective parents (Hayes 1987). The Alan Guttmacher Institute recently reported (1994) that close to half (48 percent) of American teens (ages fifteen to nineteen) say that their knowledge of sexuality and reproduction is inadequate. Even less guidance is provided to adolescents about how to resist peer pressure and the predation of older men in the case of young adolescent girls (Males 1993). While families are ideally the first source of information about parenthood, a range of institutions, including schools, religious institutions, and community-based youth-serving organizations, can educate adolescents for parenthood (Task Force on Meeting the Needs of Young Children 1994). Parent education programs should involve both genders, start no later than adolescence, but preferably begin in elementary school, and be age-appropriate and culturally sensitive (Task Force on Meeting the Needs of Young Children 1994). They should include:

- the development of infants, young children, and adolescents, and how parents, families, and communities can meet their needs;
- models of child-rearing, parenting skills, and the significance of family composition and environment on child development;
- impact of childbearing and child-rearing on the educational and occupational choices of parents, especially mothers;
- human reproduction (including the role of overall health in reproductive outcomes), methods of birth control (including abstinence), and the importance of health protection and promotion in the prenatal period;
- the causes of sexually transmitted diseases and ways of avoiding them;
- the effect of behavioral and environmental threats (including stress, poor nutrition, violence, and substance abuse) on the health of pregnant women, children, and families; and
- the availability of social services and other neighborhood supports, ranging from family planning and early intervention services for families at risk to Head Start programs and community health and social services.

Yet preparation for parenthood, which involves becoming a nurturing, caring adult for future generations whether one becomes a parent or not, constitutes a major gap in all American adolescents' current transition to adult roles. Existing programs are typically targeted toward specific groups of adolescents after they become pregnant or parents—in short, adolescent parenting programs. While effective programs of this kind are urgently needed, such programs would be optimal prior to pregnancy or the decision to have children. Part of responsible parenthood involves the decision about when, and if, to have children. Many American adolescents are having children when they are developmentally, socially, and economically unprepared for the responsibility for and caring of vulnerable babies.

Parenthood programs for young men especially need attention. Parenting education usually focuses on the adolescent mother. However, small-scale programs that pay particular attention to the role of the adolescent father have been developed to enhance father-child involvement (Hayes 1987). Interventions to encourage adolescent fathering often involve a comprehensive approach that combines parent education with community services, school activities, employment training initiatives, and life skills training. An example of such a program is Avance, a family support and education program serving Mexican American families in Texas. Evaluations show that this program improves the families' ability to provide an emotionally stimulating and nurturing environment for their young children, positively influences parents' attitudes toward child-rearing, and expands parental use of community resources (Task Force on Meeting the Needs of Young Children 1994).

Responsible parenthood must also be based on the ability of parents to provide a minimum level of economic resources to support the family unit. Barring changes in United States economic and social policies regarding income support to families and job creation, young adults must be gainfully employed at wages that are adequate to support a family unit. Thus, this aspect of responsible parenthood intersects with indicators regarding the economic capacity of the adolescent to support him/herself and dependents, related to educational attainment (Nightingale and Wolverton 1993).

Responsible Citizenship

A second aspect of adolescent roles is the preparation for responsible citizenship. A democratic society rests on an educated and informed electorate that is knowledgeable about the institutions and processes of their political system as well as a wide range of domestic and international issues. Such citizens vote regularly in elections at the local, state, and federal levels. They participate in the rich array of voluntary and community associations that are so characteristic of American society.

Citizenship indicators are part of the National Goals Initiative. Knowledge of civics is already being collected at the national level, but data collection regarding community and service learning and voter registration at age eighteen is not systematic or widespread. Of these indicators, voter registration is the best candidate for an outcome indicator of likely participation as an adult citizen.

The National Education Goals Panel's Resolution on the Assessment of Citizenship recommends three indicators as relevant assessments of citizenship: knowledge of civics, involvement in community service, and voter registration at age eighteen.

Civics Knowledge   Readiness for responsible citizenship is one positive aspect of adolescent growth. Historically, the goal of educational institutions, both public and private, has been to prepare young people for responsible participation in a democratic society by teaching appropriate curricula on political theory and processes and the responsibilities of American citizens.

American schools today appear to have failed to educate young people in civics. In 1988, less than half of all twelfth grade students understood specific governmental structures and functions, and only 6 percent understood well the role of various political institutions (National Education Goals Panel 1992). According to the State Assessment Center of the Council of Chief State School Officers, only two or three states assess high school students' knowledge of citizenship (National Education Goals Panel 1992).

The National Assessment of Education Progress (NAEP) is a state-by-state assessment in specific subject areas occurring every three years at the fourth-, eighth-, and twelfth-grade levels. The National Education Goals Panel recommends that knowledge of citizenship, including an understanding of the political, legal, and economic systems, be assessed by state and be aggregated at the national level by the NAEP. The pressures on NAEP to collect a broad array of information are great, and consideration of the inclusion of additional data must be carefully weighed against costs and strains on students and the educational testing system. However, to the extent that the United States is committed to broad participation of knowledgeable citizens in its democratic form of government, some means of assessing basic knowledge of civics seems advisable.

Community Service and Volunteer Work   Participation in community service and service learning is another potential positive indicator of adolescent development. This service builds skills and discipline, provides self-respect and elicits respect from others, and contributes to a vigorous public life. The National and Community Service Trust Act of 1993 recognized that "Residents of low-income communities, especially youth and young adults, can be empowered through their service and can help provide future community leadership" (National and Community Service Trust Act of 1993, Public Law 103-82, Sec. 2, Paragraph 6 [September 21, 1993]). The legislation, however, is not limited to youth from low-income families, and an equally compelling case can be made for more economically advantaged youth.

Information on community service is not systematically collected at this time at the local, state, or national level. The surveys that do exist reveal a range of participation in voluntary activities. Estimates of voluntary activity during adolescence range from 13 percent of the sixteen- to nineteen-year-olds according to the U.S. Department of Labor's Bureau of Labor Statistics in 1990 (National Center for Education Statistics, 1993), to an Independent Sector survey which found that 61 percent of adolescents twelve to seventeen years of age volunteered an average of three hours or more a week in 1991 (Knauft n.d.).

A major issue, prior to the collection of data, is the appropriate definition of community service and what would constitute a meaningful indicator of such service, in terms of appropriate activities, length, and nature of service (Keith 1994). There are no current data collected at the state or local level, and thus little is available to measure trends. The establishment of the omnibus Corporation for National and Community Service may provide a venue for the collection of information on community service at the national and state levels in the future.

Voter Registration   A fundamental manifestation of citizenship and a positive indicator of adolescent development is registration to vote at age eighteen. Collection of this information (registration, nonregistration) is relatively straightforward, but whether agencies that have the most regular contact with adolescents (schools, motor vehicle departments) will collect and maintain such information must be addressed. Information on voter registration and voter participation is currently collected by the U.S. Bureau of the Census and is available at the national and state levels. Specific information on adolescent voting patterns *at the local level* could be collected by the annual survey of high school seniors—*Monitoring the Future: A Continuing Study of the Lifestyles and Values of Youth*—many of whom are eighteen years old, but then it would not include school dropouts or infrequent attendees in schools. These individuals are unlikely to register to vote, since voting has been found to be related to higher levels of education (U.S. Bureau of the Census 1994).

A major issue is whether the United States wishes to collect systematic information on the registration of eligible voters, including their actual voting, on a national or state level. If such a system were to exist for adults, then instituting one for first-time registrants would naturally follow. As long as no such system exists for adult voters, collection of such information for adolescents is questionable.

RECOMMENDATIONS FOR POSITIVE INDICATORS OF ADOLESCENT DEVELOPMENT

In an ideal world with unlimited resources, information on all the above candidates for positive indicators of adolescent development would be desirable. Indeed, the list of potential indicators could be lengthened to include others of interest, such as indicators of character development. However, hard policy choices must be made, particularly with attention to the responsible use of public resources for fundamental research and for national, state, and local collection of social statistics, given the increasing competition for such resources.

With this context in mind, we recommend the further exploration of the following four indicators: perception of opportunity; involvement in postsecondary education; health-enhancing behavior; and voter registration.

Perception of Opportunity

Adolescents' perceptions of opportunity are key factors in their current behavior and future achievements. Adolescents with views of negative future outcomes are not likely to engage in prosocial behavior (Oyserman and Markus 1990). Perception of opportunity affects all aspects of an adolescent's life, including involvement in education and engaging in health-promoting activities (Wilson 1993). Adolescents who perceive future opportunities are more likely to move into constructive, positive adult roles in society.

Involvement in Postsecondary Education

A primary concern of the United States must be the educational capacities and high-level skills of its citizens. The educational attainment of a society's members is a major factor in economic development, individual involvement in the community and political life, and the adoption of healthy behavior. Currently indicators focus on the negative outcomes regarding education, such as high school dropout and illiteracy. The current global economy requires high school graduation as a minimum and postsecondary matriculation and attainment of post-high-school education or training as highly desirable.

Health-Enhancing Behavior of Adolescents

Health-enhancing environments for adolescents support them in making a successful transition to adulthood (Elliott 1993). Measurement of health-enhancing behavior requires a broad-based survey covering adolescent reports of physical and mental health status. Questions regarding exercise, eating habits, and daily activities tap into health-promoting patterns. The YRBSS could be adapted to include health-enhancing, as well as risky, behavior.

Considerable work already exists on the conceptualization of positive mental health among adolescents and identification of a research agenda (Compas 1993). However, the harnessing of this work for the development of an indicator will require research resources. As conceptualized by Compas (1993), positive adolescent mental health requires a multiaxial framework involving different perspectives or sources (adolescents, parents, teachers, peers, mental health professionals), developmental status, and sociocultural factors. Within this framework, two dimensions of positive adolescent mental health involve the development of skills to cope with stress, and the development of skills to engage in personally meaningful activities.

Health-enhancing behavior is likely to vary according to community and environmental conditions. Thus, information at the local or community level is likely to be most relevant for public policy and targeted interventions. State and national data can provide general information on the health status of adolescents, but is not likely to be informative for local, programmatic interventions.

Voter Registration

The United States is viewed as the leading democracy in the world. However, its citizens vote at comparatively low rates. As an indicator of interest in and commitment to citizenship, voter registration at age eighteen and subsequent voting would seem simple indicators to collect.

As discussed above, monitoring of the voting behavior of American citizens will require upgrading. At present, the U.S. Census Bureau collects information on voter registration for different age groups and by gender and race/ethnicity. States and local entities vary in their collection of information on voter registration. Any effort to collect information on voter registration at age eighteen should be part of a reformed data system to collect information on voter registration for the entire eligible adult population.

Unlike most indicators, voter registration and subsequent voting are relatively straightforward: either a person votes or does not, registers or does not. What is lacking is the public consensus and the will to engage in collecting this information on a systematic basis as an indicator, not only as a positive indicator of adolescent development, but also of the functioning of a democratic society.

CONCLUSION

Indicators of adolescent development must include the full range of "outcomes," from the socially desirable to problem behavior. The current imbalance toward the negative or problematic aspects of adolescent development should be redressed. Similar to the measurement of negative indicators of adolescent development, the collection of positive indicators is not straightforward and possibly more daunting. Significant barriers, depending on the specific indicator, include the paucity of basic or fundamental research related to the indicator; issues of validity, particularly construct validity; multiple sources of data and the need to triangulate among data sources; and developmental and sociocultural factors.

To the extent that the collection of specific indicators can influence their social valence, the careful identification of positive indicators of adolescent development can play an important role in changing the ways in which a society views its adolescents. This chapter provides a starting point for such a needed effort.

This paper does not reflect the views of the Carnegie Council on Adolescent Development or Carnegie Corporation of New York. Responsibility for the accuracy of the content of the paper rests with the authors.

NOTE

1. Compas 1993, pp. 166–67, italics not in original source.

REFERENCES

Alan Guttmacher Institute. 1994. *Sex and America's Teenagers*. New York: The Alan Guttmacher Institute.

Albino, Judith N., and Sandra D. Lawrence. 1993. "Promoting Oral Health in Adolescents." In *Promoting the Health of Adolescents: New Directions for the Twenty-first Century*, edited by Susan G. Millstein, Anne C. Petersen, and Elena O. Nightingale. New York: Oxford University Press.

Center for the Study of Social Policy. 1993. *Kids Count Data Book, State Profiles of Child Well-Being*. Washington, D.C.: Annie E. Casey Foundation.

Centers for Disease Control and Prevention. 1994. "Prevalence of Selected Risk Factors for Chronic Disease by Education Level in Racial/Ethnic Populations." *Morbidity and Mortality Weekly Report*, December 9, 1994.

Children's Safety Network. 1991. *A Data Book of Child and Adolescent Injury*. Washington, D.C.: National Center for Education in Maternal and Child Health.

Compas, Bruce E. 1993. "Promoting Positive Mental Health During Adolescents." In *Promoting the Health of Adolescents: New Directions for the Twenty-first Century*, edited by Susan G. Millstein, Anne C. Petersen, and Elena O. Nightingale. New York: Oxford University Press.

Cross, S. E., and Hazel R. Markus. 1994. "Self-Schemas, Possible Selves, and Competent Performance." *Journal of Educational Psychology* 86(3): 423–38.

Csikszentmihalyi, Mihalyi, and Reed Larson. 1984. *Being Adolescent: Conflict and Growth in the Teenage Years*. New York: Basic Books.

Donovan, Joseph, and Richard Jessor. 1985. "Structure of Problem Behavior in Adolescence and Young Adulthood." *Journal of Consulting and Clinical Psychology* 53: 890–904.

Dryfoos, Joy G. 1990. *Adolescents at Risk*. New York: Oxford University Press.

Elliott, Delbert S. 1993. "Health-Enhancing and Health-Compromising Lifestyles." In *Promoting the Health of Adolescents: New Directions for the Twenty-first Century*, edited by Susan G. Millstein, Anne C. Petersen, and Elena O. Nightingale. New York: Oxford University Press.

Elliott, Delbert S., and B. J. Morse. 1989. "Delinquency and Drug Use as Risk Factors in Teenage Sexual Activity." *Youth and Society* 21: 21–60.

Elster, Arthur B. 1994. "Adolescent Health Indicators." Paper prepared for the conference on Indicators of Children's Well-Being, Rockville, Md. (November 17–18, 1994).

Fagan, Jeffrey, Y.T. Cheng, and J.G. Weis. 1990. "Drug Use and Delinquency Among Inner-City Youths." *Journal of Drug Issues* 20: 349–400.

Feldman, S. Shirley, and Glen R. Elliott, Eds. 1990. *At the Threshold: The Developing Adolescent*. Cambridge, Mass.: Harvard University Press.

Gans, Judith E., Dale A. Blyth, Arthur B. Elster, and L.L. Gaveras. 1990. *America's Adolescents: How Healthy Are They?* Chicago: American Medical Association.

Hamburg, David A. 1989. *Early Adolescence: A Critical Time for Interventions in Education and Health.* New York: Carnegie Corporation of New York.

Hansell, S., and David Mechanic. 1990. "Parent and Peer Effects on Adolescent Health Behavior." In *Health Hazards in Adolescence*, edited by Klaus Hurrelmann, and F. Losel. New York: Walter de Gruyter.

Hauser, Robert M. 1994. "Indicators of High School Dropout." Paper prepared for the conference on Indicators of Children's Well-Being, Rockville, Md. (November 17–18, 1994).

Hayes, Cheryl D., Ed. 1987. *Risking the Future: Adolescent Sexuality, Pregnancy, and Childbearing.* Washington, D.C.: National Academy Press.

Hechinger, Fred M. 1992. *Fateful Choices: Healthy Youth for the 21st Century.* New York: Hill and Wang.

Kane, T. J. 1994. "Postsecondary and Vocational Education: Keeping Track of the College Track." Paper prepared for the conference on Indicators of Children's Well-Being, Rockville, Md. (November 17–18, 1994).

Keith, N. Z., ed. 1994. "School-Based Community Service." *Journal of Adolescence, Special Issue* 17(4): 311–409.

Knauft, E. B. n.d. *America's Teenagers as Volunteers.* Washington, D.C.: Independent Sector.

Kolbe, Lloyd J., L. Kann, and J. L. Collins. 1993. "Overview of the Youth Risk Behavior Surveillance System." *Public Health Reports* 108 (Suppl. 1): 2–10.

Koretz, Daniel. 1994. "Indicators of Educational Achievement." Paper prepared for the conference on Indicators of Children's Well-Being, Rockville, Md. (November 17–18, 1994).

Males, Michael. 1993. "School-Age Pregnancy: Why Hasn't Prevention Worked?" *Journal of School Health* 63: 420–32.

Markus, Hazel R., and Shinobu Kitayama. 1991. "Culture and the Self: Implications for Cognition, Emotion, and Motivation." *Psychological Review* 98: 224–53.

Merrill, J. C. 1994. *Cigarettes, Alcohol, Marijuana: Gateways to Illicit Drug Use.* New York: Center on Addiction and Substance Abuse.

Millstein, Susan G. 1993. "A View of Health from the Adolescent's Perspective." In *Promoting the Health of Adolescents: New Directions for the Twenty-first Century*, edited by Susan G. Millstein, Anne C. Petersen, and Elena O. Nightingale. New York: Oxford University Press.

Millstein, Susan G., Anne C. Petersen, and Elena O. Nightingale, eds. 1993. *Promoting the Health of Adolescents: New Directions for the Twenty-first Century.* New York: Oxford University Press.

Moore, Kristen A. 1994. "Criteria for Indicators of Child Wellbeing." Prepared for the conference on Indicators of Children's Well-Being, Rockville, Md. (November 17–18, 1994).

National Center for Education Statistics. 1993. *Youth Indicators, 1993, Trends in the Well-Being of American Youth.* Washington: U.S. Government Printing Office.

National Education Goals Panel. 1992. *The National Education Goals Report, Building a National of Learners.* Washington: U.S. Government Printing Office.

Nightingale, Elena O., and Lisa Wolverton. 1993. "Adolescent Rolelessness in Modern Society." *Teachers College Record* 94: 472–86.

Oyserman, Daphne. 1993. "Adolescent Identity and Delinquency in Interpersonal Context." *Child Psychiatry and Human Development* 23: 203–14.

Oyserman, Daphne, and Hazel R. Markus. 1990a. "Possible Selves and Delinquency." *Journal of Personality and Social Psychology* 59: 112–25.

———. 1990b. "Possible Selves in Balance: Implications for Delinquency." *Journal of Social Issues* 46: 141–57.

————. 1993. "The Sociocultural Self." In *Psychological Perspectives on the Self*, edited by J. Suls, and A.G. Greenwald. Hillsdale, N.J.: Lawrence Erlbaum Associates.

Oyserman, Daphne, and E. Saltz. 1993. "Competence, Delinquency, and Attempts to Attain Possible Selves." *Journal of Personality and Social Psychology* 65: 360–74.

Pittman, Karen, and M. Wright. 1991. "Rationale for Enhancing the Role of the Non-School Voluntary Sector in Youth Development." Carnegie Council on Adolescent Development, Washington, D.C. Unpublished manuscript.

Sallis, James F. 1993. "Promoting Healthful Diet and Physical Activity." In *Promoting the Health of Adolescents: New Directions for the Twenty-first Century*, edited by Susan G. Millstein, Anne C. Petersen, and Elena O. Nightingale. New York: Oxford University Press.

Schlossman, Stephen, and Robert B. Cairns. 1993. "Problem Girls: Observations on Past and Present." In *Children in Time and Place: Developmental and Historical Insights*, edited by Glen H. Elder, J. Model, and R. D. Parke. New York: Cambridge University Press.

Task Force on Education of Young Adolescents. 1989. *Turning Points: Preparing American Youth for the 21st Century*. Washington: Carnegie Council on Adolescent Development.

Task Force on Meeting the Needs of Young Children. 1994. *Starting Points: Meeting the Needs of Our Youngest Children*. New York: Carnegie Corporation of New York.

Task Force on Youth Development and Community Programs. 1992. *A Matter of Time: Risk and Opportunity in the Nonschool Hours*. Washington, D.C.: Carnegie Council on Adolescent Development.

U.S. Bureau of the Census. 1994a. *More Education Means Higher Career Earnings*, SB/94-17. Washington: U.S. Department of Commerce.

————. 1994b. *Statistical Abstract of the United States: 1994*, 114th ed. Washington: U.S. Government Printing Office.

U.S. Congress, Office of Technology Assessment. 1991a. *Adolescent Health—Volume I: Summary and Policy Options*, no. H-468. Washington: U.S. Government Printing Office.

————. 1991b. *Adolescent Health—Volume II: Background and the Effectiveness of Selected Prevention and Treatment Services*, no. H-466. Washington: U.S. Government Printing Office.

U.S. Department of Health and Human Services. 1991. *Healthy People 2000: National Health Promotion and Disease Prevention Objectives*, no. (PHS)91-50212. Washington: U.S. Government Printing Office.

Wilson, William Julius. 1987. *The Truly Disadvantaged: The Inner City, the Underclass, and Public Policy*. Chicago: The University of Chicago Press.

————. 1993. "Poverty, Health, and Adolescent Health Promotion." In *Promoting Adolescent Health: Third Symposium on Research Opportunities in Adolescence*. Washington, D.C.: Carnegie Council on Adolescent Development.

21

The Status of Adolescent
Problem Behavior Indicators

Bruce P. Kennedy and Deborah Prothrow-Stith

THE ADOLESCENT PERIOD is a time ripe for experimentation with different behaviors and lifestyles. The central developmental task of adolescence is to use
that experimentation to construct a coherent psychosocial identity. This emerging
identity involves an increasing independence from parents and authorities
through the development of personal, sexual, occupational, ideological, and
moral commitments. Commitments to socially approved roles and their implicit
value structures serve as the bridge between the adolescent and the social world
of the adult, providing the basis for direction and meaning in the individual's life
course (Blos 1962; Erikson 1968; Prothrow-Stith 1991).

With the emergence of increased cognitive power and physical maturity, adolescents become concerned with a variety of issues that relate to this task. They
begin to explore the meanings of the various social, occupational, and gender
roles that are presented to them, and to experiment with many of the behaviors
and lifestyles that are associated with these. During this period, peer relations
take on a greater significance in providing feedback concerning the self, and it is
often in this context that many adolescents engage in behavior that puts them at
risk for serious health and psychosocial outcomes.

Social role experimentation for most adolescents is part of normal healthy
development toward future adult roles. For some, however, it establishes patterns
of problem behavior that significantly impair their life chances. Adolescent problem behavior includes a variety of activities that are viewed as outside the norms
of conventional society and are seen as detrimental to the healthy development of
youth. Jessor and Jessor (1977) observed that alcohol and drug use, risky driving,
delinquent behavior, and precocious sexual intercourse were correlated. Based on
their research, they proposed a "syndrome of problem behavior" that indicates a
particular lifestyle characterized by risky behavior. They posit that these behaviors are anticipated by a constellation of factors that include personality, environmental, and behavioral dimensions that predispose adolescents to patterns of
risky or problem behavior. Subsequent studies of youths have generally supported
this hypothesis (Bachman, O'Malley, and Johnson 1980; Donovan, Jessor, and
Costa 1988; Elliott, Huizinga, and Menard 1989; Farrell et al. 1992), but the
degree to which these sorts of behavior co-occur across different segments of the
adolescent population is not well defined.

In a review of the problem behavior literature dealing with the overlap of juvenile delinquency, school failure, teen pregnancy, and substance abuse, Dryfoos (1990) concluded that six factors were related to all of these sorts of problem behavior: early onset of behavior problems; poor school adjustment; engagement in generally antisocial behavior; high susceptibility to peer influence; poor parenting and a general lack of parental supervision; and poverty and urban environment. She concluded that about 25 percent of youth will reach adulthood without the resources to adequately meet the demands and responsibilities of adult roles in the family and workplace.

Any full treatment of adolescent well-being must take into account the behavioral problems that place the youth at the greatest risk for mortality and morbidity, as well as for future psychosocial maladjustment. From a public health perspective, indicators of problem behavior linked to the most prevalent and serious health and social problems for adolescents should receive the first priority in the development and continuation of any statistical surveillance system. Among all of the sorts of problem behaviors, drug use (including alcohol and tobacco), risky driving, violence (both interpersonal and intrapersonal), and risky sexual behavior contribute the most to morbidity, mortality, and other social problems (including school failure) during the adolescent period, and thus will be the focus of the ensuing discussion (Kolbe, Kann, and Collins 1993).

Alcohol and Drug Use

Alcohol and other drug abuse is perhaps the most significant and pervasive problem behavior adolescents engage in, as it is implicated in a variety of other unhealthy and life-threatening types of behavior. Two legal drugs, alcohol and cigarettes, contribute significantly to the mortality and morbidity of youths and adults. The short-term consequences of cigarette use are seen in decreased physical activity by youth; for pregnant teenagers, they are related to lower infant birth weight and mortality (Public Health Service 1980). Early heavy use predicts later use which is associated with approximately four hundred thousand adult deaths each year (U.S. Department of Health and Human Services 1990). Studies of smoking conducted in Britain have shown that children who have tried cigarettes more than four times generally develop an addiction to nicotine and subsequently go on to have lengthy smoking careers (Russell 1990). Smoking also predicts other drug use and is seen as a potential stepping stone to experimentation with other substances (Kandel 1975). Recent surveys of American high school seniors indicate that about 28 percent of high school seniors currently smoke, and 10 percent, more than half a pack a day (Johnston et al. 1993).

In addition to the long-term effects on health and psychosocial functioning, heavy alcohol use also has more immediate short-term consequences for adolescent well-being and is a significant contributing factor to mortality in this population. Alcohol is implicated in much of the youth life lost due to motor vehicle crashes, drownings, homicides, and suicides, accounting for approximately half of all injuries resulting in death from these causes (Perrine, Peck, and Fell 1988). Drug and alcohol use also lead to a myriad of other sorts of problem behavior—unprotected sexual intercourse among them, which puts youth at risk for early pregnancy and for contracting STDs (including HIV). Heavy drug and alcohol use are also strongly associated with poor academic attainment and high school dropout rates which in turn put adolescents at risk for a constellation of other negative consequences (Rice et al. 1985).

Priority indicators for alcohol and drug abuse should include date for each individual on the type of drugs used, frequency and quantity of use, and age of onset.

Risky Driving Practices

Unintentional injuries are the leading cause of death for youths ages twelve to twenty-four. The vast majority of these are attributed to motor vehicle crashes, which are the leading cause of death for all persons aged one to thirty-four. Adolescents (fifteen to nineteen) are at particular risk from dying or being seriously injured in a motor vehicle crash: although they represent only 6 percent of the licensed drivers, they account for 13 percent of all motor vehicle fatalities (National Highway Traffic Safety Administration 1992).

Many of the deaths from crashes are attributable to risky driving which involves driving under the influence of alcohol, lack of occupant restraint use, competitive speed, and aggressive driving. Approximately half of all motor vehicle fatalities involve alcohol and about 30 percent of adolescents aged fifteen to twenty were intoxicated at the time of the fatal crash (National Highway Traffic Safety Administration 1992).

Among all persons killed in motor vehicle crashes, 70 percent were not wearing seatbelts. With an 83 percent nonuse rate, adolescents have the lowest seatbelt use rate of all fatally injured occupants (National Highway Traffic Safety Administration 1992). Jonah (1986) has shown that drinking and driving, no belt use, and speeding and aggressive driving cluster together, and concluded that these types of behavior could be viewed as part of a larger set of adolescent problem behavior as conceptualized by Jessor and Jessor (1977).

Priority indicators for this behavior include the prevalence and incidence of driving under the influence of alcohol and other drugs, riding with an intoxicated driver, use of seatbelts, and aggressive driving. Arrest rates for driving while intoxicated (DWI), reckless driving, and the number of alcohol-involved fatalities should also be monitored for this age group.

Violence

Intentional injuries resulting from violence make a significant contribution to the mortality and morbidity of the adolescent population. In addition to the emotional costs to the victims of violence, their families, and surrounding communities, injuries caused by violent behavior are estimated to cost society approximately twenty-six billion dollars a year (O'Carroll et al. 1993).

Homicide is the leading cause of death for young African American males and females (fifteen to thirty-four) and the second leading cause of death for all ten- to nineteen-year-olds (Hammett et al. 1992). Homicide rates among adolescents have risen since the 1980s, with an increasing number attributable to firearms (Fingerhut et al. 1992). With this rise in homicides is an increase in weapon-carrying and the use of weapons in violent altercations among youth. In a recent survey, over 26 percent of ninth- to twelfth-graders reported carrying a weapon at least once in the previous thirty days (Kann et al. 1993).

In addition to violence against others, self-directed violence in the form of suicide attempts and completions are also cause for concern in the adolescent population. Suicide rates among the young have risen steadily since the 1960s and are currently the third-leading cause of death for adolescents and young adults between the ages of fifteen and twenty-four (U.S. Department of Education 1991).

Key indicators for violent behavior are the prevalence and incidence of weapon-carrying, fighting behavior (that which results in injury and that which does not), violent victimization, suicidal ideation, suicide attempts (those that result in injury and those that do not), and the role of alcohol and other drugs in this behavior. Additional indicators to track are the actual numbers of homicides and suicides among adolescents.

Risky Sexual Behavior

Early sexual activity puts adolescents at risk for unwanted pregnancy, STDs (including HIV), and a variety of other negative health and social outcomes, both for themselves and for their children in the case of natality (Card 1981; Furstenberg et al. 1987; Hofferth and Hayes 1987). Early initiation of sexual intercourse during adolescence increases the risks for both pregnancy and STDs (Hayes 1987). Youths between the ages of 15 and 29 account for 86 percent of all cases of STDs. Infection rates of STDs vary up to 36 percent for adolescents, with those from low-income areas having the highest rates of contraction (Office of Technology Assessment 1991). About 20 percent of all AIDS cases are in the twenty- to twenty-nine-year-old age group, which indicates that many of these were infected with HIV during the early adolescent years (Centers for Disease Control and Prevention 1996). AIDS is currently the sixth-leading cause of death for all adolescents and young adults between the ages of fifteen and twenty-four (Centers for Disease Control and Prevention 1994).

About 54 percent of high school students report having had sexual intercourse; among this group around 69 percent report currently being sexually active. Eighteen percent of high school students report having had four or more sexual partners during their lifetime. Among those reporting that they were currently sexually active, 81 percent had used contraceptives. Only 46 percent report using a condom (Kann et al. 1993).

It is clear from recent surveys that risky sexual practices continue to be a major problem behavior for adolescents. Important behavioral indicators in these regards should focus on the use of contraceptives (especially condoms), age of first sexual intercourse, frequency of intercourse, number of partners, and the role of alcohol and drugs in sexual activity. Other indicators are fertility and abortion rates for adolescents.

LEVELS OF INDICATORS

Taken as a whole, the types of problem behavior reviewed above can be conceptualized as the focus for policy actions and preventative measures, and in themselves they are measurable outcomes for the national objectives put forth in *Healthy People 2000* (Public Health Service 1990). Measures that adequately track these behavioral indicators are clearly needed if we are to monitor the progress toward national goals for the health and welfare of our youth.

In addition to monitoring trends in the types of problem behavior themselves, other social indicators that contribute to these behavior patterns are also critical to measure if informed policy decisions are to be made. It is critical to know which sociodemographic groups are at greatest risk for which type of behavior and for what reasons. Simply monitoring overt behavior will not contribute to our knowledge and understanding of the social contexts and settings which shape and support such behavior. Without a complete, contextualized understanding of adolescent problem behavior, misguided policies and ineffective prevention efforts are designed and implemented. Indicators of individual-level, family-level, and community-level variables are needed if we are to develop sophisticated models of problem behavior and inform our current theories as to the causal and protective factors that lead to or away from behavior that puts adolescents at risk for maladaptations.

A basic framework for the types of indicators at each level that are crucial to a fully functional and effective indicator system is described in the following section. This description is followed by a discussion reflecting the currently available information for each of the levels with recommendations for improvements in the future.

Individual-Level Indicators

At the individual level, aside from the prevalence, incidence, and duration of all the high-risk sorts of behavior, basic demographic indicators that enable disaggregation of the data by age, gender, race/ethnicity, and socioeconomic status are critical to assist in the targeting of efforts to groups in greatest need. This point is brought home when comparing causes of mortality across different age and race/ethnic groups: While for all adolescents, the leading cause of death is motor vehicle crashes, this is not true for African American adolescents, for whom the leading cause of death is homicide (Hammett et al. 1992).

Indicators at the individual level should also assess such potential antecedent factors as: general psychological well-being, including self-esteem and perceived self-efficacy, and anxiety and depression; personality dimensions such as impulsivity, sensation-seeking, and rebelliousness; educational and vocational aspirations; academic standing and achievement; and use of leisure time.

Use of leisure time is a particularly high priority indicator as little is known about the relative contribution of different activities to the promotion of problem behavior. Indicators in this area should include data on the exposure to different types of media (television, videos, movies) with different types of content (for example, violence).

Other time-use indicators should attempt to quantify the degree of involvement in youth cultures. Youth cultures are important mediators of problem behavior. They provide the belief and value systems that structure the activities and concerns of adolescents. More detailed measures of lifestyle factors would help to create a richer portrait of the milieu in which youths present themselves and forge the meanings of their activities through the symbolic interchange of codes of speech, action, and dress. Indicators addressing these issues should be developed to include both cultural categories deemed as deviant (gangsta, freak, burnout) and those that are considered prosocial (school clubs, sports teams, church groups). Additional time-use indicators should assess the degree and availability of adult supervision in activities outside the context of school. Information on the role of these factors in influencing problem behavior is seriously lacking.

Family-Level Indicators

Indicators of family economic stability, including parents' levels of education, occupations and incomes, health insurance coverage, and other variables that capture parenting styles and parents' levels of involvement in risky behavior are vital for understanding the dynamics between the home environment and the adolescent's development.

Three critical factors that have received little attention for many of the problem behavior areas are the effects of poverty, family structure, and parental behavior. The effects of these dimensions on problem behavior are complex, not well understood, and appear to vary as a function of gender, race, and ethnicity. For example, a recent reanalysis of Gleuck's classic study of delinquency found strong effects of parenting and disciplinary styles on delinquent behavior that had been previously overlooked (Sampson and Laub 1994).

At present, the effects of race or ethnicity cannot be disentangled from the effects of socioeconomic status on most types of problem behavior (Dryfoos 1990; Huston, McLoyd, and Coll 1994). Persons with similar educational achievement and occupations may still differ as a function of ethnicity with regards to income, and especially to subjective measures of well-being such as job satisfaction. Methods of disaggregation are needed to examine these effects among youth of differing ethnic and socioeconomic backgrounds.

Other important family-level indicator variables include the type of housing (own home, apartment, public housing), the number of household members who compete for resources and parental attention, and the availability of parents or other caretakers during after-school hours.

Community-Level Variables

A number of community-level indicators have been suggested as potential antecedents to adolescent problem behavior. Among the most important of those suggested deal with the quality of the neighborhood and surrounding community. Indicators of quality are typically measured by the levels of poverty, crime, unemployment, and segregation within the community. Other community factors that are important are the quality of the schools, health care delivery systems, and the presence and involvement of other local institutions such as churches and recreational facilities.

The importance of the community-level variables should not be lost in the rush to collect individual incidence rates for specific types of problem behavior. Community factors such as levels of poverty, segregation, and unemployment create high-risk environments for youths and have been shown to have profound effects on drug abuse, violence, teen pregnancy, and school failure (National Research Council 1993).

To fully understand the trends and dynamics of adolescent problem behavior we need to collect data on all three of these levels. The importance of the family and community context in shaping and fostering healthy child and adolescent adaptations is hardly a controversial view of human development. It is a truism that socialization, and thus healthy development, is an interactional process between persons and context, yet information on these related factors is rarely integrated. While it is a difficult task to disaggregate data along all three of these levels, it is critical to develop methods that allow for such analyses and reporting. The rest of this chapter will focus on how well the current data sources on indicators of adolescent problem behavior enable such analyses.

STATUS OF ADOLESCENT PROBLEM BEHAVIOR INDICATORS WITH RECOMMENDATIONS

At present, there are several federal survey programs underway that accumulate timely data on indicators of adolescent problem behavior. There is a degree of overlap among some of these surveys as to the types of indicators collected, but not all cover the types of behavior to the same extent, nor do all collect vital information on the individual, family, and community levels discussed above. A detailed review of each of the survey programs is beyond the scope of this chapter. Instead, the focus here is on the extent to which priority indicators are measured and tracked within the federal statistical system. Recommendations for improvements conclude this chapter.

Primary data for individual-level problem behavior indicators can be obtained from several different sources. In general, the key indicators of adolescent problem behavior are being adequately monitored by various components of the statistical system, yet other individual-level variables are sorely absent.

Key indicators on the prevalence and incidence of drug use behavior are tracked on a regular basis by the Monitoring the Future Survey (MTFS), the National Household Survey of Drug Abuse (NHSDA), and the more recent Youth Risk Behavior Surveillance System (YRBSS). Indicators of risky driving practices are collected by both the MTFS and YRBSS. In addition, data on alcohol involvement and seatbelt usage in fatal motor vehicle crashes can be obtained from the Fatal Accident Reporting System (FARS), and arrest rates for driving while intoxicated (DWI) can be obtained from the Uniform Crime Reports.

Key indicators related to violence can be constructed from the YRBSS, which contains questions related to the incidence and prevalence of weapon-carrying, fighting, and suicide ideation and attempts. Data on arrests for violent behavior, victimization, and actual homicides and suicides are available from the Uniform Crime Reports, the National Crime Victimization Survey, and the Vital Statistics, respectively.

It should be acknowledged that arrest data are problematic indicators of incidence of violence. Not all episodes of violence lead to arrest, and poverty increases the likelihood of arrest. Nonfatal episodes of violence that result in injury are not adequately measured, in that emergency department assault data are not collected routinely and school suspension rates for violence or weapon-carrying are not collected in a standardized manner. Surveys such as the YRBSS and Crime Victimization Survey provide some remedy for these data needs, but there is still room for improvement. Developing more detailed e-codes for emergency rooms and trauma centers so that treatment for violence-related injuries could be better monitored would be extremely useful.[1]

Primary indicators of risky sexual behavior are also being tracked regularly by the YRBSS, which collects indicators on the frequency of sexual intercourse, number of partners, use of contraceptives, and alcohol and drug use accompanying sexual intercourse. Other sources containing more detailed information are the National Survey of Family Growth, the National Survey of Adolescent Males, and the National Longitudinal Survey of Youth. Data on fertility rates can be obtained from the Vital Statistics. The Centers for Disease Control and Prevention tabulates abortion rates and STD rates from state-provided data.

Indicators of adolescent problem behavior are generally well collected by the various government agencies that have responsibilities for specific program areas. However, there is considerable fragmentation and very little synergy from complementary efforts. The fragmentation by problem area—sexuality, violence, or drug abuse—is more a reflection of government organization than the actual occurrence of these types of behaviors in youth and has led to duplications of effort that often produce incompatible data for comparisons across problem areas. As we have argued, these sorts of adolescent problem behavior generally co-occur. To fully understand this we need to be collecting indicators of all sorts of problem behaviors in the surveys of youth.

Promotion of Interagency Coordination

Recent efforts have attempted to address this problem. Perhaps the most promising of these is the cross-agency effort spearheaded by the Centers for Disease Control and Prevention. This work has culminated in the Youth Risk Behavior Surveillance System (YRBSS). The YRBSS is a school-based survey that is conducted biennially with a national probability sample of high school students. The YRBSS redresses the fragmentation issue by collecting data in one survey framework on all the major adolescent problem behavior types. Thus, the YRBSS is a major step forward in the development of problem behavior indicators for youth.

In addition to the national probability sample, YRBSS personnel are assisting state and city health and education departments to conduct their own surveys using the core YRBSS questions. These new state and city data sources should provide local policymakers and program administrators with timely information that more accurately captures the adolescent problems in their communities. Basic surveillance systems like the YRBSS are fairly easy to implement at the local level in a cost-effective manner. We encourage its widespread use on an annual basis by state and local departments.

Development of a Truly Comprehensive Indicator System

There are still critical gaps in the adolescent problem behavior system. Monitoring various types of problem behavior within the single framework of the YRBSS has been a major improvement, and being able to track these on a regular basis will assist in the measurement of progress toward national health objectives. However, an indicator system that simply provides surveillance of behavioral outcomes will not yield other information vital for policy decision making. Monitoring trends on determinants and correlates can tell us if these problems are increasing or decreasing. But observing that rates of violence, drug use, drunk driving, and teen pregnancy go up or down will not advance our knowledge as to why these trends are happening, and will not aid in the formation of sound policies to alter negative trends.

Indicators of other individual-, family-, and community-level characteristics are either absent or are scattered among different data sources that focus on one or two types of behavior, making it difficult to assess the impact of these factors on adolescent problem behavior as a whole. The YRBSS, while collecting data on all priority problem behavior and some basic individual demographic information, does not collect data on other relevant individual-level, family-level, or community-level variables. Some of these can be found in the MTFS survey, which has a little more detail on individual- and family-level indicators, but does not sample as broad a range of problem behavior. The most detailed information for sexual practices is available from the National Family Growth Survey, the National Survey of Adolescent Males, and the National Longitudinal Survey of Youth, but this detail cannot be applied to other risky behavior for the same individuals, thus making it difficult to determine correlations among them.

It is evident that there are still some major developments to be made in this area. Despite these problems, a truly comprehensive indicator system is not beyond reach. There are several different approaches that can be further developed to address the needed data areas. The least costly approach would be to add more questions to existing data collection systems so that they provide more comprehensive coverage for all three levels of analysis. Methods for validly and cost-effectively collecting more detailed individual-level indicators such as personality, psychological well-being, participation in youth cultures, and use of leisure time have not been fully explored and this is an area for future attention. This level of individual detail may be beyond the scope of school-based questionnaires, but novel strategies could be developed to get at these important antecedents.

Consider a National Longitudinal Survey of Youth Every Decade

More costly would be the initiation of a new National Longitudinal Youth Survey that would encompass all of the problem behavior types as well as other detailed individual-, family-, and community-level indicators. Studies of this sort have the advantage over current cross-sectional surveys of being able to make more precise statements about causal and developmental factors regarding adolescent problem behavior. A difficulty with most of the past studies is that they have not included a full range of adolescent behavior, and instead focus on one or two sorts of behavior, such as alcohol and drug use or sexuality. Given the time and expense of national longitudinal studies, it is crucial that better coordination among agencies be fostered so that the data needs of each can be included in a single comprehensive survey. Due to the rapidly changing nature of society, and the impact of these changes on the development of youth, we would recommend that a major longitudinal study focusing on adolescents be implemented every ten years so that these dynamics can be better understood.

Develop and Include a Consistent Set of Family-Level Indicators

At a minimum, following the suggestions of Zill and Daly (1993), we would urge that a set of basic family-level indicators be developed and collected in a systematic and consistent fashion across surveys so that tabulations by family characteristics can be made. Family-level information that assesses the conditions of adolescent households is severely lacking in the indicator system. Adequate indices of household resources are missing in most of the surveys. Some of this data can be obtained indirectly by having the adolescent either report parent's incomes or at least occupations and educational attainment levels. Youths' reports of father's occupation have been shown to be as valid as the father's own report (Hauser and Featherman 1977). The validity of adolescents' reports of their parents' incomes is less clear; new methods of getting at this information is an area for development. Other family-level indicators such as type of housing, location of dwelling, number of persons in the home, and parental availability for supervision, should be able to be obtained through direct questions added to existing surveys.

Develop Linkages to Census Data to Obtain Community-Level Indicators

Other important data that need to be added to the present system involve community-level indicators. This is another area that represents a serious gap in many of the data collection programs. To remedy this problem, methods of linking individual surveys to census tract or block-level data should be explored. One area of promise would be simply to obtain the respondent's residence zip code which can then be linked to census blocks. This variable could easily become a standard measure across all federal data sources and would maximize the utility of other data systems currently in place. Linkages to the census data would provide valuable information concerning the levels of poverty, segregation, and population densities where the adolescents live. Community characteristics of this sort are critical if we are to create more useful disaggregations of the data.

CONCLUSION

The health and well-being of adolescents is threatened both by their risky behavior and by their family and community context. While significant progress has been made in developing indicators that track this risky behavior, there is a tremendous need for data linking risky behavior to family and community factors. Timely and reliable data is being collected on the most important sorts of adolescent problem behavior in a framework that allows for their co-occurrence to be assessed. However, the ability to link these to other possible correlates and antecedents is severely limited. The role of individual-, family-, and community-level characteristics in shaping and maintaining these types of behavior is not well understood. Data collection efforts that can link up these three levels so that individuals can be understood in the context of their families and communities are of prime importance if we are to adequately address the complex interactive forces that contribute to the tragic loss of happiness and life among American youth. Based on our overview of the adolescent problem behavior indicators system, we make the following recommendations:

1) Continue to promote interagency cooperation such as that fostered by the CDC's YRBSS program. Wherever possible, strongly encourage agencies, and their grantees, to use consistent measures for similar sorts of behavior so that results are comparable across studies.

2) Continue to provide assistance to state and city health and education departments to implement their own YRBSS; use of this consistent measure will provide the most cost-effective means for state- and local-level needs assessment and program evaluation activities.

3) Develop more comprehensive indicators so that analytic linkages can be made between individual-, family-, and community-level factors. Priority data that should be collected in all surveys are valid measures of family resources (SES). Measures of family-level indicators should be developed in collaboration among agencies so that a consistent system can be implemented across programs. Methods for making linkages to census data or other sources of community-level indicators should be further developed.

4) With interagency coordination, plan and launch another National Longitudinal Youth Survey that incorporates measures of all problem behavior as well as detailed individual-, family-, and community-level characteristics. Initiate studies of this type on a decennial basis.

NOTE

1. E-codes are supplemental diagnostic codes to the ICD-9 codes used by hospitals and emergency rooms specifically for injuries so that the cause of an injury can be clarified. For example, the primary N-code (nature of illness/injury) for a fracture would simply indicate: "head concussion." Whereas the E-code (external cause) would indicate: "head concussion sustained when assaulted at a party." The more detailed E-codes can provide data for surveillance of injury due to violence.

REFERENCES

Bachman, J. G., P. M. O'Malley, and L. D. Johnston. 1980. "Correlates of Drug Use: Part I. Selected Measures of Background, Recent Experience, and Lifestyle Orientations." *Monitoring the Future*, Occasional Paper 8. Ann Arbor, Mich.: Institute for Social Research.

Blanchen, A. J. 1993. "Measuring the Use of Alcohol and Other Drugs among Adolescents." *Public Health Reports*, 10: 25–30.

Blos, P. 1962. *On Adolescence*. New York: Free Press.

Campbell, A. 1976. "Subjective Measures of Well-Being." *American Psychologist* 31: 117–24.

Card, J. J. 1981. "Long-Term Consequences for Children of Teenage Parents." *Demography* 18: 137–56.

Centers for Disease Control and Prevention. 1990. "Weapon-Carrying among High School Students, United States, 1990." *Morbidity and Mortality Weekly Report* 40: 617–19.

———. 1994. Press Release on Prevention Marketing Initiative.

———. 1996. *HIV/AIDS Surveillance Report: 1996* 8: 13.

Donovan, J. E., R. Jessor, and F. M. Costa. "Syndrome of Adolescent Problem Behavior in Adolescence: A Replication." *Journal of Consulting and Clinical Psychology* 56: 762–65.

Dryfoos, J. G. 1990. *Adolescents at Risk: Prevalence and Prevention*. New York: Oxford University Press.

Elliott, D. S., D. Huizinga, and S. Menard. 1989. *Multiple Problem Youth: Delinquency, Substance Abuse and Mental Health Problems*. New York: Springer-Verlag.

Erikson, E. H. 1968. *Identity: Youth and Crisis*. New York: W. W. Norton.

Farrell, A. D., S. J. Danish, and C. W. Howard. 1992. "Relationship Between Drug Use and Other Problem Behaviors in Urban Adolescents." *Journal of Consulting and Clinical Psychology* 60: 705–12.

Fingerhut, L. A., D. D. Ingram, and J. J. Feldman. 1992. "Firearm and Nonfirearm Homicide Among Persons Through Nineteen Years of Age." *Journal of the American Medical Association* 267: 3048–53.

Furstenberg, F., J. Brooks-Gunn, and S. Morgan. 1987. "Adolescent Mothers and Their Children in Later Life." *Family Planning Perspectives* 19: 142–51.

Hammett, M., K. E. Powell, P. W. O'Carroll, and S. T. Clanton. 1992. "Homicide Surveillance—United States, 1979–1988." *Morbidity and Mortality Weekly Report* 41: 1–33.

Hauser, R. M., and D. L. Featherman. 1977. *The Process of Stratification*. New York: Academic Press.

Hayes, C., ed. 1987. *Risking the Future, vol. I*. Washington, D.C.: National Academy Press.

Hofferth, S., and C. Hayes, eds. 1987. *Risking the Future, vol. II*. Washington, D.C.: National Academy Press.

Huston, A. C., V. C. McLoyd, and C. Garcia-Coll. 1994. "Children and Poverty: Issues in Contemporary Research." *Child Development* 65: 275–82.

Johnston, L. D., P. M. O'Malley, and J. G. Bachman. 1993. *National Survey Results on Drug Use from the Monitoring the Future Study, 1975–1992*, series 93-3597. Washington: U.S. Government Printing Office for U.S. Department of Health and Human Services, National Institute on Drug Abuse.

Kandel, D. 1975. "Stages in Adolescent Involvement in Drug Use." *Science* 190: 912–14.

Kann, L., W. Warren, J. L. Collins, J. Ross, B. Collins, and L. J. Kolbe. 1993. "Results from the National School-Based 1991 Youth Risk Behavior Survey and Progress Toward Achieving Related Health Objectives for the Nation." *Public Health Reports* 108: 47–55.

Kolbe, L. J., L. Kann, and J. L. Collins. 1993. "Measuring the Health Behavior of Adolescents: The Youth Risk Behavior Surveillance System." *Public Health Reports* 108: 2–10.

National Highway Traffic Safety Administration. 1992. *Fatal Accident Reporting System, 1990*. Washington, D.C.: U.S. Department of Transportation.

National Research Council. 1993. *Losing Generations: Adolescents in High Risk Settings*. Washington, D.C.: National Academy Press.

O'Carroll, P. W., Y. Harel, and R. J. Waxweiler. 1993. "Measuring Adolescent Behaviors Related to Intentional Injuries." *Public Health Reports* 108: 15–19.

Office of Technology Assessment. 1991. *Adolescent Health, vol. 1: Summary and Policy Options*. Washington: U.S. Government Printing Office.

Perrine M. W., R. C. Peck, and J. C. Fell. 1989. "Epidemiological Perspective on Drunk Driving." Background paper for Surgeon General's Workshop on Drunk Driving. Rockville, Md. (December 14, 1988).

Prothrow-Stith, D. P., and M. Weissman. 1991. *Deadly Consequences: How Violence Is Destroying Our Youth and a Plan to Begin Solving the Problem*. New York: HarperCollins Publishers.

Rice, D. P., S. Kelman., L. S. Miller, and S. Dunmeyer. 1985. "The Economic Costs of Alcohol, Drug Use and Mental Illness," no. 90-1694. Washington: U.S. Government Printing Office for the Public Health Service.

Russell, M. H. 1990. "The Nicotine Addiction Trap: A Forty-Year Sentence for Four Cigarettes." *British Journal of Addictions* 85: 293–300.

Sampson, L. J., and J. H. Laub. 1994. "Urban Poverty and the Family Context of Delinquency: A New Look at Structure and Process in a Classic Study." *Child Development* 65: 523–40.

U.S. Department of Education: Office of Educational Research and Development. 1991. *Youth Indicators 1991*. Washington: U.S. Government Printing Office.

U.S. Department of Health and Human Services: Office on Smoking and Health. 1990. *Smoking and Health: A National Status Report*, Series 87-8396. Centers for Disease Control and Prevention. Washington: U.S. Government Printing Office.

Zill, N. and M. Daly, eds. 1993. *Researching the Family*. Washington, D.C.: Child Trends.

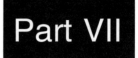

Part VII

Whither Indicators?

22

Potential and Problems in Developing Indicators on Child Well-Being from Administrative Data

Robert M. Goerge

INVESTIGATING THE POTENTIAL and problems in the development of indicators of children's well-being from administrative data is not a new activity (U.S. Department of Commerce 1981). However, during the last two decades, the subject of this activity has increasingly become *computerized* administrative data. Until the 1980s, administrative data would have been thought of as paper files rather than computerized data. It is arguable that only in the last ten years have information systems become "mature" and accessible enough to be good sources of data on children and their families. In this chapter, I discuss how administrative data are currently used for providing indicators for child well-being and how the development of these indicators could be facilitated through improved analysis and data manipulation, better data collection, and improved information and data policy.

Administrative data are data that are regularly and consistently collected in support of an organization's function and stored within that organization's information system. Administrative databases are created primarily to monitor utilization, to determine the consumption of resources, and to ascertain the capacity to supply services (U.S. Dept. of Health and Human Services 1991). Although administrative data are not collected primarily for research purposes, they can become a resource for research and statistics.

Administrative data are culled from systems that have two basic functions. A particular system may stress one of these functions over the other. The first function is reporting the purpose of accountability or reimbursement from an external or oversight agency (usually a federal one). The second is internal tracking of individuals or the services that they receive for the purpose of decision support and supporting other activities of the organization. The tracking function is what we think about when we refer to management information systems. Typically, the tracking system provides richer data, since external reporting in the human services typically is limited to eligibility of the individual for services, and tracking data assumes that one is interested in information that identifies the individual served, the individuals providing the service, the service itself, and the characteristics of these three entities.

Although there are some private sources, such as hospital and insurance records, this chapter focuses on government human services administrative data which are used for statistical purposes and which could be extremely useful in developing child indicators. They include publicly provided health care (Medicaid) utilization data; public health statistics; income maintenance (AFDC) eligibility and payment data; Food Stamps eligibility and payment data; child welfare service records; reported child abuse and neglect; primary and secondary education statistics; special education provision reporting; and family and juvenile court statistics. The use of administrative data for developing indicators will be compared to the use of social surveys, such as the National Longitudinal Survey of Youth, High School and Beyond, the Survey of Income and Program Participation, the Panel Study on Income Dynamics, and U.S. Census Bureau data. All of the administrative data are used for other research purposes—that is, basic research, evaluation, or epidemiology—but we will confine our comments to the development of statistical indicators that can provide information on the population of children at various geographic levels.

Perhaps the best example of the use of administrative data for child indicators is vital statistics—primarily data on births and deaths. While some may claim that these are collected primarily for statistical purposes, each has a clear set of administrative purposes. This is "program participation" data, but the programs are "birth" and "death," two "service" events that the entire population experiences. Many events are triggered or made possible by the fact that a birth or death certificate is issued—essentially anything that requires proof of birth or death. These two sets of data form a cornerstone of the state and federal health statistics. From these two databases, indicators of the number of births, teenage births, births to unmarried mothers, and causes of adolescent death, to name just a few, are produced.

These two data sets also provide an example of how indicators can be developed by combining data sets. When birth certificates and death certificates are linked, it is possible, for example, to calculate infant mortality statistics. The importance and value of linking databases will be stressed in this chapter as a method to develop new indicators and to increase the validity and accuracy of current indicators. This is often not possible with survey or Census Bureau data because of the lack of information, or inability (due to confidentiality restrictions) to use identifying information, on individuals needed to link records.

The 1996 Personal Responsibility and Work Opportunity Reconciliation Act changed the focus of social programs from one of federally-led cash assistance to state-led behavioral change in the form of providing incentives for welfare recipients to obtain work and get off the welfare rolls. The concern that this change may affect child well-being has put an added burden on researchers to find data that can be responsive to this concern. Surveys and administrative data are two options, though not mutually exclusive, that have potential for measuring changes in child well-being. The pros and cons of survey data are well known. While administrative data is criticized as oriented completely toward program participation, this chapter begins to address the issue of whether or not tracking program participation is an effective way of tracking child well-being.

Finally, administrative data may be the only hope to quickly develop more, timely, or new state and local indicators on child well-being. Given the data collection expense of new or new waves of social surveys—even higher when coverage of state and local populations is required—and given that much administrative data already exist, this source is ideal for the short-term development of indicators that can be used to inform the public and policymakers.

CHARACTERISTICS OF ADMINISTRATIVE DATA

Researchers and policymakers do not really know how much administrative data can contribute either to the development of indicators or to more basic research. Because very few data sets are actually mined deeply enough to understand what is available, surveys and census data are analyzed over and over again so that we know much more about what can be supported by such data. While the discussion in this chapter is not an exhaustive list of the characteristics, it provides the basis for examination and debate concerning the utility of administrative data.

Population Coverage

Although not every state and local jurisdiction has administrative databases for each topic listed in the introduction, most larger jurisdictions have them. Most jurisdictions are planning the computerization of their administrative data (Kliss and Alvey 1984). For example, as of 1993, only one state lacked a Medicaid Management Information System; and it since has been put into operation.

An administrative database typically covers the population receiving a particular service or resource, or those having a particular status. In many cases, data on all individuals who have ever been in the database is kept in the database or archived so that longitudinal information is available. One exception to this is child abuse and neglect data, which are purged at particular times depending on the outcome of the abuse and neglect investigation. However, in many states, there is a time-series available on all children who have experienced out-of-home placement (foster care) as a result of abuse or neglect. This data, when properly formatted and carefully analyzed, can provide a powerful set of indicators on how many children are so threatened within their own families that the local or state government and the courts decide to remove the children from their homes.

Because administrative data, by definition, will cover the population of individuals or families with a particular status or receiving a particular service, and the address data or some geographic data of these individuals are often available, developing indicators at the state or local level—or "small region monitoring"—is quite possible (Bannister 1994). Unlike national social surveys, which, because of cost, cannot have sampling frames that include every local region and in many cases have samples so small that even larger state indicators cannot be calculated reliably, the population coverage in administrative data allows for state and local indicators to be compiled.

Collection of Data

Unlike social surveys or census data collection, administrative data collection is done by a professional whose primary responsibility is not data collection.[1] There are both positive and negative aspects of having a professional collecting data. These workers are often affected by the results of an analysis of the administrative data, depending on how many operational or policy decisions are based on information from the Management Information System (MIS) (Leginski 1989). Also, there are issues (worker's use of time or confidentiality) other than optimal data collection that affect the data collection. Data collection can vary over time because of changes in operations or agency mandates. Finally, workers may take shortcuts or not provide certain data when they understand which data is actually used in the operation of the agency.

On the positive side, these workers may have an interest in the quality of the data they collect if they actually use the data for their own decision making (Mugford et al. 1991; Bannister 1992). It is a commonly held assumption in information systems development that the more the data are used, the better that data will be. For data items that are necessary or mandatory to complete administration functions, the amount of missing data can be minimal. There may be considerable access to the subjects so that incorrect data are more likely to be corrected than in social surveys or census data. Also, because the data are collected within the normal conduct of business, there is no interviewer inserted into the process to disrupt the lives of those studied, or to bias responses. This may be particularly important for data collection around child abuse and neglect or mental health, when it is difficult for an interviewer to be present during critical events.

Administrative data are also collected very close to the time when the event—birth, service receipt, a change in status—occurs. The date of that event is usually recorded exactly, so that the form of the data is complete in that it contains both the sequence of events and the time at which the event occurred (Coleman 1981; Tuma and Hannan 1984). This type of data allows for analyses that can get at the mechanism of how certain events happen. For example, the difference between knowing that an individual was on a welfare program in each of two different years—often how we track participation in survey data—versus knowing the exact dates of the beginning of welfare program participation across those two years is significant if one is interested in knowing how families move on and off welfare programs. When one becomes interested in why child well-being is changing, especially over a short period, having continuous-time data is preferable.

Since individual records must be accessed in administrative databases and individuals must usually be contacted in the normal course of providing service or aid, identifying information, such as names, addresses, and Social Security numbers, are usually accurate and maintained over the period during which the individual is in contact with the organization. This information allows for updating of service records, tracking individuals and families over time, and linkage of records to other administrative databases or survey data.

Reliability, Validity, and Accuracy Issues

Determining the quality of the data can be either an active or passive task. Active refers to actually checking the data with the object to which the data belongs. That could be an individual, a service recipient or agency staff member, or a paper record that is the definitive source of the data record or item. A passive data quality review refers to determining whether the data make sense or finding other sources of the same data. Active data quality review is seldom done because of cost and feasibility—it is often impossible to find a service recipient after the data are collected. However, there are instances of agencies that do have data quality assurance units that conduct this type of work. Knowing when and where that exists is key to using administrative data.

There are many parallels of these activities to survey research, even though the methods are less well established and practiced. Before administrative data can be used for statistical purposes, it is necessary to extensively review all data collection procedures and data definitions for any data that will be used for indicator development. This is not a research activity that has a clear protocol—each administrative data set is documented in its own way. Information about how "good" the data are has been seldom documented and is available only by interviewing those who maintain the database, use the data, or train those who will collect the data. There are usually multiple interviews, and knowledge about the data set is often developed in an iterative and interactive manner. In fact, finding the individuals in a bureaucracy who actually know about all the fields in a database is also an iterative process. Learning about the reliability, validity, and accuracy of data may be possible only after the data have been analyzed. For example, there may be dramatic variation among counties in a state, which may not be understood until the data actually are analyzed and experts can respond to the results.

Data that actually are used by a worker or by anyone (even a researcher) is typically more accurate. The validity of a variable is largely dependent on what a worker believes it means. For example, the handicap status of a child may be recorded without having to verify that status by a diagnostic test. In such an instance, a worker uses "behavior disorder" to signify that those adults who are in contact with the child observe that he behaves "poorly." Studying the reliability of data is seldom done for the purposes of the organization or pure research. Quality-control teams in data processing are rare. Again, as these data get used more often, or as administrators of the organizations require more data and question the source of the data, more quality assurance will take place.

If workers receive sufficient training on the collection of data, we expect the data to be more reliable and valid (Iezzoni et al. 1992). If clear and complete documentation is available, workers are more likely to provide reliable information. The less training that is available on the more complex data fields, the less these fields should be used and the more other sources of data should be used for that topic. For example, the handicap field on foster children's records is extremely poor because workers are given no training on handicap identification and verification. Thus, this data has little reliability. Data sets which have more reliable handicap data (special education, for example) can be used to improve the data on the handicaps of foster children (Goerge et al. 1991).

Units of Analysis

Administrative data of the kind discussed in this paper are typically collected at the individual level. Very often individuals within a particular family are linked with a database. For example, members of a family will share parts of their same identification number and the relationships between members will be tracked.

However, the ability to group individuals depends very much on the purpose of the data set. For example, there is usually little information on who are the parents of a child in special education, since this data is primarily used for reporting and reimbursement as opposed to tracking the child, which is more common in the classroom or regular education information systems. In these latter systems, relationships among family members are typically identified, because this information is needed to contact the family or to make the correct eligibility decision.

Focus on Negative Outcomes

The type of indicators one can most easily extract from administrative data are very much focused on problem-related outcomes and events that should not happen (Iezzoni 1990). While the following questions focus on problems, they also can be turned around to state indicators in positive ways. What percentage of children are born without their mothers having received prenatal care? How many infants die within the first months of their lives? How many children are part of AFDC grants? How many children are removed from the custody of their parents? This negative focus seems obvious since the data is collected in the course of providing services intended to ameliorate problems.

One would expect that as the use of computers moves into more everyday life situations there will be more data available on the nonproblematic aspects of children's lives. For example, as library systems become computerized, knowing how many children use libraries and borrow books can provide more information on normative aspects of children's lives. School performance data already provide such data on educational achievement. Even in these examples, however, one can understand how the problem orientation is not necessarily in the data itself, but in how the data are analyzed.

Cost

The cost of collecting administrative data is often hidden in the operational budgets of organizations (Iezzoni et al. 1992), while the high costs of collecting national data through surveys are easily determined. The costs of using administrative data for the development of indicators is not much less than that of using survey data after they have been collected. However, the organizations that collect survey data, including the census, include the cleaning of the data and the formatting of data in the costs of collection. The cleaning and formatting of administrative data often is left up to the analysts that acquire and use the data. In the experience of the author, the cost of cleaning and formatting is often half to three-quarters of the cost of a particular research project using administrative data. However, the ongoing cost of using these data in subsequent projects may be amortized because of cleaning and formatting done in previous projects.

USING STATE AND LOCAL ADMINISTRATIVE DATA

Most national indicators, other than those developed from the Bureau of the Census, are developed from data collected by state and county agencies. At the state or substate level, there is great variety and variability in the use and production of indicators from administrative data. Because of the lack of leadership in developing standards in the definitions and development of indicators, states and counties have obviously constructed indicators that address their particular context and needs. It is often possible to take administrative data and do multistate or county comparisons. But these are often limited because the definition of data fields is not comparable from one jurisdiction to the next. Also, one can use only the data fields that are comparable, and though comparable may be less rich than a particular indicator might require (Mason and Gibbs 1992; Larson and Alvarez 1990).

Comparability

How administrative data are collected is often a function of local rules and custom, but in many cases, is guided by a common federal policy. An example of this latter problem is in the no-longer operational Aids to Families with Dependent Children (AFDC) program. When measuring the duration of receipt of a particular service, such as AFDC, choosing a common unit of analysis is key. Many states track the duration of a case, which is usually defined by who the head of the household is and includes members of that household. However, individual members enter and exit that household; these exits may not be precisely recorded or they may not be archived in a way that they are easily retrievable at a later date. This ambiguity prevents knowing exactly how long, for example, certain children were parts of AFDC grants or when the family changed from being an extended family group to a two-generational household (when the grandparent separated from the household). In states where individuals are tracked, it is possible to calculate individual-level durations of service.

Another example is coding the living arrangements of children in foster care. Very few states track whether a child in foster care is living with a relative. Since these homes are often treated similarly to foster family homes, they are likely to be coded as foster family homes. However, the nature of service and the home itself is quite different, and in those states where it can be coded, we have seen large increases in home-of-relative foster care (Goerge, Wulczyn, and Harden 1994). The coding differences across states prevent the precise comparison of where foster children actually are living. This is an example, however, of where knowledge about the data and how the program is operated can result in data and indicators that can be made comparable across states.

State and County Reporting

Many different reports on service utilization are developed by state or county agencies. In health care, state or public/private agencies collect hospital discharge data to describe all individuals who are hospitalized. Common discharge forms are used which increase the probability of accurate data. The unit of analysis of these data is often the episode of service rather than the individual, due to restrictions in the reporting and use of identifying information.

Family Assistance Management Information Systems (FAMIS) and Medicaid Management Information Systems (MMIS) have provided extensive information about those families who require income and health care assistance. Indicators from these programs are often cross-sectional, so that while the FAMIS data are a tremendous source to replicate the longitudinal analysis of AFDC done by Bane and Ellwood, they have been underutilized in developing longitudinal indicators. Both of these systems were built and are maintained with matching funds from the federal government, increasing the probability that data are well maintained.

The use of child welfare service and child abuse and neglect administrative data varies tremendously from state to state, largely because of the quality of the reporting and tracking systems. As with AFDC, most state reports focus on the cross-sectional indicators of service, which are quite important for operational decision making, but less useful for understanding the outcomes of children and families in the system. A recent federal government initiative to develop better information systems in child welfare (State Automated Child Welfare Information Systems) bodes well for improving the data available to states as well as to the federal government.

Some states produce reports on students with handicapping conditions as identified through special education programs. These reports are then aggregated by the U.S. Department of Education into a yearly report (U.S. Department of Education, Office of Special Education and Rehabilitative Services 1986). There is great variation in the identification of handicaps (Knitzer et al. 1990). These indicators, however, are an excellent example of a service response to a condition as opposed to a measure of a condition in the general population. Given the general problem of accurately diagnosing handicaps other than physical ones, service provision may be a better indicator of the actual impairment that a child experiences in a particular setting (Scahill and Riddle 1990). A debate on this topic is beginning, especially in the area of child mental health. As more families of children with disabilities use Supplemental Security Income, and as families become more aware of this benefit, it may be that such administrative data will provide better (or the best) information on the disabilities of children.

Regular education is an example in which there is a fine line between what are considered research or reporting data and administrative data (Hutchison 1993). However, it is also the case that computerized management information systems are not universal and only beginning to be developed and refined in even the largest school systems. Test scores are both reported externally and maintained in administrative systems. Dropout indicators often are measured differently from one district to the next.

The area of juvenile justice is certainly of great interest, and one in which there is more comparability within and across states. Uniform crime reports are an excellent example of how administrative data can be used to provide information on a most negative set of behavior. Detention and incarceration indicators are often widely reported. A gap in reporting by states may be measures of juvenile delinquency, including status offenses.

Because of the general availability of vital statistics data, state and county health departments provide extensive reports on births, deaths, and the circumstances surrounding these events. One problem, however, that continues to plague public health as well as many other human service agencies is the lag in the reporting of the data relative to the time when the event occurred. This lag may not be as great as with surveys or census data, but when state reports are used for management purposes, the issue of the delay is magnified.

National Reporting

There are a number of national indicators developed by the federal government from administrative data. These include information from public health statistics and many of the programmatic indicators in the "Green Book." The National Center for Health Statistics, most likely the best human service example of federal use of administrative data, uses vital statistics data from states to provide an extensive set of birth, death, and population indicators (see *Monthly Vital Statistics Reports*). The Center also uses the National Hospital Discharge Survey, based on a sample of administrative data on hospital discharges, which could be expanded with today's technology to include the entire population of children who are hospitalized.

The "Green Book," produced by the U.S. House Ways and Means Committee until this year, is an example of a compendium of statistics that makes the most of analyses of administrative data, including AFDC, child welfare, and Supplemental Security Income. In many cases, the discussions of results from surveys enhance the analyses of administrative data (provided to the Federal Government by states), but more and better indicators are very much needed in many areas, including child care and child support enforcement. Much of the discussion relies on Census Bureau data or expenditure data which does not really describe the population participating in a program. A step in that direction is the development of tracking systems for child care and child support, which has already begun in many states.

The *Kids Count* project of the Annie E. Casey Foundation provides profiles of the condition of children in each of the fifty states. Areas include child health, adolescent births, juvenile crime, teen unemployment and school dropout, poverty, and household structure. These reports very much depend on analyses of administrative data since they focus on yearly changes at the state level. Vital statistics and uniform crime reports are a key to developing the comparative indicators in the *Kids Count* reports.

A few efforts in the child welfare field have been undertaken to develop comparable indicators across states. Two examples of these are the areas of child abuse and neglect and foster care. The National Child Abuse and Neglect Data System project of the National Center for Child Abuse and Neglect is a voluntary effort to include each state's aggregate- and individual-level data into a comparable structure (U.S. Department of Health and Human Services 1994). The current goal is to make the individual-level data on abuse and neglect investigations comparable across thirteen states. The Multistate Foster Care Data Archive Project of the Chapin Hall Center for Children, funded by DHHS, is a collaboration among seven states (currently) to develop comparable indicators on children in foster care from 1988 to the present (Goerge, Wulczyn, and Harden 1994). Both of these efforts require understanding how the data are collected and stored, and then calculating indicators that are valid across each of the states. The foster care project has recently completed this task for a series of the most important indicators in foster care and is expanding to include ten states.

FIVE INDICATORS

The following indicators are those which are currently able to be calculated in either all or most states with a modest investment of resources. They form a well-rounded sample of indicators upon which others could be tested and developed.

Government dependency: What percentage of the children in a particular state, county, or city are dependent on government for shelter, nutrition, parenting, or special needs at a particular point in time, not including regular education?

Out-of-home placement: What percentage of children are placed outside of their home into public custody because of abuse or neglect for the first time in a particular year?

Psychiatric hospitalization: What percentage of children are hospitalized for a psychiatric diagnosis?

High-Risk Family Formation Index: The percentage of first births, representing new families being formed, to women who have one or more of three risk factors at the time of the birth (developed by Child Trends and Westat). The risk factors are having less than a high school education, being unmarried, or being under age twenty.

Juvenile Violent Crime arrest rate: The number of arrests of youths under the age of eighteen for violent offenses.

DEVELOPING BETTER INDICATORS

Because each reporting or tracking system focuses on a limited set of outcomes and often neglects data fields that are not central to the business at hand, a potential strategy for improving indicators would be to combine administrative databases or administrative databases and survey or census data (U.S. Department of Commerce 1981). By mixing and matching fields from numerous databases, it is possible to increase the validity and accuracy of indicators. Perhaps most important, linking administrative data over years could provide both a better time-series and offer the possibility to track outcomes longitudinally (Hunter 1994; Goerge 1994). Longitudinal data, combined with a knowledge of policy and practice, could allow, at a minimum, analysis of relative child well-being over time.

An example of improving accuracy of data is the identification of racial and ethnic identifiers. These data from birth certificates are most likely better than any race or ethnicity field in any other database (though that does not mean that they are absolutely accurate, valid, or reliable). Linking birth certificate data to any data set may improve the general treatment of race and ethnicity. Another example is combining indicators of a child's disability status from school, service agency, public health and survey data, which may provide the best epidemiological estimates of childhood disability available.

Combining data from multiple sources also begins to allow investigators to study issues of service overlap and children and families who have multiple problems. The question of whether most (80 percent) of the resources are going to a few (20 percent) of the families or children (the "80/20" question) is important for welfare policy and human service management. Also, knowing how many children are poor and victims of abuse or neglect or are poor and disabled would provide those interested in improving the lives of children better information for developing policies and service programs.

Recently there has been more discussion of doing an administrative census, which would combine various types of administrative data, including AFDC and other income maintenance, income tax returns, and Social Security data, to provide an alternative to the current method of data collection for the decennial census. Such an effort could provide better information on some issues, data during intercensal years and a base population (the denominator) and measurement system to yield better prevalence and incidence rates of the host of indicators discussed during the Child Indicators Workshop.

For example, in comparing the 1990 census figures on minority infants with birth certificate data, we found a tremendous undercount in that subgroup (Goerge et al. 1993). We discovered this when we found the impossible, that over 100 percent of infants in Chicago were part of AFDC grants. It appears that, despite the adjustments made by the Census Bureau, the census data undercount the number of African American infants under one year of age living in Chicago. In order to calculate a more accurate number of children, we used Vital Statistics data on the number of live African American births in Chicago from June 1989 to June 1990 and subtracted the number of infant deaths over the same period. In this situation, an administrative census would have provided more accurate statistics.

In order to do better small-region monitoring of child indicators, increased use of geocoding (address-matching) to allow for the aggregation of records at any geographic level is very important. If addresses exist in the database, they can be geocoded and any level of spatial aggregation is possible. Individual-level data can be aggregated into census blocks and tracts, community or neighborhood areas. Geographic information also provides an additional piece of information for linking an individual's records across multiple databases.

IMPROVING ADMINISTRATIVE DATA

Universal health care offers a tremendous opportunity for the development of better indicators of child well-being. Assuming that a common health care management information system had been developed, such an MIS would provide an important basis for health and mental health indicators as well as being a major source for an administrative census (Riche 1994). However, since health care reform is either an issue of the past or one of a future that is unknown, other vehicles such as welfare reform may offer new opportunities.

We are not going to improve indicators of child well-being using administrative data until it is used more by researchers. This requires that researchers have easier access and that more uniform procedures be developed to provide this access. Researchers are too often intimidated (and often rightly so) by the bureaucratic or legal process required to acquire administrative data even when it is legally possible.

There are very few cases in which administrative data have been prepared for release for research or indicator developing (U.S. Department of Health and

Human Services 1991; Lurie 1990; Iezzoni et al. 1992). Health care data sets comprise a large fraction of these cases; recently, the state of California and University of California Data Archive and Technical Assistance (UCDATA) have made welfare program data available. However, accessing AFDC (other than the federal QC sample), child welfare, Medicaid, court, education and other human service agency data usually requires the investigator to approach the agency and make a special request. The requirements for and restrictions to access vary by the jurisdiction and the particular data set and are governed by state and local law. Researchers typically have to enter into lengthy negotiations with agencies that are certainly a disincentive to use the data.

Certainly, strong privacy protections are needed in order to improve the access by researchers. A set of mechanisms, procedures, or organizations should exist that can simplify access, link files where it would be productive, and create anonymous files that do not have identifiers (Hunter 1994). Data archives or repositories on children and families or subareas would greatly facilitate the development of better indicators (Roos et al. 1993).

Administrative data will not improve until information systems more responsive to the needs of workers are implemented. The mainframe terminal technology—in comparison to Windows, Graphical User Interface (GUI), point and click, as well as better designed relational databases—has often been intimidating to workers and has discouraged them from using the data that they regularly provide to the information system.

Much of the discussion around linking databases and privacy has centered around the use of a unique identifier used in all administrative data. There are currently severe limitations around state and local government using the Social Security number for such a purpose. However, the SSN is not the answer. Multiple pieces of identifying information are needed in order to properly match records (Newcombe 1988; Jaro 1989). A mechanism that would provide reliably linked, sterilized files to researchers or government agencies would be a major step forward in ending the ongoing discussion of a unique identifier, though there would still be an issue around the use of linked data for service-providing purposes (Soler, Shotten, and Bell 1993).

Common uniform coding schemes would also assist in better manipulation of administrative data. National reporting requirements have only partially addressed this. Common birth certificate forms, initiated and implemented by the Public Health Service, are one model. The Administration for Children and Families at the U.S. Department of Health and Human Services has taken a step in that direction with NCANDS and the Adoption and Foster Care Reporting System (AFCARS) in requiring that states provide their data in a particular format.

Better administrative data will be available when the storage of historical data is more uniform. Many states currently archive or even delete data when they become a certain age. If a client has not been a client for a number of years, their data disappears from the on-line system and may disappear altogether. Longitudinal data are critical for the development of better outcome indicators. Maintaining longitudinal files is one way in which the expense of longitudinal surveys, currently the primary tool for longitudinal analysis, can be avoided.

MAKING ADMINISTRATIVE DATA A BETTER SOURCE OF
INDICATORS FOR CHILDREN

Federal government leadership is certainly needed in order to improve both the collection and the analysis of administrative data. Some of the initiatives discussed in this chapter are an excellent beginning, but more effort in more areas would certainly allow us to better evaluate whether administrative data is a good or mediocre source of indicator development. The development of a common standard-setting protocol for each area would be an excellent start, and could be followed by each area implementing that protocol. There has been a great deal of work by private and public organizations in the development of outcome indicators that could be incorporated into the development of new information systems that are being initiated by the federal government.

Including researchers in the development of information systems would greatly improve the utility of administrative data for research and statistical purposes. Many of the definitions of data fields, form, and structure could be improved before information systems are implemented and before data have to be cleaned and manipulated in order to get basic indicators.

The legal protections against using administrative data for research purposes must be combated. Class-action suits by the American Civil Liberaties Union (ACLU) and other advocacy groups, while protecting clients, have resulted in agencies being less willing to provide data to qualified researchers. Having state child and family statistical centers may help in addressing this issue. This also may help offset the potential high costs of transforming administrative data into "research-ready" data sets.

Finally, researchers have a responsibility to make the indicators they develop from administrative data understandable to the audience of professionals in each of the disciplines that are concerned with the social policy for children and families. Indicators that are "professional-friendly" must be disseminated to larger audiences in order for the providers of the data to understand the significance of collecting the data.

NOTE

1. Service and program eligibility workers (such as for AFDC, Medicaid, child support enforcement eligibility determination) may be an exception to this, since the collection of data used to determine eligibility is their primary function.

REFERENCES

Banister, Judith. 1994. Testimony before the House subcommittee on Census, Statistics, and Postal Personnel. Congressional Testimony, 103rd Cong., 2nd sess. August 2, 1994.

Coleman, J. S. 1981. *Longitudinal Data Analysis*. New York: Basic Books.

Federal Committee on Statistical Methodology. 1981. "Report on Statistical Uses of Administrative Records." Washington: U.S. Government Printing Office for U.S. Department of Commerce.

Goerge, Robert M. 1994. "Effect of Public Child Welfare Worker Characteristics and Turnover on Discharge from Foster Care." *Child Welfare Research Review Annual*, edited by Richard P. Barth, Jill Duerr Berrick, and Neil Gilbert. New York: Columbia University Press.

Goerge, Robert M., Bong Joo Lee, Teresa Eckrich Sommer, and John Van Voorhis. 1993. "The Point-in-Time Multiple Service Use of Children and Adolescents in Illinois." Chicago: The Chapin Hall Center for Children at the University of Chicago.

Goerge, Robert M., John Van Voorhis, Stephen Grant, Katherine Casey, and Major Robinson. 1991. "Special Education Experiences of Foster Children: An Empirical Study." Chicago: Chapin Hall Center for Children at the University of Chicago.

Goerge Robert M., Fred H. Wulczyn, and Allen W. Harden. 1994. "A Report from the Multistate Foster Care Data Archive: Foster Care Dynamics, 1983–1992." Chicago: The Chapin Hall Center for Children at the University of Chicago.

Hunter, N. D. 1994a. "Department of Health and Human Services Senate Judiciary/Technology and the Law. High Tech Privacy Issues in Health Care." Testimony before the Senate Subcommittee on Technology and the Law. 103 Cong., 1st sess. January 27, 1994.

———. 1994b. Testimony before the Senate Committee on Governmental Affairs. 103rd Cong., 2nd sess. May 6, 1994.

Hutchison, D. 1993. "School Effectiveness Studies Using Administrative Data." *Educational Research* 35: 27–47.

Iezzoni, L. 1990. "Using Administrative Diagnostic Data to Assess the Quality of Hospital Care." *International Journal of Tech Assess in Health Care* 6: 272–81.

Iezzoni, L., S. Foley, T. Heeren, J. Daley, C. Duncan, E. Fisher, and J. Hughes. 1992. "A Method for Screening the Quality of Hospital Care Using Administrative Data: Preliminary Validation Results." *Quality Review Bulletin* (November): 361–71.

Jaro, M. A. 1989. "Advances in Record-Linkage Methodology as Applied to Matching the 1985 Census of Tampa, Florida." *Journal of the American Statistical Association* 84: 406, 414–20.

Kliss, B., and W. Alvey. 1984. *Statistical Uses of Administrative Records: Recent Research and Present Prospects*, vol 1. Washington: Department of the Treasury, Internal Revenue Service, Statistics of Income Division.

Knitzer, J., Z. Steinberg, and B. Fleisch. 1990. *At the Schoolhouse Door: An Examination of Program and Policies for Children with Behavioral Problems.* New York: Bank Street College.

Larson, O., J. Doris, and W. Alvarez. 1990. "Migrants and Maltreatment: Comparative Evidence from Central Register Data." *Child Abuse and Neglect* 14: 375–85.

Leginski, W., C. Croze, J. Driggers, S. Dumpman, D. Geertsen, E. Kamis-Gould, M. Namerow, R. Patton, N. Wilson, and C. Wurster. 1989. "Data Standards for Mental Health Decision Support Systems." National Institute of Mental Health, series FN, no. 10. Washington: U.S. Government Printing Office for the Department of Health and Human Services.

Lurie, N. 1990. "Administrative Data and Outcomes Research." *Medical Care* 28: 867–69.

Mason, M., and J. Gibbs. 1992. "Patterns of Adolescent Psychiatric Hospital: Implications for Social Policy." *American Journal of Orthopsychiatry* 62: 447–57.

Mugford, Miranda, Philip Banfield, and Moira O'Hanlon. 1991. "Effects of Feedback of Information on Clinical Practice: A Review." *British Medical Journal* 303(6799): 398.

Newcombe, H. B. 1988. *Handbook of Record Linkage: Methods for Health and Statistical Studies, Administration, and Business.* Oxford, England: Oxford University Press.

Riche, M. 1994. "What Health Reform Might Mean for Demographers." *Population Today* 22(1): 3.

Roos, L., C. Mustard, J. Nicol, D. McLerran, B. Comm, D. Malenka, T. Young, and M. Cohen. 1993. "Registries and Administrative Data: Organization and Accuracy." *Medical Care* 31: 201–12.

Scahill, L., and M. Riddle. 1990. "Psychiatrically Hospitalized Children: A Critical Review." *The Yale Journal of Biology and Medicine* 63: 301–12.

Soler, M., A. Shotton, and J. Bell. 1993. "Glass Walls: Confidentiality Restrictions and Inter-agency Collaboration." San Francisco, Calif.: Youth Law Center.

Tuma, N. B., and M. T. Hannan. 1984. *Social Dynamics: Models and Methods*. Orlando, Fla.: Academic Press.

U.S. Department of Education, Office of Special Education and Rehabilitative Services. 1986. *Eighth Annual Report to Congress on the Implementation of the Education of the Handicapped Act*. Washington: U.S. Government Printing Office.

U.S. Department of Health and Human Services. 1991. *The Feasibility of Linking Research-Related Data Bases to Federal and Non-Federal Medical Administrative Data Bases: A Report to Congress*. Washington: U.S. Government Printing Office.

23

Context and Connection in Social Indicators: Enhancing What We Measure and Monitor

Marc L. Miringoff and Marque-Luisa Miringoff

A BRITISH FRIEND and colleague at the United Nations, with a long career in statistical analysis at a number of United Nations agencies, once noted during an address that the United States has the best system of economic reporting in the industrialized world and the worst system of social reporting. Allowing for hyperbole, his point was well taken, particularly in terms of the comparative impact of economic and social indicators on public dialogue and public policy.

Economic indicators, unlike social indicators, are frequently and widely reported and combined into numerous indexes that give them meaning, context, and impact. Economists have created a world of barometers and gauges which continually address the question "How are we doing?" and answer it daily, weekly, monthly, quarterly, and yearly, with a large number of recognized instruments, ranging from the Dow Jones Average, to the Index of Leading Economic Indicators, to the Consumer Price Index, to the Producer Price Index. By contrast, social indicators appear infrequently—once a year at best—and are generally assessed in isolation, with little or no context, and no sense of the whole of which they are a part.

As a result of such differences, the public is far better informed about the economy than it is about social well-being. Moreover, this knowledge is closely linked to a highly visible and sophisticated economic policy apparatus. The creation of social policy, alternatively, is much less empirically based and far more vulnerable to ideology and politics.

This chapter will argue that in order for social indicators to have greater impact, they will need a more developed and holistic conceptual basis and a more direct policy link; we must examine broader concerns of theory and context as well as issues of empirical methodology and data collection. This perspective has arisen from our experience in creating and refining the Index of Social Health over the period of the past ten years (Miringoff, Miringoff, and Opdycke, forthcoming).

ECONOMIC REPORTING AND SOCIAL REPORTING: DIFFERENCES IN CONCEPT AND IMPACT

There are significant differences between economic and social indicators and how they are reported in the United States. These are apparent in the frequency and precision in which they are reported, the context in which they are presented, their connection to public policy, and the very distinct ways in which we think about economic and social well-being.

The quantity of economic data regularly before us is immense. The Dow Jones Average is communicated to the nation electronically on a minute-by-minute basis, reported throughout the day in the media, and summarized each evening on every network broadcast. Business starts, business failures, and the money supply are reported weekly. Often, these and other business indicators are presented, not in isolation, but in the context of other indicators that together form indexes which monitor different aspects of the economy. Many of these indexes are issued monthly to facilitate comparison, detect change, and provide the basis for ongoing analysis and possible intervention. The Index of Leading Economic Indicators, the Producer Price Index, the Consumer Price Index, the Index of Consumer Confidence, and others are constantly before us. They carry enormous influence because each indicator is part of the context of the rest. Interpretations of the data may vary, but there is at least a basis for discussion, debate, and policy intervention that is relatively consistent, reliable, and agreed upon.

An illustration of the variety and frequency of economic indicators and indexes is presented in table 23.1. Its findings suggest that as a society we deem this information to be of sufficient importance that we collect it, analyze it, and report it in a highly systematized manner. The frequency and accessibility of economic indicators also implies a willingness to respond and intervene. Their timeliness allows for rapid intervention and even evaluation of the impact of policy change.

Formalized communications throughout the government facilitate the process of economic reporting. Most of the weekly, monthly, and quarterly statistics and indexes in the economic arena are brought together in the annual Economic Report of the President, prepared by the Council of Economic Advisors.[1] This report, though often political in tone, summarizes the essential economic events of the previous year, proposes strategic economic plans for the future, and includes historical data on key economic indicators. Similarly, the Federal Reserve Board issues a survey of economic activity every six weeks; called the "Beige Book," this report is designed to synopsize the nation's economic health and enhance rational decision making. Through its comprehensiveness and frequency, it contributes to the routine and periodic assessment of economic conditions. The very primacy and visibility of other agencies and positions such as the Council of Economic Advisors or the Chair of the Federal Reserve Board, and the relative exactitude of their work (raising the interest rate a quarter of one percent), add legitimacy and credibility to the endeavor of economic monitoring and the importance of economic policy.

In comparison, social indicators and the endeavor of social reporting are at a still primitive state. Social indicators are far more sporadic, generally reported in isolation, and lacking a context that could be provided by other indicators and by an overall assessment of social well-being. Social indicators are rarely reported more frequently than on an annual basis and often there is a lag time of months and even years. The second half of table 23.1 summarizes the state of key social indicators and underscores the comparison with the economic indicators:

Table 23.1 Selected Economic and Social Indicators: Reporting Frequency and Lag Time

Daily	Weekly	Monthly	Quarterly	Annually
		Economic Indicators		
CRB Futures Price Index (15 sec.)	Bank Loans: Com. & Industrial (9 days)	Average Hourly Earnings Index (1–2 wks.)	Balance of Payments (75 days)	Distribution of Income (8 mo.)
Dow Jones Industrial Avg. (60 sec.)	Business Failures (5 days)	Average Weekly Earnings (1–2 wks.)	Capital Appropriations (70 days)	Intl. Investment Position of the U.S. (6 mo.)
New York Stock Exchange Composite Index (60 sec.)	Business Starts (5 days)	Average Weekly Hours (1–2 wks.)	Employment Cost Index (1 mo.)	Poverty (8 mo.)
Standard & Poor's 500 Composite Price Index (60 sec.)	Money Supply (10 days)	Balance of Trade (45 days)	Farm Parity Ratio (1 mo.)	
Wilshire 5000 Equity Index (1 day)		Capacity Utilization (2.5 wks.)	Flow of Funds (2 mo.)	
		Consumer Confidence Index (5–10 days)	GNP Price Measures (3–4 wks.)	
		Consumer Installment Credit (6 wks.)	Gross National Product (3–4 wks.)	
		Consumer Price Index (3–4 wks.)	Plant and Equipment Expenditures (2 wks.)	
		Consumer Sentiment Index (5–10 days)	Productivity (2 mo.)	
		Employment (1–2 wks.)	Unit Labor Costs (2 mo.)	
		Government Budgets and Debt (3–4 wks.)		
		Housing Starts (3 wks.)		
		Import and Export Prices Indexes (1 mo.)		
		Industrial Production Index (2.5 wks.)		
		Inventory-Sales Ratios (45 days)		

Economic Indicators	
Leading, Coincident, & Lagging Indexes	(1 mo.)
Manufacturers' Orders	(1 mo.)
Personal Income and Saving	(3–4 wks.)
Producer Price Index	(2.5 wks.)
Unemployment	(1–2 wks.)

Social Indicators

Social Indicators	
Amer. Housing Survey (biennial)	(1 yr.)
Child Abuse	(4 mo.)
Drug Abuse	(6 mo.)
Food Stamp Enrollment	(3 mo.)
Health Insurance Enrollment	(8 mo.)
High School Drop-outs	(1 yr.)
Highway Deaths Due to Alcohol	(10 mo.)
Infant Mortality	(2 yr.)
National Crime Survey	(2 yr.)
Teen Suicide	(2–3 yr.)
Uniform Crime Reports	(8–9 mo.)

Sources: Economic indicators adapted from Norman Frumkin, *Guide to Economic Indicators* 1990. Armonk, N.Y.: 1 M.E. Sharpe.
Social indicators from authors' telephone survey; analysis of data sources. Lag times are approximate. Numbers in parentheses indicate publication lag time.

It is clear from the infrequent reporting of social indicators and their lack of context and combination that their influence on the public and on public policy, almost by definition, is far less than economic indicators. This is compounded by the fact that there are few guideposts and officially sanctioned, recognized, and publicized indexes, and no governmental structures comparable to the Council of Economic Advisors in the social sphere. From the perspective of the general public, the reporting of social problems is as likely to be about a spectacular case of child abuse or teenage suicide, as about updated and current national trends. We hear far more about the "crisis in our cities" or the "crisis among youth" or "an epidemic of teenage suicide," suggesting uncontrollable situations not open to solution, than we hear anything comparable to "the economy expanded by 2.3 percent in the last quarter," which suggests a pragmatic vigilance and the possibility of rational action if trouble should occur.

As a result of these vast differences, we think very differently about economic problems than about social problems. Economic indicators reflect a coherent whole which seems to affect us all and in which all of us are invested. The parts of the economy that we monitor so closely can be viewed as moving, dynamic, touching each other, and touching the whole. The economy is about "us." Social indicators and social problems seem more isolated and separate, with little connection to each other or to the whole. Indicators such as teenage suicide, child abuse, or children in poverty, seem disconnected, measuring only the populations inside of their definitions.[2] They appear to be measures of "them."

We have a limited and fragmented perception of our social well-being because we lack common information and a common context for assessing that information. When several social problems, such as homicide, suicide, child abuse, high school dropout, and violent crime, all grow worse at the same time, each is separately portrayed as an individual and isolated crisis. We may feel the combined effects on the quality of our everyday life. We may have a gnawing sense that there is a change for the worse, but we have no systematic way to understand the extent, scope, pattern, or potential consequences of what is taking place. As a result, the quality of public discussion and policymaking about social issues is far more likely to be shaped by the passions of the day and the politics of the moment rather than by rational analysis based on accurate, timely information.

A CONCEPT OF THE WHOLE AND A NOTION OF PERFORMANCE

In order to expand the scope and impact of social indicators and to improve public education and policy deliberation, we need to establish a set of policy-oriented social measures that are generally recognized and regularly reported and to develop an underlying theory to give them context and impact. Some of the issues involved are empirical and methodological: what data will be collected and how. But considerable effort needs to be applied as well to issues of concept and theory. It is the language of economic indicators, their interconnection and the theory that binds them, that gives them their power as well as the sense that they are monitoring the dynamics of something very significant. If social indicators do not move in this direction, no matter how well conceived individually, and how well operationalized, surveyed, and reported, they will not have significant consequence for the public or the makers of policy.

In order to begin to develop a context, both for social well-being and for social indicators, two factors stand out as points of departure: an idea of the whole that connects the indicators and provides them with a context, and the notion of performance.

The notion of a whole is a difficult one. The tools of our social science trade tend to carry us in an opposite direction: toward disaggregation. Yet a social analogue for the economy is necessary to bring the discussion to the next and needed level, particularly if we are to influence public policy and public awareness and increase the use and reporting of social indicators. Economists can talk about soft spots in the economy, improvement or worsening, expanding or receding cycles or stagnation, recession, or recovery. They can point to the particular performance of specific sectors, how those sectors relate, and their place in the performance of the whole. There is a certain tension and movement, like a good story that unfolds. Without a similar notion of a whole that is being monitored, those of us who analyze and report conditions in the social sphere can point only to the worsening or improving of individual and unrelated statistics, or to a descriptive list of statistics that are not clearly linked to something larger.

In the area of child well-being, for example, we can single out a series of statistics such as child poverty or child abuse. We can say that one or both are increasing or decreasing, and we can make some tentative statements of correlation between the two. But in this state, such statistics are not really social *indicators*. An indicator, like a metaphor, carries with it a part of the whole, it is a sounding, it taps into something greater and because of its implicit connection it represents and reflects it. When Durkheim founded modern sociology through the statistical analysis of suicide rates, he wasn't merely examining suicide, but asserting that its patterns told us something about the nature and connection of society's strands, something underneath that suicide rates were signaling. Yet, a statistic like child abuse is an accounting that typically begins and ends within its own boundaries. We need to go beyond it and examine broader questions: What does child abuse indicate about our society? What does child poverty indicate? What does the improvement or worsening of these conditions tell us about other conditions and about the general condition?

Such questions sound highly theoretical, but exploring ways to expand social statistics into real indicators is a practical process. If a social statistic stands alone, disconnected, conceptually or empirically, to other indicators or to a notion of the whole, then the precise monitoring of isolated sectors of society such as children's well-being becomes problematic. Clearly, for political reasons, that sector is appealing and one needs to start somewhere, but even a superficial analysis leads to the conclusion that children's social well-being, and any individual indicator of children's well-being, is directly related to things beyond children. Isolated analysis keeps our attention on "them" as a separate sector rather than on "us," as a whole, of which they are a part. It implies, as well, that solutions or interventions should be directed toward children, when the origin of worsening conditions may very well lay elsewhere.

More than one in five children in America live in poverty, and many others close to it. It could be argued that this statistic tells us much about the condition of children in this country. But alone, it tells us little about how the condition occurred and, more important, what is to be done about it. It is merely a descriptive statement. It is possible that the most influential indicator of social well-being of children is the precipitous decline of average weekly wages in America since 1973, or the shrinking of the manufacturing employment sector, generally not included in lists of children's indicators (See Burtless 1990; Levitan, Gallo, and Shapiro 1993; Mishel and Bernstein 1993; Peterson 1993; U.S. Bureau of the Census 1993). Confining the analysis to children tells us little about the underlying dynamics involved in the well-being of that group.

Interrelated to the notion of a whole is the notion of performance. Performance is deeply embedded in the realm of economic indicators, but generally not a central aspect of social analysis. Without a notion of the whole, we cannot even pose the kind of overall question about the nation's social performance that economists do about the economy: What is our social performance as a nation? Is it improving or worsening? How does it compare to last year? What sectors are getting better? What are the soft spots? Most of us have been trained by the idea that when we build a social construct, such as authoritarianism or racism, we devise instruments to determine its relative degree of presence or absence. We generally do not think about an entity composed of some properties that are improving and some worsening at the same time, such as the factors in the Index of Leading Economic Indicators. We rarely think in terms of an individual indicator as performing against a threshold or standard.

Without developing some social analogue to the notion of economy or the whole, and without focusing on performance, the dynamic realm that characterizes economic indicators is closed to us. Ideas such as leading or lagging social indicators, or a social recession, or cycles or trends in overall social health, from which thresholds and standards can emerge, are not now possible (Miringoff, Miringoff, and Opdycke 1996). If an economic recession is defined empirically as three consecutive quarters of no growth, what would it take to declare the nation in a social recession? The absence of this kind of conceptual framework widens the gap between social indicators and public policy and public dialogue.

The creation of a theoretical thread needed to help bind the disparate data and indicators will be a difficult endeavor. The evolution of the kind of dynamic analysis and composite measures that currently characterize economic monitoring will be a slow one, which will begin and build upon the current system of data collection and reporting and its possible expansion. It required many years of research to develop the theoretical and empirical system that finally culminated in the Employment Act of 1946 that established the system of economic indicators, the Council of Economic Advisors, and the Economic Report of the President. Research on the concept of a business cycle that was the central idea of the system goes back to the beginning of the century. The theoretical and empirical aspects developed together.

The development of a notion of performance in the social sphere and the need to focus on more holistic approaches that include many indicators and begin to connect them into a context should be an important new focus for our pursuit. Advances in these areas would greatly add to the significance and impact of social indicators, which is particularly important if we are to build new corridors that connect them to policymaking and public education. When we consider how to enhance our current system of social reporting, these endeavors must have a central place.

A SYSTEM OF SOCIAL REPORTING TO IMPROVE POLICY AND HEIGHTEN PUBLIC EDUCATION

We need to explore broader, richer ties between social indicators, social policy, and the public dialogue. As currently conceived, most social indicators are not designed to frequently and regularly monitor social conditions in order to detect warning signs which require policy intervention. Bells never go off when the poverty of children reaches 20 percent, or the teenage suicide rate doubles, although the consequences for society and its future are surely as significant as a short-term rise in inflation or a slight decline in housing starts.

In determining what kind of system of data collection and reporting is needed, its frequency and its level of aggregation, we need to consider not only the realms where policy is created and technical alternatives debated and hammered out, but the public dialogue as well. We need a rational, pragmatic, and data-based approach to social issues that broadens and informs the public dialogue. Because of the way in which social indicators are reported and social problems generally portrayed in the media, the public's perception of social well-being can be hazy and courses of action very obscure.

As we have noted, the fact that social data are reported so late makes them peripheral to both the policy process and the public debate. Since data are at very best one year old and often two or more years old, changes can only be traced and analyzed years after the fact, providing a very static picture and necessitating the well worn phrase "the last year for which statistics are available." Such a phrase is rarely if ever needed in economics; few modern governments would attempt to formulate current economic policy with data on interest rates or inflation going back several years.

In order to inform policy and the public in a more timely way, to indicate significant changes in the performance of indicators that affect large numbers of the population, and to aid in the conceptual development of social indicators, we need to significantly improve our system of social reporting.

Indicators should be presented to the public as frequently as possible. Many key indicators could be reported on a quarterly basis, providing an ongoing picture of improving or worsening social conditions. Others could be reported annually, but with minimum lag time. Frequent reporting would more finely attune the public to the significance of social issues and provide meaningful opportunities for public education. Reports on the network news that child abuse or teenage suicide had increased or decreased in the past quarter, in the context of patterns over time and with experts quoted, would add weight to the reporting of these problems that their severity deserves. This would be preferable to the episodic coverage of problems such as the attention to domestic abuse brought on by the O. J. Simpson trial. Over time, this kind of systematic social reporting might change the way many social problems are viewed in the nation.

Where possible, related indicators need to be reported together, providing a greater picture of the whole. A clear, periodic, empirical portrait of the "state of" children, teenagers, the elderly, or workers would permit a deeper understanding of the issues and a greater likelihood of formulating social policies that were more comprehensive and less crisis-driven. If the state of the economy is summarized annually through the Economic Report of the President, the state of children, officially assessed by the government, could have equivalent public significance. Such assessments would reduce the isolation and lack of context that currently surround social indicators.

The reporting of changes in the performance of indicators should be stressed. We need to create a system of analysis well suited to public dialogue and policymaking, in which key findings can be readily communicated. Much economic monitoring consists only of quarterly or annual percent increases and decreases. Yet these relatively simple statistics can indicate critical swings in the economy, and over time suggest trends, patterns, points of intervention, and the ability to forecast events. Social indicators, measured more frequently and with an emphasis on changes in performance, could provide similar information, including possible warning signs and even forecasting potential.

There is a need to develop composite measures where increases or decreases signify broadly changing conditions and which include thresholds which signify the overall improvement or worsening of conditions. We need indexes such as these in the monitoring of social indicators, which are published on a periodic basis, and which have wide public dissemination. The evolution of these kind of measures, geared to an analysis of performance, requires significant theoretical and methodological development. The far more frequent collection and reporting of social data will broaden the view of social performance and suggest further approaches to their development. Without such measures that empirically combine the individual indicators and begin to provide an overall view of their performance, social reporting will remain largely confined to individual statistics and will have far less impact.

Survey and public opinion data are also a necessary complement to objective reporting. Economists use the Conference Board's Consumer Confidence Index and the University of Michigan's Index of Consumer Sentiment as an integral part of their monitoring systems. Official social reports in other countries rely heavily on social surveys to provide vital information on the "temper" of their nations regarding issues such as community cohesion, sense of safety, housing, income, problems of disability, and others.[3] In this nation, just as social problem data are fragmented, so too are methodological approaches. It is rare, but clearly desirable, to combine both types of data, giving a more integrated sense of the problem and how it is perceived.

It is also necessary to create a data base that allows for comparative analysis of states and regions. Some social indicators are not well enough developed to achieve this end. Child abuse, with its multiple state definitions, has such problems. Such data would benefit from being both defined and collected at the federal level.[4] Where surveys are involved, samples of sufficient size are needed to disseminate reliable state and regional data. Normed or adjusted measures also further the ability to compare data. While many economic measures are seasonally and regionally adjusted, few social measures are.

Such expansions and enhancements would greatly benefit our current system of social reporting. Over time, a comprehensive social reporting system, directed toward the assessment of social performance, would allow for a more informed public and a more directed social policy apparatus. As in the development of economic indicators, there is a need to develop a language that can assess cycles of achievement and decline, that includes warning signs based on agreed-upon standards and thresholds, and that accounts for the interrelationships of problems through the use of composite measures. These changes in the way we collect and report social indicators will contribute to that end.

CONCLUSION

Economic indicators have been afforded a high degree of respect throughout this chapter. Their impact and influence, the way in which they are institutionalized, their theoretical, empirical, and dynamic character are important as an analogue for the future development of social indicators. But what they lack is important as well. Economist Amartya Sen (1993) has written that if "the economic success of a nation is judged only by income and by other traditional indicators of opulence and financial soundness, as it so often is, the important goal of well-being is missed. The more conventional criteria of measuring economic success can be enhanced by including assessments of a nation's ability to extend and to improve the quality of life."

Economic indicators, despite their significant influence and relative comprehensiveness, often tell us little about social well-being. They omit much about the changing quality of life of ordinary Americans. In order to understand what is happening in the nation and what needs to be done, we need to know far more about the quality of life than what is offered by the world of economic indicators; and we need to know it with far greater accuracy and frequency than currently exists.

NOTES

1. It is interesting to note that the 1992 Economic Report of the President addresses the need for even more enhanced economic statistics, and cites an "Economic Statistics Initiative," which sought an appropriation of more that one hundred and fifty million dollars for fiscal 1993 to 1997 to develop economic reporting.

2. Poverty is generally considered to be an economic indicator. However, in this chapter we consider it to be a social indicator as well, in that it is directly connected to social problems and is not a key component of the regular and frequent monitoring system of economic indicators. Interestingly, it is also one of the very few economic indicators collected annually.

3. See for example France's Social Report, *Donnees Sociales* (Social Data); Britain's *Social Trends*, Denmark's *Levevilkar i Danmark* (Living Conditions in Denmark); Germany's *Datenreport* (Data Report); Italy's *Sintesi Della Vita Sociale Italiana* (Overview of Italian Social Life) and *Statistiche e Indicatori Sociali* (Statistics and Social Indicators); Spain's *Indicatores Sociales* (Social Indicators) and *Panoramica Social* (Social Panorama).

4. A federal monitoring system, called the National Child Abuse and Neglect Data System (NCANDS) has been developed in recent years; however, it is still primarily dependent on data which has been defined and produced at the state level. Some states include unduplicated counts of children, others duplicated, making comparative analysis problematic. A private nonprofit organization, The National Committee to Prevent Child Abuse, is currently the major source for data over time.

REFERENCES

Burtless, Gary. 1990. *A Future of Lousy Jobs: The Changing Structure of U.S. Wages.* Washington, D.C.: The Brookings Institution.

Levitan, Sar, Frank Gallo, and Isaac Shapiro. 1993. *Working But Poor: America's Contradiction.* Baltimore, Md.: Johns Hopkins University Press.

Miringoff, Marc, Marque-Luisa Miringoff, and Sandra Opdycke. Forthcoming. "Monitoring the Nation's Social Performance: The Index of Social Health." In *Children, Families, and Government: Preparing for the Twenty-First Century*, edited by Edward Zigler. New York: Cambridge University Press.

Miringoff, Marque-Luisa, Marc Miringoff, and Sandra Opdycke. 1996. "The Growing Gap Between Standard Economic Indicators and the Nation's Social Health." *Challenge* (July–Aug.): 17–22.

Mishel, Lawrence, and Jared Bernstein. 1993. *The State of Working America.* Armonk, N.Y.: M. E. Sharpe.

Peterson, Wallace. 1994. *The Silent Depression: The Fate of the American Dream.* New York: W. W. Norton and Co.

Sen, Amartya. 1993. "The Economics of Life and Death." *Scientific American.* 40.

U.S. Bureau of the Census. 1993. *The Earnings Ladder.* Statistical Brief 94, no. 3. Washington: U.S. Government Printing Office.

Children in Dire Straits: How Do We Know Whether We Are Progressing?

William R. Prosser and Matthew Stagner

IN THIS CHAPTER we outline a set of propositions about how indicators of child well-being might be created by social scientists and used by policy advocates. In particular, we are concerned with indicators for troubled children who find themselves in the social service system because of delinquency, abuse or neglect, or educational failure. We refer to these indicators as "psychosocial" indicators of child well-being.

We have four aims. First, we try to clarify terms and discuss the evolving history of indicators. Second, we look at the multiple uses of indicators. Third, we explore and critique examples of psychosocial indicators now used, noting strengths and weaknesses. Finally, we make recommendations concerning improvement of these indicators.

WHAT ARE INDICATORS AND WHY HAVE THEM?[1]

The desire to gather information to report the well-being of children and families has a long history. Foundations, advocacy groups, states, and the federal government are engaged in numerous activities to develop and refine social statistics for a host of reasons. Some or all of these activities use the word "indicators" synonymously with social statistics or as a subset of them.

Definition of Terms

We feel comfortable with the following definition of "indicators": "quantitative *descriptions* of social *conditions* that are intended to *inform* public opinion and national policymaking" (Duncan, emphasis added).[2] Indicators, generally, are a selected set of data intended to bring insights to various audiences about our country's social problems and achievements. In our opinion, indicators differ from "social statistics." Social statistics describe, while indicators purposefully inform. The *Statistical Abstract* is a collection of social statistics. A small subset of these social statistics could be called indicators. They are not measures of programmatic effort or inputs. In addition, they are not measures of programmatic outcome. As we discuss, indicators cannot determine the impact programs have made on the lives of children, except in the broadest sense of the word "indicator."

Indicators are used by different actors for different purposes and should be judged according to their purpose. While indicators most often are constructed and collected by social scientists or program administrators, they are used by many groups of people, such as analysts, advocates, government workers, politicians, the media, and the general public. Their many uses may conflict. Different standards of fairness or effectiveness apply depending on use or purpose. Social scientists have a stake in assuring that these tools are reliably constructed and in decreasing their misuse. Some purveyors of indicators—in particular, advocates—hope to spur public action. The roles of the scientist and the advocate may conflict because the two groups apply different standards to indicators. We discuss these different standards.

A Brief History of Social Indicators

Interest in social indicators has waxed and waned over the last half-century. One of the most vigorous periods was the late 1960s and early 1970s during a time of great faith in social science. Social scientists in the social indicator movement hoped to create a social index equivalent to the economic indices such as the GNP. They sought a common metric equivalent to dollars in economic analysis. The current Index of Social Health produced by Miringoff and his colleagues at Fordham University is an example of this vision (Miringoff 1993).

A review of the early literature illuminates a grandiose vision of indicators and the prospects of social science:

> Social Indicators, the tools, are needed to find the pathways through the maze of society's interconnections. They delineate social states, define social problems, and trace social trends, which by social engineering, may hopefully be guided toward social goals, formulated by social planning. (Stuart Rice, cited in Duncan 1974)

Though the fervor for social indicators has been muted over the past twenty-five years, the 1990s find a host of new applications of indicators. We have some trepidation about discussing these projects, because they do not all comport exactly with our proposed use of indicators. Yet, we feel that understanding the breadth of potential uses provides guidance to the construction of indicators and the caveats that must accompany any such enterprise.

One current use of indicators is to assist planning initiatives to target resources, evaluate the success of programs and initiatives, hold government leaders and agencies accountable, inform the public, and generate public support. The Government Performance and Results Act (GPRA) and Oregon's Benchmarks Initiative are examples of this type of effort. The recent GPRA legislation mandates the expanded use of performance measurement in the federal government. The act tries to promote strategic planning and improved resource allocation. It also requires agencies to develop outcome measures for most national programs. At the same time, the vice president's National Performance Review seeks to "reinvent" government by incorporating the use of outcome indicators into agency practice, leading agencies to become more efficient and customer-oriented.

Various states also have mounted efforts to develop measures to gauge people's lives and to set program and budget priorities. The Oregon Benchmarks Initiative, for example, involves citizens in setting goals, tracking indicators, and assessing progress. This use of indicators is now embedded in agency planning and decision making in Oregon. This is both an indicator project and an exercise in participatory democracy. The public is an integral part of the process.

Another type of project comes from outside government. For the last several years, the Annie E. Casey Foundation of Baltimore has sponsored the *Kids Count National Data Book*. The introduction to 1994 *Kids Count* states its purpose:

> *Kids Count* is a national and state-by-state effort to track the status of children in the United States. By providing policymakers and citizens with benchmarks of child well-being, *Kids Count* seeks to enrich local, state, and national discussions concerning ways to secure better futures of all children. (Annie E. Casey Foundation 1994)

The foundation also funds projects in each state that report indicators of child well-being at the county and community level.

Our assessment of *Kids Count* activities is that they are a mixture of informing and advocating. For example, *Kids Count* presents a number of social statistics, such as the percent of all births to single teens and the infant mortality rate. However, the book also ranks states from best to worst on all of the indicators. This seems to be advocacy—trying to influence the public debate within states concerning relative rankings.

The Role of Indicators in Policymaking

We believe that efforts to construct a set of indicators must consider how social science data may influence government policymaking and agenda-setting. Advocates try to convince government policymakers that problems exist, that they have potential solutions, and that resources should be allocated to support these solutions. Creating indicators and selling their importance is critical to moving an issue from merely a "condition" to the status of a "problem" (Kingdon 1984). The process by which conditions get classified as problems is unpredictable, however. Opportunities for redefinition arise for indeterminate reasons and remain viable for uncertain periods.

An advocate's selection and interpretation of problems often are subjective and change over time. A condition becomes a problem when some incident, anecdote, or indicator deviates from an ideological (or normative) goal, or when it differs from what seems possible. For example, people may perceive a problem when large differences among demographic groups occur, as with the large differences in infant mortality, out-of-wedlock childbearing, and marriage rates across the races.

The unpredictable nature of the policymaking process creates a dilemma for those of us trying to develop a set of indicators. Are indicators timeless statistics, regardless of policy priorities? Should indicators provide an information inventory that sits on a shelf to be used when needed? Or should they be selected and tailored to the advocacy objective at hand?

Advocacy and Social Science

In our opinion, using indicators for advocacy can bring conflict with social science. One point of conflict is what we call the "transparency" of indicators. In seeking to call attention to a problem, advocates prefer to use indicators that are easily understood—that is, are transparent to the general public. Social scientists, in contrast, generally feel uncomfortable with indicators that promise transparency and simplicity. They often want to develop more "opaque" indicators that control for one or several other factors and that are more accurate representations of the conditions measured. Such indicators may be more difficult for lay people to understand. Occasionally, advocates oversimplify connections between programmatic inputs and conditions measured by indicators.

For example, ranking states on raw rates of births to single teens may be a transparent method for assessing states. Yet social scientists know that these rates are strongly influenced by the economic and social conditions and the racial compositions of the population in the areas being compared. Presenting rates controlled for race/ethnicity or income may be a more balanced, but more opaque, approach. The more statistical transformation that an indicator goes through, the more opaque, but less misleading, it may become (Garbarino 1991).

Furthermore, ranking states based simply on raw rates may give a false sense of complacency to high-ranking states and inordinate blame to low-ranking states. Further investigation behind the raw numbers might show that a particular state is not doing nearly as well as would be expected given the composition of its citizens. Before policy analysts can determine whether resources should be allocated to the lowest raw-score states or lowest controlled-score states, they must know the answers to several other questions so that they can maximize the return on their resource investment.

Indicators and Evaluation

It is hard to fault efforts to hold government officials accountable for their performance. Yet, only in special circumstances can indicators be used to *evaluate* the impact of public policies. In addition, the more transparent an indicator is, the less likely it is to be directly connected to government action or inaction.

Indicators seldom pass two general evaluation requirements: understanding how program interventions relate to results; and having a valid counterfactual. First, evaluating program effectiveness requires at least a rudimentary understanding of the causal linkages among such elements as recipient characteristics, program participation, program activities, and program outcomes. Generally, given the current state of social science, we have a "causal ignorance" of these interconnections (Department of Health Education and Welfare 1973). In complex systems like local child welfare systems or state employment and training programs, simple indicators cannot provide sufficient intelligence about the causal links or counterfactuals.

Second, the lack of a valid comparison presents a serious barrier to the use of indicators for evaluating the success of programs. The essence of the scientific method is the concept of a counterfactual. Evaluations ask: how would the treatment subject (or the program recipient) have responded in the absence of the program intervention? Without appropriate counterfactuals it is easy to attribute success to programs in good times and failures in bad times without looking at whether the results are caused by the program or the environment in which it is operating. Of course, we can never know that without a doubt. We cannot turn back the clock and see the client's life again without the program intervention. Sometimes, social scientists create clinical trials with randomly selected groups, one receiving the program and the other receiving "standard care." Often, circumstances prevent us from conducting a classical experimental trial, so we use comparison groups or other methods to create counterfactuals. Indicators should have some counterfactual as well. Unless an indicator is constructed with a valid comparison, it cannot be appropriately used to evaluate the success of program policies, in our judgment.

Given our definition of indicators, evaluation results must pass a higher scientific test of appropriateness than indicators. (We discuss in the next section the tests that we believe indicators must pass.) Indicators are the products of statistical reporting systems, surveys, or administrative records. They are not the products of in-depth, multivariate studies of programs and recipients. As such, indicator trends may prompt studies of programs and policies, but the trends can never alone validate the success or failure of a policy or a program. As a consequence, we see only loose linkages between efforts to develop and use child well-being indicators and efforts to develop outcome-oriented measures of government performance, such as the National Performance Review and GPRA.

A case might be made that indicators may be used to hold government accountable in a general sense—that "things" are getting better or worse. It is possible to cite examples where the use of an indicator for this purpose makes some sense. For example, the poverty rate may have been a valid measure of the success of the "War on Poverty" in the 1960s. But the poverty statistics do not provide much evidence about who or what should be praised (or faulted) for lowering (or increasing) poverty. It is judging the performance of the President on the basis of the general state of the economy. Such judgments may be erroneous and should be made cautiously. The president has very little influence over the measure.

While indicators probably cannot prove the success of a new program, they may be able to give warning signals that things are not working as planned. Like economic leading indicators, certain measures of well-being might be able to give warning signs. Such signs should then precipitate in-depth evaluations.

PROPOSITIONS FOR INDIVIDUAL INDICATORS

We now turn to a discussion of the appropriateness of indicators used to measure the psychosocial development of children. First, we discuss specific psychosocial indicators now being used. We believe, however, that some of the concerns apply to other indicator domains. Second, we discuss some ideas about indicators in general. We hope that these propositions can guide efforts to develop indicators that tell us how well parents and communities are nurturing children and assuring satisfactory transitions to adulthood.

Table 24.1   Summary of Four Propositions About Psychosocial Indicators of Child Well-Being

Proposition	Description
Direct Measurement	An indicator should be a direct measure of children's experiences rather than measures of the performance of the human services delivery system.
Source	A child's self-report is preferable to a service system assessment for children sufficiently old enough to articulate their condition.
System Mediation	Indicators of system mediation often reflect whether the service system recognized, reported, confirmed, and responded to a psychosocial problem rather than whether children's well-being is at risk or not. System mediation may be influenced by *time constraints, supply constraints, changing community values, and reporter's perceptions of consequences* rather than children's actual well-being.
Clarity of Direction	Comparisons over time or across jurisdictions should be unambiguous concerning whether children's well-being is improving or deteriorating.
Masking Opposite Trends	Designers should assure that improvement in one indicator is not masking a deteriorating trend in a complementary indicator; for example, that decline in mortality is masking deterioration in morbidity.
Diminishing Returns	Designers should recognize that at some point the costs to children and society exceed the benefits of lowering indicators beyond it.
False Positives and False Negatives	Type I and II measurement errors may provide a false sense of child well-being because type I (false negative) errors may be misreported more frequently than type II (false positive) errors and as a result underreport the true scope of the problem.
Clear Interpretation	Indicators should provide a clear sense of appropriate corrective action. In addition, they generally should not combine two separate aspects of children's lives in one indicator.

In this section, we discuss four propositions for psychosocial indicators. By psychosocial indicators we mean indicators for troubled children who find themselves in the social service system because of delinquency, abuse or neglect, or educational failure. Table 24.1 summarizes the propositions contained in this section.

Table 24.2 lists the indicators we discuss. This list is meant to be illustrative of psychosocial indicators now used. It is *not* comprehensive, and it is *not* our proposal for a *set* of indicators. We draw most of the indicators in table 24.1 from *Kids Count* reports. The source of the indicator is listed next to the indicator. We selected examples from *Kids Count* neither to praise nor find fault with the project, but because it represents one of the most comprehensive child indicators efforts in existence.

Table 24.2   Examples of Indicators of Children's Psychosocial Well-Being Now in Use

Delinquency and crime
1. Juvenile arrest rate (CT 94) (WI 94)
2. Juvenile violent crime arrest rate (NDB 94; AR 93; AL 93; SD 93; WI 93)
3. Juveniles committed to state custody (GA 93)
4. Juvenile delinquents in secure institutions (and average days of stay) (WI 94)
5. Number of homicides and firearm homicides committed by adolescents ages 10–19 (CO 93)
6. Juvenile violent crime court referral rates (cases adjudicated per 100,000 ages 10–17 (AL 93)
7. Number of child admissions to adult jail facilities (SD 93)

Work and school
8. Percent of teens not in school and not in labor force (NDB 94; AL 94)
9. Percent graduating from high school on time (NDB 94)
10. Youth unemployment rate
11. Percent of children in special education (TN 92)
12. Rate of children retained in kindergarten (GA 93)

Substance abuse
13. Drug use by juvenile arrestees (DC 93)
14. Rate of substance use by high school students in the past month (CT 94)

Child welfare
15. Rate of children in substitute care (CO 93)
16. Rate of children entering substitute care over time (IL 93)
17. Number/rate of families investigated for CA/N (CT 94)
18. Number/rate of "confirmed" reports (by type of CA/N) (AR 93)
19. Death rate from CA/N (CO 93)

Notes: CA/N refers to child abuse/neglect; NDB refers to the *Kids Count National Data Book* and year of publication. All other references are to the state data book, identified by the two letter state abbreviation and year of publication.

Direct Measurement

First, an indicator should directly measure a factor in a child's life, originating from someone close to the child and having little mediation from the service system. Measures of child well-being should accurately reflect the true condition of the child, not features of the human service delivery system. Two issues underlie this proposition. One is the source of the report: the child, a parent, a teacher, or someone in less frequent contact with the child. A second is mediation by a service system.

Source of the Report   Some measures rely on a child's self-report of his or her condition. For example, the youth unemployment rate is determined through direct surveys of young people.[3] More often, we rely on an adult proxy to represent the well-being of the child. Sometimes a parent is the proxy respondent; at other times a professional fulfills this role.

Many types of professionals assess child well-being for the development of indicators. Teachers assess and report on children's learning ability or educational progress. Police investigate victims' reports of criminal activities of youth. Child welfare workers investigate and report on abuse and neglect. Physicians assess children's health. Psychologists assess children's emotional well-being and mental capacity. Shelters record information on the runaways they see.

It is possible to think of a continuum of sources for understanding child well-being. At one end, reports come from the child's own perceptions of his or her condition. At the other end, professionals embedded within a service system assess and report on the child's condition, such as drug use.

$$\longleftarrow \qquad\qquad\qquad\qquad\qquad\qquad\qquad\qquad \longrightarrow$$

| Child's Own Report | Parent's Report | Independent Professional Assessment | Service System Assessment |

There is no correct place on this continuum. Rather, for different domains of children's lives, different trade-offs exist at each point. Children are obviously closest to their own situation. However, they may not fully understand their condition or may not be able to communicate it (for example, if they are too young). On the other hand, they may underreport or exaggerate conditions (such as drug use). On the other side of the continuum, reporters may have professional expertise at identifying conditions, but they are removed from the child and more likely to be influenced by the service system context. Furthermore, they may only see a self-selected portion of the population with the problem. Generally, they only know about the youths who come to their facilities with drug problems, for example, not the ones who go without treatment. For each indicator it is important to consider the trade-offs at each point on the continuum.

Mediation by the Service System   If indicators are to relate to child well-being, they should measure the child's condition rather than whether the service system adequately responds to the child or has sufficient resources to identify and treat a problem. With any proxy measure from reporters within the system, the service system mediates the measure of a child's well-being.

Many indicators of psychosocial well-being do not directly measure the condition of children. Rather, they measure the *response* of the service system to the condition of children. For example, the rate of confirmed child abuse and neglect measures, in part, whether the child welfare system has enough resources and the proper tools to accept and investigate complaints of abuse and neglect. Similarly, the juvenile arrest rate measures law enforcement effort and technique as well as criminal activity by juveniles.

Mediation by the service system can occur at several points, as indicated in the flow outlined below. Community values may affect whether a problem is recognized by a potential reporter. The service system may determine whether it is then reported, whether it is confirmed, and whether it results in service. Child abuse is a good example of such a continuum.

| Problem Recognized? | → | Problem Reported? | → | Report Confirmed? | → | Service Response? |

There are at least four ways the service system mediates an indicator. First, time may constrain a reporter's action. Second, the supply of a service may constrain a reporter's action. Third, changing community values outside the service system (a change in the acceptability of spanking as proper punishment, for example) may influence a reporter's action. Fourth, various factors may affect whether the reporter senses a problem and believes it to be worth the consequences if reported. In sum, how a service system defines the problems it addresses depends in part upon what the system desires to do and is able to do.

In many service systems, actions of professionals are severely constrained by funding and *time constraints*. Assessments of child well-being may be influenced by these constraints. The true condition of children may not be discovered because professionals are too busy to conduct the necessary measurement or because they lack incentives to find the time to look for these problems.

Table 24.2 includes several examples of indicators that face this difficulty. For example, the rate of special education receipt may not be a true reflection of the rate of children with special needs. In school systems where teachers are severely overburdened, many children who may benefit from these services may not receive them because they are never properly tested. Teachers do not have the time to identify such students.

Another example comes from the juvenile justice arena. Police may have incentives *not* to charge children for some offenses. It may be easier, and faster, to release young offenders back to their parents without going through formal proceedings. Therefore, the rate of arrest of children may not reflect the true number of children committing offenses. This distortion is likely to be less severe with more violent offenses, where police may feel they must go through formal arrest proceedings.

Many indicators are influenced by *the supply of (and the demand for) services*, but the rate of service reported may be a poor proxy for the underlying condition of children. A great supply of the service, in the face of low demand, may lead to children receiving the service who do not face the underlying condition. A constrained supply of the service, in the face of high demand, may lead to far fewer children receiving the service than those who face the underlying condition. This is a problem of the *system's* resources, not of the workers' time and personal resources.

The rate of substitute care placement, for example, is an indicator where supply and demand may distort the measure of the underlying condition. Children should be placed into substitute care because workers believe that they will not be safe in their own homes. The rate of substitute care is easy to measure, but it is an indirect proxy for the rate of children who do not have parents who can properly care for them. It is, in essence, a proxy for the rate of dysfunctional parenting. A household survey of parenting behavior—a much more complicated and expensive measure—would possibly provide a very different measure of improper parenting.

In jurisdictions where the supply of foster homes is less than the demand for them, the rate of substitute care will underreport the rate of dysfunctional parenting. In areas where foster homes are relatively plentiful, the rate of substitute care may overreport the rate of improper parenting as child protection workers place children who may not truly need to be placed. This situation is now complicated by the use of "kinship" foster homes, where children are taken from their parents and placed with close relatives. The increased use of "kinship" homes has greatly increased the supply of substitute care and may distort time trends in this indicator.

Professionals within the service system are influenced by *changing community standards* over time. Differences in an indicator over time, or across jurisdictions, may reflect different community standards or values. This is perhaps best seen in the arena of child abuse and neglect. Over the past three decades, tolerance for certain parental behavior has declined dramatically. Spanking and other forms of punishment that may have been viewed as standard practice in the 1960s may now qualify as child abuse. In looking at trends over time, or in comparing jurisdictions, differences in community values may distort measures of the underlying conditions of children.

Other indicators may reflect changes in the stigma or connotation of a situation or an incident. This may be true, for example, of dropping out of school, teen pregnancy, and welfare participation rates. It can be argued that a high school diploma does not have the same meaning it had two decades ago. Welfare receipt, though it is often seen as a proxy for dependency, is subject to changing stigmas. These rates may increase or decrease because of the stigmas rather than because of changes in child well-being.

Reporters may also choose to report a condition based on their *perceptions of what will happen* when they report. For example, teachers may not want to call attention to children with problems because it may reflect poorly on their skills. Potential reporters may view the child welfare system as "antifamily." Potential reporters may not report a condition because they believe the consequences of reporting may be harmful for themselves and the families and may outweigh any potential benefit. They may prefer to work directly with the family to overcome the problem rather than involve the family in the child protection system.

Clarity of Direction

Trends in an indicator should represent, unambiguously, whether children's conditions are improving. It should be clear when an indicator moves in a particular direction that it represents an improvement (or deterioration) in children's well-being overall. For example, a decline in the percentage of youth reporting that they use drugs can be considered an improving picture. On the other hand, if juvenile arrest rates are declining, does this mean that juveniles are committing fewer crimes or that police are looking the other way more often? Likewise, comparisons made across jurisdictions at a point in time should be made in such a way to show unambiguously whether children's conditions are relatively better or worse across the various jurisdictions.

An exception to this general proposition is when an indicator is presented to provide contextual cues for more direct indicator measures. We may not know whether a change in racial composition or maternal employment rates is better or worse for children, but it may be an important control or contextual variable for other, more direct measures of well-being.

There are two reasons why an indicator may not have a clear direction. First, a change in direction with one indicator may mask changes in the opposite direction of other closely associated indicators. A decline in mortality may be accompanied by an increase in morbidity. Second, an indicator may reach a point of diminished returns, where further movement in one direction no longer represents an improvement for children's quality of life. Just as with adults, society probably should not have zero youth unemployment as a goal.

Masking Opposite Trends

A change in an indicator may disguise movement in another factor in children's lives. Without looking at both the indicator and other statistics, what appears to be a clear improvement in children's lives may in fact be a deterioration. For example, some policymakers and advocates believe that reductions in the substitute care population are desirable. Declining substitute care placement rates are viewed as a positive sign. However, without also looking at other indicators—such as the rate of child abuse and neglect—it is difficult to interpret the trend. If placements rates were declining at the time that substantiated cases of abuse and neglect were increasing, one would worry about the system's response.

The increasing divorce rate of the past three decades has been cited as a measure of the decline in child well-being. A lower proportion of children now live with both parents at any given time, and a lower proportion of children live with both parents throughout childhood. However, without knowing the rate of children harmed by living in households with high levels of conflict among the parents, it is difficult to say that this trend has made children worse off. Though the recent trend in divorce rates may imply that children are worse off, evidence would be stronger if this indicator were presented with other trends in children's well-being.

Several indicators of children's psychosocial well-being have this problem. For example, improvements in the kindergarten retention rate (that is, fewer children being retained) implies that children are doing better. However, without looking at a number of other indicators (such as whether the children not retained are successful in later school years or score better on tests of achievement), it is difficult to interpret whether a change in the retention rate in fact shows that children are doing better. Fewer children may be retained at this point in their school careers, only to find that they are retained in later years or eventually drop out from the frustration of being behind their peers.

Point of Diminishing Returns

Some indicators may show improvements in children's lives over certain parts of the scale but then reach a point of diminishing returns, where further movement in that direction leads to little or no improvement in children's well-being or may come only with huge investments.

The example of infant mortality may illustrate the point. Reducing infant mortality may come with some great expense, saving the lives of children who have high health care costs and poor quality of life. This creates a difficult moral issue. If one can create the correct scale to weigh such things (admittedly no easy task), the costs to society may outweigh the lives saved.

This issue suggests the need for a better understanding of the costs and benefits of society's attempts to "move" an indicator. With most indicators, naive users may assume that improvement at any point on the scale has the same cost and benefit. Yet with many indicators, at some point the costs of improvement may greatly exceed the benefits.

False Positives and False Negatives

Indicators should balance the costs of false positives and false negatives. Many indicators appear to tell us something important *if* we assume that the appropriate population has been captured in the indicator. However, as with statistical hypothesis testing, two types of errors may occur. Children may be labeled as *having* a condition when their true status is *not having* the condition (false positives or type II error). Or children may be assessed as *not having* a condition when, in fact, they do *have* it (false negatives or type I error). Errors of either type can lead to misinterpretation of an indicator. Type I and type II errors may be overt where there are incentives for people to misreport, or they may be unknown or unintentional.

Table 24.1 lists several indicators with this problem. For example, the rate of children in substitute care is often viewed as a proxy for children with severely abusive and neglectful parents. The increase in the rate of children in substitute care is generally interpreted as an indicator of a decline in the well-being of children. But we do not know if we have the "right" children in substitute care. There are false positives (children in care who do not need to be) and false negatives (children not in care who need to be). Workers in child welfare systems usually do not know which foster children fit which category. If they did, they would correct the mistakes. The mistakes arise partly from training and individual skills of the workers and partly from the unreliability of the measure—the poor "state of the art."

A study by Rossi, Schuerman, and Budde (1994) shows how difficult it is to avoid (or even identify) the false positives and false negatives in the child welfare arena. They asked several experts in child welfare to read case studies and indicate whether they believed the child in the case study should be placed into substitute care. They found little agreement among the experts on the sample of cases. The interobserver reliability was quite low. This study points to another problem as well: the lack of agreement among professionals about what constitutes the problem. It is difficult for professionals to agree on when child well-being is so threatened that substitute care is a better alternative.

Several other indicators have similar problems, such as juveniles committed to state custody, the percent of children in special education, rate of children retained in kindergarten, and the rate of reported or confirmed abuse and neglect. In each of these examples, false positives and false negatives are likely. Variation in practice and difference in definitions exacerbate the difficulty of determining whether child well-being is changing over time or determining whether jurisdictions are better or worse than one another. Using any of these indicators to imply something about the well-being of children is problematic.

Clear Interpretation

The reasons for indicator improvement or deterioration should be interpretable without raising confusion about the trends or issues behind the indicator. There are two issues here. First, one might think that, if possible, indicators should give clear inferences about an appropriate action to take. We note that linking indicators to policy is seldom straightforward. Yet some possible causes and consequences of trends or differences should be clear to the audience in mind.

Second, indicators should not combine two separate aspects of children's lives unless there is a clear rationale. One example of such an indicator from table 24.1 is the percent of teens not in school and not in the labor force. A decrease in the percentage of young people not in school and not in the labor force may be related to changes in the number of young people pushed out of school, leaving school voluntarily, refusing existing jobs, not being able to find jobs, or all of the above. When this indicator is not broken out or displayed with other indicators—and without a clear understanding of causal relationships within and between the education system and the labor market—it is difficult to make sense of it. Such an indicator can do little more than pique the curiosity of the reader.

As a final note, these indicators did not include direct measures of child psychosocial well-being through the administration of psychometric scales in surveys. Though we applaud the efforts of those who are using survey techniques to gather such measures for a large number of children, we do not believe these measures yet provide indicators of child well-being for a broad population. If that becomes possible, such indicators may replace some of those we have critiqued here.

PROPOSITIONS ABOUT DEVELOPING A SET OF INDICATORS

In this final section we discuss some general principles that might apply to a *set of indicators* to monitor child well-being. This discussion augments the discussion of Moore (Chapter 2, this volume).

Balanced Reporting   Our first concern is balanced reporting. Patton (1986) discusses balanced reporting in the following manner:

> [It] means considering multiple possible interpretations and analyzing various kinds of indicators. Single indicators are seldom adequate in the search for balance. Multiple indicators, multiple analytical approaches, and multiple perspectives are required for balance. Balance positive and negative findings as appropriate. Be clear about definitions. Make comparisons carefully and appropriately.

We believe a set of indicators should relate individual variables to each other and to a larger theoretical model. Our current state of knowledge makes this difficult, but we should strive toward the development of clearer models that link the various domains of children's lives.

Potential for Misinterpretation   A second concern is potential for misinterpretation. Social scientists can never prevent indicators from being misused, abused, or manipulated (Rainwater and Yancey 1967). We can, however, try to minimize *unintended* misuse. We can try to inform the general public and media about what indicators might mean and what they do not. We can strive for an appropriate balance between simple and complex indicators. We can try to keep both lay people and the agenda-setters in mind.

Data cannot speak for themselves. Therefore, interpretations always should accompany indicators. These interpretations should include possible counterinterpretations or rebuttals. In early stages, indicators may be more opaque than transparent to the lay public. Yet, media coverage and public education programs may lead to broader awareness and acceptance of difficult concepts.

A set of indicators should report data that compare geographic areas in a context and form in which readers can reasonably sense the relative risks and outcomes for children in those areas. We agree with Zill (1991) that, if states are to be compared, state rankings should be replaced by calculations of whether states are performing better or worse than expected. (Of course, the statistical model for "leveling the playing field" should be made transparent.) Alternatively, data can be presented in cross-tabular fashion using major variables known to make a difference—such as parents' education, income, and race/ethnicity (Zill 1991)—allowing an informed reader to adjust the rankings himself or herself.

SPECIAL CONDITIONS IN USING INDICATORS FOR EVALUATION

In our view of the role indicators play as data to inform the public debate, indicators are more like early warning signals—canaries in the mines or swallows in the spring—not designed for evaluation. Since the GPRA, according to our interpretation of the current discussion, intends to design indicators to evaluate programs, we present special conditions that seem to us might apply in such situations.

Indicators could be used to evaluate programs or hold officials accountable when the following conditions hold:

1. A program goal has been articulated in measurable terms.

2. An official has accepted responsibility for the achievement of that goal or has been designated responsible by executive or legislative direction. Furthermore, she or he has control of most (perhaps all?) of various government programs associated with the "treatment."

3. A program treatment or set of activities can be defined and measured. Some sense of the relationships among client attributes, treatment, and outcomes can be articulated.

4. An appropriate research design and counterfactual (what would have happened in absence of the program) can be demonstrated.

5. A rough cost-benefit (in a broad sense, including quantitative and qualitative dimensions) analysis can be calculated.

6. External factors that may contribute to the outcome are identified and controlled for in the analysis.

Though some may believe this is far too conservative a test for indicators to pass, we believe this is a reasonable test. It is one that indicators will seldom pass.

CONCLUSIONS AND RECOMMENDATIONS

In conclusion, we believe is it important to continue to improve our measures of the psychosocial well-being of children. Indicators of children's psychosocial well-being in some cases can help define policy problems and help redefine the public agenda, but they also can be misused by advocates and misunderstood by policymakers.

Throughout this chapter we have critiqued several indicators drawn from service system administrative data. We have not offered these critiques because we believe surveys should be used to create all indicators of psychosocial well-being. Rather, we believe indicators from social service data must be used, should be used, and can be improved. We offer two suggestions for improvement. First, we believe indicators are best when used together in ways that present several sides of the same problem. This is similar to Patton's (1986) recommendation for a multidisciplinary approach that considers multiple variables, paradigms, and interpretations. Second, we believe we can create better quality-assurance mechanisms for indicators drawn from the service systems. Quality-assurance checks can measure whether certain types of errors in an indicator are becoming more or less prevalent. This can help us understand, and possibly reduce, both intentional and unintentional errors when we follow this indicator across time and place, thus improving our ability to interpret indicator trends and differences.

Finally, we would like suggest a short list of the indicators we see as the best in this field at this time:

- youth unemployment rate
- rate of child poverty
- birth rates for single teens
- juvenile *violent* crime arrest rate
- death rate from child abuse and neglect

Each of these indicators has its problems. However, we believe that each avoids the most common and most serious flaws for indicators in this field.

The first two display the problems of service system mediation. Police and child protection personnel make mistakes in identifying (or not identifying) children. However, by focusing on the most serious problems—*violent* crimes and *death* from abuse or neglect—we believe the indicators minimize those problems. The chances for type I and type II errors are lessened by picking the more severe problems.

The third indicator—the youth unemployment rate—also exhibits numerous problems. However, by relying on surveys of youth and letting them identify their presence in the labor market and their work activity, it overcomes the problems of service system mediation.

The final two indicators are not, strictly speaking, indicators that measure psychosocial well-being. However, we believe we must track the social context of children. Poverty rates and rates of births to teenage mothers are clearly related to children's psychosocial problems.

This paper reflects the views of the authors. It does not necessarily reflect the views or policies of the U.S. Department of Health and Human Services Office of the Assistant Secretary for Planning and Evaluation. We appreciate the thoughtful and constructive comments we have received from Brett Brown, Tom Corbett, Sheldon Danziger, Walton Francis, Kris Moore, Richard Silva, and Nick Zill.

NOTES

1. The discussion that follows is intended to relate to indicators in general, not just psychosocial indicators.

2. The Government Performance Review Act (GPRA) discusses indicators and associates them with several types of data: an *outcome* is an assessment of the results of a program compared to its intended purpose. An *output* is a measure of an activity or effort that can be expressed in quantitative or qualitative terms. An *impact* is the comparison of program effects/consequence/ outcomes with estimates of outcomes that would have occurred in absence of the program. We have encountered a great deal of confusion concerning whether the GPRA is part of or substantially different from the general interest in promoting the general use of indicators.

3. In national surveys we seldom interview children. Fear of youths truthfulness and maturity or parental resistance are serious concerns. Child Trends' National Survey of Children is a rare exception.

REFERENCES

Annie E. Casey Foundation. 1994. "*Kids Count Data Book*: State Profiles of Child Well-being." Working paper. Baltimore, Md.: The Annie E. Casey Foundation.

Brandon, Richard N. 1992. "A Conceptual Framework for Measuring Child/Family Well-Being." Seattle, Wa.: Institute for Public Policy and Management.

Child Trends. 1993. *Researching the Family: A Guide to Survey and Statistical Data on U.S. Families*, Washington, D.C.: Child Trends.

Duncan, Otis Dudley. 1969. *Social Science Frontiers*, Newbury Park, Calif.: Sage Publications.

———. 1974. "Developing Social Indicators." *Proceedings of the National Academy of Science*, 71(12): 5096–5102.

Garbarino, James. 1991. "Conceptual Issues in the Search for Social Indicators of Child Well-Being." Source Unknown.

Kingdon, John W. 1984. *Agendas, Alternatives, and Public Policies*. Boston: Little, Brown and Company.

Miringoff, Marc L. 1993. "Index of Social Health: Monitoring the Social Well-Being of the Nation." Working paper. Tarrytown, N.Y.: Fordham Institute for Innovation in Social Policy, Fordham Graduate Center.

Oregon Progress Board. 1992. "Oregon Benchmarks: Standards for Measuring Statewide Progress and Government Performance." Report to the 1993 Legislature, Portland, Ore.

Patton, Michael Quinn. 1986. *Utilization-Focused Evaluation*. Newbury Park, Calif.: Sage Publications.

Rainwater, Lee, and William L. Yancey. 1967. *The Moynihan Report and the Politics of Controversy*. Cambridge, Mass.: The M.I.T. Press.

Rossi, Peter H., and Howard E. Freeman. 1989. *Evaluation: A Systematic Approach*. Newbury Park, Calif.: Sage Publications.

Rossi, Peter, John Schuerman, and Stephen Budde. 1994. "Understanding Child Placement Decisions and Those Who Make Them." Working paper. Chapin Hall Center for Children, University of Chicago.

Zill, Nicholas. 1991. "Improving *Kids Count*: Review of an Annual Data Book on the Condition of Children in the Fifty States of the U.S." Working paper. Washington, D.C.: Child Trends, Inc.

Aber, J. Lawrence, 133

Achenbach Behavior Problems Checklist, 14

achievement domains, 212–14

achievement indicators: adjustment for demographic differences, 219–21; building, 216–21; characteristics of, 212–14; function and use of, 209–10; recommendations for, 216–21, 227–31; status of current, 221–27

achievement tests: deriving indicators from, 212–21; functions of, 210–11; limitations of, 214–16; as measure of achievement, 212–21; minimum-competency state-level testing, 211

ACOG. See American College of Obstetricians and Gynecologists (ACOG).

Adequacy of Prenatal Care Utilization Index (APNCU Index), 63–66

administrative data; characteristics of, 459–62; defined, 457; describing deprivation or dependence, 263–64; in developing child indicators, 458–59, 462; state and local, 462–65

adolescent behavior: health-enhancing, 431–33; targeted by YRBSS, 113

adolescent health indicators: criteria for, 117–19; identifying, 115, 431; recommended, 119–20

adolescents: data collection related to health-risk behavior, 431–32; high school dropout

or completion rates by cohort, 177–78; high school dropouts, 153–59; indicators of preparation for adult roles, 433–37; potential indicator of development, 436; proposed health-enhancing behavior, 431; trends and measurement of high school completion, 160–64

Aid to Families with Dependent Children (AFDC): heterogeneity of experience, 259–61; TANF as replacement for, 10

alcohol and drug abuse: as adolescent problem behavior, 443–44; current tracking and data collection, 448–49; MFS data, 448; NHSDA data, 13, 448; YRBSS data, 448

American College of Obstetricians and Gynecologists (ACOG), 63

American Communities Survey (ACS), 11

American Housing Survey, 9, 245

Annie E. Casey Foundation: high school dropout measure (1995), 170; indicator of school environments, 8; *Kids Count* child profiles, 465; *Kids Count Data Book* (1994, 1995), 155, 169, 485

APNCU Index. See Adequacy of Prenatal Care Utilization Index (APNCU Index).

Armed Forces Qualifying Test scores, 198

Bales, Susan Nall, 76

Bane, Mary Jo, 259–61

behavior, adolescent problem: current indicator tracking, 448–49; needed community-level indicators, 447–48; needed family-level indicators, 447; needed individual-level indicators, 446–47; recommended community-level indicators, 451; recommended expanded family-level indicators, 451. *See also* risky driving practices; risky sexual behavior

behavior, problem: indicators in early childhood, 410–14; limitations of indicators for, 14–15; recommendations to improve, 424; sources of data, 13; surveys measuring, 414–20

behavior, prosocial, 13–15

Behavior Problems Index (BPI), 14, 397, 412

birth certificates: data on, 54–55; as low birth weight data source, 58–59

birth weight, low: current measurement techniques, 57–61; data sources of, 58–59; as indicator of prenatal and infant health, 49–50; indicators produced on, 61–62

birth weight data collection, 60–61

Blake, J., 321

BPI. See Behavior Problems Index (BPI).

Bronson, M. D., 133

Brooks-Gunn, Jeanne, 403
Bureau of Labor Statistics: educational attainment data, 199; *Employment and Earnings*, 197
Bureau of the Census: American Communities Survey, 11; 1990 census race and national origin data, 314–15; dropout rates of dependent family members, 172; family structure reports, 339–40; income data, 243; *Money Income of Households, Families, and Persons in the United States*, 197; Population Estimates Branch, 11; population reports, 328; proposed Survey of Program Dynamics, 136, 137; Public Use Microdata, 312, 382; question asked about educational attainment, 162–64

California Greater Avenues for Independence (GAIN), 143
Casey Foundation. *See* Annie E. Casey Foundation.
Census of the United States. *See* Bureau of the Census.
Centers for Disease Control and Prevention (CDC): abortion and STD rates, 449; Behavioral Risk Factor Survey, 112; blood lead concentration levels, 90; Division of Adolescent and School Health, 4; Youth Risk Behavior Surveillance System, 113
CEX. *See* Consumer Expenditure Survey (CEX).
Chapin Hall Center for Children, Foster Care Data Archive Project, 465
child abuse: inadequate data collection, 329; incidence of, 338; research related to, 338
Child Behavior Checklist (CBCL), 412
child care: costs of, 143; educational significance of preschool, 138–39; National Child Care Survey, 301n4; parental employment in context of, 295; parent and nonparent, 250; Profile of Child Care Settings, 301n4; quality

and characteristics, 140–41; self-care or latchkey situations, 142–43; Swedish longitudinal studies, 295
Child Care and Development Block Grant (1990), 281
child care indicators: proposed, 140, 143–44; related to well-being, 139–40
child development: indicators of early childhood development, 404–6; indicators of early positive, 396–97; influence of neighborhoods, 347–52; measurement of, 365; PSID Child Development Supplement, 294, 298; psychosocial indicators of, 487–89; recommendations for indicators for, 404–6; in relation to home environment, 293–94; sources of data on social, 13. *See also* Infant Health and Development Program; National Institute of Child Health and Human Development (NICHD)
child health: conditions reported, 5–6; criteria to judge measures of, 77–78; data related to, 4; data sources of preschool-age, 78; indicators of prenatal and infant, 47–52; low birth weight as indicator of, 50; potential indicators, 90; prenatal care as indicator of, 51; recommendations for future data collection, 90–92. *See also* adolescent health indicators; infant mortality; low birth weight; prenatal care
Child Health and Illness Profile-Adolescent Edition (CHIP-AE), 96
child health status: environmental factors, 85, 88–89; impairments, 85–88; international comparison, 100, 103t; measures of, 95–98; medical care utilization, 82–85; other conditions, 85, 88; overall, 79–82; purpose and types of measures, 95–98. *See also* adolescent health
childhood, early: improvement of indicators of child development, 397–404; indicators of

positive development, 396–97; indicators of problems of, 410–14; six areas of, 415; state-salient tasks of, 398–404
child neglect: inadequate data collection, 329; incidence of, 338; research related to, 338
children: data related to race and ethnicity, 313; in early education intervention programs, 142; effect of divorce on, 331–32; effect of immigrant status on life chances of, 317–18; effect of mother's employment on, 23–87; effect of parental employment on, 249–50; evaluation of immigrant status of, 319–20; extremely low birth weight, 413; indicators of economic well-being, 237–49; psychosocial indicators used to measure, 487–89; research on neighborhood influence on, 352–55; social and emotional adjustment, 331–32. *See also* school readiness
children in foster care: Foster Care Data Archive Project, 465; inadequate data collection, 329
children in school: high school dropout or completion rates by cohort, 177–78; high school dropouts, 153–59; indicators for early schooling, 144–47; instruction in native language, 136–37; latchkey children, 142–43; measuring high school completion, 165–67; preadolescent latchkey children, 142–43; predictors of motivation and performance, 136; proposed dropout or persistence rates, 170–76; proposed priority indicators, 147; recommended health indicators for preadolescent, 104–10; trends in high school completion, 160–62
Children's Vaccine Initiative, 85
child well-being: criteria to evaluate indicators of, 37–44, 421; economic security indicators, 24–26t; education-related indicators of, 20–24t; family structure indicators for,

343; health-related indicators of, 16–19t; indicators of educational well-being, 7; indicators of prenatal and infant health, 47–52; indicators of social development and problem behavior, 30–32t; indicators related to social and family environment, 27–29t

Chitose, Yoshimi, 318–20

citizenship indicators, 435

Coleman, James S., 349

Common Core of Data (CCD) survey, 179

communities: categories of resources in, 287–88; social organization of, 375

community-level indicators: analysis and interpretation, 385–86; contextual orientation, 374–76, 379–81; dissemination of, 386–88; error and bias reporting, 383–84; methodology, 381; outcome orientations, 374–79; recommendations for, 388–89; standardization, 385

community service as potential indicator, 436

Conflict Tactics Scale, 339

Consumer Expenditure Survey (CEX), 243–45

Consumer Price Index (CPI), 240–44

consumption: trends in children's households, 243–44

CPI. See Consumer Price Index (CPI).

CPS. See Current Population Survey (CPS).

crime: FBI Uniform Crime Reports, 13, 448, 464; National Crime Victimization Survey, 246–47; trends in, 246–47

Crouter, A. C., 294

Current Population Survey (CPS): annual March data used by Kids Count, 340; college enrollment data, 187–89; data used by Bureau of the Census, 339; distinction among students attending college and vocational schools, 203; educational attainment data, 162–64, 198–99; high school completion estimates, 167; high school completion

rates (March data), 160–61; income and consumption data, 243–45; Income and Demographic Supplement, 9, 11; information on family structure, 335; labor force data, 295–96; mean earnings by years of college (1990), 199–201; nursery or day care data, 301n4; poverty rate data, 241, 268; problems of data collection and use, 268–69; recommendations for data collection, 185; School Enrollment Supplement, 7

data: indicators as, 483; limitations of state, local, and private, 225–26; longitudinal, 290, 295–98

data collection: of administrative data, 459–62; American Housing Survey, 245; information on race and ethnicity, 313; on neighborhood institutions, 362; recommendations for CPS, 185; recommended indicators for future, 90–92; related to college age youth, 185; related to neighborhood influence, 357–58; seat belt use among adolescents, 432

death rates, international comparisons, 100, 103t

dependence. See economic dependence.

deprivation. See economic deprivation.

Dodge, K. A., 404–5

Dryfoos, J. G., 443

Dubay, Lisa C., 76–77

dynamic processes: accounting period and observation window, 263–64; longitudinal patterns, 259–63

Early Childhood Longitudinal Survey (ECLS), 128–29, 132, 134, 135; future data in, 147; planned extension of, 141; recommendations related to, 138

Early Screening Inventory, 135

earned income tax credit (EITC), 281

ECLS. See Early Childhood Longitudinal Survey (ECLS).

economic dependence: CPS data to measure, 269; indicators of long-term, 261; intergenerational indicators, 275; patterns of, 259–64; short-and long-run, 274–75; SIPP data to measure, 269–70

economic deprivation: CPS data to measure, 268–69; effect of duration of, 264–67; patterns of, 259–64; PSID and NLSY data to measure, 271; SIPP data to measure, 269–70

economic resources: effect of family structure on child's, 331; of one-and two-parent families, 330–31

economic security: factors in children's, 279; indicators of, 9–11; relation to parental employment, 280; sources of data related to, 9–10

economic well-being: children's, 239–49; indicators of, 237–49; parents', 238; value of home production for, 249

education: early intervention programs, 141–42; home learning environment, 130–38; indicators related to, 7–9; maternal, 294; payoffs for dropouts and short-term students to, 198–99; reform initiatives, 211–12; sources of data, 6–7. See also National Assessment of Educational Progress (NAEP); National Center for Education Statistics (NCES); National Educational Goals Panel (NEGP); schools; school readiness

education, high school: completion, 162–70; CPS educational attainment data, 162–64; estimates of high school completion, 168–70; future measurement of dropout and retention, 179–80; High School and Beyond (HSB) surveys, 177, 230; high school dropouts, 153–59; measuring high school completion, 165–67; proposed dropout or persistence rates, 170–76; recommendations for measuring

education, high school (*cont.*)
completion of, 178–79; trends
in high school completion,
160–62. *See also* adolescents
education, postsecondary: college admissions tests, 225;
costs of, 191–97; CPS college
enrollment estimates, 187–90;
data identifying returns to,
186; data on college enrollment, 187; educational attainment as indicator of, 189,
191–92; foregone earnings as
cost of, 195–96; identification
of payoffs, 197–99; IPEDS
estimates, 187; National Longitudinal Study of High
School Class of 1972, 197–
98, 226; National Postsecondary Student Aid Surveys
(NPSAS), 194–95, 203; payoffs to different types of,
197–98; Pell Grant assistance,
193–94; as potential indicator,
437; recommendations for
measures related to, 185–86;
student financial aid, 192–94
Education, U.S. Department of:
longitudinal data on high
school graduating classes, 191,
226; National Goals for Education, 152; Office of Educational Research and
Improvement (OERI), 128;
Prospects study, 135
educational agencies, state-level,
179
educational attainment: BLS
data, 199; CPS data, 162–64,
198–99; effect of family
structure on, 332–33; as indicator of postsecondary education, 189, 191–92
educational development tests,
214, 225
educational indicators: characteristics of, 209–10; criteria
for high school completion or
dropout, 159; educational
achievement indicators, 208;
OECD *Education at a Glance*,
137; proposed annual dropout
or persistence rates, 170–76;
proposed priority indicators,
138
Educational Testing Service
(ETS), 137, 224

*Education Counts: An Indicator
System to Monitor the Nation's
Educational Health*, 125
Elementary and Secondary Education Act (ESEA), 210, 227
Elliott, Delbert S., 431
Ellwood, David, 259–61, 264
employment, parental: assessment of father's, 281, 292; in
context of child care, 295; in
context of home, 292–94; in
context of work, 289–93; data
to assess mother's, 289–92;
effect on child of mother's,
283–88; effects on children,
287; indicators of, 249–55;
recommendations for data
collection, 299–300; studying
effects of, 287–89; of women
with children, 280–81
ethnicity: in measurement of
child well-being, 312–14; recommendations related to data
for, 316–17; reporting of,
312–13

families: economic resources of
one-parent, 330–31; economic
resources of single-mother,
330; economic resources of
two-parent, 330; factors influencing formation of, 333–34;
indicators related to, 12–13;
National Survey of Family
Growth, 64; residential patterns and relationships, 329;
SIPP and NSFH data related
to, 328; sources of data for,
11–12. *See also* children;
households; parents
Family Assistance Management
Information Systems
(FAMIS), 463–64
Family Leave Bill (1992), 281
family resources: categories of,
287; relation to employment
and child outcome, 288–89.
See also parents
family size: recommendations
related to measurement of,
325; relation to child's well-
being, 321–25
family stability: defined, 329; effects on child well-being, 329;
measurement of, 330–31;
measures of, 337–38; recom-

mendations to improve indicators of, 340–42
family structure: defined, 329;
effect on educational attainment, 332–33; effects on
child well-being, 329; indicators for child well-being, 343;
measurement of, 330–31;
measures of, 335–37; recommendations to improve indicators of, 340–42
FAMIS. *See* Family Assistance
Management Information
Systems (FAMIS).
Fatal Accident Reporting System (FARS), 448
Federal Bureau of Investigation
(FBI): Uniform Crime Re-
ports fatal accident and DWI
arrests from, 448; Uniform
Crime Reports information
on negative behaviors, 464;
Uniform Crime Report sys-
tem, 13; Uniform Crime Report youth arrest data, 13
Federal Interagency Forum on
Child and Family Statistics,
xxiv
Food Stamp program, 260–61
Foster Care Data Archive Proj-
ect, 465

Goal 1 Technical Planning
Group. *See* National Educa-
tional Goals Panel (NEGP).
good parent model, 238
Gottschalk, Peter, 264, 267
Government Performance and
Results Act (GPRA), 484,
496
Greater Avenues for Indepen-
dence (GAIN), California,
143
"Green Book." *See* U.S. Congress,
House of Representatives.

Head Start: non-English speaking children, 137; quality of
child care, 141–42; questions
to parents, 136
health: adolescent health-
enhancing behavior, 437–38;
health-risk behavior data collection, 431–32. *See also* adolescent health

health care: for children, 248; National Center for Health Statistics (NCHS), 53, 58, 64, 98; prenatal care, 62. *See also* National Health and Nutrition Examination Survey (NHANES); National Health Interview Survey (NHIS); prenatal care

health indicators: child mortality rates and causes of death, 5; children's health care, 5; children's health conditions, 5; commonly used, 100–102; defined, 96; health-related behavior, 5–6; international comparisons, 100, 103t; limitations, 6; major sources of, 98–99; problems related to, 113–14; recommended for preadolescent school children, 104–9

health indices, 96–98

Health Insurance Study, Rand Corporation, 78

Health Interview Survey, 248

health status profiles, 96–97

Healthy People 2000: National Health Promotion and Disease Prevention Objectives, 47–48, 117–18, 431

Healthy Start Program, Cleveland, 384

Hernandez, Donald J., 318, 322, 323, 331

Higher Education Reauthorization Act (1992), 202

High School and Beyond (HSB) surveys, 177, 230

Himes, 315–16

Hogan, Dennis P., 315

Home Observation Measure of the Environment (HOME) scale, 132, 293

households: census data collection, 322; consumption trends, 243–44; family structure in and out of, 335–37; indicators related to, 12–13; National Household Education Survey (NHES), 6–9, 13, 147, 414–20; National Household Survey of Drug Abuse, 13, 448; National Longitudinal Survey of Youth (NLSY), 132, 266, 271, 285, 295–98, 336–37, 397, 414–

20; National Survey of Families and Households (NSFH), 78, 328, 337, 397, 414–20; trends in incomes of, 241–43

Howes, Carollee, 295

HSB. *See* High School and Beyond (HSB) surveys.

ICD. *See* International Classification of Diseases (ICD).

immigration status: effect on child's life chances, 317–18; measurement of, 318–19; recommendations related to child well-being, 320–21

IMR. *See* infant mortality rate (IMR).

income: data collection related to, 290; Panel Study of Income Dynamics (PSID), 9, 219, 253–55, 271, 294–98; poverty threshold, 239–41; Survey of Income and Program Participation (SIPP), 9, 11, 78, 132, 141–43, 146, 219, 269–70, 328; trends in children's household, 241–43

income, parental: effect on children's life chances, 279; indicators of, 239–49

indicators: approach to identifying, 125–26; of child poverty, 10; as data, 496; definition and uses, 483–84; developed from administrative data, 465; function and use of, 209; of housing quality, 11; to monitor child well-being, 495–96; of parental and youth employment, 10–11; of prenatal and infant health, 48; related to government support programs, 10

Infant Health and Development Program, 266, 267

infant mortality: cause of death information, 54; data for population subgroups, 55; data sources used to compute, 52–53; as indicator of child health, 49–50; as indicator of prenatal and infant health, 49–50; measures of, 52; national statistics, 53; recommended data improvements,

56–57; state and county statistics, 53. *See also* death rates, international comparison

infant mortality rate (IMR): computing, 53; data source for, 55; defined, 52; neonatal and postneonatal, 52, 55; trend analysis of, 55–56, 57

information sources: for health indicators, 98–99; related to family stability, 337

institutions, neighborhood, 362–63

Integrated Postsecondary Education Data System (IPEDS): college enrollment data, 187; financial aid to college students reporting, 192; vocational school student data, 202–3

International Association for the Evaluation of Educational Achievement (IEA), 137

International Classification of Diseases (ICD), 98

investment model, 237–38, 279

Iowa Test of Educational Development (ITED), 214, 225

Iowa Tests of Basic Skills (ITBS), 214

IPEDS. *See* Integrated Postsecondary Education Data System (IPEDS).

Jacobson, Louis S., 202

Jasso, Guillermina, 318, 320

Jencks, Christopher, 346–49, 367

Jensen, Leif, 318–20

Job Training Partnership Act (JTPA), 199, 202

Johns Hopkins Ambulatory Care Case Mix System, 96

Kenney, Genevieve M., 76–77

Kentucky Education Reform Act (KERA), 211–12

Kessner Index, 62–63, 65, 66

Kids Count Data Book. See Annie E. Casey Foundation.

Kominski, Robert, 170–71

Kotelchuck's index. *See* Adequacy of Prenatal Care Utilization Index (APNCU Index).

labor force participation: effect of family structure on, 334; as indicator of parents' employment, 250–53; of women, 280–87, 294, 298
Lalonde, Robert, 202
last menstrual period (LMP) data, 60, 62
Lichter, Daniel T., 315
low birth weight: current measurement of, 57–61; as indicator of child health, 50; recommendation for improved indicators, 61–62

MacArthur Network on Adolescents at Risk, 356
McHales, S. M., 294 McKay, Henry D., 348
McLanahan, Sara, 330–34
Mayer, Susan, 346–49, 367
Medicaid: covering pregnancy and infant care, 112; Medicaid Management Information Systems (MMIS), 463–64
medical care. See health care.
Meyers, M. K., 143
MFS. See Monitoring the Future Survey (MFS).
Michigan Time Use Studies, 293
MMIS. See Medicaid.
Moffitt, Robert, 264
Monitoring the Future Survey (MFS): adolescent health data, 113; drug use behavior data, 448; social development and problem behavior data, 13, 113
Moore, Kristin A., 398, 421–24

NAEP. See National Assessment of Educational Progress (NAEP).
National Academy of Sciences, Panel on Research on Child Abuse and Neglect, 338–39
National Ambulatory Medical Care Survey (NAMCS), 78
National Assessment of Educational Progress (NAEP), 6; achievement assessment function, 210–11, 215, 217–19; data on education-related behavior, 8; recommendations for data collection, 435; sampling design and trend assessment, 223–25; student achievement data, 221, 223–30; student achievement indicator data, 145; Trial State Assessment, 229
National Association of State Scholarship and Grant Programs surveys, 195
National Center for Child Abuse and Neglect, Child Abuse and Neglect Data System, 338, 465
National Center for Education Statistics (NCES): Condition of Education (1994, 1995, 1996), 156–58; dropout reports, 177; Early Childhood Longitudinal Survey, 128, 135; high school completion rates, 168; high school dropout data, 155, 177; post-1990 education indicator initiative 139; Schools and Staffing Surveys, 137
National Center for Health Statistics (NCHS): Child Health Supplement, 98; Monthly Vital Statistics Report, 64; National Vital Statistics System, 53; report on maternal and infant health, 58
National Child Care Survey (NCCS), 301n4
National Community Service Trust Act (1993), 436
National Crime Victimization Survey, 246
National Educational Goals Panel (NEGP), 130; 1994, 1995, 1996 reports, 152, 168; Goal 1 Technical Planning Group, 129–30, 133; high school completion estimates, 165–67; Resolution on the Assessment of Citizenship, 434
National Educational Longitudinal Study (NELS): 1988, 177; achievement measures in, 226, 230
National Goals for Education, 152
National Health and Nutrition Examination Survey (NHANES): adolescent health issues, 113; data collection and reporting, 4, 78, 90, 100; examination data, 98; NHANES III, 69, 85
National Health Interview Survey (NHIS): Child Health Supplement, 14, 100, 109, 397, 414–20; child safety information, 88; data and social class in, 104; data collection for and derivation from, 78, 104; monitoring task of, 4; proposed child and family topical module, 15; Youth Risk Behavior Supplement, 432
National Hospital Ambulatory Medical Care, 113, 120
National Hospital Discharge Survey, 78
National Household Education Survey (NHES), 6–7; data related to preschool environments, 9; indicators of school readiness, 8; parent interview data, 147; problem behavior measurement in, 414–20; social development and problem behavior data, 13
National Household Survey of Drug Abuse (NHSDA), 13, 448
National Income and Product Accounts (NIPA), Personal Consumption Expenditures, 240–42
National Institute of Child Health and Human Development (NICHD): Family and Child Well-Being Research Network, xxiv; sibling comparison study, 294; Study of Early Child Care, 141, 301n3
National Longitudinal Study of High School Class of 1972 (NLS-72), 197–98, 226
National Longitudinal Survey of Youth (NLSY), 64, 78; adolescent health issues, 113; child's living arrangement data, 337; Child Supplement data, 336; data on deprivation and dependence, 271; data to compare family income and cognitive development, 266; family residential histories (1979 cohort), 329; fringe

benefit data, 291; mother-child data, 132, 285, 295–98, 397, 414–20; recommendation for adolescent-oriented, 450–51

National Maternal and Infant Health Survey (NMIHS), 64

National Medical Expenditures Survey (NMES), 78

National Natality Survey (NNS), 63, 64

National Opinion Research Center, 339

National Postsecondary Student Aid Surveys (NPSAS), 194–95; data on students attending proprietary schools, 203

National Survey of Children (NSC), 397, 414–20

National Survey of Families and Households (NSFH), 78; child's living arrangement data, 337; data related to child development, 397; data related to families, 328; problem behavior measurement in, 414–20

National Survey of Family Growth (NSFG), 64

NCES. See National Center for Education Statistics (NCES).

neighborhoods: assessment of research, 352–55; indicators related to, 12–13; research designs to test for influence of, 355–59; social organization of, 363–64; sources of data for, 11–12; theories related to, 347–52

New Standards Project, 214

NHANES. See National Health and Nutrition Examination Survey (NHANES).

NHES. See National Household Education Survey (NHES).

NICHD. See National Institute of Child Health and Human Development (NICHD).

NIPA. See National Income and Product Accounts (NIPA).

NLSY. See National Longitudinal Survey of Youth (NLSY).

NMIHS. See National Maternal and Infant Health Survey (NMIHS).

NNS. See National Natality Survey (NNS).

Nord, Christine W., 328

NPSAS. See National Postsecondary Student Aid Surveys (NPSAS).

NSFG. See National Survey of Family Growth (NSFG).

NSFH. See National Survey of Families and Households (NSFH).

Obstetrician's best estimate (OBE), 60

Office of Educational Research and Improvement (OERI), 128

Oregon Benchmarks Initiative, 484–85

Organisation for Economic Co-operation and Development (OECD): *Education at a Glance*, 137

Panel Study of Income Dynamics (PSID), 9; Child Development Supplement, 294, 298; data on deprivation and dependence, 271; data on employment and family resources, 295–96; family structure data, 329; home production data, 253–55; poverty measures, 219

parents: indicators of employment, 249–55; parental resources in child's social and emotional adjustment, 331; participation in child's schooling, 136; Survey of Parents of Children under Three, 78. See also employment, parental; good parent model; income, parental

Peabody Picture Vocabulary Test (PPVT), 397

Peabody Picture Vocabulary Test-Revised (PPVT-R), 285

Pell Grants, 193–94

perception of opportunity: as potential indicator, 437

performance: assessments to shape instruction, 214; Government Performance and Results Act, 484, 496; predictors of, 136

Personal Responsibility and Work Opportunity Recon-ciliation Act (1996), xix, 259, 270, 458

policymaking: role of indicators in, 485

population: indicators related to, 12–13; sources of data for, 11–12

poverty: among immigrant children, 319; children's outcomes related to, 279; trends in rates of child, 239–41

poverty indicators: child, 10; derived from CPS data, 268, 271; intergenerational, 273–74; short-and long-run, 272–73

poverty threshold, 239–41

prenatal care: current measurement of use, 62–68; current use measurement, 62–68; definition of, 62–63; as indicator of child health, 49, 51; production of indicators, 67–68; recommendation for improved indicators, 67–68; use as indicator of prenatal and infant health, 49–51

PSID. See Panel Study of Income Dynamics (PSID).

psychosocial indicators, 487–89

Public Health Service (PHS): *Healthy People 2000* objectives, 431; identified health objectives, 117–18

public policy: indicators to evaluate, 486–87

Quality of Adjusted Life Years Scale (QALYS), 96

race: in measurement of child well-being, 312–14; recommendations related to data for, 316–17; reporting of, 312–13

Rand Health Insurance Study (Rand HIS), 78

risky driving practices: as adolescent problem behavior, 444; data collected by MTFS and YRBSS, 448

risky sexual behavior: as adolescent problem behavior, 445; tracking and data collection, 449

Rosenzweig, Mark R., 318, 320

Sandefur, Gary, 330–34
SAS. *See* Statistical Analysis System (SAS).
SASS. *See* School and Staffing Surveys (SASS).
Schoenborn, Charlotte A., 411
Scholastic Assessment Test (SAT): test data, 225; trends, 220
School and Staffing Surveys (SASS), 7–9, 137
School Archival Records Search, 136
school readiness: conceptualization of, 127–28; indicators of, 130–38; measurement of, 128–30; unready kindergarteners, 135–36
schools: assessment of, 146; enrollment indicators, 7; proposed indicators of early schooling, 145; vocational, 202–4
security. *See* economic security.
Seltzer, Judith A., 331 Sen, Amartya, 481
Shaw, Clifford, 348
SIPP. *See* Survey of Income and Program Participation (SIPP).
SLICHS. *See* State and Local Area Immunization Coverage and Health Surveys (SLICHS).
Smith, Judith R., 266, 295
social capital, 363
social development: data sources, 13, 116; indicators of child, 30–32t; limitations to indicators of, 14–15
social indicators: history of, 484; reporting of, 473–76; uses of, 484–85
social statistics, 483
State and Local Area Immunization Coverage and Health Surveys (SLICHS), 78
Statistical Analysis System (SAS), 64

Strange Situation Paradigm (Ainsworth), 284, 301n1
Sullivan, Daniel G., 202
Supplemental Security Income program (SSI), 260–61
Survey of Income and Program Participation (SIPP), 9, 11, 78; child care module of, 141–43; Child Well-Being Module, 132, 146; data related to families, 328; data to measure deprivation and dependence, 269–70; poverty measures, 219; proposed Survey of Program Dynamics, 142, 146, 147, 269
Survey of Parents of Children Under Three (SPCU3), 78
Survey of Program Dynamics (SPD). *See* Survey of Income and Program Participation (SIPP).

TANF. *See* Temporary Assistance for Needy Families (TANF).
Taskforce on Meeting the Needs of Young Children (1944), 433–34
Temporary Assistance for Needy Families (TANF): assistance under, 270; as replacement for AFDC, 10; time limits, 281, 298–99
Trial State Assessment (TSA), 229

Uniform Crime Reports. *See* Federal Bureau of Investigation (FBI).
U.S. Congress, House of Representatives, "Green Book," 465
University of Michigan, Monitoring the Future surveys, 13, 113, 448

violence: as adolescent problem behavior, 444–45; constructing indicators from YRBSS, 448
Vital Statistics System: as child health data source, 4, 50; use in development of child indicators, 458. *See also* birth certificates
voter registration: as indicator of adolescent development, 436–38

welfare caseload statistics, 270–71
Welfare Indicators Act (1994), 259
well-being. *See* child well-being; economic well-being.
Wilson, William Julius, 346, 348–49
Wojtkiewicz, Roger, 337
women: conditions related to employment, 289–92; in home production, 253–55; labor force participation, 254, 281–87, 294, 298
Women's, Infant, and Children (WIC) Program, 112
World Health Organization (WHO): selection rule bias, 54

Year 2000. *See Healthy People 2000: National Health Promotion and Disease Prevention Objectives.*
Youth Risk Behavior Surveillance System (YRBSS), 113, 431–32; data related to adolescent problem behavior, 4, 449–50; drug use behavior data, 448

Zill, Nicholas, 328, 411